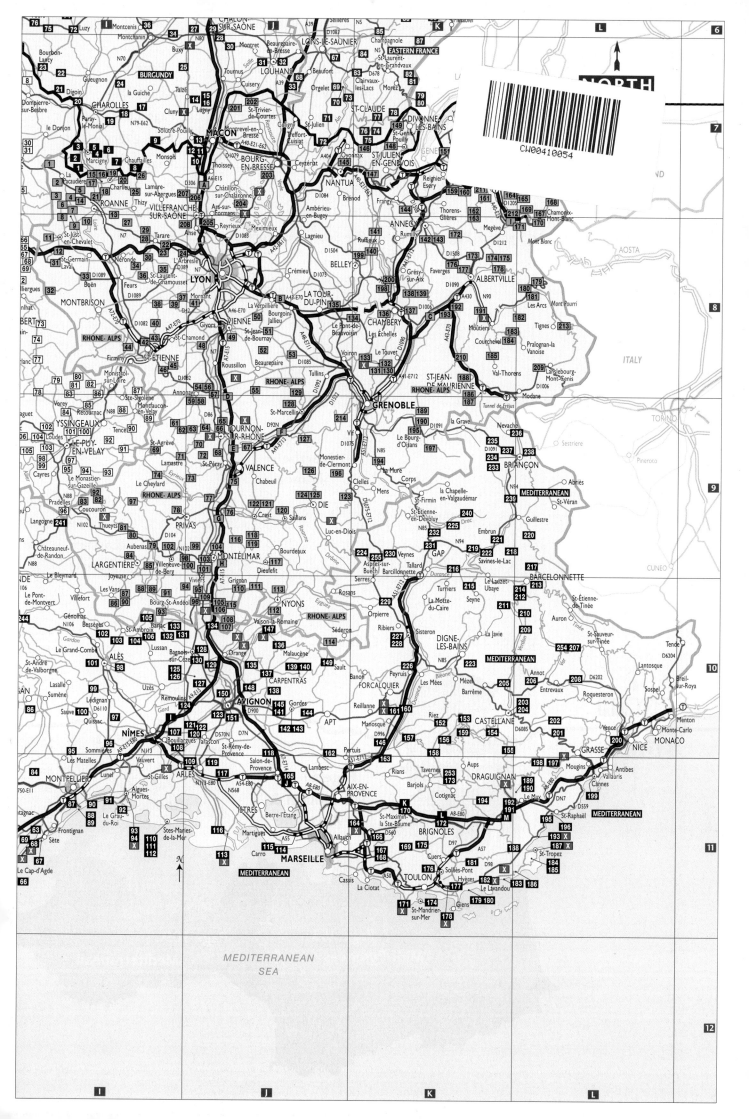

CONTENTS

Going north?
Remember to take
All the Aires
France North with you

Northern France

Normandy

Champagne

Eastern France

Brittany

Pays de Loire

Centre

Burgundy

NORTH

SOUTH

Page 195
Poitou

Page 61
Limousin & Auvergne

Page 231
Rhone-Alps

Page 19
Atlantic

Page 153
Midi-Pyrenees

Page 109
Mediterranean

Freedom of France

French Aires symbolise the freedom of motorhoming and campervanning because Aires enable you to travel all year and park overnight without constraint. France has nearly 3000 municipally provided motorhome parking areas, most of which also provide fresh and waste water facilities. French Aires range from small grassy car parks located in remote mountain villages to large motorhome only parking areas at popular tourist destinations. Use the All the Aires France North and South guides to make informed choices about where to stay and what to see.

1643 Inspections

Over half the Aires featured in the 2015 volumes were inspected by the editors, Meli and Chris. They scrutinised 1214 Aires in 2014 and 393 during the summer of 2013. Customer submissions updated hundreds more Aires. The strategy for inspections was to go to all the popular areas following the transitory routes favoured by motorhomers. Every Aire near the Atlantic and Mediterranean coasts was appraised. Canals and rivers were targeted including the Ardèche, Dordogne, Loir, Loire, Moselle, Rhône, Rhine and Tarn. Vineyards were visited all over France and quite by chance the last day of inspections was celebrated in Champagne. Special thanks goes to Total who provided their LPG fuel station list in 2012.

Front cover main image: Leucate.

First published in Great Britain by Vicarious Books LLP, 2007. This edition published for 2015.
© Vicarious Media Ltd 2014.
Copyright © text Vicarious Media Ltd. All rights reserved.
Copyright © photographs Vicarious Media Ltd unless otherwise stated.
ISBN: 978-1-910664-01-8

Editorial Team, Vicarious Media, 62 Tontine Street, Folkestone, Kent, CT20 1JP. Tel: 0131 2083333
Chief Editor: Meli George
Editors: Chris Doree and Pami Hoggatt
Editorial assistants: Caroline Stacey, Rosie Peaches Spain
Design and Artwork: Chris Gladman Design Tel: 07745 856652

HOW TO USE THIS GUIDE

Page 12. Useful information.

Before you depart read the introduction.

Avant votre départ, lisez l'introduction.

Lesen Sie die Einführung, bevor Sie abfahren.

Prima di partire leggi l'introduzione.

Antes de partir, lea la introducción.

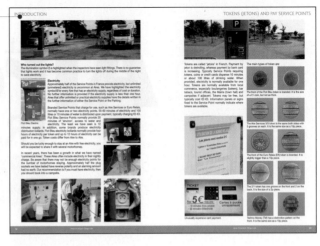

Outer cover flaps.
Key to symbols.
l'explication des symbols.
Erklärung der Symbole.
Spiegazione dei simboli.
Explicación de los símbolos.

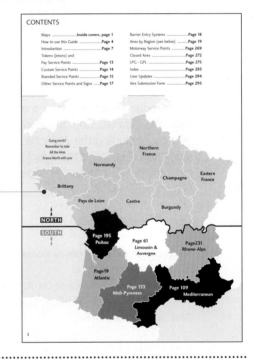

Page 2. Colour-coded regional overview map with page numbers.

Seite 2. Carte avec couleurs codées régions et numéros de page.

Seite 2. Karte mit farbcodierten Regionen und Seitenzahlen.

Pagina 2. Mappa con colori codificati regioni e numeri di pagina.

Página 2. Mapa con códigos de color de las regiones y números de página.

Step by step

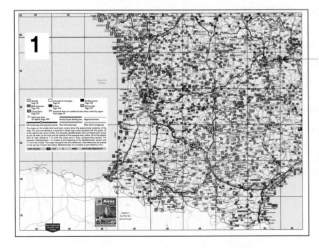

Inside covers. Maps colour-coded by region. All Aires numbered 1-2-3... in each region.

Cartes codées par couleur selon la région. Toutes les aire de service numérotées 1-2-3... dans chaque région.

Karten farblich nach Regionen codiert. Alle stellplätze nummeriert 1-2-3... in jeder Region.

Mappe a colori di un codice regionale. Tutti le aree di sosta numerati 1-2-3... in ciascuna regione.

Mapas codificados por color según la región. Todos área de servicio numerados 1-2-3... en cada región.

Page 19-268. Colour coded chapters by region.
All regions use map numbers 1-2-3…

Code couleur chapitres par région. Toutes les
régions utilisent des numéros de carte 1-2-3...

Farbcodierte Kapiteln nach Region. Alle Regionen
verwenden Zahlen auf der karte 1-2-3…

Codice colore capitoli per regione. Tutte le regioni
usare i numeri 1-2-3…

Código de colores capítulos según la región. Todas
las regiones utilizar los números del mapa 1-2-3…

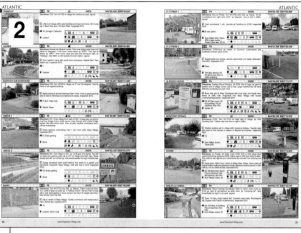

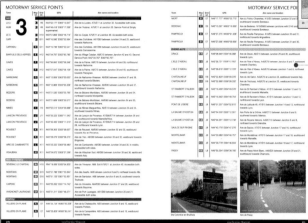

**Page 269-271. Autoroute Aires with motorhome
Service Points. Identified with letters on the maps.**

**Autoroute aires de services avec borne camping car
identifié avec lettres sur les cartes.**

**Autoroute Service-Bereich mit Wohnmobil
Abwasserentsorgung auf der Karte identifiziert mit
Buchstaben.**

**Autoroute area diservizio con servizi igienico-sanitari
per camper identificato con lettere sulle mappe.**

**Autoroute área de servicio con saneamiento de
autocaravanas identificado con letras en los mapas.**

Page 272-274. Closed Aires [X] **on maps.**

Aires de services fermé [X] **sur les cartes.**

Wohnmobilstellplätze geschlossen [X] **auf der Karte.**

Aree di sosta chiuso [X] **sulle mappe.**

Area para autocaravan cerrado [X] **en los mapas.**

Page 275-282. Fuel stations with LPG by region.

Stations d'essence au GPL par région.

Tankstellen mit Flüssiggas nach Region.

Stazioni di servizio con GPL per regione.

Estaciones de combustible con GLP por región.

Page 283-293. Alphabetical index by town name.

Index alphabétique par nom de ville.

Alphabetischer Index nach Ort Name.

Indice alfabetico per nome paese.

Indice alfabético por nombre de ciudad.

Explanation of an entry

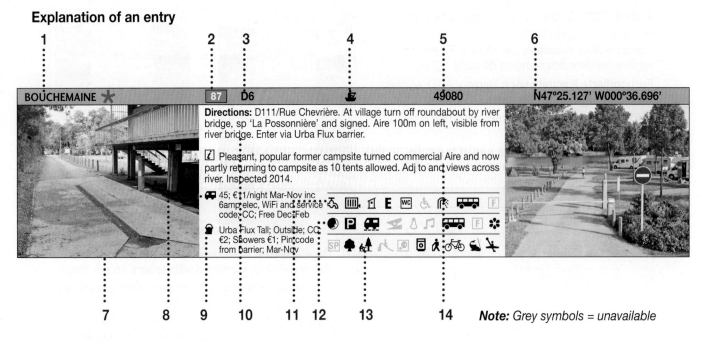

Note: *Grey symbols = unavailable*

1 Town Name.
✱ The inspectors have star rated the Aire or location. Often the view or surrounding area is of interest.
2 Map reference number.
3 Map grid reference.
4 Surroundings. Key on cover flaps.
5 Postcode. Further information on page 9.
6 GPS coordinates. Further information on page 9.

7 Photograph of Aire.
8 Number of parking spaces; Cost per night; Time limit; Open dates.
9 Service Point type; Payment type if not cash; Cost; Open dates.
10 Directions. Further information on page 9.
11 Service Point details. Key on cover flaps.
12 Parking details. Key on cover flaps.
13 Local amenities. Key on cover flaps.
14 Description of Aire and surrounding area.

Abbreviations and Glossary of Terms

5 mins	Estimated walking times.
Adj	Adjacent.
Alt	Altitude in metres.
Beau Village	Designated as one of the most beautiful. villages in France www.les-plus-beaux-villages-de-france.org/en.
CC	Credit card
CL style	Small grass parking area.
Commerce	
Local commerce	One or more: bar, baker, restaurant, convenience store, hair dresser.
Small town commerce	As above plus a mini market and bank.
Tourist commerce	Kiss me quick or seasonal restaurants and boutiques.
Town commerce	Big enough to have a wedding dress shop.
Commercial Aire	Set up for profit, often pay at barrier or Service Point.
Dead quiet	Peaceful location adj to cemetery.
Grass parking	Will not be marked as open all year, but can be used whenever conditions allow.
Hell's bells	Especially noisy church bells that chime all night or go like the clappers at 6am
Inc	Included in price.
Inside barrier	Service Point behind barrier at pay Aire. Access may be free or reduced cost for short duration.

May feel isolated if alone	Normally locations without habitation nearby, but don't lose sleep over it.
Open access	No fence or barrier.
Opp	Opposite.
Oversubscribed	Aire unlikely to have space.
Popular	Aire likely to be busy.
Poss	Possible.
Private Aire	Run by an individual, often at home or business.
pp	Per person.
Sp	Signposted 'Town name'.
Signed	Aire signed with symbol or text.
'text'	Extracts from signs.
TO	Tourist Office.
Tolerated	Unofficial motorhome parking.
Trucking hell	Noisy trucks hurtling past day and night.
Inspected	Inspected by Vicarious Media staff.
Visited	Customer submission.
Submitted	Owner supplied information.
Updated	Previously inspected but updated by customer.

1643 inspections and 300 new Aires

Over half the Aires featured in the 2015 volumes were inspected by the editors, Meli and Chris. They scrutinised 1250 Aires during 2014 and 393 in the summer of 2013. Customer submissions updated hundreds of Aires. The strategy for inspections was to go to all the popular areas following the transitory routes. Every Aire near the Atlantic and Mediterranean coasts was appraised. Canals and rivers were targeted including the Ardèche, Dordogne, Loir, Loire, Moselle, Rhône, Rhine and Tarn. Vineyards were visited all over France and, quite by chance, the last day of inspections was celebrated in Champagne. Along the way, over 300 new Aires were inspected which highlights just how important motorhome tourists are perceived to be in France.

Easy come, easy go

Aires provide motorhome travellers with the freedom to come and go as they please. Aires do not have a reception, so you cannot reserve a space and there is no booking in. Most Aires should be considered a convenient en-route stopover rather than a holiday destination. This does not mean to say that you cannot have a motorhome holiday when stopping at Aires, just that you should be motorhoming from place to place.

What are Aires and what does Aire mean?

The English translation of 'Aire' is 'area', and many French facilities have 'Aire' in their name. The full title for French motorhome Aires is 'Aire de service/stationnement pour Camping Car', which translates to 'Service area/parking for motorhomes' and are referred to as Aires in this publication. Aires are frequently signed with the motorhome service point symbol, and it is common for these signs to also refer to parking. A maximum of 48 hours parking is the national standard at Aires and this is assumed unless local signs or the articles in Mairie regulations state otherwise. Facilities differ significantly, but normally include a Service Point for water collection and disposal of waste fluids.

Motorway Aires. Do not park overnight at motorway service stations and rest areas!

French motorway services are also named "Aire 'something or other'". Motorhomes, trucks and cars are frequently broken into at motorway rest areas. Often the occupants of motorhomes are asleep during the burglary; surely a situation you would not want to be in. For completeness, a list of motorway services with Service Points has been provided at the back of the guide.

Who can use Aires?

French traffic law forbids caravans and tents from using the Aires in this guide. The law permits motorhome users to park and to cook, eat and sleep within the confines of their vehicle. This law actually enabled Aires to develop in the first place. French law does not permit camping activities at Aires, such as winding out awnings or putting out tables and chairs. We see countless examples of the rules being broken and often by French nationals, many of whom seem completely unaware of the written rules and unwritten etiquette. Thus, following their example may be unwise. Camping is permitted at all 10,500 French campsites.

Operation evasion

Over the past ten years there has been a rapid increase in the number of motorhomes on French roads, and 95 per cent of them are local camping cars. We have observed that, like birds of a feather, motorhomers flock together. For example, French motorhomers rarely venture off the main trunking routes. Consequently, overcrowding can occur at any Aire which is a short distance from a main road and is likely at those that are also in a quiet or pleasant location. Motorhomers from all nations appear compelled to drive to the coast and the sheer number of motorhomes has forced coastal authorities to put measures in place to manage parking. Motorhome parking is often controlled at well-known tourist attractions, lakes, rivers and canals. With control comes cost, so expect to pay if you want to stopover in popular areas. Freedom seekers should plan to end their day off the beaten track. We recommend that you travel with regional guidebooks, such as the Michelin green guides, in order to make the most of your visits to the lesser-known tourist attractions and villages.

Offsite parking

Some of the Aires in this guide are Service Points only without any parking. These are provided so that motorhomers can discharge waste responsibly. Motorhoming changed in France during 2012; this was not due to a change in the law but a change in attitude. As explained above, French law permits offsite parking and French motorhomers embraced this freedom. However, we have noticed that most French motorhomers were parking overnight at official places. Presumably they realised that because they congregate en masse they were spoiling it for themselves. We believe that you should continue to enjoy offsite parking, but make sure you are away from the popular motorhome destinations.

Vicarious Media champions responsible tourism

Motorhoming is booming in France and more than 300 new Aires have opened in the past two years. Some act as control measures, but many more were paid for by the local community in the hope that extra tourism would help to keep the local shops, restaurants or fuel stations open. Over the past ten years motorhomes have become much bigger, typically occupying 50 per cent more space. Bear this in mind when you park during siesta in a sleepy town square or in an empty Aire, because you are unlikely to remain alone. When parking somewhere for free you should at least try to spend what you are saving in camping fees. We would all like to see the Aires network continue to grow and this will happen if motorhomers are perceived as valuable visitors.

We can all be valued visitors if we are RESPONSIBLE and:

R espect the environment
E lect to use un-crowded Aires
S pend locally
P ark sensibly
O rganise your recycling
N o camping
S ave water
I mpeccable behaviour
B e quiet
L eave before you outstay your welcome
E valuate your impact

Finding Aires

Forward planning is advised, especially if you intend to drive late into the night. Select an area where there are two or more Aires nearby because Aires can be full, occupied by the funfair, or simply closed for maintenance. Vicarious Media is not responsible for any Aires. This book is a guide only and was correct at the time of going to press. Should you have any complaints about an Aire or wish to know why an Aire has closed, please speak to the local Mairie and remember to let us know about any changes.

Directions: The directions are written to assist you with map navigation. As far as is practical, the simplest route, that is free of height and weight restrictions, has been selected. Where possible, you should follow signs and be aware of any obstacles or diversions.

GPS navigation: The GPS coordinates provided in this guide were taken on site and it should be possible to drive to the spot where they were taken. However, this does not mean to say that your navigator will get you there. Check the directions against your printed map and look at the suggested route on your navigator. Should you not be able to use the coordinates, be aware that French postcodes cover at least a 10km radius; therefore you will need to input the town and street, too.

Signs: When provided, it is advisable to follow the motorhome symbols to the Aire. Signs and symbols differ widely, so you will need to look carefully. Unfortunately, campsites have taken to displaying motorhome Aire symbols on their direction and advertising signs. Often there is no indication that the signs are referring to campsite facilities. It is safe to assume that all campsites have sanitary facilities and this deception is unwelcome. Please do not submit campsite details to us unless the Service Point is in an accessible location outside of the campsite.

Parking

Aires operate on a first come, first served basis. Generally they are unsupervised, thus it is not possible to reserve a space. The available parking may be impractical for many reasons and parking your motorhome may make the situation worse, so always consider others first. Use bays when provided. In unmarked parking areas it is normal to park close to your neighbour when necessary, so try to leave enough space for another motorhome to slot in if the need arises. Everybody enjoys a view, so share them as much as possible. Never park overnight on the Service Point or obstruct roadways.

Large motorhomes (RVs) >7.5m: Many Aires have been designed to accommodate motorhomes up to 7m long. The highlighted coach symbols 🚌 identify Aires where the inspectors believe it should be possible for motorhomes over 7.5m to access the parking. In many cases, parking large motorhomes is only possible when there are few or no other motorhomes. Remember to put your responsible tourist hat on when you are making parking decisions. During busy periods Service Point access may not be possible. There are very few Service Points suitable for emptying fixed tank toilet systems. We strongly recommend you have a macerator fitted and travel with a long length of pipe.

Using Aires all year: Aires make suitable night stops all year round and, unlike campsites, few close for the winter. Most Aires have a hard surface. Grass covered parking areas often have compacted gravel underneath. The open all year ✿ symbol is not highlighted on grass parking, but it can usually be accessed as long as weather conditions allow. Drinking water is frequently turned off during the winter to prevent frost damage; 'Hors Gel' signs indicate this, whereas 'Hors Service' indicates out of order. Flot Bleu, Euro and Pacific Service Points normally stay in service all year because they are heated and insulated. Many of the Aires in this guide have been inspected during winter and the water was found to be on, unless otherwise stated. However, there is no guarantee that water will be on, so plan to visit several Service Points.

Time limits: Known time restrictions are provided in the listings. Many Aires restrict use to 48hrs, which is logical because it should be enough time to visit the local attractions. Aires not displaying time limits should be assumed to be 48hrs.

Service Points

There are several professionally manufactured Service Point brands. The most common are Euro Relais (Raclet) and Aire Services followed by Urba Flux, see page 15. Approximately half the Service Points in France are custom made, see page 14. Service Points normally facilitate three vital functions:

Drinking water: French tap water is very palatable, and consistent countrywide. Thoughtless users are known to contaminate taps when rinsing toilet cassettes. Using disinfectant wipes or spray before drawing water will improve hygiene. Taps are normally threaded to assist connection of hoses. Flot Bleu, Euro and Pacific Service Points have all the facilities located in one enclosed space increasing the risk of cross contamination. In addition, we have found the drinking water hose down the toilet emptying point on several occasions, so consider disinfection essential.

Waste water: Drive over drains differ widely in construction. Typically a metal grid is set in concrete near to the Service Point. Some drains are so badly designed or located that it is necessary to use a length of flexible pipe to direct waste water accurately. Some Service Points do not have a drain, but it is often possible to direct a pipe to the toilet emptying point. Flot Bleu, Euro and Pacific Service Points often have a short flexible pipe instead of a drive over drain.

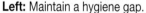

Left: Maintain a hygiene gap.

Toilet cassette emptying: Cassette emptying points differ so widely you may have to think about it before you work out the correct place. It may be necessary to remove a grid. Some drains are too small, notably Aire Services, so do not rush this operation as spillage will occur. Often two taps are provided; as a general rule toilet rinsing taps are unthreaded. Euro Relais Service Points often have a toilet rinsing tap that will flow even if tokens are required for other services. We often see small amounts of toilet contents on grids. This is not deliberate but as a result of rinsing and assuming that the cassette has liquids only. Flot Bleu, Euro and Pacific Service Points have to be unlocked before the toilet emptying point is accessible.

Who turned out the lights?

The illumination symbol ☿ is highlighted when the inspectors have seen light fittings. There is no guarantee that lights work and it has become common practice to turn the lights off during the middle of the night to save electricity.

Flot Bleu Electric

Electricity

Approximately half of the Service Points in France provide electricity, but unlimited (unmetered) electricity is uncommon at Aires. We have highlighted the electricity symbol **E** for every Aire that has an electricity supply, regardless of cost or duration. No further information is provided if the electricity supply is less than one hour. Aires that offer unlimited or practical electricity supplies have the details written in the further information of either the Service Point or the Parking.

Branded Service Points that charge for use, such as Aire Services or Euro Relais, normally have one or two electricity points. 55-60 minutes of electricity and 100 litres or 10 minutes of water is distributed upon payment, typically charging €2-€3.

Flot Bleu Service Points normally provide 20 minutes of 'environ', access to water and electricity. The least we have seen is 12 minutes supply. In addition, some brands produce electricity distribution bollards. Flot Bleu electricity bollards normally provide four hours of electricity per token and up to 12 hours of electricity can be paid for in one go. Token costs differ from Aire to Aire.

Should you be lucky enough to stay at an Aire with free electricity, you will be expected to share it with several motorhomes.

In recent years, there has been a growth in what we have named 'commercial Aires'. These Aires often include electricity in their nightly charge. Be aware that there may not be enough electricity points for the number of motorhomes staying. Approximately half the plug sockets we have tested have reverse polarity and an alarming amount had no earth. Our recommendation is if you must have electricity, then you should book into a campsite.

Tokens are called 'jetons' in French. Payment by jeton is dwindling, whereas payment by bank card is increasing. Typically Service Points requiring tokens, coins or credit cards dispense 10 minutes or about 100 litres of drinking water. When provided, electricity is normally available for one hour. Tokens are normally available from local commerce, especially boulangeries (bakers), bar tabacs, tourist offices, the Mairie (town hall) and campsites if adjacent. Tokens may be free, but typically cost €2-€3. Information panels or signs fixed to the Service Point normally indicate where tokens are available.

The main types of token are:

 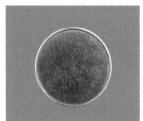

The front of the Flot Bleu token is branded. It is the size of a £1 coin, but not as thick.

The Aire Services 3/3 token is the same both sides with 3 grooves on each. It is the same size as a 10p piece.

The front of the Euro Relais (ER) token is branded. It is slightly bigger than a 10p piece.

 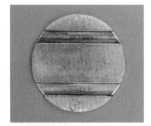

The 2/1 token has one groove on the front and 2 on the back. It is the size of a 2p piece.

Unusually expensive card payment.

Techno Money (TM) has a distinctive pattern on the front. It is the same size as a 10p piece.

CUSTOM SERVICE POINTS

Half of the Service Points in France have been custom-built by local craftsmen with inevitable differences in design and construction. Most are simple but durable and electricity is rarely provided. This has several benefits; they are rarely broken, they normally have a ground level drain, they don't require tokens and are normally free to use all year round. Sometimes the layout of a Service Point is confusing or a facility is a little way from where you expect it to be. Occasionally instructions state that cassettes should be emptied in the adjacent public toilet. However, we have seen more signs stating that cassettes must not be emptied in public toilets.

Euro Relais and Raclet: Euro Relais and Raclet are the same. All Raclet units are at least 12 years old. Euro Relais has manufactured various sizes, but they are all basically the same. In general they are easy to use, but are often in a bad state of repair. Intentional damage is common on unsupervised units that take tokens or coins. Often there are two water taps. The one for toilet rinsing normally works without payment. The toilet tap is usually marked 'Eau non potable' for hygiene reasons, but it is in fact plumbed to the same supply. When tokens or payment is required, 100 litres of water and one hour of electricity is dispensed. A lift up cover at the base enables access to the toilet emptying chamber. The hole is big enough to lose the cap from your Thetford cassette.

Mini

Junior stainless steel

Maxi

Box

Stainless steel

White plastic

Aire Services: The Aire Services brand of Service Point functions in much the same way as Euro Relais units, but is a little more confusing due to the press button operation. The robust stainless steel units are common and normally charge a fee. Credit card payment is the norm for new units. The plastic units are generally free, and thus are less likely to be damaged. Pay units generally have one or two CEE electricity points and all have fresh water and toilet rinsing taps. A small WC disposal drain is located at the front. Water is normally distributed for 10 minutes and electricity for 55 minutes. Waste water is usually disposed of in a separate drain.

Concrete

Electricity

BRANDED SERVICE POINTS

Urba Flux: Urba Flux Tall are becoming more common each year, especially for barrier entry or parking ticket payment. The Service Points are simple and robust units that distribute water and electricity. Toilet and waste water is usually disposed of in drains at the base.

Urba Flux

Tall

Barrier

Photo: John Watts

Male hozelock connector required

Euro, Pacific, Station Sanitaire

Flot Bleu inside

Flot Bleu: There are several models in the range but only two designs. Mostly they are blue, but they can also be green, white or burgundy. Fontaine, Océane and Marine units have all the services fitted to the outside of the casing. Fontaine units are free, the others take payment by coin or token.

Euro, Pacific and Station Sanitare have services located behind a narrow door on the left-hand side of the cabinet. These units are rarely free but are very robust and are likely to be in service during winter. Euro units always take bank card payment, the others will be coin or token. These cabinets are also used to distribute tokens and operate barrier systems.

Electricity

Fontaine, Océane, Marine

Point Belle Eau

SOS

Bollard. These are old.

Signs

There are numerous signs which apply to motorhomes and should be adhered to.

Motorhomes are not allowed.

STATIONNEMENT
RÉSERVÉ AU
CAMPING-CARS
LIMITÉ À 48H
DÉBALLAGE
NON AUTORISÉ

Designated parking, no unpacking.

LIMITÉ
À 48 HEURES
LIMITED
TO 48 HOURS
7 PLACES

SAUF
CAMPING-CAR

Clearway except motorhomes.

Barrier entry systems

As previously discussed it has become necessary to control motorhome parking at popular destinations. Local authorities have taken to installing barriered entries and, to a lesser extent, rising bollards at both existing and new Aires. We have frequently observed that entering and exiting is often slow or impossible. Our greatest concern is that there is no emergency override should a fire break out. We have also observed that controlled entry systems are often broken, left in the open position or removed within a year or two.

Camping Car Park (Camping-Car-Park.com) is a new breed of commercial Aire. In December 2014 they had 36 Aires, all of which were barrier operated. These are referred to as PARKNIGHT barriers. There is a membership pre pay scheme that is explained at the barrier. There is also a helpline number. Be aware that the included electricity may only be two electric points at the Service Point. Instructions say these are intended for 1hrs battery charging.

Flot Bleu sentries

Oh bollards

Camping Car Park Chatellion Plage

Camping Car Park La Cavalerie

Navarrosse

ATLANTIC

St Pey d'Armens

BUSSEROLLES | 1 | F8 | 24360 | N45°40.620' E000°38.577'

Directions: D90. Just off D90 in centre of village adj to bar, signed.

ℹ️ Bar adj. Numerous walking trails from 5km. Pleasant spot away from the madding crowd. Inspected 2013.

🚐 5

⛽ Euro Relais Junior; Token (2/1)

ST FRONT LA RIVIERE | 2 | F8 | 24300 | N45°27.983' E000°43.450'

Directions: D83. From south on D83 Aire is on left at picnic area approximately 500m past Le Caneau going towards Saint Front la Rivière, signed.

ℹ️ Pleasant place overlooking grassy picnic area. Inspected 2013.

🚐 10; Max 72hrs; Apr-Oct

⛽ Euro Relais Junior; 2 unmetered CEE elec points

ST ESTEPHE | 3 | F8 | ☀ | 24360 | N45°35.368' E000°40.480'

Directions: C201. In St Estèphe turn off D88 onto C201, sp 'Augignac' and 'Le Grand Étang'. Follow road to lake. Service Point in 2nd car parking bay, signed. Motorhome parking: N45°35.684' E000°40.447'. Off C201, sp 'Stade'. Follow road past campsite to parking on right.

ℹ️ Service Point only adj to large leisure lake. Inspected 2012.

🚐 7; Motorhomes banned 8pm-8am

⛽ Custom

NONTRON | 4 | F8 | 24300 | N45°32.167' E000°40.000'

Directions: Ave Jules Ferry, off D675. From D675 turn onto Ave Jules Ferry, sp 'Super U' and signed. At roundabout turn left into Super U. Service Point in middle of car park facing the shop. Access may be difficult in peak shopping hours.

ℹ️ Supermarket adj. Self-service laundry on D675, 2 mins, open every day. Inspected 2013.

🚐 Poss

⛽ Euro Relais Junior; €2

JUMILHAC LE GRAND | 5 | F8 | 24630 | N45°29.525' E001°03.665'

Directions: D78. From château in village take D78, sp 'Thiviers'. Service Point on the right in 100m.

ℹ️ Large château, cafés and TO in village. No parking at Service Point, but poss to park near château. Inspected 2013.

🚐 Poss; Near château

⛽ Custom

ST JEAN DE COLE | 6 | F8 | 24800 | N45°25.185' E000°50.433'

Directions: Le Bourg. Turn off D707 south of village by Mairie, sp 'St Martin de Fs'. Turn left in 20m, just past tennis courts, signed.

ℹ️ Pretty Beau Village. Rural views from Aire. Local commerce 2 mins. Inspected 2013.

🚐 5

⛽ Euro Relais Junior; Token (ER); €2

LA COQUILLE — 7 — F8 — 24450 — N45°32.562' E000°58.689'

Directions: Place St Jacques de Compostelle. From south on N21 turn 1st right after traffic lights into Place St Jacques de Compostelle. Drive past front of church and Service Point on right-hand side at bottom of car park.

i Village with local commerce 100m. Very little level parking. Bells signal every quarter hour throughout day. Inspected 2013.

4; Very sloping

Euro Relais Mini; Landscaped; Risk of grounding

LANOUAILLE — 8 — F8 — 24270 — N45°23.533' E001°08.417'

Directions: D75. Exit village to east on D75, sp 'Pompadour' and signed. Aire 150m on left, signed.

i Small town commerce 1 min. Fire station adj. Market at Aire Tues am. Inspected 2013.

5; Max 48hrs

Euro Relais Junior; 2 unmetered CEE elec points; 2 drive over drains

HAUTEFORT — 9 — F8 — ☼ — 24390 — N45°15.607' E001°08.937'

Directions: Allées du Avril 1944, off D72. Drive into Hautefort on D62. Turn onto D72 just past château at square with TO, sp 'Flot Bleu'. Aire on left.

i At beautiful hilltop town dominated by impressive château. Worth a visit. Inspected 2013.

5

Flot Bleu Pacific

EXCIDEUIL — 10 — F8 — 24160 — N45°20.157' E001°03.157'

Directions: Allée André Maurois, off D705. Approach from Périgueux on D705. At the roundabout take 1st exit onto D705, sp 'Dussac'. Turn 1st right at statue of man. Aire in car park immediately on right.

i In town with imposing fortified château. May change due to adj building work. Inspected 2013.

4; €3/night; Collected

Urba Flux; 4 unmetered CEE elec points

PAYZAC — 11 — F8 — 24270 — N45°24.004' E001°13.171'

Directions: Rue du Parc. Turn off D75 in the centre of village opp the Credit Agricole bank. Turn 1st left for the Service Point which is located behind the Hôtel de Ville, not signed.

i Local commerce 100m. Children's play area close by. Large leisure lake with swimming and water sports 5km. Inspected 2013.

3

Euro Relais Junior; 2 unmetered CEE elec points

ANGOISSE — 12 — F8 — 24270 — N45°24.778' E001°10.072'

Directions: D80e1. From either Angoisse or Payzac follow D80, sp 'Base de Loisirs de Roufflac'. Turn off D80 onto D80e1, sp 'Base de Loisirs de Roufflac'. Take 1st turning on left, signed. Service Point in far corner (looks like a bin), signed.

i At leisure lake, 2 mins downhill, with swimming, drag water skiing and restaurant. May feel isolated out of season. Inspected 2013.

20; Max 48hrs

Custom

| AZERAT | 13 | F9 | | 24210 | N45°08.970' E001°07.512' |

Directions: Turn off D6089 in Azerat towards the church, signed. Follow road around church and turn left past Mairie, signed. Aire in car park beside/behind Mairie.

i Aire located in a small, pleasant village away from main road noise. Views over tennis courts and swimming pool. Inspected 2012.

🚐 10; €2/night; Honesty box

🛒 Custom; €3; Honesty box

| THENON | 14 | F9 | | 24210 | N45°08.459' E001°04.063' |

Directions: D6089. Service Point at the Carrefour supermarked adj to D6089. Parking on opp side of road behind the Credit Agricole bank: N45°08.491' E001°04.114'.

i Supermarket and local commerce adj. The parking is just off D6089, but the buildings screen the road noise. Rural views. Inspected 2012.

🚐 10; Sheltered from road noise

🛒 Euro Relais Box; Token (ER)

| VERGT | 15 | F9 | | 24380 | N45°01.350' E000°42.634' |

Directions: D8. From centre exit on D8, sp 'Bergerac'. Turn off D8 just before Intermarché supermarket entrance. Service Point on left adj to supermarket car park, signed.

i Supermarket adj. Inspected 2012.

🚐 Poss

🛒 Urba Flux Tall; €2

| ST LEON SUR VEZERE | 16 | F9 | | 24290 | N45°00.730' E001°05.369' |

Directions: Le Bourg. From D706 take D66 into St Léon sur Vézère. Turn 1st right, signed, and follow single track road for 400m. Aire on right, signed.

i Beau Village with TO, 1 min along river. Good facilities and restaurants. Inspected 2013.

🚐 10; €5/8pm-8am May-Sept; Free 8am-8pm

🛒 Euro Relais Mini; Token; €2; Showers €1.50

| HAVE YOU VISITED AN AIRE? | **GPS co-ordinates in this guide are protected by copyright law** |

Visit www.all-the-aires.co.uk/submissions.shtml
to upload your updates and photos.

Submit updates
• Amendments
• New Aires
• Not changed

i Directions and description.

🚐 Number of parking spaces; Cost per night; Time limit
🛒 Service Point type and details; Payment type; Cost

Take at least 5 digital photos showing
• Signs
• Service Point
• Parking
• Overview
• Amenities

| MONTIGNAC 1 | 18 | F9 | | 24290 | N45°03.668' E001°09.548' |

Directions: Avenue Aristide Briand/D65. Follow one-way street past Montignac 2. At crossroads turn left, sp 'Sarlat' and signed. Cross river bridge and turn right onto D65, sp 'Sergeac' and signed. Follow road along river for 400m and Aire on right, signed. Whole town is one-way system, can only approach this way or on D65.

i River Vézère adj. Town commerce 500m. Market Wed am. Outdoor swimming pool adj. Inspected 2010.

🚐 15

🛒 Custom

MONTIGNAC 2 | 19 | F9 | 24290 | N45°04.067' E001°09.883'

Directions: Rue des Sanges. Turn off D704 bypass at traffic lights, sp 'Montignac-Centre', 'Les Eyzies' and signed. Enter town on D704e2 one-way system. In 200m turn left, sp 'P Vieux Quartiers' and signed. Parking to left at end of road in gravel area.

ℹ️ Town 100m with local commerce. Canoe hire by river, 200m. Market Wed. Inspected 2013.

🚐 20; €3/8pm-8am inc elec; CC; Pay at machine

🔧 None; See 18

SALIGNAC EYVIGUES | 20 | F9 | 24590 | N44°58.361' E001°19.238'

Directions: Rue des Écoles. Exit village on D61, sp 'Simeyrols'. Take the 1st turning on the right. Aire in car park on right.

ℹ️ Aire adj to school so can be very busy and noisy. Far field used for school sports and football. Town centre with local commerce and supermarket 2 mins. Inspected 2012.

🚐 10; Max 2 nights

🔧 Custom

GPS Co-ordinates for SatNav

The GPS Co-ordinates published in this guide were taken onsite by our inspectors. We consider them a valuable and unique asset and at the time of publishing have decided not to publish them as electronic files for use on navigation devices. You have permission to type in the co-ordinates of an Aire you intend to visit but not to store or share them. For the security of our copyright:

- **Do not compile them into lists**

- **Do not publish, share or reproduce them anywhere in any format**

STE ALVERE | 22 | F9 | 24510 | N44°56.705' E000°48.301'

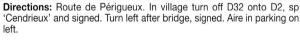

Directions: Route de Périgueux. In village turn off D32 onto D2, sp 'Cendrieux' and signed. Turn left after bridge, signed. Aire in parking on left.

ℹ️ Pleasant location adj to sports facilities on edge of the village. Local commerce 2 mins. Custom Service Point and elec points replaced by Euro Relais Box. Inspected 2012.

🚐 5

🔧 Euro Relais Box; Token (ER); €2.50

LES EYZIES DE TAYAC | 23 | F9 | T | 24620 | N44°56.325' E001°00.552'

Directions: Promenade de la Vézère, off D47. Turn off D47 in village, sp 'Pde la Vézère'. Follow road to right and under railway bridge. Aire at end of car park on right, signed.

ℹ️ Tourist commerce and restaurants 2 mins. Near prehistory museum. Grotte de Font de Gaume and Musée de l'Abri Pataud worth a visit. Inspected 2013.

🚐 25; €5/24hrs; Collected

🔧 Raclet; €2

LE BUGUE | 24 | F9 | 24260 | N44°54.980' E000°55.577'

Directions: Place Léopold Salme, off D31e. Exit town on D31e, sp 'Fumel'. After crossing river bridge turn left by Credit Agricole bank, signed. Aire signed in 50m. Gravel/grass parking adj to river. For Service Point follow road along river edge, then turn right: N44°54.976' E000°55.706'.

ℹ️ Parking under trees on hardstanding or on open grass when dry. Town commerce 100m, older part of town across river. Inspected 2013.

🚐 100; €7/night; Pay at machine; Max 72hrs

🔧 Custom

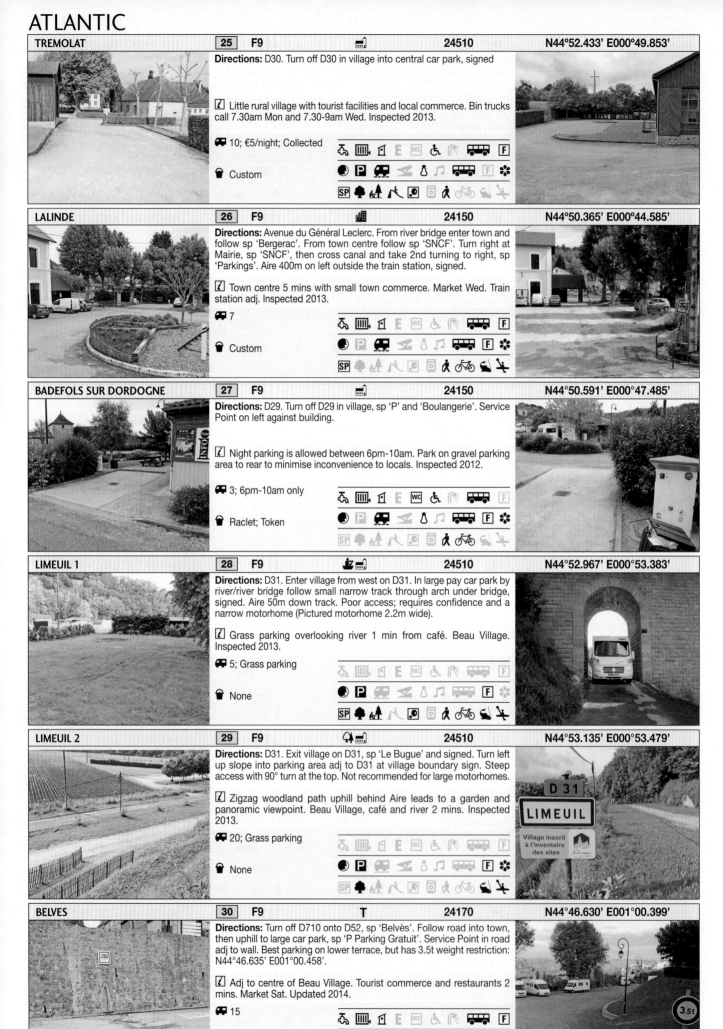

| TREMOLAT | 25 | F9 | | 24510 | N44°52.433' E000°49.853' |

Directions: D30. Turn off D30 in village into central car park, signed

i Little rural village with tourist facilities and local commerce. Bin trucks call 7.30am Mon and 7.30-9am Wed. Inspected 2013.

10; €5/night; Collected

Custom

| LALINDE | 26 | F9 | | 24150 | N44°50.365' E000°44.585' |

Directions: Avenue du Général Leclerc. From river bridge enter town and follow sp 'Bergerac'. From town centre follow sp 'SNCF'. Turn right at Mairie, sp 'SNCF', then cross canal and take 2nd turning to right, sp 'Parkings'. Aire 400m on left outside the train station, signed.

i Town centre 5 mins with small town commerce. Market Wed. Train station adj. Inspected 2013.

7

Custom

| BADEFOLS SUR DORDOGNE | 27 | F9 | | 24150 | N44°50.591' E000°47.485' |

Directions: D29. Turn off D29 in village, sp 'P' and 'Boulangerie'. Service Point on left against building.

i Night parking is allowed between 6pm-10am. Park on gravel parking area to rear to minimise inconvenience to locals. Inspected 2012.

3; 6pm-10am only

Raclet; Token

| LIMEUIL 1 | 28 | F9 | | 24510 | N44°52.967' E000°53.383' |

Directions: D31. Enter village from west on D31. In large pay car park by river/river bridge follow small narrow track through arch under bridge, signed. Aire 50m down track. Poor access; requires confidence and a narrow motorhome (Pictured motorhome 2.2m wide).

i Grass parking overlooking river 1 min from café. Beau Village. Inspected 2013.

5; Grass parking

None

| LIMEUIL 2 | 29 | F9 | | 24510 | N44°53.135' E000°53.479' |

Directions: D31. Exit village on D31, sp 'Le Bugue' and signed. Turn left up slope into parking area adj to D31 at village boundary sign. Steep access with 90° turn at the top. Not recommended for large motorhomes.

i Zigzag woodland path uphill behind Aire leads to a garden and panoramic viewpoint. Beau Village, café and river 2 mins. Inspected 2013.

20; Grass parking

None

| BELVES | 30 | F9 | T | 24170 | N44°46.630' E001°00.399' |

Directions: Turn off D710 onto D52, sp 'Belvès'. Follow road into town, then uphill to large car park, sp 'P Parking Gratuit'. Service Point in road adj to wall. Best parking on lower terrace, but has 3.5t weight restriction: N44°46.635' E001°00.458'.

i Adj to centre of Beau Village. Tourist commerce and restaurants 2 mins. Market Sat. Updated 2014.

15

Custom; Adj to road

ST CYPRIEN 1 — 31 — F9 — 24220 — N44°52.102' E001°02.663'

Directions: Rue du Priolat. Turn off D703 onto D49, sp 'Siorac'. At the roundabout turn right onto C201, sp 'Meyrals'. Aire on left in 300m, signed.

ⓘ Town commerce 1 min. Laundry at Carrefour on D703. Inspected 2013.

🚐 8; Max 24hrs

🚰 Euro Relais Mini; Token (ER); 8 elec points; 1 Token/12hrs elec; €3.50

ST CYPRIEN 2 — 32 — F9 — 24220 — N44°51.789' E001°02.430'

Directions: D703/Voie de Vallée, at Carrefour supermarket just southwest of town adj to D703.

ⓘ Supermarket and stores, laundry, pizza kiosk and tapas restaurant. Free WiFi. Inspected 2013.

🚐 Poss

🚰 Flot Bleu Marine; €2; No drive over drain or toilet emptying

LA ROQUE GAGEAC — 33 — F9 — T — 24250 — N44°49.500' E001°11.017'

Directions: Parking Place Publique, off D703. Aire in large car park at eastern end of village centre, adj to river. Large motorhomes will have difficulty accessing car park if full.

ⓘ Busy Aire adj to River Dordogne with boat trips and kayak hire. Views of cliffs with Troglodyte fort. Beau Village with tourist commerce/restaurants. Inspected 2013.

🚐 20; €7/7pm-noon; €3 day parking; Pay at machine; Max 10m

🚰 Raclet; €2

MONTFORT (VITRAC) — 34 — F9 — 24200 — N44°50.125' E001°14.912'

Directions: D703. Turn off D703 on west side of village, sp 'Aire Camping-Car'. Follow road and Aire on right in 200m.

ⓘ Shaded parking adj to village with imposing château. Touristy area and poss to hire canoes in season in Beynac-et-Cazenac. Inspected 2012.

🚐 15

🚰 Euro Relais Junior; Token (ER)

DOMME — 35 — F9 — T — 24250 — N44°48.050' E001°13.300'

Directions: Le Pradal, off D46e. From D703, D46 or D50 follow blue coach/motorhome signs (not GPS). Follow signs to D50, then D46e for 8km. This route is well signed and motorhomes are banned from entering the town.

ⓘ Rural views. 500m from centre of hilltop Beau Village. Some parts of original fortified walls and gateways remain; Gateways became prisons in 14th century, can be visited all year. Inspected 2013.

🚐 20; €5/night (from 6pm); Pay at machine; Free day parking; Apr-Nov

🚰 Euro Relais Junior; €2

SARLAT LA CANEDA — 36 — F9 — 24200 — N44°53.747' E001°12.747'

Directions: Place Flandres Dunkerque 1940, on D704. From north on D704 go right at roundabout as enter town, sp 'Camping-Car'. Aire immediately on right in car park, signed.

ⓘ Town 15 mins, large market Sat. Constant road noise. Boulangerie adj. Popular with French motorhomers. Inspected 2013.

🚐 20; €7/24hrs; €15/48hrs; Pay at machine; 2hrs free

🚰 Euro Relais Junior; €2

STE NATHALENE

37 | **F9** | ⛺ | **24200** | **N44°54.788' E001°15.902'**

Directions: From Ste Nathanlene follow sp 'Camping de Maillac' through the lanes. Aire at campsite.

ℹ️ Aire at campsite entrance. Shop and swimming pool adj. Campsite in a very rural location. Inspected 2012.

🚐 4; €12/night Jun-Sept; €10/night Oct-May; Collected

🛢️ Euro Relais Mini; €5

MONPAZIER

38 | **F9** | **T** | **24540** | **N44°41.107' E000°53.619'**

Directions: Between D53 and D660. Turn off D660 onto D53 in town centre, sp 'Belvès' and signed. Turn 1st left onto 3.5t weight restricted road, then 1st right, signed. Aire at rear of Sapeurs Pompiers (fire station), signed.

ℹ️ Bastide Beau Village 500m. Inspected 2013.

🚐 7

🛢️ Custom

BEAUMONT DE PERIGORD

39 | **F9** | 🔒 | **24440** | **N44°46.479' E000°45.937'**

Directions: D660. Approach on D660 from north. Turn left as enter Beaumont du Périgord, sp 'Salle des Fêtes' and signed. Aire behind Salle des Fêtes building.

ℹ️ This is a large parking area located just off a main trunking route but is always likely to have space. Inspected 2012.

🚐 10

🛢️ Flot Bleu Fontaine

BIRON

40 | **F9** | 🔒 | **24540** | **N44°37.843' E000°52.247'**

Directions: C203. In village turn off D53 onto C203, sp 'Vergt de Biron'. Aire in car park on left as exit village.

ℹ️ Pleasant Aire with rural views and views of château, 5 mins. Market Wed am. Inspected 2013.

🚐 10

🛢️ Flot Bleu Pacific; Token (3/3); €2

ST SAUVEUR DE BERGERAC

41 | **E9** | 🔒 | **24520** | **N44°52.112' E000°35.289'**

Directions: Route de la Rafraigne. Turn off D21, main route through, into car park past Mairie, signed.

ℹ️ Located in a small, sloping car park in the village centre. Limited local commerce 1 min. Dordogne river nearby. Inspected 2012.

🚐 3; 7m bays

🛢️ Custom

MONBAZILLAC

42 | **E9** | 🔒 | **24240** | **N44°47.321' E000°29.751'**

Directions: D13. Follow D13 through village following sp 'Domaine de la Lande'. Aire at vineyard adj to D13, sp 'Domaine de la Lande' and signed.

ℹ️ Views across vines. Motorhomers are welcomed for an aperitif (wine tasting) at 6pm, lasts up to 1hr. Deliveries are made at 8.30 each morning, except Sun. Inspected 2013.

🚐 5; Grass parking

🛢️ Custom

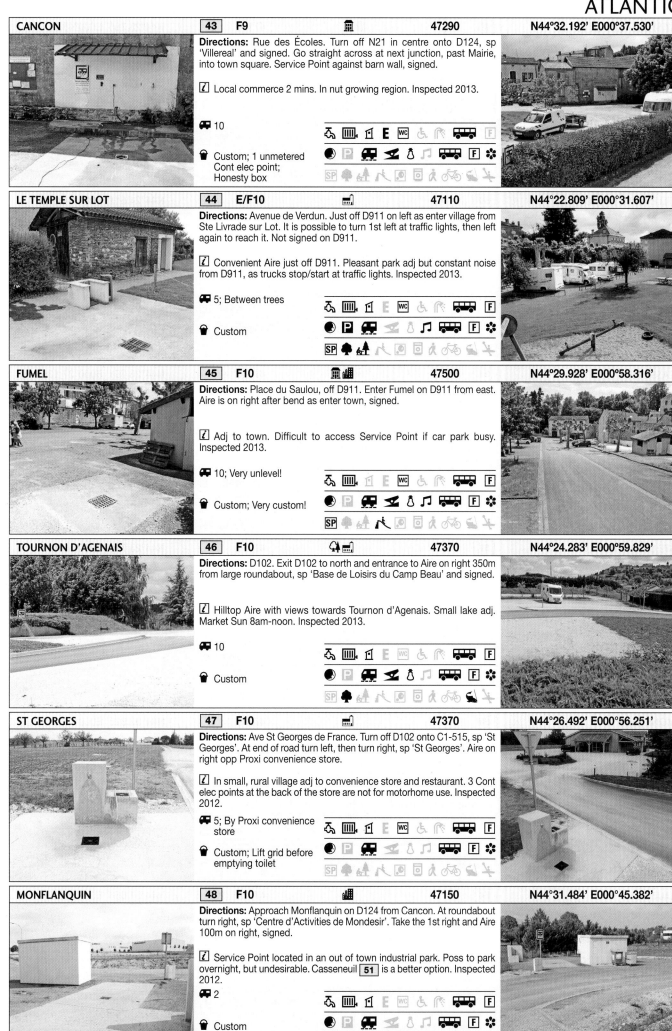

CANCON	43	F9		47290	N44°32.192' E000°37.530'

Directions: Rue des Écoles. Turn off N21 in centre onto D124, sp 'Villereal' and signed. Go straight across at next junction, past Mairie, into town square. Service Point against barn wall, signed.

ⓘ Local commerce 2 mins. In nut growing region. Inspected 2013.

🚐 10

⛲ Custom; 1 unmetered Cont elec point; Honesty box

LE TEMPLE SUR LOT	44	E/F10		47110	N44°22.809' E000°31.607'

Directions: Avenue de Verdun. Just off D911 on left as enter village from Ste Livrade sur Lot. It is possible to turn 1st left at traffic lights, then left again to reach it. Not signed on D911.

ⓘ Convenient Aire just off D911. Pleasant park adj but constant noise from D911, as trucks stop/start at traffic lights. Inspected 2013.

🚐 5; Between trees

⛲ Custom

FUMEL	45	F10		47500	N44°29.928' E000°58.316'

Directions: Place du Saulou, off D911. Enter Fumel on D911 from east. Aire is on right after bend as enter town, signed.

ⓘ Adj to town. Difficult to access Service Point if car park busy. Inspected 2013.

🚐 10; Very unlevel!

⛲ Custom; Very custom!

TOURNON D'AGENAIS	46	F10		47370	N44°24.283' E000°59.829'

Directions: D102. Exit D102 to north and entrance to Aire on right 350m from large roundabout, sp 'Base de Loisirs du Camp Beau' and signed.

ⓘ Hilltop Aire with views towards Tournon d'Agenais. Small lake adj. Market Sun 8am-noon. Inspected 2013.

🚐 10

⛲ Custom

ST GEORGES	47	F10		47370	N44°26.492' E000°56.251'

Directions: Ave St Georges de France. Turn off D102 onto C1-515, sp 'St Georges'. At end of road turn left, then turn right, sp 'St Georges'. Aire on right opp Proxi convenience store.

ⓘ In small, rural village adj to convenience store and restaurant. 3 Cont elec points at the back of the store are not for motorhome use. Inspected 2012.

🚐 5; By Proxi convenience store

⛲ Custom; Lift grid before emptying toilet

MONFLANQUIN	48	F10		47150	N44°31.484' E000°45.382'

Directions: Approach Monflanquin on D124 from Cancon. At roundabout turn right, sp 'Centre d'Activities de Mondesir'. Take the 1st right and Aire 100m on right, signed.

ⓘ Service Point located in an out of town industrial park. Poss to park overnight, but undesirable. Casseneuil 51 is a better option. Inspected 2012.

🚐 2

⛲ Custom

ST SYLVESTRE SUR LOT
49 F10 47140 N44°23.765' E000°48.281'

Directions: Rue Jean Moulin. Access from D103 or D911. Turn off D103 between D911 and river bridge. Aire behind Intermarché, designated parking by green space. Service Point by fuel station at: N44°23.733' E000°48.333'.

[i] Intermarché adj. Town 2 mins. Nice deep spaces for big motorhomes. River Lot 100m. Riverside walking path. Market Wed am. Inspected 2013.

🚐 20

🔓 Custom

VILLENEUVE SUR LOT
50 F10 47300 N44°24.511' E000°44.062'

Directions: D911. Enter town on D911 from Fumel. Service Point in E'Leclerc fuel station in retail park on right. Drive through 24/24 fuel pumps to access.

[i] Supermarket and commerce adj. Inspected 2012.

🚐 Poss

🔓 Aire Services

CASSENEUIL
51 F10 47440 N44°26.791' E000°37.136'

Directions: Place St Pierre. Exit town on D133, sp 'Cancon' and signed. At roundabout take D225, sp 'P Tourisme'. Aire immediately on left in P Tourisme car park, opp cemetery before village exit, signed.

[i] Pleasant parking on edge of town overlooking river. Town centre with local commerce 2 mins across river. Inspected 2012.

🚐 15

🔓 Custom

STE LIVRADE SUR LOT
52 F10 47110 N44°23.760' E000°35.490'

Directions: Place du Lieutenant Colonel Jean-François Calas. From south on D113 turn right at roundabout with Casino supermarket down 3.5t weight restricted road lined with plane trees, sp 'Trésor Public', 'Sapeurs Pompiers' and signed. Aire at end of road, past Terres du Sud.

[i] 2 mins to town. Aire backs onto old railway station building. Voie Verte cycle path adj. Inspected 2013.

🚐 5

🔓 Custom

MONBAHUS
53 E9 47290 N44°32.825' E000°32.101'

Directions: Rue du Château d'Eau. Turn off D124 in village centre to view point, signed. Drive up very steep, single lane hill. Aire in car park just past footpath to view point. There is very little space to turn around at top, so will be difficult for large motorhomes.

[i] Superb 360° view with interpretation 1 min uphill via footpath. Village with local commerce 2 mins downhill. Inspected 2013.

🚐 2

🔓 Custom; 2 unmetered CEE elec points (Not working)

LAUZUN
54 E9 47410 N44°37.658' E000°27.589'

Directions: Rue St Colomb. Turn off D1 at village boundary, sp 'Camping'. Follow road around past sports facilities and campsite and take the 1st turning on the left. Parking on left just before village, signed.

[i] Adj to lake and recreational area. Village centre 1 min, dominated by château, with local commerce and restaurants. Inspected 2012.

🚐 2; Max 48hrs; 7m bays

🔓 Custom; Water tap and toilets only

ST PARDOUX ISAAC | 55 | E9 | 47800 | N44°36.816' E000°21.585'

Directions: C201, at Intermarché. Exit Miramont-de-Guyenne to north on D933 and turn right onto C201, sp 'St Pardoux Isaac' and 'Intermarché'. Aire on right adj to car wash at Intermarché supermarket.

i Supermarket, fuel station and self-service laundry. Inspected 2013.

Poss

Custom

DURAS | 56 | E9 | 47120 | N44°40.678' E000°10.639'

Directions: From south on D708 follow road around village, passing château. Turn next left into C6 and follow road downhill. After 150m fork left, sp 'Aire de Camping-Car' and 'Camping Municipal'. Aire before campsite entrance.

i Campsite open May-Aug, no services or toilets rest of year. Château adj. Updated 2014.

9; €7/night May-Aug

Custom; Only when campsite open; 12 elec points

PORT STE FOY ET PONCHAPT | 57 | E9 | 33220 | N44°50.532' E000°12.547'

Directions: From west on D936 go straight over roundabout onto D936e2, sp 'Port Ste Foy et Ponchapt'. Cross railway, then go straight over 2nd roundabout onto D708, signed. Turn right before traffic lights, signed. Service Point is straight on: N44°50.513' E000°12.463'. For parking turn left, then right by church, signed.

i Adj to river, partial views. Wine/boat museum 1 min. Ste-Foy 5 mins over river bridge with town commerce. Riverside walk adj along Dordogne. Inspected 2013.

4; Marked bays

Custom

PELLEGRUE | 58 | E9 | 33790 | N44°44.694' E000°04.483'

Directions: D16e/Rue du Lavoir. Clearly signed at the D15/D16 crossroads north of town. Signed from all directions.

i Aire in small lay-by adj to old wash house and peaceful village road. Town 5 mins. Inspected 2012.

4

Raclet; 2 unmetered CEE elec points

MONSEGUR | 59 | E9 | 33580 | N44°39.056' E000°05.038'

Directions: Ave Porte des Tours. From east turn off D668 as enter town and go straight on as main road bears left, sp 'Centre Ville' and 'Halte Camping-Car'. Turn 1st left opp park. Service Point to right and parking at end, signed. Do not attempt to drive through town.

i Park with view over town. Interesting covered market. Town 2 mins. Inspected 2013.

5; Max 48hrs

Custom

LA REOLE | 60 | E9 | 33190 | N44°34.847' W000°01.815'

Directions: D1113. From town centre head east on D1113, sp 'Langon'. Aire on right by small, round tower, signed.

i Town 10 mins with local commerce. View point adj. Some road noise. Inspected 2013.

10; €4/night Jun-Sept; Collected; Grass parking

Custom

FONTET | 61 | E9 | 33190 | N44°33.721' W000°01.406'

Directions: Halte Nautique. Turn off D9 onto D9e6, sp 'Fontet' and 'Base de Loisirs Halte Nautique'. Follow road and turn left, sp 'Base de Loisirs Halte Nautique'. Follow lane to end and turn left, then immediately right. Park outside gate and enquire for entry.

i Directly adj to canal basin at marina. Swimming lake. Restaurant. Ideal long stay base. Inspected 2013.

10; €9/night inc elec; €200/month; €250/Oct-Mar; Pay at marina
Custom; Showers €1

MARMANDE 1 | 62 | E9 | 47200 | N44°29.904' E000°09.626'

Directions: Place du Moulin. From south exit D933 at roundabout onto D933e1, sp 'Marmande-Centre Ville'. Cross river and turn right at traffic lights, signed. Follow road past river and after 225m turn left into Quai des Capucins. Service Point immediately on right, signed.

i Motorhomes are only allowed to park here Nov-Mar, see | 63 |. Inspected 2013.

Nov-March only

Custom

MARMANDE 2 | 63 | E9 | 47200 | N44°29.696' E000°09.769'

Directions: From south exit D933 at roundabout onto D933e1, sp 'Marmande-Centre Ville'. Cross river and turn right at traffic lights, signed. Follow road past river and after 330m turn right, sp 'Aire Camping Car Filhole', and follow road past height barriered car parks. At roundabout turn right into Route de la Filhole, signed. Aire at end of road on left just before barrier.

i Aire on old campsite in pleasant woodland setting. Pony rides and cycle hire avail on site. 5 mins to town. Inspected 2013.

36; €8 inc 16amp elec; Collected; Apr-Oct; Grass parking
Custom; Inc

PONT DES SABLES | 64 | E10 | 47200 | N44°27.657' E000°08.334'

Directions: D933, at Emeraude Navigation. From Marmande drive 3.5km south on D933 and Aire on left immediately over canal bridge.

i Right beside canal but lots of road noise. Bike and canoe hire adj. Inspected 2013.

2; Very unlevel

Custom

CAUMONT SUR GARONNE ★ | 65 | E10 | 47430 | N44°26.506' E000°10.781'

Directions: D143, on right by canal as enter the village from north on D143. Cross canal bridge and Aire on right on hairpin bend. Access made difficult by canal bridge and trees, best to reverse in.

i Beautiful location overlooking canal. Village adj. Pizza van Wed and Fri pm. Inspected 2013.

12

Custom; €1; 6 elec points; €1/2hrs elec

VILLETON | 66 | E10 | 47400 | N44°21.844' E000°16.376'

Directions: D120, by river bridge. Aire located behind Mairie at small marina, sp 'Musée de la Mémoire Paysanne', 'Aire Camping Car', and 'Restaurant la Fluviale'.

i Canal adj, no views. Pizza restaurant and museum (€4pp) adj. Pay shower. Inspected 2013.

4

Flot Bleu Fontaine; €2; 4 elec points; Elec €2

STE BAZEILLE | 67 | E9 | | 47180 | N44°31.670' E000°06.178'

Directions: D813. Turn off D813 at roundabout as exit town towards Marmande. Service Point behind the fuel station and car wash at the Super U supermarket, signed.

ℹ️ Supermarket adj. Self-service laundry adj. Inspected 2013.

🚐 Poss

🚰 Euro Relais Mini; €2

Photo: Janet & John Watts

CASTELJALOUX | 68 | E10 | | 47700 | N44°18.657' E000°04.760'

Directions: Rue de St Michel. From D933 turn off south of town onto D291, sp 'St Michel de Castelnau' and signed. Aire 120m on left.

ℹ️ 10 mins to thermal town centre. E'Leclerc supermarket 1 min. Aire advertised at Lac les Clarens is a holiday village charging €10/night: N44°17.567' E000°04.416'. Inspected 2013.

🚐 4; Max 48hrs

🚰 Custom

BUZET SUR BAISE | 69 | E10 | | 47160 | N44°15.473' E000°18.329'

Directions: D12, at Port de Buzet. From village follow sp 'Port Fluval' and 'Aquataine Navigation'. Aire at Port de Buzet. Parking with permission, call at office. Parking on grass or car park.

ℹ️ Former tolerated parking turned Aire at pleasure marina. Inspected 2013.

🚐 15; €7/night; Collected

🚰 Euro Relais Box; Token

MONTETON | 70 | E9 | | 47120 | N44°37.377' E000°15.407'

Directions: D423. Aire just off D423 as enter village from north, signed. Service Point past recycling bins.

ℹ️ Adj to pleasant hilltop village. No designated parking but motorhomes parked on grass at time of inspection. Inspected 2012.

🚐 5; Grass parking

🚰 Raclet; 1 unmetered CEE elec point (Not working)

CASTELCULIER | 71 | F10 | | 47240 | N44°10.488' E000°41.680'

Directions: Rue du Champ de Baze. From N113 turn onto D215. Take 4th left (at roundabout) and then 1st right to Aire, signed. 3.5t weight restriction.

ℹ️ Pleasant Aire in small town with local commerce. Agen town has every possible commerce avail in easy to access retail parks. Inspected 2013.

🚐 2 adj; Other parking avail

🚰 Custom; Token; €2; Tap has been removed

LAYRAC | 72 | F10 | | 47390 | N44°07.938' E000°39.573'

Directions: Rue du 19 Mars 1962, off N21. Turn off N21 at traffic-lighted junction opp D17 down road beside war memorial (rusty metal cross), signed. Then turn right, signed. Aire on left, signed.

ℹ️ Although there are 5 bays, some will be too small for most motorhomes. Small town commerce 1 min. Market Friday am. Inspected 2013.

🚐 5; Max 3 days

🚰 Custom

NERAC | 73 | E10 | 🏛 | 47600 | N44°08.040' E000°20.134'

Directions: Boulevard Jean Darlan. Turn off D930 in town centre at traffic lights onto D656, sp 'Mézin'. At next traffic lights turn left, sp 'P du Foirail (Gratuit)'. Aire on far side of barns, on left, signed.

ⓘ Large car park/exhibition area. Supermarket adj. Town commerce 2 mins. River (other side of D930) with medieval buildings, inc castle for Henry IV. Inspected 2013.

🚐 5

🛒 Custom

LAVARDAC 1 | 74 | E10 | 🏢 | 47230 | N44°10.235' E000°17.595'

Directions: D408. From town follow D930, sp 'Nérac'. After exit roundabout on D930, turn right onto D408 at Super U. Turn right into Super U supermarket car park and the Service Point is located between the fuel station and car wash, signed.

ⓘ Supermarket and fuel station with car wash for high vehicles. Inspected 2013.

🚐 Poss

🛒 Euro Relais Junior; €2

LAVARDAC 2 | 75 | E10 | 🏨 | 47230 | N44°10.734' E000°17.954'

Directions: Rue de la Victoire. Turn off D930, main road through, onto D258, sp 'Stade-Tennis', 'Salle Polyvalente' and signed. The Aire is 200m on the left, signed. Parked cars may make it difficult to manoeuvre large motorhomes into Service Point.

ⓘ Parking poss along Rue de la Victoire about 300m from the Aire: N44°10.635' E000°18.167'. Local commerce 1 min. Inspected 2013.

🚐 3; 6m bays and obstructed by trees

🛒 Custom

ST HILAIRE DE LUSIGNAN | 76 | E10 | 🏢 | 47450 | N44°13.495' E000°30.814'

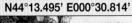

Directions: D813, between Porte Ste Marie and Agen on D813. Service Point adj to D183 and river at the southern edge of St Hilaire-de-Lusignan.

ⓘ There is limited parking provision and all parking is close to the noisy road. Inspected 2013.

🚐 2; Max 24hrs

🛒 Custom; CC; €3/10 mins

BERNOS BEAULAC | 77 | E10 | | 33430 | N44°22.181' W000°14.556'

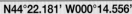

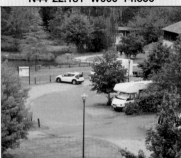

Directions: N524, at Halte Nautique. From Bazas take N524 south and the Aire is just south of village on left, sp 'Aire Touristique'.

ⓘ Lovely spot with BBQ area overlooking pond, may be noisy with revellers. Kayak hire adj. Gorges du Ciron adj. Inspected 2013.

🚐 5

🛒 Custom

LABASTIDE D'ARMAGNAC | 78 | E10 | 🏨 | 40240 | N43°58.321' W000°11.159'

Directions: D11. Turn off D626 in the village onto D11, sp 'Betbezer d'Arc' and signed. In 400m turn left into Aire, signed.

ⓘ Pleasant, large, open grass/sand parking. 1 min from village centre with local commerce. Voie Verte cycle route through village. Inspected 2012.

🚐 30; Grass/sand parking

🛒 Custom

ROQUEFORT | 79 | E10 | ⛺ | 40120 | N44°02.850' W000°19.321'

Directions: Allée de Nauton. Exit village on D932n, sp 'Bordeaux'. Turn left, sp 'Camping' and signed. Aire 50m on right past campsite, signed.

ℹ️ Aire adj to municipal campsite in small residential area. Local commerce 4 mins down D932n. Inspected 2012.

🚐 10; Grass/sand parking; Max 48hrs

🚰 Custom; Lift grid before toilet emptying

MONT DE MARSAN | 80 | D10 | 🏃 | 40000 | N43°54.394' W000°28.542'

Directions: D1. Turn off D932/D932e roundabout east of town onto D932, sp 'Mont de Marsan-Centre' and signed. Follow road towards town for 2km, then turn right at edge of park, signed. Entrance through Urba Flux barrier.

ℹ️ Pleasant landscaped commercial Aire adj to animal petting park. Town 20 mins. Inspected 2013.

🚐 41; €0.50/1hr; €7/24hrs Jun/Sept; €5/24hrs Oct-May; CC

🚰 Urba Flux Tall; €1/5 mins; 16amp elec; CC; €0.50/hr

ST SEVER | 81 | D10 | 🏛 | 40500 | N43°45.544' W000°34.547'

Directions: Allée des Anciens Combattants. Exit D933s onto D944, sp 'St Sever-Ville'. After 1km turn left, sp 'Centre Ville'. Follow for 1.2km, then turn left, sp 'Sortie de Ville' and signed. In car park take road to left, then turn left beside war memorial. Service Point in gravel car park outside school building, signed.

ℹ️ Small town commerce and historic centre adj. Suggested parking: N43°45.694' W000°34.529'. Exit car park to left and follow road to car park on left. Inspected 2013.

🚐 5

🚰 Custom

GRENADE SUR L'ADOUR | 82 | D10 | 🏢 | 40270 | N43°46.483' W000°26.100'

Directions: Place 19 Mars 1962. Approach on D824 from Mont-de-Marsan. Turn right before town centre after Carrefour Contact, sp 'P Rugby' and signed. At end of road go straight on and Service Point is on right adj to cemetery, signed.

ℹ️ Town 5 mins with restaurants, cafés and commerce. Inspected 2013.

🚐 30; Max 24hrs

🚰 Custom

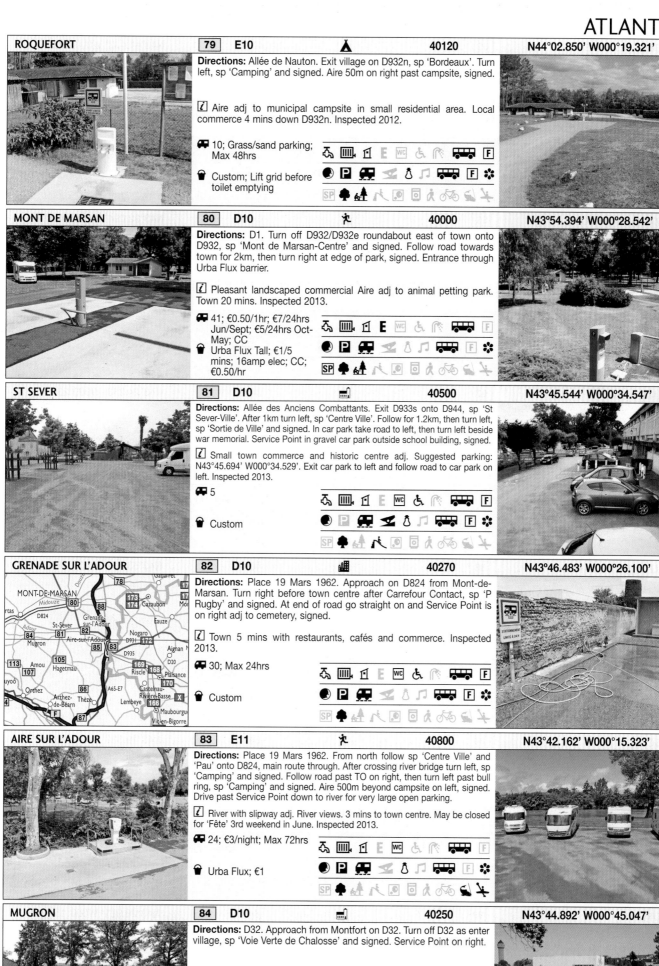

AIRE SUR L'ADOUR | 83 | E11 | 🏃 | 40800 | N43°42.162' W000°15.323'

Directions: Place 19 Mars 1962. From north follow sp 'Centre Ville' and 'Pau' onto D824, main route through. After crossing river bridge turn left, sp 'Camping' and signed. Follow road past TO on right, then turn left past bull ring, sp 'Camping' and signed. Aire 500m beyond campsite on left, signed. Drive past Service Point down to river for very large open parking.

ℹ️ River with slipway adj. River views. 3 mins to town centre. May be closed for 'Fête' 3rd weekend in June. Inspected 2013.

🚐 24; €3/night; Max 72hrs

🚰 Urba Flux; €1

MUGRON | 84 | D10 | 🏭 | 40250 | N43°44.892' W000°45.047'

Directions: D32. Approach from Montfort on D32. Turn off D32 as enter village, sp 'Voie Verte de Chalosse' and signed. Service Point on right.

ℹ️ Adj to designated cycle path to St Sever (17.9km) and Dax (31.6km). Picnic area adj. Town with local commerce 400m. Inspected 2012.

🚐 4

🚰 Aire Services; 4 unmetered 16amp CEE elec points

EUGENIE LES BAINS | 85 | E11 | 40320 | N43°41.432' W000°22.370'

Directions: Route du Mouliot. Follow sp 'Camping' in village. Designated parking 50m past campsite entrance.

i Designated motorhome parking adj to campsite which was being used as caravan storage in May 2013. Recommend 83 as a better option. Inspected 2013.

🚐 5; €3/night; Pay at campsite

🛒 Inside campsite; €3; Elec €3/night

ARZACQ ARRAZIGUET | 86 | D11 | 64410 | N43°32.094' W000°24.624'

Directions: Place du Marcadieu. Aire in car park on corner near D32/D944 junction. Drive to rear of car park and Service Point behind building, signed.

i Local commerce adj. Bastide town. Adj to covered market building. Always likely to have space. Inspected 2013.

🚐 20

🛒 Custom

SAUVAGNON | 87 | D11 | 64230 | N43°24.233' W000°23.176'

Directions: D216, near junction with D616. From south on D216 drive through town and Aire is past the church in car park on right before you reach D616, signed. Service Point behind Centre Festif. Some narrow corners but passable, walk first if unsure.

i Small town commerce adj. Centre Festif has many events, but Aire is peaceful afterwards. Inspected 2013.

🚐 8; Large bays

🛒 Custom

VILLENEUVE DE MARSAN | 88 | E10 | 40190 | N43°53.239' W000°18.355'

Directions: Rue Roger Lamothe. Approach on D1 from Mont de Marsan. Turn right as enter town, signed. Follow road and Aire on left, signed. Well signed from all directions.

i Landscaped Aire adj to sports facilities on edge of town. Small town commerce 2 mins. Inspected 2013.

🚐 7; In marked bays

🛒 Custom; 2 CEE elec points

LESCAR | 89 | D11 | 64230 | N43°19.537' W000°26.550'

Directions: Avenue du Vert Galant. From Artix (northwest) on D817 take 1st exit at roundabout onto D501, sp 'Saragosse'. Pass ALDI and turn right into Impasse du Vert Galant (GPS is at this turning for clarity). Service Point on right of turning circle, signed.

i Service Point only. Tolerated parking at P Verdun central Pau: N43°17.951' W000°22.581'. Inspected 2013.

🚐 None; See 87

🛒 Custom

MORLAAS | 90 | E11 | 64160 | N43°20.971' W000°15.760'

Directions: Avenue Gaston IV Le Croise. From Pau enter Morlaàs on D943, then D923. Follow through centre and at traffic lights turn left, sp 'Piscine'. Follow road and Service Point on left outside municipal campsite.

i Service Point only adj to municipal campsite, €10.50-€12.50/night. Inspected 2013.

🚐 None; See 87

🛒 Urba Flux Tall; €2

OLORON STE MARIE | 91 | D11 | | 64400 | N43°11.032' W000°36.511'

Directions: Rue Adoue. From Asasp Arros in south enter town on N134. Follow road straight on over 2 roundabouts. Aire after Total fuel station on right, signed. Entrance is restricted on both sides by wall, but is possible for most motorhomes.

Pleasant parking. Token from TO, 800m. Town commerce. River adj, but no views. Inspected 2013.

7; Max 48hrs

Aire Services; Token; €4; 8 CEE elec points

OGEU LES BAINS | 92 | D11 | | 64680 | N43°09.210' W000°30.130'

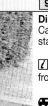
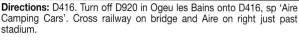

Directions: D416. Turn off D920 in Ogeu les Bains onto D416, sp 'Aire Camping Cars'. Cross railway on bridge and Aire on right just past stadium.

Village centre 800m with local commerce. Small supermarket 650m from Aire on D920 towards Oloron. Inspected 2013.

6

Custom; Token

ARUDY / SEVIGNACQ MEYRACQ | 93 | D11 | | 64260 | N43°06.430' W000°24.962'

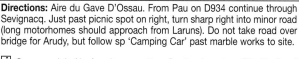

Directions: Aire du Gave D'Ossau. From Pau on D934 continue through Sevignacq. Just past picnic spot on right, turn sharp right into minor road (long motorhomes should approach from Laruns). Do not take road over bridge for Arudy, but follow sp 'Camping Car' past marble works to site.

Commercial Aire/rural campsite. Onsite laundry, €6. Regional products for sale. Close to small town of Arudy. Inspected 2013.

20; €10/night; Collected; Feb-Nov

Custom; €3; Elec €2

ARUDY | 94 | D11 | | 64260 | N43°06.322' W000°25.357'

Directions: Rue Baulong. Exit D934 onto D287, sp 'Arudy'. Cross river bridge and follow road for 800m. Turn right up small road, sp 'Piscine' and 'Camping'. In 200m at end of football pitch turn right. Follow road straight on and Aire in car park next to fire station, signed.

Located adj to sports facilities and river just 2 mins from local commerce. Inspected 2013.

5

Euro Relais Junior; €2

Photos: Carol Weaver

GOURETTE | 95 | E12 | SKI | 64440 | N42°57.784' W000°20.352'

Directions: Parking de Recommande, adj to D918. Turn off D918 before Gourette, sp 'Parking de Recommande' and signed. Follow road downhill towards gondola, then turn right. Parking in summer campsite/winter Aire.

This Aire is situated at the bottom of the gondola station. Inspected 2013.

50; €8/night; €12/night inc elec; Collected

Custom

LARUNS | 96 | D12 | | 64440 | N42°59.300' W000°25.500'

Directions: Avenue de la Gare, off D934. Aire in town centre at rear of car park. Reports suggest a barriered entry system is being installed.

Restaurants adj. Market Sat am. Inspected 2013.

22; €6; CC; Pay at machine; 6pm-9am only; In designated bays

Euro Relais Junior; Token; €3.50

LES EAUX CHAUDES | 97 | D12 | 64440 | N42°57.117' W000°26.417'

Directions: D934. In small lay-by beside D934, signed.

Aire and area subject to change. Tokens from Larun or Fabrèges TO. For parking see Laruns 96 or Artouste Fabrèges 98. Inspected 2013.

Poss; Out of season

Euro Relais Junior; Token (2/1); €3.50

ARTOUSTE FABREGES | 98 | E12 | SKI | 64440 | N42°52.817' W000°23.917'

Directions: D431. From south on D934 turn right onto D431 after dam, sp 'Artouste Fabrèges'. Cross bridge and follow road to left for 1.5km. Follow road to left, past car park and Service Point is on right, signed.

Motorhomes are now being discouraged. Night parking must not obstruct residents. Ski resort adj. Mini mountain railway in summer. Inspected 2013.

40; 7pm-7am only

Euro Relais Junior; Token (2/1)

HAVE YOU VISITED AN AIRE? GPS co-ordinates in this guide are protected by copyright law

Submit updates
• Amendments
• New Aires
• Not changed

Visit www.all-the-aires.co.uk/submissions.shtml
to upload your updates and photos.

Directions and description.

Number of parking spaces; Cost per night; Time limit
Service Point type and details; Payment type; Cost

Take at least 5 digital photos showing
• Signs
• Service Point
• Parking
• Overview
• Amenities

ARETTE PIERRE ST MARTIN | 100 | D12 | SKI | 64570 | N42°58.733' W000°44.883'

Directions: Braca de Guilhers, off D132 at ski station. Turn off D132 and follow to ski station, sp 'Station de Ski Pierre St Martin'. Pass through large car park and turn right at 1st roundabout into Aire.

Ski station adj. Adj to ski lift. Free WiFi at TO. Inspected 2013.

40; €10/night inc unmetered elec; Collected
Custom; Inc; 44 elec points

Photo: Keith & Sue Lawrence

ST JEAN PIED DE PORT | 101 | D11 | 64220 | N43°09.923' W001°13.948'

Directions: D933/Ave du Jai Alai. Turn off D933 at roundabout, sp 'P Jai Alai'. Aire is on right at end of road near Carrefour supermarket and sports facilities, signed. Service Point behind building, signed.

This is the only car park in town that allows motorhomes. Toilets in sports hall. Inspected 2013.

40; €5.50; Pay at machine

Custom; Inc

ST PALAIS | 102 | D11 | 64120 | N43°19.733' W001°01.933'

Directions: Place Sante-Elisabeth. Turn off D933 at roundabout, sp 'St Palais'. Follow road across river and straight on into town. Turn right into 2nd car park with covered market building. Drive past 1st building and the Service Point is on the rear of the 2nd building, signed. Adj parking is not designated and is popular with locals.

Covered animal market adj. Busy town car park. Town commerce adj. Inspected 2013.

5; No parking Thurs pm-Fri am (Market)

Custom

SAUVETERRE DE BEARN | 103 | D11 | | 64390 | N43°24.073' W000°56.343'

Directions: Sauterisse. Turn off D933 at roundabout north of the town, sp 'Mairie'. Follow road and Service Point is on the left as enter town, signed. Parking adj to tennis court. Turn right opp Service Point, sp 'Stade', and parking 100m: N43°24.053' W000°56.497'.

i Peaceful village with riverside walks and medieval centre. Boulangerie 100m. Inspected 2013.

🚐 20

🛒 Custom

SALIES DE BEARN | 104 | D11 | | 64270 | N43°28.393' W000°56.033'

Directions: Lieu-Dit Herre. In town centre turn off D17 at roundabout, sp 'Office Notarial'. Pass Casino Hotel and turn right at next roundabout, sp 'Office Notarial' and signed. Turn left after Office Notarial, sp 'Aire Camping-Cars'. In 100m turn left into Aire, signed.

i Commercial Aire on outskirts of small spa town. Very low amp elec. Inspected 2013.

🚐 24; €6/night inc elec; CC

🛒 Custom; Inside barrier; CC; €2

HAGETMAU | 105 | D11 | | 40700 | N43°39.247' W000°35.898'

Directions: Rue de Piquette. Turn off D933s bypass, sp 'ZI de Piquette' and signed. Follow road and turn 1st right into Rue de Piquette. Aire in car park on right, signed. Note: Very complicated one-way system through town and limited parking.

i Located in industrial area, most of which is not in use. Adj to river, limited views but good for fishing. Town commerce 4 mins. Inspected 2012.

🚐 15

🛒 Custom

NAVARRENX | 106 | D11 | T | 64190 | N43°19.205' W000°45.426'

Directions: Turn off D936 onto D947, sp 'Navarrenx'. Follow road around walled town and at roundabout turn right, sp 'Monein'. Follow road, signed, then turn left onto D2, sp 'Monein' and signed. Immediately turn right in front of Carrefour Express, signed. Service Point 50m on right opp fuel station gas bottles, signed.

i Frustratingly this is a Service Point only in a pretty, walled town. There is suitable parking in the town, suggest: N43°19.270' W000°45.657'. Inspected 2013.

🚐 Poss; Unrestricted car parks in town

🛒 Custom; Difficult access, may be better to reverse in

AMOU | 107 | D11 | ⛺ | 40330 | N43°35.350' W000°44.583'

Directions: Ave de la Digue. Turn off D13 at roundabout, sp 'Hagetmau' and signed. Go straight over next roundabout, sp 'Camping'. Turn right as exit town onto D346, sp 'Camping'. Turn right again, sp 'Camping'. Follow road through sports facilities and drive through campsite behind stadium stands and Service Point on left, signed.

i Riverside campsite in pleasant woodland setting. Hardstanding parking at stadium out of season. Inspected 2013.

🚐 €6/night; Collected

🛒 Custom; Apr-Oct

POUILLON | 108 | D11 | | 40350 | N43°36.595' W000°59.514'

Directions: D322. Follow sp 'Camping' in town and exit town on D322, sp 'Mimbaste' and 'Camping'. Service Point outside municipal campsite, opp large 'Maïsadour' building as exit village, signed.

i Service Point outside municipal campsite. Tolerated parking at lake, off D22, follow sp 'Lac du Luc': N43°35.639' W001°00.942'. Inspected 2013.

🚐 Tolerated

🛒 Custom

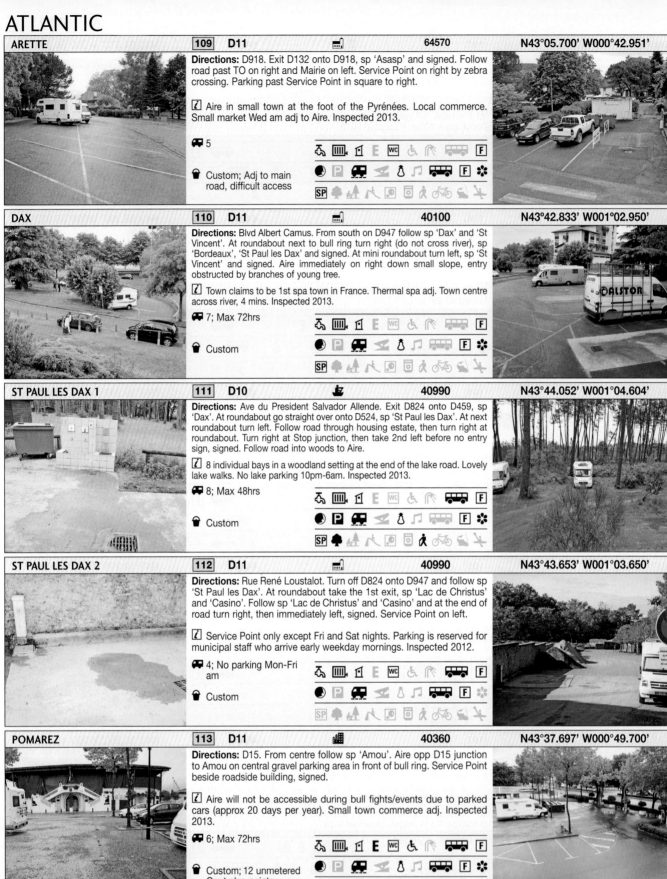

ARETTE | 109 | D11 | | 64570 | N43°05.700' W000°42.951'

Directions: D918. Exit D132 onto D918, sp 'Asasp' and signed. Follow road past TO on right and Mairie on left. Service Point on right by zebra crossing. Parking past Service Point in square to right.

Aire in small town at the foot of the Pyrénées. Local commerce. Small market Wed am adj to Aire. Inspected 2013.

5

Custom; Adj to main road, difficult access

DAX | 110 | D11 | | 40100 | N43°42.833' W001°02.950'

Directions: Blvd Albert Camus. From south on D947 follow sp 'Dax' and 'St Vincent'. At roundabout next to bull ring turn right (do not cross river), sp 'Bordeaux', 'St Paul les Dax' and signed. At mini roundabout turn left, sp 'St Vincent' and signed. Aire immediately on right down small slope, entry obstructed by branches of young tree.

Town claims to be 1st spa town in France. Thermal spa adj. Town centre across river, 4 mins. Inspected 2013.

7; Max 72hrs

Custom

ST PAUL LES DAX 1 | 111 | D10 | | 40990 | N43°44.052' W001°04.604'

Directions: Ave du President Salvador Allende. Exit D824 onto D459, sp 'Dax'. At roundabout go straight over onto D524, sp 'St Paul les Dax'. At next roundabout turn left. Follow road through housing estate, then turn right at roundabout. Turn right at Stop junction, then take 2nd left before no entry sign, signed. Follow road into woods to Aire.

8 individual bays in a woodland setting at the end of the lake road. Lovely lake walks. No lake parking 10pm-6am. Inspected 2013.

8; Max 48hrs

Custom

ST PAUL LES DAX 2 | 112 | D11 | | 40990 | N43°43.653' W001°03.650'

Directions: Rue René Loustalot. Turn off D824 onto D947 and follow sp 'St Paul les Dax'. At roundabout take the 1st exit, sp 'Lac de Christus' and 'Casino'. Follow sp 'Lac de Christus' and 'Casino' and at the end of road turn right, then immediately left, signed. Service Point on left.

Service Point only except Fri and Sat nights. Parking is reserved for municipal staff who arrive early weekday mornings. Inspected 2012.

4; No parking Mon-Fri am

Custom

POMAREZ | 113 | D11 | | 40360 | N43°37.697' W000°49.700'

Directions: D15. From centre follow sp 'Amou'. Aire opp D15 junction to Amou on central gravel parking area in front of bull ring. Service Point beside roadside building, signed.

Aire will not be accessible during bull fights/events due to parked cars (approx 20 days per year). Small town commerce adj. Inspected 2013.

6; Max 72hrs

Custom; 12 unmetered Cont elec points

ANGLET 1 | 114 | C11 | | 64600 | N43°30.427' W001°32.059'

Directions: Parking des Corsaires, off D405/Blvd des Plages. From Anglet follow sp 'Anglet-Océan' or 'Plages' and signed. At the sea turn right onto D405, sp 'La Barre'. Turn left into Aire, signed. Entrance up steep slope. Service Point and ticket machine to right, parking to left.

Surfing beach 5 mins downhill. Police inspect tickets. Inspected 2013.

60; €10/night Jul-Aug; €6/night Apr-June/Sept-Nov; Pay at machine; Max 48hrs

Custom

ANGLET 2 | 115 | C11 | | 64600 | N43°31.584' W001°30.900'

Directions: Parking des Barre. Follow D405 past 114, straight over roundabouts and past La Barre parking area. The Aire will be visible to the left. At the next roundabout turn left (almost right around), signed. The Service Point is straight on and parking is past the Service Point almost adj to La Barre parking.

ℹ️ Large, open level space, some bays with water views. Road noise. Inspected 2013.

🚐 50; €10/night Jul-Aug; €6/night Apr-Jun/Sept-Nov; CC; Pay at meter beside Service Point

🚽 Custom

CAPBRETON | 116 | C11 | | 40130 | N43°38.143' W001°26.809'

Directions: Allée des Ortolans, at beach. On D28 follow sp 'Centre Ville'. Pass the Mairie on the left, then go straight over roundabout, sp 'P Le Piste'. At next roundabout go straight on, sp 'Les Plages'. Turn left, signed, and cross carriageway, signed. Turn right, signed. Turn right again, signed. Aire at beach on left.

ℹ️ Sand dune beach; Sea and surfing adj. No shade. Inspected 2013.

🚐 200; €10/night inc CEE elec; Pay at hut/Collected

🚽 Custom; Inside/past hut

LABENNE OCEAN | 117 | C11 | | 40530 | N43°35.685' W001°27.278'

Directions: D126. From D810 at Labenne take D126, sp 'Labenne-Océan'. Turn right as enter Labenne-Océan, sp 'Parc Aquatique'. Drive straight on and Aire in 150m, signed.

ℹ️ Parking on either grass, sand or gravel. Adventure park adj with waterslide and ropes course. Inspected 2013.

🚐 70; €8/night; Collected; Mid Jun-mid Sept

🚽 Custom

ONDRES PLAGE | 118 | C11 | | 40440 | N43°34.589' W001°29.215'

Directions: D26/Ave de la Plage. From Ondres follow D26, sp 'Ondres Plage'. In car parks at end of road drive to far end, then turn left into Parking 3, signed. Barriers have been built, but were removed at the time of inspection; could be reinstated.

ℹ️ Sandy surfing beach 2 mins. Restaurant. Inspected 2013.

🚐 41; €7/night Sept-Jun; €9/night Jul-Aug; Collected; Max 48hrs

🚽 Customised Flot Bleu Pacific; 12 16amp Cont elec points on left

PEYREHORADE | 119 | D11 | | 40300 | N43°32.584' W001°05.996'

Directions: D817/Quai du Sablot. From river bridge exit town on D817, sp 'Pau'. Aire on left in town parking opp river near Carrefour market, signed.

ℹ️ Road noise. Carrefour supermarket adj. Ideal night halt only 5 mins from motorway. Inspected 2013.

🚐 10

🚽 Custom; Water tap missing in 2014

BIARRITZ | 120 | C11 | | 64200 | N43°27.990' W001°34.302'

Directions: Avenue de la Milady. To avoid central Biarritz enter from south by following sp 'Bidart'. In Bidart turn left at roundabout onto D655, sp 'Biarritz'. At end of road turn right then follow D655 to Biarritz, where it becomes D911. Turn right at roundabout, opp Hôtel de Milady, signed.

ℹ️ Very popular Aire, busy all year. Beach and supermarket 5 mins; Biarritz centre 20 mins. Inspected 2013.

🚐 50; €12/night; Collected, but barrier being installed

🚽 Custom (x2); 24 16amp CEE elec points on 6 bollards

ST JEAN DE LUZ | **121** C11 | 64500 | N43°23.112' W001°39.780'

Directions: Pont Charles de Gaulle, on D810. From south on D810 cross river bridge and Aire immediately on right before roundabout.

i Very popular Aire in noisy location. Inspected 2013.

🚐 20; Max 48hrs

🚰 Raclet; 2 unmetered CEE elec points

HENDAYE PLAGE | **122** C11 | 64700 | N43°22.213' W001°45.887'

Directions: Rue d'Ansoenia. Enter town from south on D912. Turn right onto Rue des Rosiers and follow to end. Turn right again and left at roundabout. Aire is on left by train station.

i Town 10 mins. Popular, arrive early. Nicer stop than St Jean de Luz **121**. Updated 2014.

🚐 15; €10/24hrs; Pay at machine

🚰 Custom

Photo: Keith & Sue Lawrence

ST PEE SUR NIVELLE | **123** C11 | 64310 | N43°20.983' W001°31.283'

Directions: Promenade du Parlement de Navarre. On east side of town turn off D918 at roundabout, sp 'Le Lac'. At next 2 mini roundabouts go right and follow road along lake edge, signed. Aire adj to lake, access via Flot Bleu Park barrier.

i Lake adj with pleasant walk, swimming and pedalos. Services outside parking area, but elec inside. Inspected 2013.

🚐 62; €5/12hrs; €9/24hrs; CC; 8m bays

🚰 Flot Bleu Fontaine; Token or CC; €2; Flot Bleu Elec; Token or CC; 3 tokens/12hrs elec

SARE | **124** C11 | 64310 | N43°18.794' W001°34.621'

Directions: From the east edge of village turn off D4, sp 'Sare' and signed. Aire is on left in car park before the village.

i Picturesque Basque Beau Village. Inspected 2013.

🚐 15; €6/night; Pay at machine; Max 48hrs

🚰 Custom

COL D'IBARDIN | **125** C11 | 64122 | N43°18.583' W001°41.133'

Directions: D404, at Ibardin on the border of France and Spain. From Urrugne take D4 to Col d'Ibardin and follow signs to the border along D404. Border at the summit of the hill. Turn right and parking on the right adj to road and shops.

i Parking on Spanish border. Numerous commerce and cheap fuel. Worth a look. Inspected 2013.

🚐 20; Tolerated

🚰 None

ESPELLETTE | **126** C11 | 64250 | N43°20.319' W001°26.854'

Directions: D918. Adj to D918/D249 roundabout on main route through, signed.

i Motorhome and bus parking adj to chocolate shop and other local producers. Inspected 2013.

🚐 6

🚰 None

VIEUX BOUCAU LES BAINS 1 | **127** | C10 | ⚓ | 40480 | N43°46.815' W001°24.071'

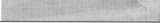

Directions: Avenue des Pêcheurs. From south on D652 turn left at large roundabout, sp 'Port d'Albret entrée Nord' and 'Aire de Camping Car'. Entrance to Aire 350m on right, no option to turn around at barrier. Enter through barrier; pay on exit. No trailers and no motorhomes over 3.5t.

ℹ Local commerce and golf course adj. Wind and kite surfing on lake; Beach 5 mins. Inspected 2013.

🚐 120; €12/night inc elec May-Sept; €6/night inc elec Oct-Apr; Max 48hrs

🚻 Custom; Inside barrier; Inc

VIEUX BOUCAU LES BAINS 2 | **128** | C10 | ⚓ | 40480 | N43°47.675' W001°24.322'

Directions: Blvd du Marensin, north of town near Plage des Sablères. Follow sp 'Municipal Camping des Sablères'. Go past the entrance to small parking area. Take ticket, pay on exit.

ℹ Uninspiring and undesirable. Inspected 2013.

🚐 35; €12 Summer; €6 Winter; Max 48hrs

🚻 Custom; Inside barrier; Inc

SEIGNOSSE | **129** | C11 | ⛺ | 40510 | N43°41.447' W001°25.536'

Directions: Adj to D79 coast road, signed. Pay at ticket machine and enter through bollards.

ℹ Commercial Aire located between noisy D79 coast road and a large campsite. Grass parking under evergreen trees. Inspected 2012.

🚐 30; €8/night; CC; Grass parking

🚻 Custom; WC emptying outside barrier

SOUSTONS PLAGE | **130** | C11 | ⚓ | 40140 | N43°46.518' W001°24.628'

Directions: Ave de la Petre. From D652 turn off at roundabout, sp 'Soustons Plage' and signed. Follow road to end, signed. Entrance through barrier.

ℹ Very pleasant commercial Aire. Direct access to beach. Nicest Aire in area. Inspected 2013.

🚐 50; €12.50/night inc elec May-Sept; €6.50/night inc elec Oct-Apr; Pay at machine

🚻 Euro Relais Junior; Inside barrier; Inc

MOLIETS PLAGE | **131** | C/D10 | ⚓ | 40660 | N43°51.040' W001°22.952'

Directions: Rue du Tuc. Exit Moliets-et-Maa to west on D117, sp 'Moliets Plages' and signed. Turn left, sp 'Le Tuc', cross road and Aire immediately on left. Entry through barrier, signed.

ℹ Sea 5 mins; Restaurants and bars at sea; Golf adj. Low trees. Inspected 2013.

🚐 40; €11/24hrs Apr-Sept; €5/24hrs Oct-Mar

🚻 Custom; Inside barrier

LEON | **132** | D10 | ⚓ | 40550 | N43°53.037' W001°19.086'

Directions: D409/Route de Puntaou. At roundabout in Léon turn onto D409, sp 'Le Lac'. At lake turn left and follow road around campsite. Parking area signed 250m from lake.

ℹ Large grass parking area with partial lake views; Swimming. Inspected 2013.

🚐 50; €10/night; Pay at machine

🚻 Custom

LAC DE VIELLE ST GIRONS | 133 | D10 | 40560 | N43°54.178' W001°18.572'

Directions: At the lake, opp campsite 'Le Col Vert'. Turn off D652, sp 'Plage de Vielle' and 'Le Lac'. Follow sp 'Le Lac' to lake. Opp campsite turn left and drive through car park. Aire on grass area behind campsite, signed.

ℹ️ Lake 2 mins. Rural views. Mini golf. Bar/restaurant. Beach. Inspected 2013.

🚐 20; €12/24hrs Jul-Aug; €9/24hrs Sept-Jun; +€0.61pp; Dogs €4.80; Collected; Max 48hrs

🛢️ Custom; Inc; 3amp elec €4.70

VIELLE ST GIRONS | 134 | D10 | 40560 | N43°57.185' W001°21.478'

Directions: Aire Camping-Car Les Tourterelles, off D42. Turn off D652 onto D42, sp 'St Girons-Plage'. Follow road towards sea, then turn right at roundabout, signed. Turn right again to Aire, signed. Entrance to Aire through barrier.

ℹ️ Commercial Aire 2 mins from sandy beach. Inspected 2012.

🚐 48; €14.10/night Aug; €13.90/night Jul; €9.30/night May/Jun/Sept

🛢️ Aire Services Box; Inside barrier; Token (3/3)

CONTIS PLAGE | 135 | D10 | 40170 | N44°05.600' W001°19.117'

Directions: Ave du Phare. Turn off D652 at roundabout onto D41, sp 'Contis Plage'. After entering Contis Plage turn left, sp 'Parking Plage' and signed. Aire on right, signed. Enter through CC operated barrier.

ℹ️ Beach 4 mins over dune (uphill). Town commerce 5 mins. Inspected 2013.

🚐 80; €11/night Jun-Sept; €7/night Mar-May/Oct-Nov; Free Dec-Feb; CC; Max 48hrs

🛢️ Euro Relais; Inside barrier; €2; 26 elec points for 1hr battery charging!

AZUR | 136 | D11 | 40140 | N43°47.307' W001°18.718'

Directions: Route du Lac. Turn off D50 onto Route du Lac at the hexagonal roundabout, sp 'Le Lac d'Azur' and signed. At the lake turn left and follow signs to Aire. Enter through PARKNIGHT barrier.

ℹ️ Commercial Aire near the northern edge of lake Soustons. Submitted 2014.

🚐 30; €12/night; CC

🛢️ Euro Relais Junior; Inside barrier; Inc

Info/photos: camping-car-park.com

ST VINCENT DE TYROSSE | 137 | D11 | 40230 | N43°40.113' W001°16.888'

Directions: D810, at Netto supermarket. Enter in front of McDonald's at the E'Leclerc supermarket roundabout and follow road around to Netto.

ℹ️ Service Point only. Self-service laundry. Inspected 2013.

🚐 None

🛢️ Custom; Token (2/2)

MIMIZAN | 138 | D10 | 40200 | N44°13.178' W001°13.786'

Directions: D87. Adj to D87 as exit town to north at municipal campsite.

ℹ️ Commercial Aire operated by and run like a campsite with prices to match. Inspected 2013.

🚐 20; See campsite price board

🛢️ Flot Bleu Pacific; €2

MIZIMAN PLAGE 1 — 139 — D10 — ! — 40200 — N44°12.839' W001°16.938'

Directions: D626. Turn right at roundabout as enter Mimizan Plage from Mimizan, sp 'Camping Municipal' and signed. Entrance to Aire 230m on right.

ℹ️ Not open and height barriered in May 2013, but still signed in town. Municipal campsite, next right, is being renovated and Aire may move there. Inspected 2013.

🚐 50; €6/night; Pay at machine

🛒 Custom

MIMIZAN PLAGE 2 — 140 — D10 — ⚓ — 40200 — N44°12.291' W001°17.829'

Directions: Rue des Gourbets. From Mimizan follow sp 'Plage' along D626 to Mimizan Plage. Turn left, sp 'Station Camping Car', and follow sp 'Station Camping Car' over bridge. Follow road to end and Aire in large car park adj to beach. Entrance through Flot Bleu Park barrier.

ℹ️ Sand dune adj; Sandy beach 2 mins; Seaside resort with cafés/restaurant; Surfing beach. Inspected 2013.

🚐 80; €12/night; CC

🛒 Flot Bleu Pacific; Inside barrier; Inc elec

STE EULALIE EN BORN — 141 — D10 — 🚣 — 40200 — N44°18.362' W001°10.915'

Directions: Route du Port, off D652. Turn off D652 onto Route du Lac, sp 'Camping Municipal', and follow for 1.9km, then turn left opp campsite. Aire on left and Service Point at end of road on left. Pay at campsite reception opp.

ℹ️ Informal Aire overlooking marina. Parking on grass on left, do not park on right. Café in season. No services when free. Inspected 2013.

🚐 40; €4/night Apr/Oct; €6.50/night May-Sept; Free Nov-Mar
🛒 Custom

GASTES ★ — 142 — D10 — 🚣 — 40160 — N44°19.714' W001°09.057'

Directions: Ave du Lac. From Gastes head north and turn off at roundabout, sp 'Le Lac'. At end of road turn left. Parking on grass, sp 'Aire Naturelle Camping Car'. Bollarded entry/exit, credit card system.

ℹ️ Small town with local commerce. Aire overlooking boats adj to lake. Sandy beach. Inspected 2013.

🚐 50; €7/night mid Jun-mid Sept; €4.50 Apr-mid Jun/mid Sept-Oct; €2 Nov-Mar; CC
🛒 Custom; Inside barrier; Inc

PARENTIS EN BORN 1 — 143 — D10 — 🏢 — 40160 — N44°20.920' W001°03.950'

Directions: D43, at Super U. Service Point in Super U car park adj to pizza kiosk near car wash.

ℹ️ Supermarket adj. Inspected 2013.

🚐 Poss

🛒 Raclet; €2; No drive over drain

PARENTIS EN BORN 2 — 144 — D10 — 🚣 — 40160 — N44°20.653' W001°05.907'

Directions: Route des Campings. From centre follow sp 'Le Lac'. Just before lake turn right, sp 'La Paillotte et Le Pipiou'. Aire 100m on right. Entrance bollarded, entry by CC.

ℹ️ No lake view. Marina, lake and restaurants 2 mins. Inspected 2013.

🚐 20; €7/night inc CEE elec; CC

🛒 Euro Relais Junior; Inside barrier; Inc; 12 CEE elec points

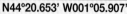

MORCENX
145 | D10 | 🏃 | 40110 | N44°02.321' W000°54.576'

Directions: Chemin de L'Abattoir. From town follow D77 towards Sabres. In 200m turn right, signed. Follow road to end and the Service Point is on left.

ℹ️ Service Point behind sports facilities and adj to noisy mainline train track. Town centre with small town commerce, 3 mins. Inspected 2012.

🚐 5; Grass/sand parking

⚲ Custom

NAVARROSSE
146 | D10 | ⚓ | 40600 | N44°25.920' W001°09.958'

Directions: Port de Navarrosse. Turn off D652 onto D305 at roundabout, sp 'Lac Mayotte'. Follow road then turn right, signed. Follow road and parking on right, signed. Entry through barrier. Take ticket, pay on exit.

ℹ️ Overlooking small marina. Shop in summer. Free day parking in low season. Inspected 2013.

🚐 30; €8 Sept-Jun; €15 Jul-Aug; CC

⚲ Custom; €4

BISCARROSSE PLAGE
147 | D10 | 🏄 | 40600 | N44°27.422' W001°14.449'

Directions: Aire du Vivier, Rue du Tit. From Arcachon follow D218. At 1st roundabout at Biscarrosse Plage turn right, signed. At next roundabout turn left, then turn right, signed. Entry through barrier. Take ticket, pay on exit.

ℹ️ Parking among pine trees on soft surface. Beach adj, through trees. Local commerce 1 min. Inspected 2013.

🚐 80; €8 Sept-Jun; €15 Jul-Aug; CC

⚲ Custom; €4

SANGUINET 1
148 | D9 | ⚓ | 40460 | N44°29.037' W001°05.495'

Directions: Aire des Bardets, Ave de Losa. From town follow sp 'Le Lac'. Turn left at lake, past **149**. Follow road around past campsite and turn left, sp 'Camping Car', into designated motorhome parking.

ℹ️ Sailing school, campsite and lake adj. Further from beach and day-trippers. Inspected 2013.

🚐 10; €8/night

⚲ Custom

SANGUINET 2
149 | D9 | ⚓ | 40460 | N44°29.160' W001°05.049'

Directions: Ave de Losa, at lake. From town follow sp 'Le Lac'. Turn left at lake, then take 1st turning to left by Le Pavillion restaurant opp beach, sp 'Parking'.

ℹ️ Small pleasant parking shared with cars under overhanging trees. Lake and beach adj. Restaurant. Some soft ground. Inspected 2013.

🚐 10; €8/night

⚲ None; See **148**

HAVE YOU VISITED AN AIRE?
GPS co-ordinates in this guide are protected by copyright law

Visit www.all-the-aires.co.uk/submissions.shtml
to upload your updates and photos.

Submit updates
- Amendments
- New Aires
- Not changed

ℹ️ Directions and description.

🚐 Number of parking spaces; Cost per night; Time limit

⚲ Service Point type and details; Payment type; Cost

Take at least 5 digital photos showing
- Signs
- Service Point
- Parking
- Overview
- Amenities

DUNE DU PYLA (PILAT) | 151 | D9 | ☼ | 33115 | N44°35.833' W001°11.900'

Photo: Carol Weaver

Directions: From Arcachon follow signs to Pyla sur Mer. Follow D218, main route, south through town following sp 'Dune de Pyla'. Turn off D218 at roundabout, sp 'P Dune de Pyla'. Access via entry barrier, pay on exit. Motorhome parking area in main car park.

ℹ️ Largest sand dune in Europe. To avoid crowds continue down road towards Biscarrosse for roadside parking with access to dune. Inspected 2013.

🚐 €8/4hrs; €10/day; Overnight parking fine €40

🛒 None

LE TEICH | 152 | D9 | 🏛 | 33470 | N44°37.984' W001°01.585'

Photo: Ian Jackson

Directions: Rue de l'Industrie. Exit A660 at Junction 3 onto D650e1, sp 'Le Teich'. Go straight over 2 roundabouts, 2nd sp 'Gare SNCF' and 'Centre Ville'. Go over level crossing and turn immediately left, sp 'Gare SNCF'. With railway on left cross over mini roundabout and Aire on left at end of car park, signed.

ℹ️ Railway adj, electric trains cause some noise. Frequent trains to Arcachon. Parc Ornithologique worth a visit. Inspected 2013.

🚐 5; Poss at Parc Ornithologique

🛒 Urba Flux; €5

Info/Photo: John Watts

AUDENGE | 153 | D9 | ⛺ | 33980 | N44°41.066' W001°00.293'

Directions: D5e5, in municipal campsite car park. From D3 turn onto D5e5 at roundabout, sp 'Camping Municipal'. At next roundabout turn into campsite adj to roundabout.

ℹ️ Service Point outside municipal campsite. Camping €14-€24/night. Tokens available from TO or campsite. Inspected 2013.

🚐 None

🛒 Euro Relais Junior; Token (ER); €4

ARCACHON | 154 | D9 | 🏢⚓ | 33120 | N44°39.096' W001°08.893'

Directions: D650. Enter Arcachon from La Teste de Buch on D650. Pass LIDL on left and turn around at next roundabout, turn right opp Citroën/Total garage in front of sp 'Parking Ralentissez'.

ℹ️ Not ideal, on busy main road. Noisy. Stadium adj. Inspected 2013.

🚐 10; Max 24hrs

🛒 Raclet

ANDERNOS LES BAINS | 155 | D9 | ⚓ | 33510 | N44°44.652' W001°06.516'

Directions: Ave du Commandant Allègre. Enter Andernos les Bains on D3 from Arès. Turn right off D3 at roundabout, sp 'Port'. Turn right into harbour, sp 'Aire de Camping Car'. Turn right and Service Point 100m on left. Parking 100m past Service Point under pine trees.

ℹ️ Adj to small working harbour, no view. Seafront 5 mins. Motorhomes banned in all other town parking. Inspected 2013.

🚐 50; €7.93/night; CC; Pay at Service Point; Max 48hrs

🛒 Urba Flux; €2.10/20 mins; CC

TAUSSAT | 156 | D9 | ⚓ | 33138 | N44°43.035' W001°04.180'

Directions: Avenue Albert Pitres. Turn off D3 south of Andernos les Bains into lane, sp 'Tous Commerce Taussat Centre' and signed. At restaurant turn left then immediately right, sp 'Taussat Port'. Aire 100m on left in small parking area before port, signed.

ℹ️ Next to small tidal fishing harbour. Beach 50m. Village with local commerce 300m. Inspected 2013.

🚐 6

🛒 None

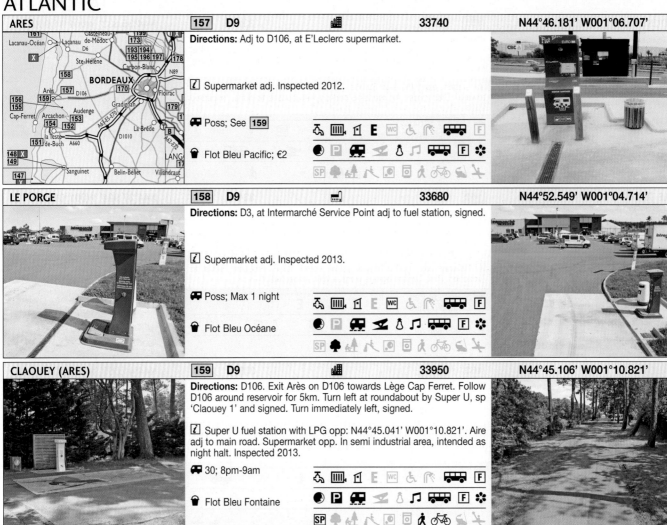

| **ARES** | 157 | D9 | | 33740 | N44°46.181' W001°06.707' |

Directions: Adj to D106, at E'Leclerc supermarket.

i Supermarket adj. Inspected 2012.

🚐 Poss; See 159

🚰 Flot Bleu Pacific; €2

| **LE PORGE** | 158 | D9 | | 33680 | N44°52.549' W001°04.714' |

Directions: D3, at Intermarché Service Point adj to fuel station, signed.

i Supermarket adj. Inspected 2013.

🚐 Poss; Max 1 night

🚰 Flot Bleu Océane

| **CLAOUEY (ARES)** | 159 | D9 | | 33950 | N44°45.106' W001°10.821' |

Directions: D106. Exit Arès on D106 towards Lège Cap Ferret. Follow D106 around reservoir for 5km. Turn left at roundabout by Super U, sp 'Claouey 1' and signed. Turn immediately left, signed.

i Super U fuel station with LPG opp: N44°45.041' W001°10.821'. Aire adj to main road. Supermarket opp. In semi industrial area, intended as night halt. Inspected 2013.

🚐 30; 8pm-9am

🚰 Flot Bleu Fontaine

GPS Co-ordinates for SatNav

The GPS Co-ordinates published in this guide were taken onsite by our inspectors. We consider them a valuable and unique asset and at the time of publishing have decided not to publish them as electronic files for use on navigation devices. You have permission to type in the co-ordinates of an Aire you intend to visit but not to store or share them. For the security of our copyright:

- **Do not compile them into lists**

- **Do not publish, share or reproduce them anywhere in any format**

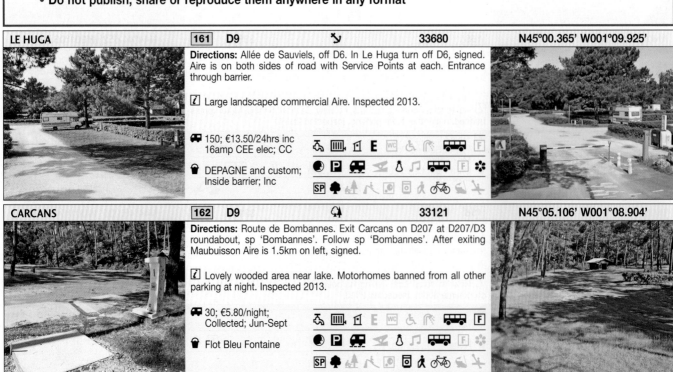

| **LE HUGA** | 161 | D9 | | 33680 | N45°00.365' W001°09.925' |

Directions: Allée de Sauviels, off D6. In Le Huga turn off D6, signed. Aire is on both sides of road with Service Points at each. Entrance through barrier.

i Large landscaped commercial Aire. Inspected 2013.

🚐 150; €13.50/24hrs inc 16amp CEE elec; CC

🚰 DEPAGNE and custom; Inside barrier; Inc

| **CARCANS** | 162 | D9 | | 33121 | N45°05.106' W001°08.904' |

Directions: Route de Bombannes. Exit Carcans on D207 at D207/D3 roundabout, sp 'Bombannes'. Follow sp 'Bombannes'. After exiting Maubuisson Aire is 1.5km on left, signed.

i Lovely wooded area near lake. Motorhomes banned from all other parking at night. Inspected 2013.

🚐 30; €5.80/night; Collected; Jun-Sept

🚰 Flot Bleu Fontaine

HOURTIN PORT | 163 | D9 | 33990 | N45°10.841' W001°04.885'

Directions: Avenue du Lac. From south on D3 turn left in Hourtin onto D4, sp 'Hourtin Port'. Continue over roundabout and follow road for 2km. 500m after Camping les Ormes, turn left to Aire, signed. Entry through barrier.

ℹ️ Beach and marina adj. Individual pitches. Pay for elec at cycle hire adj to mini golf. Self service laundry in Hourtin centre. Inspected 2013.

🚐 54; €8.30/night; CC

🚰 SISTAL; Inside barrier; Elec €2/24hrs

GRAYAN ET L'HOPITAL | 164 | D8 | 33590 | N45°25.995' W001°08.625'

Directions: Route de l'Océan. Turn off D101 onto C202, sp 'Le Gurp' and 'Camping Municipal du Gurp'. Follow C202 all the way towards sea, going straight over roundabout, and the Service Point is on the right adj to Camping Municipal du Gurp, signed.

ℹ️ Parking on a large, level grassy verge alongside road adj to municipal campsite and facilities. 700m from a vast sandy beach with WWII bunkers, small store, beach commerce and restaurants. Inspected 2013.

🚐 12; Max 48hrs

🚰 Euro Relais Junior; Token (ER); €3.50

MONTALIVET LES BAINS 1 | 165 | D8 | 33930 | N45°22.230' W001°08.658'

Directions: Avenue de L'Europe. From east on D102 turn left at traffic lights by ALDI, signed, onto Ave de l'Europe. Drive past ALDI and the Aire is on the left immediately before Camping Municipal, signed.

ℹ️ Parking under trees in a shaded, sheltered spot. Beach and town 700m. Campsite and children's activities adj, no access. Inspected 2013.

🚐 20; €8/night inc elec; €5/night without elec; Collected

🚰 Custom; Inc

MONTALIVET LES BAINS 2 | 166 | D8 | 33930 | N45°22.120' W001°08.657'

Directions: Aire La Forestier, Avenue de l'Europe. From east on D102 turn left at traffic lights by ALDI, signed, onto Ave de l'Europe. Drive past ALDI, 165, and the Camping Municipal. Aire on left immediately past campsite, signed.

ℹ️ Small woodland Aire with parking area around central picnic area. Appears to be more of an overflow/afterthought. Inspected 2013.

🚐 20; €4/night; Collected

🚰 None; See 165

MONTALIVET LES BAINS 3 | 167 | D8 | 33930 | N45°22.535' W001°09.431'

Directions: Aire Plage Sud, adj to seafront. From north enter town on D102e1. Follow road straight on along sea past miles of unrestricted parking. At Montalivet go straight on along seafront. Aire in car park on right as road bends away from sea, signed.

ℹ️ Closest Aire to beach but no shade. Beach adj. 1 min to town. Sun market in town. Inspected 2013.

🚐 60; €5/night Jul-Aug; €3/night May/Jun/Sept; Collected

🚰 None; Poss Service Point between boules court and ALDI: N45°22.505' W001°08.643'

SOULAC SUR MER | 168 | D8 | 33780 | N45°30.001' W001°08.325'

Directions: Blvd de l'Amélie. Follow sp 'L'Amélie', then sp 'Camping Les Sables'. Aire on right adj to and sp 'Camping les Sables d'Argent'. Enter through Aire Service Barrier, Service Point outside barrier.

ℹ️ Direct access to beach and tourist town accessible via cycle path. 164 only 7 mins drive. Inspected 2013.

🚐 45; €8/24hrs Jun-Sept; €4/24hrs Oct-May

🚰 Euro Relais Junior; Outside barrier; Token; €3.50

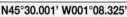

LE VERDON SUR MER | 169 | D8 | 33123 | N45°32.722' W001°03.263'

Directions: Allée des Baines/D1e4. From south on D1215 turn right onto D1e4, sp 'Le Verdon sur Mer'. Follow road to end (later part on cobbles). Aire in parking areas A and B on left, enter through barrier. Service Point outside barriers. Aire well signed through town.

ℹ️ Sandy beach opp. Motorhomes banned from everywhere in town. Local commerce 1 min. Ferry to Royan. Inspected 2013.

🚐 56; €5/night Oct-May, €8/night Jun-Sept; CC; Max 72hrs
🚰 Urba Flux Tall; CC; €2

ST JEAN D'ILLAC | 170 | D9 | 33127 | N44°48.615' W000°46.495'

Directions: Allée JJ Rousseau, off D106 roundabout at the Casino supermarket. Near LIDL, signed. Service Point in fuel station. 3 designated bays to the left of the Casino supermarket, signed.

ℹ️ LIDL and supermarket adj. No parking at sports centre. Inspected 2013.

🚐 3
🚰 Flot Bleu Euro; CC; €2

HAVE YOU VISITED AN AIRE? | GPS co-ordinates in this guide are protected by copyright law

Visit www.all-the-aires.co.uk/submissions.shtml
to upload your updates and photos.

Submit updates
• Amendments
• New Aires
• Not changed

ℹ️ Directions and description.

🚐 Number of parking spaces; Cost per night; Time limit
🚰 Service Point type and details; Payment type; Cost

Take at least 5 digital photos showing
• Signs
• Service Point
• Parking
• Overview
• Amenities

ST ESTEPHE ✳ | 172 | D8 | 33180 | N45°15.850' W000°45.483'

Directions: D2e2. From Ste Estèphe follow D2e2 through village to estuary, all roads are quiet and passable. Turn right and Aire on left of road on grassy area overlooking Gironde estuary, signed.

ℹ️ Lovely parking area with 180° views along Gironde estuary. Some noise from adj road and restaurant. Local commerce 1.3km. Inspected 2013.

🚐 100; Grass parking

🚰 Euro Relais Junior; Token (ER); Free from local bar

MACAU | 173 | D9 | 33460 | N45°00.433' W000°36.767'

Directions: Chemin du Mahoura. From D2 turn into Macau at the roundabout, sp 'Macau-Centre', and follow the road straight on. At the crossroads in the centre turn right onto D210, sp 'Ludun'. Take the next left, sp 'P Mahoura' and signed. The Aire is in the car park on the left, signed.

ℹ️ Small car park with small bays and very sloping. Very old Service Point. Inspected 2013.

🚐 4; 6m bays

🚰 Flot Bleu Océane; Token (required for elec only)

CAPIAN | 174 | E9 | 33550 | N44°42.769' W000°19.775'

Directions: D13. From Créon take D13, sp 'Cadillac' and 'Capian'. Turn left as enter village into 1st car park, signed. Aire at far end of car park, signed.

ℹ️ Landscaped Aire overlooking vines. Village 2 mins. Local sports and community facilities adj. Inspected 2013.

🚐 4

🚰 Aire Services; €2; 4 CEE elec points; €2/55 mins elec

SAUTERNES | 175 | E9 | 33210 | N44°32.050' W000°20.617'

Directions: D125e1. From Langon take D8 south. Turn right onto D125, sp 'Sauternes'. At village square/one-way system continue into village on D125e1, sp 'Bommes'. Service Point at far end of 1st car park on right immediately past church, signed. Designated parking in 2nd car park on right, signed.

ℹ️ Pretty tourist village with local commerce and wine tasting. Inspected 2013.

🚐 7

🔧 Custom; Lift front cover for WC

BAZAS | 176 | E11 | 33430 | N44°26.022' W000°12.912'

Directions: D655e1/Cours Gambetta. From south on N524 turn right onto D932e9, sp 'Bazas'. In town follow one-way system for 300m, staying to the left. Service Point on left adj to disused weighbridge. Turn left just after the Service Point into Rue du 11 Novembre 1918 and parking in adj car park. Easy to miss.

ℹ️ Aire in town centre car park. Town noise at night. Cathedral in centre. Inspected 2013.

🚐 10; 7.30pm-7am only Mon-Fri; No restriction at weekends
🔧 Euro Relais Mini

CADILLAC | 177 | E9 | 33410 | N44°38.319' W000°19.011'

Directions: Ave du Parc. Turn off D10 at roundabout onto D11, sp 'Targon' and signed. Turn left, signed, and follow one-way street. Aire located in the 2nd car park. Designated parking signed at far end. Access difficult due to parked cars Sat am (market).

ℹ️ Cadillac is a beautiful walled town surrounded by vines, 2 mins. Popular market Sat am. Inspected 2013.

🚐 8; Max 3 nights

🔧 Custom; 4 5amp elec points; €2/3hrs elec

ST ROMAIN LA VIRVEE | 178 | E10 | 33240 | N44°57.827' W000°24.106'

Directions: Route de Asques. From village centre on D737 follow sp 'Asques' and signed. Turn right as exit village, sp 'Salle des Fêtes' and signed. Follow road to bottom and the Service Point is on the left and the parking is on the right, signed.

ℹ️ On edge of village at sports facilities. Local commerce 1 min uphill. Only 5 mins from A10 but peaceful and always likely to have space. Inspected 2013.

🚐 6

🔧 Custom

CREON | 179 | E9 | 33670 | N44°46.578' W000°20.920'

Directions: Blvd Victor Hugo. In Créon follow D121e5 ring road. Aire in car park adj to ring road, signed. Drive to far end of car park. May be barriered to keep cars out; replace barrier after entry.

ℹ️ Boulangerie adj. Town 2 mins. Next village, La Sauve, has a ruined abbey. Voie Verte cycle route adj. Road noise. Inspected 2013.

🚐 5; Max 5 nights

🔧 Flot Bleu Océane; 2 unmetered CEE and Cont elec points

JUGAZAN | 180 | E9 | 33420 | N44°46.914' W000°08.576'

Directions: D128. Follow D128 east from town for 3km and Aire just after junction with D119 in lay-by on D128 at Labric, small hamlet adj to Jugazan.

ℹ️ Parking in lay-by on D128 in Labric, hamlet next to Jugazan. For services see 187. Better parking at 181. Inspected 2013.

🚐 4

🔧 None; See 187

GREZILLAC | 181 | E9 | | 33420 | N44°49.034' W000°12.989'

Directions: Le Bourg, off D11. Turn off D936 onto D11, sp 'Grézillac'. In village turn left after church opp Foyer Rural and Mairie, signed. Aire in gravel parking area on left.

i Pleasant parking overlooking vines and open countryside. Inspected 2013.

🚐 10

🚰 None; See **187**

NAUJAN ET POSTIAC | 182 | E9 | | 33420 | N44°47.223' W000°10.755'

Directions: Off D128. From Branne follow D19 south for 4.5km. Turn left onto D128, sp 'Naujan et Postiac'. Drive through village and turn right, sp 'Stade' and signed. Aire in small gravel parking area on left adj to stadium and grass area, opp vines.

i Cycle track from Bordeaux to Sauvetere de Guyenne signed in village. Stadium adj. Surrounded by vines. Inspected 2013.

🚐 3

🚰 None; See **187**

HAVE YOU VISITED AN AIRE? | GPS co-ordinates in this guide are protected by copyright law

Visit www.all-the-aires.co.uk/submissions.shtml
to upload your updates and photos.

Submit updates
- Amendments
- New Aires
- Not changed

i Directions and description.

🚐 Number of parking spaces; Cost per night; Time limit
🚰 Service Point type and details; Payment type; Cost

Take at least 5 digital photos showing
- Signs
- Service Point
- Parking
- Overview
- Amenities

FRONTENAC | 184 | E9 | | 33760 | N44°44.225' W000°09.772'

Directions: D231. In centre of village turn opp church and next to Mairie. Aire behind Mairie, signed. Service Point next to hexagonal building. More parking at end of road on grass.

i Beautiful 10 hectares of communal land adj to village and local commerce. Toilet block with outdoor sinks in high season. Inspected 2013.

🚐 30; Grass and hardstanding

🚰 Custom; Apr-Sept

SAUVETERRE DE GUYENNE | 185 | E9 | | 33540 | N44°41.400' W000°05.183'

Directions: Rue de la Gare, off D670. On south side of D670 ring road (one-way) turn right onto Rue de la Gare, sp 'Halte de Camping-Car'. Aire on right before Cave Co-operative (large wine vats). 3.5t weight limit on Aire.

i Tokens from Casino 'Maison de la Presse'. Cycle path to Créon. Inspected 2013.

🚐 5

🚰 Custom; Token; €1.50

ST PEY D'ARMENS | 186 | E9 | | 33330 | N44°51.176' W000°06.406'

Directions: Château Gerbaud, off D936e7. At St Pey D'Armens turn right onto D936e7, sp 'Château Gerbaud' and signed. Turn left, signed, then right past building and Aire in vines in 150m, very well signed.

i St Emillion wine area, tasting onsite. Very pretty town. Inspected 2013.

🚐 20; €5/night; Max 48hrs; Grass or gravel parking

🚰 Custom; 8 5-20amp CEE elec points; Elec €3

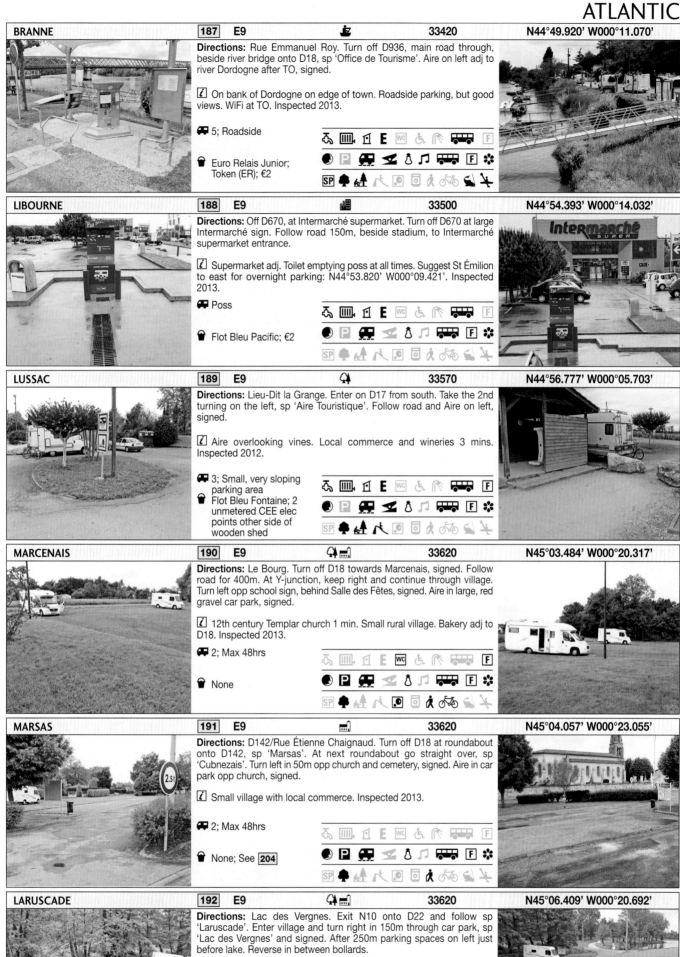

BRANNE | 187 | E9 | ⚓ | 33420 | N44°49.920' W000°11.070'

Directions: Rue Emmanuel Roy. Turn off D936, main road through, beside river bridge onto D18, sp 'Office de Tourisme'. Aire on left adj to river Dordogne after TO, signed.

ⓘ On bank of Dordogne on edge of town. Roadside parking, but good views. WiFi at TO. Inspected 2013.

🚐 5; Roadside

🚰 Euro Relais Junior; Token (ER); €2

LIBOURNE | 188 | E9 | 🏢 | 33500 | N44°54.393' W000°14.032'

Directions: Off D670, at Intermarché supermarket. Turn off D670 at large Intermarché sign. Follow road 150m, beside stadium, to Intermarché supermarket entrance.

ⓘ Supermarket adj. Toilet emptying poss at all times. Suggest St Émilion to east for overnight parking: N44°53.820' W000°09.421'. Inspected 2013.

🚐 Poss

🚰 Flot Bleu Pacific; €2

LUSSAC | 189 | E9 | 🍇 | 33570 | N44°56.777' W000°05.703'

Directions: Lieu-Dit la Grange. Enter on D17 from south. Take the 2nd turning on the left, sp 'Aire Touristique'. Follow road and Aire on left, signed.

ⓘ Aire overlooking vines. Local commerce and wineries 3 mins. Inspected 2012.

🚐 3; Small, very sloping parking area

🚰 Flot Bleu Fontaine; 2 unmetered CEE elec points other side of wooden shed

MARCENAIS | 190 | E9 | 🍇🏠 | 33620 | N45°03.484' W000°20.317'

Directions: Le Bourg. Turn off D18 towards Marcenais, signed. Follow road for 400m. At Y-junction, keep right and continue through village. Turn left opp school sign, behind Salle des Fêtes, signed. Aire in large, red gravel car park, signed.

ⓘ 12th century Templar church 1 min. Small rural village. Bakery adj to D18. Inspected 2013.

🚐 2; Max 48hrs

🚰 None

MARSAS | 191 | E9 | 🏠 | 33620 | N45°04.057' W000°23.055'

Directions: D142/Rue Étienne Chaignaud. Turn off D18 at roundabout onto D142, sp 'Marsas'. At next roundabout go straight over, sp 'Cubnezais'. Turn left in 50m opp church and cemetery, signed. Aire in car park opp church, signed.

ⓘ Small village with local commerce. Inspected 2013.

🚐 2; Max 48hrs

🚰 None; See 204

LARUSCADE | 192 | E9 | 🍇🏠 | 33620 | N45°06.409' W000°20.692'

Directions: Lac des Vergnes. Exit N10 onto D22 and follow sp 'Laruscade'. Enter village and turn right in 150m through car park, sp 'Lac des Vergnes' and signed. After 250m parking spaces on left just before lake. Reverse in between bollards.

ⓘ Shady parking adj to lake with partial views. Attended swimming in lake Jul-Aug. Village 1 min. Market days Thurs and Sat. Inspected 2013.

🚐 5; Max 48hrs

🚰 None; See 204

ST MARIENS | 193 | E9 | | 33620 | N45°06.915' W000°23.947'

Directions: D22, just off D18/D22 roundabout. Exit St Mariens on D22 towards Laruscade. After crossing D22/D18 roundabout turn 1st right and 1st right again, both sp 'Aire des Lagunes'. Designated parking in Aire de Repos.

ⓘ Toilet block with outdoor sink and picnic area adj. Some road noise. Inspected 2013.

🚐 2; Max 48hrs

🚰 None

CUBNEZAIS | 194 | E9 | | 33620 | N45°04.507' W000°24.529'

Directions: D248. Exit N10 and follow sp 'Cubnezais'. Enter village on D248. Turn left opp boulangerie, sp 'Cezac'. Turn right opp Foyer Communal building, signed. Aire on right in 100m, signed. Turn round in large car park on left if Aire is missed!

ⓘ Small designated area with small park adj. Large car park adj to recycling with views of vines. Bus stop adj. Local winery 300m offers motorhome parking. Inspected 2013.

🚐 2; Max 48hrs

🚰 Tap in WC; See 204

CEZAC | 195 | E9 | | 33620 | N45°05.475' W000°25.201'

Directions: Le Bourg. In village at traffic-lighted crossroads turn off D249 onto D248 towards church, sp 'St Mareins'. Turn left immediately in front of church, sp 'Mairie'. In 200m turn right in front of no entry sign into car park. Aire in car park, signed.

ⓘ Parking adj to bibliothèque overlooking football pitch. Village centre with convenience store 1 min. Inspected 2013.

🚐 2; Max 48hrs

🚰 None; See 204

CAVIGNAC | 196 | E9 | | 33620 | N45°06.009' W000°23.507'

Directions: Rue de la Paix. Turn left off D18 into Rue de la Paix next to La Poste, sp 'Eglise' and signed. Turn left in 150m, sp 'Rue de la Paix 80 places'. Aire behind Maison de la Petite Enfance, signed.

ⓘ Parking next to cemetery overlooking vines. Small town commerce 1 min and LIDL at north end of town. Super U south of town. Inspected 2013.

🚐 2; Max 48hrs

🚰 None; See 204

CIVRAC DE BLAYE | 197 | E9 | | 33920 | N45°06.736' W000°26.691'

Directions: D135/Parc de Mairie. From St Mariens take D135, sp 'Civrac de Blaye'. 300m after entering Civrac de Blaye turn right beside cross into 'Parc de Mairie', signed.

ⓘ Football pitches and tennis courts adj. Poss up to 10 spaces at stadium. Inspected 2013.

🚐 2; Max 48hrs

🚰 Tap at stadium; See 204

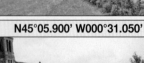

ST VIVIEN DE BLAYE | 198 | D9 | | 33920 | N45°05.900' W000°31.050'

Directions: D132. From St Christoly follow D132 south, sp 'St Vivien de Blaye'. At end of road turn right onto D135, sp 'Bourg'. At church turn left onto D132, signed. Aire next to church, signed.

ⓘ Gravel/grass parking area by church. Pond adj. May feel isolated if alone. Inspected 2013.

🚐 2; Max 48hrs

🚰 None; See 204

| BOURG | 199 | D9 | ⛺ | 33710 | N45°02.323' W000°33.606' |

Directions: Turn off D669, sp 'Le Port' and 'Halte Nautique', and follow road downhill. Turn right at the crossroads, sp 'Camping', and follow road to end. Service Point adj to campsite. Parking: Go straight on at crossroads at bottom of hill to large open area alongside river: N45°02.279' W000°33.456'.

ℹ️ Service Point at small, pleasant campsite, €8-€16/night. Citadel adj. Market Sun am. Steep climb from parking area to local commerce. Inspected 2013.

🚐 20; €5/10pm-8am; Pay at machine

🛒 Raclet; Token (ER); €2

| ST CHRISTOLY DE BLAYE 1 | 200 | D9 | | 33920 | N45°07.804' W000°30.473' |

Directions: Le Bourg, off D22. Turn off D22 in village centre by church. Drive past church and Service Point is on left by sports field, signed.

ℹ️ Parking restricted to 30 mins. Local commerce adj. Inspected 2013.

🚐 Max 30 mins; See 201

🛒 Custom

| ST CHRISTOLY DE BLAYE 2 | 201 | D9 | | 33920 | N45°09.202' W000°28.526' |

Directions: Lacs de Moulin Blanc. From St Christoly de Blaye/St Savin follow signs to 'Lacs du Moulin Blanc'. Both routes have 3.5t weight restriction. Once at lake follow signs to swimming beach. 2 marked bays, signed.

ℹ️ Lovely woodland area by swimming lake, partial views. Fishing in smaller lake. May feel isolated if alone. Inspected 2013.

🚐 2; Max 48hrs

🛒 None; See 200

| ST GIRONS D'AIGUEVIVES | 202 | D9 | | 33920 | N45°08.383' W000°32.567' |

Directions: Place du 19 Mars 1962. Aire in car park behind war memorial, opp church.

ℹ️ Lovely peaceful Aire overlooking grassy area. Inspected 2013.

🚐 2; Max 48hrs

🛒 None; See 204

| SAUGON | 203 | D9 | | 33920 | N45°10.678' W000°30.281' |

Directions: D252. Follow sp 'Saugon' on country roads. Aire adj to D252, main route, behind church and Mairie, adj to tennis courts, signed.

ℹ️ Rural village. Aire adj to playing fields and laundry in centre. Inspected 2013.

🚐 2; Max 48hrs

🛒 Custom

| ST SAVIN 1 | 204 | E9 | | 33920 | N45°08.396' W000°26.516' |

Directions: Rue des Vignes, off D23e2. Approach St Savin from east on D250. At roundabout in St Savin take 1st exit onto D23e2, sp 'Reignac' and signed. Turn 1st left, then left again, both signed. Aire behind TO, signed.

ℹ️ TO adj has free internet connection, must take own computer. Intermarché, 250m, has self-service laundry. Inspected 2013.

🚐 Max 30 mins; See 205

🛒 Custom

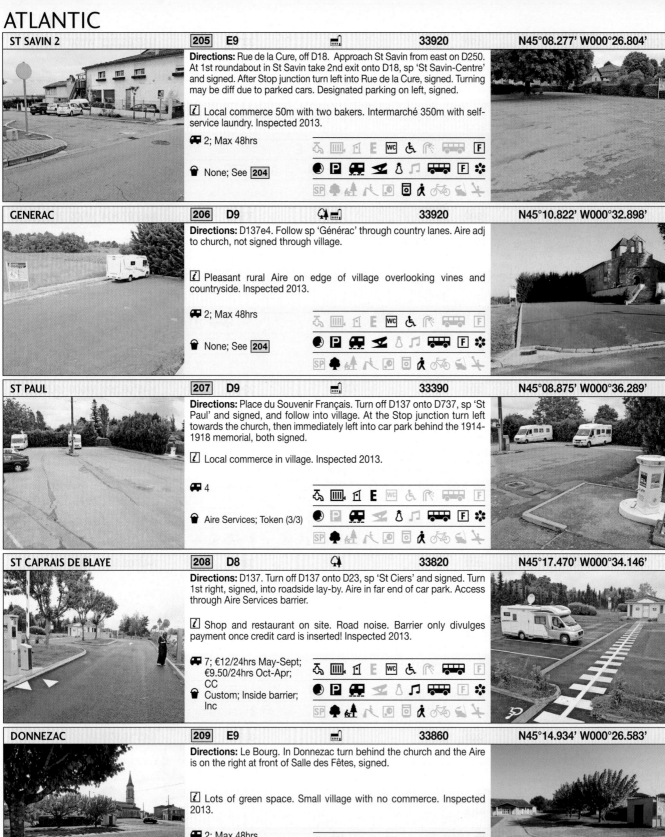

ST SAVIN 2	205	E9		33920	N45°08.277' W000°26.804'

Directions: Rue de la Cure, off D18. Approach St Savin from east on D250. At 1st roundabout in St Savin take 2nd exit onto D18, sp 'St Savin-Centre' and signed. After Stop junction turn left into Rue de la Cure, signed. Turning may be diff due to parked cars. Designated parking on left, signed.

i Local commerce 50m with two bakers. Intermarché 350m with self-service laundry. Inspected 2013.

2; Max 48hrs

None; See 204

GENERAC	206	D9		33920	N45°10.822' W000°32.898'

Directions: D137e4. Follow sp 'Générac' through country lanes. Aire adj to church, not signed through village.

i Pleasant rural Aire on edge of village overlooking vines and countryside. Inspected 2013.

2; Max 48hrs

None; See 204

ST PAUL	207	D9		33390	N45°08.875' W000°36.289'

Directions: Place du Souvenir Français. Turn off D137 onto D737, sp 'St Paul' and signed, and follow into village. At the Stop junction turn left towards the church, then immediately left into car park behind the 1914-1918 memorial, both signed.

i Local commerce in village. Inspected 2013.

4

Aire Services; Token (3/3)

ST CAPRAIS DE BLAYE	208	D8		33820	N45°17.470' W000°34.146'

Directions: D137. Turn off D137 onto D23, sp 'St Ciers' and signed. Turn 1st right, signed, into roadside lay-by. Aire in far end of car park. Access through Aire Services barrier.

i Shop and restaurant on site. Road noise. Barrier only divulges payment once credit card is inserted! Inspected 2013.

7; €12/24hrs May-Sept; €9.50/24hrs Oct-Apr; CC

Custom; Inside barrier; Inc

DONNEZAC	209	E9		33860	N45°14.934' W000°26.583'

Directions: Le Bourg. In Donnezac turn behind the church and the Aire is on the right at front of Salle des Fêtes, signed.

i Lots of green space. Small village with no commerce. Inspected 2013.

2; Max 48hrs

None; See 204

ST YZAN DE SOUDIAC	210	E9		33920	N45°08.432' W000°24.613'

Directions: D250. From St Savin take D250 east, sp 'St Yzan de Soudiac'. Aire on left in 3.5t restricted car park in village centre, opp school and next to Mairie.

i Small village with market on Wed am. Numerous commerce at St Savin. Inspected 2013.

2; Max 48hrs

None; See 204

ST MEDARD DE GUIZIERES	211	E9		33230	N45°00.925' W000°03.472'

Directions: D1089/Rue de la République. From Libourne follow D1089 east. At St Medard de Guizieres pass church and turn right opp junction with D21, sp 'P Mairie' and signed. Aire on left in small car park with difficult entrance, signed.

ⓘ Just off main shopping area with local commerce. Church adj. Inspected 2013.

2; Max 8m

Custom; Empty toilet under tap

LA ROCHE CHALAIS	212	E9		24490	N45°08.788' E000°00.340'

Directions: D674. Turn off D674 in town into the Intermarché supermarket. The Service Point is adj to the car wash. Access is difficult.

ⓘ Supermarket and self-service laundry adj. Inspected 2012.

Poss

Euro Relais Junior; €2; Drive over drain in car wash

BLAYE ✳	213	D9	T	33390	N45°07.536' W000°39.961'

Directions: Cours du Port. Follow D669 through Blaye, sp 'Citadelle'. Once alongside citadel walls turn off, sp 'Halte Nautique'. Designated motorhome parking in car park closest to river, signed.

ⓘ Popular Aire. River views from some bays. Citadel adj, free access. Town commerce 1 min. Pay Service Point and parking at Château Le Cone: N45°08.156' W000°39.864'. Inspected 2013.

50; Max 48hrs

None

Photo: Janet & John Watts

ST VINCENT JALMOUTIERS	214	E9		24410	N45°12.022' E000°11.440'

Directions: Moulin de Rafalie. Turn off D44 in village, sp 'Village Vacances' and signed. Cross river bridge and immediately turn right into Aire.

ⓘ Pleasant, peaceful Aire adj to shallow river and grassland. Village centre 2 mins with limited local commerce. Inspected 2012.

15

Custom; 2 unmetered Cont elec points under shed roof

ST ANTOINE CUMOND	215	E9		24410	N45°15.350' E000°12.031'

Directions: D43. Adj to D43 to the rear of the village car park.

ⓘ In village centre. Inspected 2012.

5

Custom

SOURZAC	216	E9		24400	N45°03.097' E000°23.715'

Directions: Ave du 11 Juin 1944, at junction of D6089 and D3e5. Aire adj to church and river bridge. Near A89/E70; ideal stopover.

ⓘ Views of either church or across river over surrounding countryside. Restaurant adj. Inspected 2013.

10; Max 24hrs

Euro Relais Junior; Token (ER); 6 5amp elec points (Not working)

VANXAINS | 217 | E9 | ⚲ | 24600 | N45°12.710 E000°17.036

Directions: D708. Exit Vanxains on D708 to south. 450m after exiting the village turn right into parking area, sp 'Stade' and signed. Aire on right above boules court, signed.

ℹ️ Adj to residential area, boules court and recycling point. Bus stop adj. Local commerce 4 mins. Inspected 2013.

🚐 3

🚰 Euro Relais Junior; 1 unmetered CEE elec point

ST AQUILIN | 218 | E9 | ⚲ | 24110 | N45°11.154' E000°29.315'

Directions: D43. Turn left as exit village on D43 to west, sp 'P'. Aire 20m on right at municipal service building.

ℹ️ A forgotten Aire at a municipal works building in a remote village. Service Point dilapidated; May fall out of use. Local commerce 2 mins. Inspected 2012.

🚐 5

🚰 Custom, on right side of building

ST LEON SUR L'ISLE | 219 | E9 | 🏢 | 24110 | N45°06.904' E000°30.029'

Directions: Route de la Lande. Turn off D3 onto D41e2, sp 'St Leon s l'Isle'. Turn right after crossing river bridge into parking adj to river: N45°07.202' E000°29.781'. For Service Point follow road through village and Service Point is adj to Maison des Associations, signed.

ℹ️ Located in peaceful village with some local commerce. Fishable river adj to parking north of village. Skateboard park adj. Inspected 2012.

🚐 5; Also 15 adj to river

🚰 Custom

RIBERAC | 220 | E9 | 🚢 | 24600 | N45°15.416' E000°20.545'

Directions: Aux Deux Ponts Ouest, off D708 outside municipal campsite. Follow D708 north out of Ribérac, sp 'Nontron'. Turn 1st left after crossing river Dronne, signed. Then turn left onto Aire, signed.

ℹ️ River adj, obscured view. Road noise. Kayak hire adj in peak season. Town centre commerce 5 mins. Inspected 2013.

🚐 20

🚰 Custom

DOUCHAPT | 221 | E9 | 🚶 | 24350 | N45°15.083' E000°26.600'

Directions: C1/Beauclair, off D710. From Ribérac take D710 east for 8km, sp 'Périgueux'. After passing through village of St Méard de Drône turn left, sp 'Village de Beauclair' and signed. Follow lane for 500m and Aire on right through gates, signed. Aire 1st turning on right after gates.

ℹ️ In grounds of holiday village. Swimming lake, no view. Washing machine available. Inspected 2013.

🚐 5; €5; Pay at Accueil (bar)

🚰 Euro Relais Junior; Token; €2

MENSIGNAC | 222 | F9 | 🏢 | 24350 | N45°13.378' E000°33.931'

Directions: Rue du Stade, off D710. From Périgueux take D710 towards Ribérac. Just before Mensignac boundary turn left, sp 'Aire de Service'. Aire straight ahead, adj to stadium.

ℹ️ 3 10m concrete patches in shade of trees surrounded by grass. Inspected 2013.

🚐 3

🚰 Flot Bleu Fontaine; €2; No drive over drain

CHATEAU L'EVEQUE `223` F9   24460   N45°14.667' E000°41.233'

Directions: Place du Jardin Public. Approach on D939 from south. Turn left at roundabout, sp 'Centre Ville'. Cross railway line and turn 1st right into car park. Then Service Point is on the left and the parking is on the right past the railway station.

i Landscaped area with gardens and footpath. Train station adj. Some train and road noise. Village with local commerce 2 mins. Inspected 2013.

🚐 8

🚰 Raclet; Token (ER); €2

TOCANE ST APRE `224` E/F9   24350   N45°15.436' E000°29.676'

Directions: D103/Rte de Montagrier, adj to stadium/municipal campsite. In village turn off D710 onto D103, sp 'Montagrier' and signed. After 250m, Aire on right through gate before village boundary, signed.

i Campsite open mid Jun-Aug. Token from campsite and village commerce. River Dronne 2 mins. Inspected 2013.

🚐 10

🚰 Euro Relais Junior; Token (ER); €2

LISLE `225` F8   24350   N45°16.878' E000°32.408'

Directions: Les Sonneries, off D1. Exit town north on D78 then turn left onto D1, sp 'Grand Brassac'. In 300m turn right, sp 'Camping Municipal'. The Service Point is on left outside municipal campsite.

i Token from campsite, open May-Sept. Service Point inoperable when campsite closed. Inspected 2013.

🚐 Poss when campsite closed

🚰 Euro Relais Junior; Token (ER); €2; May-Sept

BOURDEILLES `226` F8   24310   N45°19.383' E000°35.000'

Directions: D106. From Brantôme take D78/D106e2 to Bourdeilles. In village turn left off D106, sp 'Plaine des Loisirs'. Turn right after Service Point and follow signs around football pitch to grass parking by river on edge of village.

i River adj. Some hardstanding near Service Point. Fishing permits from Tabac. Market Sun am. Canoe hire. Inspected 2013.

🚐 50; €4/night; Collected; Grass parking

🚰 Euro Relais Mini; Token (ER)

PAUSSAC ST VIVIEN `227` E8   24310   N45°20.865' E000°32.309'

Directions: Le Bourg. From Bourdeilles follow sp 'Paussac St Vivien'. At the church turn left, sp 'Leguillac de C'. In 60m turn right, signed. Aire 20m on right.

i Small Aire at former Aire Naturelle. Inspected 2013.

🚐 3; Free 1st 24hrs, then €3.70/24hrs; + €1.60pp; Collected

🚰 Euro Relais Junior; Token (2/1); €2; 4 unmetered elec points

BRANTOME 1 `228` F8   24310   N45°22.700' E000°38.733'

Directions: Font-Vendôme. From south on D939 follow Brantôme bypass north. At roundabout take 2nd exit onto D675, sp 'Brantôme' and signed. Turn 1st left onto C417, sp 'Déchètterie' and signed. Aire on left down slope before motorhome dealer.

i Landscaped Aire. Motorhome dealer adj, parts/accessories available. Washroom. Inspected 2013.

🚐 4; €2; Collected

🚰 Custom; €1; Honesty box; 4 elec points

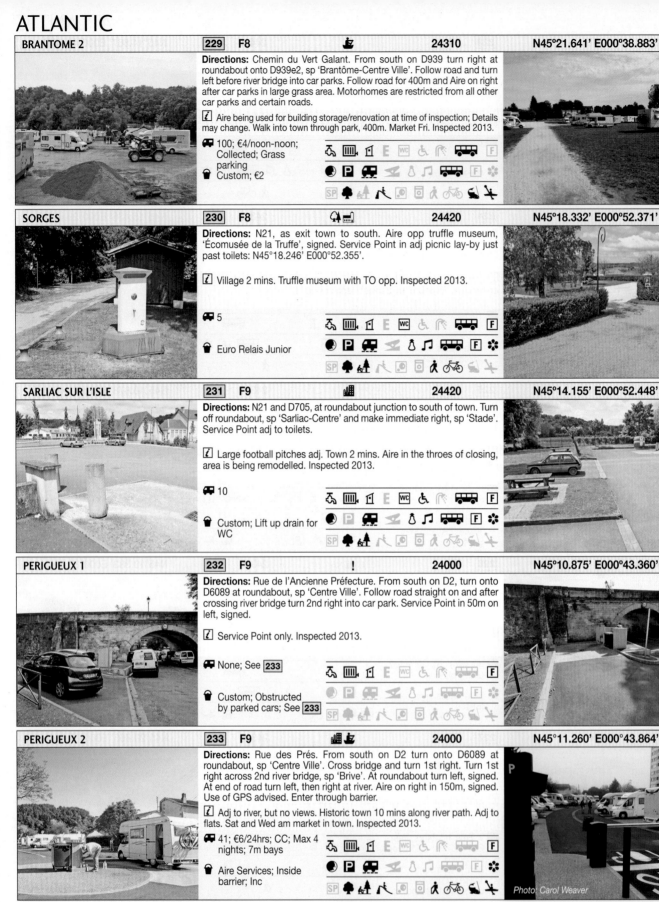

BRANTOME 2	229	F8		24310	N45°21.641' E000°38.883'

Directions: Chemin du Vert Galant. From south on D939 turn right at roundabout onto D939e2, sp 'Brantôme-Centre Ville'. Follow road and turn left before river bridge into car parks. Follow road for 400m and Aire on right after car parks in large grass area. Motorhomes are restricted from all other car parks and certain roads.

ℹ️ Aire being used for building storage/renovation at time of inspection; Details may change. Walk into town through park, 400m. Market Fri. Inspected 2013.

🚐 100; €4/noon-noon; Collected; Grass parking

🛢️ Custom; €2

SORGES	230	F8		24420	N45°18.332' E000°52.371'

Directions: N21, as exit town to south. Aire opp truffle museum, 'Écomusée de la Truffe', signed. Service Point in adj picnic lay-by just past toilets: N45°18.246' E000°52.355'.

ℹ️ Village 2 mins. Truffle museum with TO opp. Inspected 2013.

🚐 5

🛢️ Euro Relais Junior

SARLIAC SUR L'ISLE	231	F9		24420	N45°14.155' E000°52.448'

Directions: N21 and D705, at roundabout junction to south of town. Turn off roundabout, sp 'Sarliac-Centre' and make immediate right, sp 'Stade'. Service Point adj to toilets.

ℹ️ Large football pitches adj. Town 2 mins. Aire in the throes of closing, area is being remodelled. Inspected 2013.

🚐 10

🛢️ Custom; Lift up drain for WC

PERIGUEUX 1	232	F9	!	24000	N45°10.875' E000°43.360'

Directions: Rue de l'Ancienne Préfecture. From south on D2, turn onto D6089 at roundabout, sp 'Centre Ville'. Follow road straight on and after crossing river bridge turn 2nd right into car park. Service Point in 50m on left, signed.

ℹ️ Service Point only. Inspected 2013.

🚐 None; See 233

🛢️ Custom; Obstructed by parked cars; See 233

PERIGUEUX 2	233	F9		24000	N45°11.260' E000°43.864'

Directions: Rue des Prés. From south on D2 turn onto D6089 at roundabout, sp 'Centre Ville'. Cross bridge and turn 1st right. Turn 1st right across 2nd river bridge, sp 'Brive'. At roundabout turn left, signed. At end of road turn left, then right at river. Aire on right in 150m, signed. Use of GPS advised. Enter through barrier.

ℹ️ Adj to river, but no views. Historic town 10 mins along river path. Adj to flats. Sat and Wed am market in town. Inspected 2013.

🚐 41; €6/24hrs; CC; Max 4 nights; 7m bays

🛢️ Aire Services; Inside barrier; Inc

Photo: Carol Weaver

PUGNAC	234	D9		33710	N45°04.537' W000°29.912'

Directions: D249. Turn off D137 onto D249 at a roundabout, sp 'Tauriac'. Turn 1st right into the Intermarché supermarket and the Service Point is immediately on the left, signed.

ℹ️ Service Point only. Visited 2013.

🚐 None

🛢️ Aire Services Box; Token; €3

Info/Photos: Janet & John Watts

| LEMBRAS | 235 | E/F9 | | 24100 | N44°53.003' E000°31.510' |

Directions: Aire du Caudeau. In Lembras turn off N21 between two bus stops. Aire 100m on left, signed.

i Landscaped Aire away from main road. Local commerce 100m on N21. Visited 2013.

🚐 10

Custom; Free; Aire Services CEE elec; Token; €4/12hrs

Info/photos: Alan Greenwood/Rod & Liz Sleigh

| VILLEREAL | 236 | E10 | | 47210 | N44°38.271' E000°44.451' |

Directions: D104. Turn off D104 on west side of town, sp 'Aire de Jeux'. Drive to the rear of the car park for the Service Point.

i Aire in a peaceful location off main road. Town centre 200m with small town commerce and historic covered market. Market Sat am. Visited 2013.

🚐 30

Custom

Info/photos: Dave Wybrow

| LE MAS D'AGENAIS | 237 | E10 | | 47430 | N44°24.384' E000°13.204' |

Directions: D143. Turn off D6 onto D143, sp 'Lagruère'. Turn left in 300m to Aire.

i Aire adj to football ground. Village with local commerce 5 mins. Canal nearby. Visited 2014.

🚐 8

Custom; 2 unmetered CEE elec points

Info/photo: Peter Smith

| MERCULOT | 238 | E10 | | 24220 | N44°50.579' E001°02.019' |

Directions: Lieu dit Merculot. Turn off D703 onto D48, sp 'Berbiguières'. Turn off D48, sp 'Merculot'. Follow road for 400m uphill, then turn left into farm.

i Private farm Aire 3km from St Cyprien with lovely views across pastured valleys. Visited 2014.

🚐 6; €5

Custom; Inc; Elec €2.50

Info/photo: Martin & Joanne Rennie

Gastes

Vicarious Shop

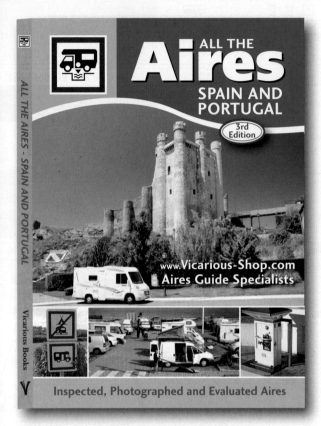
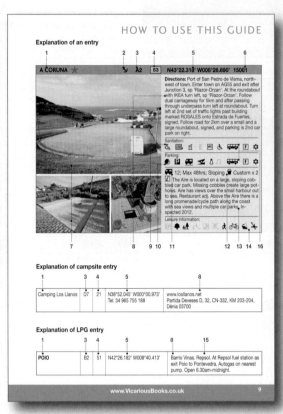
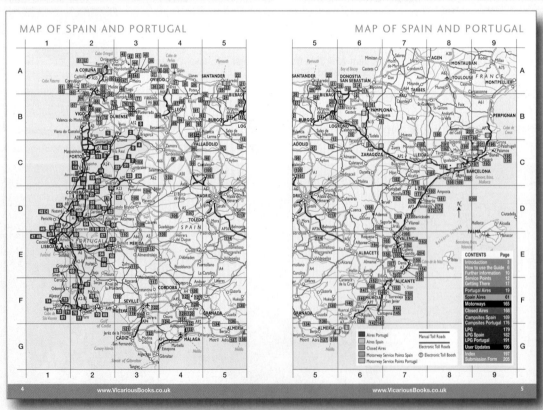

Vieille Brioude

LIMOUSIN & AUVERGNE

Turenne

| AINAY LE CHATEAU | | 1 | H7 | | 03360 | N46°42.322' E002°41.654' |

Directions: D953. South of the village adj to D953 at Internarche supermarket. Signed.

i Supermarket adj. Self-service laundry adj €9/18kg, €6/8kg, tumble dryer €1/10mins. Inspected 2012.

Poss

Flot Bleu Ocean; €2

| ST BONNET TRONCAIS | | 2 | H7 | | 03360 | N46°39.609' E002°41.824' |

Directions: D39. Enter village from south on D39. Service Point is on left at sports ground. Parking on grass behind the car park in the village, opp TO: N46°39.530' E002°41.538'.

i In Tronçais forest, a large forest with marked trails. Inspected 2013.

10; Max 48hrs; Grass parking
Custom; Token; €1.50/50L water; 1 unmetered Cont elec point

| LURCY LEVIS ★ | | 3 | H7 | | 03320 | N46°44.293' E002°56.336' |

Directions: Plan d'Eau des Sezeaux, Rue du Fontgroix. Turn onto Rue du Fontgroix at junction of D1 and D144, sp 'Plan d'Eau des Sezeaux' and signed. Follow to lake.

i Aire overlooking leisure lake. Small town close to Nevers and Loire river. 5 mins from town centre. Inspected 2012.

6; 7m bays

Aire Services; Token (3/3)

| AVERMES | | 4 | H7 | | 03000 | N46°35.218' E003°18.907' |

Directions: Rue Alphonse Daudet off D707, at the E'Leclerc fuel station. Well signed from town centre. Follow sp 'Nevers' from south.

i Supermarket; LPG at fuel station. Inspected 2010.

Poss

Flot Bleu Euro; CC; €2

Photo: Keith & Sue Lawrence

| MOULINS | | 5 | H7 | | 03000 | N46°33.506' E003°19.506' |

Directions: Chemin de Halage. Approach Moulins on D13 from Montilly. At roundabout go straight over, sp 'Montlucon' and signed. In 100m turn left, signed. Turn left again, signed, and follow road to Aire. Service Point on right. Parking accessed through Flot Bleu Park barrier.

i Former municipal campsite turned commercial Aire. Town centre 5 mins across river bridge. Inspected 2012.

30; €2.40/24hrs; CC; Pay at Flot Bleu Park; Grass parking
Flot Bleu Pacific; Token (FB) or CC; €2/4hrs elec or 20 mins servicing

---

| PARAY LE FRESIL | | 6 | H7 | | 03220 | N46°39.282' E003°36.775' |

Directions: D238, adj to roundabout by church. From Chevanges take D238 to Paray-le-Fresil. At Paray-le-Fresil follow sp 'St Martin des Lais' around church. Aire located off roundabout opp church, signed.

i Located adj to church, with daytime bells, in a small rural village. Inspected 2012.

3

Aire Services Box; CC; €2

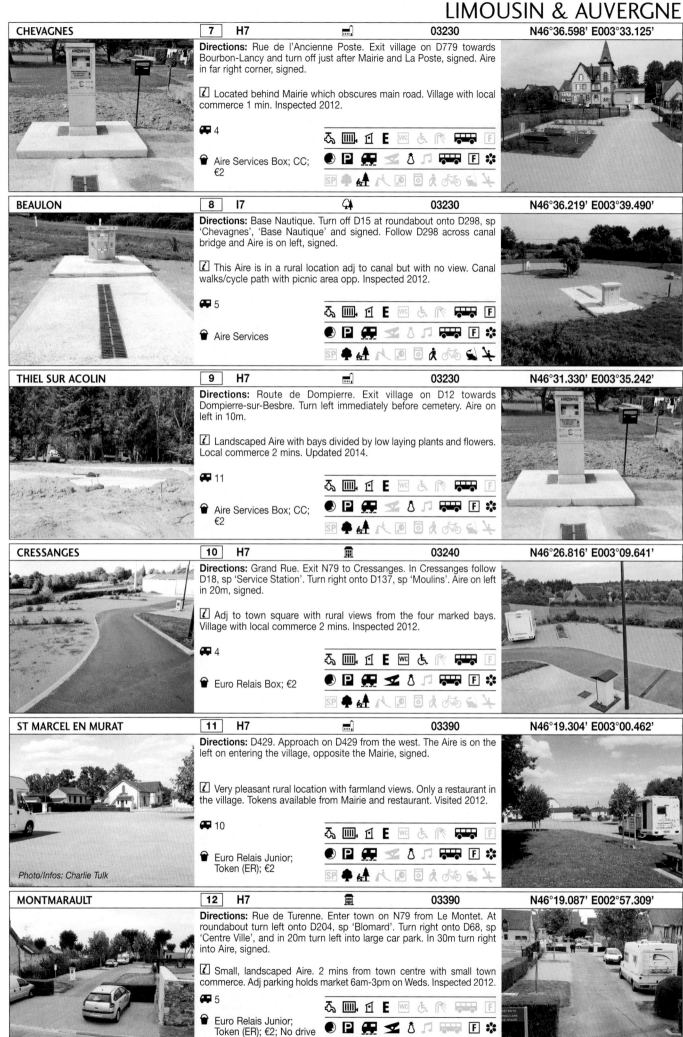

CHEVAGNES | 7 | H7 | 03230 | N46°36.598' E003°33.125'

Directions: Rue de l'Ancienne Poste. Exit village on D779 towards Bourbon-Lancy and turn off just after Mairie and La Poste, signed. Aire in far right corner, signed.

ⓘ Located behind Mairie which obscures main road. Village with local commerce 1 min. Inspected 2012.

🚐 4

🛒 Aire Services Box; CC; €2

BEAULON | 8 | I7 | 03230 | N46°36.219' E003°39.490'

Directions: Base Nautique. Turn off D15 at roundabout onto D298, sp 'Chevagnes', 'Base Nautique' and signed. Follow D298 across canal bridge and Aire is on left, signed.

ⓘ This Aire is in a rural location adj to canal but with no view. Canal walks/cycle path with picnic area opp. Inspected 2012.

🚐 5

🛒 Aire Services

THIEL SUR ACOLIN | 9 | H7 | 03230 | N46°31.330' E003°35.242'

Directions: Route de Dompierre. Exit village on D12 towards Dompierre-sur-Besbre. Turn left immediately before cemetery. Aire on left in 10m.

ⓘ Landscaped Aire with bays divided by low laying plants and flowers. Local commerce 2 mins. Updated 2014.

🚐 11

🛒 Aire Services Box; CC; €2

CRESSANGES | 10 | H7 | 03240 | N46°26.816' E003°09.641'

Directions: Grand Rue. Exit N79 to Cressanges. In Cressanges follow D18, sp 'Service Station'. Turn right onto D137, sp 'Moulins'. Aire on left in 20m, signed.

ⓘ Adj to town square with rural views from the four marked bays. Village with local commerce 2 mins. Inspected 2012.

🚐 4

🛒 Euro Relais Box; €2

ST MARCEL EN MURAT | 11 | H7 | 03390 | N46°19.304' E003°00.462'

Directions: D429. Approach on D429 from the west. The Aire is on the left on entering the village, opposite the Mairie, signed.

ⓘ Very pleasant rural location with farmland views. Only a restaurant in the village. Tokens available from Mairie and restaurant. Visited 2012.

🚐 10

🛒 Euro Relais Junior; Token (ER); €2

Photo/Infos: Charlie Tulk

MONTMARAULT | 12 | H7 | 03390 | N46°19.087' E002°57.309'

Directions: Rue de Turenne. Enter town on N79 from Le Montet. At roundabout turn left onto D204, sp 'Blomard'. Turn right onto D68, sp 'Centre Ville', and in 20m turn left into large car park. In 30m turn right into Aire, signed.

ⓘ Small, landscaped Aire. 2 mins from town centre with small town commerce. Adj parking holds market 6am-3pm on Weds. Inspected 2012.

🚐 5

🛒 Euro Relais Junior; Token (ER); €2; No drive over drain; 5 CEE elec points; Token

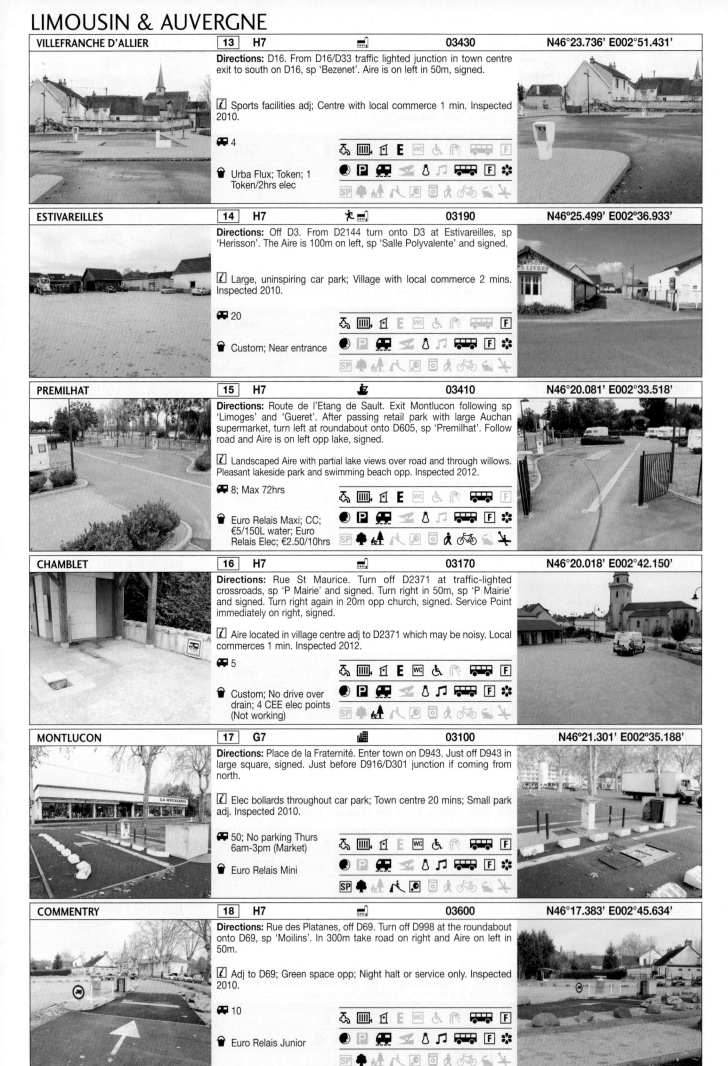

VILLEFRANCHE D'ALLIER | 13 | H7 | 03430 | N46°23.736' E002°51.431'

Directions: D16. From D16/D33 traffic lighted junction in town centre exit to south on D16, sp 'Bezenet'. Aire is on left in 50m, signed.

i Sports facilities adj; Centre with local commerce 1 min. Inspected 2010.

🚐 4

🚰 Urba Flux; Token; 1 Token/2hrs elec

ESTIVAREILLES | 14 | H7 | 03190 | N46°25.499' E002°36.933'

Directions: Off D3. From D2144 turn onto D3 at Estivareilles, sp 'Herisson'. The Aire is 100m on left, sp 'Salle Polyvalente' and signed.

i Large, uninspiring car park; Village with local commerce 2 mins. Inspected 2010.

🚐 20

🚰 Custom; Near entrance

PREMILHAT | 15 | H7 | 03410 | N46°20.081' E002°33.518'

Directions: Route de l'Etang de Sault. Exit Montlucon following sp 'Limoges' and 'Gueret'. After passing retail park with large Auchan supermarket, turn left at roundabout onto D605, sp 'Premilhat'. Follow road and Aire is on left opp lake, signed.

i Landscaped Aire with partial lake views over road and through willows. Pleasant lakeside park and swimming beach opp. Inspected 2012.

🚐 8; Max 72hrs

🚰 Euro Relais Maxi; CC; €5/150L water; Euro Relais Elec; €2.50/10hrs

CHAMBLET | 16 | H7 | 03170 | N46°20.018' E002°42.150'

Directions: Rue St Maurice. Turn off D2371 at traffic-lighted crossroads, sp 'P Mairie' and signed. Turn right in 50m, sp 'P Mairie' and signed. Turn right again in 20m opp church, signed. Service Point immediately on right, signed.

i Aire located in village centre adj to D2371 which may be noisy. Local commerces 1 min. Inspected 2012.

🚐 5

🚰 Custom; No drive over drain; 4 CEE elec points (Not working)

MONTLUCON | 17 | G7 | 03100 | N46°21.301' E002°35.188'

Directions: Place de la Fraternité. Enter town on D943. Just off D943 in large square, signed. Just before D916/D301 junction if coming from north.

i Elec bollards throughout car park; Town centre 20 mins; Small park adj. Inspected 2010.

🚐 50; No parking Thurs 6am-3pm (Market)

🚰 Euro Relais Mini

COMMENTRY | 18 | H7 | 03600 | N46°17.383' E002°45.634'

Directions: Rue des Platanes, off D69. Turn off D998 at the roundabout onto D69, sp 'Moilins'. In 300m take road on right and Aire on left in 50m.

i Adj to D69; Green space opp; Night halt or service only. Inspected 2010.

🚐 10

🚰 Euro Relais Junior

NERIS LES BAINS | 19 | H7 | | 03310 | N46°17.207' E002°39.137'

Directions: D155, at Camping du Lac. Follow sp 'Camping du Lac' through town. Located directly on D155 on west side of town.

i In thermal spa town. Beautiful town centre 10 mins, worth a visit. Parking available when campsite open. Inspected 2010.

🚐 6; €7 inc 10amp elec and showers; Pay at campsite
🚰 Raclet; Token (2/1); €2.50

CHAMBON SUR VOUEIZE | 20 | G7 | | 23170 | N46°11.170' E002°26.035'

Directions: Rue du Stade, off D915. Exit village on D915, sp 'Evaux les B' and 'Camping Municipal'. Turn off at Intermarché supermarket, signed. Service Point in 200m on left at entrance to the campsite.

i Service Point outside campsite. Nice village with 2 rivers and local commerce. Inspected 2010.

🚐 5

🚰 Euro Relais Junior; €2

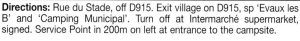

Photo: Vicky and Nick Church

MARCILLAT EN COMBRAILLE | 21 | H7 | | 03420 | N46°09.785' E002°38.240'

Directions: D1089 Rue de Combrailles. In village centre at roundabout take D1089, sp 'Poinsat'. Aire next to Gendarmerie (Police Station) on Rue de l'Économique, Adj to D1089 signed.

i A lovely, typical French village with local commerce and convenience store. Visited 2012.

🚐 18

🚰 Custom

Info/Photo: Roy Geddes

MONTAIGUT | 22 | H7 | | 63700 | N46°10.624' E002°48.376'

Directions: Off D988. In town turn south onto D988 at traffic light junction, sp 'Pionsat' and to truck parking. Turn left as exit town, sp 'Tennis'. Aire adj to tennis courts.

i On edge of village; Sport facilities adj; Town centre 3 mins. Inspected 2010.

🚐 5

🚰 Flot Bleu Pacific; Token; €2

ST ELOY LES MINES | 23 | H7 | | 63700 | N46°09.337' E002°50.152'

Directions: D2144. Adj to D2144 as enter from south, signed. Parking overlooking large lake.

i Views over lake possible; Town centre 5 mins. Swimming, boating, fishing adj. Inspected 2010.

🚐 20; Max 48hrs

🚰 Euro Relais Junior; €2

Photo: Carol Weaver

BELLENAVES | 24 | H7 | | 03330 | N46°12.325' E003°04.666'

Directions: D68. Exit Bellenaves on D68, sp 'Louroux de Bouble' and 'Vernusse'. Service Point adj to D68 on left outside campsite.

i Service Point only. Adj campsite charges €6.40 inc 2 adults. Inspected 2012.

🚐 None

🚰 Aire Services; €2

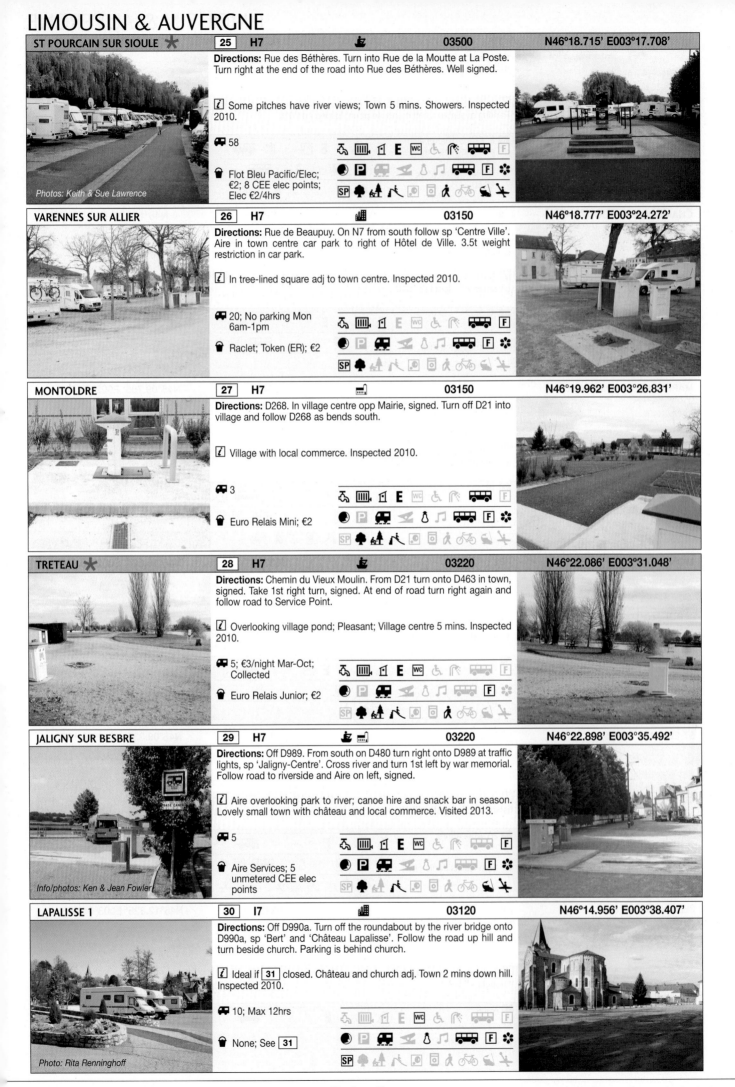

ST POURCAIN SUR SIOULE ★ | 25 | H7 | 03500 | N46°18.715' E003°17.708'

Directions: Rue des Béthères. Turn into Rue de la Moutte at La Poste. Turn right at the end of the road into Rue des Béthères. Well signed.

i Some pitches have river views; Town 5 mins. Showers. Inspected 2010.

58

Flot Bleu Pacific/Elec; €2; 8 CEE elec points; Elec €2/4hrs

Photos: Keith & Sue Lawrence

VARENNES SUR ALLIER | 26 | H7 | 03150 | N46°18.777' E003°24.272'

Directions: Rue de Beaupuy. On N7 from south follow sp 'Centre Ville'. Aire in town centre car park to right of Hôtel de Ville. 3.5t weight restriction in car park.

i In tree-lined square adj to town centre. Inspected 2010.

20; No parking Mon 6am-1pm

Raclet; Token (ER); €2

MONTOLDRE | 27 | H7 | 03150 | N46°19.962' E003°26.831'

Directions: D268. In village centre opp Mairie, signed. Turn off D21 into village and follow D268 as bends south.

i Village with local commerce. Inspected 2010.

3

Euro Relais Mini; €2

TRETEAU ★ | 28 | H7 | 03220 | N46°22.086' E003°31.048'

Directions: Chemin du Vieux Moulin. From D21 turn onto D463 in town, signed. Take 1st right turn, signed. At end of road turn right again and follow road to Service Point.

i Overlooking village pond; Pleasant; Village centre 5 mins. Inspected 2010.

5; €3/night Mar-Oct; Collected

Euro Relais Junior; €2

JALIGNY SUR BESBRE | 29 | H7 | 03220 | N46°22.898' E003°35.492'

Directions: Off D989. From south on D480 turn right onto D989 at traffic lights, sp 'Jaligny-Centre'. Cross river and turn 1st left by war memorial. Follow road to riverside and Aire on left, signed.

i Aire overlooking park to river; canoe hire and snack bar in season. Lovely small town with château and local commerce. Visited 2013.

5

Aire Services; 5 unmetered CEE elec points

Info/photos: Ken & Jean Fowler

LAPALISSE 1 | 30 | I7 | 03120 | N46°14.956' E003°38.407'

Directions: Off D990a. Turn off the roundabout by the river bridge onto D990a, sp 'Bert' and 'Château Lapalisse'. Follow the road up hill and turn beside church. Parking is behind church.

i Ideal if 31 closed. Château and church adj. Town 2 mins down hill. Inspected 2010.

10; Max 12hrs

None; See 31

Photo: Rita Renninghoff

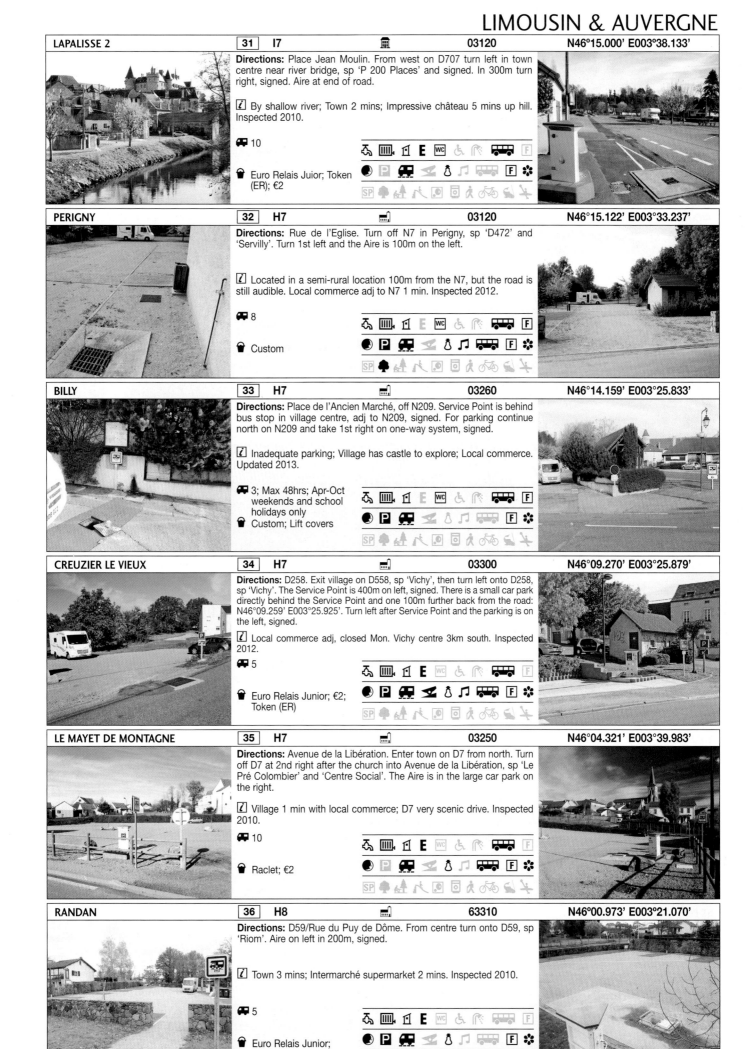

LAPALISSE 2 · 31 · I7 · 03120 · N46°15.000' E003°38.133'

Directions: Place Jean Moulin. From west on D707 turn left in town centre near river bridge, sp 'P 200 Places' and signed. In 300m turn right, signed. Aire at end of road.

By shallow river; Town 2 mins; Impressive château 5 mins up hill. Inspected 2010.

10

Euro Relais Juior; Token (ER); €2

PERIGNY · 32 · H7 · 03120 · N46°15.122' E003°33.237'

Directions: Rue de l'Eglise. Turn off N7 in Perigny, sp 'D472' and 'Servilly'. Turn 1st left and the Aire is 100m on the left.

Located in a semi-rural location 100m from the N7, but the road is still audible. Local commerce adj to N7 1 min. Inspected 2012.

8

Custom

BILLY · 33 · H7 · 03260 · N46°14.159' E003°25.833'

Directions: Place de l'Ancien Marché, off N209. Service Point is behind bus stop in village centre, adj to N209, signed. For parking continue north on N209 and take 1st right on one-way system, signed.

Inadequate parking; Village has castle to explore; Local commerce. Updated 2013.

3; Max 48hrs; Apr-Oct weekends and school holidays only

Custom; Lift covers

CREUZIER LE VIEUX · 34 · H7 · 03300 · N46°09.270' E003°25.879'

Directions: D258. Exit village on D558, sp 'Vichy', then turn left onto D258, sp 'Vichy'. The Service Point is 400m on left, signed. There is a small car park directly behind the Service Point and one 100m further back from the road: N46°09.259' E003°25.925'. Turn left after Service Point and the parking is on the left, signed.

Local commerce adj, closed Mon. Vichy centre 3km south. Inspected 2012.

5

Euro Relais Junior; €2; Token (ER)

LE MAYET DE MONTAGNE · 35 · H7 · 03250 · N46°04.321' E003°39.983'

Directions: Avenue de la Libération. Enter town on D7 from north. Turn off D7 at 2nd right after the church into Avenue de la Libération, sp 'Le Pré Colombier' and 'Centre Social'. The Aire is in the large car park on the right.

Village 1 min with local commerce; D7 very scenic drive. Inspected 2010.

10

Raclet; €2

RANDAN · 36 · H8 · 63310 · N46°00.973' E003°21.070'

Directions: D59/Rue du Puy de Dôme. From centre turn onto D59, sp 'Riom'. Aire on left in 200m, signed.

Town 3 mins; Intermarché supermarket 2 mins. Inspected 2010.

5

Euro Relais Junior; Token (ER)

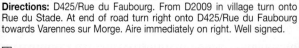

LE CHEIX | 37 | H8 | 63200 | N45°57.088' E003°10.695'

Photo: Keith & Sue Lawrence

Directions: D425/Rue du Faubourg. From D2009 in village turn onto Rue du Stade. At end of road turn right onto D425/Rue du Faubourg towards Varennes sur Morge. Aire immediately on right. Well signed.

i Countryside setting within walking distance of village. Beautiful spot. Updated 2013.

6

Custom

AIGUEPERSE | 38 | H8 | 63260 | N46°01.561' E003°12.192'

Photo: Keith & Sue Lawrence

Directions: From Grande Rue/D2009 turn onto D984 at roundabout. Turn right at next roundabout and take 2nd left into Rue de la Porte aux Boeufs. Aire situated at junction with Boulevard Charles de Gaulle.

i Town 2 mins. Inspected 2010.

10

Raclet; €2

Serviers le Chateau

POUZOL | 40 | H7 | 63440 | N46°06.189' E002°55.854'

Directions: Le Pont de Menat. Turn off D2144 near Pouzol, sp 'La Passerelle' and signed. The entrance is quite steep. Drive through the gates into Le Pont de Menat. Take the 1st turning on the left, signed, and follow the road to the right, signed.

i Aire in a pleasant rural location adj to the Gorges de la Sioule and Gorges de la Chouvigny. Distant road noise. Inspected 2012.

8; May-Oct

Flot Bleu Pacific; €2/20mins

EBREUIL | 41 | H7 | 03450 | N46°06.656' E003°04.855'

Directions: Chemin du Vieux Bard. From D998 through town follow sp 'Camping Municipal'. Service Point outside camping municipal. For parking continue 300m past the Service Point and at the end of the road turn left, then right into parking for the playing fields: N46°06.590' E003°04.537'.

i Tourist village. Playing fields adj. Inspected 2010.

20; At sports stadium

Euro Relais Junior

ST PARDOUX ★ | 42 | H7 | 63440 | N46°03.624' E002°59.710'

Directions: D2144. Enter village on D2144 from St Eloy. Turn right, sp 'Accueil Camping-Car'. Drive 1.5km and turn left onto track, sp 'Etang des Cayers' and 'Accueil Camping-Car'. Follow track down hill and around lake. GPS at turn onto track for clarity.

i A beautiful, remote and rural location. Not suitable for RVs. May feel isolated if alone. Inspected 2010.

4

Euro Relais Junior; Token (ER)

ST GERVAIS D'AUVERGNE — 43 — H8 — 63390 — N46°02.203' E002°49.107'

Directions: Follow sp 'Base de Loisirs - Etang Philippe' through town. The Service Point is at Base de Loisirs - Etang Philippe. Parking is off D534 in the car park opp the Carrefour supermarket and Sapeurs Pompiers (fire station) in the village centre: N46°01.845' E002°49.249'.

i Service Point at very pleasant leisure lake; Campsite open Apr-Sept. Parking in very ordinary town centre car park. Inspected 2012.

15; In village centre

Euro Relais Junior; €2

SAURET BESSERVE — 44 — H8 — 63390 — N45°59.544' E002°48.441'

Directions: D523. Near the church, adj to D523 in tiny village.

i Tiny village near Gorges de la Sioule. Inspected 2010.

5

Euro Relais Junior

ST GEORGES DE MONS — 45 — H8 — 63780 — N45°56.393' E002°50.573'

Directions: Place des Anciens Combattants. Turn off D19 onto D19 ring road. Turn off before town centre, sp 'Camping'. Service Point directly outside camping municipal.

i Town centre adj. Adj to large car park. Inspected 2010.

Poss, when campsite closed (Oct onwards)

Euro Relais Junior; €2

BROMONT LAMOTHE — 46 — H8 — 63230 — N45°50.394' E002°48.821'

Directions: Off D941. Turn off D941 to west of village, sp 'Camping' and signed. The Service Point is outside the campsite.

i Service Point only outside campsite. Inspected 2010.

None

Raclet; Token (2/1); €3

CHARBONNIERES LES VARENNES — 47 — H8 — 63410 — N45°53.076' E002°58.814'

Directions: D90. Turn off D943 west of Volvic onto D16, sp 'Paugnat' and signed. Follow road for 4km to roundabout taking 2nd exit onto D90. In 500m turn left, signed.

i Although close to habitation the Aire is shielded by trees and feels remote. In national park famous for springs, inc Volvic mineral water. Inspected 2012.

4; Between trees

Aire Services; Token (3/3); €2

MANZAT — 48 — H8 — 63410 — N45°57.724' E002°56.296'

Directions: D148. Turn off D19/D227, onto D418, sp 'Pulverieres' and signed. Aire 50m on right, signed.

i Large gravel car park; Town centre and local commerce 2 mins. Inspected 2010.

20

Custom

| ST BONNET PRES RIOM | 49 | H8 | | 63200 | N45°55.635' E003°06.832' |

Directions: Place de la Liberté, off D2144. Turn off D2144 at church into Place de la Liberté and stay to right at fork (higher road). Aire between church and Salle Municipal.

ⓘ Town adj with local commerce. Views of countryside. Updated 2014.

🚐 5; Max 24hrs

🛒 Custom

| CHATEL GUYON | 50 | H8 | | 63140 | N45°55.394' E003°03.962' |

Directions: Avenue du Général de Gaulle. Located just off D15 on town ring road in car park with plane trees. Sp 'Centre Ville' through town. Also parking at Parking des Roches and Parking Dupré Morand.

ⓘ In thermal town. Town 2 mins with plenty of commerce. Inspected 2010.

🚐 7; €5/night; Pay police municipal

🛒 Flot Bleu Pacific; Token

| RIOM | 51 | H8 | | 63200 | N45°53.680' E003°07.497' |

Directions: Route d'Ennazat. From Volvic approach on D986 and follow sp 'Riom', then turn left at traffic lights, sp 'Riom-Centre'. Follow sp 'Ennazat', 'A71' and signed. Cross railway bridge and the Aire is directly across the roundabout, signed.

ⓘ Adj to road which can be noisy during the day. Old town centre 8 mins. Inspected 2012.

🚐 4

🛒 Urba Flux; €2/15 mins elec and water

| CHATEAUGAY | 52 | H8 | | 63119 | N45°50.964' E003°05.077' |

Directions: Place Charles de Gaulle. Turn off D402, main route through, opp La Poste into car park just before exit village towards Volvic, sp 'Ecole Maternelle'. Service Point in far right corner, signed.

ⓘ Adj to school, no designated parking should be poss out of school hrs and at weekends. Inspected 2012.

🚐 Poss; Busy during school run

🛒 Aire Services; €2

| VOLVIC | 53 | H8 | | 63530 | N45°52.355' E003°02.813' |

Directions: Rue de Chancelas. Turn off D986, sp 'Camping'. Aire is outside the campsite.

ⓘ Designated parking located directly outside campsite; €10.50/2 people. Volvic has walking trails. Inspected 2012.

🚐 5; Max 6m

🛒 Aire Services; €2

| ORCINES | 54 | H8 | | 63870 | N45°47.271' E003°00.578' |

Directions: D941. The Service Point is located adj to D941 as exit the town towards Pontgibaud. Service Point near electricity pylon beside road.

ⓘ Service Point only outside campsite. Inspected 2012.

🚐 None

🛒 Euro Relais Junior; €2

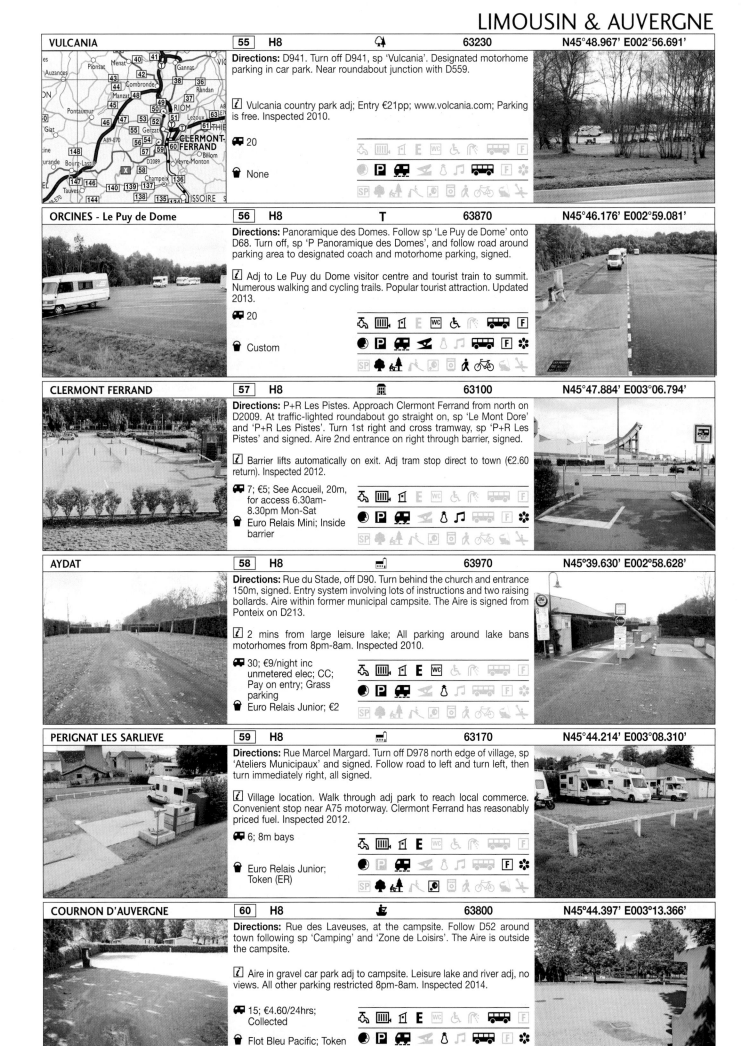

| VULCANIA | 55 | H8 | | 63230 | N45°48.967' E002°56.691' |

Directions: D941. Turn off D941, sp 'Vulcania'. Designated motorhome parking in car park. Near roundabout junction with D559.

Vulcania country park adj; Entry €21pp; www.volcania.com; Parking is free. Inspected 2010.

20

None

| ORCINES - Le Puy de Dome | 56 | H8 | T | 63870 | N45°46.176' E002°59.081' |

Directions: Panoramique des Domes. Follow sp 'Le Puy de Dome' onto D68. Turn off, sp 'P Panoramique des Domes', and follow road around parking area to designated coach and motorhome parking, signed.

Adj to Le Puy du Dome visitor centre and tourist train to summit. Numerous walking and cycling trails. Popular tourist attraction. Updated 2013.

20

Custom

| CLERMONT FERRAND | 57 | H8 | | 63100 | N45°47.884' E003°06.794' |

Directions: P+R Les Pistes. Approach Clermont Ferrand from north on D2009. At traffic-lighted roundabout go straight on, sp 'Le Mont Dore' and 'P+R Les Pistes'. Turn 1st right and cross tramway, sp 'P+R Les Pistes' and signed. Aire 2nd entrance on right through barrier, signed.

Barrier lifts automatically on exit. Adj tram stop direct to town (€2.60 return). Inspected 2012.

7; €5; See Accueil, 20m, for access 6.30am-8.30pm Mon-Sat

Euro Relais Mini; Inside barrier

| AYDAT | 58 | H8 | | 63970 | N45°39.630' E002°58.628' |

Directions: Rue du Stade, off D90. Turn behind the church and entrance 150m, signed. Entry system involving lots of instructions and two raising bollards. Aire within former municipal campsite. The Aire is signed from Ponteix on D213.

2 mins from large leisure lake; All parking around lake bans motorhomes from 8pm-8am. Inspected 2010.

30; €9/night inc unmetered elec; CC; Pay on entry; Grass parking

Euro Relais Junior; €2

| PERIGNAT LES SARLIEVE | 59 | H8 | | 63170 | N45°44.214' E003°08.310' |

Directions: Rue Marcel Margard. Turn off D978 north edge of village, sp 'Ateliers Municipaux' and signed. Follow road to left and turn left, then turn immediately right, all signed.

Village location. Walk through adj park to reach local commerce. Convenient stop near A75 motorway. Clermont Ferrand has reasonably priced fuel. Inspected 2012.

6; 8m bays

Euro Relais Junior; Token (ER)

| COURNON D'AUVERGNE | 60 | H8 | | 63800 | N45°44.397' E003°13.366' |

Directions: Rue des Laveuses, at the campsite. Follow D52 around town following sp 'Camping' and 'Zone de Loisirs'. The Aire is outside the campsite.

Aire in gravel car park adj to campsite. Leisure lake and river adj, no views. All other parking restricted 8pm-8am. Inspected 2014.

15; €4.60/24hrs; Collected

Flot Bleu Pacific; Token (FB); Lift cover for waste water disposal

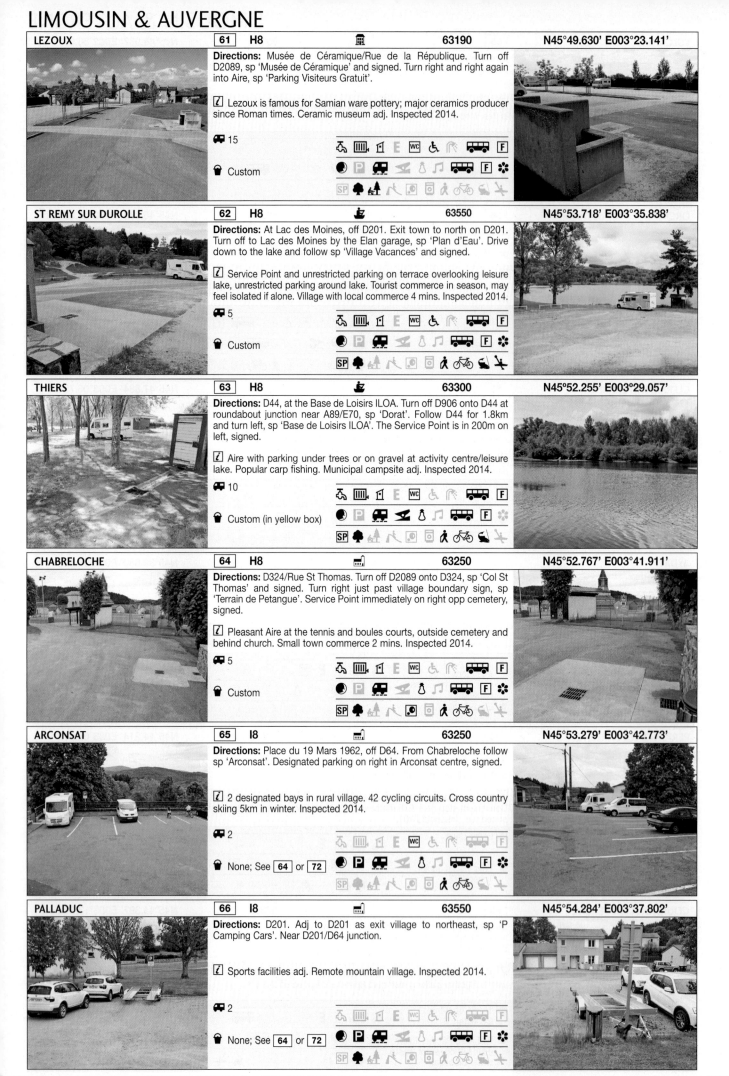

| LEZOUX | 61 | H8 | | 63190 | N45°49.630' E003°23.141' |

Directions: Musée de Céramique/Rue de la République. Turn off D2089, sp 'Musée de Céramique' and signed. Turn right and right again into Aire, sp 'Parking Visiteurs Gratuit'.

i Lezoux is famous for Samian ware pottery; major ceramics producer since Roman times. Ceramic museum adj. Inspected 2014.

🚐 15

🛒 Custom

| ST REMY SUR DUROLLE | 62 | H8 | | 63550 | N45°53.718' E003°35.838' |

Directions: At Lac des Moines, off D201. Exit town to north on D201. Turn off to Lac des Moines by the Elan garage, sp 'Plan d'Eau'. Drive down to the lake and follow sp 'Village Vacances' and signed.

i Service Point and unrestricted parking on terrace overlooking leisure lake, unrestricted parking around lake. Tourist commerce in season, may feel isolated if alone. Village with local commerce 4 mins. Inspected 2014.

🚐 5

🛒 Custom

| THIERS | 63 | H8 | | 63300 | N45°52.255' E003°29.057' |

Directions: D44, at the Base de Loisirs ILOA. Turn off D906 onto D44 at roundabout junction near A89/E70, sp 'Dorat'. Follow D44 for 1.8km and turn left, sp 'Base de Loisirs ILOA'. The Service Point is in 200m on left, signed.

i Aire with parking under trees or on gravel at activity centre/leisure lake. Popular carp fishing. Municipal campsite adj. Inspected 2014.

🚐 10

🛒 Custom (in yellow box)

| CHABRELOCHE | 64 | H8 | | 63250 | N45°52.767' E003°41.911' |

Directions: D324/Rue St Thomas. Turn off D2089 onto D324, sp 'Col St Thomas' and signed. Turn right just past village boundary sign, sp 'Terrain de Petangue'. Service Point immediately on right opp cemetery, signed.

i Pleasant Aire at the tennis and boules courts, outside cemetery and behind church. Small town commerce 2 mins. Inspected 2014.

🚐 5

🛒 Custom

| ARCONSAT | 65 | I8 | | 63250 | N45°53.279' E003°42.773' |

Directions: Place du 19 Mars 1962, off D64. From Chabreloche follow sp 'Arconsat'. Designated parking on right in Arconsat centre, signed.

i 2 designated bays in rural village. 42 cycling circuits. Cross country skiing 5km in winter. Inspected 2014.

🚐 2

🛒 None; See 64 or 72

| PALLADUC | 66 | I8 | | 63550 | N45°54.284' E003°37.802' |

Directions: D201. Adj to D201 as exit village to northeast, sp 'P Camping Cars'. Near D201/D64 junction.

i Sports facilities adj. Remote mountain village. Inspected 2014.

🚐 2

🛒 None; See 64 or 72

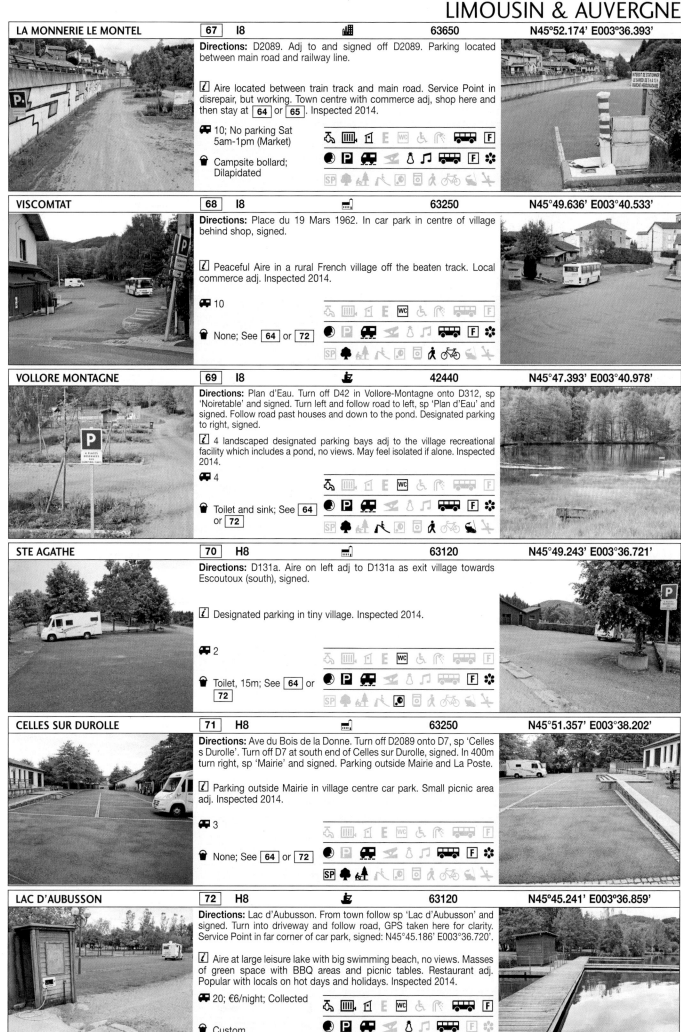

| LA MONNERIE LE MONTEL | 67 | I8 | | 63650 | N45°52.174' E003°36.393' |

Directions: D2089. Adj to and signed off D2089. Parking located between main road and railway line.

i Aire located between train track and main road. Service Point in disrepair, but working. Town centre with commerce adj, shop here and then stay at 64 or 65. Inspected 2014.

🚐 10; No parking Sat 5am-1pm (Market)

🚰 Campsite bollard; Dilapidated

| VISCOMTAT | 68 | I8 | | 63250 | N45°49.636' E003°40.533' |

Directions: Place du 19 Mars 1962. In car park in centre of village behind shop, signed.

i Peaceful Aire in a rural French village off the beaten track. Local commerce adj. Inspected 2014.

🚐 10

🚰 None; See 64 or 72

| VOLLORE MONTAGNE | 69 | I8 | | 42440 | N45°47.393' E003°40.978' |

Directions: Plan d'Eau. Turn off D42 in Vollore-Montagne onto D312, sp 'Noiretable' and signed. Turn left and follow road to left, sp 'Plan d'Eau' and signed. Follow road past houses and down to the pond. Designated parking to right, signed.

i 4 landscaped designated parking bays adj to the village recreational facility which includes a pond, no views. May feel isolated if alone. Inspected 2014.

🚐 4

🚰 Toilet and sink; See 64 or 72

| STE AGATHE | 70 | H8 | | 63120 | N45°49.243' E003°36.721' |

Directions: D131a. Aire on left adj to D131a as exit village towards Escoutoux (south), signed.

i Designated parking in tiny village. Inspected 2014.

🚐 2

🚰 Toilet, 15m; See 64 or 72

| CELLES SUR DUROLLE | 71 | H8 | | 63250 | N45°51.357' E003°38.202' |

Directions: Ave du Bois de la Donne. Turn off D2089 onto D7, sp 'Celles s Durolle'. Turn off D7 at south end of Celles sur Durolle, signed. In 400m turn right, sp 'Mairie' and signed. Parking outside Mairie and La Poste.

i Parking outside Mairie in village centre car park. Small picnic area adj. Inspected 2014.

🚐 3

🚰 None; See 64 or 72

| LAC D'AUBUSSON | 72 | H8 | | 63120 | N45°45.241' E003°36.859' |

Directions: Lac d'Aubusson. From town follow sp 'Lac d'Aubusson' and signed. Turn into driveway and follow road, GPS taken here for clarity. Service Point in far corner of car park, signed: N45°45.186' E003°36.720'.

i Aire at large leisure lake with big swimming beach, no views. Masses of green space with BBQ areas and picnic tables. Restaurant adj. Popular with locals on hot days and holidays. Inspected 2014.

🚐 20; €6/night; Collected

🚰 Custom

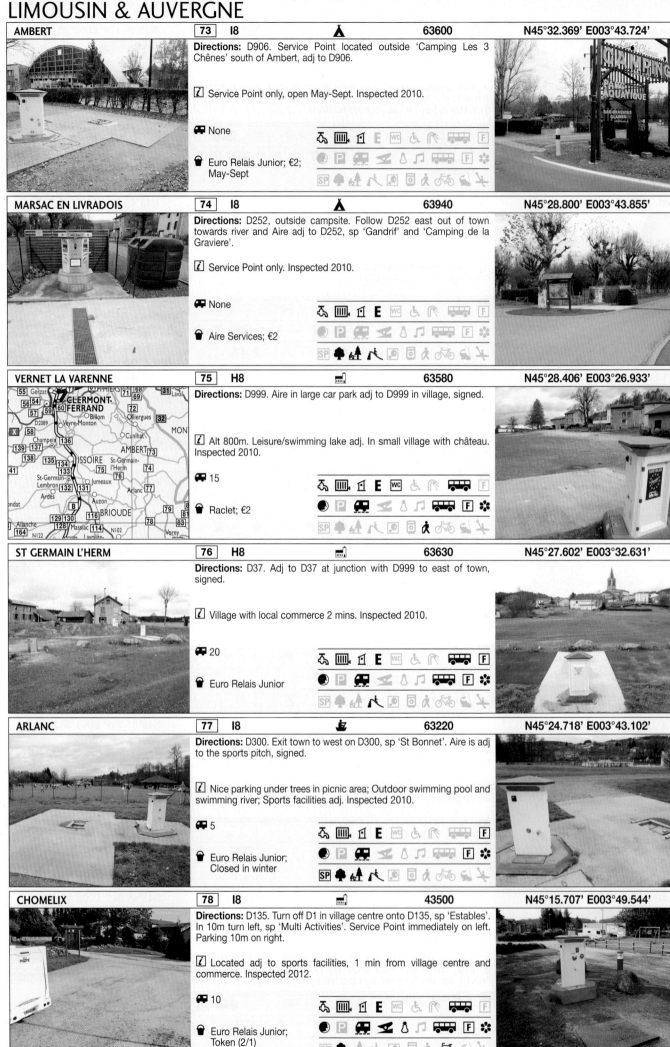

AMBERT	73	I8	⛺	63600	N45°32.369' E003°43.724'

Directions: D906. Service Point located outside 'Camping Les 3 Chênes' south of Ambert, adj to D906.

ℹ️ Service Point only, open May-Sept. Inspected 2010.

🚐 None

🛒 Euro Relais Junior; €2; May-Sept

MARSAC EN LIVRADOIS	74	I8	⛺	63940	N45°28.800' E003°43.855'

Directions: D252, outside campsite. Follow D252 east out of town towards river and Aire adj to D252, sp 'Gandrif' and 'Camping de la Graviere'.

ℹ️ Service Point only. Inspected 2010.

🚐 None

🛒 Aire Services; €2

VERNET LA VARENNE	75	H8	🛏️	63580	N45°28.406' E003°26.933'

Directions: D999. Aire in large car park adj to D999 in village, signed.

ℹ️ Alt 800m. Leisure/swimming lake adj. In small village with château. Inspected 2010.

🚐 15

🛒 Raclet; €2

ST GERMAIN L'HERM	76	H8	🛏️	63630	N45°27.602' E003°32.631'

Directions: D37. Adj to D37 at junction with D999 to east of town, signed.

ℹ️ Village with local commerce 2 mins. Inspected 2010.

🚐 20

🛒 Euro Relais Junior

ARLANC	77	I8	🎣	63220	N45°24.718' E003°43.102'

Directions: D300. Exit town to west on D300, sp 'St Bonnet'. Aire is adj to the sports pitch, signed.

ℹ️ Nice parking under trees in picnic area; Outdoor swimming pool and swimming river; Sports facilities adj. Inspected 2010.

🚐 5

🛒 Euro Relais Junior; Closed in winter

CHOMELIX	78	I8	🛏️	43500	N45°15.707' E003°49.544'

Directions: D135. Turn off D1 in village centre onto D135, sp 'Estables'. In 10m turn left, sp 'Multi Activities'. Service Point immediately on left. Parking 10m on right.

ℹ️ Located adj to sports facilities, 1 min from village centre and commerce. Inspected 2012.

🚐 10

🛒 Euro Relais Junior; Token (2/1)

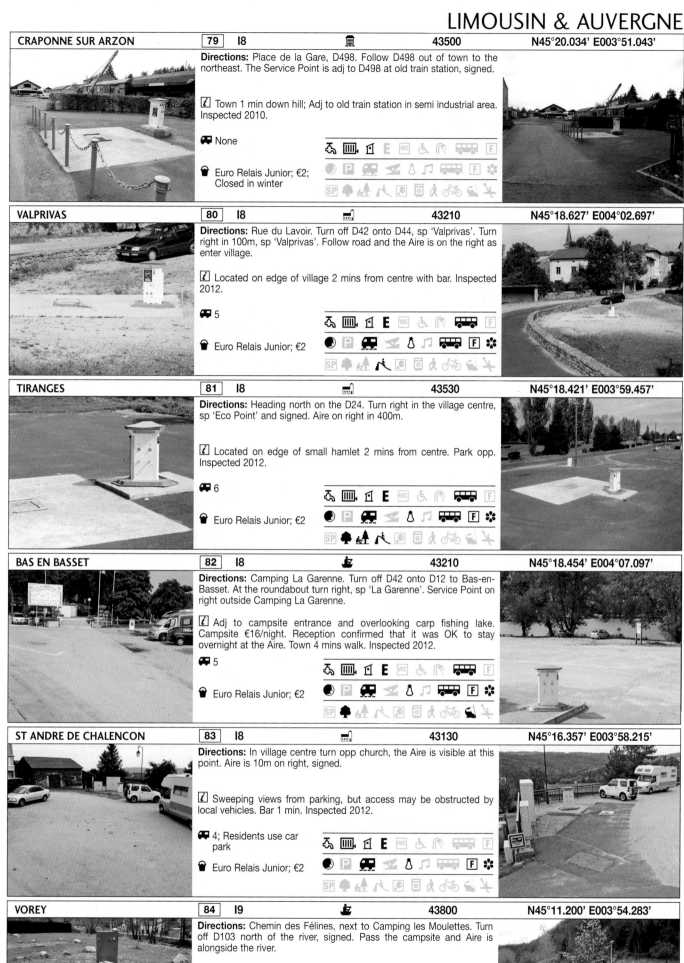

| CRAPONNE SUR ARZON | 79 | I8 | | 43500 | N45°20.034' E003°51.043' |

Directions: Place de la Gare, D498. Follow D498 out of town to the northeast. The Service Point is adj to D498 at old train station, signed.

ℹ Town 1 min down hill; Adj to old train station in semi industrial area. Inspected 2010.

🚐 None

🚰 Euro Relais Junior; €2; Closed in winter

| VALPRIVAS | 80 | I8 | | 43210 | N45°18.627' E004°02.697' |

Directions: Rue du Lavoir. Turn off D42 onto D44, sp 'Valprivas'. Turn right in 100m, sp 'Valprivas'. Follow road and the Aire is on the right as enter village.

ℹ Located on edge of village 2 mins from centre with bar. Inspected 2012.

🚐 5

🚰 Euro Relais Junior; €2

| TIRANGES | 81 | I8 | | 43530 | N45°18.421' E003°59.457' |

Directions: Heading north on the D24. Turn right in the village centre, sp 'Eco Point' and signed. Aire on right in 400m.

ℹ Located on edge of small hamlet 2 mins from centre. Park opp. Inspected 2012.

🚐 6

🚰 Euro Relais Junior; €2

| BAS EN BASSET | 82 | I8 | | 43210 | N45°18.454' E004°07.097' |

Directions: Camping La Garenne. Turn off D42 onto D12 to Bas-en-Basset. At the roundabout turn right, sp 'La Garenne'. Service Point on right outside Camping La Garenne.

ℹ Adj to campsite entrance and overlooking carp fishing lake. Campsite €16/night. Reception confirmed that it was OK to stay overnight at the Aire. Town 4 mins walk. Inspected 2012.

🚐 5

🚰 Euro Relais Junior; €2

| ST ANDRE DE CHALENCON | 83 | I8 | | 43130 | N45°16.357' E003°58.215' |

Directions: In village centre turn opp church, the Aire is visible at this point. Aire is 10m on right, signed.

ℹ Sweeping views from parking, but access may be obstructed by local vehicles. Bar 1 min. Inspected 2012.

🚐 4; Residents use car park

🚰 Euro Relais Junior; €2

| VOREY | 84 | I9 | | 43800 | N45°11.200' E003°54.283' |

Directions: Chemin des Félines, next to Camping les Moulettes. Turn off D103 north of the river, signed. Pass the campsite and Aire is alongside the river.

ℹ Adj to river overlooking sports field; Town centre 2 mins. Inspected 2010.

🚐 3

🚰 Custom; Token; €3

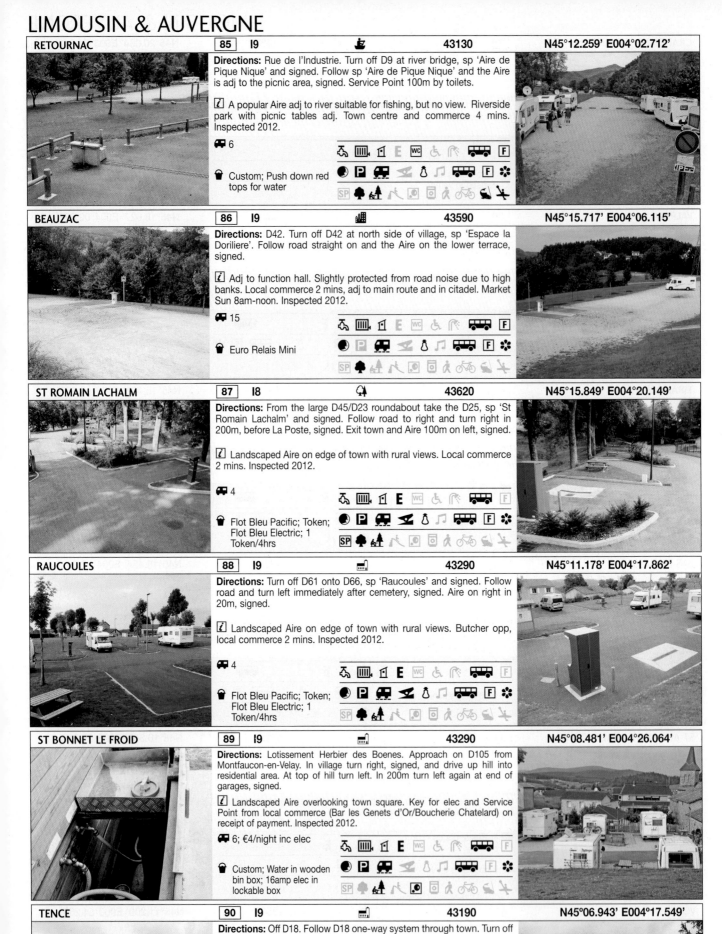

RETOURNAC | 85 | I9 | | 43130 | N45°12.259' E004°02.712'

Directions: Rue de l'Industrie. Turn off D9 at river bridge, sp 'Aire de Pique Nique' and signed. Follow sp 'Aire de Pique Nique' and the Aire is adj to the picnic area, signed. Service Point 100m by toilets.

ℹ️ A popular Aire adj to river suitable for fishing, but no view. Riverside park with picnic tables adj. Town centre and commerce 4 mins. Inspected 2012.

🚐 6

🚰 Custom; Push down red tops for water

BEAUZAC | 86 | I9 | | 43590 | N45°15.717' E004°06.115'

Directions: D42. Turn off D42 at north side of village, sp 'Espace la Doriliere'. Follow road straight on and the Aire on the lower terrace, signed.

ℹ️ Adj to function hall. Slightly protected from road noise due to high banks. Local commerce 2 mins, adj to main route and in citadel. Market Sun 8am-noon. Inspected 2012.

🚐 15

🚰 Euro Relais Mini

ST ROMAIN LACHALM | 87 | I8 | | 43620 | N45°15.849' E004°20.149'

Directions: From the large D45/D23 roundabout take the D25, sp 'St Romain Lachalm' and signed. Follow road to right and turn right in 200m, before La Poste, signed. Exit town and Aire 100m on left, signed.

ℹ️ Landscaped Aire on edge of town with rural views. Local commerce 2 mins. Inspected 2012.

🚐 4

🚰 Flot Bleu Pacific; Token; Flot Bleu Electric; 1 Token/4hrs

RAUCOULES | 88 | I9 | | 43290 | N45°11.178' E004°17.862'

Directions: Turn off D61 onto D66, sp 'Raucoules' and signed. Follow road and turn left immediately after cemetery, signed. Aire on right in 20m, signed.

ℹ️ Landscaped Aire on edge of town with rural views. Butcher opp, local commerce 2 mins. Inspected 2012.

🚐 4

🚰 Flot Bleu Pacific; Token; Flot Bleu Electric; 1 Token/4hrs

ST BONNET LE FROID | 89 | I9 | | 43290 | N45°08.481' E004°26.064'

Directions: Lotissement Herbier des Boenes. Approach on D105 from Montfaucon-en-Velay. In village turn right, signed, and drive up hill into residential area. At top of hill turn left. In 200m turn left again at end of garages, signed.

ℹ️ Landscaped Aire overlooking town square. Key for elec and Service Point from local commerce (Bar les Genets d'Or/Boucherie Chatelard) on receipt of payment. Inspected 2012.

🚐 6; €4/night inc elec

🚰 Custom; Water in wooden bin box; 16amp elec in lockable box

TENCE | 90 | I9 | | 43190 | N45°06.943' E004°17.549'

Directions: Off D18. Follow D18 one-way system through town. Turn off D18 down a narrow road which quickly widens, sp 'Parking le Fieu' and 'Maison de Retraite'. Aire in car park on left.

ℹ️ Large car park at rear of town; Service Point turned off in winter, but elec points working when inspected in Nov. Inspected 2010.

🚐 10

🚰 Raclet; 2 unmetered CEE elec points

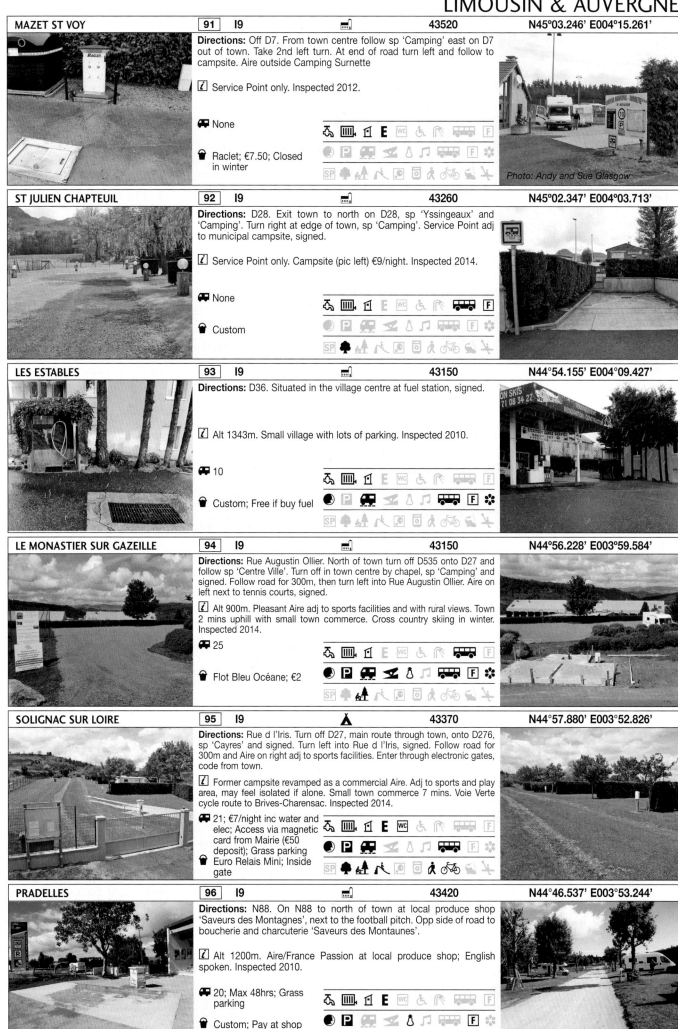

| **MAZET ST VOY** | 91 | I9 | | 43520 | N45°03.246' E004°15.261' |

Directions: Off D7. From town centre follow sp 'Camping' east on D7 out of town. Take 2nd left turn. At end of road turn left and follow to campsite. Aire outside Camping Surnette

i Service Point only. Inspected 2012.

🚐 None

🛢 Raclet; €7.50; Closed in winter

Photo: Andy and Sue Glasgow

| **ST JULIEN CHAPTEUIL** | 92 | I9 | | 43260 | N45°02.347' E004°03.713' |

Directions: D28. Exit town to north on D28, sp 'Yssingeaux' and 'Camping'. Turn right at edge of town, sp 'Camping'. Service Point adj to municipal campsite, signed.

i Service Point only. Campsite (pic left) €9/night. Inspected 2014.

🚐 None

🛢 Custom

| **LES ESTABLES** | 93 | I9 | | 43150 | N44°54.155' E004°09.427' |

Directions: D36. Situated in the village centre at fuel station, signed.

i Alt 1343m. Small village with lots of parking. Inspected 2010.

🚐 10

🛢 Custom; Free if buy fuel

| **LE MONASTIER SUR GAZEILLE** | 94 | I9 | | 43150 | N44°56.228' E003°59.584' |

Directions: Rue Augustin Ollier. North of town turn off D535 onto D27 and follow sp 'Centre Ville'. Turn off in town centre by chapel, sp 'Camping' and signed. Follow road for 300m, then turn left into Rue Augustin Ollier. Aire on left next to tennis courts, signed.

i Alt 900m. Pleasant Aire adj to sports facilities and with rural views. Town 2 mins uphill with small town commerce. Cross country skiing in winter. Inspected 2014.

🚐 25

🛢 Flot Bleu Océane; €2

| **SOLIGNAC SUR LOIRE** | 95 | I9 | | 43370 | N44°57.880' E003°52.826' |

Directions: Rue d l'Iris. Turn off D27, main route through town, onto D276, sp 'Cayres' and signed. Turn left into Rue d l'Iris, signed. Follow road for 300m and Aire on right adj to sports facilities. Enter through electronic gates, code from town.

i Former campsite revamped as a commercial Aire. Adj to sports and play area, may feel isolated if alone. Small town commerce 7 mins. Voie Verte cycle route to Brives-Charensac. Inspected 2014.

🚐 21; €7/night inc water and elec; Access via magnetic card from Mairie (€50 deposit); Grass parking

🛢 Euro Relais Mini; Inside gate

| **PRADELLES** | 96 | I9 | | 43420 | N44°46.537' E003°53.244' |

Directions: N88. On N88 to north of town at local produce shop 'Saveurs des Montagnes', next to the football pitch. Opp side of road to boucherie and charcuterie 'Saveurs des Montaunes'.

i Alt 1200m. Aire/France Passion at local produce shop; English spoken. Inspected 2010.

🚐 20; Max 48hrs; Grass parking

🛢 Custom; Pay at shop

Info/photos: Keith & Sue Lawrence

COUBON
97 | I9 | ⚓ | 43700 | N44°59.836' E003°55.006'

Directions: D37/Route du Plan d'Eau. In Coubon centre by the river bridge at the village car park, beside the church and cemetery.

ℹ️ Aire in popular local car park adj to river and lovely park. Small town commerce adj. Inspected 2014.

🚐 10; Max 6m; Must park in marked bays

🛒 Custom; €2.50; Mar-Nov

LE PUY EN VELAY 1
98 | I9 | 🏙 | 43000 | N45°02.979' E003°53.394'

Directions: D13/Boulevard de Cluny. From N88 turn onto D13, sp 'Vichy'. Service Point 200m on right before Super U fuel station, signed.

ℹ️ Service Point only. Inspected 2014.

🚐 None; See 99

🛒 Euro Relais Mini; Token (ER); No drive over drain

LE PUY EN VELAY 2
99 | I9 | T | 43000 | N45°02.634' E003°53.574'

Directions: Rue de la Gazelle. Follow signs in Puy centre. Parking outside the train station, signed, in the coach station.

ℹ️ Aire located in Puy centre at bus and train station. Busses drive through parking area. Large town commerce adj. Puy's medieval centre 10 mins downhill, then uphill. Inspected 2014.

🚐 8; €4.50/24hrs; Pay at machine to right of entrance against wall; Max 48hrs

🛒 None; See 98

AIGUILHE
100 | I9 | T | 43000 | N45°03.038' E003°53.017'

Directions: N102. Drive past 98. At roundabout go straight on, sp 'Vichy'. Go all the way around the next elongated roundabout, then turn right into car park. Designated parking on left, signed.

ℹ️ Adj to busy main road in parking at bottom of religious pilgrimage site Rocher St Michel, €3.50pp, www.rochersaintmichel.fr. Footpath to top with many steps. Puy centre 10 mins. Inspected 2014.

🚐 6; Max 24hrs; Max 9m

🛒 None; See 98

BEAULIEU
101 | I9 | 🏛 | 43800 | N45°07.602' E003°56.815'

Directions: Lois Saux. Turn off D103 at traffic lights in Lavoûte-sur-Loire onto D7, sp 'Beaulieu'. In Beaulieu turn off D7 just after Elan fuel station, sp 'La Galoche' and signed. Aire immediately on right.

ℹ️ This Aire has moved and is adj to the main road. Village centre with local commerce 4 mins. Updated 2014.

🚐 6

🛒 Custom

AIRE de SERVICE
RESERVEE UNIQUEMENT
aux CAMPING-CARS

Cette aire de stationnement vous est proposée gratuitement
MERCI de la laisser propre pour les futurs occupants

BEAULIEU VOUS ACCUEILLE A TITRE GRACIEUX
Vous trouverez au bourg:
- une boulangerie épicerie
- un bar-tabac-journaux
- une coiffeuse
- un médecin ..... Merci de penser à eux ...

Pour tous renseignements complémentaires
s'adresser à la MAIRIE: 04.71.08.53.60

ST PAULIEN
102 | I9 | ⛺ | 43350 | N45°07.223' E003°47.607'

Directions: D25. Turn off D906 in St Paulien by the church onto D13, sp 'Allegre'. Turn left onto D25, sp 'Loudes' and 'Camping'. Service Point on left outside campsite entrance.

ℹ️ Service Point only. Inspected 2012.

🚐 None

🛒 Urba Flux Tall; €3

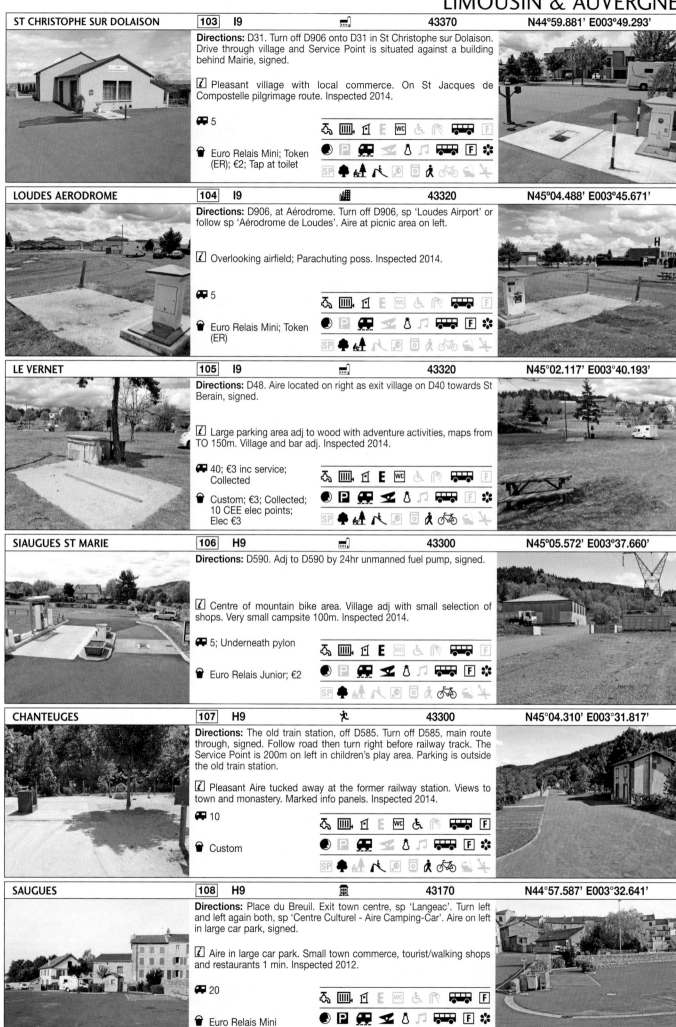

| ST CHRISTOPHE SUR DOLAISON | 103 | I9 | | 43370 | N44°59.881' E003°49.293' |

Directions: D31. Turn off D906 onto D31 in St Christophe sur Dolaison. Drive through village and Service Point is situated against a building behind Mairie, signed.

ⓘ Pleasant village with local commerce. On St Jacques de Compostelle pilgrimage route. Inspected 2014.

🚐 5

🛒 Euro Relais Mini; Token (ER); €2; Tap at toilet

| LOUDES AERODROME | 104 | I9 | | 43320 | N45°04.488' E003°45.671' |

Directions: D906, at Aérodrome. Turn off D906, sp 'Loudes Airport' or follow sp 'Aérodrome de Loudes'. Aire at picnic area on left.

ⓘ Overlooking airfield; Parachuting poss. Inspected 2014.

🚐 5

🛒 Euro Relais Mini; Token (ER)

| LE VERNET | 105 | I9 | | 43320 | N45°02.117' E003°40.193' |

Directions: D48. Aire located on right as exit village on D40 towards St Berain, signed.

ⓘ Large parking area adj to wood with adventure activities, maps from TO 150m. Village and bar adj. Inspected 2014.

🚐 40; €3 inc service; Collected

🛒 Custom; €3; Collected; 10 CEE elec points; Elec €3

| SIAUGUES ST MARIE | 106 | H9 | | 43300 | N45°05.572' E003°37.660' |

Directions: D590. Adj to D590 by 24hr unmanned fuel pump, signed.

ⓘ Centre of mountain bike area. Village adj with small selection of shops. Very small campsite 100m. Inspected 2014.

🚐 5; Underneath pylon

🛒 Euro Relais Junior; €2

| CHANTEUGES | 107 | H9 | | 43300 | N45°04.310' E003°31.817' |

Directions: The old train station, off D585. Turn off D585, main route through, signed. Follow road then turn right before railway track. The Service Point is 200m on left in children's play area. Parking is outside the old train station.

ⓘ Pleasant Aire tucked away at the former railway station. Views to town and monastery. Marked info panels. Inspected 2014.

🚐 10

🛒 Custom

| SAUGUES | 108 | H9 | | 43170 | N44°57.587' E003°32.641' |

Directions: Place du Breuil. Exit town centre, sp 'Langeac'. Turn left and left again both, sp 'Centre Culturel - Aire Camping-Car'. Aire on left in large car park, signed.

ⓘ Aire in large car park. Small town commerce, tourist/walking shops and restaurants 1 min. Inspected 2012.

🚐 20

🛒 Euro Relais Mini

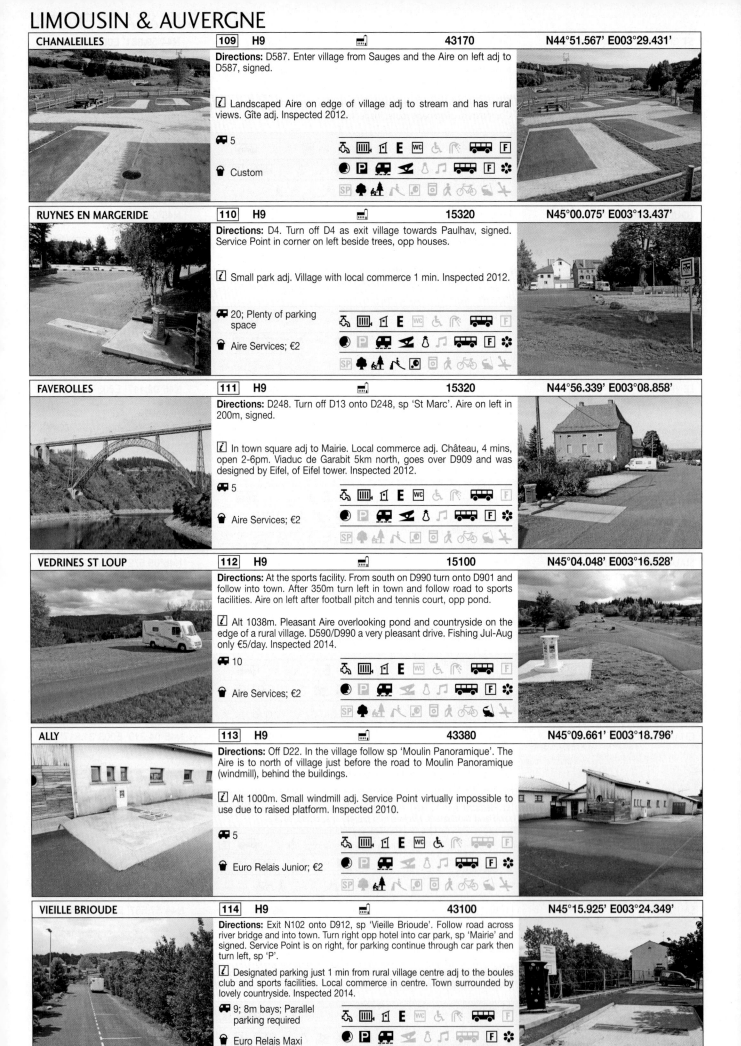

| CHANALEILLES | 109 | H9 | | 43170 | N44°51.567' E003°29.431' |

Directions: D587. Enter village from Sauges and the Aire on left adj to D587, signed.

i Landscaped Aire on edge of village adj to stream and has rural views. Gîte adj. Inspected 2012.

5

Custom

| RUYNES EN MARGERIDE | 110 | H9 | | 15320 | N45°00.075' E003°13.437' |

Directions: D4. Turn off D4 as exit village towards Paulhav, signed. Service Point in corner on left beside trees, opp houses.

i Small park adj. Village with local commerce 1 min. Inspected 2012.

20; Plenty of parking space

Aire Services; €2

| FAVEROLLES | 111 | H9 | | 15320 | N44°56.339' E003°08.858' |

Directions: D248. Turn off D13 onto D248, sp 'St Marc'. Aire on left in 200m, signed.

i In town square adj to Mairie. Local commerce adj. Château, 4 mins, open 2-6pm. Viaduc de Garabit 5km north, goes over D909 and was designed by Eifel, of Eifel tower. Inspected 2012.

5

Aire Services; €2

| VEDRINES ST LOUP | 112 | H9 | | 15100 | N45°04.048' E003°16.528' |

Directions: At the sports facility. From south on D990 turn onto D901 and follow into town. After 350m turn left in town and follow road to sports facilities. Aire on left after football pitch and tennis court, opp pond.

i Alt 1038m. Pleasant Aire overlooking pond and countryside on the edge of a rural village. D590/D990 a very pleasant drive. Fishing Jul-Aug only €5/day. Inspected 2014.

10

Aire Services; €2

| ALLY | 113 | H9 | | 43380 | N45°09.661' E003°18.796' |

Directions: Off D22. In the village follow sp 'Moulin Panoramique'. The Aire is to north of village just before the road to Moulin Panoramique (windmill), behind the buildings.

i Alt 1000m. Small windmill adj. Service Point virtually impossible to use due to raised platform. Inspected 2010.

5

Euro Relais Junior; €2

| VIEILLE BRIOUDE | 114 | H9 | | 43100 | N45°15.925' E003°24.349' |

Directions: Exit N102 onto D912, sp 'Vieille Brioude'. Follow road across river bridge and into town. Turn right opp hotel into car park, sp 'Mairie' and signed. Service Point is on right, for parking continue through car park then turn left, sp 'P'.

i Designated parking just 1 min from rural village centre adj to the boules club and sports facilities. Local commerce in centre. Town surrounded by lovely countryside. Inspected 2014.

9; 8m bays; Parallel parking required

Euro Relais Maxi (Burgundy); CC

HAVE YOU VISITED AN AIRE?

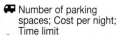

Submit updates
• Amendments
• New Aires
• Not changed

Visit www.all-the-aires.co.uk/submissions.shtml
to upload your updates and photos.

ℹ️ Directions and description.

🚐 Number of parking spaces; Cost per night; Time limit

🚰 Service Point type and details; Payment type; Cost

Take at least 5 digital photos showing
• Signs
• Service Point
• Parking
• Overview
• Amenities

BRIOUDE	116	H8	🏛️	43100	N45°17.679' E003°23.256'

Directions: D588. From N102 enter Brioude on D588 from roundabout. Go under 4m bridge following sp 'Centre Ville', then turn right, sp 'P Centre Historique' and signed. Service Point 50m on right, parking adj. Sp 'P Centre Historique' throughout town.

ℹ️ Adj to city wall. Town 3 mins uphill or via lift. Nearby Lavaudieu is a Beau Village with parking: N45°15.840' E003°27.501'. Inspected 2014.

🚐 20

🚰 Flot Bleu Pacific (Burgundy); Token

LA CHAPELLE LAURENT	117	H9		15500	N45°10.830' E003°14.635'

Directions: D10. On D10 as exit town towards St-Laurent-Chabreuges (north). 20 mins from Junction 25 on A75.

ℹ️ Alt 970m. Grass parking adj to sports facilities on edge of town. Local commerce, 2 mins, includes a very large cheese shop. Car park, 300m, provides good winter parking. Inspected 2014.

🚐 10; Grass parking

🚰 Custom; €1; Turned off in winter

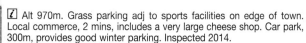

ST FLOUR 1	118	H9	🏢	03100	N45°02.157' E003°05.905'

Directions: Rue Marie-Aimée Méraville. Exit A75 at Junction 28, sp 'St Flour'. At roundabout follow sp 'St Flour'. Follow road until enter town (at bottom of hill). Turn right, signed. Follow road, turning left across bridge, and Aire is then on right.

ℹ️ Quieter Aire than 119 in residential area with views of hilltop town. Only likely to be busy when events on at 119. Lower town commerce 2 mins. Inspected 2014.

🚐 10

🚰 Euro Relais Maxi; €2

ST FLOUR 2	119	H9	🏢	15100	N45°02.059' E003°05.251'

Directions: Cours Chazerat. Take D926 up hill, sp 'Haute Ville'. At top of hill go straight on at roundabout and through car park. Turn left at roundabout and then next left into Cours Chazerat. Service Point in Cours Chazerat, outside hospital.

ℹ️ Service Point located in centre of hilltop town with town commerce adj. Large car park, but parking subject to local events. Inspected 2014.

🚐 50

🚰 Euro Relais Maxi; €2

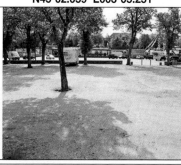

CHAUDES AIGUES	120	H9	🏢	15110	N44°50.986' E003°00.182'

Directions: Off D981. Turn off D921 onto D989 in town, signed. Do not cross river bridge, but drive straight on through gap into large car park behind.

ℹ️ Town 2 mins; Natural spring water 87°F. Aire in unglamorous, but well located car park. Inspected 2010.

🚐 20

🚰 Raclet; €2

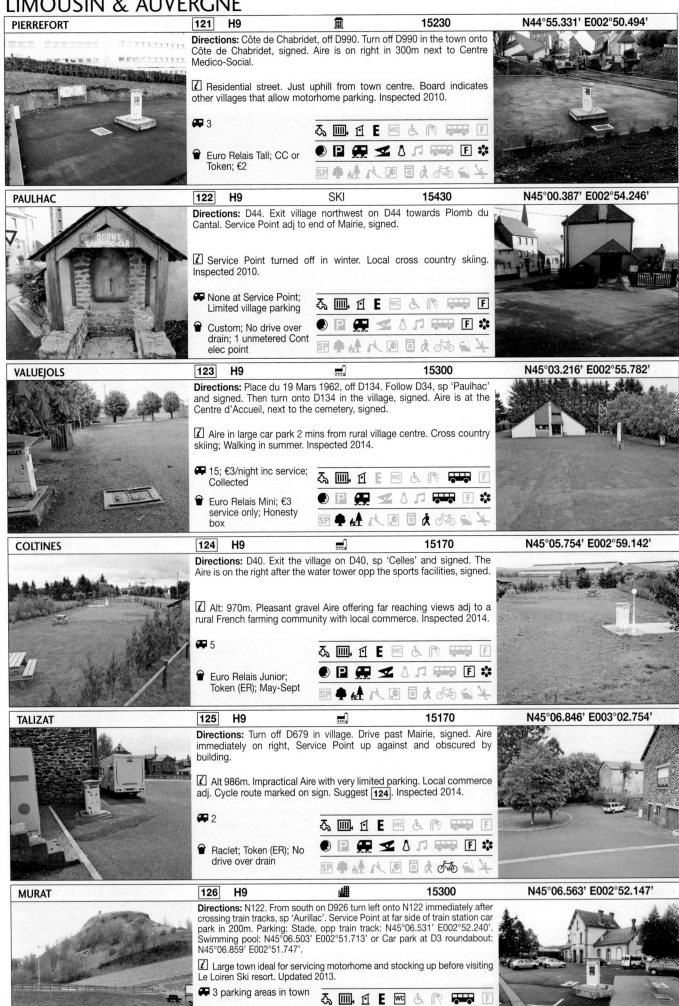

PIERREFORT | 121 | H9 | | 15230 | N44°55.331' E002°50.494'

Directions: Côte de Chabridet, off D990. Turn off D990 in the town onto Côte de Chabridet, signed. Aire is on right in 300m next to Centre Medico-Social.

i Residential street. Just uphill from town centre. Board indicates other villages that allow motorhome parking. Inspected 2010.

🚐 3

🛒 Euro Relais Tall; CC or Token; €2

PAULHAC | 122 | H9 | SKI | 15430 | N45°00.387' E002°54.246'

Directions: D44. Exit village northwest on D44 towards Plomb du Cantal. Service Point adj to end of Mairie, signed.

i Service Point turned off in winter. Local cross country skiing. Inspected 2010.

🚐 None at Service Point; Limited village parking

🛒 Custom; No drive over drain; 1 unmetered Cont elec point

VALUEJOLS | 123 | H9 | | 15300 | N45°03.216' E002°55.782'

Directions: Place du 19 Mars 1962, off D134. Follow D34, sp 'Paulhac' and signed. Then turn onto D134 in the village, signed. Aire is at the Centre d'Accueil, next to the cemetery, signed.

i Aire in large car park 2 mins from rural village centre. Cross country skiing; Walking in summer. Inspected 2014.

🚐 15; €3/night inc service; Collected

🛒 Euro Relais Mini; €3 service only; Honesty box

COLTINES | 124 | H9 | | 15170 | N45°05.754' E002°59.142'

Directions: D40. Exit the village on D40, sp 'Celles' and signed. The Aire is on the right after the water tower opp the sports facilities, signed.

i Alt: 970m. Pleasant gravel Aire offering far reaching views adj to a rural French farming community with local commerce. Inspected 2014.

🚐 5

🛒 Euro Relais Junior; Token (ER); May-Sept

TALIZAT | 125 | H9 | | 15170 | N45°06.846' E003°02.754'

Directions: Turn off D679 in village. Drive past Mairie, signed. Aire immediately on right, Service Point up against and obscured by building.

i Alt 986m. Impractical Aire with very limited parking. Local commerce adj. Cycle route marked on sign. Suggest 124. Inspected 2014.

🚐 2

🛒 Raclet; Token (ER); No drive over drain

MURAT | 126 | H9 | | 15300 | N45°06.563' E002°52.147'

Directions: N122. From south on D926 turn left onto N122 immediately after crossing train tracks, sp 'Aurillac'. Service Point at far side of train station car park in 200m. Parking: Stade, opp train track: N45°06.531' E002°52.240'. Swimming pool: N45°06.503' E002°51.713' or Car park at D3 roundabout: N45°06.859' E002°51.747'.

i Large town ideal for servicing motorhome and stocking up before visiting Le Loiren Ski resort. Updated 2013.

🚐 3 parking areas in town

🛒 Raclet; €2

NEUSSARGUES MOISSAC | 127 | H9 | | 15170 | N45°08.065' E002°58.881'

Directions: N122/D679 junction. Turn off N122 to Neussargues-Moissac and Aire is on the right, signed.

i On edge of village near main road. Local commerce 100m. Inspected 2013.

🚐 5

🚰 Euro Relais Tall; CC/Token (ER)

MASSIAC | 128 | H9 | | 15500 | N45°15.209' E003°11.599'

Directions: Rue Jacques Chaban Delmas. In town follow sp 'Murat' onto N122. Cross railway track and river then turn 1st right onto D21, sp 'Allanche' and signed. Turn 1st right, sp 'Gymnase' and signed. Follow road along river where there are 10 marked bays, signed. Service Point and hardstanding parking 100m on left.

i Pleasant Aire with 10 bays adj to shallow river in a peaceful location just 4 mins across pedestrian bridge to town. Town commerce includes numerous cafés. Inspected 2014.

🚐 10 grass; 5 hardstanding

🚰 Custom; 2 elec points; Elec €2

BLESLE | 129 | H8 | T | 43450 | N45°19.013' E003°10.461'

Directions: D8. Exit A75 at Junction 23 and at roundabout turn right, sp 'Blesle'. Turn off D909 onto D8 and follow sp 'Blesle'. As enter Blesle turn left into parking, signed.

i Designated parking at entrance to medieval Beau Village. Only 10 mins from A75, so ideal stop en route. Inspected 2014.

🚐 6; Max 48hrs; Large motorhomes dependent on parking

🚰 None; See 128

CHALET (MASSIAC) | 130 | H8 | | 43450 | N45°16.332' E003°11.933'

Directions: Chapelle Ste Madeliene. Exit Massiac to north following sp 'Claremont Ferrand'. At roundabout by A75 and Intermarché supermarket, turn right onto C55, sp 'Chalet' and signed. Follow lane up hill to end. Parking in large grass area at top.

i Alt 700m. Parking at scenic view point. Chapelle Ste Madeliene, 2 mins, is perched on the clifftop overlooking Massiac. Ideal lunch stop but may feel isolated if alone overnight. Inspected 2014.

🚐 30

🚰 None; See 128

BRASSAC LES MINES | 131 | H8 | | 63570 | N45°24.811' E003°20.118'

Directions: Place du Muse, by D34/D34a junction. Follow sp 'Jumeaux' and signed as exit town to east on D34. Service Point on right.

i Service Point adj to main road. Inspected 2014.

🚐 None

🚰 Flot Bleu Pacific (Green); €2

ST GERMAIN LEMBRON | 132 | H8 | | 63340 | N45°27.331' E003°14.208'

Directions: Rue de la Ronzière, off D214. Turn off D909, main route through, onto D214, sp 'Ardes s/ Cruze'. Turn left in 200m, sp 'Salle Polyvalente' and signed. Service Point on left adj to the Salle Polyvalente, signed.

i Aire in community building car park. Small town commerce 3 mins. Preferable stop to 133. Inspected 2014.

🚐 10

🚰 Custom; Lift cover

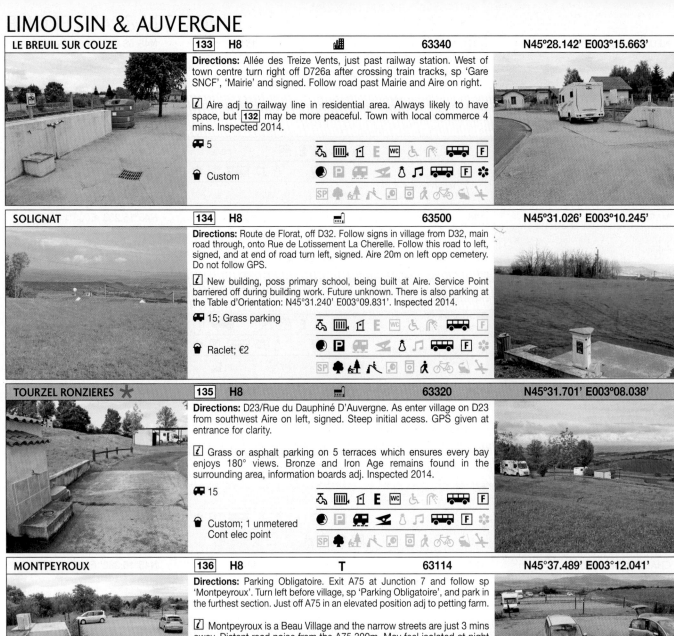

LE BREUIL SUR COUZE
133 H8   63340   N45°28.142' E003°15.663'

Directions: Allée des Treize Vents, just past railway station. West of town centre turn right off D726a after crossing train tracks, sp 'Gare SNCF', 'Mairie' and signed. Follow road past Mairie and Aire on right.

i Aire adj to railway line in residential area. Always likely to have space, but **132** may be more peaceful. Town with local commerce 4 mins. Inspected 2014.

5

Custom

SOLIGNAT
134 H8   63500   N45°31.026' E003°10.245'

Directions: Route de Florat, off D32. Follow signs in village from D32, main road through, onto Rue de Lotissement La Cherelle. Follow this road to left, signed, and at end of road turn left, signed. Aire 20m on left opp cemetery. Do not follow GPS.

i New building, poss primary school, being built at Aire. Service Point barriered off during building work. Future unknown. There is also parking at the Table d'Orientation: N45°31.240' E003°09.831'. Inspected 2014.

15; Grass parking

Raclet; €2

TOURZEL RONZIERES ★
135 H8   63320   N45°31.701' E003°08.038'

Directions: D23/Rue du Dauphiné D'Auvergne. As enter village on D23 from southwest Aire on left, signed. Steep initial acess. GPS given at entrance for clarity.

i Grass or asphalt parking on 5 terraces which ensures every bay enjoys 180° views. Bronze and Iron Age remains found in the surrounding area, information boards adj. Inspected 2014.

15

Custom; 1 unmetered
Cont elec point

MONTPEYROUX
136 H8   T   63114   N45°37.489' E003°12.041'

Directions: Parking Obligatoire. Exit A75 at Junction 7 and follow sp 'Montpeyroux'. Turn left before village, sp 'Parking Obligatoire', and park in the furthest section. Just off A75 in an elevated position adj to petting farm.

i Montpeyroux is a Beau Village and the narrow streets are just 3 mins away. Distant road noise from the A75 300m. May feel isolated at night and suffers cold winds. Inspected 2012.

10; Large motorhomes poss if not busy

Aire Services; Token (3/3)

CHAMPEIX
137 H8   63320   N45°35.293' E003°06.886'

Directions: D996. Exit town to west on D996 towards Mont Dore. Turn left after Gendarmerie and cross bridge, signed. Follow road to right. Service Point on left in compound, parking past compound, signed.

i Aire in roadside lay-by sheltered from road by trees, may feel isolated if alone. Service Point in fenced compound, closed Oct-Apr. Town 3 mins. Market Fri am. Inspected 2014.

10

Raclet; Token (2/1); Lift cover for drive over drain; May-Sept

CHAMBON SUR LAC
138 H8   63790   N45°34.209' E002°54.285'

Directions: Off D996. In Chambon sur Lac turn off D996, main route, sp 'Camping les Bombes' and signed. Service Point directly adj to campsite entrance. Designated parking is 100m on left, signed.

i 5 mins to lake; No views of lake; All lakeside parking bans motorhomes. Updated 2013.

50; €6/night; Collected

Flot Bleu Fontaine; Token; €3

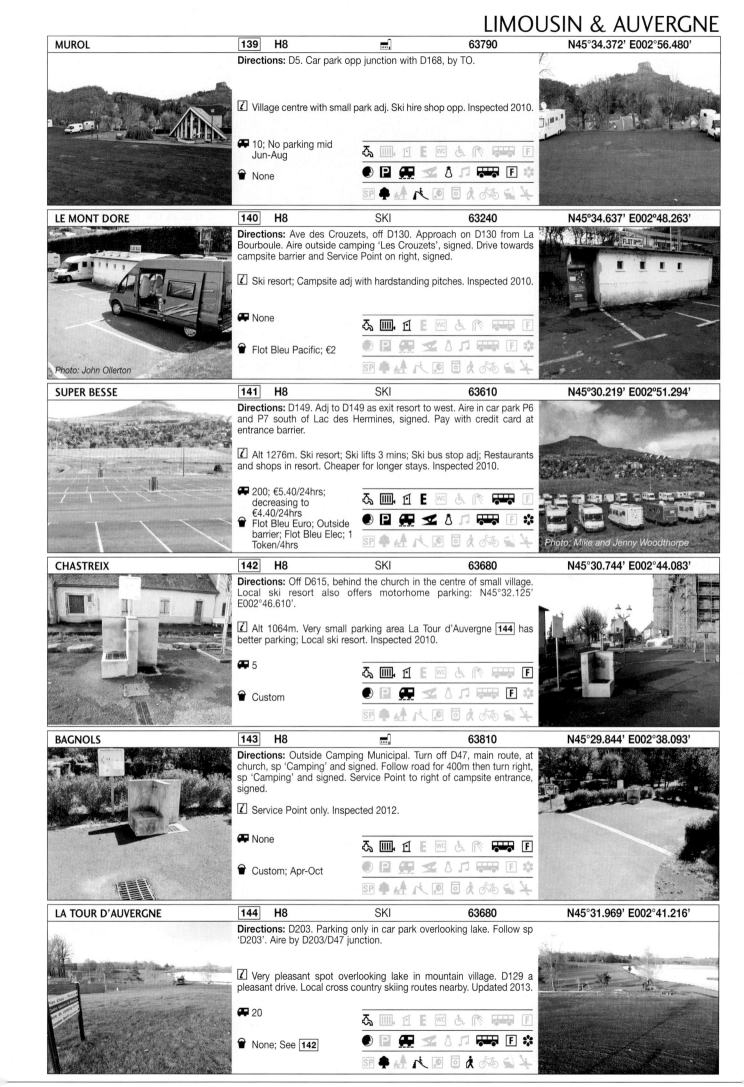

| MUROL | | 139 | H8 | | 63790 | N45°34.372' E002°56.480' |

Directions: D5. Car park opp junction with D168, by TO.

i Village centre with small park adj. Ski hire shop opp. Inspected 2010.

10; No parking mid Jun-Aug

None

| LE MONT DORE | | 140 | H8 | SKI | 63240 | N45°34.637' E002°48.263' |

Directions: Ave des Crouzets, off D130. Approach on D130 from La Bourboule. Aire outside camping 'Les Crouzets', signed. Drive towards campsite barrier and Service Point on right, signed.

i Ski resort; Campsite adj with hardstanding pitches. Inspected 2010.

None

Flot Bleu Pacific; €2

Photo: John Ollerton

| SUPER BESSE | | 141 | H8 | SKI | 63610 | N45°30.219' E002°51.294' |

Directions: D149. Adj to D149 as exit resort to west. Aire in car park P6 and P7 south of Lac des Hermines, signed. Pay with credit card at entrance barrier.

i Alt 1276m. Ski resort; Ski lifts 3 mins; Ski bus stop adj; Restaurants and shops in resort. Cheaper for longer stays. Inspected 2010.

200; €5.40/24hrs; decreasing to €4.40/24hrs

Flot Bleu Euro; Outside barrier; Flot Bleu Elec; 1 Token/4hrs

Photo: Mike and Jenny Woodthorpe

| CHASTREIX | | 142 | H8 | SKI | 63680 | N45°30.744' E002°44.083' |

Directions: Off D615, behind the church in the centre of small village. Local ski resort also offers motorhome parking: N45°32.125' E002°46.610'.

i Alt 1064m. Very small parking area La Tour d'Auvergne 144 has better parking; Local ski resort. Inspected 2010.

5

Custom

| BAGNOLS | | 143 | H8 | | 63810 | N45°29.844' E002°38.093' |

Directions: Outside Camping Municipal. Turn off D47, main route, at church, sp 'Camping' and signed. Follow road for 400m then turn right, sp 'Camping' and signed. Service Point to right of campsite entrance, signed.

i Service Point only. Inspected 2012.

None

Custom; Apr-Oct

| LA TOUR D'AUVERGNE | | 144 | H8 | SKI | 63680 | N45°31.969' E002°41.216' |

Directions: D203. Parking only in car park overlooking lake. Follow sp 'D203'. Aire by D203/D47 junction.

i Very pleasant spot overlooking lake in mountain village. D129 a pleasant drive. Local cross country skiing routes nearby. Updated 2013.

20

None; See 142

St Mathieu

MURAT LE QUAIRE | 146 | H8 | 63150 | N45°36.174' E002°44.251'

Photos/Info: John Cox

Directions: Route de la Banne d'Ordanche. Turn off D219 opposite church in centre of Murat le Quaire. Follow road and Aire is on right before the lake. Enter through Urba Flux popup barrier.

ℹ️ Near lake up in the hills. Shower and toilet block onsite; shower €1 for 10 mins. Local commerce 12 mins. Visited 2012.

🚐 37; €8/night; CC

🚰 Urba Flux Tall; €1/10 mins water or 2hrs elec

LES GANNES (MESSEIX) | 147 | G8 | 63750 | N45°36.935' E002°33.389'

Directions: Place des Pins. Turn off D987 at Les Gannes onto D73c, sp 'Messeix' and signed. Aire in car park 200m on left, signed.

ℹ️ Located in a small hamlet adj to small park (no dogs) and local commerce. Inspected 2012.

🚐 7

🚰 Aire Services; Token (3/3)

ST GERMAIN PRES HERMENT | 148 | G8 | 63470 | N45°43.716' E002°32.711'

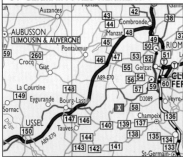

Directions: D98. Visible and signed off D98 between Lastic and Verneugheol on one of two roads to the lake etang. Service Point 30m on left.

ℹ️ Lake 100m and restaurant perhaps open in season. Very nice place off beaten track. May feel isolated out of season. Visited 2012.

🚐 5

🚰 Flot Bleu Pacific; €2

Photo/Info: Carol Weaver

LA COURTINE | 149 | G8 | 23100 | N45°42.351' E002°15.545'

Directions: Impasse Jacques Bayle. From La Courtine take the D982 towards Aubusson. Turn right to the side of the Casino convenience store, signed. Follow road for 250m and turn left into Impasse Jacques Bayle and Aire on right, signed.

ℹ️ Local commerce 5 mins. Large lake 2 mins. Visited 2013.

🚐 10; Max 24hrs

🚰 Euro Relais Junior; Token; €2

Photo/Info: John Cox

USSEL | 150 | G8 | 19200 | N45°32.865' E002°17.013'

Directions: D157/Rte de Ponty. After crossing river take D157 northwest towards Meymac. Aire is at Centre Touristique de Ponty at the lake to the west of Ussel, opp Camping Municipal de Ponty.

ℹ️ Service Point only. Inspected 2010.

🚐 None

🚰 Raclet; €2

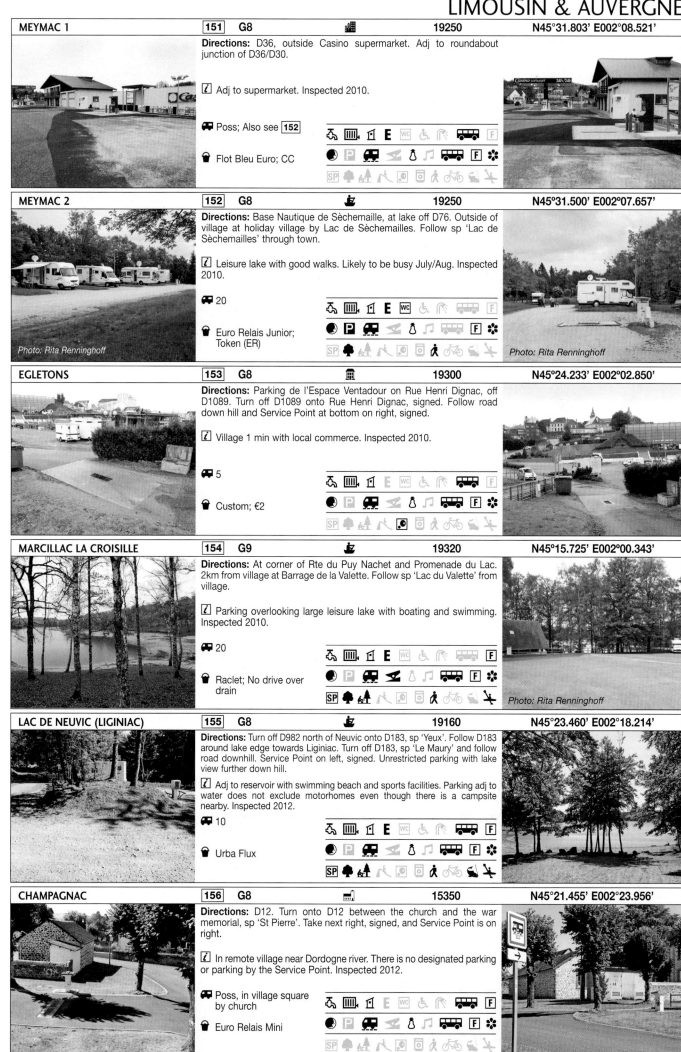

| MEYMAC 1 | 151 | G8 | | 19250 | N45°31.803' E002°08.521' |

Directions: D36, outside Casino supermarket. Adj to roundabout junction of D36/D30.

ℹ️ Adj to supermarket. Inspected 2010.

🚐 Poss; Also see 152

🚰 Flot Bleu Euro; CC

| MEYMAC 2 | 152 | G8 | | 19250 | N45°31.500' E002°07.657' |

Directions: Base Nautique de Sèchemaille, at lake off D76. Outside of village at holiday village by Lac de Sèchemailles. Follow sp 'Lac de Sèchemailles' through town.

ℹ️ Leisure lake with good walks. Likely to be busy July/Aug. Inspected 2010.

🚐 20

🚰 Euro Relais Junior; Token (ER)

Photo: Rita Renninghoff

Photo: Rita Renninghoff

| EGLETONS | 153 | G8 | | 19300 | N45°24.233' E002°02.850' |

Directions: Parking de l'Espace Ventadour on Rue Henri Dignac, off D1089. Turn off D1089 onto Rue Henri Dignac, signed. Follow road down hill and Service Point at bottom on right, signed.

ℹ️ Village 1 min with local commerce. Inspected 2010.

🚐 5

🚰 Custom; €2

| MARCILLAC LA CROISILLE | 154 | G9 | | 19320 | N45°15.725' E002°00.343' |

Directions: At corner of Rte du Puy Nachet and Promenade du Lac. 2km from village at Barrage de la Valette. Follow sp 'Lac du Valette' from village.

ℹ️ Parking overlooking large leisure lake with boating and swimming. Inspected 2010.

🚐 20

🚰 Raclet; No drive over drain

Photo: Rita Renninghoff

| LAC DE NEUVIC (LIGINIAC) | 155 | G8 | | 19160 | N45°23.460' E002°18.214' |

Directions: Turn off D982 north of Neuvic onto D183, sp 'Yeux'. Follow D183 around lake edge towards Liginiac. Turn off D183, sp 'Le Maury' and follow road downhill. Service Point on left, signed. Unrestricted parking with lake view further down hill.

ℹ️ Adj to reservoir with swimming beach and sports facilities. Parking adj to water does not exclude motorhomes even though there is a campsite nearby. Inspected 2012.

🚐 10

🚰 Urba Flux

| CHAMPAGNAC | 156 | G8 | | 15350 | N45°21.455' E002°23.956' |

Directions: D12. Turn onto D12 between the church and the war memorial, sp 'St Pierre'. Take next right, signed, and Service Point is on right.

ℹ️ In remote village near Dordogne river. There is no designated parking or parking by the Service Point. Inspected 2012.

🚐 Poss, in village square by church

🚰 Euro Relais Mini

BORT LES ORGUES | 157 | G8 | | 19110 | N45°23.950' E002°29.833'

Directions: Rue Font Grande. Best access via D979. Turn off D979 into town. Turn right before river bridge by Gendarmerie, sp 'Complex Sportif' and signed. Follow road along river to Aire. Aire is signed on all routes through town. Some routes are narrow with difficult turns.

River views. Town commerce 1 min; Hypermarket within walking distance. Updated 2013.

5

Custom

Photo: Rita Renninghoff

CHAMPS SUR TARENTAINE MARCHAL | 158 | G8 | | 15270 | N45°23.672' E002°33.486'

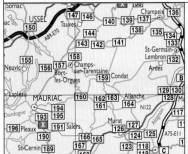

Directions: D679. Adj to D679 through gate to house 16, signed. Nearly opp Elan garage, specializing as HGV mechanic.

Start of Gorges de la Rhue drive. Village 1 min with local commerce. Inspected 2010.

1 hardstanding; Additional grass parking

Euro Relais Mini

CONDAT | 159 | H8 | | 15190 | N45°20.335' E002°45.766'

Directions: D678. Adj to D678 just beside roundabout junction with D679, by river bridge. The Service Point is visible from roundabout.

Sign suggests for your security you should stay in campsite but does not ban motorhomes. Inspected 2010.

5

Flot Bleu Pacific; Token

VALETTE | 160 | H9 | | 15400 | N45°16.198' E002°36.135'

Directions: Off D678. Turn off D678 in village, signed. Aire in 100m in new housing development.

Landscaped Aire in rural location; On cheese route. Inspected 2010.

5; 8m bays

Euro Relais Junior; €2

SEGUR LES VILLAS | 161 | H9 | | 15300 | N45°13.390' E002°49.111'

Directions: Turn off D3 into Segur-les-Villas. Turn off main route through at Vival convenience store and drive along side of store, signed. In 250m turn right, signed.

Alt 1200m. Aire located adj to sports pitch in an isolated mountain village with local commerce. Inspected 2012.

8; Grass parking

Euro Relais Junior; Token (ER)

ROIM ES MONTAGNES | 162 | H9 | | 15400 | N45°17.059' E002°39.263'

Directions: Between D3 and Rue du Champ de Foire. Turn off D49 at roundabout by old train station, signed. Cross the tracks and turn immediately right, signed. Service Point on right, opp cattle market.

Service Point only but there is lots of local unrestricted parking. Inspected 2010.

Local parking

Flot Bleu Pacific; €2; No drive over drain

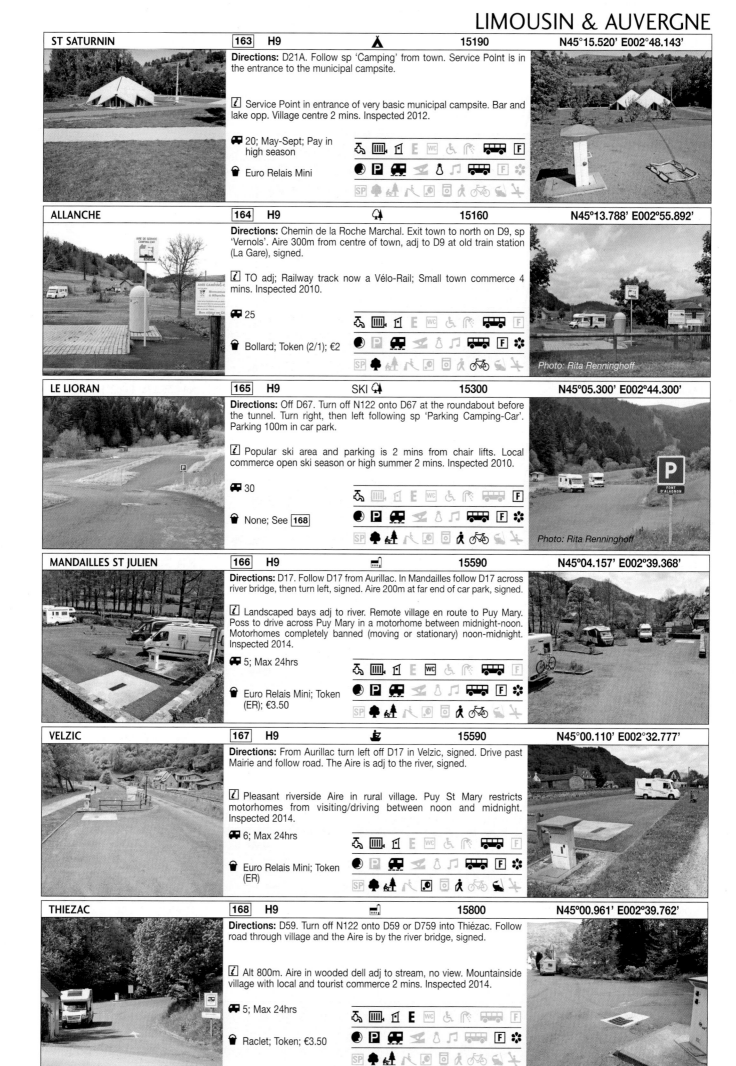

| ST SATURNIN | 163 | H9 | ⛺ | 15190 | N45°15.520' E002°48.143' |

Directions: D21A. Follow sp 'Camping' from town. Service Point is in the entrance to the municipal campsite.

ℹ Service Point in entrance of very basic municipal campsite. Bar and lake opp. Village centre 2 mins. Inspected 2012.

🚐 20; May-Sept; Pay in high season

🚰 Euro Relais Mini

| ALLANCHE | 164 | H9 | 🚲 | 15160 | N45°13.788' E002°55.892' |

Directions: Chemin de la Roche Marchal. Exit town to north on D9, sp 'Vernols'. Aire 300m from centre of town, adj to D9 at old train station (La Gare), signed.

ℹ TO adj; Railway track now a Vélo-Rail; Small town commerce 4 mins. Inspected 2010.

🚐 25

🚰 Bollard; Token (2/1); €2

Photo: Rita Renninghoff

| LE LIORAN | 165 | H9 | SKI 🚲 | 15300 | N45°05.300' E002°44.300' |

Directions: Off D67. Turn off N122 onto D67 at the roundabout before the tunnel. Turn right, then left following sp 'Parking Camping-Car'. Parking 100m in car park.

ℹ Popular ski area and parking is 2 mins from chair lifts. Local commerce open ski season or high summer 2 mins. Inspected 2010.

🚐 30

🚰 None; See 168

Photo: Rita Renninghoff

| MANDAILLES ST JULIEN | 166 | H9 | 🏭 | 15590 | N45°04.157' E002°39.368' |

Directions: D17. Follow D17 from Aurillac. In Mandailles follow D17 across river bridge, then turn left, signed. Aire 200m at far end of car park, signed.

ℹ Landscaped bays adj to river. Remote village en route to Puy Mary. Poss to drive across Puy Mary in a motorhome between midnight-noon. Motorhomes completely banned (moving or stationary) noon-midnight. Inspected 2014.

🚐 5; Max 24hrs

🚰 Euro Relais Mini; Token (ER); €3.50

| VELZIC | 167 | H9 | 🎿 | 15590 | N45°00.110' E002°32.777' |

Directions: From Aurillac turn left off D17 in Velzic, signed. Drive past Mairie and follow road. The Aire is adj to the river, signed.

ℹ Pleasant riverside Aire in rural village. Puy St Mary restricts motorhomes from visiting/driving between noon and midnight. Inspected 2014.

🚐 6; Max 24hrs

🚰 Euro Relais Mini; Token (ER)

| THIEZAC | 168 | H9 | 🏭 | 15800 | N45°00.961' E002°39.762' |

Directions: D59. Turn off N122 onto D59 or D759 into Thiézac. Follow road through village and the Aire is by the river bridge, signed.

ℹ Alt 800m. Aire in wooded dell adj to stream, no view. Mountainside village with local and tourist commerce 2 mins. Inspected 2014.

🚐 5; Max 24hrs

🚰 Raclet; Token; €3.50

VIC SUR CERE | 169 | H9 | 15800 | N44°58.942' E002°37.891'

Directions: Place de l'Egalité, Avenue des Tilleuls. Turn off N122, sp 'Camping' and 'Aire de Camping-Car'. Turn left in front of cemetery, signed. Follow road past campsite and the Aire is on the right.

ℹ Pleasant Aire with landscaped bays. Peaceful location with river and park adj, no views. Small town commerce 2 mins. Inspected 2014.

🚐 10

Euro Relais Junior; Token (ER)

AURILLAC | 170 | G9 | 15000 | N44°55.790' E002°26.971'

Directions: Champ de Foire, off D17. Follow sp 'Puy Mary' through town, then 'Aire de Camping Car'. In town near river, well signed.

ℹ Designated parking under nesting rooks in a popular town centre car park near river, obstructed views. Town commerce 2 mins. Route to Puy Mary adj. Inspected 2014.

🚐 10; Max 24hrs

Euro Relais Junior; Token (ER)

LACAPELLE VIESCAMP | 171 | G9 | 15150 | N44°55.275' E002°15.820'

Directions: D18, on the outskirts of the village at the entrance to municipal campsite opp local shop. Turn into campsite between hedges and Service Point is to the right.

ℹ Large reservoir with limited parking considering its size. No parking has lakeside views. Lake predominantly used by fishermen. Inspected 2014.

🚐 4; Only when campsite closed

Euro Relais Junior; Token (ER); €2

VEZAC | 172 | G9 | 15130 | N44°53.425' E002°31.073'

Directions: D206. Turn off D990 onto D206, sp 'Labrousse', 'Golf' and signed. The Aire is on the left in 600m, signed.

ℹ Golf course opp. Restaurant 1 min. Inspected 2014.

🚐 2; Max 24hrs

Euro Relais Mini; Token (ER)

MARCOLES | 173 | G9 | 15220 | N44°46.818' E002°21.248'

Directions: D66. Follow D66 through village. Turn off into sports facilities, signed. Service Point on the right and parking 20m further on the right, signed.

ℹ Aire at sports facilities adj to municipal camping field. 4 designated bays are unlevel, but there is plenty of other parking. Views over open access sports facility. Inspected 2014.

🚐 4; €8.40/night; mid Jun-Sept

Custom; 4 CEE elec points at Service Point (long lead needed)

MONTSALVY | 174 | G9 | 15120 | N44°42.477' E002°29.792'

Directions: Off D19. From north turn off D920 onto D19 into town. Aire 250m on left before Centre de Secours.

ℹ Very landscaped Aire adj to amenity space. Bays have grass and hedges giving optimum privacy. Hedge dictates which way to park. Old bays now turn around/overflow area. Local commerce 2 mins. Inspected 2014.

🚐 10; plus 10 overflow

Euro Relais Junior; €2; Showers €1

VIEILLEVIE 175 G9 15120 N44°38.662' E002°25.064'

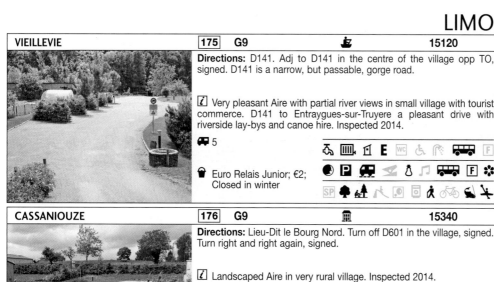
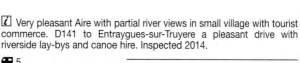

Directions: D141. Adj to D141 in the centre of the village opp TO, signed. D141 is a narrow, but passable, gorge road.

i Very pleasant Aire with partial river views in small village with tourist commerce. D141 to Entraygues-sur-Truyère a pleasant drive with riverside lay-bys and canoe hire. Inspected 2014.

🚐 5

Euro Relais Junior; €2; Closed in winter

CASSANIOUZE 176 G9 15340 N44°41.629' E002°22.949'

Directions: Lieu-Dit le Bourg Nord. Turn off D601 in the village, signed. Turn right and right again, signed.

i Landscaped Aire in very rural village. Inspected 2014.

🚐 6

Euro Relais Junior; €2; Closed in winter

CALVINET 177 G9 15340 N44°42.607' E002°21.526'

Directions: Adj to Camping Municipal de Calvinet and sports fields, off D66. Turn off D66 in town, sp 'Tennis' and signed. Turn left past tennis courts, signed, and the Aire is on the left.

i A confused Aire adj to camping field overlooking open access sports fields. Prices quoted are for the campsite. Inspected 2014.

🚐 Parking: 6; €6/night; Collected

Euro Relais Junior; €2; Elec €2/night

MONTMURAT 178 G9 15600 N44°37.685' E002°11.860'

Directions: D345. From Maurs on D663 turn right onto D45 at St Constant. Turn right onto D345, sp 'Montmurat'. Follow D345 and Aire on left just before village. DO NOT take motorhome into village, very narrow and steep.

i Picnic area and viewpoint above Aire with 360° views. May feel isolated if alone. Inspected 2014.

🚐 20

Flot Bleu Fontaine; €2

MAURS LA JOLIE 179 G9 15600 N44°42.872' E002°11.762'

Directions: D19/Route de Quézac. Enter Maurs from north on N122 and turn off in town, signed. Follow road beside Hotel Bar Le Plaisance and continue for 500m. Aire on left outside cemetery, signed.

i Adj to cemetery with additional parking opp. 3 mins from town commerce. Inspected 2014.

🚐 6

Euro Relais Junior; Token (ER)

CAYROLS 180 G9 15290 N44°49.803' E002°13.973'

Directions: D51, at sports facilities. On main route through village, signed. Parking has 5.5t weight restriction.

i Pleasant location by community sports facilities with plenty of parking. Local commerce in village. Inspected 2014.

🚐 30

Euro Relais Junior; Token (2/1)

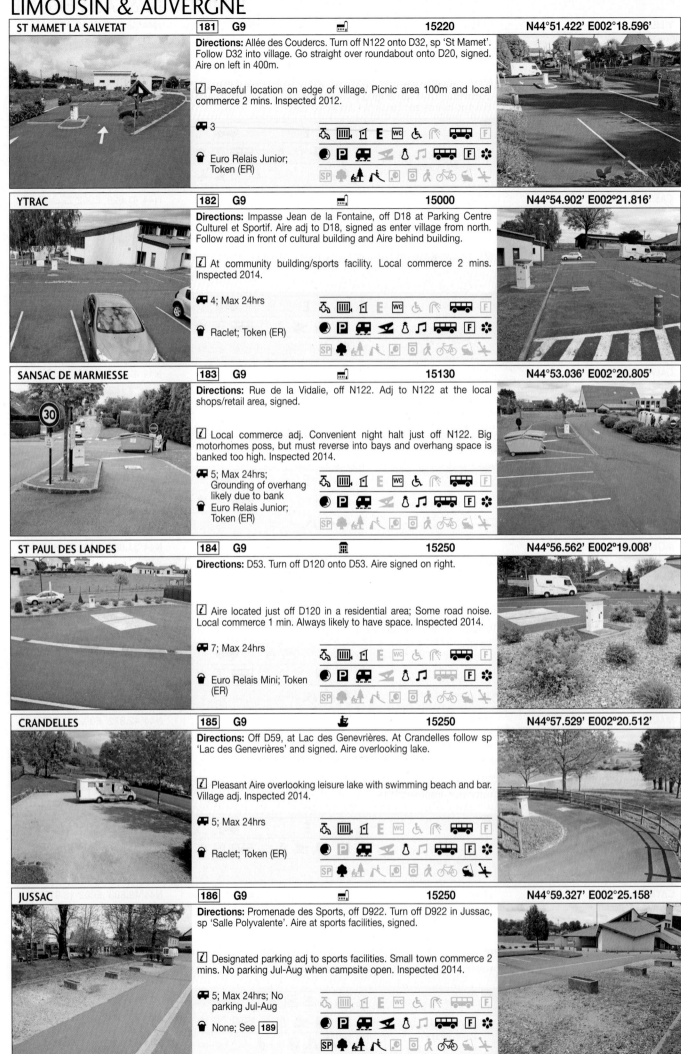

ST MAMET LA SALVETAT | 181 | G9 | 15220 | N44°51.422' E002°18.596'

Directions: Allée des Coudercs. Turn off N122 onto D32, sp 'St Mamet'. Follow D32 into village. Go straight over roundabout onto D20, signed. Aire on left in 400m.

ℹ️ Peaceful location on edge of village. Picnic area 100m and local commerce 2 mins. Inspected 2012.

🚐 3

Euro Relais Junior; Token (ER)

YTRAC | 182 | G9 | 15000 | N44°54.902' E002°21.816'

Directions: Impasse Jean de la Fontaine, off D18 at Parking Centre Culturel et Sportif. Aire adj to D18, signed as enter village from north. Follow road in front of cultural building and Aire behind building.

ℹ️ At community building/sports facility. Local commerce 2 mins. Inspected 2014.

🚐 4; Max 24hrs

Raclet; Token (ER)

SANSAC DE MARMIESSE | 183 | G9 | 15130 | N44°53.036' E002°20.805'

Directions: Rue de la Vidalie, off N122. Adj to N122 at the local shops/retail area, signed.

ℹ️ Local commerce adj. Convenient night halt just off N122. Big motorhomes poss, but must reverse into bays and overhang space is banked too high. Inspected 2014.

🚐 5; Max 24hrs; Grounding of overhang likely due to bank
Euro Relais Junior; Token (ER)

ST PAUL DES LANDES | 184 | G9 | 15250 | N44°56.562' E002°19.008'

Directions: D53. Turn off D120 onto D53. Aire signed on right.

ℹ️ Aire located just off D120 in a residential area; Some road noise. Local commerce 1 min. Always likely to have space. Inspected 2014.

🚐 7; Max 24hrs

Euro Relais Mini; Token (ER)

CRANDELLES | 185 | G9 | 15250 | N44°57.529' E002°20.512'

Directions: Off D59, at Lac des Genevrières. At Crandelles follow sp 'Lac des Genevrières' and signed. Aire overlooking lake.

ℹ️ Pleasant Aire overlooking leisure lake with swimming beach and bar. Village adj. Inspected 2014.

🚐 5; Max 24hrs

Raclet; Token (ER)

JUSSAC | 186 | G9 | 15250 | N44°59.327' E002°25.158'

Directions: Promenade des Sports, off D922. Turn off D922 in Jussac, sp 'Salle Polyvalente'. Aire at sports facilities, signed.

ℹ️ Designated parking adj to sports facilities. Small town commerce 2 mins. No parking Jul-Aug when campsite open. Inspected 2014.

🚐 5; Max 24hrs; No parking Jul-Aug

None; See 189

AYRENS | 187 | G9 | | 15250 | N44°59.138' E002°19.627'

Directions: Off D53c. At D52/D53 junction in village turn onto D53, sp 'Jassac'. Follow road behind church and turn left, sp 'Terrain de Sports'. Aire in 100m.

i Limited parking in tiny village adj to small wood yard. Local commerce 1 min. Inspected 2014.

🚐 5; Try 185 1st

🚰 Euro Relais Mini; Token (ER); No drive over drain

NAUCELLES | 188 | G9 | | 15000 | N44°57.393' E002°25.044'

Directions: Rue du Terrou. Turn off D922 onto D253 at roundabout south of Naucelles, sp 'Crandelles'. In 200m turn right, sp 'Mairie'. At the Stop junction turn right, signed. Turn right at next junction and Service Point is on left side of car park.

i Located 300m from D922 in centre of village but is surrounded by sports facilities and amenity grass. Local commerce 2 mins. Inspected 2014.

🚐 20

🚰 Euro Relais Mini; Token (ER)

ST CERNIN | 189 | G9 | | 15310 | N45°03.191' E002°25.584'

Directions: D160. Follow main route south out of town. At 1st fork, stay left, sp 'Aurillac'. At next fork stay left onto D160, sp 'Route des Crêtes'. Aire on right in 600m.

i Really just a Service Point with picnic area and small boules court adj. Inspected 2014.

🚐 1

🚰 Euro Relais Junior

ST MARTIN VALMEROUX | 190 | G9 | | 15140 | N45°06.958' E002°25.231'

Directions: D37/Rue de Montjoly. Turn off D922 in the village onto D37, sp 'Loupiac' and 'Camping'. The Service Point is in 450m past the campsite, signed. 3.5t weight restriction on car park.

i Aire adj to pleasant riverside campsite on the edge of town. Small town commerce 3 mins. Inspected 2014.

🚐 10

🚰 Euro Relais Maxi

SALERS | 191 | G9 | | 15140 | N45°08.909' E002°29.927'

Directions: Off D680. Follow sp 'Camping' through village. Service Point is outside Camping Le Mourial, sp 'Camping Municipal'. Parking is adj to campsite and sports facilities, signed. Day parking on D680 ring road to north of town, signed: N45°08.417' E002°29.676'.

i Alt 992m. Day parking avail for visiting pretty cobbled Beau Village. Aire a pleasant 1.5km walk from village. Cold Sept-May due to altitude. May feel isolated if alone. Inspected 2014.

🚐 30; €5.50; Pay at campsite; 9 (day parking); €3; Pay at machine

🚰 Aire Services; Token; €2

LAROQUEBROU | 192 | G9 | | 15150 | N44°57.892' E002°11.803'

Directions: D653. Enter town from east on D653. Service Point is against the road on the right opp D18 turning to 'Lacapelle V.' and campsite.

i Service Point near pleasant riverside municipal campsite on edge of riverside town. Parking possible in lay-by opp. Inspected 2014.

🚐 1 designated; 10 opp

🚰 Flot Bleu Fontaine; €2

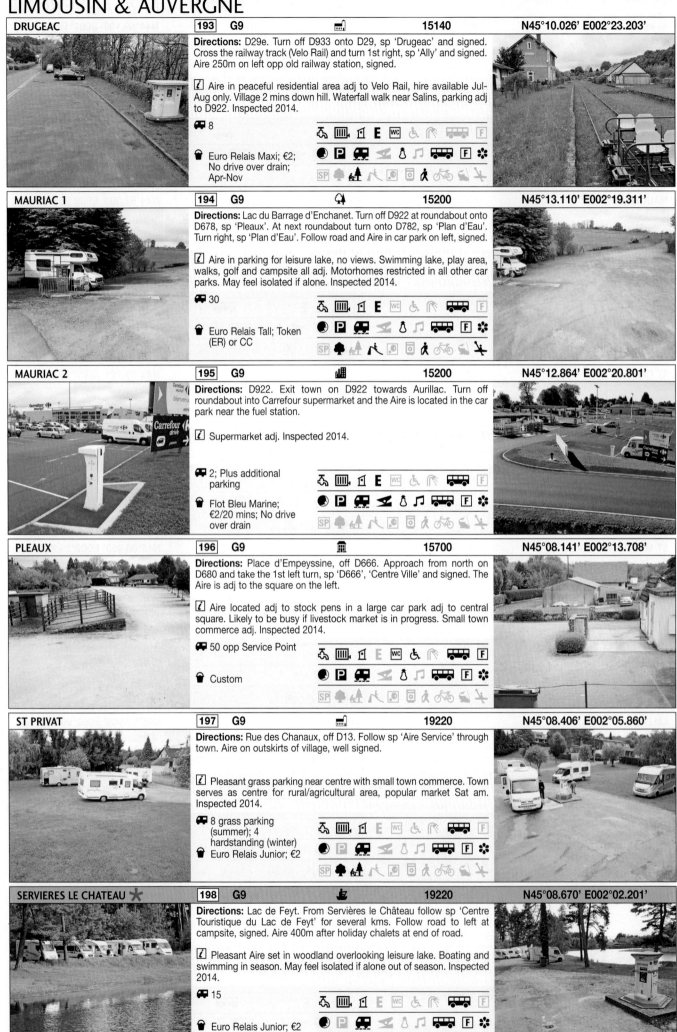

DRUGEAC
193 G9   15140   N45°10.026' E002°23.203'

Directions: D29e. Turn off D933 onto D29, sp 'Drugeac' and signed. Cross the railway track (Velo Rail) and turn 1st right, sp 'Ally' and signed. Aire 250m on left opp old railway station, signed.

ℹ️ Aire in peaceful residential area adj to Velo Rail, hire available Jul-Aug only. Village 2 mins down hill. Waterfall walk near Salins, parking adj to D922. Inspected 2014.

🚐 8

🚰 Euro Relais Maxi; €2; No drive over drain; Apr-Nov

MAURIAC 1
194 G9   15200   N45°13.110' E002°19.311'

Directions: Lac du Barrage d'Enchanet. Turn off D922 at roundabout onto D678, sp 'Pleaux'. At next roundabout turn onto D782, sp 'Plan d'Eau'. Turn right, sp 'Plan d'Eau'. Follow road and Aire in car park on left, signed.

ℹ️ Aire in parking for leisure lake, no views. Swimming lake, play area, walks, golf and campsite all adj. Motorhomes restricted in all other car parks. May feel isolated if alone. Inspected 2014.

🚐 30

🚰 Euro Relais Tall; Token (ER) or CC

MAURIAC 2
195 G9   15200   N45°12.864' E002°20.801'

Directions: D922. Exit town on D922 towards Aurillac. Turn off roundabout into Carrefour supermarket and the Aire is located in the car park near the fuel station.

ℹ️ Supermarket adj. Inspected 2014.

🚐 2; Plus additional parking

🚰 Flot Bleu Marine; €2/20 mins; No drive over drain

PLEAUX
196 G9   15700   N45°08.141' E002°13.708'

Directions: Place d'Empeyssine, off D666. Approach from north on D680 and take the 1st left turn, sp 'D666', 'Centre Ville' and signed. The Aire is adj to the square on the left.

ℹ️ Aire located adj to stock pens in a large car park adj to central square. Likely to be busy if livestock market is in progress. Small town commerce adj. Inspected 2014.

🚐 50 opp Service Point

🚰 Custom

ST PRIVAT
197 G9   19220   N45°08.406' E002°05.860'

Directions: Rue des Chanaux, off D13. Follow sp 'Aire Service' through town. Aire on outskirts of village, well signed.

ℹ️ Pleasant grass parking near centre with small town commerce. Town serves as centre for rural/agricultural area, popular market Sat am. Inspected 2014.

🚐 8 grass parking (summer); 4 hardstanding (winter)

🚰 Euro Relais Junior; €2

SERVIERES LE CHATEAU ✴
198 G9   19220   N45°08.670' E002°02.201'

Directions: Lac de Feyt. From Servières le Château follow sp 'Centre Touristique du Lac de Feyt' for several kms. Follow road to left at campsite, signed. Aire 400m after holiday chalets at end of road.

ℹ️ Pleasant Aire set in woodland overlooking leisure lake. Boating and swimming in season. May feel isolated if alone out of season. Inspected 2014.

🚐 15

🚰 Euro Relais Junior; €2

FORGES | `199` | G9 | ▲ | 19380 | N45°09.205' E001°52.265'

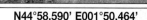

Directions: Rue Pierre et Marie Curie. Exit D1120, sp 'Camping Municipal'. Aire on left. Enter through PARKNIGHT barrier.

ℹ Commercial barriered Aire replacing former municipal campsite and being installed at time of inspection. Inspected 2014.

🚐 31; €12/night; CC

♛ Euro Relais Junior; Inside barrier

BEAULIEU SUR DORDOGNE | `200` | G9 | ⛴ | 19120 | N44°58.590' E001°50.464'

Directions: Rue Gontrand Roye. Turn off D940 near TO onto D41, sp 'Astaillac'. Turn left off D41 as exit town, sp 'Du Pont (Municipal)'. Aire 50m.

ℹ Aire adj to canoe slalom course. Town centre 3 mins bans motorhomes but has town commerce. Inspected 2012.

🚐 20; €5/night Sept-Jun, €10/night Jul-Aug; Collected
♛ Custom; Tap under green cover, hose connection needed; Turned off in Oct

---

BEYNAT | `201` | G9 | 🔓 | 19190 | N45°07.338' E001°43.534'

Directions: Rue de la Châtaigne. Turn off D921 at roundabout onto D169, sp 'Beynat Centre Bourg' and signed. In 700m turn right at Stop junction onto D130, sp 'Meyssac'. Turn right into car parks, signed. Aire on left.

ℹ Aire in large car park by school adj to woods. Local commerce 2 mins uphill. Inspected 2014.

🚐 30

♛ Euro Relais Mini; Token (ER); Tokens free from commerce

LANTEUIL | `202` | G9 | 🔓 | 19190 | N45°07.731' E001°39.698'

Directions: Le Doux. Turn off D921 at roundabout by telephone box, sp 'Le Doux'. Cross bridge and Aire is on right, signed.

ℹ Aire adj to main route in small village. Small stream adj. Local commerce 2 mins. Inspected 2014.

🚐 10

♛ Aire Services; Toilets and bins locked

TURENNE | `203` | F9 | T | 19500 | N45°03.233' E001°34.837'

Directions: Turn off D8 at Turenne and drive behind TO, signed. Follow lane down hill then turn right into parking, signed. Be careful not to tail swipe wall at bottom of hill.

ℹ Views from Aire of hilltop Beau Village with château at top open to public, €4.80, www.chateau-turenne.com. A pleasant place to wander for a few hours. Inspected 2014.

🚐 14; Max 48hrs

♛ Euro Relais Junior; 2 unmetered CEE elec points

COLLONGES LA ROUGE | `204` | F9 | T | 19500 | N45°03.523' E001°39.551'

Directions: P Le Marchadial. From Meyssac follow D38 west towards Brive. Turn off D38, sp 'P Le Marchadial'. Turn 1st right, signed. Follow lane and Aire on left, signed.

ℹ Pretty Beau Village 700m with tourist commerce; very popular with French tourists. Maison de la Sirène museum and guided village tour, €3; must book, www.tourismecorreze.com. Small town commerce at Meyssac. Inspected 2014.

🚐 40; €5/24hrs; Collected

♛ Custom

DAMPNIAT | 205 | G9 | 19360 | N45°09.763' E001°38.258'

Directions: From church in Dampniat centre follow signs to Aire. Located down narrow lane at sports facilities, 1km from centre.

ℹ️ Aire located in pleasant rural location adj to a few houses with panoramic rural views. Most parking reserved for adj sports facilities. Local commerce 1 min. Inspected 2014.

🚐 5

Euro Relais Junior; €4; 2 unmetered CEE elec points

BRIVE LA GAILLARDE | 206 | F9 | 19100 | N45°09.903' E001°32.500'

Directions: Blvd Michelet. On D1089 on north side of river turn off roundabout by cinema, sp 'Park des Sports'. In 100m turn left, just past Mr Bricologe, signed. Aire 10m on right. Enter through Flot Bleu Park barrier.

ℹ️ Commercial Aire adj to riverside walk/park. Town 2 mins across bridge. Adj commerce includes supermarket and cinema. May feel vulnerable if alone. Inspected 2014.

🚐 10; €8/24hrs; CC

Flot Bleu Pacific; Token/CC; €2; Flot Bleu Elec; Token; €2/6hrs; All inside barrier

LISSAC SUR COUZE | 207 | F9 | 19600 | N45°05.933' E001°27.810'

Info/photos: David Statham

Directions: Le Bourg. In Lissac sur Couze turn off roundabout, sp 'Le Soulier' and 'Table du Lac'. Follow road down hill and fork right towards lake. Fork right again, sp 'Parking des Peupliers'. Aire in parking on right. Enter via CC barrier.

ℹ️ Aire adj to lake which is run by adj campsite. May feel isolated if alone. Visited 2014.

🚐 10; €4; CC

Euro Relais Mini; Token; €4

TULLE | 208 | G9 | 19000 | N45°16.494' E001°46.440'

Directions: Quai Victor Continsouza. Exit town centre to north on D23, sp 'Correze'. In 200m turn right across river bridge into retail park. Service Point in fuel station of Intermarché supermarket, signed.

ℹ️ Supermarket and retail park adj. Inspected 2012.

🚐 Poss

Euro Relais Box; Token (ER) or €2

DONZENAC | 209 | F9 | 19270 | N45°13.126' E001°31.140'

Directions: Off D170. Exit A20 at Junction 48 and follow sp 'Donzenac'. In town turn right onto D920, sp 'Ussac'. Follow road out of town and at roundabout turn right onto D170, sp 'Ussac' and 'La Rivière'. Turn right in 300m and Aire just before campsite barrier on left, signed.

ℹ️ River adj, no view. Campsite adj; Showers €2 avail Apr-Oct. Intermarché supermarket 300m. Historic town 1.5km up hill. Inspected 2014.

🚐 10

Euro Relais Mini; Elec €3.40/night (Not working)

ALLASSAC | 210 | F8 | 19240 | N45°15.531' E001°28.410'

Directions: Ave du Saillant, off D9 opp train station. Follow sp 'Gare SNCF' in town. Aire opp train station, 200m from centre.

ℹ️ Pretty town centre with small town commerce 4 mins. Train station adj. Inspected 2014.

🚐 4; Max 3 days; 6m bays, no overhang

Euro Relais Junior; 2 unmetered CEE elec points

SADROC | 211 | F8 | 19270 | N45°16.983' E001°32.918'

Directions: D9, in the village centre by the church. Follow sp 'Sadroc' from A20. In Sadroc centre turn right by tabac, signed, and right again to Aire, signed.

ℹ️ Aire located in a small well maintained village centre; Church adj. Local commerce adj. Inspected 2014.

🚐 6; Max 24hrs; 8m bays

🔌 Custom; 4 unmetered CEE elec points

VIGEOIS - Lac de Pontcharal | 212 | F8 | 19410 | N45°22.049' E001°32.037'

Directions: D7. Exit A20 at Junction 45 and follow sp 'Vigeois' onto D3. In Vigeois turn left onto D7, sp 'Lac de Pontcharal'. Aire on left adj to D7, signed.

ℹ️ Leisure lake adj, no views from parking adj to Service Point. Other parking unrestricted with views over beach and diving platform. Lovely area but may feel isolated if alone. Inspected 2014.

🚐 10

🔌 Euro Relais Junior; Token (ER); €2

UZERCHE ★ | 213 | G8 | 19140 | N45°25.471' E001°33.968'

Directions: D3, at Place de la Petite Gare. Turn off A20 at Junction 44 and follow sp 'Uzerche' onto D920. In town turn left off D920, sp 'Treignac'. Follow road and at the roundabout turn left onto D3, signed. Aire 150m on right, signed.

ℹ️ Very popular Aire at old train station; Cycle/walk along old track. Sat market on Aire; No parking Sat am, 20th of each month or during fair. River adj, no views. Small town commerce 3 mins. Inspected 2014.

🚐 20; Max 48hrs; No parking Sat (Market)

🔌 Custom; WC emptying in toilets at special point; 40 unmetered CEE elec points

TREIGNAC | 214 | G8 | 19260 | N45°32.608' E001°47.949'

Directions: Parking des Rivieres, off D940 in large gravel area by river. Adj to D940 north of Treignac, towards Gueret. At roundabout with industrial park turn off, signed.

ℹ️ Rural location too far to walk to village; Shallow river with canoe club boat launch adj. Inspected 2010.

🚐 50

🔌 Custom

CHAMBERET | 215 | G8 | 19370 | N45°34.767' E001°43.236'

Directions: Route de la Font Blanche. Exit village to west on D3, sp 'Masseret' and 'M.A.S. Stade'. Turn left onto Rte de la Font Blanche, signed. Aire at sports ground, opp cemetery.

ℹ️ Overlooking sports field; Village centre with local commerce adj. Inspected 2010.

🚐 4; 12m bays

🔌 Custom; Toilet disposal at WC

ST VITTE SUR BRIANCE | 216 | F8 | 87380 | N45°37.526' E001°32.762'

Directions: Place de la Mairie, adj to D31. Just off D31 next to the Mairie in the centre of the village. Service Point behind Mairie.

ℹ️ Small village centre parking area. Service Point may be obstructed by parked cars. Nearby St German les Belles signs motorhomes, but Centre de Tourism Montréal is a campsite. Inspected 2014.

🚐 2; Max 5 days; €5/day over 5 days

🔌 Custom; 4 unmetered CEE elec points (long cable needed)

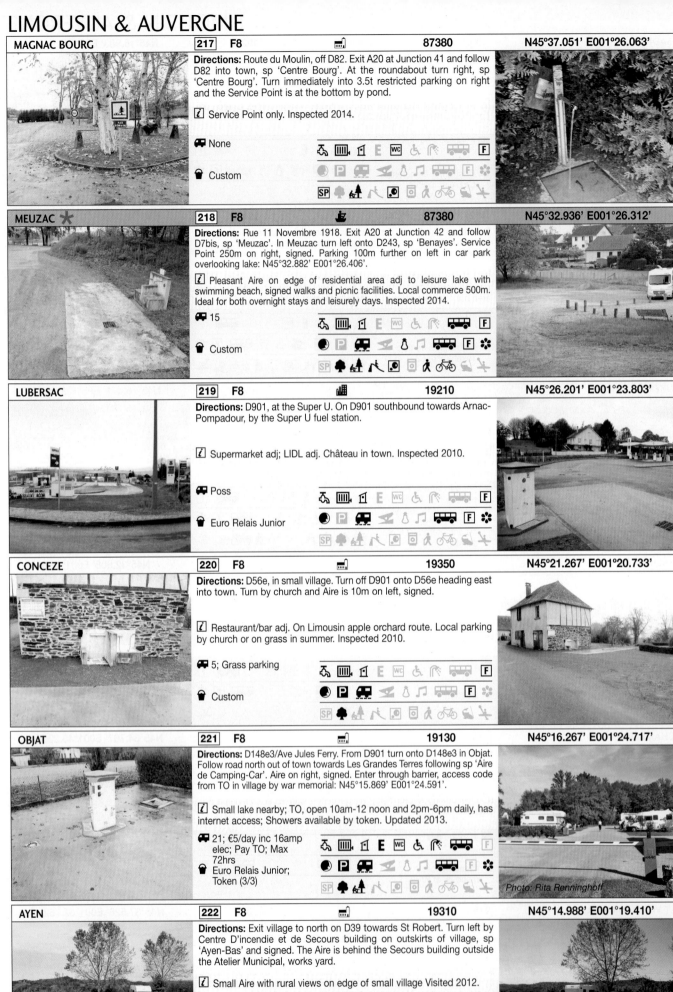

MAGNAC BOURG
217 F8   87380   N45°37.051' E001°26.063'

Directions: Route du Moulin, off D82. Exit A20 at Junction 41 and follow D82 into town, sp 'Centre Bourg'. At the roundabout turn right, sp 'Centre Bourg'. Turn immediately into 3.5t restricted parking on right and the Service Point is at the bottom by pond.

i Service Point only. Inspected 2014.

None

Custom

MEUZAC ★
218 F8   87380   N45°32.936' E001°26.312'

Directions: Rue 11 Novembre 1918. Exit A20 at Junction 42 and follow D7bis, sp 'Meuzac'. In Meuzac turn left onto D243, sp 'Benayes'. Service Point 250m on right, signed. Parking 100m further on left in car park overlooking lake: N45°32.882' E001°26.406'.

i Pleasant Aire on edge of residential area adj to leisure lake with swimming beach, signed walks and picnic facilities. Local commerce 500m. Ideal for both overnight stays and leisurely days. Inspected 2014.

15

Custom

LUBERSAC
219 F8   19210   N45°26.201' E001°23.803'

Directions: D901, at the Super U. On D901 southbound towards Arnac-Pompadour, by the Super U fuel station.

i Supermarket adj; LIDL adj. Château in town. Inspected 2010.

Poss

Euro Relais Junior

CONCEZE
220 F8   19350   N45°21.267' E001°20.733'

Directions: D56e, in small village. Turn off D901 onto D56e heading east into town. Turn by church and Aire is 10m on left, signed.

i Restaurant/bar adj. On Limousin apple orchard route. Local parking by church or on grass in summer. Inspected 2010.

5; Grass parking

Custom

OBJAT
221 F8   19130   N45°16.267' E001°24.717'

Directions: D148e3/Ave Jules Ferry. From D901 turn onto D148e3 in Objat. Follow road north out of town towards Les Grandes Terres following sp 'Aire de Camping-Car'. Aire on right, signed. Enter through barrier, access code from TO in village by war memorial: N45°15.869' E001°24.591'.

i Small lake nearby; TO, open 10am-12 noon and 2pm-6pm daily, has internet access; Showers available by token. Updated 2013.

21; €5/day inc 16amp elec; Pay TO; Max 72hrs

Euro Relais Junior; Token (3/3)

Photo: Rita Renninghoff

AYEN
222 F8   19310   N45°14.988' E001°19.410'

Directions: Exit village to north on D39 towards St Robert. Turn left by Centre D'incendie et de Secours building on outskirts of village, sp 'Ayen-Bas' and signed. The Aire is behind the Secours building outside the Atelier Municipal, works yard.

i Small Aire with rural views on edge of small village Visited 2012.

5

Custom

Info/photos: John & Janet Thay

GLANDON — 223 — F8 — 87500 — N45°28.621' E001°13.718'

Directions: D18. Exit town to south on D18. Aire is adj to D18 just past the sports facilities by the weigh bridge.

ℹ️ Village 2 mins; Local parking available. Inspected 2010.

🚐 2

🚰 Euro Relais Mini; Token (2/1); €3.50

ST YRIEIX LA PERCHE — 224 — F8 — 87500 — N45°30.753' E001°12.380'

Directions: D704/Ave Gutenberg. Turn off at the roundabout junction of D704/D901 and the Aire is in the car park on the left, adj to roundabout, signed.

ℹ️ Really just a Service Point in a very unlevel town car park; Medieval town 5 mins. Inspected 2010.

🚐 Poss

🚰 Euro Relais Mini; Token (2/1); €3.50

PIERRE BUFFIERE — 225 — F8 — 87260 — N45°41.370' E001°22.260'

Directions: Turn off A20 at Junction 40, sp 'Pierre Buffiere', then follow sp 'Stade'. Drive through the building complex and the Aire is on the left.

ℹ️ Service Point with two parking bays opp municipal camping field (May-Sept €10.50/night) and gîtes. More parking before campsite at stade. Only minutes from A20, convenient night/lunch halt. May feel isolated if alone. Inspected 2014.

🚐 10; Park at stade when campsite open

🚰 Custom; 1 CEE elec point (Not working)

NEXON — 226 — F8 — 87800 — N45°40.255' E001°10.866'

Directions: D15a1, near Etang de la Lande. Turn off D11 in town onto D15, sp 'Etang de la Lande'. In 1.6km turn left onto D15a1, signed. Follow road towards lake and Aire on left.

ℹ️ Service Point outside campsite near small lake/swimming pond. Less commercial than 227. Inspected 2010.

🚐 3

🚰 Custom

ST HILAIRE LES PLACES — 227 — F8 — 87800 — N45°38.053' E001°09.700'

Directions: At Lac Plaisance. Turn off D11, sp 'Lac Plaisance' and follow sp 'Lac Plaisance'. At campsite entrance keep left through gates. Travel down hill past car park on right and Aire in bottom of car park on left.

ℹ️ At leisure/swimming lake; Lake views from bottom and top car park. Inspected 2010.

🚐 10; €1.50pp Jul-Aug; Pay at campsite

🚰 Raclet; Token (2/1)

Photo: Geoff Myatt

CHALUS — 228 — F8 — 87230 — N45°39.656' E000°59.286'

Directions: N21. Exit town on N21 towards Limoges. Aire on right, sp 'Aire des Energies' and signed. Designated parking behind building, signed.

ℹ️ Adj to N21 but sheltered by banks. This is a motorway style fuel station which also appeals to trucks. There is a small shop and café onsite. Updated 2014.

🚐 15

🚰 Custom; €2; Showers €2

PAGEAS | 229 | F8 | 87230 | N45°40.690' E001°00.135'

Directions: N21. From north on N21 turn right at bottom of hill before village onto D141a, sp 'Pageas'. Aire immediately on right in large, flat grass parking area. Limited hardstanding for winter use.

ℹ️ Lake; Play area in adjoining park. Well kept; Easy walk to village. Restaurant next to Aire. Inspected 2012.

🚐 10; Grass parking

⛲ Euro Relais Junior; Token (ER); €2

ORADOUR SUR VAYRES | 230 | F8 | 87150 | N45°43.963' E000°51.942'

Directions: Rue Jean Giraudeau, off D901.Turn off D901 by the Hotel de Ville/Mairie, opp D75 junction, sp 'Relais de la Vaynes' and signed. Service Point 50m on left, undesignated parking opp.

ℹ️ Local commerce 1 min. Hell's Bells all night. Voie Verte cycle/walking route to Chalus from town. Inspected 2014.

🚐 5

⛲ Custom

CUSSAC | 231 | F8 | 87150 | N45°42.318' E000°50.957'

Directions: Rue du 8 Mai 1945, off D73. From west on D669 turn right alongside cemetery onto D73, sp 'Marval'. Turn 1st left opp cemetery parking. The Aire is 75m on right, signed.

ℹ️ Very small Aire adj to boules court. Pleasant village with local commerce adj. Inspected 2014.

🚐 3

⛲ Euro Relais Junior; Token (ER); €2

ST MATHIEU | 232 | F8 | 87440 | N45°42.912' E000°47.242'

Directions: C65. Turn off D675 in St Mathieu onto D699, sp 'Limoges'. Turn off D699 onto D127, sp 'Centre Tourisme du Lac'. Turn off D127 onto C65, sp 'Centre Tourisme du Lac'. Turn left into Centre Tourisme du Lac. Aire is on right, signed.

ℹ️ Aire adj to leisure lake with walks and boat hire. Views of lake from the very uneven parking. Adj campsite open May-Sept. Inspected 2014.

🚐 20

⛲ Depagne; €2

ST LAURENT SUR GORRE | 233 | F8 | 87310 | N45°45.922' E000°57.390'

Directions: Allée des Lilas. Exit town on D34, sp 'Vayres' and signed. Turn left in front of Gendarmerie, sp 'La Cote' and signed. After passing the stade municipal turn left and follow road to lake. Aire in former municipal campsite, sp 'Accueil Camping-Cars Les Chenes'.

ℹ️ Former campsite turned commercial Aire beside small leisure lake and park. Local commerce 7 mins, partially uphill. Inspected 2012.

🚐 30; €6/night; Collected; Grass parking between trees

⛲ Custom; Numerous unmetered Cont elec points

LES SALLES LAVAUGUYON | 234 | F8 | 87440 | N45°44.412' E000°42.037'

Directions: D33. Exit village on D33, sp 'St Mathieu'. Turn right after cemetery, signed. Aire in 20m on lower road.

ℹ️ Pleasant country Aire located on the Richard the Lionheart route. Covered picnic area adj. Village with local commerce 4 mins. Inspected 2014.

🚐 6; €4/24hrs; Honesty box

⛲ Flot Bleu Fontaine; 1 CEE elec point on timer (Not working)

ROCHECHOUART | 235 | F8 | T | 87600 | N45°49.320' E000°49.208'

Directions: Place du Château. Turn off D675, sp 'P Hotel de Ville' and 'Château'. Follow road up hill and Service Point is in car park opp château and adj to Hotel de Ville.

ℹ️ Central car park which will be busy in summer on château open days. Château open Wed-Mon, €4.60pp, www.museum-rochecouart.com. Alternative adj roadside parking may be more practical or car park on D675: N45°49.454' E000°49.316'. Inspected 2014.

🚐 5 in adj car park marked with 5m bays; Other parking avail

⛲ Flot Bleu Océane; Token; €2; Toilets 150m

JAVERDAT | 236 | F8 | R | 87520 | N45°57.145' E000°59.158'

Directions: C8. Turn off D711 in village centre by church onto C8, signed. Aire on right as exit village, signed.

ℹ️ Landscaped Aire in a small village. Onsite toilet block. Local commerce 1 min, tokens free from Auberge bar. Inspected 2014.

🚐 4; Max 72hrs

⛲ Aires Services; Token; Aire Services Electric; 1 Token/55 mins

ORADOUR SUR GLANE | 237 | F8 | | 87520 | N45°56.129' E001°01.531'

Directions: From north on D3 turn right on entering town, signed. Follow road, then turn right, signed. Aire in 50m on one-way loop. Always popular, each bay is designed for two motorhomes.

ℹ️ Memorial at opp end of town (1.3km) commemorating 642 people killed during a Nazi attack on the town on June 10, 1944: N45°55.727' E001°02.114'. Open Feb-mid Dec 9am-5pm, later in spring/summer; €7.80pp. Inspected 2014.

🚐 27; Double bays

⛲ Euro Relais Junior; €2

NIEUL | 238 | F8 | | 87510 | N45°55.553' E001°10.318'

Directions: Rue de la Gare. Turn off D28 into car park opp château, signed. Service Point in car park, parking on grass behind car park.

ℹ️ Pleasant parking area with views of château, which has open access gardens, in one direction and grassland in the other. Local commerce 2 mins. Updated 2014.

🚐 22; Max 72hrs; Grass parking

⛲ Custom; Empty toilet down toilet

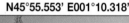

ST PRIEST TAURION | 239 | F8 | | 87480 | N45°53.172' E001°23.785'

Directions: Stade Municipal. Follow D29 through town towards Royeres. After crossing river bridge turn right in 100m into stade municipal, signed. Drive to the right and the Service Point is close to the river.

ℹ️ Adj to river with limited views but does have interesting water management ruins. Fishing is private. Sports ground adj. Local commerce 1 min on D29. Inspected 2012.

🚐 17

⛲ Custom

RAZES - Lac de St Pardoux | 240 | F8 | | 87640 | N46°02.050' E001°17.892'

Directions: Lac de St Pardoux. From Razes follow D44, sp 'Lac de St Pardoux'. Turn off D44, sp 'Lac de St Pardoux', and Service Point is in 1st parking area on left.

ℹ️ Large leisure lake adj and partial views from parking. Swimming beach, boating, walk/cycle around lake 24km (6hrs). Inspected 2012.

🚐 15; Max 1 night

⛲ Aire Services; Token (3/3); €3.50

Photo: Donna Garner

BESSINES SUR GARTEMPE | 241 | F7 | 87250 | N46°06.568' E001°22.183'

Directions: Parking Champ de Foire, Rue d'Ingolsheim. In village turn beside Mairie, signed. Aire in car park in 100m.

Aire located in the central square parking. Constant comings and goings of vehicles when commerce open. Local commerce 2 mins. Inspected 2014.

5

Euro Relais Junior; No drive over drain; 2 unmetered CEE elec points

CIEUX | 242 | F8 | 87520 | N45°59.500' E001°02.966'

Directions: Allée Bel Air, off D711. Follow D711 east through the village towards Nantiat. As exit village turn right off D711 onto Allée Bel Air, sp 'Aire Naturelle'. Aire is adj to Aire Naturelle municipal campsite.

Village with local commerce 200m. Down a lane directly opp is a very large lake with fishing available; permits from Mairie. Visited 2013.

20; Grass parking

Euro Relais Box; Token (ER)

Info/photos: Chris & Di Ruoff

BELLAC 1 | 243 | F7 | 87300 | N46°06.956' E001°03.086'

Directions: Rue des Tanneries. Approach from south on N147. Exit roundabout onto D947, sp 'Bellac'. Turn left onto D3, sp 'Blond' and signed. Turn right, signed. Follow road to Service Point on right, signed. Parking is on left before Service Point: N46°06.891' E001°03.128'.

Beautiful riverside park in tranquil setting. Roman bridge and marked walks adj. Town with commerce 5 mins uphill. Market Sat. Inspected 2014.

5

Custom

BELLAC 2 | 244 | F7 | 87300 | N46°07.283' E001°02.764'

Directions: Rue Louis Jouvet. From north turn off N147 at roundabout onto D947, sp 'St Junien' and 'Bellac'. After 4.3kms turn 1st right past village boundary sign, signed. Designated parking in car park 700m on right opp Hotel de Ville, signed. Other designated 3.5t parking adj to D947 by Maison de Association and TO: N46°07.253' E001°03.034'.

Two designated parking areas in town centre. School opp 1st, TO opp 2nd. Town commerce adj. Inspected 2014.

5+5

None; See 243

BUSSIERE POITEVINE | 245 | F7 | 87320 | N46°14.187' E000°54.103'

Directions: D942. Turn off N147 onto D942, sp 'Gueret'. Turn right in 700m, just past village boundary sign. Service Point in 10m, behind toilets. Parking adj to road and on other side of lake.

Pleasant parking adj to park with pond and walk. Distant road noise from N147. Ideal stop if transiting along N147. Local commerce 2 mins. Inspected 2014.

20

Euro Relais Box; Token (ER)

RANCON | 246 | F7 | 87290 | N46°07.653' E001°10.885'

Directions: D1. Exit village on D1 towards Bellac (south). Aire on right in lay-by as exit village, signed. Parking is in the stade (sports stadium) through adj gate and up steep slope: N46°07.698' E001°10.830'.

Slightly isolated parking on edge of small village avail summer only. Limited local commerce 2 mins. Sports facilities adj. 12th century Lanterne des Morts in town at former cemetery: N46°07.933' E001°10.950'. Inspected 2014.

10; Grass and gravel; Summer only

Custom

| MARSAC | 247 | G7 | | 23210 | N46°05.995' E001°34.780' |

Directions: Off D42. Follow sp 'Camping' northwest out of village on D42. At campsite entrance take road to right, signed. Service Point 100m on left, signed.

i Small parking area at stadium 100m past Service Point. Campsite adj. Inspected 2010.

🚐 5

🚰 Custom; €5

| ST DIZIER LEYRENNE | 248 | G8 | | 23400 | N46°01.390' E001°43.032' |

Directions: D912. From south follow D912 to St Dizier Leyrenne. Aire on right adj to D912 when enter village, next to municipal campsite and Etang de la Valodie.

i Village 10 mins; Lake walk adj. Inspected 2010.

🚐 3

🚰 Custom

| CHATELUS LE MARCHEIX | 249 | G8 | | 23430 | N45°59.931' E001°36.198' |

Directions: Off D8. Exit the village to the west on D8 towards Villemaumy. Turn off at the edge of the village, sp 'Camping'. The Service Point is in 50m on the left, outside municipal campsite.

i Lovely rural views. Adj campsite open Jul-Aug, €11.50/night. Inspected 2010.

🚐 5; When campsite closed

🚰 Raclet; €2

| BOURGANEUF | 250 | G8 | | 23400 | N45°57.265' E001°45.460' |

Directions: D912. Enter town from north on D912. Turn left in front of turreted building, signed. Turn right in car park, signed.

i Pleasant town with multiple commerce 200m uphill. Inspected 2010.

🚐 5

🚰 Euro Relais Mini

| MONTBOUCHER | 251 | G8 | | 23400 | N45°57.089' E001°40.866' |

Directions: Off D36, in village centre. Turn off D941 onto D36, sp 'Montboucher'. Follow signs to Aire. In village centre follow road behind church and to right.

i Located in a rural village. Tennis court adj. Inspected 2010.

🚐 10

🚰 Euro Relais Mini

| SAUVIAT SUR VIGE | 252 | G8 | | 87400 | N45°54.559' E001°36.911' |

Directions: N141. Adj to N141 as enter village from northeast, signed. Aire on left in large parking area.

i Town adj. Inspected 2010.

🚐 20

🚰 Urba Flux; €2; No drive over drain

ST JUNIEN LA BREGERE | 253 | G8 | 23400 | N45°52.950' E001°45.190'

Directions: D13, off D940. In village turn off D940 onto D13. Turn right in 200m, signed.

*Rural views; Village 2 mins. Some road noise from D940. Inspected 2010.

3

Custom

PEYRAT LE CHATEAU | 254 | G8 | 87470 | N45°48.881' E001°46.251'

Directions: Place du Pré de l'Age. Turn off D940 main road in town centre opp TO. Aire 100m on left.

*Rural views; Village 1 min with local commerce, museum and lake. Inspected 2010.

10

Custom; Token; €1; Nov-Mar

BUJALEUF | 255 | G8 | 87460 | N45°48.297' E001°38.207'

Directions: D16. Exit village to northeast on D16, sp 'Cheissoux' and 'Lac de Ste Helene'. Parking adj to Lake Ste Helene 1.5km from the village, signed. Service Point on Rue du Champ du Foire. Turn off D14 as exit village towards Eymoutiers, signed: N45°47.856' E001°37.893'.

*Parking adj to large open space and leisure lake/reservoir. Village has local commerce. Inspected 2010.

5

Custom

EYMOUTIERS | 256 | G8 | 87120 | N45°44.293' E001°44.108'

Directions: D979. Exit town to west on D979 towards Limoges. The Service Point is located at the Casino supermarket fuel station on the left as exit town.

*Service Point removed Sept 2014. Future uncertain. Inspected 2014.

Poss; No long term parking near Service Point

Flot Bleu Fontaine; 1 unmetered elec point; No drive over drain

LAC DE VASSIVIERE | 257 | G8 | 87470 | N45°47.188' E001°52.134'

Directions: Traveling east go through Beaumont-du-Lac to north on D43. Turn left in 1km onto D43b sp 'Lac Vassiviere'. At D222 T-junction turn right then in 100m turn left and re-join the D43B both sp 'Peirrefitte' and signed. Follow road straight on, sp 'Plage' and signed to lake, The Service Point is on the left after the campsite.

*Peaceful lakeside Aire with views of lake and a swimming beach adj. There is a holiday village behind the Aire but no other commerce. Great area to discover by boat, bike or on foot. Updated 2014.

Tollerated

Euro Relais Junior; €2

ROYERE DE VASSIVIERE | 258 | G8 | 23460 | N45°50.403' E001°54.668'

Directions: D3. Exit the village to south on D3, sp 'Gentious'. The Aire is adj to D3 in the car park by the Proxi mini market, signed.

*Pleasant village with local commerce adj. Updated 2014.

5; Closed Tues pm for market Wed am

Euro Relais Mini

FELLETIN | 259 | G8 | 23500 | N45°52.923' E002°10.546'

Directions: Rue des Fosses. Located off D10 and D982, sp 'Crocq'. Well signed from all directions. Service Point accessible from slope at rear of car park.

ℹ️ Town with commerce 200m. Inspected 2010.

🚐 5

⚲ Euro Relais Mini

CROCQ | 260 | G8 | 23260 | N45°51.812' E002°22.125'

Directions: Route de la Bourboule. Follow D996, main route, through Crocq towards Giat. The Aire is at the sports facilities adj to D996, signed. Entrance is narrow but passable with care.

ℹ️ Located adj to sports facilities and fire station. Local commerce 3 mins. Inspected 2012.

🚐 6; Grass parking but other hardstanding parking poss

⚲ Euro Relais Junior; Token (ER)

AUBUSSON | 261 | G8 | 23200 | N45°57.407' E002°10.514'

Directions: Place du Champ de Foire, off D988, signed. Enter town from north on D990. Turn onto D988, sp 'Aubusson D94a'. Follow road past Intermarché and Aire is in car park 100m on left, signed.

ℹ️ Large town 2 mins; Do not attempt to drive through town in anything but van-style motorhome. Inspected 2010.

🚐 20

⚲ Euro Relais Junior; €2

AHUN | 262 | G7 | 23150 | N46°04.797' E002°02.648'

Directions: Route de Limoges. Turn off D942 onto D13, sp 'Camping Municipal' and signed. Service Point on left outside municipal campsite, signed.

ℹ️ Service Point outside small, pleasant municipal campsite that charges €6.50 inc 2 people. Village with local commerce 2 mins. Inspected 2012.

🚐 Poss, when campsite closed

⚲ Euro Relais Mini

CHENERAILLES | 263 | G7 | 23130 | N46°06.641' E002°10.683'

Directions: D990. Exit town towards Aubusson and the Aire is on the left, signed.

ℹ️ Next to housing estate; Adj to main road; Village centre 2 mins with local commerce. Inspected 2010.

🚐 5

⚲ Euro Relais Junior; Token (ER)

CRESSAT | 264 | G7 | 23140 | N46°08.363' E002°06.610'

Directions: Off D990. As enter Cressat from Chénérailles, Aire just past lake on left, signed.

ℹ️ Lake adj, but no view; Village 2 mins uphill. Inspected 2010.

🚐 5; 8m bays

⚲ Raclet; Token (2/1)

GOUZON | 265 | G7 | 23230 | N46°11.486' E002°14.412'

Directions: Place du Champ de Foire, Rue d'Alcantera. Drive out of Gouzon on D997, sp 'Aubusson'. Turn off, sp 'Camping'. Before road splits turn left, sp 'Parking Ombragé: Pique-Nique' and signed.

i Shaded parking under trees. Town and restaurants 2 mins. Updated 2013

🚐 10

🔧 Raclet

JARNAGES | 266 | G7 | 23140 | N46°11.064' E002°04.870'

Directions: D65. In Jarnages turn right at La Poste onto D65, sp 'Accueil Camping Car'. Service Point adj to play area and lake.

i Lake, mini golf, village/shops 3 mins; Level walk to town. Inspected 2010.

🚐 5

🔧 Euro Relais Junior; €2

ST LAURENT | 267 | G7 | 23000 | N46°09.983' E001°57.700'

Directions: D3. Turn onto D3 in village centre at rear of church, sp 'Bourne Camping-Car'. Aire 50m on right in car park, adj to church.

i Good stopover. Local commerce nearby. Inspected 2010.

🚐 4; 8m bays

🔧 Euro Relais Junior; 2 unmetered elec points

GUERET - AIRE DES MONT DE GUERET | 268 | G7 | 23000 | N46°10.945' E001°50.918'

Directions: D942/DN145. Exit N145 at Junction 45, sp 'Gueret Ouest', and follow sp 'Aire des Mont de Gueret'. Aire located at motorway services behind main building, signed.

i Motorway services with shop/café that is technically off the motorway but as with all motorway Aires we advise you not to stay overnight. Inspected 2012.

🚐 10; Not Recommended

🔧 Euro Relais Junior; €2

LA CELLE DUNOISE | 269 | G7 | 23800 | N46°18.534' E001°46.459'

Directions: D48a/Rte du Canard. Exit village to south on D22, sp 'Gueret' and signed. Turn left onto D48a, signed. Service Point is on left outside municipal campsite.

i Service Point only. Inspected 2010.

🚐 None

🔧 Euro Relais Junior; €2

BOUSSAC | 270 | G7 | 23600 | N46°20.867' E002°13.242'

Directions: D997. Follow D997 through town towards Gueret. Aire on left adj to large car park/livestock market, signed.

i Adj to livestock market and D997, both of which can be busy and noisy. Small town commerce 1 min. Inspected 2012.

🚐 10

🔧 Euro Relais Box

LIMOISE | 271 | H7 | | 03320 | N46°40.540' E003°03.071'

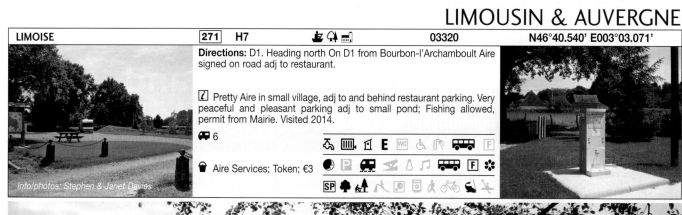

Directions: D1. Heading north On D1 from Bourbon-l'Archamboult Aire signed on road adj to restaurant.

ℹ️ Pretty Aire in small village, adj to and behind restaurant parking. Very peaceful and pleasant parking adj to small pond; Fishing allowed, permit from Mairie. Visited 2014.

🚐 6

🚿 Aire Services; Token; €3

Info/photos: Stephen & Janet Davies

Bellac

Aiguilhe

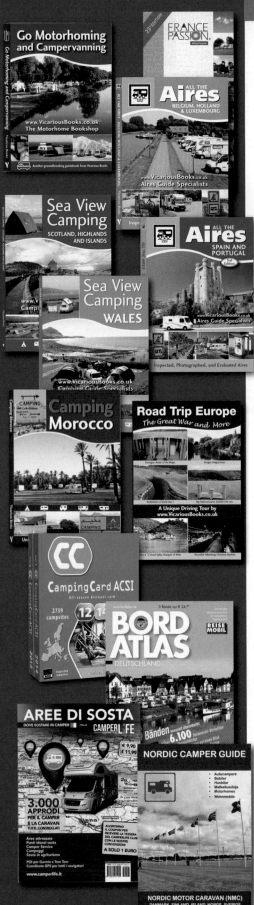

Ste Croix du Verdon

MEDITERRANEAN

Carro

CASTELNAUDARY — 1 — G11 — 11490 — N43°18.843' E001°56.947'

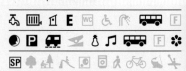

Directions: D624. Approach on D624 from south to avoid driving through town. Aire adj to D624 on left before Gendarmerie, signed. Enter through PARKNIGHT barrier.

i Uninspiring commercial Aire in noisy location adj to Canal du Midi, no views. Small town commerce 2 mins. Day parking adj to Canal du Midi at: N43°21.130' E001°49.442'. Inspected 2014.

9; €12/24hrs; CC; Discounts for pass holders

Euro Relais Junior; Inside barrier; Inc; 7 CEE elec points; Inc

SALLES SUR L'HERS — 2 — G11 — 11410 — N43°17.534' E001°47.259'

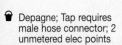

Directions: Rue des Écoles. From south on D625 turn right past La Poste, sp 'Borne Camping Car'. Follow road to bottom of hill on one-way system. Aire in 70m outside sports grounds, signed.

i Sloping parking adj to sports stadium on edge of village. Stream adj and footpaths into open countryside. Very pleasant shady spot. Inspected 2013.

10

Depagne; Tap requires male hose connector; 2 unmetered elec points

BELPECH — 3 — G11 — 11420 — N43°11.915' E001°44.709'

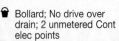

Directions: Rue du Stade. Approach on D502 from Marty (west). At Stop junction turn left onto D102, sp 'Belpech'. Turn right opp CA bank into Rue du Stade. Follow road and turn left into sports stadium after houses. Aire to right, not signed. Counter lever barrier should be open.

i If the barrier is closed there is hardstanding space avail outside. Open access sports ground adj. Small town commerce 2 mins. Inspected 2013.

5; Grass parking

Bollard; No drive over drain; 2 unmetered Cont elec points

FANJEAUX — 4 — G11 — 11270 — N43°11.154' E002°01.933'

Directions: Chemin des Fontanelles. From Carcassonne on D119 enter village and pass through arch then take 1st right. Take the last left at a complicated junction, sp 'Borne Camping Cars', and follow road up the hill. In 300m turn left by the crucifix, signed. Aire immediately on left.

i Popular Aire at medieval hilltop village. Small town commerce and TO, all 300m downhill. Inspected 2013.

12; Max 48hrs

Bollard; No drive over drain

PEZENS — 5 — G11 — 11170 — N43°15.329' E002°15.813'

Directions: Place de la Liberté. Traveling towards Carcassonne on D6113 Aire is in car park on left just after crossing the river in town. Difficult access, reverse in if possible.

i Adj to shops and restaurants. Noise from road. No river views. Inspected 2013.

4

Bollard; No drive over drain; 1 unmetered elec point

Photo: Keith & Sue Lawrence

CARCASSONNE — 6 — G11 — T — 11000 — N43°12.324' E002°22.362'

Directions: P2, Chemin de Montlegun. Approach from east on D6113. Exit D6113, sp 'La Cité'. Follow sp 'La Cité' up hill and turn right. Take 1st right, sp 'P2' and signed. Aire 50m on right through barrier, signed.

i This is a large out of town parking area for buses and motorhomes just 4 mins from the fairytale city of Carcassonne. Inspected 2013.

50; 1st hr free; 2-6hrs €5, then €1/hr; Pay on exit; Free 8pm-8am

Custom; Inside barrier; In disrepair

ROUTIER | 7 | G11 | 🏛 | 11240 | N43°06.492' E002°07.391'

Directions: Place du Malepere, off D702/Ave de Madailhan. From D623 turn onto D309, sp 'Routier'. Continue through village, D309 becomes D702. Turn left into Place du Malepere, sp 'Caravanning'. In 10m turn right. Service Point on right and parking on right past Service Point.

ℹ Individual bays with rural views. Wine growing region. Very peaceful. Inspected 2013.

🚐 5

🏧 Bollard; 2 unmetered elec points; Lift cover for WC

VILLENEUVE MINERVOIS | 8 | G11 | 🏛 | 11160 | N43°18.900' E002°27.850'

Directions: D111. From D111 turn into the car park in the town centre, opp Mairie and next to the Spar shop. Once in car park, turn right and Service Point in far right corner. Designated parking before Service Point, signed.

ℹ Small, peaceful village. Local commerce adj. Shaded parking in summer. Inspected 2013.

🚐 5; Max 48hrs; Designated bays

🏧 Bollard

ESPERAZA | 9 | G12 | 🏭 | 11260 | N42°56.028' E002°12.949'

Directions: Avenue François Mitterrand. Turn off D118 onto D46, sp 'Espéraza' and 'Camping'. Follow D46 into town and turn left before river bridge, signed. Follow road along river for 400m and parking is on the right under pine trees. Service Point on left, signed.

ℹ Pleasant parking under trees adj to suburb and small river, partial views but access adj. Town 4 mins. Inspected 2013.

🚐 20; On grass under trees

🏧 Custom

LAGRASSE | 10 | H11 | T | 11220 | N43°05.563' E002°37.245'

Directions: At 'Parking 2', Avenue des Condomines. Follow D3 through village towards Trèbes. Turn right just before exit village, sp 'P2'. Turn next left into car park. Service Point and parking down slope, signed.

ℹ Grass and hardstanding parking. Beau Village with abbey and tourist commerce 1 min. Inspected 2013.

🚐 40; €5/24hrs high season; €3/24hrs low season; Collected

🏧 Custom

VILLEROUGE TERMENES | 11 | H11 | 🏭 | 11330 | N43°00.287' E002°37.601'

Directions: D613. Aire adj to D613 at rear corner of parking for château, beside shop, signed.

ℹ Shop selling local products adj. Entrance to château opp side of road, signed. Inspected 2013.

🚐 3

🏧 None; See 12

FELINES TERMENES | 12 | H12 | 🏛🛐 | 11330 | N42°59.225' E002°36.776'

Directions: D613. Aire in village car park on left as exit towards Mouthoumet just before D39 junction, not signed.

ℹ Pleasant car park under trees. Village centre 1 min. Very old Service Point, elec working but water off June 2013. Inspected 2013.

🚐 5

🏧 Bollard; No drive over drain

QUILLAN — 13 — G12 — 11500 — N42°52.450' E002°10.950'

Directions: La Gare, D117. Turn off D117, main route through, into car park, sp 'Le Gare' and signed. Parking also for railway station and buses.

i Parking under trees. Market in parking Sat am. Small town commerce opp. Train to Carcassone. Inspected 2013.

🚐 5

Custom; Token (2/0); €3.20

LAPRADELLE PUILAURENS — 14 — G12 — 11140 — N42°48.583' E002°18.517'

Directions: Rue de la Devèze, off D117. Turn off D117 at viaduct. Aire between viaduct and fire station, signed. Be careful to avoid bollard in entrance.

i Poss parking adj to fire station. Views of mountains and château. Inspected 2013.

🚐 Poss

Custom

DUILHAC SOUS PEYREPERTUSE — 15 — G12 — 11350 — N42°51.683' E002°33.917'

Directions: D814. From Maury take D19, sp 'Château de Queribus'. After passing the château turn left onto D14, sp 'Duilhac-s/s-P'. At entrance to village turn left onto D814, sp 'Duilhac-s/s-Peyrepertuse 0.7' and 'Château de Peyrepertuse'. Follow road past cafés and Aire is in car park on left, signed.

i Beautiful views of surrounding mountains. Village centre with cafés 250m. Castle 3.5km by road; adults from €6. Medieval fête in town 2nd week of Aug. Inspected 2013.

🚐 20

Custom

PUYVALADOR — 16 — G12 — SKI — 66210 — N42°39.076' E002°04.622'

Directions: Rue des Sources. Turn off D118 onto D32g and follow signs to Puyvalador ski station. Aire on left in 'Parking 3'. Access road in poor condition.

i Service Point in very poor condition. Tap missing at time of 2010 inspection. Unable to reinspect in 2013 as D118 being resurfaced and closed.

🚐 20

Custom

LES ANGLES PLA DEL MIR — 17 — G12 — 66210 — N42°33.787' E002°04.008'

Directions: Pla del Mir ski lift station. Turn off D118 onto D32, sp 'Les Angles'. D32 is a very wide road and a scenic drive. In Les Angles turn off D32 opp large car park banning motorhomes, sp 'Parc Animaler' and 'Parking Camping Car'. Follow road up hill and Service Point is to the left of the ski lift, signed. Designated parking is to the right, signed.

i Alt 1791m. Ski lift station adj; 3 ski runs finish adj to Aire. Tokens from adj animal park. May feel isolated if alone out of season. Inspected 2013.

🚐 40

Customised Aire Services; Token; €3

MONT LOUIS ✶ — 18 — G12 — T — 66210 — N42°30.409' E002°07.345'

Directions: Parking des Remparts. Turn off N116 into car park, sp 'Parking Entrée', on right-hand side of arched entrance into town (do not drive through arch into town). Pass through barriers, not in use at time of inspection, and Aire is at rear of car park. Also possible to walk to town from N116 lay-by.

i Parking adj to impressive citadel walls, numerous shops/cafés inside citadel. Town in the foothills of the Pyrénées. Inspected 2013.

🚐 20; €5/4pm-10am; Pay at machine

Custom; Under arch; Inc

THUES ENTRE VALLS — 19 — G12 — 66360 — N42°31.333' E002°13.283'

Directions: Turn off N116, sp 'Gorges de la Carança'. Cross 3.5t weight restricted bridge, turn left and follow sp 'Gorges de la Carança'. Enter car park through barrier, then follow signs to large grass area on left. Go with flow by entering in morning/departing in afternoon as approach roads narrow with few passing places.

i Adj to cool gorge walk to grotto. Café in car park in season. Inspected 2013.

10; €8/day; Pay at machine

Custom; Inside barrier; Inc

EGAT — 20 — G12 — 66120 — N42°29.850' E02°00.800'

Directions: D618, at Super U in Égat. Located at the roundabout junction of D618 and D33f, southwest of Égat. Service Point at the supermarket fuel station, signed. For parking follow service road behind supermarket, sp 'Parking 2 110 places': N42°29.876' E002°00.670'.

i At supermarket that feels more like a service station. Ski shop adj. Toilets and free WiFi in supermarket. Inspected 2013.

Poss

Euro Relais Junior; €2; No drive over drain

SAILLAGOUSE — 21 — G12 — 66800 — N42°27.467' E002°02.250'

Directions: Lieu-Dit Village. Turn off N116, opp Hôtel de Ville, by fun statues in village centre, signed. Aire 10m on left in car park.

i Town centre adj, small cheese market Wed am. There are 3 Flot Bleu elec points dotted about town, but this is the only signed parking. Inspected 2013.

5

Flot Bleu Pacific; Token; €4; Flot Bleu Elec (Not working)

LIMOUX — 22 — G11 — 11300 — N43°03.475' E002°12.888'

Directions: Rue Louis Braille. Best approached from north on D118. On entering town fork left following sp 'Centre Ville', then turn left into Rue Louis Braille, sp 'Gamm Vert'. The Aire is on the left, signed. Not signed from other directions.

i Town centre 5 mins. Large market Fri am. LPG available at E'Leclerc on D118 at Centre Commercial. Visited 2013.

20

Custom

Info/photos: Janet & John Watts/David Abbott

BOLQUERE PYRENEES 2000 — 23 — G12 — 66210 — N42°30.867' E002°03.733'

Directions: D618, at Casino supermarket. Located on D618, Mont Louis to Égat road, north of Bolquère.

i Service Point only. Motorhomes banned from previous parking areas. Inspected 2013.

None

Flot Bleu Euro; CC; €2

CASTEIL — 24 — G12 — 66820 — N42°32.017' E002°23.517'

Directions: D116. Small parking area on left before village adj to D116, signed.

i Pleasant woodland setting. Tap and toilet up steps in car park but not accessible by motorhome due to height barrier. Inspected 2013.

10

None; See 25 and 26

MEDITERRANEAN

VERNET LES BAINS 1

| 25 | G12 | | 66820 | N42°33.395' E002°23.043' |

Directions: D116, at Intermarché supermarket. On right as enter town on D116, opp campsite. Service Point adj to fuel station.

i Supermarket adj, campsite opp. Inspected 2013.

🚐 Poss

🚰 Euro Relais Mini; Token (ER); €2.50; Drive over drain in car wash poss

VERNET LES BAINS 2

| 26 | G12 | | 66820 | N42°32.567' E002°23.433' |

Directions: Chemin de la Laiterie. Turn off D116 at roundabout at far end of village, signed. Cross river bridge and turn left, sp 'Aire Camping Car', past pink hotel. Follow road to right of car park. Aire at end of road, signed.

i Parking on two levels overlooking thermal spa town. Inspected 2013.

🚐 20

🚰 Flot Bleu Océane; Token (FB); €2

BELESTA

| 27 | H12 | | 66720 | N42°42.925' E002°36.562' |

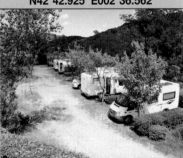

Directions: D21. Exit Ille-sur-Têt , sp 'Belesta' and follow sp 'Belesta'. As enter village turn right, signed, down narrow road on 20% hill. At bottom of hill turn left, signed. Service Point on right, parking past tennis court and children's play area, signed. Actual GPS: N42°42.982' E002°36.477'.

i Aire adj to picnic area on outskirts of village. Drive up on D21 has some unusual rocky landscape. Inspected 2013.

🚐 8; €5/night; Collected; Hedged bays

🚰 Flot Bleu Pacific; Token (FB); Flot Bleu Elec; 1 Token/4hrs elec

ST MARSAL

| 28 | H12 | | 66110 | N42°32.250' E002°37.400' |

Directions: D618. From Amélie-les-Bains-Palalda take D618 to St Marsal; this road is a shorter, easier drive than from Bouleternère. Turn right into village car park and take road to right, signed. Turn 1st left and Aire on left, signed.

i Isolated village with just a village shop. Showers €1, but sign does not indicate location. Inspected 2013.

🚐 5; €3/night; Pay at shop

🚰 Tap

AMELIE LES BAINS

| 29 | H12 | | 66110 | N42°28.717' E002°40.433' |

Directions: Rue des Lledoners. Turn off D115, sp 'Camping Municipal'. Aire on right adj to campsite, signed

i Next to popular campsite. Short walk to pretty spa town nestled in wooded hills. Inspected 2013.

🚐 5; €6/night; Max 48hrs

🚰 Raclet Maxi; Token (ER); €4; No drive over drain

ST PAUL DE FENOUILLET

| 30 | H12 | | 66220 | N42°48.633' E002°30.267' |

Directions: Place St Pierre. Turn off D117 into car park in town centre, sp 'Gare SNCF' and signed. Service Point against road edge.

i Service Point in small town centre car park. Also used as bus stop. Inspected 2013.

🚐 Poss in town car park

🚰 Flot Bleu Euro; CC; €3; No drive over drain

LE BOULOU — 31 H12 — 66160 — N42°31.636' E002°50.229'

Directions: Chemin du Moli Nou. Exit Boulou towards Perpignan on D900 and turn right, sp 'P. Cimetière' and signed. Take next left turn, signed. Aire in 50m by the cemetery.

i Very popular Aire adj to stadium with football pitch. Town with numerous commerce 2 mins. Market Thurs/Sun am. Inspected 2013.

🚐 21; Max 24hrs

🚰 Aire Services; €2

ST ANDRE — 32 H12 — 66690 — N42°33.135' E002°58.396'

Directions: Rue de Taxo. Exit D914 at Junction 11, sp 'St André'. Follow sp 'St André'. Turn right into Intermarché supermarket car park, signed. Drive behind supermarket and turn left, signed. Aire 100m past cemetery, signed. If approaching from other directions, do not follow GPS off main route through town.

i Supermarket 200m. Town 2 mins. Inspected 2013.

🚐 6; €2.30/night; Collected; Free during day; Max 3 nights

🚰 Flot Bleu Océane; Token; €2; Flexi hose for waste water

COLLIOURE — 33 H12 — 66190 — N42°31.517' E003°04.100'

Directions: D86/Route de Madeloc. Turn off D914 at Junction 14, sp 'Collioure'. Follow road straight across roundabout, sp 'Camping'. Aire on left adj to tennis club, entry through barrier.

i Shuttle bus to village every 30 mins May-Sept. Elec points suggest use should be 2hrs. Inspected 2013.

🚐 40; €10/24hrs Oct-Apr; €15/24hrs May-Sept; Pay at kiosk

🚰 Custom; Inside barrier; 12 CEE elec points on lower terrace

PORT VENDRES — 34 H12 — 66660 — N42°31.063' E003°06.815'

Directions: Route de la Jetée. Turn off D914 onto D86b, sp 'Port de Commerce' and signed. Follow road to port entrance and turn right at roundabout. Aire 100m on right, signed. May need to reverse in/out.

i Popular Aire adj to sea and harbour but no views. Beach adj but swimming banned. Town 5 mins. Updated 2014.

🚐 40; €10/night; Collected

🚰 Sani Station; Inc; Token (provided on payment)

ST CYPRIEN — 35 H12 — 66750 — N42°37.076' E003°02.103'

Directions: Rue Jean de la Fontaine. Turn off D81 at roundabout, sp 'St Cyprien-Le Port'. At roundabout turn right, sp 'Le Port'. Follow road past LIDL, then turn right. At roundabout turn left, sp 'P Le Port'. Follow road to left along marina edge and Aire on left, signed. Entry through Flot Bleu Park barriers.

i Adj to and partially overlooking marina. Restaurants adj. Inspected 2013.

🚐 50; €1/hr, €6/24hrs Dec-Mar; €3/hr, €8/24hrs Apr-Jun/Sept-Nov; €4/hr, €10/24hrs Jul-Aug; CC

🚰 Flot Bleu Océane; Inside barrier; Flot Bleu Elec; Token

LATOUR BAS ELNE — 36 H12 — 66200 — N42°35.998' E003°00.438'

Directions: Parking Camping Cars Rousillon. Turn off D81 at roundabout, sp 'Latour Bas Elne' and signed. Follow road for 1.5km and Aire on left, signed.

i Motorhome dealers, some English spoken. Workshop. Security gates locked at night. Inspected 2013.

🚐 40; €10/night inc elec; Collected; Grass parking

🚰 Custom; Inc

CANET EN ROUSSILLON | 37 | H12 | 66140 | N42°41.967' E003°01.335'

Directions: D617. Turn off D617 at the roundabout into the Hyper Casino, sp 'Hyper Casino Entree'. The Service Point is adj to the fuel station, adj to McDonald's.

i Supermarket adj. Inspected 2013.

🚐 Poss

🛒 Euro Relais Junior; €2

LE BARCARES 1 - Port | 38 | H12 | ⚓ | 66420 | N42°48.000' E003°01.883'

Directions: Quai Alain Colas. From south on D83 exit at Junction 11, sp 'Port'. At roundabout go straight on. Cross next roundabout, then turn left at roundabout, sp 'Le Port'. Go straight over next roundabout, then turn left at roundabout, sp 'P Bassin de la Tourette'. Aire at end of road, enter through PARKNIGHT barrier.

i Views across boats in marina (Bassin de la Tourette). Also see **39 40 41 42 43**. Submitted 2014.

🚐 28; €12/night; CC; Discounts for pass holders

🛒 Euro Relais Junior; Inside

Library photo

LE BARCARES 2 | 39 | H12 | ☼ | 66420 | N42°48.667' E003°02.067'

Directions: Rue André Malraux. From south on D83 exit at Junction 12 and at the roundabout take 3rd exit, sp 'Le Lydia'. Aire at far end of parking on left adj to pine woodland.

i 2 dedicated parking spaces adj to pine woodland (La Grande Pinede). Also see **38 40 41 42 43**. Inspected 2013.

🚐 2; Max 4hrs (8am-9pm); Max 6m

🛒 None

LE BARCARES 3 | 40 | H12 | ☼ | 66420 | N42°47.350' E003°02.033'

Directions: Rue Annibal. Leave D83 at Junction 10, sp 'Village'. Go straight over roundabout, sp 'Le Barcares-Village'. Take 2nd right into Rue Annibal, sp 'P Place les Pins'. Aire in small car park 200m on right, parking signed in far corner.

i In small car park at rear of town hall. Only 600m from beach. Inspected 2013. Also see **38 39 41 42 43**.

🚐 3; Max 4hrs (8am-9pm)

🛒 None

LE BARCARES 4 | 41 | H12 | ☼ | 66420 | N42°50.067' E003°02.267'

Directions: Rue des Marines. From south on D83 exit at Junction 14, sp 'Grande Plage Nord'. At roundabout turn left, sp 'Cap de Front', and follow road which runs parallel to D83. Aire 400m in parking bays on left, just past bus stop opp junction.

i Adj to D83 so some road noise. Cycle track adj. Also see **38 39 40 42 43**. Inspected 2013.

🚐 3; Max 4hrs (8am-9pm)

🛒 None

LE BARCARES 5 | 42 | H12 | ☼ | 66420 | N42°49.454' E003°01.823'

Directions: Avenue de l'Ile de la Coudalère. From north on D83 exit at Junction 13 and at roundabout take 1st exit, sp 'Nautica'. Aire on right overlooking lake, signed.

i Dedicated parking spaces overlooking lake, kite/windsurfers etc. Also see **38 39 40 42 43**. Inspected 2013.

🚐 3; Max 4hrs (8am-9pm)

🛒 None

LEUCATE — 43 — H12 — 11370 — N42°54.817' E003°01.200'

Directions: D327. From south exit D627, sp 'Leucate village'. Turn left onto D327, sp 'Caves'. Pass under road bridge and Aire on left, signed. Enter through Urba Flux barrier.

i Terraced Aire overlooking lake with distant views of mountains beyond. Windsurf school and café. Pay WiFi. Popular with windsurfers. Inspected 2013.

🚐 100; €7.20/24hrs; CC

🚰 Flot Bleu Fontaine; Inside barrier; €2

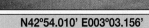

LEUCATE PLAGE — 44 — H12 — ⚓ — 11370 — N42°54.010' E003°03.156'

Directions: From south on D627 turn onto D327, sp 'Leucate Plage', and then turn right, sp 'Leucate Plage' and signed. Turn right in 500m, sp 'Leucate Plage', then follow road to right, signed. Aire past campsite, on both sides of road. Enter through Urba Flux barrier.

i 15 sea/beach view bays. Direct access to beach on left side. No shade. Inspected 2013.

🚐 200; €7.20/24hrs Apr-Oct; No services Nov-Apr; CC

🚰 Flot Bleu Fontaine; Inside barrier; €2

LA FRANQUI PLAGE — 45 — H12 — 11370 — N42°56.625' E003°01.830'

Directions: Chemin de las Pitchinos. From D627 turn off, sp 'La Franqui'. Then follow sp 'Les Cousseles'. Follow road across bridge onto island and round to right. Service Point adj to campsite entrance.

i Service Point only. Inspected 2013.

🚐 None

🚰 Custom; Token; €5

PORT LA NOUVELLE 1 — 46 — H11 — 11210 — N43°00.977' E003°02.958'

Directions: Rue Vincent Auriol. From south take D709 to Port la Nouvelle. At the roundabout turn right, sp 'Centre Ville 3.5t'. Go straight on, past 47 and 48, go over roundabout and at the next roundabout turn left. Service Point at far end of Super U car park near self-service laundry.

i Supermarket adj. Self service laundry adj. Inspected 2013.

🚐 None; See 48

🚰 Aire Services; €2

PORT LA NOUVELLE 2 — 47 — H11 — ⚓ — 11210 — N43°00.890' E003°02.779'

Directions: Blvd Francis Vals, outside the municipal campsite. From south take D709 to Port la Nouvelle. At the roundabout turn right, sp 'Centre Ville 3.5t'. After crossing railway on bridge, turn left at next roundabout, sp 'Le Golfe'. Service Point on left outside camping Le Golfe, in 3.5t weight restricted area.

i Service Point only. Inspected 2013.

🚐 None

🚰 Flot Bleu Euro; CC

PORT LA NOUVELLE 3 — 48 — H11 — 11210 — N43°00.817' E003°02.450'

Directions: Chemin des Vignes. From south take D709 to Port la Nouvelle. At the roundabout turn right, sp 'Centre Ville 3.5t'. After crossing railway on bridge, turn left, signed. Turn left again, sp 'Gare SNCF', and Aire on left, signed. Entrance through counter lever barrier, open when Aire open.

i 3 mins to town centre. Adj to railway and main road so noisy at times. Flot Bleu Fontaine for toilet emptying. Inspected 2013.

🚐 100; €4/day Apr-Oct; €7/day Jul-Aug; Collected

🚰 Flot Bleu Euro; CC; €2; Flot Bleu Fontaine

MEDITERRANEAN

PEYRIAC DE MER
49   H11   11440   N43°05.551' E002°57.749'

Directions: D105. Turn off D6009, sp 'Peyriac de Mer'. Follow road through village, signed. Exit village on D105, sp 'Bages'. Aire on left, signed.

ⓘ Adj basic campsite. Inland sea and beach opp but no view. Village has local commerce and 30 min motorhome parking is allowed. Inspected 2012.

🚐 6; €5/night; Collected

🚰 Custom; Adj to 1st building

GRUISSAN PORT
50   H11   11430   N43°06.256' E003°05.983'

Directions: Quai de la Tramontane. Enter Gruissan from north on D32. Go straight over roundabout, sp 'Gruissan-Centre'. Follow road to right, sp 'Gruissan-Village' and 'Le Port'. At roundabout turn left then left again, both sp 'Aire des 4 Vents'. Follow road to end and Aire on left at marina. Entry has manned hut and manual barrier.

ⓘ Adj to marina with views across water/boats. Town 5 mins. Showers. Inspected 2013.

🚐 100; €8.50/noon-noon; Pay at kiosk; Mar-Nov

🚰 Urba Flux; Inside barrier; Inc

GRUISSAN PLAGE
51   H11   11430   N43°05.754' E003°06.591'

Directions: Avenue de la Jetée. Enter Gruissan from north on D32. Go straight over roundabout, sp 'Gruissan-Centre'. Follow road to right, sp 'Gruissan-Village' and 'Le Port'. Go straight over roundabout, past **50**, following sp 'Plage de Chalets'. Parking is 1.9km at end of road, signed. Barrier manned by guardian in adj hut.

ⓘ Ideal beach holiday location; Sandy beach adj. Popular area for water sports, inc kite surfing, windsurfing. Cycle path to town adj. Inspected 2013.

🚐 100; €8.50/noon-noon; Pay at kiosk; Mar-Nov

🚰 Custom; Inside barrier; Inc

VINASSAN
52   H11   11110   N43°12.278' E003°04.451'

Directions: D31/Ave du Docteur Etienne Montestruc. Follow D31 through town towards Salles d'Aude and Aire is on left through Aire Services barrier, signed.

ⓘ Aire located under trees providing deep shade. Village with local commerce 1 min. Inspected 2012.

🚐 10; €8/24hrs inc elec; CC

🚰 Aire Services; Inside barrier; 16amp elec inc

OUVEILLAN
53   H11   11590   N43°17.533' E002°58.208'

Directions: Rue de la Coopérative, off D13. As exit town to north exit roundabout, sp 'Cave Coopérative' and signed. Take road to left and turn left in 10m next to orange house, signed. Access road is narrow and may be obstructed by bushes. Walk in first and check there is space.

ⓘ Aire popular with French motorhomers. Local wine production adj. Local commerce in village. Inspected 2013.

🚐 5

🚰 Custom

NARBONNE 1
54   H11   11100   N43°10.550' E002°59.656'

Directions: Ave du Général Leclerc. From south on D6009 dual carriageway follow sp 'Centre Ville'. Service Point is at the Casino supermarket just after turning sp 'Narbonne Plage'.

ⓘ Supermarket adj. Many shops within walking distance. Inspected 2013.

🚐 Poss

🚰 Flot Bleu Euro; CC; €2

NARBONNE 2 | 55 | H11 | 11100 | N43°10.834' E003°01.419'

Directions: Ave de la Mer, at parking 'La Narbonette'. Enter Narbonne from east on D168 (road also goes to Narbonne Plage). Aire opp Parc des Expositions, signed. Enter via Flot Bleu Park barrier.

ℹ️ Free bus to Narbonne every 15 mins from theatre. Cycle hire €15. 5 mins to busy lively town. Inspected 2013.

🚐 34; €9 inc elec; CC; Max 72hrs

🚰 Flot Bleu Euro; Inside barrier; CC; €2

NARBONNE PLAGE | 56 | H11 | 11100 | N43°08.828' E003°09.249'

Directions: Off D332. At D168/D332 roundabout south of town turn onto D332, sp 'Gruissan'. Turn left, sp 'Aire Camping Car' and 'Aqua jet'. Aire on right in 20m. Barrier at entry, opened by warden 8am-8pm.

ℹ️ Commercial Aire adj to vast beach which is popular with wind/kite surfers. Aqua park adj. No facilities 8pm-8am. Inspected 2013.

🚐 100: €10/night; Pay at kiosk; Accessible 8am-8pm; Apr-Oct

🚰 Custom; Inside barrier; 8am-7pm

LES CABANES DE FLEURY | 57 | H11 | 11560 | N43°12.910' E003°14.088'

Directions: Ave Eric Tabarly, off D718. From Fleury follow D718, sp 'Les Cabanes de Flery'. Follow road to right, then straight on past campsite into marina. Aire on right past marina, signed.

ℹ️ Small river/creek marina adj, partial views. Beach adj, no views. Local commerce adj. Inspected 2013.

🚐 50; €6.50/night; Collected; Free 9am-3pm

🚰 Flot Bleu Océane; Token; €2

VALRAS PLAGE | 58 | H11 | 34350 | N43°14.600' E003°16.903'

Directions: Boulevard Pierre Giraud. Enter town on D19. At the roundabout turn right, sp 'Casino'. At the traffic lights turn right, sp 'Casino'. Turn right before road bends to sea, Service Point on right in 10m. Follow road as bends to sea for unofficial parking in 100m: N43°14.529' E003°16.906'.

ℹ️ Motorhomes banned from parking in town Apr-Oct. Resort along sandy beach with restaurants. Inspected 2013.

🚐 Tolerated; Nov-Mar

🚰 Aire Services; €2/50L water

ST PIERRE LA MER | 59 | H11 | 11560 | N43°11.388' E003°11.805'

Directions: Enter town from Narbonne on D1118. Turn left on Blvd des Embruns and follow it along the seafront. At the roundabout turn right, signed. Follow road past municipal campsite and Aire is adj to the height barriered car park, signed. Enter via Flot Bleu Park barrier.

ℹ️ Commercial Aire with informal feel. Sailing school adj. In sea marsh with footpaths through to beach/naturist beach. Inspected 2013.

🚐 100; 1st 2hrs free; €7/24hrs; CC

🚰 Flot Bleu Océane; Inside barrier; Token; €2; Elec 1 Token/4hrs

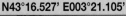

PORTIRAGNES PLAGE | 60 | H11 | 34420 | N43°16.527' E003°21.105'

Directions: Avenue de la Grande Maïre. Turn off D37 at roundabout north of town, sp 'Plage OUEST'. Turn right, sp 'Plage OUEST'. Follow road to left, sp 'Plage Ouest Parking', and go straight over roundabout. Aire on left, signed. Service Point at: N43°16.781' E003°21.096'.

ℹ️ Large sandy beach 200m. Toilet 150m. Large wetland area with paths adj, no view. Roadside parking banned. Updated 2014.

🚐 20; €8/night; Pay at TO for access code; Max 72hrs

🚰 Custom; 500m from parking

MEDITERRANEAN

SERIGNAN
61 H11   34410   N43°16.140' E003°17.020'

Directions: D64. Approach from north on D64. At roundabout turn right off D64 towards Super U supermarket. At next roundabout turn left. Drive past fuel station, follow road to left, then turn left into fuel station. Service Point on right, signed.

ℹ️ Supermarket adj. Self-service laundry adj. Inspected 2012.

🚐 Poss

⛲ Aire Services; €2

VILLENEUVE LES BEZIERS
62 H11   34420   N43°18.994' E003°17.076'

Directions: Promenade des Vernets, adj to canal outside Camping des Berges du Canal. From town centre cross canal on D37e13 and turn immediately right, sp 'Les Berges du Canal'. Follow road along canal and Service Point 100m on left.

ℹ️ Campsite adj. All parking restricted. Inspected 2013.

🚐 None

⛲ Custom; €2

BALARUC LES BAINS
63 I11   34540   N43°26.739' E003°40.665'

Directions: Turn off D2 onto D2e11, sp 'Balaruc les Bains' and signed. At roundabout turn left, signed. In 800m turn right, signed. Additional 6 places: N43°26.711' E003°40.510'. Exit parking and turn right, then right again at roundabout at end of road. Turn right at end of road and additional parking 100m on left, signed.

ℹ️ Thermal spa adj. Updated 2014.

🚐 6+6; €7/night; Collected

⛲ Aire Services; Token (3/3)

MONTAGNAC
64 H11   34530   N43°28.517' E003°29.467'

Directions: At D613/D5e11 junction. Approach town from Mèze. Turn right onto 5e11 1.8km after dual carriageway starts at Montagnac boundary sign, signed. Turn immediately right to Aire, signed.

ℹ️ Small parking area, but always likely to have space. Overlooks dual carriageway so some road noise, but tolerable. Inspected 2013.

🚐 4

⛲ Custom

LE CAP D'AGDE
65 H11   34300   N43°17.148' E003°31.037'

Directions: Parking de la Bavière. Exit D612, sp 'Le Cap d'Agde'. At 1st roundabout turn left, then turn right at 2nd roundabout. Aire 20m on right, signed. Entry phone at barrier. Pay at Camping de la Clape, 100m. Service Point outside barrier.

ℹ️ Adj to road, overlooked by residential flats. Sea 10 mins walk. Inspected 2013.

🚐 22; €10/24hrs Apr-Oct; €5/24hrs Nov-Mar; Pay at campsite, 100m; 7m bays

⛲ Flot Bleu Euro; CC; €2

AGDE
66 H11   34300   N43°17.954' E003°28.259'

Directions: Route de Guiraudette, at Hyper U. Exit D612, sp 'Grau d'Agde'. At roundabout turn left, crossing over D612, sp 'Grau d'Agde'. At next roundabout turn right, then right again into Hyper U.

ℹ️ Supermarket, self-service laundry, garden centre and McDonald's adj. Inspected 2013.

🚐 Poss

⛲ Euro Relais Mini; Token (ER); €2.50

SETE | 67 | I11 | | 34200 | N43°22.019' E003°36.962'

Directions: N112. From Agde follow N112 beach road for 6km towards Sète. Aire on right off roundabout.

ℹ️ Isolated Aire off main road adj to railway. Large sandy beach adj via footpath. Updated 2013.

🚐 35

🚰 Aire Services; CC; €1

MARSEILLAN PLAGE | 68 | I11 | | 34340 | N43°19.149' E003°32.928'

Directions: Rue des Goélands. From Sète on D612 turn off at roundabout, sp 'Plage-Centre'. Turn left in 50m, signed. Aire on left, Service Point past Urba Flux barrier entrance.

ℹ️ Former municipal campsite turned Aire. Town and beach 7 mins. Inspected 2012.

🚐 €4/24hrs Jan-Mar/Nov-Dec; €6/24hrs Apr-Jun/Sept-Oct; €10/24hrs Jul-Aug; CC

🚰 Urba Flux Tall; CC; €2/10 mins

MEZE | 69 | I11 | | 34140 | N43°26.453' E003°35.700'

Directions: Avenue du Stade. From roundabout on D613 west of village turn onto D158, sp 'Loupian'. In 1.2km turn right, sp 'Parc de Sesquier'. Follow road straight on for 1km and Aire is just past football pitch adj to road, signed.

ℹ️ Road adj with poor surface increasing traffic noise. Town 15 mins. Next to sports facilities. Inspected 2013.

🚐 20

🚰 Custom

VAILHAN | 70 | H11 | | 34320 | N43°33.324' E003°17.930'

Directions: Lieu Dit l'Eglise. Approach Vailhan from Roujan. Follow D125 through the village, sp 'Fournols' and signed. Aire on left, adj to the church before the village exit, signed.

ℹ️ Remote village near reservoir. Walking paths adj. Restaurant nearby. Inspected 2013.

🚐 5; €5/night; Collected

🚰 Custom

SALASC | 71 | H11 | | 34800 | N43°37.068' E003°19.027'

Directions: D148. Turn off D908 onto D148, sp 'Salasc'. Follow the road to the village and turn right into parking area as enter village, sp 'P'. Two bays in the middle of the car park are assigned to motorhomers. D8 between Salasc and Mourèze has a 2.2m width restriction.

ℹ️ Salasc is a pretty picture postcard French village with local commerce. Walking trails. Inspected 2013.

🚐 2; Max 1 night; Grass parking, but hardstanding available

🚰 None

BEDARIEUX | 72 | H11 | | 34600 | N43°36.644' E003°09.206'

Directions: Quai de la Passerelle. From east on D908 follow sp 'Centre Ville' through a series of roundabouts. As approach town turn left, sp 'P Av. J. Moulin' and signed. Follow road to right, then turn left. Follow road straight on along river edge and the Aire is on the right, opp a college, signed.

ℹ️ Parking obstructed by trees, manoeuvre with care. Small town commerce 5 mins along shallow river. Inspected 2013.

🚐 15; Max 72hrs; Sign suggests €5 and pay at machine but machine removed

🚰 Urba Flux Tall

Sete

LAC DU SALAGOU - Rives de Clermont `74` H11 34800 N43°38.811' E003°23.350'

Directions: Lac du Salagou/Rives de Clermont. From Clermont l'Hérault turn off D908 onto D156e4, sp 'Lac du Salagou'. Follow sp 'Rives de Clermont'. Turn right before height barriered car park, sp 'Base de Plein Air' and signed. Service Point on right and parking beyond, signed.

i Adj to the busiest part of the lake. Café adj. Lake 150m with swimming beach. Inspected 2013.

6; €5/night Oct-May; €6/night Jun-Sept; €7/night Jul-Aug; Elec inc; Pay at campsite

Custom; Token; €2; 4 16amp CEE elec points

LAC DU SALAGOU - Rives de Liausson `75` H11 34800 N43°38.609' E003°23.278'

Directions: Rives de Liausson. Before right turning for `74` turn left onto D156e7, sp 'Lac du Salagou' and 'Rives de Liausson'. Designated parking on right in 300m, signed.

i Level ground adj to road. No view of lake. May feel isolated if alone. Inspected 2013.

10; Max 1 night

None

LAC DU SALAGOU - Rives d'Octon `76` H11 34800 N43°39.065' E003°19.484'

Directions: Rives d'Octon. On east side of Lac du Salagou turn off D148, sp 'Rives d'Octon'. Follow road and motorhome parking is next to the day car park, signed.

i Designated parking in a natural area, access lumpy and bumpy. Café, boat hire adj. Access to lake, no views. May feel isolated if alone. Inspected 2013.

10; Max 1 night

None

LAC DU SALAGOU - Village des Arts `77` H11 34800 N43°39.253' E003°19.069'

Directions: Off D148, adj to picnic area. Turn off D148, sp 'Village des Arts'. Designated parking just past picnic area on left, signed.

i Small parking area adj to picnic area. No lake views. Inspected 2013.

4; Max 1 night

None

LAC DU SALAGOU - Rives des Vailhes `78` H11 34700 N43°40.268' E003°21.280'

Directions: D148e5. On north of Lac du Salagou turn off D148/D148e4 onto D148e5, sp 'Les Vailhés'. Turn left in 600m before lakeside parking, sp 'Les Vailhés', then take 1st right. Aire on left before campsite, signed.

i Partial lake views. Lake has slipway and swimming beach. Basketball hoop and table tennis table. Inspected 2013.

16; €5/night low season; €8/night high season; Max 48hrs

Custom; Tap, drain, toilet disposal destroyed; Elec not working

MOUREZE `79` H11 34800 N43°37.040' E003°21.661'

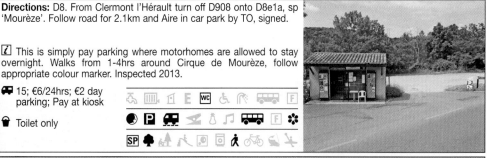

Directions: D8. From Clermont l'Hérault turn off D908 onto D8e1a, sp 'Mourèze'. Follow road for 2.1km and Aire in car park by TO, signed.

ℹ️ This is simply pay parking where motorhomes are allowed to stay overnight. Walks from 1-4hrs around Cirque de Mourèze, follow appropriate colour marker. Inspected 2013.

🚐 15; €6/24hrs; €2 day parking; Pay at kiosk

🚰 Toilet only

FRAISSE SUR AGOUT ⭐ `80` H11 34330 N43°36.267' E002°47.750'

Directions: Chemin de la Salvetat á Fraisse. From west on D14 turn right just before village, sp 'Île sur l'Agout' and signed. Aire on right in 180m.

ℹ️ Pleasant riverside Aire. Riverside park includes BBQ point. TO and local commerce 2 mins. Aire can flood in winter. Inspected 2014.

🚐 10; €7/24hrs; Collected; Grass parking

🚰 Flot Bleu Compact; 6 unmetered CEE elec points

LA SALVETAT SUR AGOUT `81` H11 34330 N43°36.021' E002°40.749'

Directions: Sailing school car park. Turn off D907 south of La Salvetat-sur-Agout onto D14e1, sp 'Lac de la Raviège' and 'Base Touristique des Bouldouïres'. In 2.8km turn left, sp 'Base Touristique des Bouldouïres'. Follow road past the campsite to the sailing school car park adj to lake.

ℹ️ Aire on sloping parking adj to large leisure lake/reservoir, no views. Sailing and sandy beach, swimming poss. May feel isolated out of season. Inspected 2014.

🚐 20; Max 48hrs; Grass parking close to lake, hardstanding in previous lay-by

🚰 Custom; Open Apr-Oct

LUNAS `82` H11 34650 N43°42.351' E003°11.179'

Directions: D35. On right as approach Lunas from Le Bousquet d'Orb, sp 'Base de Loisirs' and signed. Approach from east is very narrow and winding with a sheer drop.

ℹ️ Popular Aire adj to small leisure lake, entry €4/pp. Café adj. Footpath to village with local commerce. Inspected 2013.

🚐 30

🚰 Custom; Toilets inside leisure lake facility

GIGNAC `83` H11 34150 N43°39.716' E003°33.522'

Directions: Chemin de la Meuse, outside Camping La Meuse. Take D32 north out of village, sp 'Aniane'. Turn left, sp 'La Meuse' with the campsite symbol. Service Point to the left of campsite entrance.

ℹ️ Service Point only. Inspected 2013.

🚐 None; See `84`

🚰 Euro Relais Mini; Token (ER)

ANIANE `84` I11 34150 N43°41.183' E003°34.950'

Directions: D32. In Aniane follow D32 towards St Jean de Foz. Turn left, sp 'Sapeurs Pompiers'. Turn left, then immediately right, and follow road to end. Aire in parking at end of road, signed. Also signed from 'P Centre Ville' parking by La Poste in town.

ℹ️ Large parking area suitable for all motorhomes, always likely to have space. Local commerce 200m. Inspected 2013.

🚐 12

🚰 None; See `83`

ARRE | 85 | H10 | 30120 | N43°58.055' E003°31.262'

Directions: D999. Aire adj to D999 at eastern end of the village, 200m from Mairie, signed.

ℹ Local commerce within 500m. Walking and cycling on old railway track 100m. Inspected 2013.

🚐 5

Euro Relais Mini; €2

AVEZE | 86 | I10 | 30120 | N43°58.545' E003°35.931'

Directions: Le Pouchounet. Turn off D999 onto D48, sp 'Avèze'. Turn right before river bridge, sp 'Salle Polyvalente' and signed. Service Point on approach road, unrestricted parking adj.

ℹ Pleasant area with access to shallow river. Café and municipal facilities adj inc sports facilities and campsite. Inspected 2013.

🚐 5

Euro Relais Mini

VILLENEUVE LES MAGUELONE | 87 | I11 | 34750 | N43°31.769' E003°52.092'

Directions: Rue René Bert. From Palavas les Flots approach on D185. Turn left at roundabout, sp 'Villeneuve M Centre'. Turn left again, sp 'Plage' and signed. Follow road for 400m, then turn left alongside cycle path on gravel track, sp 'Arenes' and signed. Aire straight on after Stop junction, enter through gate.

ℹ Commercial Aire with clearly defined bays on asphalt. Partial view of water from 2 bays. Favoured by large motorhome users as no obstacles to impede access. Inspected 2014.

🚐 26; €14/night May-Sept; €9/night Oct-Apr; 16amp elec inc; CC; Pay at barrier

Custom; 26 16amp CEE elec points

PALAVAS LES FLOTS 1 | 88 | I11 | 34250 | N43°31.808' E003°55.471'

Directions: Rue Frédéric Mistral. On D986 from north go straight over roundabout, sp 'Halte Camping Cars'. Take next left, sp 'Halte Camping Cars', which turns back on itself under 3.7m bridge. GPS taken from top of road. Exact GPS: N43°31.855'E003°55.438'.

ℹ Large commercial Aire at pleasure boat marina, many bays have marina views. Road noise in some areas. Bike hire at reception. Inspected 2014.

🚐 126; €11/4pm-4pm Oct-May; €14 Jun-Sep; +€3 if over 8m; +€0.22/pp tax; Pay at reception

Custom; Inc; Inside; Elec €2

PALAVAS LES FLOTS 2 | 89 | I11 | 34250 | N43°31.948' E003°55.630'

Directions: Ave de l'Abbé Brocardi. From D986 turn off at roundabout, sp 'Office de Tourisme' and signed. Cross bridge and turn off at roundabout with multi-storey car park, signed. Turn left, signed, and follow signs to Aire. Guardian will direct you to a pitch, on a Segway.

ℹ Large municipally run commercial Aire that resembles an airport car park. The adj multi-storey car park provides shaded parking. 24hr guardian. www.palavaslesflots.com. Inspected 2014.

🚐 130+; €11.70/night; Pay guardian

Custom; 12amp elec €2

CARNON PLAGE | 90 | I11 | 34280 | N43°33.033' E003°59.633'

Directions: From Palavas les Flots take D62e2, sp 'Carnon'. In Carnon turn onto D59, sp 'Carnon Est'. Follow road to end, then turn left, sp 'Le Grand Motte'. Turn left in 150m, sp 'Les Saladelles'. Turn right into Camping Les Saladelles. Aire to left of campsite, enter through barrier.

ℹ Only 80m from sandy Mediterranean beach with snack bars, boardwalks and popular with kite surfers. Price includes use of showers and campsite facilities. Inspected 2014.

🚐 18; €13/night Jul-Aug; €11.50/night Sept-Jun; Elec inc; CC

Custom; Inside barrier

LA GRANDE MOTTE | 91 | I11 | 34280 | N43°34.033' E004°04.467'

Directions: Ave de la Petite Motte. From Le Grau du Roi follow D255 west across bridge and onto D59. Follow road to left, sp 'Centre Ville' and signed. At traffic lights turn left, then 1st right at traffic lights, then right again at 2nd set of traffic lights, all sp 'Petite Motte' and signed. Aire on right at end of road past campsites.

ℹ 5-10 mins from sea. Showers. Looks like part of a campsite dedicated to motorhomes. Inspected 2013.

🚐 30; €16 Jun-Aug; €13 May/Sept; €11 Oct-Apr; CC

♁ Custom; Inside barrier; Inc; Plenty of 16amp elec points

LE GRAU DU ROI | 92 | I11 | 30240 | N43°32.437' E004°08.011'

Directions: D62a. Enter town on D62a following sp 'Port de Pêche'. Aire just off large roundabout, visible from road and signed. Enter through barrier, take ticket and pay at machine. Height barrier prevents motorhomes entering during busy periods; check access before turning off roundabout as road past car park passable but not ideal.

ℹ Beach and water park adj. Town gets very busy during weekends and holidays. Inspected 2013.

🚐 50; Up to €19.10/24hrs; Pay by hr at machine

♁ Aire Services; €2

AIGUES MORTES 1 | 93 | I11 | 30220 | N43°33.950' E004°11.117'

Directions: Rue du Port, parking at port. Enter town from south on D62. At roundabout turn right, sp 'Aigues Mortes'. Follow road to Aigues Mortes then turn right before river bridge, signed. Follow road for 300m, Aire on left. Barrier not working at time of inspection, but payment still possible at machine. Motorhomes banned from everywhere but the official Aire.

ℹ Aire overlooks port. Walled city with pristine walls, views of walls from Aire. Central square has cafés and restaurants. Worth a visit. Inspected 2013.

🚐 30; €16/24hrs; Barrier; Pay at machine

♁ Custom; Inside barrier; Inc

AIGUES MORTES 2 | 94 | I11 | 30220 | N43°34.640' E004°11.978'

Directions: D979, parking at Intermarché. On northern outskirts of town at roundabout junction of D62/D979/D46. On entering car park turn right and parking signed at rear of Intermarché against grass bank.

ℹ Aigues Mortes 5 mins. Ideal parking if day visiting as motorhomes banned from all car parking in town. Supermarket with LPG adj. Inspected 2013.

🚐 10

♁ None; See 92; Toilet key avail after purchase

ST MATHIEU DE TREVIERS | 95 | I10 | 34270 | N43°45.733' E003°51.634'

Directions: Chemin de la Ville. Turn off D17 at roundabout, sp 'St Mathieu-Village de Haut' and signed. Follow road straight on for 200m, then at stop junction go straight over and turn diagonally left and drive through white gate. Aire on right through additional gate. Gate locked 10pm-8am.

ℹ Aire adj to sports centre in gravel car park with unmarked bays. Very quiet. Market Sun am. Inspected 2013.

🚐 10; €5/24hrs; Collected

♁ SOS; 9 16amp elec points

SOMMIERES | 96 | I10 | 30250 | N43°47.183' E004°05.233'

Directions: Outside Camping Municipal Le Garanel. Turn off D6110 onto D40, sp 'Nîmes'. At roundabout turn right, sp 'Nîmes', and follow road onto 3.5t one-way system through town. Turn right at river, sp 'Camping Municipal'. Follow road to right, then turn left, sp 'Camping Municipal'. Road opens into large parking area. Service Point in far corner to the right of the campsite entrance.

ℹ Medieval riverside town. Campsite open Apr-Sept. River 1 min with stepping stone causeway. Inspected 2014.

🚐 5

♁ Euro Relais Mini; Token (ER); €3.30

ST MAMERT DU GARD — 97 — I10 — 30730 — N43°53.084' E004°11.418'

Directions: Rue du Gres, off D1. Turn off D999 onto D22, sp 'St Mamert du G'. In 4km turn left onto D1, sp 'St Mamert du Gard'. Service Point 300m on left behind recycling, signed. Parking: N43°53.381' E004°11.422'. Exit Service Point to left onto D1. Turn right in centre, sp 'Mairie' and 'P Gratuit'. Turn 1st left, then 1st left again, both signed. Parking on right, signed.

i Village with local commerce. Peaceful parking with no shade. Inspected 2013.

🚐 5

🪣 Custom; Reverse in

ALES — 98 — I10 — 30100 — N44°07.208' E004°04.927'

Directions: Ave Jules Guesde. To avoid town approach from south on N106. At roundabout turn left, sp 'Alès-Centre' and 'La Prairie'. After crossing river bridge turn right, sp 'Centre Ville' and 'La Prairie'. Follow road along river. Go straight over roundabout, sp 'La Brésis' and signed. Aire 100m on right, signed.

i 3 end bays suit larger motorhomes. Adj river is more of a storm drain. Large town commerce 1 min. Inspected 2014.

🚐 12

🪣 Depagne

ANDUZE — 99 — I10 — T — 30140 — N44°02.890' E003°59.110'

Directions: Place de la Gare. Follow D907 through town and turn into train station car park, sp 'Gare'. For Service Point follow road to left through car park. Service Point on left: N44°03.001' E003°59.090'. For parking follow signs behind building, signed.

i At train station for tourist steam train to St Jean du Gard (40 mins), runs Apr-Oct. Tourist commerce 4 mins. St Jean du Gard **101** a more charming town. Inspected 2013.

🚐 30

🪣 Euro Relais Junior; €2

SAUVE — 100 — I10 — T — 30610 — N43°56.390' E003°57.160'

Directions: D999. Turn off D999 in village into roadside car park, signed. Turn left and Aire on left adj to road wall, signed. Car park floods.

i Pleasant parking under plane trees. Must park in designated space. Local commerce adj. Medieval village access via archway opp Service Point. Inspected 2013.

🚐 10

🪣 Custom

ST JEAN DU GARD ★ — 101 — I10 — T — 30270 — N44°06.094' E003°53.042'

Directions: Rue Beaux de Maguielle. Turn off D907 at traffic lights into St Jean du Gard, sp 'Lasalle', 'Centre Ville' and 'Gare'. Follow road for 600m straight on through town. After crossing river go straight on and to the left in the train station car park. Service Point on left next to the bus parking, signed.

i Gard steam train to Anduze adj, 40 mins. Unrestricted parking beyond Service Point and very shaded parking adj to road below. Tourist commerce 1 min. Inspected 2013.

🚐 10

🪣 Raclet

VILLEFORT — 102 — I10 — 48800 — N44°26.033' E003°55.833'

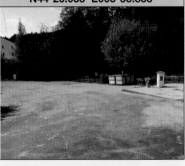

Directions: Rue du 19 Mars 1962. From south on D901 turn left just before village, sp 'Les Sédariès'. Aire on left just past Gendarmerie.

i Roadside parking but very quiet road. D901 from south is very scenic. Inspected 2010.

🚐 5

🪣 Euro Relais Junior; €2

Photo: Keith & Sue Lawrence

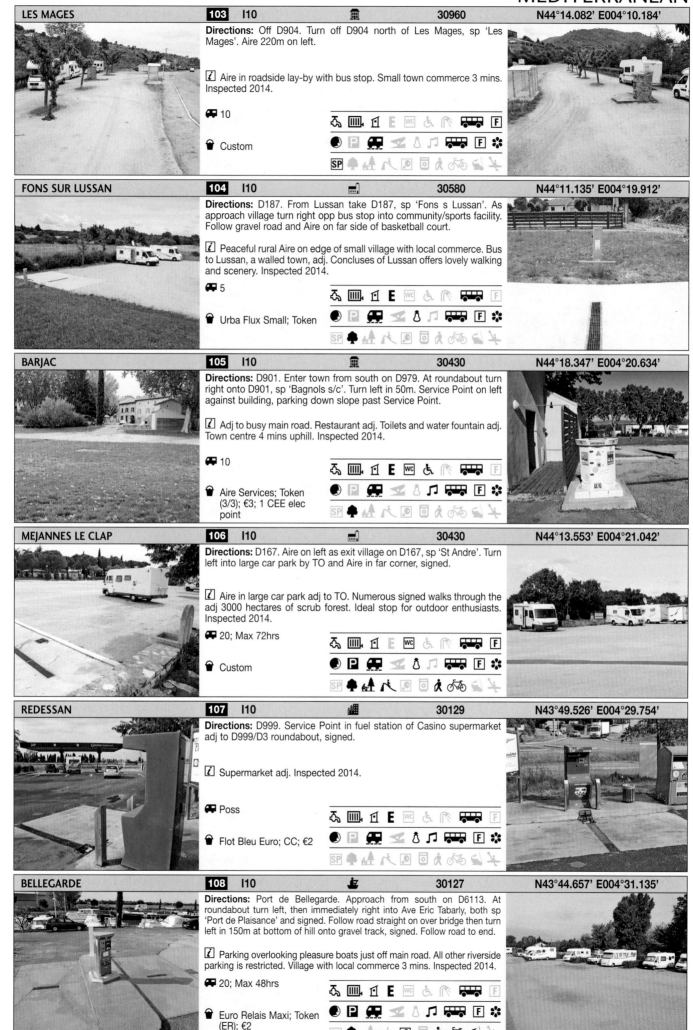

| LES MAGES | **103** | I10 | | 30960 | N44°14.082' E004°10.184' |

Directions: Off D904. Turn off D904 north of Les Mages, sp 'Les Mages'. Aire 220m on left.

ℹ️ Aire in roadside lay-by with bus stop. Small town commerce 3 mins. Inspected 2014.

🚐 10

⛲ Custom

| FONS SUR LUSSAN | **104** | I10 | | 30580 | N44°11.135' E004°19.912' |

Directions: D187. From Lussan take D187, sp 'Fons s Lussan'. As approach village turn right opp bus stop into community/sports facility. Follow gravel road and Aire on far side of basketball court.

ℹ️ Peaceful rural Aire on edge of small village with local commerce. Bus to Lussan, a walled town, adj. Concluses of Lussan offers lovely walking and scenery. Inspected 2014.

🚐 5

⛲ Urba Flux Small; Token

| BARJAC | **105** | I10 | | 30430 | N44°18.347' E004°20.634' |

Directions: D901. Enter town from south on D979. At roundabout turn right onto D901, sp 'Bagnols s/c'. Turn left in 50m. Service Point on left against building, parking down slope past Service Point.

ℹ️ Adj to busy main road. Restaurant adj. Toilets and water fountain adj. Town centre 4 mins uphill. Inspected 2014.

🚐 10

⛲ Aire Services; Token (3/3); €3; 1 CEE elec point

| MEJANNES LE CLAP | **106** | I10 | | 30430 | N44°13.553' E004°21.042' |

Directions: D167. Aire on left as exit village on D167, sp 'St Andre'. Turn left into large car park by TO and Aire in far corner, signed.

ℹ️ Aire in large car park adj to TO. Numerous signed walks through the adj 3000 hectares of scrub forest. Ideal stop for outdoor enthusiasts. Inspected 2014.

🚐 20; Max 72hrs

⛲ Custom

| REDESSAN | **107** | I10 | | 30129 | N43°49.526' E004°29.754' |

Directions: D999. Service Point in fuel station of Casino supermarket adj to D999/D3 roundabout, signed.

ℹ️ Supermarket adj. Inspected 2014.

🚐 Poss

⛲ Flot Bleu Euro; CC; €2

| BELLEGARDE | **108** | I10 | | 30127 | N43°44.657' E004°31.135' |

Directions: Port de Bellegarde. Approach from south on D6113. At roundabout turn left, then immediately right into Ave Eric Tabarly, both sp 'Port de Plaisance' and signed. Follow road straight on over bridge then turn left in 150m at bottom of hill onto gravel track, signed. Follow road to end.

ℹ️ Parking overlooking pleasure boats just off main road. All other riverside parking is restricted. Village with local commerce 3 mins. Inspected 2014.

🚐 20; Max 48hrs

⛲ Euro Relais Maxi; Token (ER); €2

ARLES

| 109 | J11 | | 13200 | N43°41.026' E004°37.821' |

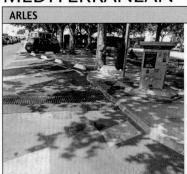
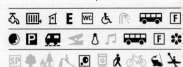

Directions: Exit N113 at Junction 7, sp 'Arles-ZI Port'. Turn left at roundabout, sp 'Arles-Centre'. After 1.7km turn right at traffic lights by city wall, sp 'Gare SNCF'. Go straight over roundabout into car park, signed. Follow road to river and turn right. Service Point immediately on right, signed. Parking 100m along river at lion statues, signed.

ℹ️ Oversubscribed Aire; expect change. Beautiful historic town with Roman amphitheatre, historic monuments and commerce. Inspected 2014.

🚐 6; Do not park in bus bays

🛒 Euro Relais Junior; 2 unmetered CEE elec points

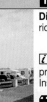

LES STES MARIES DE LA MER 1

| 110 | I11 | | 13460 | N43°27.326' E004°25.649' |

Directions: Rue Crin Blanc, adj to D570/Ave d'Arles. At end of pony rides/ranches go across roundabout. Turn left in 20m, opp pond.

ℹ️ Aire in town centre with tourist commerce. Beach 3 mins. Local area promotes pony rides. Gypsy Fair closes Aire for 2 weeks mid May. Inspected 2014.

🚐 30; €10/night <7.5m; €20/night >7.5m; Collected; Max 48hrs

🛒 Custom

Photo: Keith & Sue Lawrence

LES STES MARIES DE LA MER 2

| 111 | I11 | | 13460 | N43°27.222' E004°26.231' |

Directions: Vallée des Lys, Ave Jacques-Yves Cousteau. At end of pony rides/ranches turn left at roundabout. Follow road straight over next roundabout, then turn left onto Ave Jacques-Yves Cousteau. Aire just off roundabout after campsite turning, sp 'Plage Est'.

ℹ️ Parking adj to beach and sea, no view due to sea wall. Sea wall is promenade to town (closer than **112**). Exposed to wind. Pony rides in area. Gypsy Fair closes Aire for 2 weeks mid May. Inspected 2014.

🚐 30; €10/night <7.5m; €20/night >7.5m; Collected; Max 48hrs

🛒 Custom

LES STES MARIES DE LA MER 3

| 112 | I11 | | 13460 | N43°26.997' E004°24.344' |

Directions: D38. From town exit to west on D38. Turn left off D38, sp 'Camping Front de Mer'. Aire in large car park on left, signed. Pay guardian upon entering.

ℹ️ Parking adj to beach and Mediterranean sea, but no view due to sea wall. Sea wall is promenade to town. Exposed to wind. Local area promotes pony rides. Inspected 2014.

🚐 30; €10/night <7.5m; €20/night >7.5m; Collected; Max 48hrs

🛒 Custom; Inside barrier

PORT ST LOUIS DU RHONE

| 113 | J11 | | 13230 | N43°23.062' E004°49.155' |

Directions: Avenue de la 1ère D.F.L. From north follow D35 through town on main road, signed. At marina follow road to right then take 2nd left. Cross lift bridge and go straight over roundabout, signed. Aire 800m on left, signed. Enter through Urba Flux bollard.

ℹ️ Aire located in an exposed riverside location in the desolate old dock area. 4 riverside bays. 1km to marina, 1.5km to town. May feel isolated if alone. Inspected 2014.

🚐 70; €6.25/24hrs; CC; Pay at barrier

🛒 Urba Flux; Inside barrier

SAUSSET LES PINS

| 114 | J11 | | 13960 | N43°20.294' E005°06.513' |

Directions: Stade Michel Hidalgo. Enter Sausset les Pins from north on D5. At roundabout turn left, sp 'Stade M Hidalgo'. The Aire is 450m on the left, sp 'Stade M Hidalgo' and signed.

ℹ️ Very sloping Aire in a small space shared with truck parking. Harbour 7 mins downhill. Inspected 2014.

🚐 16; Max 72hrs

🛒 Urba Flux Tall; €2; No drive over drain

CARRO | 115 | J11 | 13500 | N43°19.758' E005°02.416'

Directions: Quai Jean Vérandy. Turn off D49b into Carro and follow main route through town to marina. Follow road around marina and Aire on right. Enter through Urba Flux barrier.

ℹ️ Aire located on the harbour end with 40 bays with views to sea one side or marina the other. Exposed spot popular with windsurfers. Local commerce 1 min. Inspected 2014.

🚐 60; €12/24hrs Jul-Aug; €10/24hrs Jun-Sept; €8/24hrs Oct-May; CC; Pay at barrier

🚽 Depagne; Inside barrier

SALIN DE GIRAUD | 116 | J11 | 13129 | N43°24.739' E004°43.851'

Directions: Rue de la Bouvine. From Arles follow D36. 400m after traffic lights turn right, sp 'Centre Ville' and signed. Turn left at Medi@site and then right just before fire station, signed.

ℹ️ Aire on designated gravel car park tucked away from town. Local commerce 1 min. Local rice growing area. Chain ferry (takes all vehicles) across Rhone €5. Inspected 2014.

🚐 20

🚽 Custom WC disposal; Flot Bleu Elec/Water; Token (FB)

ST MARTIN DE CRAU | 117 | J11 | 13310 | N43°38.309' E004°48.823'

Directions: N1453. Enter from east on D113. At roundabout follow sp 'St Martin de Crau'. Go straight over next roundabout. At traffic lights turn right, sp 'Mouries', then immediately left opp Gendarmerie. Aire in large car park adj to toilets, signed.

ℹ️ Despite being a large car park, only 3 bays have been allocated to motorhomes. Town centre, 2 mins, has 3.5t weight restriction. Library opp. Inspected 2014.

🚐 3; Max 24hrs

🚽 Urba Flux Tall

SENAS | 118 | J10 | 13560 | N43°44.644' E005°04.853'

Directions: Ave des Jardins. Turn off D7n at roundabout, sp 'La Capellette', 'Centre de Secours' and signed. Follow road and the Aire is on left alongside school, signed.

ℹ️ Outside school, best avoided during school hours. Village 4 mins. Inspected 2014.

🚐 10

🚽 Euro Relais Junior; Token (ER)

FONTVIEILLE | 119 | J11 | 13900 | N43°43.174' E004°42.703'

Directions: P Moulin de Daudet. In Fontvieille centre turn off D17 onto D33, sp 'Moules', 'Moulin de Daudet' and signed. Follow road for 750m then turn left, sp 'Moulin de Daudet' and signed. Aire on right through Urba Flux barrier.

ℹ️ Very pleasant Aire in former quarry with a very Mediterranean feel. Steps to Moulin de Daudet. Château 10 mins. Town centre with tourist commerce 3 mins. Inspected 2014.

🚐 30; €5/24hrs; CC

🚽 Urba Flux Tall; Inside barrier; Inc

BEAUCAIRE | 120 | J10 | 30300 | N43°48.371' E004°38.250'

Directions: Quai de la Paix Nord. From Redessan follow D999 into town. In town turn right at roundabout onto D986l, sp 'Arles' and 'Centre Historic'. Follow D986l aross river bridge and turn 1st right, signed. Aire 150m on right, signed.

ℹ️ Small Aire adj to river marina. Large motorhomes subject to space. Unrestricted car park at Château de Tarascon: N43°48.338' E004°39.297'. Inspected 2014.

🚐 9; Subject to Rhône flooding

🚽 Euro Relais Junior Tall; Token (ER)

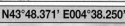
Château de Tarascon

COMPS ✳

| 121 | J10 | | 30300 | N43°51.257' E004°36.488' |

Directions: Rue St Nicolas. From D986l turn into town at traffic lights, sp 'Stade' and signed. Turn right, sp 'Stade' and signed. Follow road straight on, sp 'Bouladrome' and signed. Town narrow but passable. Turning right through white wall into bullfighting arena, continue straight on for riverside parking or turn 1st right for services and winter parking within flood barrier, signed.

ℹ Popular grass parking under trees at riverside or hardstanding parking adj to Service Point. River can flood. Local commerce 2 mins. Inspected 2013.

🚐 50; €3/24hrs; Collected

🚰 Aire Services; CC; €3

VALLABREGUES

| 122 | J10 | | 30300 | N43°51.464' E004°37.586' |

Directions: D183a/Route d'Aramon. Exit Vallabrègues to north on D183a, sp 'Avignon'. Aire is 300m on left, signed. Service Point in entrance, parking beyond.

ℹ Landscaped Aire with plenty of space adj to road. River Gard nearby, but no views. Very basic crazy golf and picnic area adj. Inspected 2013.

🚐 6

🚰 Euro Relais Junior, Token (ER); €2

BARBENTANE

| 123 | J10 | | 13570 | N43°54.202' E004°44.481' |

Directions: Turn off D35 near bull ring, sp 'Arenes Stade' and signed. Aire is 300m on right, signed.

ℹ Aire located in gravel car park at rear of sports facility adj to municipal storage area. Large car park adj to Abbaye St Michel de Frigolet on D81: N43°51.602' E004°43.707'. Inspected 2014.

🚐 20; €5/night; CC; Pay at Service Point

🚰 Urba Flux Tall; CC

REMOULINS

| 124 | I10 | | 30210 | N43°56.258' E004°33.321' |

Directions: D981. Turn off at roundabout with D986l and D6086, signed. Service Point on D981.

ℹ Service Point only. Unrestricted parking across bridge on right: N43°56.287' E004°33.521'. Inspected 2013.

🚐 Tolerated

🚰 Flot Bleu Euro; CC; €5

LAUDUN L'ARDOISE 1

| 125 | J10 | | 30290 | N44°06.476' E004°39.327' |

Directions: Place du 19 Mars 1962. From D6086 turn onto D9 at roundabout, sp 'L'Ardoise'. After 3.5km turn left onto D9ex, sp 'Laudun'. Follow road straight over roundabout. Turn left, follow road uphill and turn left again, both sp 'Camp de César'. Aire in car park on right, signed.

ℹ 2 mins downhill to pretty town. Côtes du Rhône producing area. Always likely to have space. Inspected 2013.

🚐 3

🚰 Customised Flot Bleu; No drive over drain

LAUDUN L'ARDOISE 2

| 126 | J10 | | 30290 | N44°06.228' E004°39.829' |

Directions: Vignerons de Laudun, D121. Exit village on D121, sp 'Roquemaure' and 'Cave de Laudun' on wall. Aire 200m on left on the far side of Vignerons de Laudun, signed. Parking past Service Point under trees.

ℹ Pleasant grass/gravel parking under trees at wine producer. Will fill your bottles with wine (price/litre or kg). Worth the experience, open 9am-noon/2-6.30pm. Inspected 2013.

🚐 10; Max 24hrs

🚰 Custom

| L'ARDOISE | **127** J10 | 30290 | N44°05.717' E004°42.083' |

Directions: Place de la Resistance, off N580. Turn off N580 by La Poste, signed. Follow road through square past Mairie and La Poste. Service Point adj to tennis court, signed.

ℹ️ Conveniently located just 100m off N580 with a building to park behind to reduce road noise. Inspected 2013.

🚐 6

Custom

| CHUSCLAN | **128** J10 | 30200 | N44°08.733' E004°40.644' |

Directions: D138. From N580 turn onto D138 at roundabout, sp 'Chusclan'. Turn right to stay on D138, sp 'Chusclan'. Follow road for 1.7km and Aire on left opp Côtes du Rhône producer, signed.

ℹ️ Private Aire belonging to Côtes du Rhône seller; Open 9am-noon and 4-6.30pm all year. Tasting at 7pm. Views across vines. Inspected 2013.

🚐 6

Custom

| ST LAURENT DES ARBRES | **129** J10 | 30120 | N44°03.554' E004°42.672' |

Directions: D101. Turn off N580 at roundabout northeast of St Laurent des Arbres onto D101, sp 'Roquemaure'. At next roundabout turn left. Service Point located at the fuel station of the Casino supermarket, signed.

ℹ️ Supermarket adj. Inspected 2014.

🚐 Poss

Flot Bleu Euro; CC

| BAGNOLS SUR CEZE | **130** J10 | 30200 | N44°10.102' E004°37.178' |

Directions: Rue du Moulinet. Enter town from north on N86. At roundabout turn left, sp 'Avignon' and signed. Turn right in 100m, signed, then right again, signed. Follow road for 200m to Aire on right, signed.

ℹ️ Adj to noisy main road, but it is an acceptable stop close to town. Commerce 4 mins. Inspected 2013.

🚐 6; Max 24hrs

Flot Bleu Fontaine

| ST ALEXANDRE | **131** I10 | 30130 | N44°13.648' E004°37.369' |

Directions: Route des Remparts. Turn off N86 and follow sp 'St Alexandre' onto D311. Follow D311 to St Alexandre, drive past cemetery and turn left into car park adj to cemetery. Aire at far end of car park, signed.

ℹ️ Views over vines and hills from Aire. Local commerce in village. France Passion site signed on other side of cemetery. Inspected 2013.

🚐 3

Custom

| ST LAURENT DE CARNOLS | **132** I10 | 30200 | N44°12.612' E004°31.853' |

Directions: D166. Turn off D980 onto D166, sp 'St Laurent de Carnols' and signed. Aire 700m on right, signed.

ℹ️ Landscaped Aire in Côtes du Rhône wine area. Adj to wine seller. Rhône and Ardèche rivers nearby. Inspected 2014.

🚐 4; Max 48hrs; Need to reverse out

Urba Flux Tall; Token; €2

MEDITERRANEAN

ST PAULET DE CAISSON
133   I10   🏢   30130   N44°15.947' E004°35.861'

Directions: Chemin du Plane. Turn off D256, sp 'Cave Cooperative' and signed. Follow road behind cave and Service Point at rear, signed.

ℹ️ Service Point adj to Cave Cooperative. May be diff to access during the harvest period. Inspected 2014.

🚐 None

🚰 Urba Flux; Token; €2

BOLLENE
134   J10   🏢   84500   N44°19.317' E004°44.650'

Directions: D26, at E'Leclerc supermarket. Turn off D26 at roundabout north of town, sp 'Centre Commercial'. Drive around past fuel station to rear of supermarket and Service Point is in a roadway within the parking.

ℹ️ E'Leclerc supermarket and fuel station adj with LPG, cheap diesel, car wash and hypermarket. Can be noisy until late. Inspected 2013.

🚐 Poss

🚰 Flot Bleu Pacific

SARRIANS
135   J10   ⛺   84260   N44°04.776' E004°58.671'

Directions: Off D221, at Camping de la Ste Croix. Turn off D950 at Intermarché roundabout at southern edge of town, sp 'Camping Municipal' and signed. Turn right into campsite and drive past entrance into parking area, signed.

ℹ️ Campsite adj. BMX bike track. Inspected 2013.

🚐 10; €3/night; Collected

🚰 Euro Relais Junior; Token (3/1); €2

MALAUCENE
136   J10   🏛️   84340   N44°10.652' E005°07.792'

Directions: Ave Charles De Gaulle, off D938. Turn left off D938 between plane trees as enter town, signed. Follow road for 200m to Aire at rear of Gendarmerie near sports facilities, signed.

ℹ️ Large open Aire. Motorhomes must park here. Market Wed. Inspected 2013.

🚐 20; €3/day; Collected

🚰 Custom

CARPENTRAS
137   J10   🏢   84200   N44°02.653' E005°03.284'

Directions: Ave Pierre de Coubertin, adj to Camping Lou Comtadou. Heading towards St Didier on D4 turn right at Y-junction before roundabout, sp 'Complexe Sportif' and 'Parking'. After 850m turn left through outer gate of municipal campsite, sp 'P de Coubertin'. Aire on right, signed.

ℹ️ Adj to municipal facilities around 10 mins walk from town with numerous commerce. Bus stop adj. Municipal campsite adj. Inspected 2013.

🚐 10

🚰 Aire Services

PERNES LES FONTAINES
138   J10   ⛺   84210   N43°59.989' E005°04.097'

Directions: Chemin du Camping, adj to Camping Municipal Coucourelle. Exit town on D28, sp 'St Didier'. Turn left, sp 'Camping Municipal Coucourelle'. Turn right, sp 'Camping' and signed, and follow road behind sports facilities. Service Point is just prior to campsite.

ℹ️ Service Point only. Inspected 2013.

🚐 Poss

🚰 Flot Bleu Fontaine; Mid Mar-mid Oct

BEDOIN 1

139 J10   🏛   84410   N44°07.483' E005°10.333'

Directions: Chemin de Bédoin á Malaucène. From south on D974 turn left at roundabout onto D138, sp 'P Municipal Gratuit'. Follow road left, then turn right, sp 'Camping Municipal' and signed. Follow road to left and Service Point on right. Parking 150m by entrance to municipal campsite, signed.

ℹ️ Municipal swimming pool adj. 2 mins from tourist village with local commerce. D19 popular with cyclists. Inspected 2013.

🚐 40; €3/night; Collected; Max 72hrs

👕 Aire Services; €2

BEDOIN 2

140 J10   🏛   84410   N44°07.927' E005°10.239'

Directions: D19. From Bédoin follow D19 north for 1.3km. Service Point is on left of road outside Camping le Pastory.

ℹ️ Service Point only. Inspected 2013.

🚐 None; See **139**

👕 Euro Relais Mini; Token; €2

FONTAINE DE VAUCLUSE ⭐

141 J10   🏊   84800   N43°55.218' E005°07.453'

Directions: D24. Follow D25 through town. Pass car parks and cross river. Aire 500m on right. Enter through PARKNIGHT barrier. Alternatively turn off D25 before town onto D57, sp 'Camping'. Turn left onto D24, sp 'Camping'; this route is sometimes temporarily no entry.

ℹ️ Village centre 3 mins with restaurants around a pretty weir. Canoe hire in season. Popular at weekends. Mysterious source of river Sorgue (water highest in spring). Petrarch's house, now a museum; Apr-Oct from €1.50. Inspected 2014.

🚐 27; €12/24hrs Apr-Oct; €9.60/24hrs Nov-Mar; CC

👕 Euro Relais Junior; Inside; Inc; 2 unmetered elec points

GORDES 1

142 J10   T   84220   N43°54.961' E005°11.857'

Directions: Off D15, approx 2km from D15/D2 junction. Aire is at far end of car park, sp 'Bus Parking'. Approaching from other directions requires navigating narrow village roads.

ℹ️ Aire in large car park 3 mins from the city, a stunning Beau Village clinging to the side of a cliff. Best viewed from viewpoint on D15. Inspected 2014.

🚐 30; €8/24hrs; Collected

👕 Aire Services; Inside; €3; To access, tell attendant you wish to service

GORDES 2

143 J10   ⛺   84220   N43°54.067' E005°11.583'

Directions: D2. From D900 turn onto D2 at Coustellet, sp 'Gordes' from west and 'Musée de la Lavande' from east. Aire on left after 5.6km, just before Village des Bories, signed.

ℹ️ Large gravel car park near Village des Bories, a pleasant undulating 1.5km walk on lanes, entrance €6. Gourdes 20 mins uphill on main road. Inspected 2014.

🚐 50

👕 None; See **142**

ROUSSILLON

144 J10   T   84220   N43°53.782' E005°17.760'

Directions: D149. Turn off D4 onto D104, sp 'Roussillon'. Follow road to village and at roundabout turn left onto D149, signed. Designated car park immediately on left, enter through barrier.

ℹ️ Designated parking outside a Beau Village. Motorhomes banned from village centre. Tourist commerce in centre, 3 mins. Ochre dye museum on D104. Inspected 2014.

🚐 10; €2/8am-10pm; €5/10pm-8am; CC; Pay at machine; Max 48hrs

👕 Toilets and water tap in bus car park opp

L'ISLE SUR LA SORGUE · 145 · J10 · 84800 · N43°55.059' E005°02.841'

Directions: Gare SNCF. Approach on D901 from Avignon as other roads have 3.1m height restrictions. Turn off D901 at roundabout, sp 'Gare SNCF'. At next roundabout turn right. Parking in large car park adj to train track. Access diff Sunday due to market in town.

i Large car park adj to train station. Town has numerous antique shops and halls and a market/brocante every Sun which is very popular. Arrive Sat and do not expect to depart until Mon. Inspected 2014.

🚐 30

⚲ Toilets outside train station

STE TULLE · 146 · K10 · 04220 · N43°47.073' E005°45.824'

Directions: Parc Municipal des Sports. Enter St Tulle on D996/D4096 from Mirabeau (south). Turn 1st left on entering town, then turn right at Stop junction, sp 'Parc des Sports'. Turn into 1st car park on the left. Service Point against building.

i Parking under plane trees in municipal sports area. Park, boules court, and other sports facilities adj. Town centre 3 mins. Inspected 2012.

🚐 10

⚲ Custom

VAISON LA ROMAINE · 147 · J10 · T · 84110 · N44°14.786' E005°04.445'

Directions: Avenue André Coudray. Turn off D975, main route through, at roundabout opp amphitheatre, signed. At T-junction at end of road turn left and the Aire is 150m on left, signed. Motorhomes banned from all other car parks.

i Modern village 3 mins. Medieval village nearby, motorised tourist train in summer from centre of village. Voie Verte cycle route nearby. Inspected 2013.

🚐 30; €10/24hrs; Collected

⚲ Custom

BEDARRIDES · 148 · J10 · 84370 · N44°02.347' E004°54.191'

Directions: Chemin des Sences. From town centre turn left at roundabout before old river bridge, signed. Aire 200m on right, signed.

i Designated parking in a peaceful location adj to scent garden which leads to river. Small town commerce 2 mins. Châteauneuf du Pape wine village nearby: N44°03.357' E004°49.910'. Inspected 2014.

🚐 4; Max 72hrs; Max 9m

⚲ Aire Services Box; Token (3/3); No drive over drain or toilet point

SAULT · 149 · J10 · 84390 · N44°05.718' E005°24.703'

Directions: D950. Enter town from north on D950 and go straight over roundabout. Turn left opp Saupers Pompiers, sp 'P P3' and 'Cimitière'. Aire in Parking P3, signed.

i The Aire is 5 mins walk from the lovely old town with local commerce. Good base for exploring Mont Ventoux and Gorges de Nesque. Updated 2014.

🚐 20

⚲ Euro Relais Mini; €2

Info/Photos: Jean & Ken Fowler

AVIGNON 1 · 150 · J10 · ☀ · 84000 · N43°57.111' E004°47.621'

Directions: Park & Ride Ile Poit. From Aramon (south) on D2 go straight on past A7 'Avignon' turning, then take next left, sp 'Avignon'. Turn right onto D900 and cross river bridge. Turn 1st right, sp 'P&R Ile Poit'. Aire is on right before P&R barrier, signed.

i Free, frequent shuttle bus to walled city from adj bus stop. Area under video surveillance during day. Inspected 2013.

🚐 13; This area may no longer be accessible, see 151

⚲ None

AVIGNON 2 — 151 — J10 — 84000 — N43°57.335' E004°47.947'

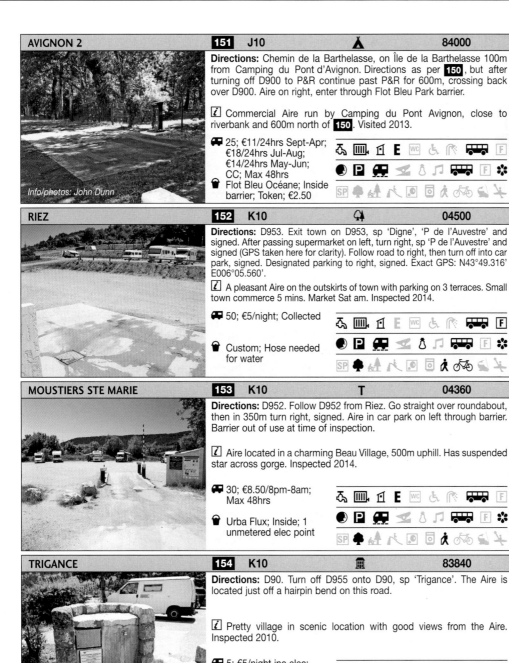

Info/photos: John Dunn

Directions: Chemin de la Barthelasse, on Île de la Barthelasse 100m from Camping du Pont d'Avignon. Directions as per **150**, but after turning off D900 to P&R continue past P&R for 600m, crossing back over D900. Aire on right, enter through Flot Bleu Park barrier.

ℹ️ Commercial Aire run by Camping du Pont Avignon, close to riverbank and 600m north of **150**. Visited 2013.

🚐 25; €11/24hrs Sept-Apr; €18/24hrs Jul-Aug; €14/24hrs May-Jun; CC; Max 48hrs

💧 Flot Bleu Océane; Inside barrier; Token; €2.50

RIEZ — 152 — K10 — 04500 — N43°49.445' E006°05.634'

Directions: D953. Exit town on D953, sp 'Digne', 'P de l'Auvestre' and signed. After passing supermarket on left, turn right, sp 'P de l'Auvestre' and signed (GPS taken here for clarity). Follow road to right, then turn off into car park, signed. Designated parking to right, signed. Exact GPS: N43°49.316' E006°05.560'.

ℹ️ A pleasant Aire on the outskirts of town with parking on 3 terraces. Small town commerce 5 mins. Market Sat am. Inspected 2014.

🚐 50; €5/night; Collected

💧 Custom; Hose needed for water

MOUSTIERS STE MARIE — 153 — K10 — T — 04360 — N43°50.617' E006°13.100'

Directions: D952. Follow D952 from Riez. Go straight over roundabout, then in 350m turn right, signed. Aire in car park on left through barrier. Barrier out of use at time of inspection.

ℹ️ Aire located in a charming Beau Village, 500m uphill. Has suspended star across gorge. Inspected 2014.

🚐 30; €8.50/8pm-8am; Max 48hrs

💧 Urba Flux; Inside; 1 unmetered elec point

TRIGANCE — 154 — K10 — 83840 — N43°45.611' E006°26.495'

Photo: Keith & Sue Lawrence

Directions: D90. Turn off D955 onto D90, sp 'Trigance'. The Aire is located just off a hairpin bend on this road.

ℹ️ Pretty village in scenic location with good views from the Aire. Inspected 2010.

🚐 5; €5/night inc elec; Collected; Apr-Oct; Max 72hrs

💧 Custom

COMPS SUR ARTUBY — 155 — K10 — 83840 — N43°42.375' E006°30.392'

Directions: D955. South of Comps-Sur-Artuby at bend in D955.

ℹ️ Token available from Le Rouable Pizzeria on site. 500m to village. Views over valley. Inspected 2010.

🚐 19; Max 24hrs

💧 Custom; Token; €3

Photo: Keith & Sue Lawrence

STE CROIX DE VERDON — 156 — K10 — 04500 — N43°45.651' E006°09.058'

Directions: D111a. From Quinson on D11 drive past lavender fields and turn onto D111. Follow sp 'Ste Croix du Verdon' onto D111a and downhill towards lake. Do not turn right to village, continue downhill, sp 'Camping Municipal'. Aire on right, signed.

ℹ️ A peaceful Aire offering views of the large Lac de Ste Croix for 8 motorhomes. Local commerce 2 mins. Canyon du Verdon nearby. Lavender flowering June, harvested mid July. Inspected 2014.

🚐 22; €6.50/10pm-8am; Collected; Free in winter; Max 48hrs

💧 Custom; Turned off in winter; 2 unmetered elec points by boules court

GREOUX LES BAINS | 157 | K10 | 04800 | N43°45.336' E005°53.314'

Directions: Chemin de la Barque. On D952 from Riez turn left at roundabout onto D8, sp 'St Julien'. Follow road for 500m then turn right immediately before river bridge, signed. Follow road uphill for 200m and turn right, signed. Turn right again, signed, and enter through barrier.

ℹ️ Former municipal campsite turned commercial Aire offering shaded parking on multiple treed terraces. Town is a spa resort with tourist commerce and casino. Inspected 2014.

🚐 71; €9/24hrs inc 6amp elec; Pay at machine; Max 3.5t/8m; No trailers/cars

🚰 Custom; Inside; Inc

QUINSON | 158 | K10 | 04500 | N43°41.881' E006°02.347'

Directions: P du Musée. From south on D13 turn right after passing lake, sp 'Parking du Musée'. Turn left, sp 'P du Musée'. Aire on left before height barrier. Parking must not obstruct car park entrance or coach parking; large motorhomes subject to space. May need to reverse out.

ℹ️ Parking near Prehistoric museum. River Verdon with tourist commerce 200m. Hire a canoe (€8/hr), pedalo (€12) or electric boat (€23) and meander through the Gorges du Verdon to Lac d'Esparron. Inspected 2014.

🚐 7

🚰 Custom; Water marked non potable

LES SALLES SUR VERDON | 159 | K10 | 83630 | N43°46.617' E006°12.844'

Directions: D957. Parking adj to D957 southbound, signed. Private Service Point 450m south of parking at L'Heritage Hotel/Restaurant: N43°46.455' E006°13.070'. Adj to D957 near junction with D71, signed.

ℹ️ Service Point at private establishment that also allows overnight parking for a fee. Municipal designated parking near a delightful lake and beach, easy walk down 'No entry' road. Visited 2013.

🚐 25

🚰 Custom; €6 service only; €8 inc parking at hotel

Info/photos: Joy & Bob Podesta

LA BRILLANNE | 160 | K10 | 04700 | N43°55.922' E005°53.409'

Directions: D4096. Adj to main route through town at the fuel station of the Carrefour supermarket. 3m height barrier avoidable.

ℹ️ Supermarket adj. Inspected 2012.

🚐 Poss

🚰 Flot Bleu Pacific; 1 Token/20 mins

VILLENEUVE | 161 | K10 | 04180 | N43°53.773' E005°51.705'

Directions: Cimetière. Turn off D4096 at roundabout, sp 'Villeneuve'. Follow sp 'P Cimetière' and signs up the hill then out of village. Turn right towards cemetery then follow road and signs downhill around the cemetery, signed.

ℹ️ Popular Aire under trees next to cemetery; dead quiet. Hilly walk to village centre 4 mins which has local commerce and convenience store. Inspected 2014.

🚐 12; Max 48hrs

🚰 Custom; No water Dec-Feb

PUYVERT | 162 | J10 | 84160 | N43°44.828' E005°20.247'

Directions: D973, behind Super U car wash. At roundabout south of Puyvert turn right onto D27, sp 'Lauris'. At next junction turn left onto D973. Enter Super U car park and Aire on right behind car wash adj to laundry.

ℹ️ Supermarket adj. Can be noisy. Self-service laundry adj. Inspected 2010.

🚐 Poss

🚰 Raclet; 2 unmetered elec points

Photo: Keith & Sue Lawrence

ST PAUL LES DURANCE | 163 | K11 | 🏛 | 13115 | N43°41.255' E005°42.243'

Directions: Chemin du Retour. Cross river at Pont St Roch, signed. DO NOT use 2nd river bridge closest to Cadarache military base as town is one-way and impassable. Turn 1st left, signed, and follow road to end. Turn into residential campsite and follow road to right. Aire at end of road. Actual GPS: N43°41.241' E005°42.336'.

ℹ One of the most unusually located Aires in France! Residential caravans in all states make the area resemble a shanty town. Inspected 2014.

🚐 6; Marked bays

🚰 Flot Bleu Fontaine

GREASQUE | 164 | K11 | 🏭 | 13850 | N43°25.996' E005°32.044'

Directions: Route de la Chapelle. At D46/D46a roundabout turn off, sp 'Gardanne'. At next roundabout turn off, sp 'Hély d'Oissel' and signed. Follow road uphill to mine, well signed.

ℹ Official parking to left beside skateboard ramps, motorhomes banned from all other parking in a 12km radius. Mining museum adj. Inspected 2014.

🚐 20

🚰 Custom

PELISSANNE | 165 | J11 | 🏭 | 13330 | N43°37.699' E005°09.225'

Directions: Chemin de la Prouvenque, near D15h/D17 junction. Enter town from south on D17. Just past junction with D15h turn left, sp 'Prouvenque' and signed. Aire at sports facilities.

ℹ Town 3 mins. Football pitch and skate park adj. Elec decommissioned since 2010. Inspected 2012.

🚐 5

🚰 Custom

Photo: Keith & Sue Lawrence

AURIOL | 166 | K11 | 🏢 | 13390 | N43°22.081' E005°38.483'

Directions: D560, at Casino supermarket entrance. Exit Auriol towards Péage on D560. Aire at supermarket.

ℹ Supermarket adj. Inspected 2014.

🚐 Poss

🚰 Flot Bleu Pacific (Green); Token

GEMENOS | 167 | K11 | 🏭 | 13420 | N43°17.877' E005°37.760'

Directions: Cours Sudre. From D396, main route through town, turn off, sp 'La Ste Baume' and signed. At end of road go straight on into left car park and follow road around car park. Turn right in front of La Poste, signed. Aire is behind La Poste; Service Point to left, parking to right.

ℹ Aire in tucked away location that can be difficult to access due to badly parked cars. Local commerce adj. Market Wed am. Inspected 2014.

🚐 3; Max 24hrs

🚰 Custom

LE BEAUSSET | 168 | K11 | 🏢 | 83330 | N43°11.900' E005°48.371'

Directions: DN8, at Casino supermarket.

ℹ Very difficult to access, in small busy car park. Avoid if poss. Supermarket adj. Inspected 2014.

🚐 Poss

🚰 Flot Bleu Euro; CC; €2

CUGES LES PINS ✱ | 169 | K11 | | 13780 | N43°16.868' E005°42.350'

Directions: Le Cros Reynier. Turn off D8n in Cuges les Pins at the traffic lights by the TO, sp 'Espace Socioculturel' and signed. Follow road straight on up rough but very passable roads with passing places, signed. Follow road to left around park and Aire on left, signed.

ℹ️ A commercial Aire in the wooded hills with parking on terraces. Pleasant park adj with walking trails. Local commerce 5 mins through park. Inspected 2014.

🚐 20; €3/24hrs (noon-noon); €4/24hrs Jul-Aug; +€3 large motorhome; +€3/trailer; Collected

🚰 Custom; €1.50; Elec avail from generator

STE MAXIMIN LA STE BAUME | 170 | K11 | | 83470 | N43°27.420' E005°51.196'

Directions: D560. Follow sp 'Aix en Pce' through town. Service Point adj to D560/DN7 at the Hyper U. To locate Service Point enter supermarket parking and drive beside car wash, then turn right. Service Point on left.

ℹ️ Supermarket, retail park, McDonald's and bank adj. Inspected 2012.

🚐 Poss

🚰 Flot Bleu Pacific; €2

SIX FOURS LES PLAGES | 171 | K11 | | 83140 | N43°06.752' E005°48.714'

Directions: Sq Hippolyte Cesmat. In town follow sp 'Six Fours' onto one-way dual carriageway along seafront of Six-Fours-les-Plages. After TO turn left, sp 'Bureau de Poste', and immediately left again. Accessible only from behind TO. After servicing have to reverse out into road.

ℹ️ All non-height barriered parking is unrestricted and night parking is allowed. Tourist resort with large shingle beach. Inspected 2014.

🚐 Poss

🚰 Custom; Unhygienic and tricky; No access Sun am May-Sept

BRIGNOLES | 172 | K11 | | 83170 | N43°24.579' E006°03.722'

Directions: D2007. From DN7 at roundabout take D1007 towards town centre. At traffic lights turn right onto D2007 and 1st right into Casino supermarket. Service Point at fuel station.

ℹ️ Town centre 2 mins. Supermarket adj. Inspected 2014.

🚐 Poss

🚰 Flot Bleu Pacific; Token

SILLANS LA CASCADE | 173 | K11 | | 83690 | N43°34.047' E006°10.932'

Directions: D560/Route de Salernes, on main road south of village. 3.5t weight restriction on Aire.

ℹ️ Aire in roadside lay-by. 30 mins walk to famous waterfall. Walled town 2 mins. On historic villages cycle route. Inspected 2014.

🚐 10; Max 24hrs

🚰 Urba Flux; Token; €3

ST MANDRIER SUR MER | 174 | K11 | | 83430 | N43°04.636' E005°54.326'

Directions: Ancienne Route de Saint-Mandrier, off D18. From west on D18 turn right 200m after tennis courts, sp 'Tennis' and signed. Follow road to right, signed. Service Point on right just past football pitches outside tennis club. Parking next right turn, sp 'Parking Est': N43°04.661' E005°54.262'.

ℹ️ Popular but difficult parking, may have to reverse out onto road. Additional parking on seafront: N43°04.742' E005°54.013'. Inspected 2014.

🚐 6; Max 48hrs; Max 8m

🚰 SOS

LA ROQUEBRUSSANNE | 175 | K11 | 83136 | N43°20.164' E005°58.775'

Directions: Ave St Sébastien, off D5. Approach from south on D5. Turn right off D5, as enter village, onto D64, sp 'Neoules'. Turn immediately right and Aire on right, signed.

ℹ Adj to noisy road. Wine seller opp. Village centre, 2 mins, has 3.5t weight restriction and is too narrow for most motorhomes to drive through. Inspected 2012.

🚐 6

🔧 Euro Relais Maxi; Token; €2; No drive over drain

SOLLIES PONT | 176 | K11 | 83210 | N43°12.137' E006°02.813'

Directions: Ave Jean Brunet. Heading south on A57 exit at Junction 8. At roundabout turn left, sp 'Centre Commercial'. Turn right, then drive through car park and turn left, then right. Service Point adj to Casino fuel station.

ℹ Supermarket adj. Motorway adj. Inspected 2012.

🚐 Poss but very noisy

🔧 Flot Bleu Euro; CC; €2

HYERES 1 | 177 | K11 | 83400 | N43°06.478' E006°07.710'

Directions: D559/Ave Geoffroy St Hilaire, at the Casino supermarket. From Toulon go across roundabout on A570 then at traffic lights turn right onto D559. The Aire is down this road on right. Narrow access. Not signed from road.

ℹ Supermarket adj. Inspected 2014.

🚐 None

🔧 Flot Bleu Euro (Green); CC; €3

HYERES 2 | 178 | K11 | 83400 | N43°06.782' E006°06.952'

Directions: Hyper E'Leclerc. From Toulon turn right off A570 at roundabout, then fork right. At roundabout take 2nd exit and follow advert to the Hyper E'Leclerc. Service Point adj to fuel station.

ℹ Supermarket adj. Inspected 2014.

🚐 Poss

🔧 Flot Bleu Euro; CC; €1.50; Can lift grid to empty WC

LA LONDE LES MAURES 1 | 179 | K11 | 83250 | N43°07.905' E006°13.836'

Directions: Rond Point Ducourneau. Turn off N98, sp 'La Londe Les Maures'. At next roundabout go straight over, sp 'Port-Plages' and signed. Service Point and parking adj to roundabout 'Ducourneau'.

ℹ Adj to road and roundabout. Local commerce 5 mins. Inspected 2014.

🚐 4; Max 24hrs

🔧 Flot Bleu Euro; CC

LA LONDE LES MAURES 2 | 180 | K11 | 83250 | N43°08.303' E006°14.259'

Directions: D559, at Casino supermarket fuel station. Aire on right on D559 as exit town towards Bormes les Mimosas.

ℹ Supermarket adj. Town centre adj. Inspected 2014.

🚐 Poss

🔧 Flot Bleu Euro (Green; not working); CC

Photo: Keith & Sue Lawrence

COLLOBRIERES
181 K11 T 83610 N43°14.237' E006°18.170'

Directions: D14. From west on D14 turn right at village boundary, sp 'Sapeurs Pompiers' and signed. Aire 20m, signed. Parking on other side of village: N43°14.198' E006°18.886', well signed through village. Alternative approaches are along narrow, twisting roads with no barriers!

ℹ Pleasant tourist village with restaurants and craft shops 2 mins. Park at Aire and walk in. Inspected 2014.

🚐 30

🪣 Euro Relais Box; €2

LA FAVIERE
182 K11 ⚓ 83230 N43°07.494' E006°21.708'

Directions: Blvd du Port, off D198. From west on D198 follow sp 'Port' through town. At port turn left, sp 'Toutes Directions', and follow road to 'Le Lavandou'. Service Point 100m from port, adj to road and park.

ℹ Raised up; Only enough stopping space for 1 motorhome; Difficult. Inspected 2014.

🚐 Motorhomes restricted from all parking Apr-Oct

🪣 Raclet; Token (ER); €2

CAVALIERE
183 K11 ⚓ 83980 N43°09.124' E006°25.842'

Directions: D559, adj to main road. From west on D559 parking on left at rear of large gravel car park when sea is visible on right, entrance sp 'Camping-Car'.

ℹ Large partially terraced commercial Aire. Sea across road. Local and tourist commerce 1 min. Inspected 2014.

🚐 100; €16/24hrs inc 16amp elec; Collected

🪣 Custom; Inside; Inc

RAMATUELLE 1
184 L11 ⚓ 83350 N43°12.676' E006°39.731'

Directions: Route de Bonne-Terrasse. From D93, St Tropez to La Croix Valmer, turn off, sp 'Déchetterie' and signed. Follow road, crossing bridge, signed. Aire entrance is on left before beach. 5.5t weight restriction on road.

ℹ Large open commercial Aire ideal for a beach holiday. Cove with sandy beach and tourist commerce 1 min. Inspected 2014.

🚐 50; €8/night Apr-Oct; €5/night Nov-Mar; Pay at kiosk/collected; Max 48hrs

🪣 Custom; Inside; Inc; 7.30am-5pm; Cold water showers

RAMATUELLE 2
185 L11 ⚓ 83350 N43°14.341' E006°39.693'

Directions: Route des Tamaris. Turn off D93 between St Tropez and Pampelonne, sp 'Les Tamaris'. Parking on left near end of road.

ℹ Large open landscaped commercial Aire adj to beach with numerous tourist commerce and activities. Ideal for a beach holiday. Inspected 2014.

🚐 56; €10 Sept-Jun; €18 Jul-Aug; 9am-9am (day parking half price)

🪣 Custom; Inside; 1 Token/100L water; €2; 6amp elec €5 Sept-June; €7 Jul-Aug; Cold water shower on beach

CAVALAIRE SUR MER
186 L11 🏛 83240 N43°11.700' E006°32.844'

Directions: From La Croix Valmer take D559, sp 'Cavalaire'. Turn right just past Total Access fuel station, sp 'Cimetière'. Follow road through cemetery car park and up hill. At Stop junction turn left, then left again. Follow road for 350m and Service Point is on left.

ℹ Service Point only near recycling/municipal yard. Parking at cemetery is not restricted but will be if abused. May feel isolated if alone. Inspected 2014.

🚐 Tolerated in cemetery car park; Arrive late, depart early

🪣 Euro Relais Mini; €2

ST TROPEZ | 187 | L11 | | 83990 | N43°15.819' E006°40.303'

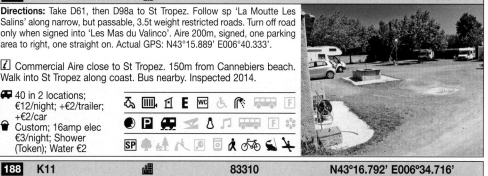

Directions: Take D61, then D98a to St Tropez. Follow sp 'La Moutte Les Salins' along narrow, but passable, 3.5t weight restricted roads. Turn off road only when signed into 'Les Mas du Valinco'. Aire 200m, signed, one parking area to right, one straight on. Actual GPS: N43°15.889' E006°40.333'.

ⓘ Commercial Aire close to St Tropez. 150m from Cannebiers beach. Walk into St Tropez along coast. Bus nearby. Inspected 2014.

🚐 40 in 2 locations; €12/night; +€2/trailer; +€2/car

🛒 Custom; 16amp elec €3/night; Shower (Token); Water €2

PORT GRIMAUD | 188 | K11 | | 83310 | N43°16.792' E006°34.716'

Directions: N98. From St Tropez on D98 Aire is signed after junction with D14.

ⓘ Aire located in lay-by adj to busy, noisy main road. Boulangerie and restaurant adj. Suggest beachside campsite 500m towards Ste Maxime instead. Inspected 2014.

🚐 10; €13/24hrs; Pay at machine

🛒 Euro Relais Maxi; 2 unmetered CEE elec points

LA MOTTE 1 | 189 | L11 | | 83920 | N43°29.318' E006°32.521'

Directions: Off D47/Route de Trans. From Le Muy exit onto D25 towards Callas. Turn left at D25/D47 roundabout, sp 'La Motte'. Follow road to tennis courts, turning left before the town, signed. Drive around the tennis courts and Aire through gateway and on left, signed.

ⓘ Aire located at sports facility in a residential area. Local commerce 3 mins. Popular walking and cycling area. Inspected 2014.

🚐 10

🛒 Euro Relais Box; Token (ER); €2; Also see **190**

LA MOTTE 2 | 190 | L11 | | 83920 | N43°29.776' E006°31.879'

Directions: D47/Route de Trans. From Le Muy exit onto D25 towards Callas. Turn left at D25/D47 roundabout, sp 'La Motte'. Follow road through town, max 10m long, then turn left, sp 'Trans'. Aire on right, not signed.

ⓘ Aire on edge of village en route to Gorges de Verdon. Local commerce 4 mins. New Aire nearby, this Aire may close. Inspected 2014.

🚐 10; Max 24hrs

🛒 Urba Flux Tall

LES ARCS SUR ARGENS | 191 | K11 | | 83460 | N43°27.161' E006°29.463'

Directions: D555. Turn off DN7 onto D555, sp 'Draguignan'. At the next roundabout turn left, sp 'ZA le Pont Rout'. At either of the next two roundabouts turn left into the Hyper U supermarket complex. The Service Point is at the rear of the fuel station.

ⓘ Supermarket adj. Inspected 2014.

🚐 Poss

🛒 Flot Bleu Euro; CC; €2

LES ARCS | 192 | K11 | | 83460 | N43°27.292' E006°28.644'

Directions: Ave des Laurons, at Cellier des Archers. From Draguignan (north) on D555 turn off at roundabout junction with D91, sp 'Gare'. Follow road along train tracks, past station, and across T-Junction, sp 'Cellier des Archers'. Aire in 100m.

ⓘ A popular private Aire at Côtes de Provence wine cellar. Large shop selling wine and alcohol starting at €1.50/litre (supply own bottle). Inspected 2014.

🚐 25; Max 3 nights

🛒 Custom; Trees overhang drive over drain

STE MAXIME

193 L11 — 83120 — N43°19.025' E006°37.799'

Directions: D25, just off large roundabout with McDonald's. If approach from St Tropez (south) on N98 follow sp 'Le Muy' to large roundabout and turn off roundabout before McDonald's, signed. Aire on left, enter through Vinci barrier.

ℹ️ Large gravel Aire adj to ring road and McDonald's. LIDL 3 mins. Town and beach 8 mins. Water taxi from harbour to St Tropez, €13.50 return in high season. www.bateauxverts.com. Inspected 2014.

🚐 30; €10 Apr-Sept; €5 Oct-Mar; Max 48hrs; Pay at machine
⛽ Urba Flux; Outside

LE THORONET

194 K11 — 83340 — N43°27.052' E006°18.253'

Directions: D79. Service Point adj to D79 at TO, signed.

ℹ️ Token from TO. Parking in car sized bays with no overhang. Suitable as a transitory night halt. Abbaye du Thoronet nearby. Inspected 2014.

🚐 5; 5m bays on far side of car park: N43°27.059' E006°18.162'
⛽ Custom; Token

LA GAILLARDE

195 L11 — 83370 — N43°21.934' E006°42.720'

Directions: N98/D1098, Chez Marcel. Signed off N98; 100m from main road at La Gaillarde. Pay guardian at entrance.

ℹ️ Well located commercial Aire in a good location for a beach holiday with a sandy beach and sea view snack bar just across the road. Shower €0.50. Washing machine €5. Inspected 2014.

🚐 50; €11/24hrs inc service; €1.50/hr day parking; Pay at kiosk
⛽ Custom; 4amp elec €3/night

FREJUS

196 L11 — 83600 — N43°26.367' E006°44.671'

Directions: D100/Avenue André Léotard, at Casino supermarket. As enter Fréjus from north on D37 take 3rd exit at roundabout onto DN7, sp 'Fréjus-Centre'. Supermarket on left at next junction. Service Point adj to fuel station.

ℹ️ Supermarket adj. Overnight parking not permitted. Inspected 2014.

🚐 None

⛽ Flot Bleu Euro; CC; €5

FAYENCE

197 L11 — 83440 — N43°37.380' E006°41.412'

Directions: Off D563 roundabout. Enter town from south on D19 or D563. At roundabout follow D563, sp 'Mons' and 'Centre Ville'. Turn immediately left, signed. Service Point on left, 2 designated bays on right but one obstructed by tree. See info for additional parking.

ℹ️ Parking la Ferrage, from roundabout signed off 1st hairpin bend towards centre: N43°37.314' E006°41.589'. Parking P3, signed off D563: N43°37.481' E006°41.802' (3 bays, closest to town). Hilltop town. Inspected 2012.

🚐 2; Max 48hrs; Max 8m

⛽ Urba Flux; €4/15 mins; Diff access

CALLIAN

198 L11 — 83440 — N43°36.251' E006°45.290'

Directions: Off D562. Turn off D562 east of town at roundabout towards McDonald's. Pass McDonald's and turn left at the roundabout. Service Point on left adj to car wash.

ℹ️ Service Point only. Inspected 2012.

🚐 None

⛽ Urba Flux; Token; €2

CANNES | 199 | L11 | 06150 | N43°33.002' E006°58.236'

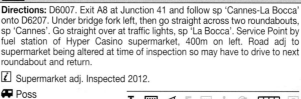

Directions: D6007. Exit A8 at Junction 41 and follow sp 'Cannes-La Bocca' onto D6207. Under bridge fork left, then go straight across two roundabouts, sp 'Cannes'. Go straight over at traffic lights, sp 'La Bocca'. Service Point by fuel station of Hyper Casino supermarket, 400m on left. Road adj to supermarket being altered at time of inspection so may have to drive to next roundabout and return.

ℹ️ Supermarket adj. Inspected 2012.

🚐 Poss

🚰 Flot Bleu Euro; €2

ST LAURENT DU VAR | 200 | L10 | 06700 | N43°41.119' E007°11.116'

Directions: Route des Pugets. Exit A8 at Junction 49 and follow sp ' St Laurent-Centre'. Go straight on at roundabout, sp 'Cimetière St Marc' and signed. At next roundabout go straight on, sp 'Parc d'Activities'. Turn left at next roundabout, sp 'Cimetière St Marc' and signed. Turn left at roundabout, sp 'Cimetière', then left again, sp 'Cimetière St Marc'. Aire 400m on right, signed.

ℹ️ Hillside location opp cemetery and overlooking industrial park. Popular Aire with difficult access. Town 4 mins. Updated 2013.

🚐 7; Not suitable for motorhomes with trailers

🚰 Custom

CAILLE | 201 | L10 | 06750 | N43°46.733' E006°43.997'

Directions: Junction of Rue St Pons and Rue des Ecuries, off D79/D80. Turn off D6085 onto D79, sp 'Caille'. Enter village and follow motorhome signs sp with 'Bas du Ville'. Aire on left, signed. Very small Aire, not suitable for large motorhomes.

ℹ️ Ancient village. Local commerce and 2 restaurants. Inspected 2010.

🚐 3

🚰 Flot Bleu Pacific; €4; No drive over drain

Photo: Keith and Sue Lawrence

LAC DE THORENC | 202 | L10 | 06750 | N43°47.967' E006°48.500'

Directions: Lac de Thorenc. Turn off D2 at parking, signed.

ℹ️ Lovely peaceful spot. Pony rides. Woodland walks around lake. Inspected 2010.

🚐 20

🚰 Custom

Photo: Keith & Sue Lawrence

CASTELLANE 1 | 203 | L10 | 04120 | N43°50.763' E006°30.950'

Directions: D4085/D952. Aire on right as enter town on D4085 from Grasse, next to river under big rock with chapel on top, sp 'Parking Obligatoire Camping Cars'. Insert payment into machine barrier which lifts to enter; correct Euros needed.

ℹ️ Very popular Aire with good facilities. Beneath Notre Dame du Roc. Close to town with local commerce. Updated 2014.

🚐 40; €6; Max 48hrs

🚰 Custom; Inside barrier; Inc

Photo: goexploremotorhomehire.co.uk

CASTELLANE 2 | 204 | K10 | 04120 | N43°51.150' E006°30.500'

Directions: D955, at Casino supermarket. On northern edge of town at roundabout junction of D955 and D4085. Flot Bleu machine at fuel station.

ℹ️ Too small for overnight parking. Narrow access. Inspected 2012.

🚐 Poss

🚰 Flot Bleu Pacific; Token

ST ANDRE LES ALPES | 205 | K10 | 04170 | N43°57.921' E006°30.439'

Directions: D2/Grand Rue. From south on N202 take 2nd exit onto D2, turning back on yourself onto D2/Grand Rue, signed. Aire 100m on left.

i Large tarmac parking area. No shade. Inspected 2010.

🚐 20

🚰 Flot Bleu Euro; Token or CC; €3

Info/photos: Keith & Sue Lawrence

ANNOT | 206 | L10 | 04240 | N43°57.793' E006°39.860'

Directions: Chemin de la Colle Basse. From south on D908 turn left in village centre, sp 'Aire de Camping Car'. Cross river and follow signs for 300m. Aire on left in woodland area on edge of village.

i Lovely woodland setting. Some bays not hardstanding. Washing sink. Market Tues. Station for summer mountain railway to Nice. Visited 2014.

🚐 10

🚰 Custom

Info/photos; Keith & Sue Lawrence

VALBERG | 207 | L10 | SKI | 06470 | N44°05.766' E006°56.204'

Directions: Follow 'Aire Accueil' signs through town. Turn off D28, sp 'Ecole des Neiges'. Go past a tall stone bell tower. Turn right, signed, just before the road widens for parking. Turn immediately right as go around bend, signed. Follow this road and the Aire is on the right, clearly signed.

i Stunning scenery through Gorges de Daluis on approach via D2202. Lovely alpine views from Aire. Well worth the drive. Inspected 2010.

🚐 21; €10 inc services and elec

🚰 Custom; 24 elec points

Info/photos: Keith & Sue Lawrence

PUGET THENIERS | 208 | L10 | 06260 | N43°57.207' E006°53.943'

Directions: Avenue Bischoffsheim. Turn off D6202 in Puget Théniers onto D2211a, sp 'La Penne' and 'Col St Raphaël'. After crossing river bridge turn 1st left, sp 'Hôpital' and 'Le Fraget'. Aire on right in 260m, past hospital.

i Aire in car park opp river. Small village set in French Alps with a few shops and a visitor centre for the steam train. Visited 2012.

🚐 20; €3.50/night; Max 48hrs

🚰 Urba Flux Tall; Token; €2

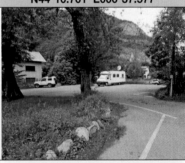

Info: Michelle Swan. Library photos

COLMARS LES ALPES | 209 | L10 | 04370 | N44°10.761' E006°37.577'

Directions: Turn off D908 opp the Garage des Alps, signed. In 50m turn left before the river bridge. The Service Point is on the left. Approach from north via Col d'Allos not advised.

i Interesting, well preserved walled town, well worth a look. Footpath to Cascade de la Lance. Inspected 2010.

🚐 5

🚰 Flot Bleu Euro; CC; €3

Info/photos: Keith & Sue Lawrence

ALLOS | 210 | L10 | SKI | 04260 | N44°14.583' E006°37.367'

Directions: Park de Loisirs, off D908. From south on D908 go through town and turn left immediately before river bridge, sp 'Park de Loisirs' and signed. Approach from north via Col d'Allos not advised. Enter via Flot Bleu Park barrier.

i At base of ski lift. Inspected 2010.

🚐 20; €5 1st night, then €4/night; CC; Max 72hrs

🚰 Flot Bleu Standard Plus; Inside Barrier; Inc 8 600w elec points

Info/photos: Keith & Sue Lawrence

LA FOUX D'ALLOS | 211 | K10 | SKI | 04260 | N44°17.738' E006°34.135'

Directions: D908. From south on D908, the Service Point is on left immediately after exiting the tunnel. Approach from north via Col D'Allos not advised due to 3.5t weight and 7m length restriction for 24km of virtually single track road.

ℹ️ Flot Bleu behind wooden toilet block, under ski lift. Only really a roadside Service Point, but parking poss if desperate. Inspected 2010.

🚐 Poss

🚰 Flot Bleu Euro; CC

Info/photos: Keith & Sue Lawrence

UVERNET FOURS | 212 | L10 | | 04400 | N44°22.091' E006°37.668'

Directions: D902, Lotissement le Bachelard. From Barcelonnette follow D902 south for 3km. Aire on right before village of Uvernet-Fours.

ℹ️ Shady Aire among pine trees alongside river. Rural setting with mountain views. Inspected 2010.

🚐 6; Not in 'storm conditions' due to flooding
🚰 Flot Bleu Pacific; €2

Info/photos: Keith & Sue Lawrence

BARCELONNETTE | 213 | L10 | | 04400 | N44°22.917' E006°39.483'

Directions: Chemin des Alpages. From west on D900 turn right to cross river on D902. Immediately after crossing river turn left onto Digue de la Gravette. After 600m turn right. Aire on left behind stadium. Well signed from D900.

ℹ️ Rural location on edge of town. Parking on grass among trees. Token machine onsite. Mountain views. Updated 2014.

🚐 15

🚰 Euro Relais Junior; Token (ER)

Info/photos: Keith & Sue Lawrence

PRA LOUP 1600 | 214 | L10 | SKI | 04400 | N44°22.054' E006°36.367'

Directions: D109. Roadside Aire next to bottom gondola station 'Choupettes'. Good access road, signed.

ℹ️ Alt 1600m. Ski resort. Free bus/ski lift adj to Aire. Not a pretty resort but good skiing. www.praloup.com Inspected 2010.

🚐 20

🚰 Flot Bleu Standard Plus; €3

Info/photos: Keith & Sue Lawrence

SELONNET | 215 | K10 | | 04140 | N44°22.101' E006°18.912'

Directions: From south on D900 turn left onto D900c, sp 'Selonnet'. Turn left onto D1, then left again. Aire 400m on left. Signed from D900.

ℹ️ Aire on edge of village. Pleasant, rural location adj to river with lovely views of surrounding mountains. Updated 2014.

🚐 7

🚰 Aire Services; Token (3/3)

Info/photos: Keith & Sue Lawrence

LA BREOLE | 216 | K9 | | 04340 | N44°27.466' E006°17.518'

Directions: D707. From west on D900b turn left onto D707, sp 'La Breole'. Aire 40m on left, signed.

ℹ️ Rural views from Aire. Large reservoir nearby. Local commerce 2 mins. Visited 2012.

🚐 5

🚰 Flot Bleu Fontaine

Photo: Alan Hoida

Info/Photo: Kevin Holley

MEDITERRANEAN

JAUSIERS
217 L9   04850   N44°24.712' E006°43.750'

Directions: D900. Aire adj to D900 as enter village from Barcelonnette. If full, further parking over river bridge on right.

Small rough parking area. Border with Italy via Col de Larche on D900. Inspected 2010.

4

Flot Bleu Euro; CC; €3

Info/photos: Keith & Sue Lawrence

LES ORRES
218 K9   SKI   05200   N44°29.980' E006°33.435'

Directions: Parking Bas de Champs Lacas, off D40. From Embrun follow D40 approx 16km. Aire in large parking area, sp 'Parking B', below chairlift ticket office. Well signed.

Alt 1564m. Ski resort/summer walking in alps. Inspected 2010.

50; Max 15 days

Flot Bleu Pacific; €3;
Showers at TO: Pay

Info/photos: Keith & Sue Lawrence

CHORGES
219 K9   05230   N44°32.750' E006°16.800'

Directions: Chemin la Butte. From southeast on N94 turn right onto D9/Ave d'Embrun, sp 'Chorges' and signed. After 800m turn right into Place du Champ de Foire. Continue between Gendarmerie and Salles des Fêtes and Aire on right in 150m.

BMX bike park adj. Inspected 2010.

20; Max 12hrs

None

Info/photos: Keith & Sue Lawrence

VARS LES CLAUX ✳
220 L9   SKI   05560   N44°34.534' E006°40.675'

Directions: Off D902, in car park P5 at the top of the resort.

Alt 1600m. Free chairlift adj. Good for walking. Free WiFi at TO. Updated 2014.

50

Flot Bleu Pacific in
building; Elec 15 mins;
No drive over drain

Info/photos: Keith & Sue Lawrence

EMBRUN
221 K9   05200   N44°32.773' E006°28.815'

Directions: N94, at Intermarché supermarket. From Embrun take N94 south. After crossing river turn right at roundabout, sp 'Centre Commercial'. Flot Bleu on left as road bends, outside Intermarché fuel station.

Laundry at fuel station. Free WiFi at McDonald's. Inspected 2010.

Poss

Flot Bleu Pacific; €2

Info/photos: Keith & Sue Lawrence

SAVINES LE LAC
222 K9   05160   N44°31.483' E006°24.033'

Directions: D954/Avenue Faubourg. From west on N94, after crossing lake on long bridge, take 1st right onto D954/Avenue Faubourg, sp 'P Camping Cars'. Aire on left in 180m.

100m from village by lake with beach (water freezing in summer!) and boat trips available. Updated 2012.

17; €7/24hrs (noon-noon) inc elec

Custom; €2; 14 unmetered elec points

Photo: Carol Weaver

DIGNE LES BAINS | 223 | K10 | 🏛 | 04000 | N44°04.796' E006°15.637'

Directions: D20/Ave des Thermes. In town follow sp 'Les Thermes' and 'Piscine les Eaux Chaudes' onto D20. Pass Intermarché supermarket and drive a further 1.5km. Aire is on right near thermal spa, signed. Riverside day parking (8am-10pm): N44°05.419' E006°13.718'. Between the two road bridges on other side of river.

ℹ️ Adj to thermal baths. Pleasant 3km walk to town. Updated 2013.

🚐 30

⛽ Euro Relais Junior; Token (ER); €2.50

LA BEAUME DES ARNAUDS | 224 | K9 | ⛺🏢 | 05140 | N44°33.127' E005°38.164'

Directions: D993. Adj to D993 on the eastern edge of the village.

ℹ️ Aire in car park adj to D993 and railway line (trains 6am-10pm). Lovely mountain village. Local commerce nearby. Visited 2013.

🚐 10

⛽ Flot Bleu Standard Plus; €2

Info/photos: Joy & Bob Podesta

PONT DU FOSSE ✶ | 225 | K9 | ⚓ | 05260 | N44°40.200' E006°14.317'

Directions: Off D944. From the river bridge in Pont du Fosse follow D944 northeast for 900m. Ignore sign to Aire that crosses 3.5t weight restricted bridge. Continue and take next right turn adj to Toyota garage (The GPS given is at this turning for clarity). Follow road to right and Aire is in 500m.

ℹ️ Very pleasant Aire in woodland setting. Located adj to river with beautiful mountain views. Updated 2014.

🚐 20; Apr-Oct

⛽ Euro Relais Junior; Token (ER); €2; 8 elec points

Info/photos: Keith & Sue Lawrence

CHATEAU ARNOUX ST AUBAN | 226 | K10 | 🏛 | 04160 | N44°05.762' E006°00.603'

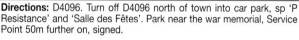

Directions: D4096. Turn off D4096 north of town into car park, sp 'P Resistance' and 'Salle des Fêtes'. Park near the war memorial, Service Point 50m further on, signed.

ℹ️ Adj to a busy and very noisy road. Small town commerce 2 mins walk through adj park. Inspected 2012.

🚐 15

⛽ Custom; Push down hard on red tops

SISTERON | 227 | K10 | 🏢 | 04200 | N44°12.019' E005°56.631'

Directions: D4085/Cours Melchior Donnet. From south follow D4085 through town. Aire in car park on right, below picturesque citadel.

ℹ️ Castle adj. Close to main road but only a few minutes walk from town and has lovely views at night of floodlit rocks. Inspected 2012.

🚐 10

⛽ Flot Bleu Standard Plus; €2

SISTERON (NORTH) | 228 | K10 | 🏢 | 04200 | N44°14.208' E005°54.701'

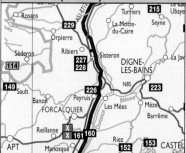

Directions: Follow D4085 north out of Sisteron. At roundabout junction with E712/D4075 turn right to stay on D4085, sp 'Gap'. At next roundabout turn left, sp 'Zone Commercial'. At next roundabout turn left into Super U. Service Point is near fuel station adj to car wash, signed.

ℹ️ Supermarket adj. Self-service laundry adj, €0.50/kg. 10 mins drive from town. Inspected 2012.

🚐 Poss

⛽ Flot Bleu Pacific; Token/20 mins

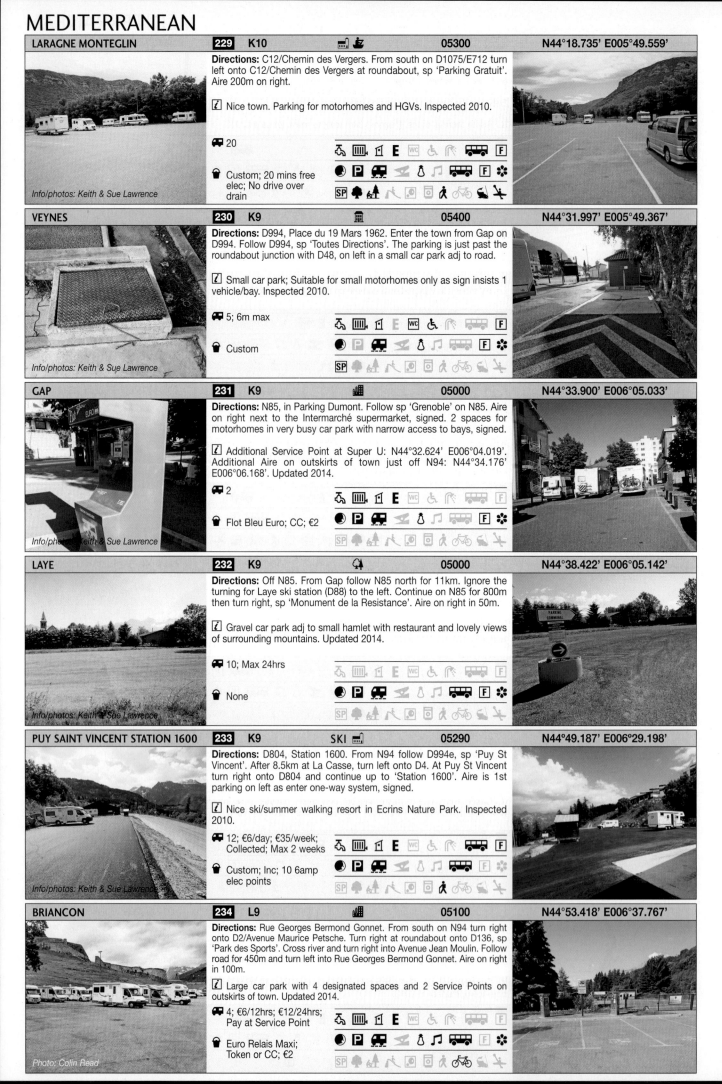

LARAGNE MONTEGLIN | 229 | K10 | 05300 | N44°18.735' E005°49.559'

Directions: C12/Chemin des Vergers. From south on D1075/E712 turn left onto C12/Chemin des Vergers at roundabout, sp 'Parking Gratuit'. Aire 200m on right.

i Nice town. Parking for motorhomes and HGVs. Inspected 2010.

🚐 20

🚰 Custom; 20 mins free elec; No drive over drain

Info/photos: Keith & Sue Lawrence

VEYNES | 230 | K9 | 05400 | N44°31.997' E005°49.367'

Directions: D994, Place du 19 Mars 1962. Enter the town from Gap on D994. Follow D994, sp 'Toutes Directions'. The parking is just past the roundabout junction with D48, on left in a small car park adj to road.

i Small car park; Suitable for small motorhomes only as sign insists 1 vehicle/bay. Inspected 2010.

🚐 5; 6m max

🚰 Custom

Info/photos: Keith & Sue Lawrence

GAP | 231 | K9 | 05000 | N44°33.900' E006°05.033'

Directions: N85, in Parking Dumont. Follow sp 'Grenoble' on N85. Aire on right next to the Intermarché supermarket, signed. 2 spaces for motorhomes in very busy car park with narrow access to bays, signed.

i Additional Service Point at Super U: N44°32.624' E006°04.019'. Additional Aire on outskirts of town just off N94: N44°34.176' E006°06.168'. Updated 2014.

🚐 2

🚰 Flot Bleu Euro; CC; €2

Info/photos: Keith & Sue Lawrence

LAYE | 232 | K9 | 05000 | N44°38.422' E006°05.142'

Directions: Off N85. From Gap follow N85 north for 11km. Ignore the turning for Laye ski station (D88) to the left. Continue on N85 for 800m then turn right, sp 'Monument de la Resistance'. Aire on right in 50m.

i Gravel car park adj to small hamlet with restaurant and lovely views of surrounding mountains. Updated 2014.

🚐 10; Max 24hrs

🚰 None

Info/photos: Keith & Sue Lawrence

PUY SAINT VINCENT STATION 1600 | 233 | K9 | SKI | 05290 | N44°49.187' E006°29.198'

Directions: D804, Station 1600. From N94 follow D994e, sp 'Puy St Vincent'. After 8.5km at La Casse, turn left onto D4. At Puy St Vincent turn right onto D804 and continue up to 'Station 1600'. Aire is 1st parking on left as enter one-way system, signed.

i Nice ski/summer walking resort in Ecrins Nature Park. Inspected 2010.

🚐 12; €6/day/€35/week; Collected; Max 2 weeks

🚰 Custom; Inc; 10 6amp elec points

Info/photos: Keith & Sue Lawrence

BRIANCON | 234 | L9 | 05100 | N44°53.418' E006°37.767'

Directions: Rue Georges Bermond Gonnet. From south on N94 turn right onto D2/Avenue Maurice Petsche. Turn right at roundabout onto D136, sp 'Park des Sports'. Cross river and turn right into Avenue Jean Moulin. Follow road for 450m and turn left into Rue Georges Bermond Gonnet. Aire on right in 100m.

i Large car park with 4 designated spaces and 2 Service Points on outskirts of town. Updated 2014.

🚐 4; €6/12hrs; €12/24hrs; Pay at Service Point

🚰 Euro Relais Maxi; Token or CC; €2

Photo: Colin Read

LE MONETIER LES BAINS | 235 | K9 | SKI | 05220 | N44°58.285' E006°30.748'

Directions: Off D1091. From Briançon (south) enter town on D1091. Just after the town boundary sign turn left, sp 'Espace Loisirs'. Follow lane to parking, across bridge, adj to river, signed.

ⓘ Pleasant Aire in picturesque valley. Ski station 1 min. Very scenic drive over Col du Lautaret (2058m). Updated 2014.

🚐 50; €4.80/day; Collected

⛲ Euro Relais Maxi

Info/photos: Keith & Sue Lawrence

NEVACHE | 236 | K9 | ⛺ | 05100 | N45°01.004' E006°38.177'

Directions: D994g. From N94 turn onto D994g, sp 'La Vachette'. Follow road for approximately 15km. Road very narrow through villages. Service Point is on left on gravel track, opp D1 turning to Col Echelle, signed.

ⓘ Camping Municipal de la Lame 500m further towards Névache. Camping in low season: Motorhome €3, Adults €1. Inspected 2010.

🚐 At campsite

⛲ Custom

Info/photos: Keith & Sue Lawrence

LA SALLE LES ALPES | 237 | K9 | SKI | 05240 | N44°56.867' E006°33.333'

Directions: Chemin des Preras. From south on D1091 turn left into Allée des Peupliers 700m after roundabout, sp 'Plan d'Eau'. Keep left and follow road for 300m. Cross river and turn right at roundabout. Aire immediately on left.

ⓘ Adj to ski lift and small swimming lake. Updated 2014.

🚐 20; €8/24hrs inc elec; Register at TO for electronic gate key, pay when key returned

⛲ Raclet

Info/photos: Keith & Sue Lawrence

MONTGENEVRE | 238 | L9 | SKI | 05100 | N44°56.074' E006°44.185'

Directions: Off N94. Large purpose built Aire well signed in town. Italy 1 mile by road. Need snow chains for Col du Lautaret coming from Grenoble. Also access via Fréjus tunnel.

ⓘ Summer walking resort. Excellent skiing. 100m to slopes. Free shuttle bus to/from Aire. Inspected 2010.

🚐 280; €10/day decreases day by day; Pay on exit; 10amp elec inc

⛲ Custom; €3; Pay at machine

Info/photos: Keith & Sue Lawrence

ST CREPIN | 239 | K9 | ✈ | 05600 | N44°42.250' E006°36.055'

Directions: D138. From south on N94 turn left onto D138, sp 'Aerodrome'. Turn left immediately after river bridge towards aerodrome buildings. Aire on left. Signed on N94 from south, but not from north.

ⓘ Rural location between river and campsite charging €6/night. Visited 2011.

🚐 None

⛲ Custom

Info/photos: Keith & Sue Lawrence

ORCIERES | 240 | K9 | SKI | 05170 | N44°41.704' E006°19.562'

Directions: Les Balcons d'Orcières. From west take D944 to Orcières, then follow D76 up to Orcières-Merlette ski resort. Follow sp 'Parking P2'.

ⓘ Dramatic top floor car park on top of ski area. Lots of signed walks and stunning mountain views. May be free in summer. Inspected 2010.

🚐 24; €12/24hrs inc elec; Pay warden

⛲ Raclet

Info/photos: Keith & Sue Lawrence

LANGOGNE
241 | I9 | 48300 | N44°44.250' E003°50.050'

Photo: Camping-Car-Park.com

Directions: Parking at Lac de Naussac, off D26. Turn off N88 in town between the pharmacy and cinema, sp 'Office du Tourisme'. Follow this road for 2.2km (joins D26) to Aire, sp 'Lac de Naussac' and 'Base Nautique'. Enter through PARKNIGHT barrier.

Lake adj, some views. Hotel, restaurants and snack bar adj. Sailing school adj. Updated 2014.

40; €12/night; CC

Euro Relais Maxi; Inside barrier

Library photo

MENDE
242 | H10 | 48000 | N44°31.248' E003°29.724'

Directions: Rue du Faubourg Montbel. Follow N88 into town from west. At D42/N88 roundabout turn left, sp 'Base de Canoë-Kayak' and signed. Follow road along river and Aire in car park just after river bridge, signed. Service Point near exit, signed, and parking in far corner, signed.

Aire located adj to river weir and old bridge. Large town adj. On transitory route to Gorges du Tarn and Med coast. Locals park in spare bays during day when adj car park full. Inspected 2014.

25; 9 riverside; Max 96hrs

Aire Services; €2

ISPAGNAC
243 | H10 | 48320 | N44°22.256' E003°32.202'

Directions: Chemin des Plots. As enter village from north turn right off D907bis (Gorges du Tarn) at the 'Information' sign into car park, signed. Aire is through car park and on the left just beyond the WC, signed. 3.5t weight restriction on parking.

Service Point in town centre car park. Parking moved near to campsite: N44°22.313' E003°31.773'. On start/end Gorges du Tarn, a must see (subject to height restrictions). Inspected 2014.

None; See info

Custom; Token (2/1); Difficult access

FLORAC
244 | I10 | 48400 | N44°19.528' E003°35.414'

Directions: D16. From north on N106 turn off, sp 'Florac', and cross river. At roundabout turn right, sp 'Les Vignes' and signed. Turn left, signed, and follow road onto one-way system, turning right, left and right at end of road onto D16, sp 'Les Vignes' and signed. Follow road up hill and Aire on right, signed.

Popular Aire located in a peaceful location on a terraced car park above the town. Parking on Service Point terrace can take all sized motorhomes. Inspected 2014.

20; Max 24hrs

Raclet; €2

LA CANOURGUE
245 | H10 | 48500 | N44°25.993' E003°12.705'

Directions: D998. Exit A75 at Junction 40 and follow sp 'Banassac' and 'La Canourgue' onto D998. Follow road into La Canourgue and Aire 500m on right through gateway, signed.

Very convenient Aire to A75 with plenty of parking. Supermarket 300m. Local commerce adj. Inspected 2014.

25; Max 24hrs

Custom

ST GERMAIN DU TEIL
246 | H10 | 48340 | N44°28.746' E003°10.311'

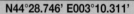

Directions: D52. Exit A75 at Junction 40 and follow sp 'St Germain du Teil' onto D809 then D52. Follow D52 to village then turn right in front of 8 à Huit, sp 'Gendarmerie'. Aire in car park behind 8 à Huit.

Alt 800m. Aire in car park between commerce and community hall, always likely to have space. Pleasant rural community with local commerce adj. Cross country skiing nearby in winter. Inspected 2014.

10

Custom

MARVEJOLS

247 H9 T 48100 N44°33.244' E003°17.216'

Directions: Lotissement Pre de Suzon. Enter Marvejols from south on D809. At city wall gatehouse turn left. Follow road and when it bends to the right, go straight on. Service Point adj to toilets, signed, car park to left has 115 spaces.

ℹ️ Quiet residential area; marked with car bays, 5 bays with poss overhang. Medieval walled city 500m, laundry in gatehouse. Wolf park 8.6km north in Ste Lucie, adults from €7.80. www.loupsdugevaudan.com. Inspected 2014.

🚐 30

🔱 Custom

ST CHELY D'APCHER

248 H9 🏢 48200 N44°48.050' E003°16.473'

Directions: Avenue de la Gare, adj to D809. Turn off D809/Blvd Guerin d'Apcher into car park adj to roundabout, signed. Service Point on right.

ℹ️ Small, busy town centre car park. Tokens from TO 200m. Supermarket 400m. Local commerce adj. Inspected 2010.

🚐 2

🔱 Euro Relais Junior; Token (ER)

Info/photos: Keith & Sue Lawrence

LE MALZIEU VILLE

249 H9 🏛️ 48140 N44°51.302' E003°20.003'

Directions: Place du Foirail. From D989 follow signs into Rue du Barry. At end of road turn left and the Aire is on right.

ℹ️ Pleasant spot on edge of pretty, medieval walled town adj to river. Medieval festival in May/June. Updated 2014.

🚐 6

🔱 Custom

Info/photos: Keith & Sue Lawrence

LE MONASTIER

250 H10 🏢 48100 N44°30.534' E003°15.104'

Directions: N809, at the train station. From A75 turn off at Junction 39, sp 'Le Monastier', and follow road down hill. At roundabout turn left onto D809. Aire is 150m on right at train station, signed.

ℹ️ Landscaped Aire located between main road and train station. Builder's yard adj. Likely to have space. Inspected 2014.

🚐 4

🔱 Raclet

HOMPS

251 H11 🏭 11200 N43°16.191' E002°43.063'

Directions: Rue du Lac. From east turn off D610, sp 'Homps'. Turn right, sp 'Olonzac'. After crossing the canal, take the 1st left, sp 'Lac de Jouarres'. At the roundabout turn left and follow the rough road. Park where detailed on sign.

ℹ️ Parking adj to boat marina on the Canal du Midi. Visit the port Capitainerie for local produce and TO. Day parking at Lac de Jouarres: N43°16.473' E002°42.585'. Visited 2013.

🚐 20; Max 24hrs

🔱 None

Info/photos: Janet & John Watts/Chris de Wet

FITOU

252 H12 🏢 11510 N42°53.578' E002°59.796'

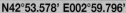

Directions: D900/D6009, at hotel. Aire adj to D900/D6009 south of the D50/D6009 junction, signed.

ℹ️ Commercial Aire on D900/D6009 main road, which can be noisy. Bar/restaurant adj. Visited 2013.

🚐 10; €5/12hrs; €7/24hrs; Collected

🔱 Flot Bleu Océane; Inside; Token; €2

Info/photos: Barry Mills

SALERNES

| 253 | K11 | | 83690 | N43°33.529' E006°14.011' |

Directions: Route des Quatre Chemins. Exit town on D31, sp 'Entrecasteaux' and 'Terra Rosa'. Turn 1st right and cross bridge, then follow road to left. Aire 150m on left just past entrance to Terra Rossa ceramic museum.

ℹ Peaceful Aire. Town centre 10 mins with small town commerce. Ceramic museum adj. Visited 2014.

🚐 5

Custom

Info/photos: Lynne Watson

GUILLAUMES

| 254 | L10 | | 06470 | N44°05.308' E006°51.178' |

Directions: D2202. Turn off D2202 by pharmacy, signed. Aire at end of road on left.

ℹ Mountain village in deep valley. Small town commerce 300m. Aire has unfenced steep drops to rivers on 2 sides. Visited 2014.

🚐 40

Euro Relais Junior; €2

Info: Robin H Ford

ASPRES SUR BUECH

| 255 | K9 | | 05140 | N44°31.214' E005°45.241' |

Directions: Avenue de la Gare. Turn off D1075, sp 'Office du Tourisme' and signed. Follow road past the TO and alongside the railway line and the Aire is on left, signed.

ℹ Small town commerce and TO 200m. Visited 2014.

🚐 5

Custom

Info/photos: Rod & Liz Sleigh

Quinson

Bozouls

MIDI-PYRENEES

Albi

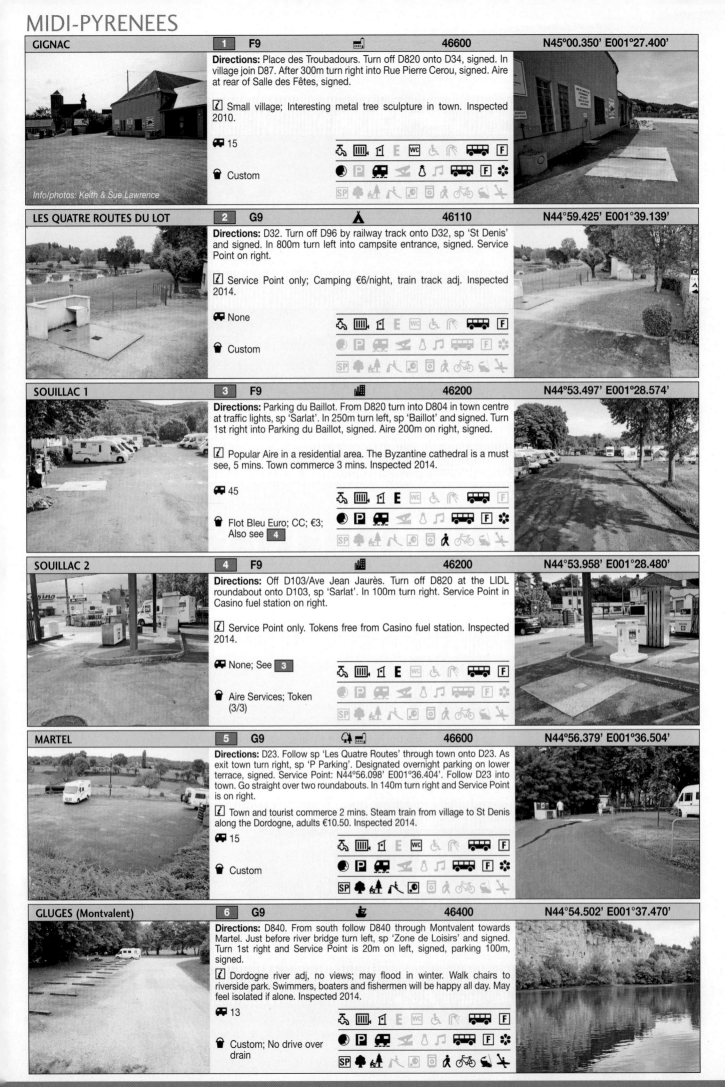

GIGNAC	**1**	F9		46600	N45°00.350' E001°27.400'

Directions: Place des Troubadours. Turn off D820 onto D34, signed. In village join D87. After 300m turn right into Rue Pierre Cerou, signed. Aire at rear of Salle des Fêtes, signed.

ℹ️ Small village; Interesting metal tree sculpture in town. Inspected 2010.

🚐 15

🪣 Custom

Info/photos: Keith & Sue Lawrence

LES QUATRE ROUTES DU LOT	**2**	G9	⛺	46110	N44°59.425' E001°39.139'

Directions: D32. Turn off D96 by railway track onto D32, sp 'St Denis' and signed. In 800m turn left into campsite entrance, signed. Service Point on right.

ℹ️ Service Point only; Camping €6/night, train track adj. Inspected 2014.

🚐 None

🪣 Custom

SOUILLAC 1	**3**	F9	🏢	46200	N44°53.497' E001°28.574'

Directions: Parking du Baillot. From D820 turn into D804 in town centre at traffic lights, sp 'Sarlat'. In 250m turn left, sp 'Baillot' and signed. Turn 1st right into Parking du Baillot, signed. Aire 200m on right, signed.

ℹ️ Popular Aire in a residential area. The Byzantine cathedral is a must see, 5 mins. Town commerce 3 mins. Inspected 2014.

🚐 45

🪣 Flot Bleu Euro; CC; €3; Also see **4**

SOUILLAC 2	**4**	F9	🏢	46200	N44°53.958' E001°28.480'

Directions: Off D103/Ave Jean Jaurès. Turn off D820 at the LIDL roundabout onto D103, sp 'Sarlat'. In 100m turn right. Service Point in Casino fuel station on right.

ℹ️ Service Point only. Tokens free from Casino fuel station. Inspected 2014.

🚐 None; See **3**

🪣 Aire Services; Token (3/3)

MARTEL	**5**	G9		46600	N44°56.379' E001°36.504'

Directions: D23. Follow sp 'Les Quatre Routes' through town onto D23. As exit town turn right, sp 'P Parking'. Designated overnight parking on lower terrace, signed. Service Point: N44°56.098' E001°36.404'. Follow D23 into town. Go straight over two roundabouts. In 140m turn right and Service Point is on right.

ℹ️ Town and tourist commerce 2 mins. Steam train from village to St Denis along the Dordogne, adults €10.50. Inspected 2014.

🚐 15

🪣 Custom

GLUGES (Montvalent)	**6**	G9		46400	N44°54.502' E001°37.470'

Directions: D840. From south follow D840 through Montvalent towards Martel. Just before river bridge turn left, sp 'Zone de Loisirs' and signed. Turn 1st right and Service Point is 20m on left, signed, parking 100m, signed.

ℹ️ Dordogne river adj, no views; may flood in winter. Walk chairs to riverside park. Swimmers, boaters and fishermen will be happy all day. May feel isolated if alone. Inspected 2014.

🚐 13

🪣 Custom; No drive over drain

LABASTIDE MURAT   `7`   G9   🔔   46240   N44°39.004' E001°34.237'

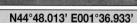

Directions: D677. Exit town on D677, sp 'Gramat'. Turn left as exit town into Carrefour supermarket car park. Service Point located behind supermarket in what is believed to be municipal space.

ℹ️ This Aire feels different to most supermarket stops because of the views, and rural location. Pleasant town centre with local commerce 2 mins. Inspected 2012.

🚐 5; Closest to Service Point

🛒 Custom

ROCAMADOUR   `8`   G9   T   46500   N44°48.013' E001°36.933'

Directions: Parking Le Château. From west on D673 turn right onto D200 in L'Hospitalet, sp 'Parking Le Château' and 'Remparts'. Parking at coach park in 700m just beyond funicular railway station. DO NOT attempt to drive through lower Rocamadour village.

ℹ️ Must see amazing town clinging onto cliff. Walk or funicular railway to village adj, €4.20 return. Grotto in town adj to TO. All local parking unrestricted. Inspected 2014.

🚐 25; Tolerated

🛒 None; See `9`

ALVIGNAC   `9`   G9   🏛️   46500   N44°49.502' E0001°41.827'

Directions: D673/Route de Padirac. From south on D840 turn right onto D673, sp 'Alvignac'. Follow road through centre and Aire on right on inside of bend 150m after junction with D20, signed.

ℹ️ Aire located on edge of town adj to a pleasant park, poss campsite in summer. Local commerce 2 mins. Rocamadour `8` should be visited. Inspected 2014.

🚐 15

🛒 Raclet

GRAMAT   `10`   G9   🏛️   46500   N44°46.789' E001°43.705'

Directions: Avenue Paul Mazet. From D840 turn onto D807 at roundabout, sp 'Gramat Centre'. At roundabout turn left, signed. Follow road and Aire on left.

ℹ️ Aire located on a quiet residential street. Town commerce 5 mins. Inspected 2014.

🚐 20; Max 48hrs

🛒 Euro Relais Junior; 2 unmetered elec points

ST CERE   `11`   G9   🏨   46400   N44°51.685' E001°53.128'

Directions: Chemin du Stade. Follow ring road around town following sp 'A20' and 'Figeac'. Turn off ring road, sp 'Stade' and signed. Follow road for 150m into car park. Service Point and designated parking at far end of car park.

ℹ️ Aire in large unrestricted car park that will only be busy if the sports ground has an event. Town commerce 3 mins. Views of medieval hilltop castle from designated parking. Inspected 2014.

🚐 3; Plus additional parking

🛒 Flot Bleu Fontaine; No drive over drain

SOUSCEYRAC   `12`   G9   🏨   46190   N44°52.361' E002°02.201'

Directions: D653. Adj to D653 in village centre car park facing La Poste and Mairie. Service Point behind toilet block, not visible from road.

ℹ️ Aire located in centre of town adj to small town commerce. Plenty of parking, but parking closest to Service Point may be obstructed at times. Tiny medieval centre adj. Inspected 2014.

🚐 10

🛒 Euro Relais Junior; 1 unmetered elec point; No drive over drain

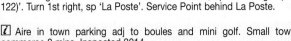

| LATRONQUIERE | 13 | G9 | | 46210 | N44°47.951' E002°04.741' |

Directions: Place du 19 Mars 1962. Follow D31 through town centre towards Figeac. Turn left before Salle des Fêtes, sp 'Le Rouget (RN 122)'. Turn 1st right, sp 'La Poste'. Service Point behind La Poste.

ℹ️ Aire in town parking adj to boules and mini golf. Small town commerce 2 mins. Inspected 2014.

🚐 15

Euro Relais Junior; 1 unmetered CEE elec; No drive over drain

| MONTET ET BOUXAL | 14 | G9 | | 46210 | N44°44.471' E002°01.169' |

Directions: D653. From north on D653 the Service Point is on the right between car wash and 24hr fuel station.

ℹ️ Aire in small rural village. Parking behind Service Point is large but mostly sloping. It is possible to level near the top. Inspected 2014.

🚐 15

Euro Relais Junior; Potable water near fuel pumps; 1 unmetered CEE elec point; No drive over drain

| LEYME | 15 | G9 | | 46120 | N44°47.001' E001°54.044' |

Directions: From south on D39 Service Point at 24hr fuel station on right at entry to village, opp church. Parking: Continue towards village for 140m and turn left. 'Parking Tennis' 200m on left: N44°47.042' E001°53.878'. Further parking other side of football pitch in Allées des Platanes: N44°47.127' E001°53.846'.

ℹ️ Parking is roadside but little used roads. Lots of green space adj and around village. Inspected 2010.

🚐 8 by tennis courts; 5 in Allée des Platanes

Aire Services

Info/photos: Keith & Sue Lawrence

| LACAPELLE MARIVAL | 16 | G9 | | 46120 | N44°43.685' E001°55.799' |

Directions: D653/Place Larroque. From D840 turn onto D940, sp 'Lacapelle Marival'. In town turn right onto D653, sp 'Latronquière'. Follow road to large parking area. Aire on right at rear of car park.

ℹ️ Pretty town with 13th century château in centre, 2 mins. Thriving market Mon in centre, does not affect Aire. Inspected 2014.

🚐 30

Euro Relais Junior; €2; No drive over drain

| THEMINES | 17 | G9 | | 46120 | N44°44.466' E001°49.784' |

Directions: D40, outside the church. Turn onto D40 at Thémines, sp 'Halle de Thémines'. Turn left at covered market, opp Mairie. Service Point at top of hill just past church.

ℹ️ Church adj. Small village with local commerce. Slope too steep to sleep. Night halt only, must depart by midday. Inspected 2014.

🚐 Max 12hrs

Euro Relais Junior; 1 unmetered elec point; No drive over drain

| CARDAILLAC | 18 | G9 | T | 46100 | N44°40.755' E001°59.874' |

Directions: Off D15, by the church in village centre. Signed from D15 main route through village. 100m of narrow turns to access. May be difficult to manoeuvre on busy days when car park full.

ℹ️ Well maintained, pretty, medieval fortified Beau Village 3 mins down main street. Adj village has shabby chic charm, ensure you wander down the alleys and back streets. Inspected 2014.

🚐 10

Euro Relais Junior; €2; No drive over drain

AUTOIRE | 19 | G9 | T | 46400 | N44°51.358' E001°49.316'

Directions: Lieu-Dit La Roque Maynard, adj to D38. Turn off D30 onto D38, sp 'Autoire'. Follow road for 2.3km and the Aire is on the right as enter village, signed. Drive down slope and Service Point is on right adj to toilets. Additional parking on D30 at KM30 in Aire de Repos d'Autoire.

ℹ Aire adj to a Beau Village, 2 mins up path. Walk to Autoire waterfall and Cirque d'Autoire, visible from village. Inspected 2014.

🚐 30

Euro Relais Box; €2

FIGEAC | 20 | G9 | ▦ | 46100 | N44°36.661' E002°02.213'

Directions: From N122 or D13 at roundabout exit onto D19, signed. Service Point is 300m on right in small car park with trees against town wall, signed. For better parking continue across next roundabout into Parking du Foirail: N44°36.721' E002°02.095'.

ℹ Service Point difficult to access if car park busy. Large town. Motorhomes can park anywhere. Inspected 2014.

🚐 40

Euro Relais Junior; €2

BOUILLAC | 21 | G9 | ▦ | 12300 | N44°34.372' E002°09.459'

Directions: Adj to D840. From Figeac on D840 the Aire is on the right in roadside lay-by 280m after 'Bienvenue à Aveyron' sign, signed.

ℹ Aire in attractive roadside picnic area alongside noisy main road. River views and access. Inspected 2014.

🚐 10; Max 24hrs

Custom; Token; €3

BOISSE PENCHOT | 22 | G9 | ▦ | 12300 | N44°35.517' E002°12.333'

Directions: Off D42. Turn off D840 onto D42, sp 'Boisse Penchot' and signed. After 1.3km turn left, signed, and Aire on right in 125m.

ℹ Pleasant Aire with 8 landscaped bays. River Lot and riverside park 10m, partial view from some bays. Local commerce adj. Inspected 2014.

🚐 8

Euro Relais Junior; Token (ER); €3

CRANSAC LES THERMES | 23 | G10 | ▦ | 12110 | N44°31.367' E002°16.433'

Directions: Avenue de la Gare. Turn off D11 in town onto Ave de la Gare. The Aire is before you cross the railway track.

ℹ 6 landscaped bays separated by shrubs. Pleasant Aire in thermal town. Inspected 2010.

🚐 6; €5; Max 48hrs

Custom

Info photos: Keith & Sue Lawrence

NAUSSAC | 24 | G9 | ⛺ | 12700 | N44°31.293' E002°04.774'

Directions: Aire de Loisirs de Naussac/Lieu Dit le Causse Naut. From D922 turn onto D88 at Loupiac. Follow road towards Naussac for 5.5km. Turn left off D88 into Lieu Dit le Causse and Aire on right in 400m.

ℹ Nice Aire among trees. Inspected 2010.

🚐 8; €4/night

Custom; 6 unmetered elec points

Info photos: Keith & Sue Lawrence

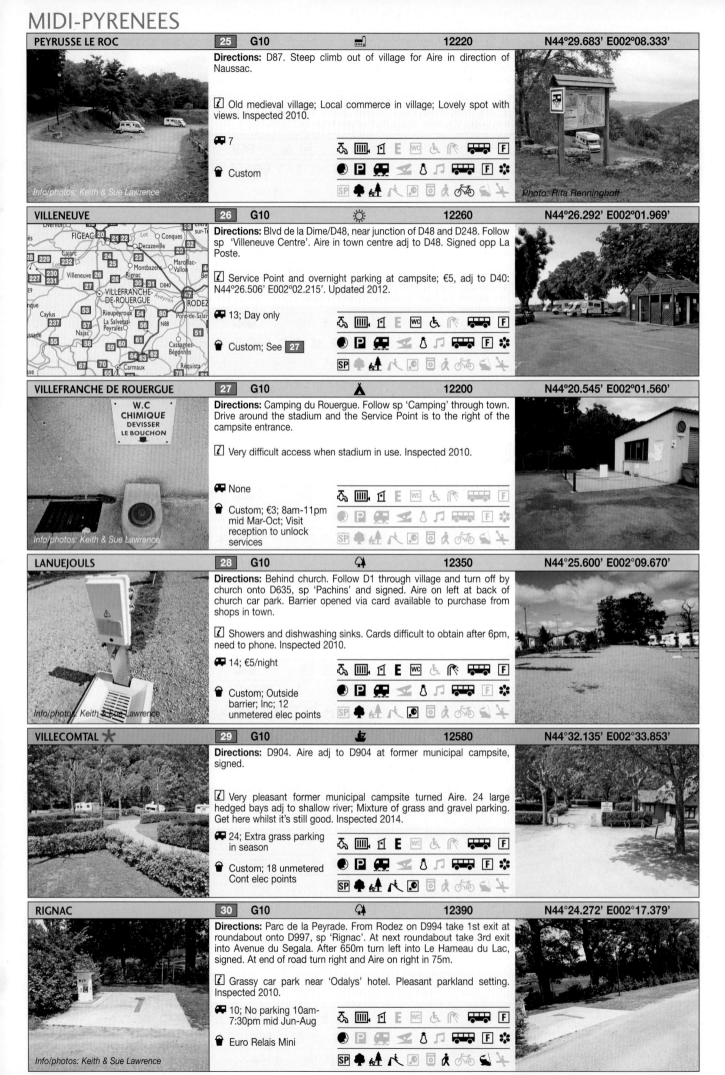

PEYRUSSE LE ROC 25 G10 12220 N44°29.683' E002°08.333'

Directions: D87. Steep climb out of village for Aire in direction of Naussac.

ℹ️ Old medieval village; Local commerce in village; Lovely spot with views. Inspected 2010.

🚐 7

Custom

Info/photos: Keith & Sue Lawrence

Photo: Rita Renninghoff

VILLENEUVE 26 G10 12260 N44°26.292' E002°01.969'

Directions: Blvd de la Dime/D48, near junction of D48 and D248. Follow sp 'Villeneuve Centre'. Aire in town centre adj to D48. Signed opp La Poste.

ℹ️ Service Point and overnight parking at campsite; €5, adj to D40: N44°26.506' E002°02.215'. Updated 2012.

🚐 13; Day only

Custom; See 27

VILLEFRANCHE DE ROUERGUE 27 G10 12200 N44°20.545' E002°01.560'

Directions: Camping du Rouergue. Follow sp 'Camping' through town. Drive around the stadium and the Service Point is to the right of the campsite entrance.

ℹ️ Very difficult access when stadium in use. Inspected 2010.

🚐 None

Custom; €3; 8am-11pm mid Mar-Oct; Visit reception to unlock services

Info/photos: Keith & Sue Lawrence

LANUEJOULS 28 G10 12350 N44°25.600' E002°09.670'

Directions: Behind church. Follow D1 through village and turn off by church onto D635, sp 'Pachins' and signed. Aire on left at back of church car park. Barrier opened via card available to purchase from shops in town.

ℹ️ Showers and dishwashing sinks. Cards difficult to obtain after 6pm, need to phone. Inspected 2010.

🚐 14; €5/night

Custom; Outside barrier; Inc; 12 unmetered elec points

Info/photos: Keith & Sue Lawrence

VILLECOMTAL ⭐ 29 G10 12580 N44°32.135' E002°33.853'

Directions: D904. Aire adj to D904 at former municipal campsite, signed.

ℹ️ Very pleasant former municipal campsite turned Aire. 24 large hedged bays adj to shallow river; Mixture of grass and gravel parking. Get here whilst it's still good. Inspected 2014.

🚐 24; Extra grass parking in season

Custom; 18 unmetered Cont elec points

RIGNAC 30 G10 12390 N44°24.272' E002°17.379'

Directions: Parc de la Peyrade. From Rodez on D994 take 1st exit at roundabout onto D997, sp 'Rignac'. At next roundabout take 3rd exit into Avenue du Segala. After 650m turn left into Le Hameau du Lac, signed. At end of road turn right and Aire on right in 75m.

ℹ️ Grassy car park near 'Odalys' hotel. Pleasant parkland setting. Inspected 2010.

🚐 10; No parking 10am-7:30pm mid Jun-Aug

Euro Relais Mini

Info/photos: Keith & Sue Lawrence

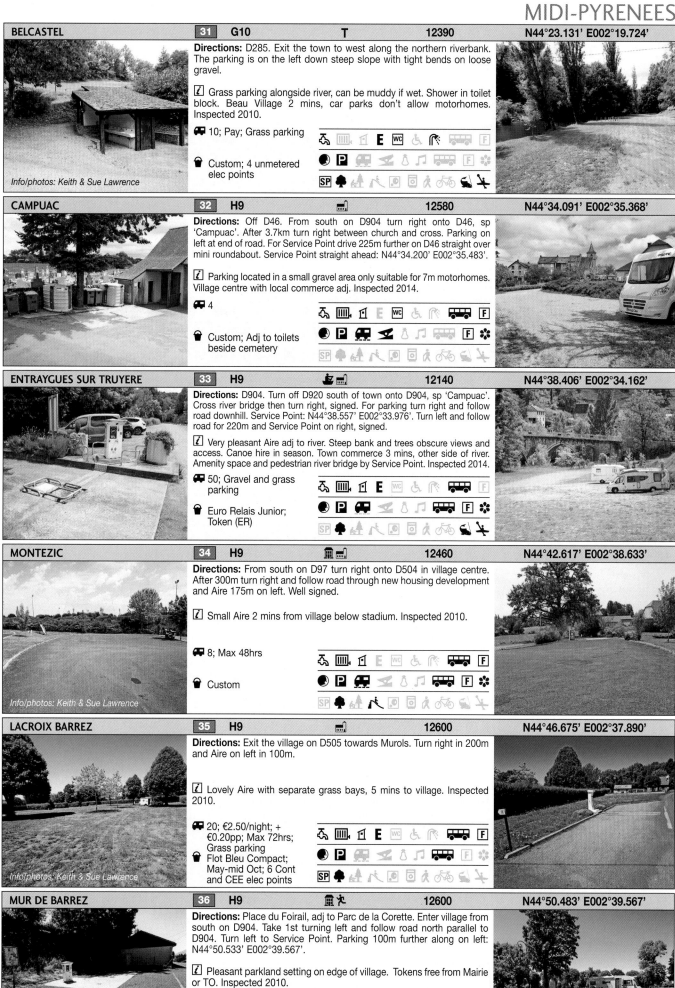

BELCASTEL
31 | G10 | T | 12390 | N44°23.131' E002°19.724'

Directions: D285. Exit the town to west along the northern riverbank. The parking is on the left down steep slope with tight bends on loose gravel.

i Grass parking alongside river, can be muddy if wet. Shower in toilet block. Beau Village 2 mins, car parks don't allow motorhomes. Inspected 2010.

🚐 10; Pay; Grass parking

🔧 Custom; 4 unmetered elec points

Info/photos: Keith & Sue Lawrence

CAMPUAC
32 | H9 | | 12580 | N44°34.091' E002°35.368'

Directions: Off D46. From south on D904 turn right onto D46, sp 'Campuac'. After 3.7km turn right between church and cross. Parking on left at end of road. For Service Point drive 225m further on D46 straight over mini roundabout. Service Point straight ahead: N44°34.200' E002°35.483'.

i Parking located in a small gravel area only suitable for 7m motorhomes. Village centre with local commerce adj. Inspected 2014.

🚐 4

🔧 Custom; Adj to toilets beside cemetery

ENTRAYGUES SUR TRUYERE
33 | H9 | | 12140 | N44°38.406' E002°34.162'

Directions: D904. Turn off D920 south of town onto D904, sp 'Campuac'. Cross river bridge then turn right, signed. For parking turn right and follow road downhill. Service Point: N44°38.557' E002°33.976'. Turn left and follow road for 220m and Service Point on right, signed.

i Very pleasant Aire adj to river. Steep bank and trees obscure views and access. Canoe hire in season. Town commerce 3 mins, other side of river. Amenity space and pedestrian river bridge by Service Point. Inspected 2014.

🚐 50; Gravel and grass parking

🔧 Euro Relais Junior; Token (ER)

MONTEZIC
34 | H9 | | 12460 | N44°42.617' E002°38.633'

Directions: From south on D97 turn right onto D504 in village centre. After 300m turn right and follow road through new housing development and Aire 175m on left. Well signed.

i Small Aire 2 mins from village below stadium. Inspected 2010.

🚐 8; Max 48hrs

🔧 Custom

Info/photos: Keith & Sue Lawrence

LACROIX BARREZ
35 | H9 | | 12600 | N44°46.675' E002°37.890'

Directions: Exit the village on D505 towards Murols. Turn right in 200m and Aire on left in 100m.

i Lovely Aire with separate grass bays, 5 mins to village. Inspected 2010.

🚐 20; €2.50/night; + €0.20pp; Max 72hrs; Grass parking

🔧 Flot Bleu Compact; May-mid Oct; 6 Cont and CEE elec points

Info/photos: Keith & Sue Lawrence

MUR DE BARREZ
36 | H9 | | 12600 | N44°50.483' E002°39.567'

Directions: Place du Foirail, adj to Parc de la Corette. Enter village from south on D904. Take 1st turning left and follow road north parallel to D904. Turn left to Service Point. Parking 100m further along on left: N44°50.533' E002°39.567'.

i Pleasant parkland setting on edge of village. Tokens free from Mairie or TO. Inspected 2010.

🚐 5

🔧 Euro Relais Junior; Token (ER)

Info/photos: Keith & Sue Lawrence

THERONDELS | 37 | H9 | 12600 | N44°53.900' E002°45.567'

Info/photos: Keith & Sue Lawrence

Directions: From Mur de Barrez take D900, sp 'Barrage de Sarrans'. In Brommat turn right onto D18, sp 'Thérondels'. Take the 1st right after D236 and Service Point is 200m on right.

i Grass parking around the Service Point but notice on Service Point also invites parking in village centre. Inspected 2010.

🚐 5; Max 24hrs

💧 Flot Bleu Pacific

STE GENEVIEVE SUR ARGENCE | 38 | H9 | 12420 | N44°48.117' E002°45.733'

Info/photos: Keith & Sue Lawrence

Directions: Rue de l'Argence. From D900 heading south, or D78 heading east, turn into Rue de l'Argence (which connects the two roads). The parking is adj to the river, signed.

i Pleasant spot adj to small river; Village 5 mins. Tokens from TO, Mairie, and shops. BBQ point. WiFi at TO. Inspected 2010.

🚐 10

💧 Flot Bleu Pacific; Token; €2

LAGUIOLE | 39 | H9 | 12210 | N44°40.917' E002°51.250'

Info/photos: Keith & Sue Lawrence

Directions: Outside Camping Les Monts D'Aubrac, off D921. From south turn right off D921, signed. Follow road to campsite.

i Service Point only outside entrance to campsite. Inspected 2010.

🚐 None; See 40

💧 Custom

LAGUIOLE SKI STATION | 40 | H9 | SKI | 12210 | N44°40.367' E002°55.633'

Info/photos: Keith & Sue Lawrence

Directions: Lieu-Dit le Bouyssou, off D15. From Laguiole take D15, sp 'Aubrac' and 'Station de Ski de Laguiole'. Follow road for 9.8km and Aire on right at 'Station de Ski de Laguiole'. Location labelled on map as 'Chalets du Bouyssou', but not on signposts.

i Alt 1360m. Large parking area at ski station. Lots of summer walks, well marked footpaths. Dog sledge rides all year. Inspected 2010.

🚐 20

💧 None; See 39

AUBRAC | 41 | H9 | 12470 | N44°37.233' E002°59.200'

Info/photos: Keith & Sue Lawrence

Directions: D533. From north on D987 turn left in village centre onto D533, sp 'St Chely D'Aubrac'. Aire on right in 150m on edge of village.

i Alt 1345m. Pleasant parking area on the edge of the village. Botanical gardens. Toilets 150m towards village. Inspected 2010.

🚐 20

💧 Flot Bleu Fontaine

ST GENIEZ D'OLT | 42 | H10 | 12130 | N44°28.183' E002°59.000'

Info/photos: Keith & Sue Lawrence

Directions: D503/Route de la Cascade. From village centre head northeast on D509/Rte de la Cascade and Service Point is 500m, outside campsite.

i Service Point only outside entrance to campsite. Campsite open April-Sept. Inspected 2010.

🚐 None

💧 Aire Services; €1

STE EULALIE D'OLT — 43 — H10 — T — 12130 — N44°27.883' E002°56.950'

Directions: Rue de la Grave. From east on D988 turn right at start of village onto D597. After 700m turn right into Route de la Passerelle, then right into Rue de la Grave. Aire at end of road outside Camping Municipal La Grave. Enter through barrier.

ℹ️ Machine outside campsite office gives tokens for entrance barrier (correct money needed). Pretty historic Beau Village. Inspected 2010.

🚐 13; €8/night; mid May-mid Sept; Purchase token to lift barrier

🚰 Custom; Inc; 16amp CEE elec inc

Info/photos: Keith & Sue Lawrence

BOZOULS — 44 — G/H10 — T — 12340 — N44°28.326' E002°43.264'

Directions: Rue Marc André Fabre, adj to D20. Turn off D20, sp 'Bibliothèque' and 'Mediathèque'. Aire immediately on left in large car park, signed.

ℹ️ Well located Aire. Continue down lane on foot into pedestrianised street and follow to left for commerce, gorge and views across to a cliff top commune. Poss to walk past waterfall and up through gorge. Inspected 2014.

🚐 10

🚰 Custom

CAMPAGNAC — 45 — H10 — 🏨 — 12560 — N44°25.185' E003°05.313'

Directions: Off D37. In village centre turn off D202 onto D37, sp 'St Laurent d'Olt' and 'Gendarmerie'. Turn 1st right past Gendarmerie and the Aire is on the right directly behind the Gendarmerie.

ℹ️ Peaceful village with local commerce. Unmetered elec in grassed area, long cable needed. Inspected 2014.

🚐 5; €3/night; Collected

🚰 Custom

LAISSAC — 46 — H10 — 🏢 — 12310 — N44°23.140' E002°49.282'

Directions: From N88 turn onto D28, sp 'Laissac'. Take 1st right, signed. Drive around Intermarché and turn right, signed.

ℹ️ Intermarché supermarket 2 mins. Adj to N88, road noise. Town 5 mins. Livestock market Tue am in adj parking area. Inspected 2014.

🚐 6

🚰 Custom; €2; Honesty box

RODEZ — 47 — H10 — 🏢🌳 — 12000 — N44°21.467' E002°35.647'

Directions: D162, opp ZI Cantaranne. Turn off N88 at roundabout onto D217/Ave de la Roquette. After 2km do not turn left over railway line, but carry straight on, sp 'Rodez'. After a further 1.6km turn left at large junction, sp 'Ste Radegonde'. Aire 750m on right, signed.

ℹ️ Pleasant landscaped Aire surrounded by green fields with walk/cycle to Rodez adj. Rodez historic centre 30 mins uphill. Inspected 2014.

🚐 6; Max 72hrs

🚰 Custom

SEGUR — 48 — H10 — ⛽🏠 — 12290 — N44°17.441' E002°50.104'

Directions: Rue de la Mairie, off D95. From Rodez take D29 28km to Ségur. In village turn right onto D95 then left into Rue de la Mairie. Service Point signed.

ℹ️ Parking not designated but poss on grass to right of Service Point or hardstandings past Service Point on left. Showers at Service Point, €2, token. Inspected 2010.

🚐 Poss; Max 48hrs

🚰 Custom

Info/photos: Keith & Sue Lawrence

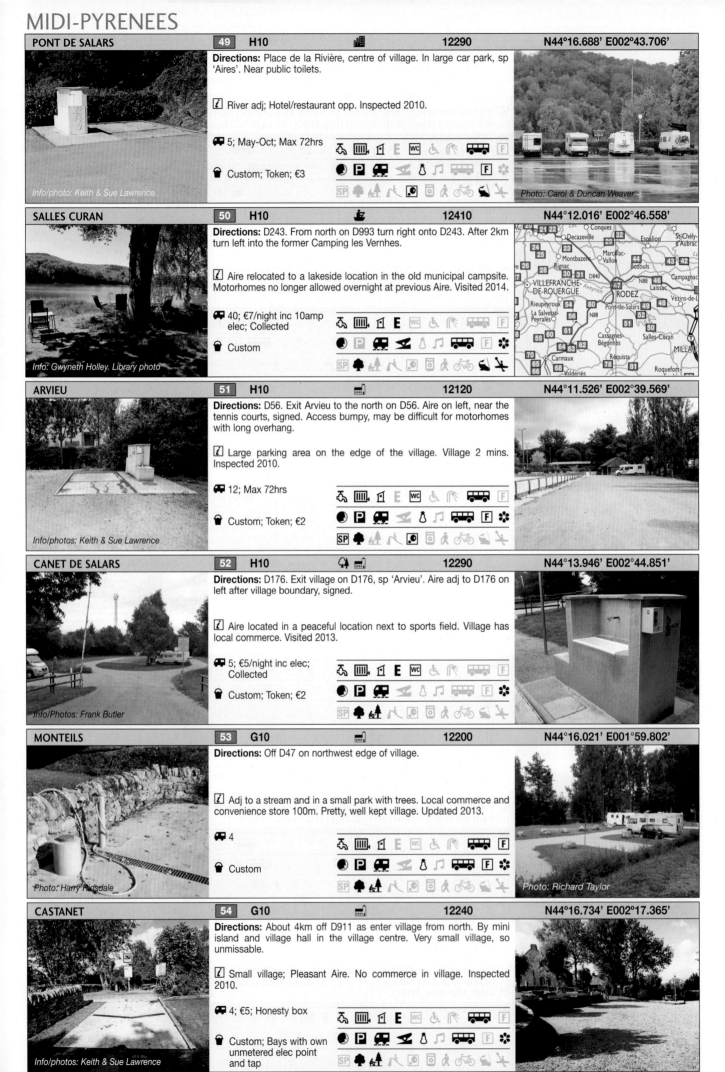

PONT DE SALARS — 49 — H10 — 12290 — N44°16.688' E002°43.706'

Directions: Place de la Rivière, centre of village. In large car park, sp 'Aires'. Near public toilets.

ℹ️ River adj; Hotel/restaurant opp. Inspected 2010.

🚐 5; May-Oct; Max 72hrs

⛲ Custom; Token; €3

Info/photo: Keith & Sue Lawrence

Photo: Carol & Duncan Weaver

SALLES CURAN — 50 — H10 — 12410 — N44°12.016' E002°46.558'

Directions: D243. From north on D993 turn right onto D243. After 2km turn left into the former Camping les Vernhes.

ℹ️ Aire relocated to a lakeside location in the old municipal campsite. Motorhomes no longer allowed overnight at previous Aire. Visited 2014.

🚐 40; €7/night inc 10amp elec; Collected

⛲ Custom

Info: Gwyneth Holley. Library photo

ARVIEU — 51 — H10 — 12120 — N44°11.526' E002°39.569'

Directions: D56. Exit Arvieu to the north on D56. Aire on left, near the tennis courts, signed. Access bumpy, may be difficult for motorhomes with long overhang.

ℹ️ Large parking area on the edge of the village. Village 2 mins. Inspected 2010.

🚐 12; Max 72hrs

⛲ Custom; Token; €2

Info/photos: Keith & Sue Lawrence

CANET DE SALARS — 52 — H10 — 12290 — N44°13.946' E002°44.851'

Directions: D176. Exit village on D176, sp 'Arvieu'. Aire adj to D176 on left after village boundary, signed.

ℹ️ Aire located in a peaceful location next to sports field. Village has local commerce. Visited 2013.

🚐 5; €5/night inc elec; Collected

⛲ Custom; Token; €2

Info/Photos: Frank Butler

MONTEILS — 53 — G10 — 12200 — N44°16.021' E001°59.802'

Directions: Off D47 on northwest edge of village.

ℹ️ Adj to a stream and in a small park with trees. Local commerce and convenience store 100m. Pretty, well kept village. Updated 2013.

🚐 4

⛲ Custom

Photo: Harry Ridsdale

Photo: Richard Taylor

CASTANET — 54 — G10 — 12240 — N44°16.734' E002°17.365'

Directions: About 4km off D911 as enter village from north. By mini island and village hall in the village centre. Very small village, so unmissable.

ℹ️ Small village; Pleasant Aire. No commerce in village. Inspected 2010.

🚐 4; €5; Honesty box

⛲ Custom; Bays with own unmetered elec point and tap

Info/photos: Keith & Sue Lawrence

ST ANTONIN NOBLE VAL | 55 | G10 | 82140 | N44°09.144' E001°45.085'

Directions: Chemin de Roumegous. Entering town on D5/D958 from Caussade turn 1st right onto Blvd de la Condamine, sp 'P Gratuit'. Turn right again onto Rte des Fours Á Chaux then left into Chemin de Roumegous. Service Point at entrance to car park.

ⓘ Town centre 2 mins; Gorges adj. Inspected 2010.

🚐 20

🔱 Custom

Info/photos: Keith & Sue Lawrence

SAUVETERRE DE ROUERGUE | 56 | G10 | T | 12800 | N44°12.960' E002°19.014'

Directions: D997. On right of D997 as enter town from Naucelle, signed.

ⓘ Shower €1.50. On edge of Beau Village, 5 mins. Free municipal campsite. Inspected 2010.

🚐 11; May-Oct; Grass parking

🔱 Custom; Elec €2/24hrs

Info/photos: Keith & Sue Lawrence

NAJAC | 57 | G10 | 12270 | N44°13.289' E001°58.041'

Directions: From Najac follow D39 to Mazerolles, following signs to campsite/Aire. Go past campsite, left over bridge, then left towards swimming pool and tennis courts. Aire on left 400m after bridge.

ⓘ Aire by river next to campsite. 1.5km steep climb to Beau Village with château and church. Beautiful spot. Updated 2013.

🚐 10

🔱 Euro Relais Junior; Token (ER); €2

Info/photos: Keith & Sue Lawrence

LAGUEPIE | 58 | G10 | 82250 | N44°08.693' E001°58.317'

Directions: Quai de la Libération. Turn off D958 just south of river L'Aveyron into Quai de la Libération, signed. Service Point against wall on right.

ⓘ In small cul de sac above river. Road used as car park so could be difficult to access/turn around. Inspected 2010.

🚐 Poss

🔱 Custom

Info/photos: Keith & Sue Lawrence

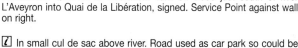

LE SEGUR | 59 | G10 | 81640 | N44°06.533' E002°03.517'

Directions: Mairie and Maison du Temps Libre. Just off D27 in small village 6km northwest of Monestiés.

ⓘ In tiny village. Inspected 2010.

🚐 Poss

🔱 Custom; Large bore flexi hose for waste water

Info/photos: Keith & Sue Lawrence

MIRANDOL BOURGNOUNAC | 60 | G10 | 81190 | N44°08.513' E002°10.000'

Directions: Place du Foirail. Turn off D905 in centre of the village, signed. The Aire is in the car park and the Service Point is to the rear of the car park against a building, signed.

ⓘ Car park in village centre. Inspected 2010.

🚐 5

🔱 Custom; Flexi hose for waste water

Info/photos: Keith & Sue Lawrence

NAUCELLE | 61 | G10 | 12800 | N44°11.830' E002°20.510'

Directions: Place du Ségala, at back of village square. From D997 turn onto D52 by water fountain, public toilets and La Poste, sp 'Crespin'. Service Point 100m on left, signed.

ℹ️ The parking is very impractical, so really just a Service Point. Inspected 2014.

🚐 Impractical

👤 Custom

ST JUST SUR VIAUR | 62 | G10 | 12800 | N44°07.433' E002°22.533'

Directions: Parking at Place des Fêtes. From N88 take D10 south to Castelpers. Turn right onto D532, sp 'St Just'. Aire on left in 2km.

ℹ️ Pleasant rural location with BBQ site. On the Gorges du Viaur road and close to the Viaduc du Viaur. Inspected 2010.

🚐 5; Max 48hrs

👤 Euro Relais Junior; 2 unmetered elec points

Info/photos: Keith & Sue Lawrence

TANUS | 63 | G10 | 81190 | N44°06.150' E002°19.006'

Directions: Rue de Tanus le Vieux. The Aire is by the cattle market as you exit the village on D688 towards Rodez. Turn off N88, sp 'Tanus'. At roundabout turn left, sp 'Tanus'. Follow the main route to left at church, then turn left into car park/cattle market. Service Point to left.

ℹ️ Aire in a large gravel car park which will only be busy when cattle market on. Both shaded and unshaded parking. Always likely to have space. Local commerce nearby. Inspected 2014.

🚐 40

👤 Custom; No drive over drain, flexi hose missing

PAMPELONNE | 64 | G10 | 81190 | N44°07.334' E002°14.651'

Directions: Place du Foirail. Follow D78 through village and turn onto D53, sp 'Tanus'. The Aire is on right at edge of village green, with weighbridge and public toilets.

ℹ️ Pleasant. Restaurant adj. Inspected 2010.

🚐 5

👤 Custom; Flexi hose for waste water

Info/photos: Keith & Sue Lawrence

LE GARRIC (Carmaux) | 65 | G10 | 81400 | N44°00.858' E002°08.080'

Directions: Off D25. Exit Carmaux to south on D988, sp 'Cap' Découverte'. In 3.8km at roundabout turn right onto D25, sp 'Cap' Découverte'. At next roundabout turn left into Cap' Découverte. Follow road past car parks and across roundabout, signed. Service Point on left before campsite.

ℹ️ Service Point outside campsite at Cap' Découverte activity centre with zip lining, dry skiing, swimming, etc; adults €24.50/day. May feel isolated if alone. Inspected 2014.

🚐 Poss on grass opp or before Service Point

👤 Custom

CARMAUX | 66 | G10 | 81400 | N44°03.021' E002°09.879'

Directions: Turn off N88 onto D91 and follow sp 'Carmaux'. Follow road to right, then turn right into Rue Gambetta. Drive round main square and turn off, sp 'Aire Camping-Car'. Follow road to right, sp 'Rosières'. As road bends left, go straight on and Aire is on left, signed.

ℹ️ The Aire is located adj to sports facilities, 2 mins from town centre with town commerce. Market Friday am. Some noise from local industry during day. Inspected 2014.

🚐 20

👤 Custom

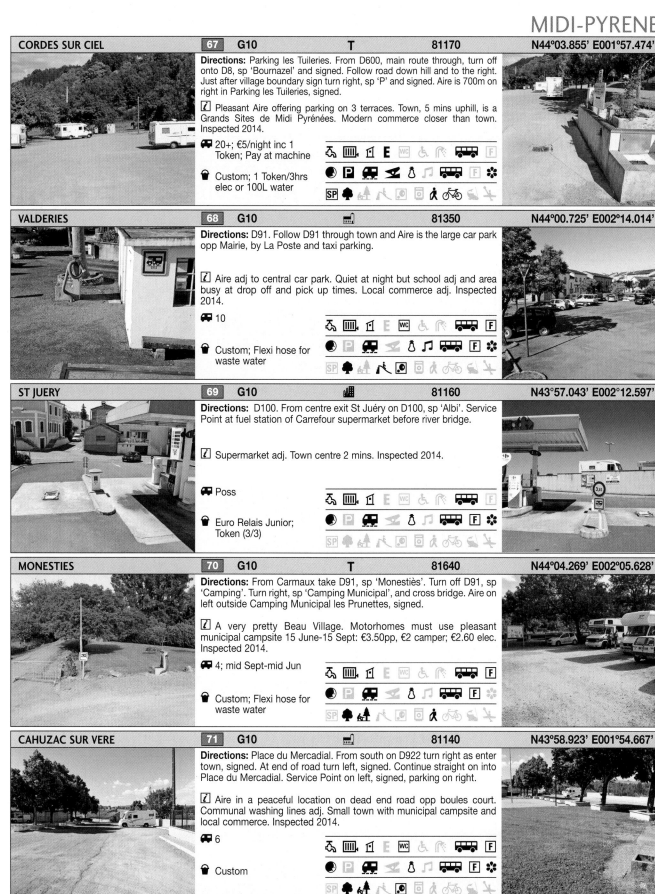

| CORDES SUR CIEL | 67 | G10 | | T | | 81170 | | N44°03.855' E001°57.474' |

Directions: Parking les Tuileries. From D600, main route through, turn off onto D8, sp 'Bournazel' and signed. Follow road down hill and to the right. Just after village boundary sign turn right, sp 'P' and signed. Aire is 700m on right in Parking les Tuileries, signed.

ℹ️ Pleasant Aire offering parking on 3 terraces. Town, 5 mins uphill, is a Grands Sites de Midi Pyrénées. Modern commerce closer than town. Inspected 2014.

🚐 20+; €5/night inc 1 Token; Pay at machine

🚰 Custom; 1 Token/3hrs elec or 100L water

| VALDERIES | 68 | G10 | | 🛏️ | | 81350 | | N44°00.725' E002°14.014' |

Directions: D91. Follow D91 through town and Aire is the large car park opp Mairie, by La Poste and taxi parking.

ℹ️ Aire adj to central car park. Quiet at night but school adj and area busy at drop off and pick up times. Local commerce adj. Inspected 2014.

🚐 10

🚰 Custom; Flexi hose for waste water

| ST JUERY | 69 | G10 | | 🏢 | | 81160 | | N43°57.043' E002°12.597' |

Directions: D100. From centre exit St Juéry on D100, sp 'Albi'. Service Point at fuel station of Carrefour supermarket before river bridge.

ℹ️ Supermarket adj. Town centre 2 mins. Inspected 2014.

🚐 Poss

🚰 Euro Relais Junior; Token (3/3)

| MONESTIES | 70 | G10 | | T | | 81640 | | N44°04.269' E002°05.628' |

Directions: From Carmaux take D91, sp 'Monestiès'. Turn off D91, sp 'Camping'. Turn right, sp 'Camping Municipal', and cross bridge. Aire on left outside Camping Municipal les Prunettes, signed.

ℹ️ A very pretty Beau Village. Motorhomes must use pleasant municipal campsite 15 June-15 Sept: €3.50pp, €2 camper; €2.60 elec. Inspected 2014.

🚐 4; mid Sept-mid Jun

🚰 Custom; Flexi hose for waste water

| CAHUZAC SUR VERE | 71 | G10 | | 🛏️ | | 81140 | | N43°58.923' E001°54.667' |

Directions: Place du Mercadial. From south on D922 turn right as enter town, signed. At end of road turn left, signed. Continue straight on into Place du Mercadial. Service Point on left, signed, parking on right.

ℹ️ Aire in a peaceful location on dead end road opp boules court. Communal washing lines adj. Small town with municipal campsite and local commerce. Inspected 2014.

🚐 6

🚰 Custom

| ALBI 1 | 72 | G10 | | 🏢 | | 81000 | | N43°55.856' E002°10.669' |

Directions: Rue Jean Rostand, at Kercher branded car wash. Service Point directly behind 2.8m car wash bays. Safest entrance is through exit; must reverse out.

ℹ️ Service Point only, difficult access. Motorhome wash bay 3.5m Inspected 2014.

🚐 None; See 74

🚰 Flot Bleu Océane; Token; €2

ALBI 2 — 73 — G10 — 81000 — N43°55.159' E002°06.458'

Directions: Z.I. Fonlabour. Turn off N88 at Junction 13 and follow sp 'Z.A. Fonlabour'. In 1200m turn left at roundabout. Service Point outside E'Leclerc Express Drive, signed.

ℹ️ Supermarket and retail shops adj. Inspected 2014.

🚐 Poss; See 74

⛲ Aire Services; CC; €2

ALBI 3 — 74 — G10 — 81000 — N43°55.886' E002°08.152'

Directions: Rue René Cassin. From large traffic-lighted roundabout by river bridge turn off, sp 'Base de Loisirs de Pratgraussals' and signed. Turn right at end of road, then left and after following road around sewerage works turn right, all signed. Service Point immediately on right, parking around corner on left.

ℹ️ Roadside parking adj to cemetery and leisure park. View of Albi cathedral steeple, Albi 20 mins along river Tarn. Leisure park attracts youthful behaviour. May feel isolated if alone. Inspected 2014.

🚐 10

⛲ Aire Services; 2 unmetered CEE elec points (push button)

ALBI 4 — 75 — G10 — 81000 — N43°56.761' E002°09.071'

Directions: D988. From north on N88 turn onto D988 at roundabout, sp 'Albi Centre'. Service Point is on the right in 700m, signed.

ℹ️ Road parking available but really just a Service Point. Inspected 2014.

🚐 None; See 74

⛲ Custom; Toilet waste disposal at waist height

ALBI 5 — 76 — G10 — T — 81000 — N43°55.630' E002°08.458'

Directions: P Cathédrale, Blvd du Général Sibille. From Albi 4 75 follow sp 'Centre Ville'. Cross bridge and turn right in 600m when road opens to square. At next junction turn right and follow road for 300m. Turn left at roundabout, signed, then immediately right into P Cathédrale. Follow road to left downhill, sp 'École Européenne…'. Aire on the left, sp 'Sauf Camping-Cars'.

ℹ️ Excellently located pleasant Aire at the base of Albi cathedral, the largest brick structure in world. Historic centre adj. Inspected 2014.

🚐 9; Max 48hrs

⛲ None; See 75

HAVE YOU VISITED AN AIRE? — GPS co-ordinates in this guide are protected by copyright law

Submit updates
- Amendments
- New Aires
- Not changed

Visit www.all-the-aires.co.uk/submissions.shtml
to upload your updates and photos.

ℹ️ Directions and description.

🚐 Number of parking spaces; Cost per night; Time limit

⛲ Service Point type and details; Payment type; Cost

Take at least 5 digital photos showing
- Signs
- Service Point
- Parking
- Overview
- Amenities

REQUISTA — 78 — G10 — 12170 — N44°02.073' E002°32.163'

Directions: Place François Fabié. From north on D902 turn left into Place François Fabié opp Renault garage. Aire adj to Salle des Fêtes.

ℹ️ Aire in large unlevel car park. Alternative level parking in next car park. Small town commerce 2 mins. Very scenic drive on D902 along river Tarn to 81 via Brousse le Château, a Beau Village. Inspected 2014.

🚐 6 hedged bays plus additional parking

⛲ Custom

COUPIAC | 79 | G10 | | 12550 | N43°57.100' E002°35.033'

Directions: Off D90, at rear of 'Station Service'. From D999 turn onto D33, sp 'Réquista'. After 12km turn right onto D60, sp 'Coupiac'. In village turn right onto D60, sp 'Montclar' and signed. Turn right over bridge onto D90, sp 'Martrin' and signed. Turn right again in 400m and Service Point on left adj to 24hr fuel station.

i Pleasant Aire on grass between trees. 200m from medieval village and château. Background factory noise/smells. Inspected 2014.

🚐 5; Grass parking

🚾 Custom

BARAQUEVILLE | 80 | G10 | | 12160 | N44°16.702' E002°25.976'

Directions: Rue du Val de l'Enne. From N88 turn into town car park adj to N88/D911 roundabout, signed. Follow road past Mairie then turn 1st right. Follow road for 330m to Aire.

i Pleasant landscaped Aire overlooking fields with a lake in the distance. On terrace above livestock market. Small town shops 2 mins. Inspected 2014.

🚐 12

🚾 Euro Relais Junior; Token (ER); €3

BROQUIES | 81 | H10 | | 12480 | N44°00.294' E002°41.617'

Directions: From Vabres L'Abbaye follow D25 to Broquiès. In village centre turn left onto D54. Turn next left into Place de la Mairie, then 1st right into Rte de Mazies/D200e. Aire on left in 140m as road bends left.

i Aire in a pleasant location situated on a terrace overlooking the wooded hills of the Tarn Valley. 3 further elec sockets in recycling area. Local commerce 1 min uphill. Inspected 2014.

🚐 15

🚾 Custom; 1 unmetered elec point

ROQUEFORT SUR SOULZON | 82 | H10 | T | 12250 | N43°58.867' E002°58.867'

Directions: D23, at entrance to village next to TO. From Millau take D992/D999 then D23, sp 'Roquefort'. Aire is on left as you enter village.

i Popular Aire located on a sloping car park with panoramic views. TO adj. The village is a short walk uphill with numerous Roquefort cheese cave tours. The 'Société' Roquefort cave tour is recommended. Inspected 2014.

🚐 10

🚾 Custom; Toilets down steps

LA CAVALERIE | 83 | H10 | | 12230 | N44°00.520' E003°09.145'

Directions: D277. Exit A75 at Junction 47 and follow sp 'La Cavalerie' onto D999. As approach Le Cavalerie turn right onto D277, signed. Aire immediately on right, enter through PARKNIGHT barrier.

i A landscaped commercial Aire within earshot of the A75. Ideal night halt when heading south. Village 3 mins has Templar ruins. Inspected 2014

🚐 32; €12/night; CC

🚾 Euro Relais Junior; Inside barrier; Inc

MILLAU | 84 | H10 | | 12100 | N44°05.750' E003°05.133'

Directions: Rue de la Saunerie. From south follow D809 across river, sp 'Millau-Centre'. Take 1st slip road on right, sp 'P Centre Historic' and signed. Follow under D809 and go straight on, sp 'P La Grave'. Pass Parking La Grave then turn right at mini roundabout, signed. Turn right. Enter through PARK NIGHT barrier.

i Popular landscaped commercial Aire adj to main road. Millau 2 mins. Viewpoint underneath Millau bridge: N44°04.807' E003°01.299'. Inspected 2014.

🚐 32; €12/night; CC

🚾 Euro Relais Junior; Inside barrier; Inc; 24 CEE elec points

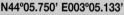

| LA COUVERTOIRADE | 85 | H10 | T | 12230 | N43°54.776' E003°18.970' |

Directions: Off D55. Enter 1st car park and follow signs to motorhome area.

ℹ Within 200m walk of large 12th century fortified Templar Beau Village. Inspected 2010.

🚐 30; €3; Pay on exit

None

photos: Keith & Sue Lawrence

| ST JEAN D'ALCAS | 86 | H10 | T | 12250 | N43°55.600' E003°00.517' |

Directions: D516. Aire next to cemetery on east/southeast edge of village, signed.

ℹ A basic Aire which is always likely to have space. The village centre, 3 mins down hill, has an amazing fortified town with info panels in English, audio tour available. Inspected 2014.

🚐 10

Custom

| VABRES L'ABBAYE | 87 | H10 | | 12400 | N43°56.728' E002°50.367' |

Directions: Rue de la Vigne. From St Affrique on D999 turn left at 1st roundabout, sp 'Vabres l'Abbaye'. Follow road, then turn left into Rue du Coustel at village hall and pharmacy, signed. Follow road to right, then turn right, signed. Service Point immediately on right.

ℹ Pleasant town Aire in large car park at rear of village hall with open and shaded parking. Bells noisy when they chime. Local commerce 2 mins. Inspected 2014.

🚐 20

Euro Relais Mini; Token (ER); €2

| CAMARES | 88 | H10 | | 12360 | N43°49.017' E002°52.883' |

Directions: Base de Loisirs, Chemin des Zizines. Turn off D902 just south of village, sp 'Plan d'Eau', 'Base de Loisirs', and signed. Cross bridge and turn right into Chemin des Zizines. After 430m turn left and Aire in car park for swimming lake.

ℹ Aire between river Dourdou and popular swimming lake with 'beach'; supervised 2-7pm in summer/weekends. Town, 4 mins, is very pleasant with a river weir and local commerce. Inspected 2014.

🚐 25; Max 72hrs

Custom

| ST SERNIN SUR RANCE | 89 | H10 | | 12380 | N43°53.205' E002°36.103' |

Directions: From east on D999 pass through village and turn right immediately before high river bridge, signed. Follow road downhill and Aire on right under bridge, signed. Access road steep with a sharp bend at end which could be difficult in icy conditions.

ℹ This is a very pleasant Aire adj to stream and away from road noise, but may feel isolated if alone. 5 mins up the road to village which has local commerce. Inspected 2014.

🚐 5; Max 72hrs

Custom

| MURAT SUR VEBRE | 90 | H11 | | 81320 | N43°41.250' E002°51.201' |

Directions: D622. Aire adj to D622 as exit village towards Lacaune. In lay-by on left, signed.

ℹ A traditional French village Aire in local parking area adj to boules court. Local commerce within 2 mins, butcher adj has interesting range of sausages and hams. Inspected 2014.

🚐 5

Custom

ALBAN | 91 | G10 | T | 81250 | N43°53.230' E002°27.545'

Directions: Rue Italo Zaccaron. From D999 turn off in Alban, sp 'Complexe Sportif' and signed. Follow road down hill and Aire on left before sports stadium. 3.5t weight restriction on some parking.

i Pleasant Aire away from the road noise overlooking open access sports ground. Small town commerce 2 mins uphill on D999. Inspected 2014.

🚐 15

🚰 Euro Relais Junior; €2

RAYSSAC | 92 | G10 | | 81330 | N43°49.067' E002°24.950'

Directions: From D81 turn onto D59, sp 'Rayssac'. Aire on right on entry to village in small car park adj to Mairie. Approach from north not advised, very narrow roads.

i Tiny village. BBQ point. Inspected 2010.

🚐 3; Max 24hrs

🚰 Flot Bleu Compact; €3.05; Pay Mairie; 2 unmetered elec points

Info/photos: Keith & Sue Lawrence

BELMONT SUR RANCE | 93 | H10 | | 12370 | N43°48.979' E002°45.164'

Directions: Adj to D32 in car park, opp Mairie.

i Popular Aire with lovely garden. No animals allowed in garden. Interesting village with old church. Local commerce adj. Inspected 2014.

🚐 3; Max 24hrs

🚰 Flot Bleu Fontaine

LAC DU LAOUZES ⭐ | 94 | H11 | | 81320 | N43°38.815' E002°46.938'

Directions: D162. From northeast on D162 the Aire is on north shore of lake 3km after junction with D162c, signed.

i Popular pleasant Aire along shore of lake, all bays with lake views. Water access for swimming, boating and fishing. Busy at weekends. Inspected 2014.

🚐 20; €6.56 Sept-Jun; €7.56 Jul-Aug; Collected

🚰 Custom; 16 CEE elec points dotted through parking

MAZAMET | 95 | G11 | | 81200 | N43°29.450' E002°22.800'

Directions: Parking Champ de la Ville, Rue du Bassin. From Labruguière follow N112 towards town. At traffic lights turn right and follow sp 'Centre Ville'. At end of road in town centre turn right at traffic lights. Then turn left, sp 'P Champ de la Ville'. At roundabout turn right into car park. Service Point on lower terrace, level parking on top terrace.

i The Aire is centrally located in a town centre car park shaded by plane trees. The car park is virtually empty at night, but busy Sat am (market). Town commerce 3 mins. Inspected 2014.

🚐 20+

🚰 Custom

MAZAMET LAC DES MONTAGNES | 96 | G11 | | 81200 | N43°27.733' E002°20.800'

Directions: Lac des Montagnes. From Mazamet take D118, sp 'Lac des Montagnes'. After 6km turn right, sp 'Lac des Montagnes' and signed. Service Point located at 'Parking 1'. Better parking available at 'Parking 2' further around lake: N43°27.917' E002°20.517'.

i Swimming lake; Beach; Outdoor showers; Green space; Crazy golf; Lake walks. Parking 2, adj to grassy area. BBQ. Inspected 2010.

🚐 10; Max 48hrs

🚰 Custom

Info/photos: Keith & Sue Lawrence

ANGLES | 97 | G11 | 81260 | N43°33.932' E002°33.924'

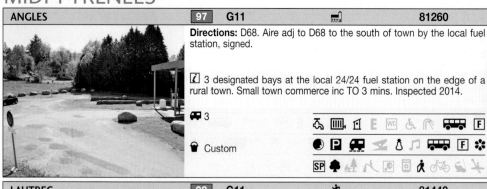

Directions: D68. Aire adj to D68 to the south of town by the local fuel station, signed.

ℹ 3 designated bays at the local 24/24 fuel station on the edge of a rural town. Small town commerce inc TO 3 mins. Inspected 2014.

🚐 3

🔧 Custom

LAUTREC | 98 | G11 | 81440 | N43°42.239' E002°07.830'

Directions: Espace Aquatique Base de Loisirs. Approach on D83 toward Castres. Turn off D83 onto D92, sp 'Vielmur', 'Base de Loisirs' and signed. Follow road then turn left, signed. Turn left again and Aire is on right, signed. Town centre has 3.5t weight restriction.

ℹ Aire on outskirts of hilltop town adj to leisure park, lakes (no views) and recreational facilities. Beau Village with local commerce 10 mins up hill. Inspected 2012.

🚐 40

🔧 Euro Relais Junior; €2; Token (ER)

LACAUNE | 99 | H11 | 81230 | N43°42.576' E002°42.446'

Directions: Rue de la Belmette. Turn off D607 in town, sp 'Les Vidals' and 'Camping'. Turn left, sp 'Camping'. Service Point on left outside campsite entrance, signed.

ℹ Service Point only. Inspected 2014.

🚐 None

🔧 Custom; Token (3/3)

CASTRES | 100 | G11 | 81100 | N43°35.431' E002°12.398'

Directions: N126. Approach Castres on N126 from south. Turn left at 2nd roundabout by Dacia showroom. Service Point on right, signed. For night parking exit town on D89. Turn right sp, 'Parc de Gourjade' and follow road to car park.

ℹ Service Point only. Restricted overnight parking Max 1 night 5pm-10am only N43°37.225' E002°15.203'. Inspected 2012.

🚐 None

🔧 Custom

Photo: Keith & Sue Lawrence

LABRUGUIERE | 101 | G11 | 81290 | N43°31.883' E002°15.317'

Directions: Parc du Montimont. Approach from Puylaurens on D621. Turn right before railway track, sp 'Domaine d'En Laure'. Follow road to right, then turn left, both sp 'Domaine d'En Laure'. Enter through gate and follow drive. Aire on left, signed, at Domaine d'En Laure.

ℹ Aire in a shaded location in a peaceful public park with fishing lake and holiday bungalows. Predominantly grass parking. Small town commerce 10 mins. Gates locked 11pm. May feel isolated if alone. Inspected 2014.

🚐 10

🔧 Urba Flux; €2

REVEL 1 | 102 | D4 | 31250 | N43°27.222' E002°00.841'

Directions: Chemin des Peupliers. From town centre ring road follow sp 'Halte Camping-Cars'. Turn left into gravel track, signed. Aire at end of track. Enter through Urba Flux barrier.

ℹ Isolated position away from town in the middle of sports fields and trout farm. Unsuitable gravel parking on some bays, remaining on grass. Free access to swimming pool, show receipt. Inspected 2014.

🚐 28; €9/night Jun-Aug; €7/night Sept-May; +tax and inc elec (16 points); CC

🔧 Custom; Inside barrier; Inc; €3

REVEL 2 — 103 G11 — 31250 — N43°27.779' E002°00.318'

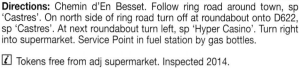

Directions: Chemin d'En Besset. Follow ring road around town, sp 'Castres'. On north side of ring road turn off at roundabout onto D622, sp 'Castres'. At next roundabout turn left, sp 'Hyper Casino'. Turn right into supermarket. Service Point in fuel station by gas bottles.

i Tokens free from adj supermarket. Inspected 2014.

🚐 Poss; See 106

🚰 Aire Services; Token (3/3); Free from supermarket

PUYLAURENS — 104 G11 — 81700 — N43°34.122' E002°00.725'

Directions: Rue Albert Thorel. From N126 turn onto D84 south of town, sp 'Puylaurens'. At roundabout take 1st exit to continue on D84 and follow road. Turn right at roundabout into Rue Édouard Vairette, signed. Follow road and Aire on left after 300m, signed.

i Pleasant peaceful landscaped Aire on part of an old campsite with some hedged pitches and some shade. Outdoor swimming pool adj. Horse fair in town on the 1st Sun of each month. Inspected 2014.

🚐 15

🚰 Custom; Tap in middle; WC in hedge

LACROUZETTE — 105 G11 — 81210 — N43°39.779' E002°20.919'

Directions: Place du Theron. Approach Lacrouzette from Roquecourbe on D30. Follow road through town, turning right onto one-way system, sp 'Toutes Directions'. Turn left, sp 'Brassac'. Turn next left, sp 'P Place du Theron'. Aire on right behind sculpture.

i Aire in large open car park with plenty of space. Local commerce 1 min. Near national park and gorges. Inspected 2012.

🚐 10

🚰 Flot Bleu Océane; Token; €2

DURFORT — 106 G11 — 81540 — N43°26.358' E002°03.909'

Directions: D44. Exit D85 onto D44, sp 'Durfort'. Follow road and as enter village turn right signed, into large car park. Service Point to left.

i Pleasant tranquil Aire in ample car park close to village centre. Local/tourist commerce 1 min. Rural views of surrounding national park. Nicknamed Cité du Cuivre (the copper city); copper museum in town. Inspected 2014.

🚐 10

🚰 Custom

SOREZE — 107 G11 — 81540 — N43°27.017' E002°03.928'

Directions: P Gratuit 250. Approach Sorèze on D85 from Revel. At roundabout adj to U Express turn right onto C18, sp 'P Gratuit 250' and 'TO'. Follow road to left and Service Point on left, parking on right before height barriered parking.

i A pleasant Aire backing onto green space. Small town commerce, TO, glass museum and monastery museum all 1 min. Walking trail around town in English. Inspected 2014.

🚐 7

🚰 Custom

VILLEFRANCHE DE LAURAGAIS — 108 G11 — 31290 — N43°23.786' E001°42.559'

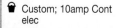

Directions: Chemin de Magnauques, No 10. From D813 turn onto D622e, sp 'Castelnaudary'. Then at the roundabout turn onto D622, sp 'Auterive'. Cross railway bridge then turn left in 450m immediately before the village boundary sign into Chemin de Magnauques. No 10 is the pink house 100m on left.

i Privately owned by motorhome owner and located behind his house. Limited English but very friendly and helpful. Washing machine €2. Free WiFi on site. Commerce 5 mins. Visited 2014.

🚐 10; €10/night; Collected

🚰 Custom; 10amp Cont elec

Info/photos: Chris & Mo Thomas

SAVERDUN | 109 | F11 | 09700 | N43°13.556' E001°36.226'

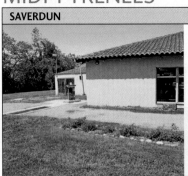

Directions: D14. Service Point located in the Aire de Repos roadside lay-by adj to D14 south of town, signed. Service Point directly behind shop.

Aire located in very pleasant roadside lay-by with large picnic area, TO and café. Tokens from TO. Noise from road and trucks parking. Recommend 114. Inspected 2014.

20

Euro Relais Junior; Token (ER); €2.50

LAVAUR | 110 | F11 | 81500 | N43°41.177' E001°49.083'

Directions: Chemin d'en Trabouillou. Exit town on D112 towards Castres. Turn off D112 onto D87, sp 'Caraman'. Go straight over roundabout, sp 'Caraman'. In 200m turn left, sp 'Cuisine Centrale' and signed. In 100m turn left, signed.

Parking behind school. Small town commerce 5 mins. Market Saturday mornings. Inspected 2012.

5

Custom

LABARTHE SUR LEZE | 111 | F11 | 31860 | N43°27.261' E001°23.696'

Directions: D4. Adj to D4 at the western edge of town near its junction with D19.

Supermarket adj with 24hr fuel and LPG by CC. Visited 2013.

Poss

Euro Relais Box; Token or €2

Info/photos: Janet & John Watts

ST LYS | 112 | F11 | 31470 | N43°30.920' E001°10.553'

Directions: Route de Saiguede. From town centre turn off by church, sp 'Fontenilles'. Turn left onto D12, sp 'L'Isle Jourdain' truck route and 'Le Moulin'. Service Point is 10m on right, poorly signed and may be obstructed by parked cars. For suitable overnight parking follow road round bend and turn left into car park.

Parking adj to boules courts. Town with numerous commerce 2 mins uphill. Service Point is very old and underused. Inspected 2012.

5

Custom; Poss obstructed by cars

VENERQUE | 113 | F11 | 31810 | N43°26.010' E001°26.406'

Directions: Base de Loisirs/Allées du Duc de Ventadour. Exit Le Vernet on D19. Cross river and enter Venerque. Turn left before river bridge, sp 'Base de Loisirs' and signed. Parking on right between trees, Service Point to left.

Pleasant parking on a plane tree lined avenue. Suitable for all motorhomes. Boules adj. Canoe hire in season. Local commerce 2 mins. Inspected 2014.

10

Custom; 2 toilets

AUTERIVE | 114 | F11 | 32550 | N43°21.100' E001°28.583'

Directions: Rue des Docteurs Basset. Turn off D820 at traffic lights onto D622, sp 'Nailloux'. Go straight over roundabout and cross river. Turn 1st right, signed, for Service Point. 100m down dead end road: N43°21.011' E001°28.637'. For parking turn 1st left after crossing river bridge into car park before D35 junction.

Pleasant canalside parking with river Ariège across adj gardens. Well maintained town with small town with commerce 2 mins. Inspected 2014.

12; 6m bays plus overhang

Custom

ST SULPICE SUR LEZE	115	F11		31410	N43°19.812' E001°18.999'

Directions: D622. Aire is adj to D622 as you enter town from A64. The Service Point is in the fuel station of the Intermarché supermarket, next to the car wash.

i Supermarket adj. Pretty town with covered arcades 3 mins. Inspected 2014.

🚐 Poss

♟ Euro Relais Junior; €2

GPS Co-ordinates for SatNav

The GPS Co-ordinates published in this guide were taken onsite by our inspectors. We consider them a valuable and unique asset and at the time of publishing have decided not to publish them as electronic files for use on navigation devices. You have permission to type in the co-ordinates of an Aire you intend to visit but not to store or share them. For the security of our copyright:

- **Do not compile them into lists**

- **Do not publish, share or reproduce them anywhere in any format**

L'ISLE JOURDAIN	117	F11		32600	N43°37.174' E001°04.335'

Directions: Allée du Lac. Exit town to west on D161. Turn right, 500m from town, onto D654, signed. Turn left in front of railway track into Allée du Lac. Service Point immediately on left, signed. Unrestricted parking before Service Point.

i At leisure lake with waterskiing, indoor swimming pool and other water related sports. No designated parking, but unrestricted parking available. Inspected 2012.

🚐 5

♟ Custom

GIMONT	118	F11		32200	N43°37.810' E000°52.187'

Directions: N124. From town on A24 follow sp 'Auch'. After crossing river bridge turn immediately right into Aire, signed.

i Trucking hell! The Aire has a lovely outlook overlooking a fishing pond, but that is completely overshadowed by the noise from the traffic within 15m. For a quieter stop, try 183. Inspected 2014.

🚐 10

♟ Bollard

SAMATAN	119	F11		32130	N43°29.296' E000°55.628'

Directions: D39. From Samatan turn onto D39, sp 'Lombez'. At the roundabout turn left into Les Rivages, signed. Turn left and the Aire is at the end, signed.

i Aire between D39 and holiday rentals. Complex has lake with walks, no views. Small town shops in centre, 3 mins. Inspected 2014.

🚐 10; €3/night; +€0.20pp/night; Collected

♟ Custom; Pay; Water tap in box

LOMBEZ	120	F11		32220	N43°28.485' E000°54.959'

Directions: D632. Enter Lombez on D634/D632 from Samatan. Aire is in car park on right just after the D626 junction and before the Gendarmerie, signed.

i Aire located in very large car park adj to sports stadium. Park opp with a walk. Busy during sporting events and used as night parking by truckers. Inspected 2014.

🚐 40

♟ Custom

AUZAS | 121 | F11 | 31360 | N43°10.200' E000°53.217'

Directions: D33r. From St Martory on D52 turn left onto D33r, sp 'Auzas'. After 900m turn left to lake, sp 'Lac'. Follow road downhill to lower terrace, signed. Service Point in 100m opp church, signed: N43°10.158' E000°53.102'.

Aire adj to small leisure lake, 3 parallel bays have lake views. Leisure facilities inc outdoor gym, mini golf and boats in summer. Best to walk WC to Service Point, 150m, as parking very impractical. Inspected 2014.

9; €4/night inc unmetered CEE elec; Collected

Custom; Lift cover by sign; Water, elec and WC at parking

MARTRES TOLOSANE | 122 | F11 | 31220 | N43°12.134' E001°00.665'

Directions: D10. From central one-way system turn onto D10, sp 'Alan'. Service Point on right opp cemetery, signed.

It is possible to night halt outside cemetery, but really this is just a Service Point. Suggest 125 and 126 as alternatives. Inspected 2014.

2

Bollard

BOUSSENS | 123 | F11 | 31360 | N43°10.666' E000°58.482'

Directions: Turn off D817 at roundabout onto D62n, sp 'Boussens' and 'Du Lac'. At roundabout turn left, sp 'Du Lac' and 'Camping'. Turn right at end of road, sp 'Camping', then left, signed. Service Point on left before campsite, signed.

Although it is possible to squeeze 2 motorhomes here, really it is only a Service Point. Try 125 and 126. Inspected 2014.

2 poss; Additional on D817 at Aire de Repos

Custom; Water at rock; Lift cover

ST CROIX VOLVESTRE | 124 | F11 | 09230 | N43°07.600' E001°10.250'

Directions: D35. Exit the village on D35 towards Latour. The Aire is at the sports fields. Signed off D35.

Small village with some local commerce 5 mins. Inspected 2010.

7

Custom

Info/photos: Keith & Sue Lawrence

MAZERES SUR SALAT ★ | 125 | F11 | 31260 | N43°08.080' E000°58.579'

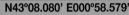

Directions: Le Pre Commune. At traffic lights in town centre turn off D13 onto D52, sp 'Cassagne'. Just before river bridge turn left. Follow road along river to Aire.

Aire in a beautiful location overlooking fish ladder and weir with views of the Pyrénées beyond. Small town commerce 3 mins. Inspected 2014.

8

Custom; 1 Cont elec point

ST MARTORY | 126 | F11 | 31360 | N43°08.507' E000°55.726'

Directions: D817, in car park adj to D817 near D52/D117 junction.

Pleasant Aire overlooking river and old river bridge. Local commerce adj and market on Aire Fri, but does not impede Aire if parked on river edge. Inspected 2014.

7

Custom; Lift grid

ST GIRONS
127 | F12 | 09200 | N42°59.303' E001°08.366'

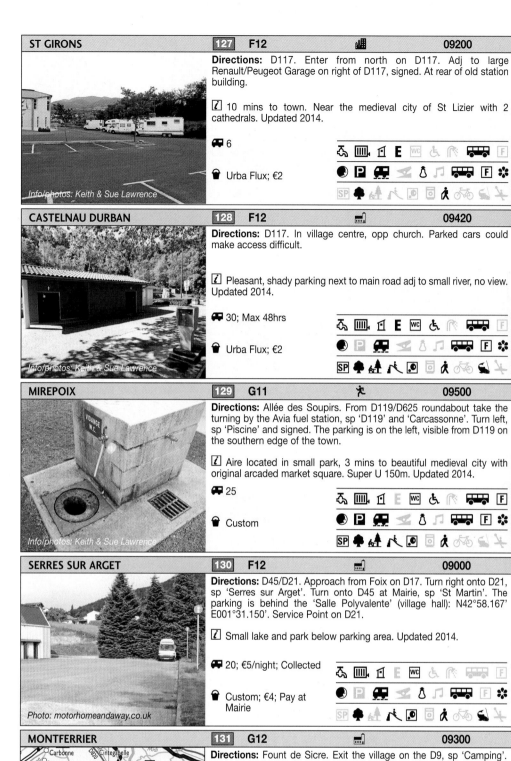

Directions: D117. Enter from north on D117. Adj to large Renault/Peugeot Garage on right of D117, signed. At rear of old station building.

i 10 mins to town. Near the medieval city of St Lizier with 2 cathedrals. Updated 2014.

🚐 6

Urba Flux; €2

Info/photos: Keith & Sue Lawrence

CASTELNAU DURBAN
128 | F12 | 09420 | N42°59.996' E001°20.398'

Directions: D117. In village centre, opp church. Parked cars could make access difficult.

i Pleasant, shady parking next to main road adj to small river, no view. Updated 2014.

🚐 30; Max 48hrs

Urba Flux; €2

Info/photos: Keith & Sue Lawrence

MIREPOIX
129 | G11 | 09500 | N43°05.097' E001°52.453'

Directions: Allée des Soupirs. From D119/D625 roundabout take the turning by the Avia fuel station, sp 'D119' and 'Carcassonne'. Turn left, sp 'Piscine' and signed. The parking is on the left, visible from D119 on the southern edge of the town.

i Aire located in small park, 3 mins to beautiful medieval city with original arcaded market square. Super U 150m. Updated 2014.

🚐 25

Custom

Info/photos: Keith & Sue Lawrence

SERRES SUR ARGET
130 | F12 | 09000 | N42°58.150' E001°31.133'

Directions: D45/D21. Approach from Foix on D17. Turn right onto D21, sp 'Serres sur Arget'. Turn onto D45 at Mairie, sp 'St Martin'. The parking is behind the 'Salle Polyvalente' (village hall): N42°58.167' E001°31.150'. Service Point on D21.

i Small lake and park below parking area. Updated 2014.

🚐 20; €5/night; Collected

Custom; €4; Pay at Mairie

Photo: motorhomeandaway.co.uk

MONTFERRIER
131 | G12 | 09300 | N42°53.554' E001°47.522'

Directions: Fount de Sicre. Exit the village on the D9, sp 'Camping'. Turn right off D9 at Camping La Fount de Sicre, signed. Drive between campsite and river to Aire on right, signed.

i Aire in small mountain village on route to mountain passes. Updated 2014.

🚐 7; Grass and gravel parking

Custom

Info/Photo: Jean & Ken Fowler

LES CABANNES
132 | G12 | 09310 | N42°47.067' E001°40.967'

Directions: Quartier la Bexane. From E9/N20 take D522, sp 'Les Cabannes'. Follow signs to Aire adj to Gendarmerie. Both well signed.

i Very scenic location. Updated 2014.

🚐 30; €6/24hrs; Collected

Custom; €2

Info/photos: Keith & Sue Lawrence

VICDESSOS

133 F12  09220 N42°46.133' E001°30.150'

Photo: Sue & Trevor Smith

Directions: Rue de l'Eglise. Turn off D8 into D708/Rue de l'Eglise, sp 'Parking Camping Cars'. Immediately turn right, passing 8 à Huit supermarket. Aire just beyond the shop.

Adj to river on outskirts of village amid beautiful scenery. Updated 2014.

20; €6; Pay at Mairie

Custom; Inc; 12 Cont unmetered elec points

AX LE THERME

134 G12 09110 N42°43.567' E001°49.884'

Info/photos: Dot Palastanga/Janet & John Watts/Phil & Julie Hutchins

Directions: La Capelette, adj to N20 on the left-hand side as approach the town. Aire is located next to railway station car park. Enter through Aire Services barrier.

Popular ski resort. Busy traffic on adj N20 to Andorra and local railway line adj. Town commerce and hot springs 10 mins. Day parking allowed in town 6am-6pm. Visited 2013.

25; €6/24hrs; €10/48hrs; €14/72hrs; CC

Aire Services; Inside barrier; 1hr elec and 100L water inc

L'HOSPITALET PRES L'ANDORRE

135 G12 09390 N42°35.335' E001°47.985'

Info/photos: Janet & John Watts

Directions: Les Fountanals. From north on N20, turn left onto N22 opp electricity plant, sp 'Pas de la Case' and 'Mairie'. Cross railway track and turn immediately left into car park, signed. The Aire is adj to railway station car park, signed.

L'Hospitalet is a village in a narrow valley amid snowy mountains near Andorra and the Spanish border. Local commerce adj. Visited 2013.

27

Euro Relais Maxi; CC; Water €2; Elec €6/6hrs

ST GAUDENS

136 F11 31800 N43°06.610' E000°42.493'

Directions: Rue des Chanteurs du Comminges. Exit St Gaudens towards Montréjeaux on D817. Turn right at roundabout junction with D39a, sp 'Le Belvédère' with the campsite symbol. Service Point in 100m.

Service Point only. Inspected 2014.

None

Custom; Jun-Sept; 1 unmetered Cont elec point

MONTREJEAU

137 E11 31210 N43°05.059' E000°34.306'

Directions: D817. Just off main road near centre of town at Place de Verdun, around octagonal, covered car park.

Well located designated parking just moments from small town commerce. Good patisserie and popular and reasonably priced restaurant adj. Viewpoint across to the Pyrénées adj. Sheltered from road noise, surprisingly peaceful stop. Inspected 2014.

5

Toilet only

GOURDAN POLIGNAN

138 E11 31510 N43°03.611' E000°35.529'

Directions: D825. Service Point at Super U just off D8/A645/D825/N125 roundabout. The Service Point is in the fuel station.

Supermarket adj. Inspected 2014.

Poss; See **137**

Euro Relais Junior; €2

BAGNERES DE LUCHON — 139 — E12 — 31110 — N42°47.706' E000°35.920'

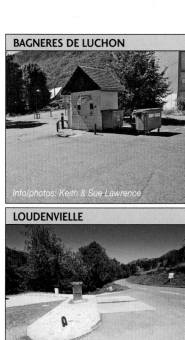

Directions: Rue Jean Mermoz. Approaching from north on D125 turn left, sp 'D125', 'Espagne', and 'Accueil Camping Car' on very small sign at road level. Take the next left and follow this road. The Aire is on the left, opp the sports ground.

i Path to Lac de Badech from Aire. LIDL nearby; Thermal baths. 10 mins to town. Tokens from TO. Updated 2014.

🚐 30; €4; Collected; 7m bays

🚰 Custom; Token; €4

Info/photos: Keith & Sue Lawrence

LOUDENVIELLE — 140 — E12 — 65510 — N42°48.083' E000°24.650'

Directions: D25/Chemin du Hourgade. From north take D618. Turn off onto D25 and continue south approx 3.5km. Aire adj to lake on right.

i Adj to Lac de Genos-Loudenvielle; Thermal baths. Inspected 2010.

🚐 20

🚰 Euro Relais Junior; Token (ER); €2

Info/photos: Keith & Sue Lawrence

ST LARY SOULAN — 141 — E12 — SKI — 65170 — N42°49.348' E000°19.397'

Directions: D19, at Parking du Stade. From north on D929 take 1st exit at roundabout as enter town onto D116. At next roundabout turn left onto D19. Aire 100m on right in car park, opp stadium.

i Ski resort with all necessary facilities. Cable car 500m from Aire. Convenient stop en route to Spain via Bielsa Tunnel. Inspected 2010.

🚐 34; €6/7pm-8am; Collected

🚰 Euro Relais Junior; €2

Info/photos: Keith & Sue Lawrence

PIAU ENGALY — 142 — E12 — SKI — 65170 — N42°47.150' E000°09.467'

Directions: D118, Parking 5 at ski station. From north on D929 turn right onto D118 after Aragnouet, sp 'Piau Engaly'. Follow road up to ski station and Aire is in Parking 5 on right, signed.

i Alt 1855m. Stunning views. Parking free in summer but no services. www.piau-engaly.com Inspected 2010.

🚐 100; €6 in ski season/Jul-Aug; Collected

🚰 Custom; €6 for 4amp elec in ski season

Info/photos: Keith & Sue Lawrence

ARREAU — 143 — E12 — 65240 — N42°54.437' E000°21.549'

Directions: Avenue de la Gare. Turn off D929 into Ave de la Gare, sp 'Volerie: Les Aigles d'Aure', and cross river bridge. Aire in car park on left within 150m.

i Pretty, small village en route to Bielsa Tunnel to Spain. Updated 2014.

🚐 15; €2/night; Collected

🚰 Custom; No drive over drain

Info/photos: Keith & Sue Lawrence

LA MONGIE 1900 STATION — 144 — E12 — SKI — 65200 — N42°54.750' E000°10.733'

Directions: Place Pène Nègre. From Ste Marie de Campan follow D918 to La Mongie ski station. Turn sharp right just before 'Le Choucas' restaurant. Follow road uphill for 500m to Place Pène Nègre. May be signed 'Parking 4' in ski season.

i Lovely views and lots of walking. Cable car to Pic du Midi de Bigorre in summer: €30. Inspected 2010.

🚐 20

🚰 None

Info/photos: Keith & Sue Lawrence

PAYOLLE | 145 | E12 | | 65710 | N42°56.309' E000°17.498'

Directions: D113. From east on D918 turn left in Payolle onto D113, sp 'Complexe Touristique du Lac de Payolle'. After 700m fork right, sp 'Hourquette D'Ancizan'. Aire on left adj to stream. Service Point above parking area at fork in road, signed.

Beautiful location alongside mountain stream in area with unfenced livestock. View of Pic du Midi de Bigorre. Updated 2014.

15

Custom

Info/photos: Keith & Sue Lawrence

STE MARIE DE CAMPAN | 146 | E12 | | 65710 | N42°58.955' E000°13.694'

Directions: D918. Follow D935 from Campan, sp 'Col d'Aspin'. In Ste Marie de Campan turn left onto D918, sp 'Arreau'. Aire 100m on left, signed.

Alt 853m. Aire adj to D918 at base of Col d'Aspin, a popular tourist drive and cycle to 1489m. Ideal stop if 157 full. Inspected 2014.

5; Max 48hrs

Custom

LA MONGIE | 147 | E12 | SKI | 65200 | N42°55.168' E000°11.403'

Directions: Just off D918 between Artigues-Campan and La Mongie. Large gravel parking area. May be signed as 'Parking 5' in ski season.

Alt 1575m. Just below ski resort of La Mongie, with cable car to summit of Pic du Midi de Bigorre with stunning scenery. Inspected 2010.

100

None

Info/photos: Keith & Sue Lawrence

GAVARNIE | 148 | E12 | SKI | 65120 | N42°44.317' W000°01.167'

Directions: D923. From Gavarnie turn onto D923 from D921. Parking on left opp monument in 3km.

Popular walk to Cirque de Gavarnie and waterfalls. Updated 2014.

50; €10 in season; Collected

Custom; In poor state of repair

Photo: motorhomeandaway.co.uk

Photo: Motorhomeandaway.co.uk

BONAC | 149 | F12 | | 09800 | N42°52.527' E000°58.489'

Directions: D4. From St Girons take D618 to Castillon-en-Couserans, then continue on D4 to Bonac. Drive through village and turn left beyond lake. Aire on opp side of lake, signed.

Landscaped commercial Aire by lake; Lovely mountain scenery. Very small village with limited local commerce. Visited 2014.

11; €6/night Sept-Jun; €7/night Jul-Aug; +0.30pp tax; Collected

Custom; 10 unmetered elec points

Info/photos: Jean & Ken Fowler

PIERREFITTE NESTALAS | 150 | E12 | | 65260 | N42°57.572' W000°04.608'

Directions: Rue Victor Hugo. From D921 turn off by the Mairie following signs to 'Aire de Pique-Nique'.

Popular Aire directly adj to foot/cycle path to Cauterets/Lourdes. Updated 2014.

14

Walther; €1

Photo: Carol Weaver

CAUTERETS 1 | 151 | E12 | SKI | 65110 | N42°53.577' W000°06.769'

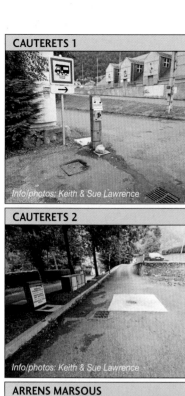

Info/photos: Keith & Sue Lawrence

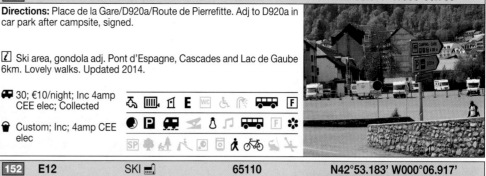

Directions: Place de la Gare/D920a/Route de Pierrefitte. Adj to D920a in car park after campsite, signed.

i Ski area, gondola adj. Pont d'Espagne, Cascades and Lac de Gaube 6km. Lovely walks. Updated 2014.

🚐 30; €10/night; Inc 4amp CEE elec; Collected

🚰 Custom; Inc; 4amp CEE elec

CAUTERETS 2 | 152 | E12 | SKI | 65110 | N42°53.183' W000°06.917'

Info/photos: Keith & Sue Lawrence

Directions: Avenue du Docteur Charles Thierry, off D920a. From north on D920a pass through the town following sp 'Pont d'Espagne'. Aire on left at rear of casino just before leaving town.

i Some shade and quieter than 151. Updated 2014.

🚐 25; €10/night; Collected; Inc CEE elec

🚰 Custom; Inc

ARRENS MARSOUS | 153 | E12 | 65400 | N42°57.483' W000°12.433'

Info/photos: Keith & Sue Lawrence

Directions: D918. Exit the village on D918 towards Argèles-Gazost. Parking area on right, turn right beside La Balaguere building. Aire is signed with a small sign on road edge. Follow road to parking area.

i Pleasant area on edge of village. Small convenience store nearby. Updated 2014.

🚐 10

🚰 Euro Relais Junior; €2

LANNEMEZAN | 154 | E11 | 65300 | N43°07.651' E000°22.859'

Directions: Espace du Nebouzan. Turn off D817 at roundabout onto D939, sp 'Galan'. Follow sp 'Galan' and 'P 200 places' (not truck route sp 'Galan'). As exiting town turn left into car park. After driving through car park turn right, then turn left, signed. Follow road through entrance and behind building.

i Aire located on a terrace behind the sports facility. May feel isolated if alone. Town commerce 5 mins. Market Wed am. Inspected 2014.

🚐 30

🚰 Aire Services; 1 unmetered CEE elec point

ARGELES GAZOST | 155 | E11 | 65400 | N43°00.562' W000°05.129'

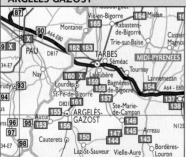

Directions: Turn off D821 at roundabout, sp 'Zone Artisanale' and signed. Turn 1st left and Service Point on right at PIKYCO, signed.

i Service Point only. Inspected 2012.

🚐 None

🚰 Flot Bleu Pacific; €2

SOULOM | 156 | E12 | 65260 | N42°57.350' W000°04.364'

Info/photos: Keith & Sue Lawrence

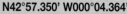

Directions: D921/Avenue des Deux Ponts. From south on D921 Aire on right 700m after roundabout junction with D13. Large rectangular parking area as enter Soulom.

i Pleasant open area with mountain views. Snack bar in corner of car park. Inspected 2010.

🚐 20

🚰 Custom

CAMPAN
157 E11   65710   N43°01.099' E000°10.687'

Directions: D8. From Bagnères de Bigorre follow sp 'Campan' onto D935. In Campan turn left off D935 just before church, signed. Follow road to left and Aire on right. Service Point on left by crucifix and parking on right, signed.

ℹ️ Alt 653m. Aire in the foothills of the Pyrénées. Small farm and its collection of machinery, fodder and cats surround the Aire and give it a quaint feel. Inspected 2014.

🚐 5; Max 48hrs

🚰 Custom; Push tap down hard

BAGNERES DE BIGORRE
158 E11   65200   N43°04.396' E000°09.139'

Directions: Off Rue René Cassin. From north on D935 enter town and turn left at roundabout, sp 'Campan'. After 600m cross river and turn right, signed. Take 1st left, signed, and Aire in parking on right.

ℹ️ This well used Aire is located in a large car park in a semi industrial area. Views of the Pyrénées mountains from all parking areas. Interesting large town with a Basque feel, 6 mins. Inspected 2014.

🚐 30

🚰 Euro Relais Mini

POUZAC
159 E11   65200   N43°04.750' E000°08.482'

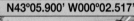

Directions: D935, at Intermarché supermarket. Traveling towards Bagnères de Bigorre from north on D935 the Aire is on the left. Service Point behind fuel station, adj to self-service laundry.

ℹ️ Supermarket and self-service laundry adj. Inspected 2014.

🚐 Poss; Large gravel parking to rear

🚰 Euro Relais Mini; €2

LOURDES
160 E11   65100   N43°05.900' W000°02.517'

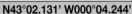

Directions: D97/Blvd du Lapacca. From north on N21 take 1st exit at roundabout onto D914, sp 'Centre Ville'. At traffic lights by railway bridge continue straight on D914. At roundabout cross straight over, staying on D914. Take 3rd turning left into Blvd du Lapacca. Parking on right in 300m by toilets.

ℹ️ This parking is undesignated, but tolerated. All parking in Lourdes is now restricted to day parking. This parking will change. Inspected 2014.

🚐 45; Tolerated

🚰 Toilets; €0.50

AGOS VIDALOS
161 E11   65400   N43°02.131' W000°04.244'

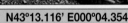

Directions: D921b. Exit D821 and follow sp 'Agos Vidalos'. Aire on right beside Camping Soleil du Pibeste. Enter through PARKNIGHT barrier.

ℹ️ Commercial Aire located in a valley surrounded by Pyrénées mountains. Submitted 2014.

🚐 29; €12/24hrs; CC; Discounts for pass holders

🚰 Euro Relais Junior; Inside barrier; Inc

Photos: Camping-Car-Park.com

TARBES 1
162 E11   65000   N43°13.116' E000°04.354'

Directions: N21. Follow sp 'Toutes Directions'. Service Point just past N21/D935 roundabout opp stadium, signed. Parking: N43°13.282' E000°04.493'. From Service Point turn right, then left at the next two roundabouts. Unrestricted parking under trees on right.

ℹ️ Parking area under trees between park and stadium. Inspected 2014.

🚐 10; Tolerated

🚰 Flot Bleu Euro; CC; €3

TARBES 2 — 163 E11 🏛 65000 N43°14.577' E000°04.080'

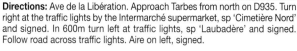

Directions: Ave de la Libération. Approach Tarbes from north on D935. Turn right at the traffic lights by the Intermarché supermarket, sp 'Cimetière Nord' and signed. In 600m turn left at traffic lights, sp 'Laubadère' and signed. Follow road across traffic lights. Aire on left, signed.

ℹ️ Aire adj to garage in a residential area. Local commerce adj. Tarbes centre 25 mins, large park near centre. Inspected 2014.

🚐 20; €10/night inc 5amp elec; €8/night inc water; Collected

🛒 Custom; €5/water+2hrs elec if not staying

MIELAN — 164 E11 🏛 32170 N43°25.994' E000°18.519'

Directions: Rue du Cubet. Approach town on N21 from Mirande. Turn left as enter town, signed. Follow road for 300m and Aire is in car park on left, signed.

ℹ️ Just off N21 but sheltered from road noise. Town with small town commerce and historic covered market 5 mins. Inspected 2014.

🚐 6; Additional parking

🛒 Custom

VIC EN BIGORRE — 165 E11 🏛 65500 N43°23.085' E000°02.956'

Directions: Rue du Stade. From town centre follow sp 'Pau'. After crossing river bridge turn left onto D61, sp 'Montaner' and signed. Turn immediately right, signed, and Aire immediately on right under plane trees, signed.

ℹ️ Parking is possible with care under low plane trees that provide excellent shade on hot summer days. Noisy main road adj. Town centre commerce 5 mins. Inspected 2012.

🚐 6; Under trees

🛒 Custom

MAUBOURGUET — 166 E11 🏢 65700 N43°26.584' E000°02.493'

Directions: D935. Turn off D935 south of town to Super U supermarket. Aire adj to fuel station, signed.

ℹ️ Designated parking at supermarket just off main route. Inspected 2012.

🚐 6

🛒 Flot Bleu Pacific; €2; Flot Bleu Electric; €1/3hrs; 4 CEE elec points

MASSEUBE — 167 E11 🏢 32140 N43°26.566' E000°34.687'

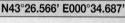

Directions: D929. Exit town to north on D929. At roundabout turn into Super U supermarket car park. Service Point adj to self-service laundry.

ℹ️ Supermarket and self-service laundry adj. Inspected 2014.

🚐 Poss

🛒 Custom

PLAISANCE — 168 E11 🏕 32160 N43°36.491' E000°02.918'

Directions: Place des Arenes. Turn off D946 by river bridge into car park, signed. Opp outdoor swimming pool. Drive behind bull ring and Service Point is on left, signed.

ℹ️ Service Point only. Inspected 2012.

🚐 Max 4hrs, no parking 8pm-6am

🛒 Euro Relais Mini

RISCLE | 169 | E11 | | 32400 | N43°39.697' W000°04.737'

Directions: Rue des Loubines. Turn off D935 at river bridge as exit town to north, signed. Follow road and Service Point is on right and parking is beyond.

i Part of former campsite with partial views over river. May feel isolated if alone. Town with local commerce 5 mins. Inspected 2012.

🚐 6; Grass parking

⛲ Custom

BEAUMARCHES | 170 | E11 | | 32160 | N43°35.243' E000°05.536'

Directions: Off D946. Turn off D3 onto D946, sp 'Beaumarchés'. Turn left, sp 'Beaumarchés Plastiques' and signed. Follow road past plastics company and Aire 2nd turning on left. Signed.

i Peaceful with views over lane to open countryside and vines. 300m to village centre. Inspected 2010.

🚐 5; Grass parking

⛲ Custom

Info/photos: Keith & Sue Lawrence

MIRANDE | 171 | E11 | | 32300 | N43°30.801' E000°24.501'

Directions: Chemin du Batardeau. Turn off N21, sp 'Chalets L'ile du Pont', and follow sp 'L'ile du Pont'. Service Point to right of campsite entrance.

i Campsite adj €15/night. Inspected 2012.

🚐 None

⛲ Custom; Token

NOGARO | 172 | E11 | | 32110 | N43°45.871' W000°01.995'

Directions: Avenue des Sports. From D931 from Eauze turn right just past glider Aerodrome down Avenue des Sports, signed.

i Adj to VIP reception for racing circuit. ALDI 2 mins. Outdoor swimming pool opp. Inspected 2010.

🚐 10

⛲ Flot Bleu Euro; CC

Info/photos: Keith & Sue Lawrence

BARBOTAN LES THERMES | 173 | E10 | | 32150 | N43°56.967' W000°02.600'

Directions: Off D656, at the casino. Turn off D656, sp 'Parking Nocturne Payant' and 'Casino'. Bear left and park in front of casino.

i Large parking area adj to town centre, ideal night stop. For longer stays see 174. Toilets and free WiFi at TO adj. Inspected 2010.

🚐 20; €6/10pm-6am; Collected

⛲ None; See 174

LAC DE L'UBY - Barbotan les Thermes | 174 | E10 | | 32150 | N43°56.150' W000°01.950'

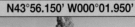

Directions: Lac de l'uby. Must apply for barrier key at TO in Barbotan les Thermes, see 173. From TO turn right onto D656 and continue over roundabout. After 500m turn left, sp 'Lac de l'uby' and signed. After 1.8km turn right onto track to height barriers. Aire in car park beyond.

i TO in Barbotan has key to barrier, €60 deposit. Lovely location. Long elec leads needed for some bays. Insufficient elec points for every bay. Inspected 2010.

🚐 50; €6/night; Collected

⛲ Custom; Inc; CEE elec inc

Info/photos: Keith & Sue Lawrence

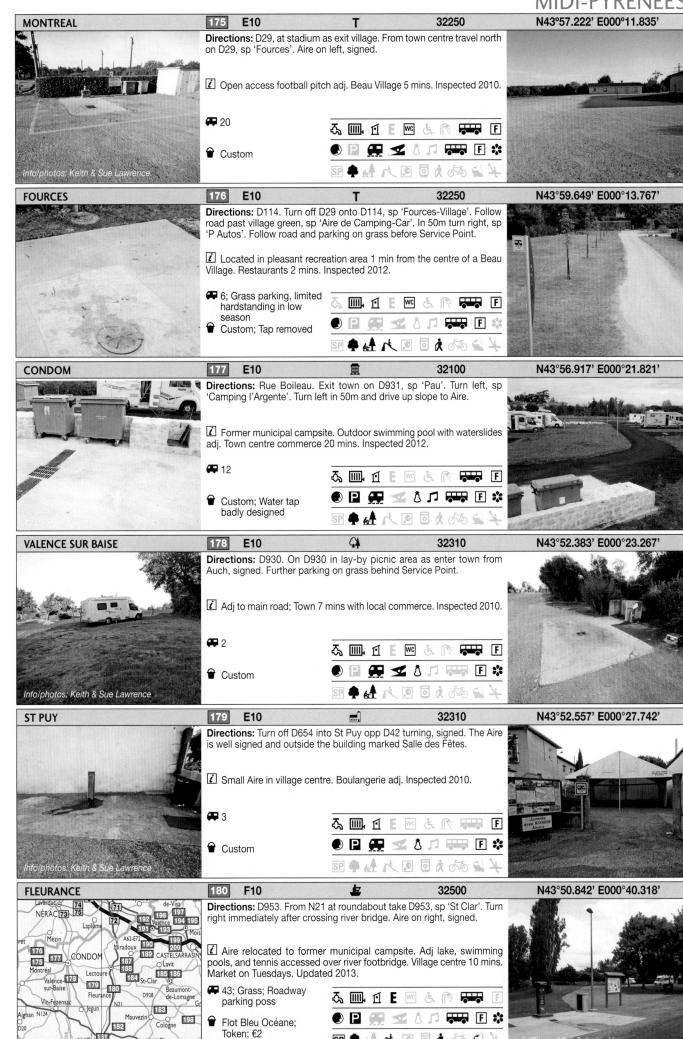

| MONTREAL | 175 | E10 | T | 32250 | N43°57.222' E000°11.835' |

Directions: D29, at stadium as exit village. From town centre travel north on D29, sp 'Fources'. Aire on left, signed.

ℹ️ Open access football pitch adj. Beau Village 5 mins. Inspected 2010.

🚐 20

🔓 Custom

Info/photos: Keith & Sue Lawrence

| FOURCES | 176 | E10 | T | 32250 | N43°59.649' E000°13.767' |

Directions: D114. Turn off D29 onto D114, sp 'Fources-Village'. Follow road past village green, sp 'Aire de Camping-Car'. In 50m turn right, sp 'P Autos'. Follow road and parking on grass before Service Point.

ℹ️ Located in pleasant recreation area 1 min from the centre of a Beau Village. Restaurants 2 mins. Inspected 2012.

🚐 6; Grass parking, limited hardstanding in low season

🔓 Custom; Tap removed

| CONDOM | 177 | E10 | 🏛️ | 32100 | N43°56.917' E000°21.821' |

Directions: Rue Boileau. Exit town on D931, sp 'Pau'. Turn left, sp 'Camping l'Argente'. Turn left in 50m and drive up slope to Aire.

ℹ️ Former municipal campsite. Outdoor swimming pool with waterslides adj. Town centre commerce 20 mins. Inspected 2012.

🚐 12

🔓 Custom; Water tap badly designed

| VALENCE SUR BAISE | 178 | E10 | 🎣 | 32310 | N43°52.383' E000°23.267' |

Directions: D930. On D930 in lay-by picnic area as enter town from Auch, signed. Further parking on grass behind Service Point.

ℹ️ Adj to main road; Town 7 mins with local commerce. Inspected 2010.

🚐 2

🔓 Custom

Info/photos: Keith & Sue Lawrence

| ST PUY | 179 | E10 | 🏛️ | 32310 | N43°52.557' E000°27.742' |

Directions: Turn off D654 into St Puy opp D42 turning, signed. The Aire is well signed and outside the building marked Salle des Fêtes.

ℹ️ Small Aire in village centre. Boulangerie adj. Inspected 2010.

🚐 3

🔓 Custom

Info/photos: Keith & Sue Lawrence

| FLEURANCE | 180 | F10 | ⚓ | 32500 | N43°50.842' E000°40.318' |

Directions: D953. From N21 at roundabout take D953, sp 'St Clar'. Turn right immediately after crossing river bridge. Aire on right, signed.

ℹ️ Aire relocated to former municipal campsite. Adj lake, swimming pools, and tennis accessed over river footbridge. Village centre 10 mins. Market on Tuesdays. Updated 2013.

🚐 43; Grass; Roadway parking poss

🔓 Flot Bleu Océane; Token; €2

Info/Photo: Mick & Jackie Varney

AUCH | 181 | E11 | ⛺ | 32000 | N43°38.192' E000°35.325'

Info/photos: Keith & Sue Lawrence

Directions: Rue du Général de Gaulle. From north on N21 follow sp 'Tarbes'. In town turn left at traffic lights (by pharmacy) into Rue du Général de Gaulle. Aire on right in 400m just before river bridge and adj to Salle de Table Tennis, sp 'Camping' and signed.

ℹ️ Service Point accessible when campsite closed. Inspected 2010.

🚐 3; €4/night; Pay at campsite

🚰 Point Belle Eau

PREIGNAN | 182 | F11 | 🏭 | 32810 | N43°42.748' E000°38.053'

Info/photos: Keith & Sue Lawrence

Directions: Rue Emile Zola. When entering from Auch turn right at 1st roundabout, sp 'Municipal Sports'. Follow road for 1.5km and Aire on right, signed.

ℹ️ Parking limited to the 5 marked bays to left of the car park. Service Point opp. Inspected 2010.

🚐 5

🚰 Custom

SARRANT | 183 | F11 | T | 32120 | N43°46.537' E000°55.679'

Directions: D165. From north on D165 the Aire is on the left as you enter village, signed.

ℹ️ Very pleasant Aire overlooking a large grass area. Small fortified Beau Village with local commerce worth a wander. Inspected 2014.

🚐 15

🚰 Custom

ST CLAR | 184 | F10 | 🌳 | 32380 | N43°53.474' E000°46.375'

Info/photos: Keith & Sue Lawrence

Directions: Leave St Clar on D13 towards Gramont. Aire to east of village on left.

ℹ️ Very nice Aire spaced out amongst fruit trees with good views. Village approx 5 mins. Updated 2013.

🚐 10; Max 24hrs

🚰 Custom

BEAUMONT DE LOMAGNE 1 | 185 | F10 | 🏢 | 82500 | N43°52.824' E000°59.452'

Directions: D3. Enter town on D928 from Larrazet. At the roundabout turn right onto D3, sp 'Centre Ville'. Cross railway track and turn 1st right. Aire on right, signed.

ℹ️ On the edge of town adj to D928 and railway track. Local cars use car park but there should always be space. Town centre 3 mins uphill. Inspected 2014.

🚐 10

🚰 Custom

BEAUMONT DE LOMAGNE 2 | 186 | F10 | 🏢 | 82500 | N43°53.543' E001°00.695'

Directions: D928, at the car wash in the Casino supermarket car park. Aire adj to D928 as enter town from Larrazet in the east.

ℹ️ Supermarket adj. Inspected 2014.

🚐 Poss

🚰 Flot Bleu Euro; CC/Token; €2/20mins

LECTOURE 1

| 187 | F10 | | 32700 | N43°56.078' E000°38.030' |

Directions: Avenue Jacques Descamps. From north on N21 turn right in Lectoure into Avenue Jacques Descamps. Service Point, fuel station, and laundry on left of road, supermarket and main car park on right.

i Laundry (open 24/7) adj to fuel pay kiosk: €8/18kg; €6/8kg inc powder; €1/16kg/12 mins drying. Updated 2012.

Poss

Euro Relais Box

Photo: Janet & John Watts

LECTOURE 2

| 188 | F10 | | 32700 | N43°56.085' E000°37.568' |

Directions: Rue Victor Hugo. Turn off roundabout near town centre into Rue Victor Hugo, signed. One-way and 3.5t. Poss to park in car park 100m on right. Or continue, then turn right at roundabout into Chemin des Amandiers. Poss to park 100m on left: N43°56.158' E000°37.573'.

i Parking in Rue Victor Hugo is convenient for town centre visit, only about 400m. Parking in Chemin des Amandiers is very pleasant. Market Fri in centre. Visited 2012.

10

None; See 187

Info/photos: Janet & John Watts

ST ANTOINE

| 189 | F10 | | 32340 | N44°02.149' E000°50.542' |

Directions: D953. Enter St Antoine from Valance on D953. As enter village turn 1st left, signed. Follow arrows behind stone barns on gravel track. Parking on right, arrowed.

i Aire in a peaceful location behind the village with views of countryside. Local commerce 2 mins in medieval streets. Pilgrims continue the centuries old tradition and pass through the village en route to Santiago. Inspected 2014.

10

Custom

BARDIGUES

| 190 | F10 | | 82340 | N44°02.316' E000°53.551' |

Directions: Between D89 and D11, outside cemetery. Signed off D11, but more easily accessible from D89 as road doesn't go through village. Exit D89 from either direction, sp 'Bardigues'. Aire at top of hill by cemetery. Open unlocked gates to enter.

i Landscaped Aire with rural views in a tranquil village. Local commerce 2 mins uphill. Inspected 2014.

4

Custom; €2

DONZAC

| 191 | F10 | | 82340 | N44°06.855' E000°49.239' |

Directions: D30, at Lac des Sources. From north on D813 turn right onto D30 at Lamagistère, sp 'Donzac' and signed. Cross river and Aire on right at lake, signed.

i Aire at pleasant picnic area with pond and arboretum. Local commerce in village centre, 2 mins. River Garonne 800m. Power station 1.4km. Inspected 2014.

20

Custom; WC down well!

VALENCE D'AGEN

| 192 | F10 | | 82400 | N44°06.342' E000°53.168' |

Directions: Rue des Tanneries. Turn off D813 to the west of town onto D11E, sp ' Centre Ville' and signed. Drive into town and turn right opp covered market, sp 'Mairie' and 'Port Canal'. Turn left, then right, signed. Cross canal and Aire on right.

i Adj to canal but no view. Showers and toilets in former abattoir. Small town commerce 2 mins. Inspected 2012.

20

Aire Services; €4/15 mins water and 2hrs elec; Showers Apr-Oct

MALAUSE | 193 | F10 | | 82200 | N44°05.483' E000°58.402'

Directions: D4. Turn off D813 at the roundabout by the church onto D4, sp 'Boudou'. Turn immediately left into the car park by the church and the Service Point is on the right.

ℹ️ Noisy as just off D830 trucking route. Local commerce adj. 191 (10 mins) a quieter stop. Inspected 2012.

🚐 5

Flot Bleu Océane; Token/30mins

MOISSAC | 194 | F10 | | 82200 | N44°05.994' E001°05.087'

Directions: Promenade Sancert. Turn off D813 at river bridge, sp 'Berges du Tarn' and 'Port-Canal'. Designated parking adj to river by large riverside hotel/restaurant, signed.

ℹ️ Views of river and bridge from some bays. Pleasant riverside park with walk adj. Town commerce 2 mins. Inspected 2014.

🚐 15

Flot Bleu Electric; Token; 4 CEE elec points; €2/24hrs

ST BENOIT (MOISSAC) | 195 | F10 | | 82200 | N44°05.776' E001°05.317'

Directions: D72/Route de Gandalou. Turn off D813 before Moissac at roundabout onto D72, signed. Follow road and Service Point on left, outside campsite, signed.

ℹ️ Service Point only. Inspected 2014.

🚐 None; See 194

Custom

MONTJOI | 196 | F10 | | 82400 | N44°11.868' E000°55.347'

Directions: D46. In village just off D46 opp church, signed.

ℹ️ Recommended off the beaten track stop not far from D813. Pleasant and peaceful, village Aire with rural views. Good walking. Inspected 2012.

🚐 10

Custom

CASTELSAGRAT | 197 | F10 | | 82400 | N44°11.008' E000°56.675'

Directions: Cooperative Agricole. Turn off D953 at the roundabout onto D7, sp 'Castelsagrat'. In 2.5km turn left onto D28, 'Castelsagrat'. At village turn right, sp 'Valance'. Turn left, sp 'Cooperative Agricole'. Turn right and Aire at end of road.

ℹ️ Pleasant Aire on large gravel area with rural views. Idyllic village centre, 2 mins, with charming covered walkways which houses local commerce. Inspected 2014.

🚐 25

Aire Services; Token (3/3)

CADOURS | 198 | F11 | | 31480 | N43°43.368' E001°02.916'

Directions: Chemin d'En Cornac. Exit town to south on D24, sp 'Garac'. At roundabout turn left down small lane, signed. Follow road to right, signed, and Aire on right, signed.

ℹ️ A small, poorly positioned Aire overlooking sports stadium. Suitable for a night halt, but might feel isolated if alone. Town commerce 7 mins. Inspected 2014.

🚐 1 hardstanding; 5 on grass

Custom

ST NICOLAS DE LA GRAVE | 199 | F10 | 82210 | N44°03.828' E001°01.494'

Directions: Rue Bouchotte, off D26. Enter town on D26, D15, or D67 and follow sp 'Centre Ville'. Drive behind church and follow signs to Aire.

ℹ️ Traditional town Aire. Town centre 2 mins with interesting architecture including the former Château Richard Coeur de Lion (Richard Lionheart). Birthplace of Lamothe Cadillac, founder of Detroit, USA; free museum open Jul-Aug. Inspected 2014.

🚐 10

🏠 Euro Relais Mini

CASTELSARRASIN | 200 | F10 | 82100 | N44°02.314' E001°06.136'

Directions: Allee de la Source. Exit E72/A62 Junction 9. Take D813 and follow sp 'Toulouse' onto one way system. Turn right into Rue du Gaz, signed. Take 1st right into Allee de la Source, signed. Aire on left, access via Aire Services barrier.

ℹ️ Aire located in residential streets 5 mins from town centre. Inspected 2012.

🚐 30; €3/24hrs; CC
🏠 Aire Services; Inside barrier; €2.50; Aire Services Electric; €2.50/24hrs; 16 CEE elec points

GRISOLLES | 201 | F10 | 82170 | N43°49.759' E001°17.884'

Directions: Chemin du Canal. Turn off D820 onto D49 at roundabout, sp 'Grisolles' and signed. Cross canal and turn 1st right, signed. Take 2nd left, signed, and Aire is behind Espace Socioculturel, signed.

ℹ️ Aire in a large car park behind social centre. Village centre 2 mins with commerce. Canal 100m for walks and cycling. Inspected 2014.

🚐 10

🏠 Custom

GRENADE | 202 | F11 | 31330 | N43°46.300' E001°17.817'

Directions: Quai de la Garonne. From D17/D29 roundabout follow D17 towards Ondes, signed. Turn left at recycling point, signed. Service Point in front of recycling. Parking: N43°46.103' E001°17.710'. At D17/D29 roundabout turn left onto D2, sp 'Toulouse'. Turn 2nd right, sp 'Salle des Fêtes'. Parking immediately on right.

ℹ️ Market Sat am and adj school can make Service Point access difficult. Parking suitable to visit town centre, 5 mins. Inspected 2014.

🚐 10

🏠 Custom

TOULOUSE | 203 | F11 | 31200 | N43°35.236' E001°29.442'

Directions: Cité de l'Espace. Approach Toulouse from Castres (east) on D826. Cross over A61, sp 'Cité de l'Espace', then turn left, sp 'Cité de l'Espace'. Go straight over the 1st roundabout, then turn right at the next roundabout into Cité de l'Espace parking, signed. Press intercom at barrier for entry.

ℹ️ Gated parking at Cité de l'Espace, a theme park based on outer space. Adult €25. Visited 2013.

🚐 Poss

🏠 None

LA MAGDELAINE SUR TARN | 204 | F10 | 31340 | N43°48.611' E001°32.407'

Directions: Chemin du Lac. Turn off D630 onto D15, sp 'La Magdelaine'. Follow road and at roundabout turn onto D61, sp 'Montjoire'. Follow road around sports facilities then turn right into Chemin du Lac. Follow road and Aire is on left, signed.

ℹ️ Adj to and overlooking leisure lake. Grass parking when dry. Local commerce 4 mins. Short Voie Verte cycle track from D630. Inspected 2012.

🚐 2; Additional grass parking
🏠 Aire Services; CC; €5/30 mins

VILLEMUR SUR TARN | 205 | F10 | 31340 | N43°51.176' E001°29.879'

Directions: Ave du Général Leclerc. Turn off D630 onto D14, sp 'Villemur sur Tarn'. Follow road and Aire adj to D14 before town on right, signed.

ⓘ Adj to main road and sports facilities. Town centre 4 mins. Inspected 2012.

🚐 3; 1 bay obstructed by tree

🚰 Aire Services; CC; €5/30 mins

CASTELNAU DE MONTMIRAL 1 | 206 | G10 | 81140 | N43°58.007' E001°48.163'

Directions: Aire privée Les Miquels. Off D964 between Castelnau de Montmiral and Puycelci. Very clearly sp 'Les Miquels' from both directions.

ⓘ Family run pleasant commercial Aire in rural location at gîte/restaurant. Use of swimming pool inc. Breakfast avail. Castelnau-de-Montmiral is visible and walking distance, 20 mins uphill. Inspected 2014.

🚐 6; €4pp Oct-May; €5pp Jun-Sept; Inc unmetered elec

🚰 Custom

CASTELNAU DE MONTMIRAL 2 | 207 | G10 | T | 81140 | N43°57.954' E001°49.119'

Directions: Turn off D964 at roundabout and follow sp 'P Bus Motorhome' (symbols) along road around outside of town. Parking on gravel partly under trees on left, not signed. These are the largest bays and parking allowed anywhere around the city walls.

ⓘ Unrestricted parking at a Beau Village. Historic hilltop town adj with tourist commerce, pedestrianised central square. Inspected 2014.

🚐 10; No overnight parking Jul-Aug

🚰 Toilets; See 209

LISLE SUR TARN | 208 | G10 | 81310 | N43°51.729' E001°49.106'

Directions: At Lac, off D988. As enter town from Gaillac on D988 turn left at roundabout before lake onto D14b, sp 'Office du Tourisme' and 'Camping Car'. Aire on southeast corner of lake by small pond.

ⓘ Adj pond, no views; BBQ. Town 7 mins; Local commerce. Inspected 2012.

🚐 15

🚰 Custom

GAILLAC | 209 | G10 | T | 81600 | N43°53.977' E001°53.696'

Directions: Parking Rives Thomas in Rue des Silos. From south on D964 follow road into town. At centre follow sp 'P Rives Thomas'. Service Point at bottom of large unrestricted car park on several levels.

ⓘ Gaillac is a pleasant traditional French town with a historic centre, 2 mins up short slope. Town commerce 2 mins. Inspected 2014.

🚐 20

🚰 Custom

MONTAUBAN | 210 | F10 | 82000 | N44°00.435' E001°20.519'

Directions: Rue Clos de Lauzun. Approach Montauban on D958 from west. Go straight over roundabout, sp 'Port-Canal'. In 900m turn right, sp 'Port-Canal'. Go under railway, 3.8m height restriction, and turn left, sp 'Port-Canal'. Take the next left, then follow road through marina. Aire on left, enter through Aire Services barrier.

ⓘ Over landscaped commercial Aire adj to small river marina, no views. The marina is very pleasant with tourist commerce and bike hire. Noisy commercial train track runs adj. Inspected 2014.

🚐 10; €6/24hrs inc elec; CC

🚰 Aire Services; Inside barrier

NEGREPELISSE | 211 | F10 | 🏛 | 82800 | N44°04.442' E001°31.582'

Directions: D958. Approach from east. At the D115/D65/D958 roundabout take D958 following sp 'Centre Ville' and signed. Turn left at next roundabout continuing on D958, signed. Entrance to Aire 200m on right between hedges, adj to D958, signed.

i Aire just 1 min from centre. Small town commerce includes a laundry. Market Wed am. Walking and cycle paths and picnic areas along river Aveyron. Inspected 2014.

🚐 6

🔧 Custom

LAUZERTE 1 | 212 | F10 | 🏕 | 82110 | N44°16.026' E001°08.447'

Directions: From Montcuq travel south on D653 which becomes D953. At D953/D2 junction go straight on into small lane. Turn immediately right into picnic area adj to junction. Service Point signed on toilets.

i Aire in shaded picnic area with BBQ area adj to river with views. Road noise from main route but no truck parking. 1.7km to Lauzerte, a Beau Village. Inspected 2014.

🚐 10

🔧 Custom

LAUZERTE 2 | 213 | F10 | T | 82110 | N44°15.251' E001°08.192'

Directions: From Montcuq travel south on D653 which becomes D953. At D953/D2 junction turn onto D2, sp 'Lauzerte-Centre'. Follow road into village, then follow to left, signed. Aire on right in small car park, signed.

i Aire in small Beau Village. No real overnight parking as car park too small and sloping, see 212. Market Wed am. Inspected 2014.

🚐 3; No parking Wed am (market)

🔧 Custom

MONTCUQ | 214 | F10 | 🏢 | 46800 | N44°20.452' E001°12.151'

Directions: D653. Aire in roadside lay-by adj to D653, signed.

i Ideal lunch stop to visit Montcuq. At night the parking is shared with trucks. Road gets noisy from trucks around 6am. 212 (15 mins) is a quieter stop. Inspected 2014.

🚐 20

🔧 Euro Relais Junior; Token (ER); €2

ROQUECOR | 215 | F10 | 🏕🏠 | 82150 | N44°19.393' E000°56.651'

Directions: On D656 from Tournon d'Agenais take 1st turning on left by two plane trees, sp 'Roquecor'. Drive into village and Aire on left, signed.

i Rural views; Village 2 mins with local commerce and convenience store. Inspected 2010.

🚐 6; 10m bays

🔧 Custom

Info/photos: Keith & Sue Lawrence

MAUROUX | 216 | F10 | 🏕🏠 | 46700 | N44°27.099' E001°02.870'

Directions: Aire de Repos 'La Garenne', D5. Approx 180m south of village in woodland, but hardcore roads and parking spots.

i Local commerce in village. Pleasant woodland Aire. Covered BBQ and kitchen area open Apr-Oct. Inspected 2010.

🚐 10; Apr-Oct

🔧 Custom

Info/photos: Keith & Sue Lawrence

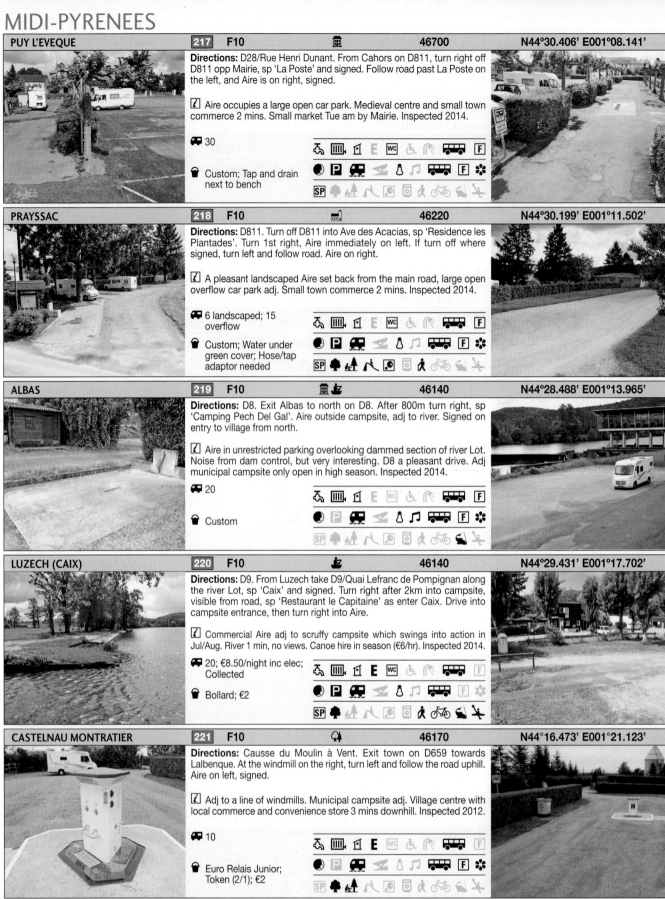

| PUY L'EVEQUE | 217 | F10 | 🏛 | 46700 | N44°30.406' E001°08.141' |

Directions: D28/Rue Henri Dunant. From Cahors on D811, turn right off D811 opp Mairie, sp 'La Poste' and signed. Follow road past La Poste on the left, and Aire is on right, signed.

ℹ️ Aire occupies a large open car park. Medieval centre and small town commerce 2 mins. Small market Tue am by Mairie. Inspected 2014.

🚐 30

Custom; Tap and drain next to bench

| PRAYSSAC | 218 | F10 | | 46220 | N44°30.199' E001°11.502' |

Directions: D811. Turn off D811 into Ave des Acacias, sp 'Residence les Plantades'. Turn 1st right, Aire immediately on left. If turn off where signed, turn left and follow road. Aire on right.

ℹ️ A pleasant landscaped Aire set back from the main road, large open overflow car park adj. Small town commerce 2 mins. Inspected 2014.

🚐 6 landscaped; 15 overflow

Custom; Water under green cover; Hose/tap adaptor needed

| ALBAS | 219 | F10 | 🏛⚓ | 46140 | N44°28.488' E001°13.965' |

Directions: D8. Exit Albas to north on D8. After 800m turn right, sp 'Camping Pech Del Gal'. Aire outside campsite, adj to river. Signed on entry to village from north.

ℹ️ Aire in unrestricted parking overlooking dammed section of river Lot. Noise from dam control, but very interesting. D8 a pleasant drive. Adj municipal campsite only open in high season. Inspected 2014.

🚐 20

Custom

| LUZECH (CAIX) | 220 | F10 | ⚓ | 46140 | N44°29.431' E001°17.702' |

Directions: D9. From Luzech take D9/Quai Lefranc de Pompignan along the river Lot, sp 'Caix' and signed. Turn right after 2km into campsite, visible from road, sp 'Restaurant le Capitaine' as enter Caix. Drive into campsite entrance, then turn right into Aire.

ℹ️ Commercial Aire adj to scruffy campsite which swings into action in Jul/Aug. River 1 min, no views. Canoe hire in season (€6/hr). Inspected 2014.

🚐 20; €8.50/night inc elec; Collected

Bollard; €2

| CASTELNAU MONTRATIER | 221 | F10 | | 46170 | N44°16.473' E001°21.123' |

Directions: Causse du Moulin à Vent. Exit town on D659 towards Lalbenque. At the windmill on the right, turn left and follow the road uphill. Aire on left, signed.

ℹ️ Adj to a line of windmills. Municipal campsite adj. Village centre with local commerce and convenience store 3 mins downhill. Inspected 2012.

🚐 10

Euro Relais Junior; Token (2/1); €2

| LABASTIDE MARNHAC | 222 | F10 | | 46090 | N44°23.163' E001°23.856' |

Directions: Between D7 and D67. Turn off D7 onto D67, sp 'l'Hospitalet' and signed. Turn immediately left, signed, then 1st right. Aire on left.

ℹ️ Adj to picnic area and tennis courts. Bar/restaurant adj. On popular GR65 walking route. Inspected 2014.

🚐 10

Custom

CAHORS 1 | 223 | F10 | | 46000 | N44°26.420' E001°26.468'

Directions: Parking St Georges. Approach Cahors from south on D820. Follow sp 'Cahors-Centre' onto D620. Turn off to P St Georges at roundabout before river bridge, signed. Service Point and 3 bays on right, signed. Additional parking: N44°26.324' E001°26.464'.

ℹ️ Limited riverside parking, additional riverside parking tolerated between Service Point and additional parking. Historic town adj with amazing pedestrianised medieval river bridge, 5 mins. Inspected 2014.

🚐 3 riverside; 40 in overflow; Max 86hrs

🔧 Custom

CAHORS 2 | 224 | F10 | | 46000 | N44°27.689' E001°27.033'

Directions: Avenue Édouard Herriot. From Cahors centre follow D911, sp 'Rodez'. 70m after Total fuel station turn left into Rue Jean Racine. Aire at Intermarché at end of road, currently in car wash on left side of car park, signed.

ℹ️ Poss being moved to new location. Token available from supermarket, free when spending over €20 in shop, not on fuel. Inspected 2014.

🚐 Poss

🔧 Custom; Token; €2

ARCAMBAL | 225 | F10 | | 46090 | N44°27.412' E001°30.966'

Directions: D8. At Arcambal centre turn onto D8 at traffic lights, sp 'St Cirq Lapopie'. Aire immediately on right behind Mairie.

ℹ️ Aire located in village centre just off D911. Boules court and park adj. Water tap by hairdressers. Inspected 2014.

🚐 10

🔧 Euro Relais Junior; Token (ER); €2

VERS | 226 | F10 | | 46090 | N44°29.131' E001°33.302'

Directions: Off D662. From St Géry on D662 turn left on entering village, sp 'Camping'. For parking turn right at tennis courts, signed. Service Point: N44°29.175' E001°33.391'. Go past tennis courts down gravel track.

ℹ️ Pleasant location at old station with access to toilets and a warm shower. Picnic park adj. Local and tourist commerce inc restaurant with river views. Market Thur am. Inspected 2014.

🚐 10; €5/night; Collected

🔧 Custom

ST GERY | 227 | G10 | | 46330 | N44°28.702' E001°34.895'

Directions: D662. Adj to D662 in village centre, signed.

ℹ️ Pleasant location just off village centre with local commerce. Miniature train and museum 2 mins. No river access. Inspected 2014.

🚐 30

🔧 Custom

CABRERETS | 228 | G10 | | 46330 | N44°30.463' E001°39.736'

Directions: D41. Follow D41 north of the village. Service Point outside Camping Familial Cantal.

ℹ️ Service Point only. Adj to basic riverside campsite set into gorge. €3.50 pitch, €2.80pp, €2.50 elec. Inspected 2012.

🚐 None

🔧 Custom; Apr-Oct

BOUZIES — 229 — G10 — 46330 — N44°28.993' E001°38.716'

Directions: D40. Turn off D662 onto 10t weight and 2.3m (wheelbase) width restricted bridge to D40, sp 'Bouziers'. Turn left and left again. Service Point in car park on left. Overnight car park to right adj to river. To avoid bridge approach from St-Cirq-Lapopie.

i Adj to river park. Partial views through trees to river. Canoe hire adj. D662, a pleasant river drive under rocky overhangs and tunnels. Inspected 2014.

🚐 15

🔧 Euro Relais Box; Token (ER)

ST CIRQ LAPOPIE 1 — 230 — G10 — T — 46330 — N44°27.864' E001°39.810'

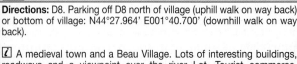

Directions: D8. Parking off D8 north of village (uphill walk on way back) or bottom of village: N44°27.964' E001°40.700' (downhill walk on way back).

i A medieval town and a Beau Village. Lots of interesting buildings, roadways and a viewpoint over the river Lot. Tourist commerce. Inspected 2014.

🚐 40; €3; Pay at machine; 9am-9pm only

🔧 None; See 231

ST CIRQ LAPOPIE 2 — 231 — G10 — 46330 — N44°28.233' E001°40.830'

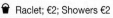

Directions: La Plage. Turn off D662 at roundabout in Tour de Faure onto D181, sp 'St Cirq Lapopie' and signed, and cross river Lot and go straight onto D8. After 150m turn right, sp 'Parking de la Plage'. At river, Service Point and shaded bays to right, open parking to left.

i Aire adj to river Lot in riverside park with views through trees to river. Canoe hire in season (€5/hr). St Cirq Lapopie a must see, see 230. Inspected 2014.

🚐 50; €7; Collected

🔧 Raclet; €2; Showers €2

CAJARC — 232 — G10 — 46160 — N44°29.075' E001°50.744'

Directions: Avenue de la Gare. Follow ring road around town turning at D117/D17 roundabout onto D17, sp 'Figeac'. Turn right immediately, sp 'P la Gare' and signed. Aire 50m, signed.

i Aire adj to old train station, now a youth centre. Town commerce 1 min. Inspected 2014.

🚐 10

🔧 Custom; €1

PRADINES — 233 — F10 — 46090 — N44°27.762' E001°25.242'

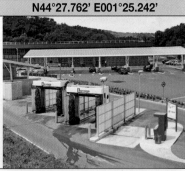

Directions: D8. Follow D820 south towards Cahors. Cross river and turn 1st right, sp 'D8' and 'Luzech'. At roundabout turn right onto D8, sp 'Cahors'. At next roundabout turn right into L'Auto fuel station. Service Point is directly on left next to car wash, to access drive behind car wash.

i Service Point only. Can pre-pay for fuel in store. Inspected 2014.

🚐 None

🔧 Flot Bleu

CATUS ★ — 234 — F9 — 46150 — N44°33.346' E001°20.344'

Directions: Off D6. In Catus at the D6/D5 junction by the old market turn onto D6, sp 'Cahors'. Turn left before river bridge, signed, and follow road along river through car park. Service Point on right.

i Aire full of French charm 2 mins from small town commerce. Small market Tue am on adj street, locals park at Aire but still accessible. Inspected 2014.

🚐 10

🔧 Custom

Photo: Tim Gibbs & Jane Wells

DEGAGNAC | 235 | F9 | | 46340 | N44°40.073' E001°18.565'

Directions: D6. From north on D6 turn left by the tennis courts towards the leisure lake. Parking is in this car park, signed. Service Point: N44°39.971' E001°18.910'. Exit parking to left and turn left in 250m onto D2, sp 'St Germain'. Take 1st left to Service Point.

ℹ️ Parking is in a large gravel car park overlooking the leisure lake. Service Point is in the village, park here to shop in the village before retiring back to the lake. Inspected 2014.

🚐 20

⚲ Euro Relais Box; Token (ER)

GOURDON | 236 | F9 | | 46300 | N44°44.067' E001°23.116'

Directions: Place du Foirail. Follow one-way system in town, sp 'Figeac' or 'Rodez' and signed. After passing the church on the right, turn right, sp 'Quartier du Foirail'. Follow signs through car park and down slope to Aire on right.

ℹ️ Pleasant landscaped Aire on edge of attractive hilltop town. Restaurant adj. Town centre 5 mins. Inspected 2014.

🚐 8

⚲ Custom; €1; 8 12amp elec points; €1/1.5hrs

CAYLUS | 237 | G10 | | 82160 | N44°14.022' E001°46.282'

Directions: D19. On D19 as exit Caylus towards St Antonin. On left opp Maison du Patrimoine, signed.

ℹ️ Adj to main road; Opp pond; BBQ; Table tennis. Pleasant place. Service Point old with surrounding concrete breaking up. Inspected 2010.

🚐 20

⚲ Custom

St Cirq Lapopie

Sarrant

Bourcefranc le Chapus

POITOU

Le Chateau d'Oleron

| MAULEON | **1** D6 | 🏛🏃 | 79700 | N46°55.070' W000°45.133' |

Directions: Rue de la Bachelette. Follow sp 'Niort' south out of town on D744. Turn right up lane after exiting town, sp 'Complexe Sportif' and signed. Follow lane into housing estate until reach sports fields. Aire signed on left.

ℹ️ Swimming pool with waterslide adj. Sports field adj. Town 20 mins. Inspected 2010.

🚐 5, Max 48hrs

⛲ Custom

| ST AMAND SUR SEVRE 1 | **2** D6 | 🏃🏨 | 79700 | N46°52.154' W000°47.998' |

Directions: Rue Fontaine, off D154. Located directly on C56.

ℹ️ Village 2 mins. Riverside 2 mins. Inspected 2010.

🚐 5; Max 48hrs; Reinforced grass parking

⛲ Custom

| ST AMAND SUR SEVRE 2 | **3** D6 | 🎣 | 79700 | N46°53.033' W000°49.546' |

Directions: C2. Sp 'Bar Moulin de Chaligny' from road. Located on C2, between St Amand-s-Sèvre and Treize-Vents. 2.5km from D34 junction.

ℹ️ Commercial Aire at bar/restaurant surrounded by fields located at beautiful riverside spot. Inspected 2010.

🚐 10; €5/night; Collected; Grass parking

⛲ Custom; €3; Unmetered elec available

| BRESSUIRE | **4** E6 | 🏛 | 79300 | N46°50.670' W000°29.489' |

Directions: Place Labate. Follow D938ter from Thouars and drive straight on into town. Turn right at 2nd roundabout, sp 'Voultegon', and Aire on right in 100m.

ℹ️ Numerous commerce in town. Parking St Jacques unrestricted: N46°50.221' W000°29.660'. Updated 2013.

🚐 30; Max 24hrs

⛲ Custom; Water tap by urinal

| ST MAURICE LA FOUGEREUSE | **5** E6 | 🏨 | 79150 | N47°01.974' W000°30.509' |

Directions: Espace de la rivière Juliot. Turn off D748 in La Fougereuse onto D161, sp 'St Maurice'. In St Maurice turn right into car park, opp D33 junction, sp 'Espace de la rivière Juliot'.

ℹ️ Aire adj to pleasant village pond and park. Local commerce 2 mins. Inspected 2012.

🚐 4

⛲ Custom; 2 unmetered CEE elec points in toilet

| BOISME | **6** E6 | ⛵ | 79300 | N46°46.655' W000°26.007' |

Directions: Rue des Essarts. From north on D139. In Boisme turn left onto D135, sp 'Chiche' and signed. Follow road around lake and Aire is in the car park at the far end of the lake, signed.

ℹ️ Aire adj to pleasant lake and park. Walk around lake to local commerce in village centre, 5 mins. Inspected 2012.

🚐 5

⛲ Custom

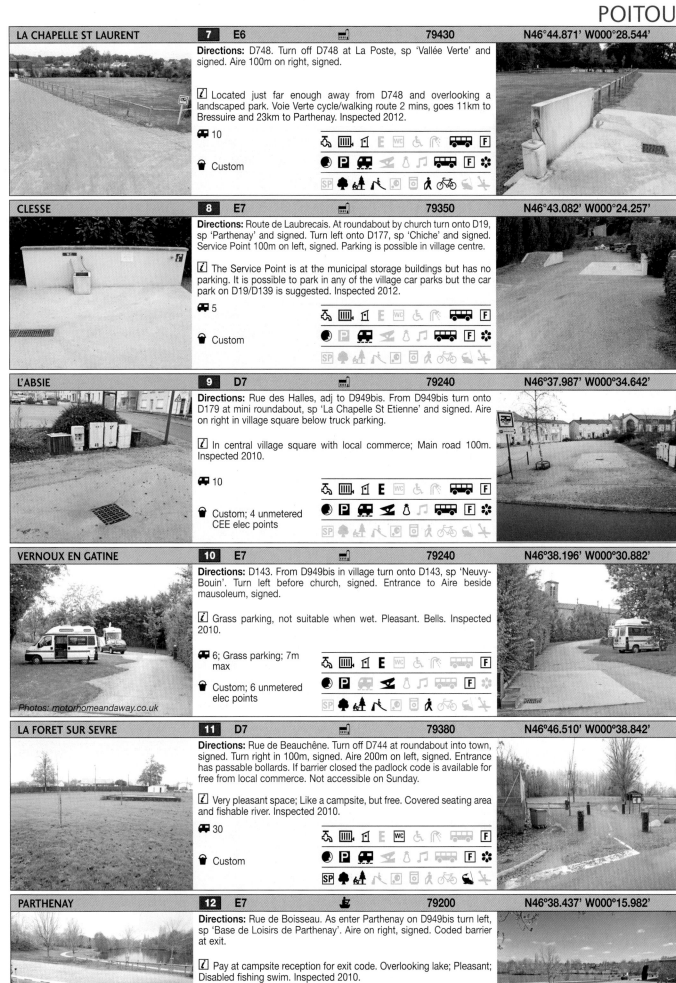

LA CHAPELLE ST LAURENT — 7 — E6 — 79430 — N46°44.871' W000°28.544'

Directions: D748. Turn off D748 at La Poste, sp 'Vallée Verte' and signed. Aire 100m on right, signed.

i Located just far enough away from D748 and overlooking a landscaped park. Voie Verte cycle/walking route 2 mins, goes 11km to Bressuire and 23km to Parthenay. Inspected 2012.

🚐 10

Custom

CLESSE — 8 — E7 — 79350 — N46°43.082' W000°24.257'

Directions: Route de Laubrecais. At roundabout by church turn onto D19, sp 'Parthenay' and signed. Turn left onto D177, sp 'Chiche' and signed. Service Point 100m on left, signed. Parking is possible in village centre.

i The Service Point is at the municipal storage buildings but has no parking. It is possible to park in any of the village car parks but the car park on D19/D139 is suggested. Inspected 2012.

🚐 5

Custom

L'ABSIE — 9 — D7 — 79240 — N46°37.987' W000°34.642'

Directions: Rue des Halles, adj to D949bis. From D949bis turn onto D179 at mini roundabout, sp 'La Chapelle St Etienne' and signed. Aire on right in village square below truck parking.

i In central village square with local commerce; Main road 100m. Inspected 2010.

🚐 10

Custom; 4 unmetered CEE elec points

VERNOUX EN GATINE — 10 — E7 — 79240 — N46°38.196' W000°30.882'

Directions: D143. From D949bis in village turn onto D143, sp 'Neuvy-Bouin'. Turn left before church, signed. Entrance to Aire beside mausoleum, signed.

i Grass parking, not suitable when wet. Pleasant. Bells. Inspected 2010.

🚐 6; Grass parking; 7m max

Custom; 6 unmetered elec points

Photos: *motorhomeandaway.co.uk*

LA FORET SUR SEVRE — 11 — D7 — 79380 — N46°46.510' W000°38.842'

Directions: Rue de Beauchêne. Turn off D744 at roundabout into town, signed. Turn right in 100m, signed. Aire 200m on left, signed. Entrance has passable bollards. If barrier closed the padlock code is available for free from local commerce. Not accessible on Sunday.

i Very pleasant space; Like a campsite, but free. Covered seating area and fishable river. Inspected 2010.

🚐 30

Custom

PARTHENAY — 12 — E7 — 79200 — N46°38.437' W000°15.982'

Directions: Rue de Boisseau. As enter Parthenay on D949bis turn left, sp 'Base de Loisirs de Parthenay'. Aire on right, signed. Coded barrier at exit.

i Pay at campsite reception for exit code. Overlooking lake; Pleasant; Disabled fishing swim. Inspected 2010.

🚐 10; €6-€8/24hrs; Pay at campsite; Apr-Oct

Custom; Inside barrier

POITOU

VASLES

13 E7  79340 N46°34.402' W000°01.394'

Directions: Rue de la Cité. From D59 follow sp 'Parking' and 'Espace Mouton Village', both with sheep heads. Aire at large parking area near stadium, between D59 and D121.

ℹ️ At Sheep Village with lots of items celebraiting sheep; Entry to park €9pp in high season. www.moutonvillage.fr. Inspected 2010.

🚐 20

🏠 Custom

MENIGOUTE

14 E7  79340 N46°29.887' W000°03.450'

Directions: Rue des Vignes. From the village centre take D21, sp 'La Pagerie'. Turn immediately right into Rue des Vignes. Drive past SPA supermarket and Aire is on left.

ℹ️ In centre of small town adj to open access sports field. SPA supermarket adj. Inspected 2012.

🚐 7

🏠 Custom

AYRON

15 E7  86190 N46°39.382' E000°05.286'

Directions: Off N149/E62, outside campsite at Etang de Fleix. Take N149/E62 east out of town. Pass barn and in 650m turn off N149, sp 'Camping' and 'Le VIP Peche'. Service Point outside the campsite, parking on right before campsite, signed.

ℹ️ Fishing lake and bait shop 2 mins; No view of lake from parking and no swimming in lake. Inspected 2010.

🚐 30; €3/8pm-8am; Pay at bar

🏠 Flot Bleu Pacific; €4

ST LOUP LAMAIRE

16 E6  79600 N46°47.128' W000°09.850'

Directions: From the west follow D46. Cross the river and after passing under the railway bridge turn off D46 onto D121, sp 'Clemille' and signed. The Aire is on the left in 100m.

ℹ️ Large grass parking on outskirts of pretty village with local commerce. Near river, but no views. Inspected 2010.

🚐 30; Grass parking

🏠 Custom

AIRVAULT

17 E6  79600 N46°49.506' W000°08.578'

Directions: Rue de la Gare. Approach from south on D46 and at the roundabout take D725E, sp 'St Varent'. Turn right across railway track onto D27, sp 'Airvault' and signed. At the next roundabout go almost right around and enter car park on left, signed. Aire at far end. Do not drive through village centre is narrow, 3.5t weight and 2.2m height restricted in places.

ℹ️ Located just off the edge of town in a peaceful car park. Market Saturday. Inspected 2012.

🚐 5

🏠 Custom; Self-cleaning toilet

ST VARENT

18 E6  79330 N46°53.857' W000°14.490'

Directions: D28. Turn off D28 beside Collage F Villon, signed. The Aire is outside the municipal campsite.

ℹ️ Parking next to sports field/centre. Supermarket 150m. Inspected 2010.

🚐 10; Max 48hrs

🏠 Custom

THOUARS | 19 | E6 | 🏛 | 79100 | N46°58.579' W000°12.702'

Directions: Place Ferdinand Buisson, outside old city wall. Turn off D938 at roundabout, sp 'Centre Ville'. Follow sp 'Centre Ville'. After passing the cemetery follow sp 'Autre Directions', then 'P Cemetery'. Aire 200m on left, signed.

ℹ️ Pleasant location against town ramparts; Motorhomes restricted to small part of car park. Town 3 mins uphill. Updated 2013.

🚐 8; 7m narrow bays

🔌 Campsite bollard

ST MARTIN DE SANZAY | 20 | E6 | ⚓ | 79290 | N47°05.529' W000°12.082'

Directions: La Zona de Loisirs La Ballastière, at Etang la Ballastière. Head north from St Martin de Sanzay on D158, following sp 'Etang la Ballastière' and signed. The Aire is at the leisure lake. Barrier entry; Access via card from local commerce, €20 deposit.

ℹ️ Leisure lake adj, but no views; Holiday place in summer, looks abandonded in winter. Inspected 2010.

🚐 50; €5/night; Collected; Grass parking

🔌 Custom; Inside barrier; Inc

OIRON | 21 | E6 | 🏛 | 79100 | N46°56.875' W000°04.954'

Directions: Salle Polyvalente, in village centre. Follow D64/D145 south, sp 'Salle Polyvalente' and signed. Parking is in Salle Polyvalente car park. Service Point is behind a building.

ℹ️ Pretty village with local commerce 2 mins. Château de Oiron in village, entry €7pp; www.oiron.fr. Inspected 2012.

🚐 10

🔌 Custom; Token

LOUDUN | 22 | E6 | 🏢 | 86200 | N47°01.108' E000°05.313'

Directions: Avenue de Ouagadougou. Enter Loudun from north on D147 and follow sp 'Z.I. Nord', then 'Ave de Ouagadougou'. Follow this road for 650m and the Service Point is at the car wash on the right.

ℹ️ In urban industrial estate at car wash; 1 car wash suitable for motorhomes. Inspected 2013.

🚐 4

🔌 Flot Bleu Standard Plus (Yellow); €2

CHALAIS | 23 | E6 | 🏢 | 86200 | N46°57.510' E000°06.279'

Directions: D347. Turn off D347, sp 'Aire de Repos de la Briande'. Aire at rear, signed. Be aware, two private Aires signed at Mirebeau, €5/night: N46°46.842' E000°11.638'. Agressais is a France Passion site. Inspected 2012.

ℹ️ This landscaped Aire with hedged bays is to rear of a roadside lay-by just off the noisy D347 main route. Café and local products for sale. Inspected 2013.

🚐 8

🔌 Custom; 4 unmetered 10amp CEE elec points

MIREBEAU | 24 | E6 | 🏛 | 86110 | N46°46.836' E000°11.639'

Directions: 14 Rue du Pas Martin. Turn off D347 at Mirebeau onto D15, signed. Drive through village and turn right onto Rue du Pas Martin. Turn into gate before no entry sign.

ℹ️ Owner lives next door, will collect money and sells regional products. Troglodyte cave nearby. Walled town of Mirebeau 1km. Visited 2013.

🚐 8; €7/night; Collected

🔌 Custom; Inside gate; Inc

Info/photos: V Whalley/Edward Wood

POITIERS - FUTUROSCOPE
25 | E7 | 86360 | N46°39.813' E000°22.094'

Directions: Avenue du Futuroscope, at Futuroscope off D20d. Aire adj to roundabout junction of D910 and D20d. Aire on right after automated barrier off smaller D20d roundabout.

i Futuroscope adj, www.futuroscope.com. Inspected 2013.

100; 1st hr free; €7/24hrs; Pay at machine
Euro Relais Maxi; €4

VENDEUVRE DU POITOU
26 | E7 | 86380 | N46°43.466' E000°17.922'

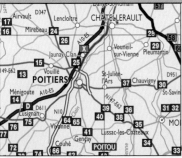

Directions: D757. Adj to D757 as exit village to south towards Poitiers. Designated parking on left adj to park, signed.

i Adj to l'Aire des Marais, a streamside picnic area. Pleasant location with some road noise. Inspected 2013.

2

Tap and Continental toilet only

LOUDUN
27 | E6 | 86200 | N47°00.815' E000°04.679'

Directions: Place de la Porte Saint Nicolas. Turn off D347 to the north west of town.

i Adj to local commerce. Short walk from a medieval town gate and a pleasant town centre. Inspected 2013.

Max 30 mins; Max 3.5t; Lots of local parking

Aires Services; €2

LA ROCHE POSAY
28 | F7 | 86270 | N46°47.630' E000°47.874'

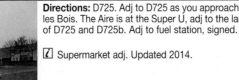

Directions: D725. Adj to D725 as you approach the town from Coussay les Bois. The Aire is at the Super U, adj to the large roundabout junction of D725 and D725b. Adj to fuel station, signed.

i Supermarket adj. Updated 2014.

Poss

Aire Services; 1 unmetered elec point

VICQ SUR GARTEMPE
29 | F7 | 86260 | N46°43.447' E000°51.719'

Directions: D5. Exit village on D5, sp 'La Roche Posay'. Aire is 300m on the left, signed.

i Large parking area by boules courts. Could have road noise. Village with local commerce 2 mins. Visited 2012.

10

Custom

Info/Photo: John Cox

ST SAVIN
30 | F7 | 86310 | N46°34.154' E000°52.110'

Directions: Rue du 8 Mai 1945. Turn off D951 in the town centre onto D11, sp 'Nalliers' and 'Camping-Kayak'. Follow D11, sp 'Camping-Kayak', then turn right into the campsite. Take the 1st left and the Service Point is behind the conifer bush.

i Service Point only at small, well kept municipal campsite surrounding water mill; Campsite charges €2/motorhome plus €2pp/night. Inspected 2014.

Poss, when campsite closed

Custom; €2; Pay at reception

MONTMORILLON 1 — 31 — F7 — 86500 — N46°25.129' E000°51.285'

Directions: D727/Route to Lussac-les-Châteaux, at E'Leclerc. At the Centre Commercial by the lavage (car wash).

ℹ Supermarket adj. Norauto adj. Inspected 2014.

🚐 10

🚰 Euro Relais Junior; 1 unmetered elec point

MONTMORILLON 2 — 32 — F7 — 86500 — N46°25.389' E000°52.069'

Directions: Rue Léon Dardant. Approach on D54 from south. At traffic lights turn left onto D727, sp 'Chauvigny'. Cross river bridge and turn right at traffic lights. Turn right again, then left, then right, signed. Some of these turns are narrow due to parked cars, large motorhome owners advised to inspect before attempting.

ℹ Parking adj to river, but no view. Town with numerous commerce 3 mins. Inspected 2012.

🚐 10; Max 24hrs

🚰 Urba Flux Tall; CC

LATHUS ST REMY — 33 — F7 — 86390 — N46°19.974' E000°57.431'

Directions: D10. Exit town on D10, sp 'St Rémy' and signed. Aire 150m on right, signed.

ℹ Pleasant Aire with hedged bays backing onto very basic camping field. Leisure pond opp is popular fishing spot. Local commerce 2 mins. Inspected 2014.

🚐 8; Hedged bays

🚰 Euro Relais Junior; 1 unmetered elec point (long lead needed)

MOULISMES — 34 — F7 — 86500 — N46°19.985' E000°48.578'

Directions: N147. Exit town on N147 north towards Lussac les Châteaux. Aire at end of town on right, sp 'Aire de Repos'; not in the truck stop in town. Service Point by toilets. Slightly more peaceful parking poss 200m away overlooking pond.

ℹ Very popular overnight stop. N147 is a very busy, noisy truck route. Suggest Bussière Poitevine 245 (Limo) as an alternative. Grass parking very boggy in wet weather. Snack bar in summer. Inspected 2014.

🚐 80

🚰 Custom; Token (ER); €3

LUSSAC LES CHATEAUX — 35 — F7 — 86320 — N46°24.165' E000°43.534'

Directions: Place de l'Amitie, D11/Rue du Quai. In main town centre parking, sp 'Aire de Repos' off N147/E62.

ℹ Service Point adj to main town square with numerous undesignated parking. Noise from N147. Town commerce and TO adj. Inspected 2014.

🚐 30; In centre square; No parking Thurs pm (Boules)/Sat am (Market)

🚰 Custom

CIVAUX — 36 — F7 — 86320 — N46°26.949' E000°40.001'

Directions: Route de la Necropole. Turn off D749 onto D83, sp 'Civaux'. Cross river bridge and turn right at the roundabout towards the power station, sp 'Morthemer'. Turn into the parking at the power station and follow road to right. The Service Point is outside the campsite entrance.

ℹ Service Point outside campsite adj to leisure facilities at the base of the power station. Swimming pool, bowling and crocodile land all have unrestricted parking. Inspected 2014.

🚐 30

🚰 Custom

CHAUVIGNY — 37 — F7 — T — 86300 — N46°34.386' E000°38.812'

Directions: Rue Porte Chevreau. Turn off D951/D749 roundabout, sp 'Camping'. Turn left onto D2, sp 'Camping' and signed. Follow road up hill, then turn left, signed. Go straight on at stop junction, then turn left, signed. Aire 50m on left beside cemetery, signed.

i Adj to medieval city with narrow streets to wander around. Campsite: N46°34.255' E000°39.206' has Service Point inside and charges motorhomes €6/night. Updated 2014.

🚐 10

🚻 Toilets only

LHOMMAIZE — 38 — F7 — 86410 — N46°26.101' E000°35.811'

Directions: Adj to junction of N147/E62 and D8. From N147 turn onto D8 in village towards Verrières. Aire on right behind Mairie, sp 'Aire de Repos'.

i River adj. Town quite pleasant. Sheltered from road. Inspected 2010.

🚐 2

🚻 Custom; 2 unmetered elec points

FLEURE — 39 — E7 — 86340 — N46°28.708' E000°31.406'

Directions: D2, northeast of village. Parking at the church. Aire signed from N147.

i Church adj; Village 2 mins. Inspected 2010.

🚐 5

🚻 None

NIEUIL L'ESPOIR — 40 — E7 — 86340 — N46°29.113' E000°27.268'

Directions: D1/Allée du Champ de Foire. On D1 as enter village from north, sp 'Camping Car'. Signed from N147.

i Very pleasant spot. Town 2 mins. Updated 2014.

🚐 10; Reinforced grass parking

🚻 Euro Relais Junior; Token

GENCAY — 41 — E7 — 86160 — N46°22.384' E000°24.373'

Directions: Rue de Civray. Follow D741 towards Civray through town. Turn left just before D1 turning to Brion. Service Point to left, in car park under trees.

i Aire located in large car park at foot of water tower. Low trees. Road noise from D741. Local commerce 2 mins. Inspected 2012.

🚐 10; Under/between trees

🚻 Aire Services; Token; Toilets and water at water tower

USSON DU POITOU — 42 — E7 — 86350 — N46°16.540' E000°31.590'

Directions: D727. Turn off D741 onto D727, sp 'Usson du Poitou'. Aire on right opp cemetery, signed.

i Aire adj to pleasant riverside picnic area, no views, in large open car park. Local commerce 2 mins. Inspected 2014.

🚐 15

🚻 Euro Relais Junior; 1 unmetered elec point

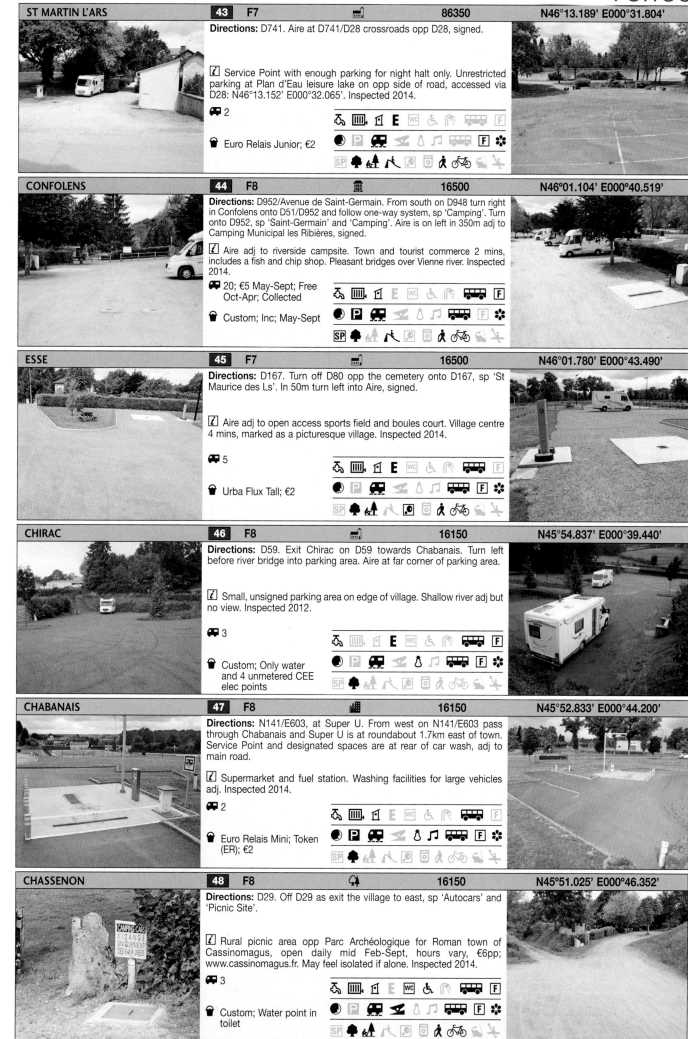

ST MARTIN L'ARS | 43 | F7 | 86350 | N46°13.189' E000°31.804'

Directions: D741. Aire at D741/D28 crossroads opp D28, signed.

ℹ Service Point with enough parking for night halt only. Unrestricted parking at Plan d'Eau leisure lake on opp side of road, accessed via D28: N46°13.152' E000°32.065'. Inspected 2014.

🚐 2

🚰 Euro Relais Junior; €2

CONFOLENS | 44 | F8 | 16500 | N46°01.104' E000°40.519'

Directions: D952/Avenue de Saint-Germain. From south on D948 turn right in Confolens onto D51/D952 and follow one-way system, sp 'Camping'. Turn onto D952, sp 'Saint-Germain' and 'Camping'. Aire is on left in 350m adj to Camping Municipal les Ribières, signed.

ℹ Aire adj to riverside campsite. Town and tourist commerce 2 mins, includes a fish and chip shop. Pleasant bridges over Vienne river. Inspected 2014.

🚐 20; €5 May-Sept; Free Oct-Apr; Collected

🚰 Custom; Inc; May-Sept

ESSE | 45 | F7 | 16500 | N46°01.780' E000°43.490'

Directions: D167. Turn off D80 opp the cemetery onto D167, sp 'St Maurice des Ls'. In 50m turn left into Aire, signed.

ℹ Aire adj to open access sports field and boules court. Village centre 4 mins, marked as a picturesque village. Inspected 2014.

🚐 5

🚰 Urba Flux Tall; €2

CHIRAC | 46 | F8 | 16150 | N45°54.837' E000°39.440'

Directions: D59. Exit Chirac on D59 towards Chabanais. Turn left before river bridge into parking area. Aire at far corner of parking area.

ℹ Small, unsigned parking area on edge of village. Shallow river adj but no view. Inspected 2012.

🚐 3

🚰 Custom; Only water and 4 unmetered CEE elec points

CHABANAIS | 47 | F8 | 16150 | N45°52.833' E000°44.200'

Directions: N141/E603, at Super U. From west on N141/E603 pass through Chabanais and Super U is at roundabout 1.7km east of town. Service Point and designated spaces are at rear of car wash, adj to main road.

ℹ Supermarket and fuel station. Washing facilities for large vehicles adj. Inspected 2014.

🚐 2

🚰 Euro Relais Mini; Token (ER); €2

CHASSENON | 48 | F8 | 16150 | N45°51.025' E000°46.352'

Directions: D29. Off D29 as exit the village to east, sp 'Autocars' and 'Picnic Site'.

ℹ Rural picnic area opp Parc Archéologique for Roman town of Cassinomagus, open daily mid Feb-Sept, hours vary, €6pp; www.cassinomagus.fr. May feel isolated if alone. Inspected 2014.

🚐 3

🚰 Custom; Water point in toilet

ST QUENTIN SUR CHARENTE (PRESSIGNAC) ✦ `49` F8   16150   N45°49.633' E000°41.287'

Directions: Lac de Lavaud. From St Quentin-sur-Charente follow D161, sp 'Pressignac' and 'Lac de Lavaud'. In 1.6km turn right onto D214, sp 'Lac de Lavaud'. Aire at end of road, signed.

ℹ️ Lovely location with reservoir views from entire car park. Slipway for non motorised boats adj. Footpaths across adj dam and around lake parkland. Isolated if alone, `51` better winter stop. Inspected 2014.

🚐 10; Max 72hrs

🛢️ Custom; 4 unmetered elec points; Apr-Oct

HAVE YOU VISITED AN AIRE?   GPS co-ordinates in this guide are protected by copyright law

Visit www.all-the-aires.co.uk/submissions.shtml
to upload your updates and photos.

Submit updates
- Amendments
- New Aires
- Not changed

ℹ️ Directions and description.

🚐 Number of parking spaces; Cost per night; Time limit

🛢️ Service Point type and details; Payment type; Cost

Take at least 5 digital photos showing
- Signs
- Service Point
- Parking
- Overview
- Amenities

LESIGNAC DURAND `51` F8   16310   N45°48.700' E000°38.283'

Directions: Off D52. Turn off D52 in village centre at the local shop, sp 'P' and signed. Drive past the vintage, but active, fuel pumps to the Aire.

ℹ️ In pleasant village which overlooks Lac de Mas Chaban, partial views from Aire. Numerous walks and activities around the reservoir. Small village with local commerce adj. Inspected 2014.

🚐 6; Max 72hrs

🛢️ Custom; 6 unmetered elec points; Apr-Oct

MASSIGNAC `52` F8   16310   N45°46.786' E000°39.304'

Directions: Off D163. In village centre turn onto D163 at church, sp 'Challains'. Turn immediately right beside church for Service Point, adj to Mairie, and small parking area. Additional parking next right in picnic area at rear of church: N45°46.805' E000°39.340'.

ℹ️ Charming rural village with local commerce and TO. Inspected 2014.

🚐 5; Large motorhomes depending on parked cars

🛢️ Custom; Lift blue cover for WC emptying; 2 unmetered CEE elec points

---

CHATAIN BESSON `53` E8   16220   N45°40.983' E000°33.579'

Directions: D699. Clearly signed off D699 in Chatain Besson, opp La Poste and Salle Municipale.

ℹ️ In village. Toilets avail at rear of Salle Municipale across road with picnic area. Inspected 2010.

🚐 10

🛢️ Euro Relais Mini

Info/photos: Keith & Sue Lawrence

LA ROCHEFOUCAULD `54` E8   16110   N45°45.053' E000°23.275'

Directions: Route de Limoges. Exit town towards N141, sp 'Taponnat'. Aire 400m on left outside E'Leclerc Drive supermarket, opp fuel station, signed. There are two E'Leclerc supermarkets in town, the other bans motorhomes.

ℹ️ Designated parking against noisy main route. All other parking has 2.5m height restriction. Supermarket adj. Inspected 2014.

🚐 7

🛢️ Euro Relais Box; €2

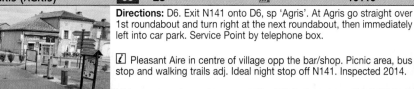

| LE PONT D'AGRIS (AGRIS) | **55** | E8 | | 16110 | N45°47.168' E000°20.343' |

Directions: D6. Exit N141 onto D6, sp 'Agris'. At Agris go straight over 1st roundabout and turn right at the next roundabout, then immediately left into car park. Service Point by telephone box.

ℹ️ Pleasant Aire in centre of village opp the bar/shop. Picnic area, bus stop and walking trails adj. Ideal night stop off N141. Inspected 2014.

🚐 5

🏧 Urba Flux Tall; €3

| CELLEFROUIN | **56** | E8 | | 16260 | N45°53.655' E000°23.179' |

Directions: Off D739, to west of village. As enter village from Mansle (west) on D739 turn off, sp 'Aire de Loisirs', 'Pique-nique' and signed. Turn right before tennis court and Service Point at toilet block in far corner of car park.

ℹ️ Very pleasant large Aire adj to leisure area, inc picnic area within park, marked walks and an open access tennis court. Local commerce in village, 2 mins. Inspected 2014.

🚐 30

🏧 Custom; Service Point behind toilets

| CHASSENEUIL SUR BONNIEURE | **57** | E8 | | 16260 | N45°49.493' E000°27.100' |

Directions: Rue du 8 Mai 1945. Turn off D942 onto D27, sp 'Montemboeuf' and signed. Follow road past the central square, then turn left just before the Intermarché, signed. Service Point near toilets.

ℹ️ In centre of town just off main route through. Small town commerce adj. Market Wed. Inspected 2014.

🚐 4

🏧 Euro Relais Junior; €2

| ROUMAZIERES LOUBERT | **58** | F8 | | 16270 | N45°52.962' E000°34.351' |

Directions: N141. Aire on N141 as exit towards La Rochefoucauld. Turn off opp D169 turning to Chantrezac, sp 'Aire de Détente' and signed.

ℹ️ Trucking hell! Aire adj to very noisy main road in a small parking area. Suitable to service but **60** much better overnight stop. Snack bar in adj picnic area. Inspected 2014.

🚐 10

🏧 Euro Relais Junior; 2 unmetered CEE elec points

| ST LAURENT DE CERIS | **59** | F8 | | 16450 | N45°56.446' E000°28.984' |

Directions: In village centre. Service Point opp Champ de Foire and next to children's play area. The Service Point is difficult to access. The Champ de Foire parking is across the road and has 4 unmetered CEE elec points.

ℹ️ Local commerce and convenience store 1 min. Inspected 2012.

🚐 7; Parking adj to Service Point impractical, park opp

🏧 Custom; Diff access; 7 unmetered CEE elec points

| VERTEUIL SUR CHARENTE | **60** | E8 | | 16510 | N45°58.788' E000°14.122' |

Directions: Rue de la Fontaine, off D26. Follow sp 'Aire de Détente' through town; narrow access through town.

ℹ️ Pretty village with château, park, and river 1 min; Pleasant spot. Local commerce 2 mins. Inspected 2013.

🚐 10; Max 48hrs

🏧 Custom; 4 elec points €2/24hrs; See Mairie

CHARROUX | 61 | E7 | T | 86250 | N46°08.573' E000°24.411'

Directions: D148/Route de Limoges. From east on D148 at roundabout do not follow ring road to right but take 3rd exit towards village centre on old D148. Aire on left in 1.2km, signed. 200m before tower.

ℹ️ Interesting abbey ruins and Beau Village 220m. Plenty of local commerce. Tokens available from local commerce. Inspected 2010.

🚐 15

Aire Services; Token (3/3); €2

LIZANT | 62 | E7 | | 86400 | N46°05.165' E000°16.697'

Directions: D104. In centre of Lizant at the D107/D104 junction around the war memorial turn off, sp 'P'. Turn right into car park in 50m, signed.

ℹ️ Pretty rural village and park with picnic area and stream adj. Walking and cycle routes. Visited 2013.

🚐 8

Euro Relais Junior

Info: Richard Hall. Library photo

ROMAGNE | 63 | E7 | | 86700 | N46°16.123' E000°18.247'

Directions: Espace Detente. From church take D25, sp 'Brux'. Then turn left on D27, sp 'Civray' and signed. Go straight on, sp 'St Romain' and signed. Aire on right at the sports facilities, signed.

ℹ️ Landscaped Aire at sports facilities. Pleasant well maintained area located 2 mins from village centre with local commerce. Inspected 2012.

🚐 6; Max 72hrs

Custom; 6 CEE 5amp elec points

VIVONNE | 64 | E7 | | 86370 | N46°25.553' E000°15.773'

Directions: Avenue de la Plage. Turn off D4, main route through, in village centre into parking area, sp 'Office de Tourisme'. Aire at far side of car park next to TO, signed.

ℹ️ Local commerce and TO adj. Interesting town with numerous waterways and sports. Inspected 2013.

🚐 3

Aire Services; €2

CHATEAU LARCHER | 65 | E7 | | 86160 | N46°24.869' E000°18.938'

Directions: Off D88. Turn off D88, sp 'Camping' and 'Stade'. Aire at sports ground. Gate has digital lock, code from TO.

ℹ️ At sports ground. River adj. Nice walk through sports ground to castle and village. Pleasant spot. Updated 2014.

🚐 10; €4/24hrs inc elec; Collected; Mar-Oct

Custom; €3

Photo: Keith & Patricia Dyer

Photo: Sid Thomas

COUHE | 66 | E7 | | 86700 | N46°17.907' E000°10.705'

Directions: Rue de Bel-Air/D26. Turn off D2 onto D26/Rue de Bel-Air at covered market. Drive through parking area and take 2nd turning on left into larger parking area. Service Point on left by toilet.

ℹ️ Views. Town commerce and lovely covered market 2 mins. Very convenient to N10. Inspected 2013.

🚐 5; In designated bays

Custom

CHAUNAY | 67 | E7 | 86510 | N46°12.356' E000°09.823'

Directions: D25/Grande Rue. Turn off D25 in centre into car park, signed. Aire are rear of car park, behind the toilets and the school, signed.

ℹ️ Local commerce adj. Lots of space in car park. Inspected 2013.

🚐 5

🔌 Urba Flux; 7 unmetered elec points

SAUZE VAUSSAIS | 68 | E7 | 79190 | N46°08.123' E000°06.399'

Directions: Place des Halles in main town square. Follow sp 'Office de Tourisme'. Aire in back corner by Sapeurs Pompiers (Fire Station).

ℹ️ In town square. TO adj. Inspected 2010.

🚐 10

🔌 Flot Bleu Océane; Token for elec only

Info/photos: Keith & Sue Lawrence

LONDIGNY | 69 | E7 | 16700 | N46°05.010' E000°08.102'

Directions: Place de l'Eglise. From D26 turn into Londigny, then turn left, sp 'Place de l'Eglise'. The Aire is at the church.

ℹ️ Rural; No facilities in village. Private château 500m. Bells 3 times/day. Trees obstruct some parking. Inspected 2013.

🚐 5; Max 48hrs

🔌 Custom; 1 unmetered elec point; Mar-Oct

CHEF BOUTONNE | 70 | E7 | 79110 | N46°06.607' W000°04.626'

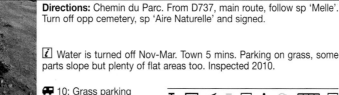

Directions: Chemin du Parc. From D737, main route, follow sp 'Melle'. Turn off opp cemetery, sp 'Aire Naturelle' and signed.

ℹ️ Water is turned off Nov-Mar. Town 5 mins. Parking on grass, some parts slope but plenty of flat areas too. Inspected 2010.

🚐 10; Grass parking

🔌 Custom

Info/photos: Keith & Sue Lawrence

MELLE | 71 | E7 | 79500 | N46°13.907' W000°08.643'

Directions: Rue de la Croix Casselin, outside municipal campsite. Turn off D737 and follow sp 'Camping'. Service Point outside campsite. Parking available in town, follow sp 'Parking du Jardin': N46°13.361'W000°08.394'.

ℹ️ Service Point only. Campsite adj. Updated 2014.

🚐 In town

🔌 Custom

CHEY | 72 | E7 | 79120 | N46°18.246' W000°02.980'

Directions: From D950, main route, turn off near church by boulangerie, signed. Aire behind boulangerie, signed.

ℹ️ Village with local commerce 1 min. Updated 2014.

🚐 4

🔌 Custom

POITOU

LEZAY
73 E7   79120   N46°15.884' W000°00.685'

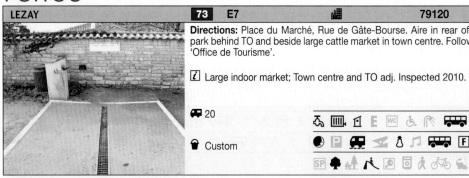

Directions: Place du Marché, Rue de Gâte-Bourse. Aire in rear of car park behind TO and beside large cattle market in town centre. Follow sp 'Office de Tourisme'.

i Large indoor market; Town centre and TO adj. Inspected 2010.

🚐 20

⚱ Custom

ROM
74 E7   79120   N46°17.463' E000°06.850'

Directions: D14, adj to river by bridge. Signed.

i River adj; Basketball court; Poss bar/restaurant in summer. War graves in adj cemetery. Updated 2014.

🚐 10

⚱ Custom; By building at far end

ROUILLE
75 E7   86480   N46°25.247' E000°02.247'

Directions: D611. Turn off D611 in town centre into 3.5t weight restricted car park opp church, signed. Service Point on right before Sapeurs Pompiers (fire station).

i Large parking area adj to very noisy road. Local commerce adj. Inspected 2012.

🚐 7

⚱ Custom

PAMPROUX
76 E7   79800   N46°23.770' W000°03.506'

Directions: D329/Rue de la Cueille. Turn off D5 or D5e to west of village centre, sp 'D329' and 'Fomperron'.

i Pleasant village centre with good selection of local commerce 2 mins; Rural views. Inspected 2012.

🚐 3; 12m bays

⚱ Flot Bleu Océane; €2

LA MOTHE ST HERAY
77 E7   79800   N46°21.589' W000°07.083'

Directions: D5/Rue du Pont l'Abbe. At junction between D737/D5 as enter village. Signed on building.

i Village 4 mins; Adj to busy main road; Washing sinks. Inspected 2010.

🚐 3

⚱ Flot Bleu Fontaine; €1

CELLES SUR BELLE
78 E7   79370   N46°15.754' W000°12.494'

Directions: Rue des Halles. Follow D948, main road, then turn off, signed. Drive down cobbled streets past church and TO. Turn left at bottom of hill opp impressive gates.

i TO and town 2 mins. Abbey adj with gardens and buildings. Goats cheese made locally. Motorbike museum at abbey. Updated 2014.

🚐 20

⚱ Custom; Water opp disposal

MONTIGNE | 79 | E7 | 🏨 | 79370 | N46°12.752' W000°14.337'

Directions: D103. Exit the village on the D103 towards Perigne. Aire on right, signed. Steep access into the Aire from road and may be difficult for larger motorhomes.

ℹ️ This Aire is in a pleasant spot amongst mature trees making it feel like a picnic area. Service Point consists of a tap and drain, water turned off Sept 2014. Suggest **78** instead. Updated 2014.

🚐 10; Grass parking

🛢️ Custom

Info/photos: Janet & John Watts

MOUGON | 80 | E7 | 🏢 | 79370 | N46°17.574' W000°17.700'

Directions: Rue René Gaillard. Turn off D948, sp 'Mougon Ouest', and take 1st right at greenhouses, sp 'Melle'. The Service Point is in the fuel station of the SPAR supermarket.

ℹ️ In commercial area in front of Spar supermarket and car wash area. Updated 2014.

🚐 Poss in village centre

🛢️ Custom

LA CRECHE | 81 | E7 | 🏛️🏃 | 79260 | N46°21.621' W000°18.389'

Directions: D7/D182 roundabout, at Stade Georges André Groussard. Sp 'Aire de Repos' and 'Camping Car' from N11 and in town. Aire on north edge of town, sp 'D7 Cherveux

ℹ️ At sports park with stream. Town centre 3 mins. Updated 2014.

🚐 10; Max 48hrs

🛢️ Flot Bleu Fontaine

NIORT | 82 | E7 | 🏛️ | 79000 | N46°19.763' W000°27.870'

Directions: Rue de Bessac, on northwest side of town centre. Enter town from west on D148/D648 following sp 'Centre Ville'. Travel south towards centre and turn left at 4th roundabout onto Blvd Main. Turn right at next roundabout and turn close left onto Rue de Bessac which is one-way. Aire in car park on right.

ℹ️ Popular Aire. River adj and can walk directly into town over bridges from Aire. Updated 2014.

🚐 15; €7.50/24hrs inc unmetered elec; Collected; Max 7 days; Must park in designated bays

🛢️ Euro Relais Junior

COULONGES SUR L'AUTIZE | 83 | D7 | 🏛️ | 79160 | N46°28.812' W000°35.629'

Directions: D744. Aire adj to D744, sp 'Aire de Repos' and signed. Large motorhomes may struggle to turn around, assess before entering.

ℹ️ Adj to busy and noisy main road. Small park adj. Town centre with small town commerce 4 mins. Inspected 2012.

🚐 2; Limited additional parking

🛢️ Custom; 4 unmetered CEE elec points

MAGNE | 84 | E7 | 🏢 | 79460 | N46°18.963' W000°33.404'

Directions: D9, at the Super U. Turn off D1 onto D9 into Magné. Aire just off large roundabout to west of town, adj to fuel station but accessible from other side.

ℹ️ Supermarket adj. Updated 2014.

🚐 Poss

🛢️ Euro Relais Junior; €2

Info/photos: Janet & John Watts

COULON | 85 | D7 | 79510 | N46°19.244' W000°35.464'

Directions: D123. Enter town on D1. Go across river and turn left at crossroads. Aire adj to D123 as exit village to west in large, open field, signed. Enter through barrier.

ℹ️ In area known as 'Green Venice'. Village centre 2 mins. Updated 2014.

🚐 80; €7.50/24hrs; CC; Apr-Oct; Grass parking

🚻 Aire Services; Inside barrier; Inc; 2 unmetered elec points

Info/photos: Janet & John Watts

MAUZE SUR LE MIGNON | 86 | D7 | 79210 | N46°11.990' W000°40.857'

Directions: Rue du Port, off Rte de Saint-Hilaire/D101. Aire across river from D101 on edge of town, sp 'Camping'. Outside campsite, but in different area.

ℹ️ Aire adj to campsite and elegant 19th century canal port. Village with local commerce 5 mins. Updated 2014.

🚐 10

🚻 Flot Bleu Pacific; Token; €3

LA LAIGNE | 87 | D7 | 17170 | N46°12.782' W000°45.226'

Directions: D114. Adj to D114 as exit village towards Noirt on right, signed.

ℹ️ Service Point in popular truck parking area. Inspected 2012.

🚐 5

🚻 Flot Bleu Océane; €2

LA RONDE | 88 | D7 | 17170 | N46°18.306' W000°48.294'

Directions: D116/Rue du Port. Follow D116 north from village and Aire is 500m on left at the Aire de Repos, signed.

ℹ️ Grass area adj to dyke. Located in area known as 'Green Venice'. Inspected 2010.

🚐 10; Grass parking

🚻 Flot Bleu Océane; €2

ARCAIS | 89 | D7 | 79210 | N46°17.786' W000°41.249'

Directions: D102. Just off D102 in car park, signed. Located on the east edge of the village. Entrance via barrier.

ℹ️ In 'Green Venice', a popular tourist destination. Updated 2013.

🚐 40; €6/night; CC; Apr-Oct; Grass parking

🚻 Custom; Outside barrier

Photos: Janet & John Watts

TAUGON | 90 | D7 | 17170 | N46°18.363' W000°50.156'

Directions: D109. Adj to D109 in front of cemetery as exit village towards St Jean de Liversay.

ℹ️ Service Point with limited parking adj. Updated 2014.

🚐 Poss

🚻 Flot Bleu Océane; €2

MARANS 1 — 91 — D7 — 17230 — N46°18.759' W000°59.895'

Directions: Quai du 11 Novembre, at the port. Turn off D105, sp 'ZI du Port'. Follow sp 'ZI du Port' and the Service Point is against a building. Motorhomes are banned from car park nearest to town. Exit town as entered to avoid narrow streets.

i Adj to river with sailing boats, restaurants, etc. Town 5 mins. Inspected 2014.

🚐 None; See 92

⛲ Custom

MARANS 2 — 92 — D7 — 17230 — N46°18.773' W000°59.529'

Directions: N137, at Super U supermarket. As exit town to north on N137 turn into Super U supermarket. Service Point is at the edge of the car park opp car wash, not in the fuel station.

i Supermarket adj. Inspected 2014.

🚐 Poss

⛲ Euro Relais Mini; €2

ST JEAN DE LIVERSAY — 93 — D7 — 17170 — N46°16.200' W000°52.349'

Directions: Rue St-Jean. In village turn off D109, sp 'St Cyr du Doret'. Service Point immediately on right. It is difficult to turn around to return to D109. From Service Point turn right past church, into 3.5t restricted road. Follow road past Mairie and parking is on right: N46°16.217' W000°52.540'.

i Over engineering makes it difficult to exit Service Point. Parking adj to sports facilities. Local commerce 1 min. Updated 2014.

🚐 5

⛲ Flot Bleu Océane; Token

HAVE YOU VISITED AN AIRE? | GPS co-ordinates in this guide are protected by copyright law

Submit updates
- Amendments
- New Aires
- Not changed

Visit www.all-the-aires.co.uk/submissions.shtml to upload your updates and photos.

i Directions and description.

🚐 Number of parking spaces; Cost per night; Time limit
⛲ Service Point type and details; Payment type; Cost

Take at least 5 digital photos showing
- Signs
- Service Point
- Parking
- Overview
- Amenities

ESNANDES — 95 — D7 — 17137 — N46°15.167' W001°07.200'

Directions: Rue de l'Ocean. Turn off D105 onto Rue de l'Ocean. The Service Point is in 400m on the right outside camping Les Misottes.

i Service Point only. Inspected 2014.

🚐 None

⛲ Raclet; Token; €1.50

RIVEDOUX PLAGE (ILE DE RE) — 96 — D7 — 17940 — N46°09.590' W001°15.978'

Directions: Camping Municipal Le Platin. As enter Rivedoux Plage turn off the D201/D735 roundabout, sp 'Camping Municipal' and signed. Aire in 20m adj to campsite, signed. Enter through barrier.

i The only Aire on the island overlooking the sea, 7 bays with excellent views. Local commerce 2 mins. Inspected 2014.

🚐 17; 45 mins free; €6/24hrs Nov-Mar; €14/24hrs Apr-Jun; €17/24hrs Jul-Aug; €13/24hrs Sept-Oct; Inc elec Apr-Sept; CC
⛲ SOS; Inside barrier; Token; €3

ST MARTIN DE RE — 97 — D7 — 17410 — N46°11.955' W001°21.905'

Directions: Rue du Rampart. From south on D735 turn into St Martin de Re at roundabout, sp 'St Martin' and 'Camping Municipal'. After driving through city wall turn left, sp 'Camping Municipal'. Follow one-way road, then turn right into Aire. Enter through barrier.

ℹ️ Fortified town with interesting ramparts; Easy walk to town with picturesque port; Cycling all around island. Inspected 2014.

🚐 17; €11/24hrs; CC; Max 72hrs; 8m bays

🚰 Custom; Inside barrier

LES PORTES EN RE 1 — 98 — D7 — 17880 — N46°13.756' W001°29.001'

Directions: D101/Route du Fier. Follow D101 through Les Portes-en-Ré. When road reaches coast it turns sharply to the south. Aire at the end of the road near the sea.

ℹ️ Parking 20m from beach, no view. Inspected 2014.

🚐 7; €10/24hrs; Pay at machine; 10m bays

🚰 SOS

LES PORTES EN RE 2 — 99 — D7 — 17880 — N46°14.534' W001°32.524'

Directions: D101. Follow D101 west from Les Portes-en-Ré. Day parking area in 3km adj to D101. Service Point outside campsite: N46°14.902' W001°29.569'.

ℹ️ Large, unrestricted parking area adj to beach, no views. Service Point in poor state of repair, see **98**. Inspected 2014.

🚐 20 (day parking); Poss day parking near Service Point

🚰 SOS (Not working)

GPS Co-ordinates for SatNav

The GPS Co-ordinates published in this guide were taken onsite by our inspectors. We consider them a valuable and unique asset and at the time of publishing have decided not to publish them as electronic files for use on navigation devices. You have permission to type in the co-ordinates of an Aire you intend to visit but not to store or share them. For the security of our copyright:

- **Do not compile them into lists**

- **Do not publish, share or reproduce them anywhere in any format**

ST CLEMENT DES BALEINES — 101 — D7 — 17590 — N46°13.662' W001°32.787'

Directions: Rue de la Forêt. From south on D735 drive past St Clements des Baleines, then turn left, signed. Drive straight on, then when straight on is no longer possible turn left. Follow road and Aire on right, signed. Enter through Aire Services bollard.

ℹ️ This is a large open Aire which is a complete sun trap. The island is popular with cyclists and there are numerous flat cycle paths across the island. Inspected 2014.

🚐 40; €11/24hrs; €18/48hrs; Inc unmetered elec; CC; Max 48hrs

🚰 Euro Relais Junior; Inside barrier; Token; €2

LA ROCHELLE 1 — 102 — D7 — 17000 — N46°09.959' W001°09.255'

Directions: Esplanade des Parcs, Parc Charruyer. Turn off N237 onto D104 into town. Stay on main road going straight across all junctions and roundabouts. After 3rd roundabout turn right, sp 'Gaston Neveur' and 'Parking'. Designated parking starts from Gaston Neveur building.

ℹ️ 10 mins walk or cycle to interesting town centre through park. Market Fri. Town parking bans motorhomes. Inspected 2014.

🚐 24; 7m bays; Must park within lines of designated bays or face €35 fine

🚰 Custom

LA ROCHELLE 2 | 103 | D7 | | 17000 | N46°09.134' W001°08.390'

Directions: Rue des Jars, on south side of railway station. Accessible from D937 ring road. Sp 'P+R Vieux Port' through town. Enter through barrier. GPS taken at entry to large parking complex.

i Motorhome parking on either grass or gravel. Frequent P&R bus to town centre inc in price, except Sun. No access 8pm-7am, closed Sun Oct-May. Inspected 2014.

50; €10.50/24hrs; CC

Aire Services; Inside barrier; Inc

LA ROCHELLE 3 | 104 | D7 | | 17000 | N46°09.060' W001°09.491'

Directions: Avenue Michel Crépeau. Follow sp 'Les Minimes', then 'Camping'. Service Point in small lay-by on main road opp Camping Le Soleil, signed.

i Service Point only. All local parking bans motorhomes. Inspected 2014.

None; See 102, 103 or 105

Custom

LA ROCHELLE 4 | 105 | D7 | | 17000 | N46°08.641' W001°10.301'

Directions: Quai du Lazaret. Follow sp 'Les Minimes', then 'Port des Minimes'. Follow road to end and designated parking in car park along back edge, closest to boats, signed.

i Popular designated parking between a marina and the sea. Views of masts. Local commerce 2 mins (motorhomes banned from this car park). Must park in designated bays or face a €35 fine. Inspected 2014.

31; Must park in designated bays

None; See 103

AYTRE (ANGOULINS) | 106 | D7 | | 17690 | N46°06.778' W001°07.381'

Directions: Route de la Plage. Exit Angoulins following sp 'Aytre Plage'. After crossing railway track turn left and follow road. Drive through restricted car parks and turn right. Follow road to Service Point (eventually). Parking is straight on over 3.5t weight restricted bridge, signed.

i Pleasant Aire in remote location adj to enclosed bay of sand and stone. No views from official parking, but good views from overflow parking. May feel isolated if alone. Inspected 2014.

30; Max 48hrs

Custom

ANGOULINS SUR MER | 107 | D7 | | 17690 | N46°06.377' W001°08.151'

Directions: Follow D111e1, main route, west through town towards coast following sp 'Tennis Club'. Cross train tracks and Service Point on left: N46°06.357' W001°06.995'. From Service Point continue straight on, pass campsite and parking on right, signed. 5 more 7m bays at end of road: N46°06.542' W001°08.279'.

i Parking opp sandy beach with limited sea views. Tourist commerce adj. popular cycling and walking paths. May feel isolated if alone. Inspected 2014.

17

Euro Relais Mini

AIGREFEUILLE D'AUNIS | 108 | D7 | | 17290 | N46°07.447' W000°54.869'

Directions: Lac de Frace. Exit village on D113, sp 'Virson'. Exit village and turn right, sp 'Lac de Frace' and signed. Follow road to Service Point on right and parking 50m on left.

i By leisure/fishing lake but no views from parking. Walk around lake. May feel isolated at night. Night fishing prohibited. Inspected 2012.

20; Max 24hrs

Urba Flux Tall; 1 unmetered elec point (Not working)

CHATELAILLON PLAGE 1 — 109 — D7 — 17340 — N46°03.768' W001°05.476'

Directions: Chemin Vert. From Chatelaillon Plage follow sp 'Les Boucholeurs'. At Les Boucholeurs follow sp 'Centre Aquatique'. Overnight parking is tolerated in the Centre Aquatique car park on the right.

ℹ️ Tolerated night parking from 10pm-9am only; €35 fine for parking during day. Local day parking on roadside. Inspected 2014.

🚐 30; 10pm-9am only

🚰 None

CHATELAILLON PLAGE 2 — 110 — D7 — 17340 — N46°04.358' W001°04.731'

Directions: Blvd Georges Clemenceau, at the race track. From centre of town follow sp 'P Hippodrome' and signed. Aire in designated section of race track parking, signed. Enter through barrier.

ℹ️ Aire to rear of car park, may be difficult to access during hippo racing! Town centre and beaches cycleable. Inspected 2014.

🚐 51; €12/24hrs; CC; Discounts for pass holders

🚰 Euro Relais Junior; Inside barrier; 2 unmetered elec points

CHATELAILLON PLAGE 3 — 111 — D7 — 17340 — N46°04.611' W001°05.317'

Directions: D202/Ave de Strasbourg. From D137/E602 turn onto D109 west towards beach in Loin-du-Bruit. Cross over 3 roundabouts, D109 becomes D202, and Aire on right by TO, opp Gendarmerie. Difficult parking to manoeuvre.

ℹ️ Small, impractical and oversubscribed designated parking. Likely to close. Inspected 2014.

🚐 5; Max 48hrs

🚰 None; See 110

ROCHEFORT 1 — 112 — D8 — 17300 — N45°55.687' W000°57.289'

Directions: Ave de la Charente. From south cross bridge and turn right onto D911, sp 'Rochefort'. At roundabout turn left onto D911, sp 'Rochefort'. At next 2 roundabouts turn right, sp 'Camping Municipal'. Turn left, sp 'Camping Municipal'. Drive past campsite and Aire is on left, signed.

ℹ️ Town centre with commerce and numerous historic buildings to leisurely wander 7 mins. May feel isolated if alone. Inspected 2014.

🚐 40; €3/24hrs; Pay at machine; Max 6 days

🚰 Custom

ROCHEFORT 2 — 113 — D8 — 17300 — N45°56.648' W000°57.443'

Directions: Off D911. Exit D137 at Junction 32 onto D5, sp 'Rochefort-Nord'. Turn onto D911, sp 'Centre Ville'. At end of road turn right, then immediately left, sp 'Capitainerie' and signed. Turn 1st left and Service Point on left, parking straight on. Overflow parking: N45°56.818' W000°57.607'.

ℹ️ Aire in pleasant Napoleonic/regency marina overlooking boats in dry storage. LIDL 2 mins, town centre commerce 4 mins. Inspected 2014.

🚐 20+15; €6/24hrs; Pay at machine

🚰 Custom

ROCHEFORT SUR MER — 114 — D8 — 17300 — N45°55.106' W000°57.850'

Directions: Pont Transbordeur. Approach from south, then follow sp 'Pont Transbordeur'. At Pont Transbordeur, follow one-way route which will take you through Aire, signed.

ℹ️ Only free overnight parking in town. 19th century Pont Transbordeur 500m, a tourist attraction lift bridge, €2.60pp return; free museum on Echillais side. May feel isolated if alone. Inspected 2014.

🚐 20; Roadside

🚰 None; See 112 and 113

MURON — 115 — D7 — 17430 — N46°02.176' W000°49.660'

Directions: Place du Champ de Foire. Exit D911, sp 'Muron'. The Aire is clearly signed in the village.

 Small village centre 1 min; Motorhome weather vane at Aire. Updated 2014.

🚐 5

🍾 Custom

Photo: Dr WTR Pryce

ST GERMAIN DE MARENCENNES 1 — 116 — D7 — 17700 — N46°04.632' W000°47.247'

Directions: Place St André. From north on D911 turn right onto Rue de Trois Ponts and follow into St Germain de Marencennes. Aire on left before village centre.

 Village 1 min. Inspected 2010.

🚐 6

🍾 Custom

ST GERMAIN DE MARENCENNES 2 — 117 — D7 — 17700 — N46°04.752' W000°46.997'

Directions: Rue de Moulin Neuf. From north on D911 turn right into Rue de Trois Ponts then 1st right into Rue du Moulin Neuf. Aire is on the left in 150m.

 Located in a leisure area in a parkland setting with specimen trees. Baker calls early am. Visited 2013.

🚐 8; €5/day; Collected; Max 72hrs; Mar-Nov

🍾 Custom

Info/photos: Janet & John Watts/Gillian Hoyle/Ken & Sylvi Oliver

ST SAVINIEN — 118 — D8 — 17350 — N45°52.682' W000°41.068'

Directions: D18. From St Jean d'Angély take D18 west, sp 'St Savinien'. Continue through town and cross river onto island following sp 'Ile aux Loisirs'. Service Point 200m on left outside campsite. Parking 100m past campsite, signed.

 Service Point outside 'Ile Aux Loisirs' campsite. Available even when campsite closed. Updated 2013.

🚐 5

🍾 Custom

Photo: Keith & Sue Lawrence

TAILLEBOURG — 119 — D8 — 17350 — N45°49.980' W000°38.800'

Directions: Les Douves, D127. Signed from the junction of D127 and D114. Service Point below château wall at the entrance to former campsite.

 Service Point only. Visited 2014.

🚐 None

🍾 Custom

Info/photos: Janet & John Watts

TONNAY CHARENTE — 120 — D8 — 17430 — N45°56.371' W000°52.897'

Directions: Quai Auriol Roy-Bry. To avoid town approach from east on D739. At the roundabout turn onto D137, sp 'Saintes'. Turn right onto D124, sp 'Tonnay-Charente'. Follow road under 4m bridge and Aire on left, signed.

 Aire outside municipal campsite, adj to river but no view. Small town 4 mins. Distant road noise. Updated 2014.

🚐 16; Max 7 days

🍾 Custom

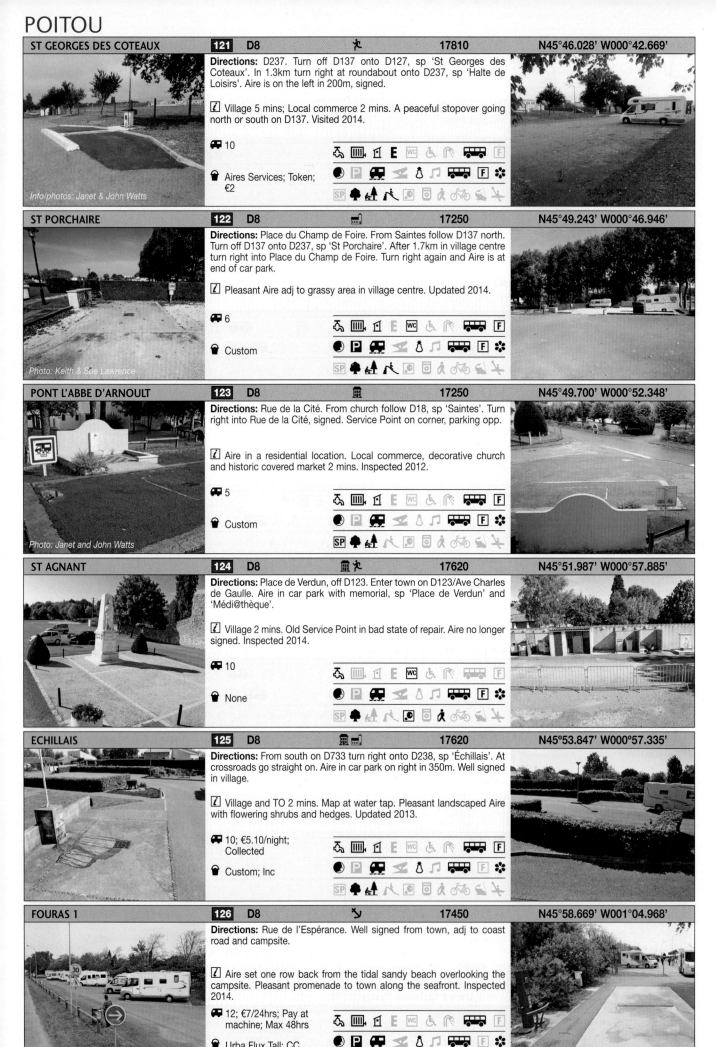

ST GEORGES DES COTEAUX | 121 | D8 | 17810 | N45°46.028' W000°42.669'

Directions: D237. Turn off D137 onto D127, sp 'St Georges des Coteaux'. In 1.3km turn right at roundabout onto D237, sp 'Halte de Loisirs'. Aire is on the left in 200m, signed.

i Village 5 mins; Local commerce 2 mins. A peaceful stopover going north or south on D137. Visited 2014.

10

Aires Services; Token; €2

Info/photos: Janet & John Watts

ST PORCHAIRE | 122 | D8 | 17250 | N45°49.243' W000°46.946'

Directions: Place du Champ de Foire. From Saintes follow D137 north. Turn off D137 onto D237, sp 'St Porchaire'. After 1.7km in village centre turn right into Place du Champ de Foire. Turn right again and Aire is at end of car park.

i Pleasant Aire adj to grassy area in village centre. Updated 2014.

6

Custom

Photo: Keith & Sue Lawrence

PONT L'ABBE D'ARNOULT | 123 | D8 | 17250 | N45°49.700' W000°52.348'

Directions: Rue de la Cité. From church follow D18, sp 'Saintes'. Turn right into Rue de la Cité, signed. Service Point on corner, parking opp.

i Aire in a residential location. Local commerce, decorative church and historic covered market 2 mins. Inspected 2012.

5

Custom

Photo: Janet and John Watts

ST AGNANT | 124 | D8 | 17620 | N45°51.987' W000°57.885'

Directions: Place de Verdun, off D123. Enter town on D123/Ave Charles de Gaulle. Aire in car park with memorial, sp 'Place de Verdun' and 'Médi@thèque'.

i Village 2 mins. Old Service Point in bad state of repair. Aire no longer signed. Inspected 2014.

10

None

ECHILLAIS | 125 | D8 | 17620 | N45°53.847' W000°57.335'

Directions: From south on D733 turn right onto D238, sp 'Échillais'. At crossroads go straight on. Aire in car park on right in 350m. Well signed in village.

i Village and TO 2 mins. Map at water tap. Pleasant landscaped Aire with flowering shrubs and hedges. Updated 2013.

10; €5.10/night; Collected

Custom; Inc

FOURAS 1 | 126 | D8 | 17450 | N45°58.669' W001°04.968'

Directions: Rue de l'Espérance. Well signed from town, adj to coast road and campsite.

i Aire set one row back from the tidal sandy beach overlooking the campsite. Pleasant promenade to town along the seafront. Inspected 2014.

12; €7/24hrs; Pay at machine; Max 48hrs

Urba Flux Tall; CC

FOURAS 2 | 127 | D8 | | 17450 | N45°59.528' W001°05.202'

Directions: D937c/Avenue du Cadoret, just off roundabout outside Camping Le Cadoret. Signed from main road. 3.5t weight restriction on Aire.

i Campsite and mini golf adj. Town 5 mins. Inspected 2014.

9; €7/24hrs; Pay at machine; Park on left

Custom; Token; €1

FOURAS 3 | 128 | D8 | | 17450 | N45°59.744' W001°06.355'

Directions: Rue du Bois Vert. From Fouras follow sp 'La Fumée'. Turn left at fort, sp 'P Gratuite' and 'Fort Voban'. Designated parking at rear of car park, signed.

i Designated parking adj to fort ruin, no access. Beaches and picnic areas nearby. Ideal to walk/cycle to Ponte de la Fumée which has a causeway at low tide. Parking there is €36/24hrs. Inspected 2014.

24; €6/24hrs; Pay at machine

None

GPS Co-ordinates for SatNav

The GPS Co-ordinates published in this guide were taken onsite by our inspectors. We consider them a valuable and unique asset and at the time of publishing have decided not to publish them as electronic files for use on navigation devices. You have permission to type in the co-ordinates of an Aire you intend to visit but not to store or share them. For the security of our copyright:

- **Do not compile them into lists**
- **Do not publish, share or reproduce them anywhere in any format**

SOUBISE 1 | 130 | D8 | | 17780 | N45°55.703' W001°00.401'

Directions: Rue Colbert. From Rochefort follow sp 'Soubise', then 'Port de Barques'. Turn right, signed, into village and after 400m turn right again. Aire on right, signed. Open barrier to enter.

i Lovely Aire with grass and gravel parking offering a very pleasant feel. Boats wind through creeks, visible at high tides. Town commerce 3 mins uphill. Inspected 2014.

40; €7/24hrs inc unmetered elec; Pay at machine

Custom; Inside barrier; Inc

SOUBISE 2 | 131 | D8 | | 17780 | N45°55.577' W001°00.911'

Directions: Ave de Soubise. Exit Soubise following sp 'Port des Barques'. Aire immediately on left by village boundary in roadside picnic area, signed.

i Pleasant, shaded roadside picnic area. Ideal as night halt or if 130 full. Inspected 2014.

5

Urba Flux Tall; CC; €2.50

PORT DES BARQUES | 132 | D8 | | 17730 | N45°56.800' W001°05.400'

Directions: At junction of D125/D125e3. Turn left off D125 at town entrance, sp 'Plage' and signed. Follow road for 1.5km. After passing cemetery on left the Aire is 100m on left. Entry through Aire Services barrier.

i Uninspiring Aire adj to boules court and sports facilities. Possible to visit Île Madame across causeway. Inspected 2014.

30; €6.20/night Mar-Nov; CC

Aire Services; Outside barrier; CC; €2

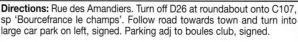

BOURCEFRANC LE CHAPUS 1 — 133 — D8 — 17560 — N45°50.755' W001°08.948'

Directions: Rue des Amandiers. Turn off D26 at roundabout onto C107, sp 'Bourcefrance le champs'. Follow road towards town and turn into large car park on left, signed. Parking adj to boules club, signed.

ℹ️ Large parking area in town centre. Boules club and pharmacy adj. Inspected 2014.

🚐 10; Max 24hrs

🚰 None; See **134**

BOURCEFRANC LE CHAPUS 2 — 134 — D8 — 17320 — N45°49.867' W001°09.048'

Directions: Barre à l'Anglais. Exit town on C107 and go straight across roundabout with D26, sp 'Plages'. Service Point 1.5km on left outside Camping La Giroflee. Parking 600m further down road on right: N45°49.564' W001°08.582'.

ℹ️ Parking adj to tidal sandy beach overlooking sea and island. Service Point on sand, some parts are deep. Tokens avail from TO. Inspected 2014.

🚐 30; €5.50/10pm-9am; Pay at machine

🚰 Euro Relais Junior; Token (ER); €4.50

HIERS BROUAGE — 135 — D8 — 17320 — N45°51.166' W001°04.636'

Directions: D3. Exit Hiers Brouage north on D3. Service Point on right at bend in road by boat. Set in small roadside municipal recycling area just before village boundary.

ℹ️ Service Point only. Service Point out of service at time of inspections in 2010 and 2014. Inspected 2014.

🚐 None

🚰 Raclet; Token (ER); €4; Water not working

ST JUST LUZAC — 136 — D8 — 17320 — N45°47.950' W001°02.900'

Directions: Avenue des Vignes, at ZI Fief de Luzac. In St Just Luzac turn off D728 at roundabout onto D241e1, sp 'Luzac'. Take 1st right into Rue des Vignes. Aire in 80m in small industrial estate.

ℹ️ In industrial estate, not picturesque, but suitable night halt. Only 1 bay but plenty of additional parking. Boulangerie adj. Inspected 2014.

🚐 1; Plus additional parking

🚰 Euro Relais Junior; Token (2/1); €4

ST TROJAN LES BAINS 1 — 137 — D8 — 17370 — N45°50.624' W001°12.533'

Directions: Place de la Liberté, off D126. Aire in centre adj to large car park near TO.

ℹ️ Designated parking adj to large height barriered car park. TO and local commerce at roundabout 50m. Inspected 2014.

🚐 10; Max 72hrs

🚰 None; See **138**

ST TROJAN LES BAINS 2 — 138 — D8 — 17370 — N45°49.632' W001°13.059'

Directions: Avenue des Bris. From D126 turn off at roundabout, sp 'Plage de Gatseau'. Follow sp 'Plage de Gatseau' and fork left when road divides. Service Point on right at ZI les Bris.

ℹ️ Service Point only. Inspected 2014.

🚐 None; See **137** and **139**

🚰 Urba Flux Tall; CC; €5

ST TROJAN LES BAINS 3 | 139 | D8 | | 17370 | N45°50.467' W001°12.331'

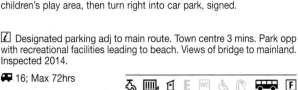

Directions: Rue Capitaine Patoiseau. Turn off main route through opp children's play area, then turn right into car park, signed.

ℹ Designated parking adj to main route. Town centre 3 mins. Park opp with recreational facilities leading to beach. Views of bridge to mainland. Inspected 2014.

🚐 16; Max 72hrs

🚰 None; See **138**

LE GRAND VILLAGE PLAGE (ILE D'OLERON) | 140 | D8 | | 17370 | N45°51.714' W001°14.436'

Directions: Allée des Pins. Follow D26 to Grand Village. Turn onto D126 at roundabout, sp 'La Cotiniere'. Turn left at next roundabout, sp 'Plage'. Turn 1st right, then left in front of Camping Les Pins to Aire, signed.

ℹ Landscaped Aire under shady pine trees. Bays are unlevel and some are impractical. Inspected 2014.

🚐 9; €6/24hrs; CC; Pay at Service Point

🚰 Urba Flux Small; CC; €4

LE CHATEAU D'OLERON | 141 | D8 | | 17480 | N45°53.791' W001°12.125'

Directions: Blvd Phillippe Daste. From bridge follow sp 'Château d'Oléron'. In Château d'Oléron follow sp 'Ors' and signed, then follow sp 'Plage' and signed. Aire on left in 1.2km, enter through Aire Services barrier.

ℹ Large commercial Aire on former campsite. Shower water is solar heated. Tidal beach with a small stretch of sand opp. Inspected 2014.

🚐 100; €10/night inc 6amp elec; CC; Pay at barrier

🚰 Euro Relais Junior; Inside barrier; Inc

ROYAN | 142 | D8 | | 17200 | N45°37.717' W001°00.751'

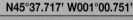

Directions: Rue Bel Air. Approach from east on N150. Turn right at roundabout just past D25 junction, sp 'Habitat 17'. Turn 1st right, sp 'Espace Commercial Royan 2'. Follow road to end, then turn left, immediately right across railway tracks and immediately right again, sp 'Scouts de France'. Aire 150m on left, enter through PARKNIGHT barrier.

ℹ Commercial Aire 10 mins from beach and town centre. Visited 2014.

🚐 40; €12/night; CC; Discounts for pass holders

🚰 Euro Relais Junior; Inside barrier

Info/photos: Peter Hesketh

DOLUS D'OLERON | 143 | D8 | | 17550 | N45°54.717' W001°15.266'

Directions: Route du Stade. Turn off D734 at roundabout in Dolus d'Oléron onto D126, sp 'Boyardville'. In 700m turn right, sp 'Parc Aquatique'. Service Point on left by tennis courts. Parking 50m past Service Point, signed.

ℹ Pleasant grass parking with approx 14 hardstanding for winter use. Pay for both services and parking by CC on Service Point, however Service Point is broken regularly. Inspected 2014.

🚐 30; €5/24hrs; Collected

🚰 Euro Relais Maxi; CC or Token (ER); €4

BOYARDVILLE | 144 | D8 | | 17190 | N45°57.805' W001°14.680'

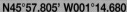

Directions: Allée de Fort Royer. Take D126 from Dolus d'Oleron to Boyardville. As enter town turn right, immediately right again into Camping Fort Royer and right again, signed. Enter Aire through barrier.

ℹ Commercial Aire adj to campsite on previous campsite ground close to main road adj. Bays marked by elec points. One of the nicest Aires on the island. Inspected 2014.

🚐 40; €9/night inc 6amp elec; CC; Pay at barrier

🚰 Custom; Inside barrier

POITOU

LA COTINIERE (ILE D'OLERON) — 145 — D8 — 🏕 — 17310 — N45°55.425' W001°20.576'

Directions: Ave des Pins. In St Pierre turn off D734 at traffic lights onto D274, sp 'La Cotinière'. Follow sp 'La Cotinière' to end of road. Turn right, sp 'Camping, and Aire is 50m past Camping Municipal de la Fauche-Prere, signed.

ⓘ Small parking area under trees next to municipal campsite. Beach 100m through campsite. Inspected 2012.

🚐 5; €9/24hrs; + tax; Collected

🚰 Raclet; Token; €4

LA MORELIERE — 146 — D7 — 🏭 — 17650 — N46°02.651' W001°23.924'

Directions: D734. North of St Denis d'Oléron adj to D734, signed.

ⓘ Service Point only. Flot Bleu provides water adj to custom WC emptying point. Flush standing behind wall if you don't want wet feet! Inspected 2014.

🚐 None; See **147**

🚰 Flot Bleu Euro (Not working) and Custom; Token or CC; €5

Photo: Trevor Mace

ST DENIS D'OLERON — 147 — D7 — 🌳 — 17650 — N46°01.659' W001°22.993'

Directions: Route des Huttes. From the south approach St Denis d'Oléran on D734. 350m after passing boundary sign turn left onto Route des Huttes, signed. Follow road and Aire is on right, signed. Enter through barrier.

ⓘ Commercial Aire on former campsite with grass and reinforced grass pitches between deciduous trees. Old amenities block. Town and seafront 1km. Inspected 2014.

🚐 160; €9 inc 5amp elec and showers; Max 4 nights; Grass parking

🚰 Custom; Inside barrier

LA BREE LES BAINS — 148 — D7 — 🏭 — 17840 — N46°00.508' W001°21.437'

Directions: D273e1, at ZA de la Brée les Bains. Turn off D734 into La Brée les Bains on D273e1. Turn right just before boundary sign. Aire in industrial area on right before you enter town.

ⓘ Adj to recycling point and caravan sales/storage. Tokens from TO, 1km. Inspected 2014.

🚐 30

🚰 Euro Relais Junior; €4.50

MARENNES 1 — 149 — D8 — 🏢 — 17320 — N45°49.399' W001°06.127'

Directions: Rue Ovide Beillard. Turn off D728, Marennes bypass, onto D3 at the traffic lights, sp 'Marennes'. Follow the road for 900m then turn left, sp 'E Leclerc'. Follow road behind fuel station and up behind gas bottles. Service Point 10m, signed.

ⓘ Supermarket adj. Inspected 2014.

🚐 5

🚰 Euro Relais Mini; Token (ER); €3

MARENNES 2 — 150 — D8 — 🏛 — 17320 — N45°49.561' W001°05.819'

Directions: Rue Jean Moulin. Turn off D728, Marennes bypass, onto D3 at the traffic lights, sp 'Marennes'. Turn left, sp 'Centre d'Animation et de loisirs'. Aire 700m in car park opp Intermarché supermarket. Do not park on the side with houses against it.

ⓘ Large, open gravel parking area in residential area. Adj to supermarket. Inspected 2014.

🚐 20

🚰 Euro Relais Junior; Token (2/1)

SAUJON · 151 · D8 · 17600 · N45°40.513' W000°55.905'

Directions: Route des Écluses. Exit N150 onto D1, sp 'Saujon-Le Lande', and follow sp 'Port de Ribérou'. Turn right, sp 'Port de Ribérou'. Aire on left, signed. 5.5t weight restriction on parking.

ℹ️ Adj to former campsite and fairly busy main road. Adj to pond and river with footpath to town, 3 mins. Inspected 2014.

🚐 20; €4/24hrs; €10/72hrs; CC; Pay at Service Point; Max 6 days

🚰 Euro Relais Maxi; CC/Token (ER); €4

LE GUA · 152 · D8 · 17600 · N45°43.538' W000°56.684'

Directions: Place 19 Mars 1962. Enter village on D1 from south. At roundabout turn left. Aire 50m on left.

ℹ️ Small parking area just off the central square. Local commerce 1 min. Market Sun. Inspected 2014.

🚐 2; Depending on parked cars

🚰 Raclet; Token (2/1)

NIEULLE SUR SEUDRE · 153 · D8 · 17600 · N45°45.153' W001°00.131'

Directions: Place de la Mairie, off D241. From Marennes take D728 southeast. Fork right onto D131. Then turn right onto D118, sp 'Nieulle sur Seudre'. At end of road turn right onto D241 and follow road straight on. Aire on right in centre of village outside school.

ℹ️ Small parking area outside school, La Poste and Mairie. Take care using services as corner of building overhangs Service Point. Local commerce 2 mins. Inspected 2014.

🚐 3

🚰 Euro Relais Junior; 2 unmetered CEE elec points

LA PALMYRE 1 · 154 · D8 · 17570 · N45°41.483' W001°11.352'

Directions: Avenue de l'Atlantique, off D25. Turn off D141e1 onto D25 at roundabout in La Palmyre, sp 'Ronce les Bains'. Turn left, sp 'Le Plage' and 'Tennis'. Aire 150m on right. Enter through Urba Flux barrier.

ℹ️ Commercial Aire located beside sand dunes in a pleasant wooded area. Sandy beach 1 min through picnic area. Town centre 5 mins. Inspected 2014.

🚐 83; €8/24hrs; CC; Max 7 days; 10m bays

🚰 Euro Relais Junior; Outside barrier; Token (ER); €2

LA PALMYRE 2 · 155 · D8 · 17570 · N45°40.982' W001°10.818'

Directions: Blvd de la Plage. Turn off D141e1/D25 at roundabout, sp 'Le Port'. Follow sp 'Le Port'. Drive through port and Aire 500m further along coast road, signed.

ℹ️ Large designated parking area which is less popular than 154. Beach and park over protective sand dune 1 min. Port with tourist commerce 1 min. Town 700m on cycle path. Inspected 2014.

🚐 56; €8/24hrs; Pay at machine

🚰 None; See 154

LES MATHES · 156 · D8 · 17570 · N45°42.848' W001°08.864'

Directions: Rue de la Garenne. Turn off at roundabout adj to SPAR supermarket onto D141, sp 'Royan'. Turn right, sp 'Espace Multi-Loisirs' and signed. Aire on right.

ℹ️ Large uninspiring commercial Aire next to pleasant recreational facilities offering poor value for money locally. Always likely to have space. Inspected 2014.

🚐 40; €8; Pay at machine; Feb-Nov

🚰 Custom; Token (ER); €4

LA TREMBLADE | 157 | D8 | 17390 | N45°46.957' W001°09.137'

Directions: Rue Marcel Gaillardon. Turn off D25 at the roundabout with paper boats (junction with D728e), sp 'La Tremblade-Centre'. In 20m turn left, sp 'Le Port a Sec' and signed. Follow road for 800m, then turn right past the Aire. Turn right again into entrance.

i Landscaped commercial Aire tucked away in a residential area. Bays are marked and the Aire is well designed. Inspected 2014.

🚐 32; €10/24hrs inc elec; Pay at machine; Max 72hrs

🚰 Urba Flux Tall

ST GEORGES DE DIDONNE 1 | 158 | D8 | 17110 | N45°36.178' W000°59.522'

Directions: Allée des Ormes. Turn off D25 at roundabout, sp 'St Georges de Didonne-Centre'. Follow road straight on, sp 'Centre Ville'. Turn left, sp 'P Gillet'. Aire is on right in 50m. Difficult entrance due to street furniture and road layout.

i Designated parking at rear of car park backing on to cemetery. More peaceful than 159. Might also be poss to park closer to beach, no views: N45°36.010' W001°00.422'. Inspected 2014.

🚐 8; €7/24hrs; Collected

🚰 None; See 159

ST GEORGES DE DIDONNE 2 | 159 | D8 | 17110 | N45°36.261' W000°59.974'

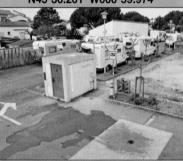

Directions: Rue du Stade. From south on D25 turn off at roundabout, sp 'St Georges de Didonne-Centre'. Follow road straight on, sp 'Centre Ville'. Turn right, sp 'Marche' on road. Follow road straight on and Aire is on right in 400m.

i 5 mins to beach and town centre. Opp sports facilities. Pleasant seaside town with large sandy beach. Inspected 2014.

🚐 19; €7/24hrs; Collected; Max 72hrs

🚰 Custom

MESCHERS SUR GIRONDE | 160 | D8 | 17132 | N45°33.377' W000°56.695'

Directions: Routes des Salines. From Talmont on D145 turn left on entry to Meschers sur Gironde, sp 'Le Port' and signed. Follow road to left and Aire and Service Point at end of road, signed.

i Aire adj to working port overlooking boats in dry storage. Restaurants/bars on quay. Cycle to Talmont sur Gironde for a day out. Inspected 2014.

🚐 12; €5/24hrs; Pay at machine

🚰 Custom; €2; 12 16amp CEE elec points

COZES | 161 | D8 | 17120 | N45°35.177' W000°49.999'

Directions: Ave de la Gare. Enter town from north on D17. Turn right after crossing railway track, sp 'Talmont'. Turn right in 50m, signed. Aire at far end of car park.

i Adj to sports facilities and velo rail. Hire a velo cart in summer and pedal along the disused railway. Inspected 2014.

🚐 8

🚰 Custom

ST SEURIN D'UZET ★ | 162 | D8 | 17120 | N45°30.061' W000°50.097'

Directions: Place du Créac, off D145 adj to river. Signed from D145 main road. Aire on opp side of marina to church, signed.

i Overlooking river marina in village centre. Pleasant grass area adj with benches. Slipway opp. Inspected 2014.

🚐 14; €7/night inc unmetered CEE elec; Collected

🚰 Custom; Token; €1

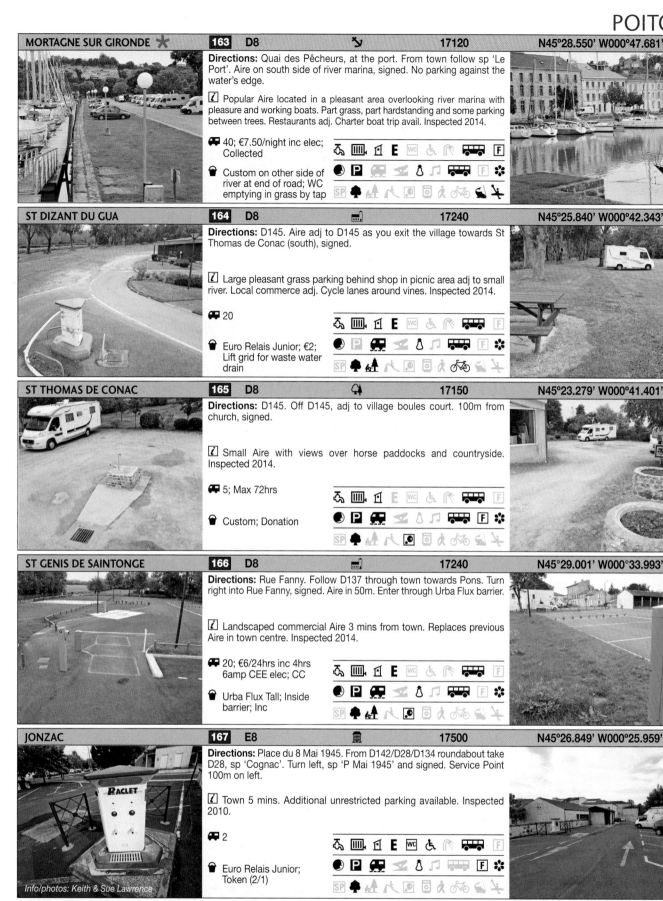

MORTAGNE SUR GIRONDE ✳	**163**	**D8**	⚓	**17120**	**N45°28.550' W000°47.681'**

Directions: Quai des Pêcheurs, at the port. From town follow sp 'Le Port'. Aire on south side of river marina, signed. No parking against the water's edge.

ⓘ Popular Aire located in a pleasant area overlooking river marina with pleasure and working boats. Part grass, part hardstanding and some parking between trees. Restaurants adj. Charter boat trip avail. Inspected 2014.

🚐 40; €7.50/night inc elec; Collected

🪣 Custom on other side of river at end of road; WC emptying in grass by tap

---

ST DIZANT DU GUA	**164**	**D8**		**17240**	**N45°25.840' W000°42.343'**

Directions: D145. Aire adj to D145 as you exit the village towards St Thomas de Conac (south), signed.

ⓘ Large pleasant grass parking behind shop in picnic area adj to small river. Local commerce adj. Cycle lanes around vines. Inspected 2014.

🚐 20

🪣 Euro Relais Junior; €2; Lift grid for waste water drain

ST THOMAS DE CONAC	**165**	**D8**		**17150**	**N45°23.279' W000°41.401'**

Directions: D145. Off D145, adj to village boules court. 100m from church, signed.

ⓘ Small Aire with views over horse paddocks and countryside. Inspected 2014.

🚐 5; Max 72hrs

🪣 Custom; Donation

ST GENIS DE SAINTONGE	**166**	**D8**		**17240**	**N45°29.001' W000°33.993'**

Directions: Rue Fanny. Follow D137 through town towards Pons. Turn right into Rue Fanny, signed. Aire in 50m. Enter through Urba Flux barrier.

ⓘ Landscaped commercial Aire 3 mins from town. Replaces previous Aire in town centre. Inspected 2014.

🚐 20; €6/24hrs inc 4hrs 6amp CEE elec; CC

🪣 Urba Flux Tall; Inside barrier; Inc

JONZAC	**167**	**E8**		**17500**	**N45°26.849' W000°25.959'**

Directions: Place du 8 Mai 1945. From D142/D28/D134 roundabout take D28, sp 'Cognac'. Turn left, sp 'P Mai 1945' and signed. Service Point 100m on left.

ⓘ Town 5 mins. Additional unrestricted parking available. Inspected 2010.

🚐 2

🪣 Euro Relais Junior; Token (2/1)

Info/photos: Keith & Sue Lawrence

LEOVILLE	**168**	**E8**		**17500**	**N45°22.752' W000°20.112'**

Directions: Off D253e3. From D142 in village turn onto D253e3, sp 'Aire de Loisirs'. Turn right in 150m. Aire on right at end of road.

ⓘ Pleasant parkland area with lake and footpath to village. Tokens avail from boulangerie facing church. Inspected 2010.

🚐 6

🪣 Euro Relais Mini; Token (ER)

Info/photos: Keith & Sue Lawrence

Photo: Joy & Bob Podesta

MONTLIEU LA GARDE — 169 — E8 — 17210 — N45°14.919' W000°15.071'

Directions: Les Coupries, off D910. Exit N10/E606 onto D730, sp 'Montlieu la Garde'. Turn left onto D910/D13 and follow signs through village to Aire. Well signed. Pay with CC on entry to lower chain barrier.

ℹ️ Automated Aire/municipal campsite on edge of village. Min of 1 night required to use Service Point. Showers avail by token, €1. Inspected 2010.

🚐 10; €8/night; CC

🚰 Custom; CC/Token; €1; Inc elec

Info/photos: Keith & Sue Lawrence

MONTGUYON — 170 — E9 — 17270 — N45°13.075' W000°10.990'

Directions: Rue de Vassiac. From Montlieu la Garde on D730 turn left at roundabout onto D910, sp 'Centre', with 3.5t restriction. Go straight across next roundabout and follow main road around right-hand bend. Turn left onto D158, sp 'Martron' and signed. Follow road straight on, signed. Aire on right in 400m at stadium, signed.

ℹ️ At stadium with comprehensive sports facilities. Town 5 mins. Inspected 2013.

🚐 10

🚰 Custom

CLERAC — 171 — E9 — 17270 — N45°10.754' W000°13.693'

Directions: D261e1/Route des Vignes. Turn off D158 in the centre of the village onto the D261e towards Cercoux. The Aire is adj to the pond, next to the boulangerie.

ℹ️ Lovely Aire on edge of village overlooking pond and countryside. Updated 2014.

🚐 5

🚰 Euro Relais Junior; 1 unmetered elec point; Excellent toilet

Info/photo: Bethan D Flowers

BROSSAC — 172 — E8 — 16480 — N45°19.974' W000°02.738'

Directions: Turn off D731 onto D7, Rue de la Gare. Turn sharp right into Rue du Château d'Eau. Aire adj to stadium.

ℹ️ Pleasant, peaceful spot by stadium; Lots of green space; Each bay has own drain; Toilet at stadium 100m. Inspected 2010.

🚐 4

🚰 Flot Bleu Euro; CC; €5

Info/photos: Keith & Sue Lawrence

AUBETERRE SUR DRONNE — 173 — E8 — 16390 — N45°16.162' E000°10.606'

Directions: D2/Route de Riberac, at Base de Loisirs. Adj to D2 to east of town after crossing river. Parking near Service Point in summer. Riverside parking allowed in winter.

ℹ️ Peaceful Aire outside municipal campsite beside river with kayak hire. Shop 300m; Short walk into beautiful Beau Village. Inspected 2012.

🚐 5

🚰 Flot Bleu Océane; €2

ST SEVERIN — 174 — E8 — 16390 — N45°18.750' E000°15.300'

Directions: Rue de la Pavancelle, off D709 in the centre of the village. Near the Mairie (town hall), opp the SPAR supermarket.

ℹ️ Aire set between D709 and Rue de la Pavacelle in well kept village. Inspected 2010.

🚐 3

🚰 Custom; Unmetered elec

Info/photos: Keith & Sue Lawrence

MOUTHIERS SUR BOEME | 175 | E8 | | 16440 | N45°33.254' E000°07.493'

Directions: Chemin de la Chauveterie. Turn off D12 at the roundabout to the north of the village into Place du Champ du Foire, signed. Follow road to right and the Aire is in front of the church, signed.

ℹ️ Pleasant Aire overlooking church. Square with convenience store, local commerce and small market on Thursday morning adj. Inspected 2012.

🚐 5

🛒 Custom

VILLEBOIS LAVALETTE | 176 | E8 | | 16320 | N45°28.900' E000°16.583'

Directions: Place du Champ de Foire, off D16. From west on D16 go straight over roundabout into town. Take next right and another immediate right and Aire on left.

ℹ️ Pleasant spot. Impressive château in town. WiFi, €0.50/30mins, at TO at end of car park. Toilets underground in road below car park. Updated 2014.

🚐 2

🛒 Urba Flux Tall; €2

Info/photos: Keith & Sue Lawrence

VOEUIL ET GIGET | 177 | E8 | | 16400 | N45°35.092' E000°09.292'

Directions: Rue de la Mairie. Turn off D674 as exit village by covered water feature. Aire 20m on right, behind church.

ℹ️ In village; Restaurant adj. Pretty church and stream adj. Updated 2014.

🚐 3

🛒 Flot Bleu Océane; €2

Info/photos: Keith & Sue Lawrence

SERS | 178 | E8 | | 16410 | N45°35.788' E000°19.298'

Directions: Rue du Champ de Foire. Turn off D25 onto Rue du Champ de Foire at either end of village, signed. Easiest entrance is from east. Aire just off central square, signed. Fencing and bushes look like they restrict entrance but it is over 3m wide.

ℹ️ Aire adj to sports facilities just off central square. Local commerce 1 min. Inspected 2012.

🚐 7; Grass parking; Max 48hrs

🛒 Euro Relais Junior; Token (ER); €3

TOUVRE | 179 | E8 | | 16600 | N45°39.657' E000°15.489'

Directions: Route du Pontil. Follow D57 to south. After crossing railway line turn 1st right onto D408, sp 'Soyaux'. Aire 20m on right, signed.

ℹ️ Landscaped Aire adj to a railway line. Bus stop adj. Aire at Plan d'Eau le Grande Prairie closed in 2010, night parking banned, but still signed from N141. Updated 2014.

🚐 7

🛒 Aire Services

LA COURONNE | 180 | E8 | | 16400 | N45°36.378' E000°06.019'

Directions: Rue de la Foucaudie. Turn of D699, main route, by chemist signed. Turn left by lovely turreted building in village centre, signed. Follow road around the block to the rear of the turreted building. Aire is next to police station, signed.

ℹ️ Lovely Aire in very nice village. Mini market 2 mins. Inspected 2013.

🚐 5; No parking Wed am (Market)

🛒 Custom

ROULLET ST ESTEPHE | **181** | E8 | 16440 | N45°34.785' E000°02.704'

Directions: Off D210. Take Exit 7 from N10 for Roullet Centre. At roundabout turn onto D210. Turn off to Aire, opp YPO Camping Cars.

ℹ️ River and park adj, town 5 mins. Popular convenient stop just off N10, always likely to have space. Inspected 2013.

🚐 20

🔧 Custom

NERSAC | **182** | E8 | 16440 | N45°37.555' E000°03.004'

Directions: Rue de la Fontaine, off D26. Follow sp 'Aire de Loisirs' and signs through town on D26. Narrow access through town due to river bridges and parked cars. Aire signed off D26, then 50m on right, signed.

ℹ️ Lovely Aire in very nice village, well worth a look around. Inspected 2013.

🚐 7; Max 48hrs

🔧 Custom; 4 unmetered elec points

HIERSAC | **183** | E8 | 16290 | N45°39.978' W000°00.022'

Directions: D14. Exit village on D14 towards Châteauneuf sur Charente. Aire on left just before village boundary.

ℹ️ Aire located on the edge of the village. Local commerce inc convenience store on N141, 4 mins. Inspected 2014.

🚐 3

🔧 Urba Flux Tall; CC; €2/20 mins

MONTMOREAU ST CYBARD | **184** | E8 | 16190 | N45°23.948' E000°07.963'

Directions: Rue de la Tude, off D674. From south on D674 turn right at mini roundabout into Rue de la Tude opp La Poste, signed.

ℹ️ Open, slightly sloping square. Grassy area between parking and river Tude. Château in town. Inspected 2010.

🚐 8

🔧 Flot Bleu Pacific; €2; 8 elec points

Info/photos: Keith & Sue Lawrence

SIREUIL | **185** | E8 | 16440 | N45°37.034' E000°00.411'

Directions: Chemin du Ponton. Turn off D7 north of village, sp 'Lavoir Ancien' and signed. At T-junction turn right and parking is immediately on right adj to river.

ℹ️ Idyllic riverside parking isolated from the village. BBQ and picnic area onsite. Village centre 2 mins. Inspected 2012.

🚐 3; Grass parking

🔧 None

CHATEAUNEUF SUR CHARENTE | **186** | E8 | 16120 | N45°35.924' W000°03.403'

Directions: Rue due Prieure. Turn off D699 opp D84 turning, sp 'Centre Ville' and 'Hôpital'. Turn right, sp 'Hôpital', then left. Follow road to right past church, sp 'P Centre Ville Prieure'. Turn left, sp 'P Centre Ville Prieure'. Aire in car park on left, signed. Access through town diff due to narrow streets.

ℹ️ This is a good town centre Aire in a car park that is unlikely to be full of local cars. Small town commerce 2 mins. Cognac producer 1 min. Inspected 2012.

🚐 4

🔧 Urba Flux Tall; CC; €2/20 mins

ST SIMON | 187 | E8 | 16120 | N45°39.168' W000°05.119'

Directions: D22. Adj to D22 on right as exit village towards Jarnac, signed.

ℹ️ Designated landscaped parking in former fenced compound on edge of village. Views over vines. In cognac region. Inspected 2014

🚐 6

🚰 Urba Flux Tall; CC

ROUILLAC | 188 | E8 | 16170 | N45°46.592' W000°03.678'

Directions: Rue de Genac. From southeast on D939 as enter town take 3rd exit at roundabout towards Super U supermarket. Aire on left opp Super U fuel station and overlooking large open grassy area.

ℹ️ Supermarket opp; Village 5 mins. Lots of open, green space adj. Noise at night from adj road. Updated 2014.

🚐 7

🚰 Euro Relais; Token (ER)

Info/photos: Keith & Sue Lawrence

AIGRE | 189 | E8 | 16140 | N45°53.603' E000°00.329'

Directions: Rue des Charrières. From west on D739 turn off, sp 'Aire de Repos' and 'Camping Car'. Aire on right.

ℹ️ Pleasant Aire in small parkland setting. €5 includes shower, toilets, all services and elec. Updated 2013.

🚐 5; €5.50 inc elec May-Oct; Collected; Free Nov-Apr

🚰 Bollard

MANSLE | 190 | E8 | 16230 | N45°52.674' E000°10.894'

Directions: Rue de Watlington. As enter Mansle from north on D18 turn left, sp 'Camping le Champion'. Service Point outside campsite.

ℹ️ Town 5 mins; Restaurant La Marmite adj. Inspected 2013.

🚐 2; In low season only

🚰 Raclet; €2

JARNAC | 191 | E8 | ☼ | 16200 | N45°40.598' W000°10.390'

Directions: Aire de Loisirs de l'Île Madame. Turn off N141 and follow sp 'Jarnac' onto D736. Turn right immediately before river bridge, sp 'Camping'. Service Point to left in riverside car park outside Camping l'Île Madame.

ℹ️ Service Point only outside campsite, must stay overnight in campsite. Campsite under renovation. Inspected 2014.

🚐 Day parking only; Banned 8pm-8am

🚰 Euro Relais Junior; Drive over drain 18cm high!; 2 unmetered elec points

SEGONZAC | 192 | E8 | 16130 | N45°36.869' W000°13.255'

Directions: Place du Jardin Public, adj to Rue Henri Gourry. From D763 turn onto Rue Gourry and follow to end. Aire on right. Signed from all directions.

ℹ️ Village 5 mins; Sign showing local cognac producers. Inspected 2010.

🚐 4 (each with elec); Max 4 days

🚰 Custom; 4 unmetered elec points

Info/photos: Keith & Sue Lawrence

LIGNIERES SONNEVILLE
193 E8 — 16130 — N45°33.413' W000°10.957'

Directions: Off D90. From D699 turn onto D90 in town. Follow D90 south for 300m then turn left and Aire on left in 100m.

Large, gravel parking area adj to football pitch and ancient restored barn. In grounds of 17th century moated château now housing Mairie. Pretty historic village. Inspected 2010.

20

Custom

CRITEUIL LA MAGDELEINE
194 E8 — 16300 — N45°32.279' W000°12.906'

Directions: Off D151. From west on D699 turn right onto D151, sp 'Criteuil'. At right-hand bend continue straight onto C2 into village. Aire on right in village centre by school and behind Mairie, signed.

No amenities in village; No real parking. Inspected 2010.

2

Euro Relais Junior; 1 unmetered elec point

Info/photos: Keith & Sue Lawrence

ARCHIAC
195 E8 — 17520 — N45°31.205' W000°18.277'

Directions: Rue du Pâtis, off D699. Aire at foot of water tower behind La Poste in village centre.

Village adj. Service Point in rear right-hand corner of car park by toilets. Small market Sat am. Inspected 2010.

5

Euro Relais Mini

Info/photos: Keith & Sue Lawrence

GENTE
196 E8 — 16130 — N45°37.732' W000°18.921'

Directions: Off D148. From Cognac (north) on D731 turn left onto D148, sp 'Gente'. After 1.2km fork right into Lieu-Dit La Vallade. Aire on right in 400m by sports field and boules pitches.

Well maintained Aire and surroundings on edge of village; Skate park adj; WCs at boules pavilion. Inspected 2010.

5; Max 2 nights

Custom; 6 unmetered elec points

Info/photos: Keith & Sue Lawrence

COGNAC
197 E8 — 16100 — N45°41.910' W000°19.962'

Directions: Place de la Levade. Enter Cognac from north on D731. At roundabout turn right, sp 'Cognac-Centre'. At roundabout turn left, sp 'St Jacques'. At roundabout turn right, sp 'Centre Ville'. In 50m turn right, sp 'Parking Gratuit' and signed. Aire at end of parking on right.

Adj to Hennessey cognac producer, walk around building for visitor centre. Pleasant riverside park adj, cross bridge for town. Inspected 2014.

3

Raclet; €2; 4 bays at Service Point limited to 2hrs

CHERVES RICHEMONT
198 E8 — 16370 — N45°44.410' W000°21.350'

Directions: Impasse du Vieux Chene. At Cherves Richemont turn off D731 onto D85, sp 'Matha'. Follow road and turn left in 500m, signed. Aire 10m on left.

5 designated bays overlooking pony paddock. Local commerce 2 mins. Ideal if **197** full. Inspected 2014.

5

Aire Services

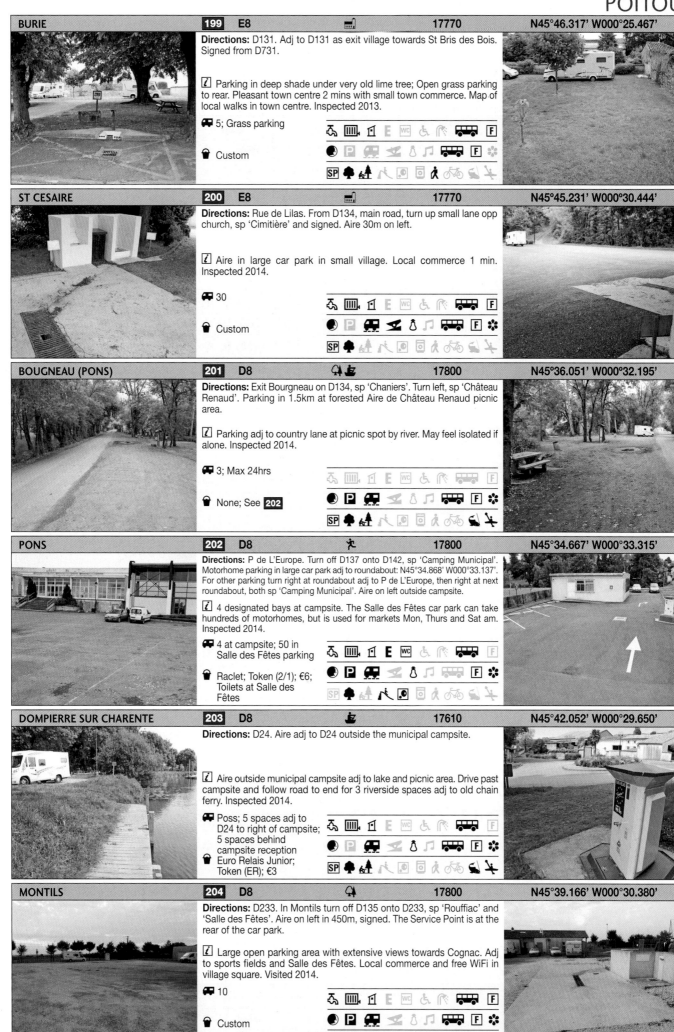

BURIE | 199 | E8 | 17770 | N45°46.317' W000°25.467'

Directions: D131. Adj to D131 as exit village towards St Bris des Bois. Signed from D731.

i Parking in deep shade under very old lime tree; Open grass parking to rear. Pleasant town centre 2 mins with small town commerce. Map of local walks in town centre. Inspected 2013.

🚐 5; Grass parking

⛲ Custom

ST CESAIRE | 200 | E8 | 17770 | N45°45.231' W000°30.444'

Directions: Rue de Lilas. From D134, main road, turn up small lane opp church, sp 'Cimitière' and signed. Aire 30m on left.

i Aire in large car park in small village. Local commerce 1 min. Inspected 2014.

🚐 30

⛲ Custom

BOUGNEAU (PONS) | 201 | D8 | 17800 | N45°36.051' W000°32.195'

Directions: Exit Bourgneau on D134, sp 'Chaniers'. Turn left, sp 'Château Renaud'. Parking in 1.5km at forested Aire de Château Renaud picnic area.

i Parking adj to country lane at picnic spot by river. May feel isolated if alone. Inspected 2014.

🚐 3; Max 24hrs

⛲ None; See 202

PONS | 202 | D8 | 17800 | N45°34.667' W000°33.315'

Directions: P de L'Europe. Turn off D137 onto D142, sp 'Camping Municipal'. Motorhome parking in large car park adj to roundabout: N45°34.868' W000°33.137'. For other parking turn right at roundabout adj to P de L'Europe, then right at next roundabout, both sp 'Camping Municipal'. Aire on left outside campsite.

i 4 designated bays at campsite. The Salle des Fêtes car park can take hundreds of motorhomes, but is used for markets Mon, Thurs and Sat am. Inspected 2014.

🚐 4 at campsite; 50 in Salle des Fêtes parking

⛲ Raclet; Token (2/1); €6; Toilets at Salle des Fêtes

DOMPIERRE SUR CHARENTE | 203 | D8 | 17610 | N45°42.052' W000°29.650'

Directions: D24. Aire adj to D24 outside the municipal campsite.

i Aire outside municipal campsite adj to lake and picnic area. Drive past campsite and follow road to end for 3 riverside spaces adj to old chain ferry. Inspected 2014.

🚐 Poss; 5 spaces adj to D24 to right of campsite; 5 spaces behind campsite reception

⛲ Euro Relais Junior; Token (ER); €3

MONTILS | 204 | D8 | 17800 | N45°39.166' W000°30.380'

Directions: D233. In Montils turn off D135 onto D233, sp 'Rouffiac' and 'Salle des Fêtes'. Aire on left in 450m, signed. The Service Point is at the rear of the car park.

i Large open parking area with extensive views towards Cognac. Adj to sports fields and Salle des Fêtes. Local commerce and free WiFi in village square. Visited 2014.

🚐 10

⛲ Custom

Info/photos: Janet & John Watts

SAINTES | 205 | E8 | 🏢 | 17100 | N45°44.427' W000°37.621'

Directions: Ave de Saintonge. From Cognac follow D24 to Saintes. Go straight on, sp 'Centre Ville', then turn left at roundabout always staying on D24, sp 'Office de Tourisme'. At next roundabout turn left, sp 'P Palu' and signed. Aire on right, signed.

ℹ️ Large designated bays in car park opp E'Leclerc supermarket. Road noise from adj main road. Riverside park access at end of Aire with foot/cycle path into Saintes centre, 4 mins. Inspected 2014.

🚐 10; €5/day; Pay at machine

🚰 Aire Services; CC; €5

ST JEAN D'ANGELY | 206 | E8 | ⚓ | 17400 | N45°56.722' W000°32.249'

Directions: Avenue de Marennes/D18. From east cross river and turn off D18 before junction with D218, sp 'Base de Plein Aire' and signed. 3 designated bays in car park at Base Nautique.

ℹ️ Lots of green space; Mini golf, skate park, table tennis, sandpit, football pitch, outdoor swimming pool and river adj, no views. Updated 2014.

🚐 3; Max 2 Nights

🚰 Custom

Info/photos: Keith & Sue Lawrence

Photo: Keith Seymour

MATHA | 207 | E8 | 🏭 | 17160 | N45°51.937' W000°19.321'

Directions: Boulevard Bossais. From west on D939 turn off at roundabout, sp 'Matha' and 'DID Centre d'Exploitation'. At 2nd roundabout turn right and Aire is on right in 200m, adj to pond.

ℹ️ Gatehouse of old château and pond adj. Toilets locked at time of inspection. Additional grass parking. Inspected 2010.

🚐 5

🚰 Custom; 5 unmetered elec points

Info/photos: Keith & Sue Lawrence

LOULAY | 208 | E7 | 🏭 | 17330 | N46°02.858' W000°30.688'

Directions: Rue des Tilleuls, off D150. From St Jean D'Angely take D150 north. At Loulay turn right into Place du Général de Gaulle. Drive around the outside of the car park/square, following sp 'P Poids Lourds' and signed. Turn left into Rue des Tilleuls (one-way and heads back to main road). Aire on left at rear of La Poste and Mairie.

ℹ️ Small roadside Aire in one-way street. Attractive small town square (up steps behind Aire) with market on Fridays. Updated 2014.

🚐 3

🚰 Custom

AULNAY 1 | 209 | E8 | 🏭 | 17470 | N46°01.344' W000°20.716'

Directions: D129/Rue de Salles. Exit town to north on D129, sp 'Chef-Boutonne'. Aire 200m on right, signed.

ℹ️ Town 3 mins; Market Thursday. Updated 2014.

🚐 15

🚰 Custom

Info/photos: Keith & Sue Lawrence

AULNAY 2 | 210 | E8 | ☀️ 🏢 | | N46°01.407' W000°21.274'

Directions: D121/Avenue de l'Église. From D950 turn into Aulnay on D121. The parking area is on the left opp the church.

ℹ️ Proximity to D950 useful for an overnight stop. Free WiFi at Maison de Tourisme. Visited 2014.

🚐 6

🚰 None; See 209

Info/photos: Janet & John Watts

Ambierle

RHONE-ALPS

Le Benisson Dieu

ST MARTIN D'ESTREAUX | 1 | I7 | 🏛 | 42620 | N46°12.434' E003°47.888'

Directions: D52. From south on N7 take 3rd exit at roundabout, sp 'St Martin D'Estréaux'. Follow road through town and turn right opp D207 onto D52, sp 'Sail les Bains' and signed. Follow road to right and Aire is on right, signed.

ℹ Aire in peaceful residential area and is a convenient stop when travelling north/south on N7. Small town commerce 3 mins. Inspected 2014.

🚐 6 in adj parking area; Max 48hrs

⚑ Custom

LE CROZET | 2 | I7 | 🏭 | 42310 | N46°10.164' E003°51.448'

Directions: D35. Exit N7 at Junction 59, sp 'La Pacaudière'. Follow road to La Pacaudière and turn right onto D35, sp 'Le Crozet'. Follow road under 3.8m arched railway bridge up towards village. Turn sharp left, signed. Aire on left, signed. Best to reverse in.

ℹ A difficult Aire to access due to its location and size. 2 mins from medieval village. Inspected 2014.

🚐 2; Max 72hrs

⚑ Custom; €2; Elec €2/4hrs

ST RIRAND | 3 | I7 | 🏭 | 42370 | N46°04.503' E003°51.015'

Directions: Le Moulin, off D41 opp church. From Renaison take D9, then turn left onto D41, sp 'St Rirand'. At start of village turn left into Lieu-Dit Le Moulin opp church, signed. Aire 100m on left.

ℹ Small Aire in lovely, rural setting on edge of village. Covered picnic benches on decking 'islands'. Small wetland park with paths or longer walk around reservoir. Inspected 2014.

🚐 3; Max 9m; See 9

⚑ Custom

AMBIERLE | 4 | I7 | 🌳🏭 | 42820 | N46°06.392' E003°53.623'

Directions: Rue du 19 Mars 1962. Turn off D8, sp 'Ambierle'. In centre by church turn right, sp 'Le Musée', 'Salle Municipale' and signed. Follow road straight on, signed. Parking on right overlooking cemetery, Service Point to the left behind municipal hall, signed.

ℹ Parking with views across cemetery to vast valley beyond. Ambierle is a village of character. Interesting Benedictine priory complex in centre with ornately tiled roof, 2 mins. Inspected 2014.

🚐 5

⚑ Custom

ST GERMAIN LESPINASSE | 5 | I7 | 🏭 | 42640 | N46°06.317' E003°57.737'

Directions: D18. From south on N7 exit onto D4, sp 'St Germain Lespinasse'. In town turn right onto D18. Aire in car park on left just beyond village centre, signed.

ℹ Small designated parking area with some shade and lovely views across open countryside. Additional parking with overhang and truck sized bays adj. Small town commerce adj. Market Thurs. Inspected 2014.

🚐 3; More parking adj

⚑ Custom

RENAISON | 6 | I7 | ⚓ | 42370 | N46°02.863' E003°55.276'

Directions: Rue des Rivières. Approach Renaison on D9 from Roanne. Follow D9 into centre, then turn left in central square, signed. Follow road downhill for 400m then turn right, signed. Aire 400m on left, signed.

ℹ Pleasant, peaceful shaded Aire by small river and weir at edge of town. Grass and gravel parking available. Small town commerce 4 mins. Inspected 2014.

🚐 8

⚑ Custom

ST ANDRE D'APCHON

| 7 | I7 | | 42370 | N46°02.040' E003°55.625' |

Directions: La Prébande. Turn off D8 at roundabout into St André d'Apchon. Turn right, sp 'Eglise' and signed. Follow road to end, then turn left, sp 'Eglise' and signed. Follow road to right at church and Aire 400m on right, signed.

ℹ️ Aire located on outskirts of village with views of Côte Roannaise grapes. Local commerce 2 mins. Church has interesting tiled roof. Inspected 2014.

🚐 3

⚱️ Custom

ARCON

| 8 | I8 | | 42370 | N46°00.557' E003°53.294' |

Directions: D51. From St André d'Apchon follow D51 to Arçon. Aire on right adj to road 100m from church, signed.

ℹ️ Really pleasant rural community Aire with space for 3 motorhomes next to Service Point and 2 more spaces with panoramic views on terrace above. Walking routes adj. Inspected 2014.

🚐 6

⚱️ Custom; Nice toilets

LES NOES

| 9 | I7 | | 42370 | N46°02.459' E003°51.105' |

Directions: D47. From Renaison on D9 turn left onto D47, sp 'Les Noes'. Follow D47 to Les Noës and Aire on left at start of village, approx 6.3km.

ℹ️ Pleasant rural village Aire near a large reservoir. Peaceful location to get away from it all; nice walk around reservoir. Local commerce 2 mins. Inspected 2014.

🚐 10

⚱️ Custom

VILLEREST ★

| 10 | I8 | | 42300 | N45°59.189' E004°02.578' |

Directions: D18. Exit D53 onto D18, sp 'Villerest'. At roundabout turn right, sp 'Lac de Villerest'. Follow road for approx 1km and Aire is on right overlooking lake, signed.

ℹ️ Terraced Aire overlooking large leisure lake near the Gorges de la Loire. Leisure lake has numerous tourist commerce, swimming beach and water slides. Inspected 2014.

🚐 20; €5/night Apr-Oct; Collected; Free Nov-Mar

⚱️ Custom; At toilet block; Inc; Apr-Oct; Flot Bleu Pacific; €4 (2 x €2); Nov-Mar

ST JUST EN CHEVALET

| 11 | I8 | | 42430 | N45°54.846' E003°50.851' |

Directions: D1. From Champoly follow D53 through town. At the end of the road turn left onto D1, sp 'Roanne'. Service Point immediately on right, signed.

ℹ️ Service Point and parking in centre adj to small town commerce. The parking is unlevel and used as local truck parking at weekends, suggest 12 instead. Inspected 2014.

🚐 15 in car park on D1/D53 junction

⚱️ Urba Flux; Elec €2; Water free

CHAMPOLY

| 12 | I8 | | 42430 | N45°51.346' E003°49.940' |

Photo: Rod Poxon

Directions: Salle des Fêtes, off D24. From Noirétable on D53 turn off D53, sp 'Champoly'. As approach town turn right, sp 'Salle de Fêtes' and signed. Follow road and Service Point on left, signed. 3.5t parking adj to Service Point and large car park around Salle des Fêtes.

ℹ️ Aire at Salle des Fêtes in a peaceful location overlooking countryside. 3 mins from centre with local commerce. Inspected 2014.

🚐 20

⚱️ Euro Relais Junior; €2

ROANNE ★   13   I7   42300   N46°02.267' E004°04.969'

Directions: Allée de l'Amiral Merveilleux Du Vignaux. From D53/D207/D482 roundabout in centre near river bridge turn off, sp 'Maison du Port'. Turn right and cross canal on bridge, sp 'Capitainerie'. Follow road to right and Aire is 200m past Capitainerie, signed.

Landscaped Aire; lovely outlook over canal basin and boats. Nicely laid out; plenty of space; grass between large level bays. Canal adj, boat hire avail. Large town commerce 4 mins. Inspected 2014.

10; €6/night; Collected; Max 6 days

Flot Bleu Euro; CC; €2.10; Elec 1 Token/12hrs

ST HAON LE CHATEL   14   I7   42370   N46°03.830' E003°54.777'

Directions: D39. Turn off D8, sp 'St Haon le Châtel'. Follow road to left, signed, and in 400m follow road to left again, sp 'St Croix' and signed. Aire 100m on right, signed.

Peaceful Aire on edge of historic town. Village of character centre 3 mins uphill. Inspected 2014.

3

Custom

POUILLY SOUS CHARLIEU 1   15   I7   42720   N46°08.589' E004°06.515'

Directions: D482/Rue de la République. From D4 turn onto D482, sp 'Roanne'. Aire 200m on left opp mini Casino market and just before D35 junction, sp 'Espace Loisirs' and signed.

Town 2 mins with commerce. Park adj. Also check 16, as may be preferred. Inspected 2014.

10; No parking Sun 6am-1pm (Market)

Aire Services

POUILLY SOUS CHARLIEU 2   16   I7   42720   N46°08.829' E004°05.998'

Directions: D4. Exit town on D487/D4 towards Briennon. Turn right into picnic area before/adj to river bridge. Designated parking in car park adj to riverside picnic area, signed.

Parking adj to riverside picnic area, an ideal spot to take your chair for a walk to enjoy some riverside views. Likely to be more peaceful than 15. Inspected 2014.

4

None; See 15

LA BENISSON DIEU   17   I7   T   42720   N46°09.053' E004°02.766'

Directions: D4. Turn off D4 in La Benisson Dieu, sp 'Abbaye Cistercienne' and signed. Drive towards church and designated parking on left overlooking church, signed.

Designated parking overlooking abbey with ornate roof and spire; free entry, €3 to climb some of the bell tower. TO at abbey. On Santiago (St Jacques) pilgrimage route. School adj, busy at drop off and collection times. Inspected 2014.

2

None; See 15; Toilets near TO

ST HILAIRE SOUS CHARLIEU   18   I7   42190   N46°06.632' E004°11.298'

Directions: Exit Pouilly sous Charlieu on D35, sp 'St Hilaire' and 'Boyer'. Follow D35, sp 'Boyer', then turn onto D49, sp 'Boyer'. Turn right into lane, sp 'Le Grand Couvert Architecture Rurale'. Designated parking in car park 50m to right, signed.

Parking adj to barn visitor attraction, for free entry press button. Enter €2 into slot and the exhibit comes to life. Bread oven being built. Rural views from parking. Inspected 2014.

2

None; See 15

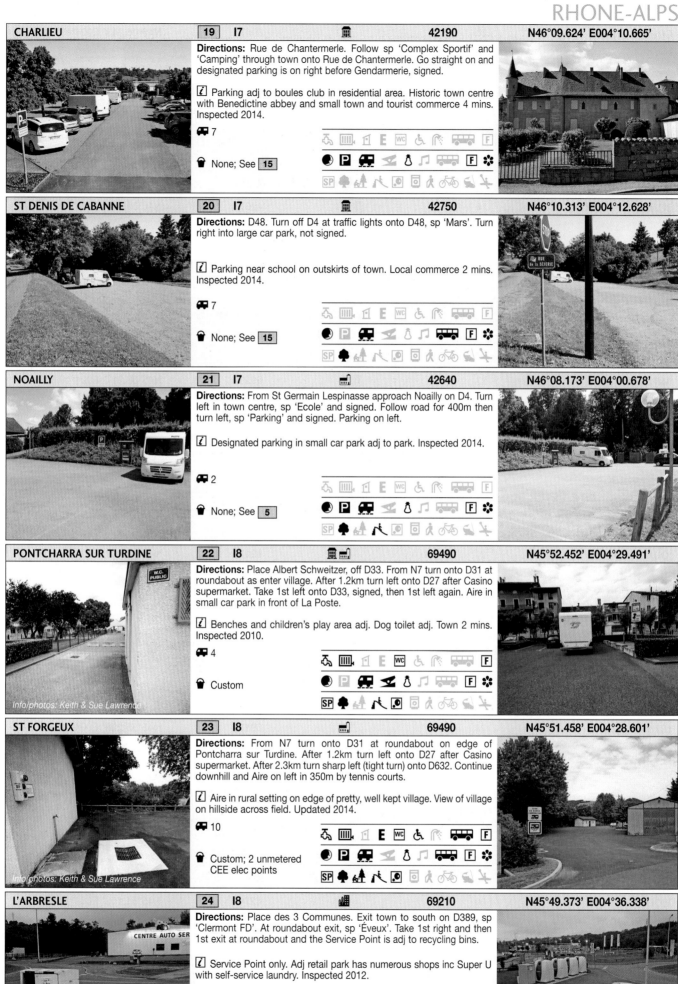

CHARLIEU | 19 | I7 | | 42190 | N46°09.624' E004°10.665'

Directions: Rue de Chantermerle. Follow sp 'Complex Sportif' and 'Camping' through town onto Rue de Chantermerle. Go straight on and designated parking is on right before Gendarmerie, signed.

Parking adj to boules club in residential area. Historic town centre with Benedictine abbey and small town and tourist commerce 4 mins. Inspected 2014.

7

None; See 15

ST DENIS DE CABANNE | 20 | I7 | | 42750 | N46°10.313' E004°12.628'

Directions: D48. Turn off D4 at traffic lights onto D48, sp 'Mars'. Turn right into large car park, not signed.

Parking near school on outskirts of town. Local commerce 2 mins. Inspected 2014.

7

None; See 15

NOAILLY | 21 | I7 | | 42640 | N46°08.173' E004°00.678'

Directions: From St Germain Lespinasse approach Noailly on D4. Turn left in town centre, sp 'Ecole' and signed. Follow road for 400m then turn left, sp 'Parking' and signed. Parking on left.

Designated parking in small car park adj to park. Inspected 2014.

2

None; See 5

PONTCHARRA SUR TURDINE | 22 | I8 | | 69490 | N45°52.452' E004°29.491'

Directions: Place Albert Schweitzer, off D33. From N7 turn onto D31 at roundabout as enter village. After 1.2km turn left onto D27 after Casino supermarket. Take 1st left onto D33, signed, then 1st left again. Aire in small car park in front of La Poste.

Benches and children's play area adj. Dog toilet adj. Town 2 mins. Inspected 2010.

4

Custom

Info/photos: Keith & Sue Lawrence

ST FORGEUX | 23 | I8 | | 69490 | N45°51.458' E004°28.601'

Directions: From N7 turn onto D31 at roundabout on edge of Pontcharra sur Turdine. After 1.2km turn left onto D27 after Casino supermarket. After 2.3km turn sharp left (tight turn) onto D632. Continue downhill and Aire on left in 350m by tennis courts.

Aire in rural setting on edge of pretty, well kept village. View of village on hillside across field. Updated 2014.

10

Custom; 2 unmetered CEE elec points

Info/photos: Keith & Sue Lawrence

L'ARBRESLE | 24 | I8 | | 69210 | N45°49.373' E004°36.338'

Directions: Place des 3 Communes. Exit town to south on D389, sp 'Clermont FD'. At roundabout exit, sp 'Éveux'. Take 1st right and then 1st exit at roundabout and the Service Point is adj to recycling bins.

Service Point only. Adj retail park has numerous shops inc Super U with self-service laundry. Inspected 2012.

None

Custom

COURS LA VILLE
25 | I7 | 🏢 | 69470 | N46°06.243' E004°19.400'

Directions: Chemin de la Rivière. From south follow D308 around north side of town, sp 'Chauffailles'. After passing the Intermarché on left, turn right, signed, and drive past sports ground. Follow road downhill and Aire on left, signed. Lift barrier to enter.

ℹ️ Aire in a residential area adj to Ambulance taxi station and tennis club. Stream adj. Hardstanding near entrance, grass parking further back. Inspected 2014.

🚐 10

🛒 Custom

BELMONT DE LA LOIRE
26 | I7 | 🏢🏭 | 42670 | N46°09.936' E004°20.787'

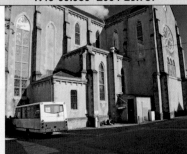

Directions: Place de l'Eglise. From west follow D4, sp 'Chauffailles', and turn left at the D31/D4 roundabout, signed. For Service Point turn left to the church, signed. Service Point against church. For parking turn right and drive past Les Arcades and the TO, parking on right: N46°10.041' E004°20.672'.

ℹ️ Parking in large car park 200m from TO. Benedictine abbey in town surrounded by some local commerce. Inspected 2014.

🚐 20 at P les Arcade; 2 at Service Point

🛒 Custom; 2 Cont elec points

AMPLEPUIS
27 | I8 | 🏢🏃 | 69550 | N45°58.217' E004°19.850'

Directions: Rue Paul de la Goutte. From south on D8, exit at D8/D10 roundabout onto D8e, sp 'Thizy'. Turn 1st right after 250m, sp 'Aire Camping Car'. Aire on right, by bus stop, in 120m at Rue Paul de la Goutte, signed. 7.5t weight restriction on Aire.

ℹ️ Parking at 'Salle des Sports Daniel Pierrefeu'. Water below ground under large red flaps, may be turned off in winter. Risk of grounding at entrance. Inspected 2010.

🚐 10; Max 48hrs

🛒 Custom

Photo: Keith & Sue Lawrence

JOUX
28 | I8 | 🏭 | 69170 | N45°53.302' E004°22.553'

Directions: At 'Salle des Fêtes' on D79. From east on N7 turn left onto D79, sp 'Joux'. Aire on left in 1.3km at start of village, sp 'Salle des Fêtes' and signed.

ℹ️ Service Point at bottom of very sloping car park with loose gravel. Adj to village hall. Better level parking at lakeside: N45°53.439' E004°22.953'. Inspected 2010.

🚐 10

🛒 Custom

Info/photos: Keith & Sue Lawrence

LES SAUVAGES
29 | I8 | 🏭 | 69170 | N45°55.238' E004°22.627'

Directions: Les Près de Sienne, off D121. From Tarare (southeast) on D8 turn left onto D121, signed. Follow road for 600m through village and turn right at village boundary sign by small memorial, sp 'Les Près de Sienne' and signed.

ℹ️ Choice of 3 parking areas: 1 adj to stadium and Service Point with some shade and 2 across road with good views adj to self-service weighbridge. Updated 2014.

🚐 20

🛒 Custom; Donation box

Info/photos: Keith & Sue Lawrence

VIOLAY
30 | I8 | 🏭 | 42780 | N45°51.153' E004°21.306'

Directions: Place Giroud. Turn off D1 opp D49 turning to Villechenève, signed. Turn left into car park, the Aire is located at the far end.

ℹ️ Adj to panoramic view but obstructed by conifers. Local commerce 1 min, adj to D1. Inspected 2012.

🚐 3

🛒 Custom; 3 Cont elec points (Not working)

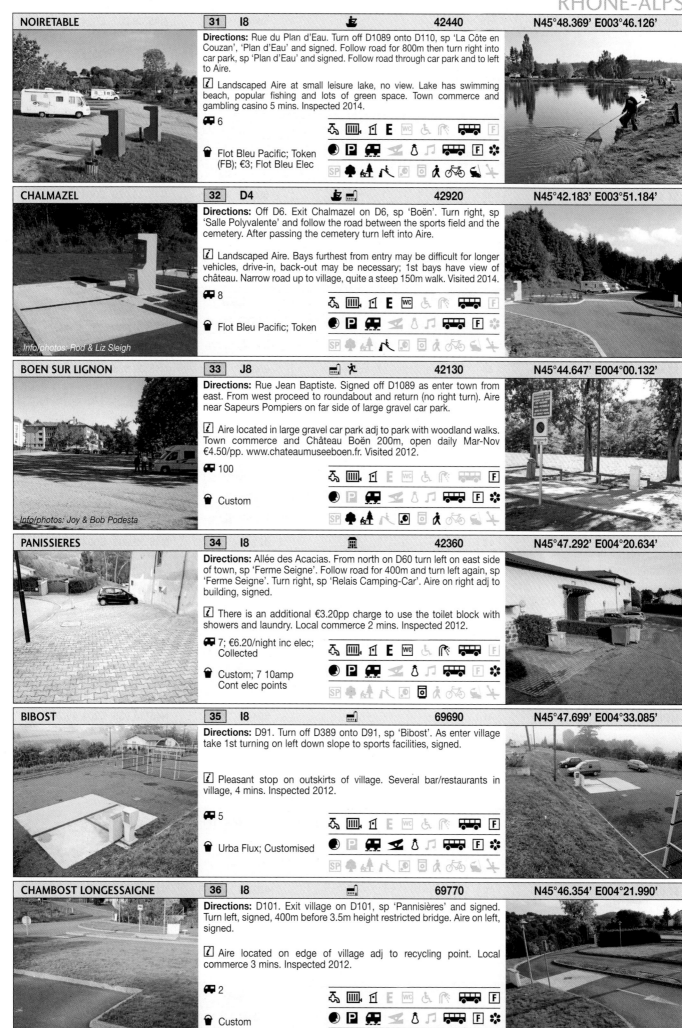

NOIRETABLE | **31** | **I8** | 42440 | N45°48.369' E003°46.126'

Directions: Rue du Plan d'Eau. Turn off D1089 onto D110, sp 'La Côte en Couzan', 'Plan d'Eau' and signed. Follow road for 800m then turn right into car park, sp 'Plan d'Eau' and signed. Follow road through car park and to left to Aire.

i Landscaped Aire at small leisure lake, no view. Lake has swimming beach, popular fishing and lots of green space. Town commerce and gambling casino 5 mins. Inspected 2014.

6

Flot Bleu Pacific; Token (FB); €3; Flot Bleu Elec

CHALMAZEL | **32** | **D4** | 42920 | N45°42.183' E003°51.184'

Directions: Off D6. Exit Chalmazel on D6, sp 'Boën'. Turn right, sp 'Salle Polyvalente' and follow the road between the sports field and the cemetery. After passing the cemetery turn left into Aire.

i Landscaped Aire. Bays furthest from entry may be difficult for longer vehicles, drive-in, back-out may be necessary; 1st bays have view of château. Narrow road up to village, quite a steep 150m walk. Visited 2014.

8

Flot Bleu Pacific; Token

Info/photos: Rod & Liz Sleigh

BOEN SUR LIGNON | **33** | **J8** | 42130 | N45°44.647' E004°00.132'

Directions: Rue Jean Baptiste. Signed off D1089 as enter town from east. From west proceed to roundabout and return (no right turn). Aire near Sapeurs Pompiers on far side of large gravel car park.

i Aire located in large gravel car park adj to park with woodland walks. Town commerce and Château Boën 200m, open daily Mar-Nov €4.50/pp. www.chateaumuseeboen.fr. Visited 2012.

100

Custom

Info/photos: Joy & Bob Podesta

PANISSIERES | **34** | **I8** | 42360 | N45°47.292' E004°20.634'

Directions: Allée des Acacias. From north on D60 turn left on east side of town, sp 'Ferme Seigne'. Follow road for 400m and turn left again, sp 'Ferme Seigne'. Turn right, sp 'Relais Camping-Car'. Aire on right adj to building, signed.

i There is an additional €3.20pp charge to use the toilet block with showers and laundry. Local commerce 2 mins. Inspected 2012.

7; €6.20/night inc elec; Collected

Custom; 7 10amp Cont elec points

BIBOST | **35** | **I8** | 69690 | N45°47.699' E004°33.085'

Directions: D91. Turn off D389 onto D91, sp 'Bibost'. As enter village take 1st turning on left down slope to sports facilities, signed.

i Pleasant stop on outskirts of village. Several bar/restaurants in village, 4 mins. Inspected 2012.

5

Urba Flux; Customised

CHAMBOST LONGESSAIGNE | **36** | **I8** | 69770 | N45°46.354' E004°21.990'

Directions: D101. Exit village on D101, sp 'Pannisières' and signed. Turn left, signed, 400m before 3.5m height restricted bridge. Aire on left, signed.

i Aire located on edge of village adj to recycling point. Local commerce 3 mins. Inspected 2012.

2

Custom

CHAUSSAN
37 | I8 | 69440 | N45°38.037' E004°38.279'

Directions: D34. In Mornant turn onto D34, sp 'Chaussan'. In Chaussan turn left at roundabout, signed.

ℹ️ Service Point only, limited use and access! Inspected 2012.

🚐 None

🛁 Custom; Dysfunctional; Tap on side of building

ST SYMPHORIEN SUR COISE
38 | I8 | 69590 | N45°38.026' E004°27.532'

Directions: D4. In town follow sp 'Lyon' to navigate one-way system onto D4 northbound. Aire in car park adj to D4, signed.

ℹ️ D4 is a busy and noisy road. Town centre with local commerce 3 mins. Tokens free from Tabac/Mairie. Inspected 2012.

🚐 5; Popular local parking

🛁 Custom; Token (See nearest toilet)

ST MARTIN EN HAUT - Larajasse
39 | I8 | 69850 | N45°38.535' E004°32.111'

Directions: Off D311. Exit St Martin en Haut on D311 towards St Symphorien sur Coise. After 2.4km turn left off D311 onto small road, sp 'Village Vacances l'Oree du Bois' and signed. Follow road downhill, across stream and up the other side, then turn 1st left. Aire on left, signed.

ℹ️ In a remote, rural location adj to vacation village with café and fishing lake. Voie Verte cycle route/walks adj. Inspected 2012.

🚐 5; Grass and gravel parking

🛁 Custom

FONTANES
40 | I8 | 42140 | N45°32.808' E004°26.408'

Directions: Hameau de Chantemerle. Approach Fontanes from south on D3. Turn left as enter village down a steep slope, signed. Follow road and Aire is on right, signed.

ℹ️ Aire adj to sports facilities in a peaceful rural village. History info panel and walking panel adj. Local shop selling regional produce 2 mins uphill. Inspected 2013.

🚐 3

🛁 Custom

MORNANT
41 | J8 | 69440 | N45°36.935' E004°40.254'

Directions: Rue Boiron, adj to D30. Outside municipal campsite, signed.

ℹ️ Service Point only. Inspected 2012.

🚐 None

🛁 Euro Relais Junior; 2 unmetered CEE elec points

ST PRIEST EN JAREZ
42 | I8 | 42270 | N45°28.721' E004°21.522'

Directions: At fuel station, off N82. From south on A72 exit at Junction 10 and turn right onto N82, sp 'St Priest en Jarez'. Aire at the fuel station of the Casino supermarket, signed.

ℹ️ Supermarket adj. Inspected 2012.

🚐 Poss

🛁 Flot Bleu Euro; CC; €2

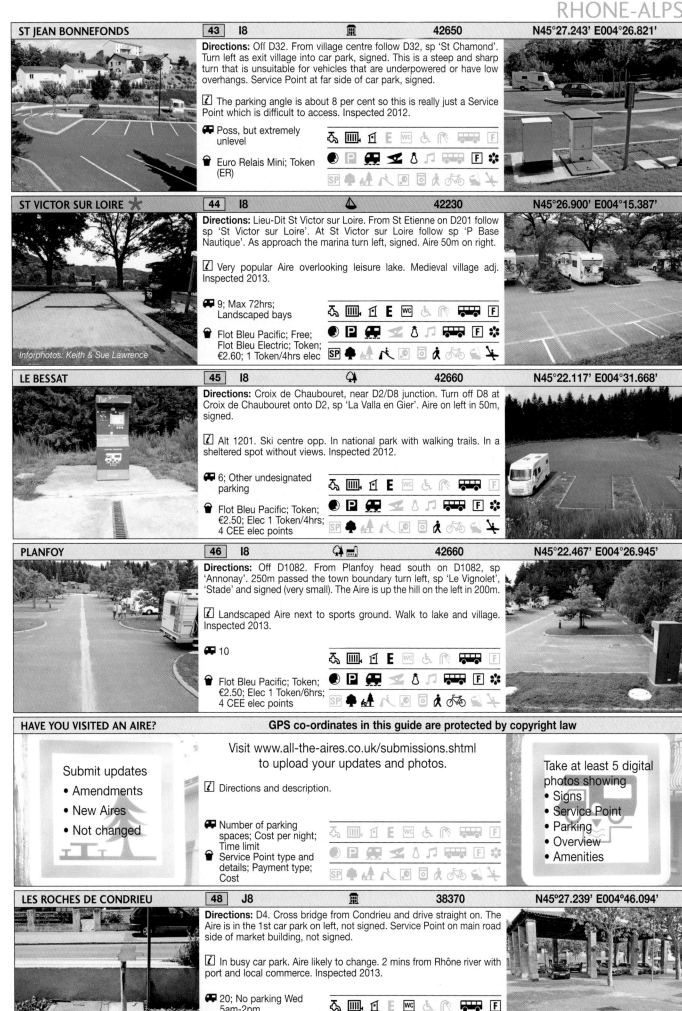

| ST JEAN BONNEFONDS | 43 | I8 | | 42650 | N45°27.243' E004°26.821' |

Directions: Off D32. From village centre follow D32, sp 'St Chamond'. Turn left as exit village into car park, signed. This is a steep and sharp turn that is unsuitable for vehicles that are underpowered or have low overhangs. Service Point at far side of car park, signed.

The parking angle is about 8 per cent so this is really just a Service Point which is difficult to access. Inspected 2012.

🚐 Poss, but extremely unlevel

🚰 Euro Relais Mini; Token (ER)

| ST VICTOR SUR LOIRE ✶ | 44 | I8 | | 42230 | N45°26.900' E004°15.387' |

Directions: Lieu-Dit St Victor sur Loire. From St Etienne on D201 follow sp 'St Victor sur Loire'. At St Victor sur Loire follow sp 'P Base Nautique'. As approach the marina turn left, signed. Aire 50m on right.

Very popular Aire overlooking leisure lake. Medieval village adj. Inspected 2013.

🚐 9; Max 72hrs; Landscaped bays

🚰 Flot Bleu Pacific; Free; Flot Bleu Electric; Token; €2.60; 1 Token/4hrs elec

Info/photos: Keith & Sue Lawrence

| LE BESSAT | 45 | I8 | | 42660 | N45°22.117' E004°31.668' |

Directions: Croix de Chaubouret, near D2/D8 junction. Turn off D8 at Croix de Chaubouret onto D2, sp 'La Valla en Gier'. Aire on left in 50m, signed.

Alt 1201. Ski centre opp. In national park with walking trails. In a sheltered spot without views. Inspected 2012.

🚐 6; Other undesignated parking

🚰 Flot Bleu Pacific; Token; €2.50; Elec 1 Token/4hrs; 4 CEE elec points

| PLANFOY | 46 | I8 | | 42660 | N45°22.467' E004°26.945' |

Directions: Off D1082. From Planfoy head south on D1082, sp 'Annonay'. 250m passed the town boundary turn left, sp 'Le Vignolet', 'Stade' and signed (very small). The Aire is up the hill on the left in 200m.

Landscaped Aire next to sports ground. Walk to lake and village. Inspected 2013.

🚐 10

🚰 Flot Bleu Pacific; Token; €2.50; Elec 1 Token/6hrs; 4 CEE elec points

| HAVE YOU VISITED AN AIRE? | GPS co-ordinates in this guide are protected by copyright law |

Submit updates
- Amendments
- New Aires
- Not changed

Visit www.all-the-aires.co.uk/submissions.shtml
to upload your updates and photos.

Directions and description.

🚐 Number of parking spaces; Cost per night; Time limit
🚰 Service Point type and details; Payment type; Cost

Take at least 5 digital photos showing
- Signs
- Service Point
- Parking
- Overview
- Amenities

| LES ROCHES DE CONDRIEU | 48 | J8 | | 38370 | N45°27.239' E004°46.094' |

Directions: D4. Cross bridge from Condrieu and drive straight on. The Aire is in the 1st car park on left, not signed. Service Point on main road side of market building, not signed.

In busy car park. Aire likely to change. 2 mins from Rhône river with port and local commerce. Inspected 2013.

🚐 20; No parking Wed 5am-2pm

🚰 Custom

Info/photos: Keith & Sue Lawrence

VIENNE — 49 — J8 — 38200 — N45°32.320' E004°52.352'

Directions: N7. From north on A7/E15 exit at Junction 9, sp 'Vienne'. Follow dual carriageway along the Rhône for 1.8km. At traffic lights turn left, sp 'St Symphorien'. Go under bridge and turn left at roundabout, sp 'St Symphorien' and signed. After 2 sets of traffic lights turn right into car park, signed. Take 3rd row on left to Aire.

i Town commerce and bank adj, but Vienne centre 10 mins walk. Market in car park Fri 12-8pm. River Rhône access restricted by road. Inspected 2012.

🚐 6

Custom

ST GEORGES D'ESPERANCHE — 50 — J8 — 38790 — N45°33.348' E005°04.504'

Directions: Chemin des Picarnus. From D75 exit roundabout onto D53, sp 'St Georges d'E. Centre'. Follow D53 4km into town, then follow sp 'St Georges Centre' over 2 roundabouts. At end of road follow signs through car park to Aire. Narrow access and 3.5t weight restriction on Aire.

i Pleasant stop. Local commerce 5 mins. Inspected 2010.

🚐 10

Custom

Info/photos: Keith & Sue Lawrence

ST JEAN DE BOURNAY — 51 — J8 — 38440 — N45°30.060' E005°08.300'

Directions: Parking 'Place du Marché' at Place François Mitterrand. From roundabout on D518 follow truck route into town on Rte de Villeneuve. Turn right onto Rue du Dr Paillard and then left on Place du Marché, signed. Aire on right.

i Small town commerce 2 mins. Inspected 2010.

🚐 50; No parking Mon 5am-2.30pm (Market)

Custom

Info/photos: Keith & Sue Lawrence

EYZIN PINET — 52 — J8 — 38780 — N45°28.481' E004°59.984'

Directions: Rue du Stade, off D38. Turn off D502 onto D38, sp 'Eyzin-Pinet'. Follow D38 into village and the Aire is on the left, signed.

i Pleasant, well located Aire adj to green space but only 1 min from village centre with local commerce. Inspected 2012.

🚐 8; Max 48hrs

Custom

ST ETIENNE DE ST GEOIRS — 53 — J8 — 38590 — N45°21.219' E005°20.097'

Directions: Chemin de la Pierre, adj to D154d. Exit St Étienne de St Geoirs towards Grenoble-Isère Airport on D519c, then D154d. Take 2nd exit at retail park roundabout, then turn immediately right into 3.5t weight restricted road. Service Point on left at end of car park before fuel station, signed.

i Supermarket adj. McDonald's adj. Inspected 2012.

🚐 Poss

Flot Bleu Standard Plus; €2

BOULIEU LES ANNONAY — 54 — J8 — 07100 — N45°16.139' E004°40.188'

Directions: Chemin du Lavoir. Turn off D820 into Rue du Musard (3.5t restricted) opp D342 turning to St Clair. Take 1st left at 1914-1918 war memorial, sp 'Aire de Camping-cars'. Take 1st right, signed, and then turn right again. At end of road turn left into Aire.

i Adj to park. Charming medieval centre 2 mins with local shops and restaurants. Inspected 2012.

🚐 6; Other undesignated parking in area

Custom; Donation

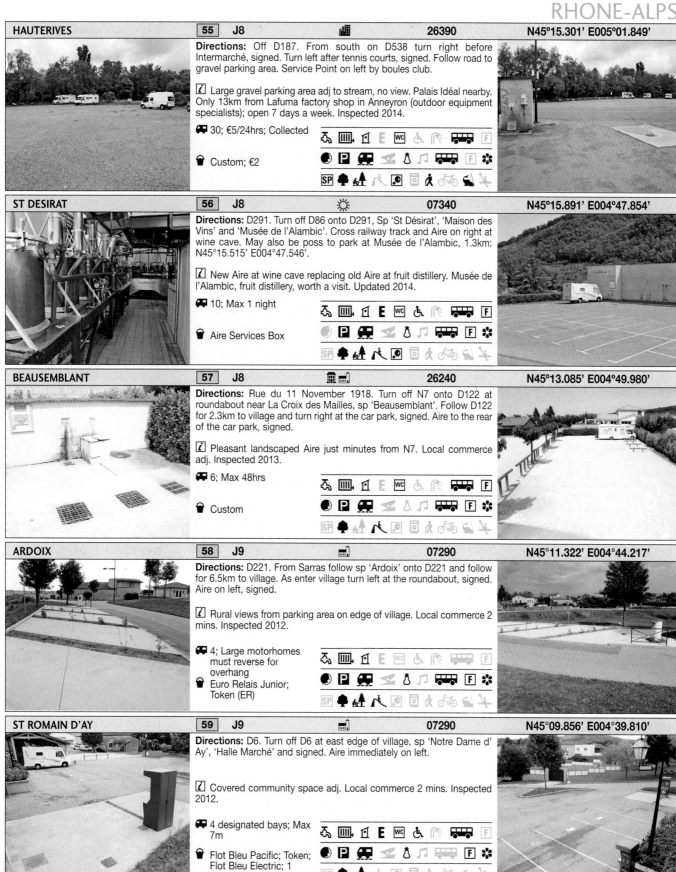

| HAUTERIVES | 55 | J8 | | 26390 | N45°15.301' E005°01.849' |

Directions: Off D187. From south on D538 turn right before Intermarché, signed. Turn left after tennis courts, signed. Follow road to gravel parking area. Service Point on left by boules club.

ℹ️ Large gravel parking area adj to stream, no view. Palais Idéal nearby. Only 13km from Lafuma factory shop in Anneyron (outdoor equipment specialists); open 7 days a week. Inspected 2014.

🚐 30; €5/24hrs; Collected

♿ Custom; €2

| ST DESIRAT | 56 | J8 | ☀ | 07340 | N45°15.891' E004°47.854' |

Directions: D291. Turn off D86 onto D291, Sp 'St Désirat', 'Maison des Vins' and 'Musée de l'Alambic'. Cross railway track and Aire on right at wine cave. May also be poss to park at Musée de l'Alambic, 1.3km: N45°15.515' E004°47.546'.

ℹ️ New Aire at wine cave replacing old Aire at fruit distillery. Musée de l'Alambic, fruit distillery, worth a visit. Updated 2014.

🚐 10; Max 1 night

♿ Aire Services Box

| BEAUSEMBLANT | 57 | J8 | | 26240 | N45°13.085' E004°49.980' |

Directions: Rue du 11 November 1918. Turn off N7 onto D122 at roundabout near La Croix des Mailles, sp 'Beausemblant'. Follow D122 for 2.3km to village and turn right at the car park, signed. Aire to the rear of the car park, signed.

ℹ️ Pleasant landscaped Aire just minutes from N7. Local commerce adj. Inspected 2013.

🚐 6; Max 48hrs

♿ Custom

| ARDOIX | 58 | J9 | | 07290 | N45°11.322' E004°44.217' |

Directions: D221. From Sarras follow sp 'Ardoix' onto D221 and follow for 6.5km to village. As enter village turn left at the roundabout, signed. Aire on left, signed.

ℹ️ Rural views from parking area on edge of village. Local commerce 2 mins. Inspected 2012.

🚐 4; Large motorhomes must reverse for overhang

♿ Euro Relais Junior; Token (ER)

| ST ROMAIN D'AY | 59 | J9 | | 07290 | N45°09.856' E004°39.810' |

Directions: D6. Turn off D6 at east edge of village, sp 'Notre Dame d' Ay', 'Halle Marché' and signed. Aire immediately on left.

ℹ️ Covered community space adj. Local commerce 2 mins. Inspected 2012.

🚐 4 designated bays; Max 7m

♿ Flot Bleu Pacific; Token; Flot Bleu Electric; 1 Token/4hrs

GPS Co-ordinates for SatNav

The GPS Co-ordinates published in this guide were taken onsite by our inspectors. We consider them a valuable and unique asset and at the time of publishing have decided not to publish them as electronic files for use on navigation devices. You have permission to type in the co-ordinates of an Aire you intend to visit but not to store or share them. For the security of our copyright:

• **Do not compile them into lists**

• **Do not publish, share or reproduce them anywhere in any format**

LALOUVESC

| **61** | I9 | | 07520 | N45°07.277' E004°32.036' |

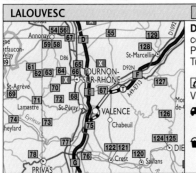

Directions: D532. Turn off D532 in centre onto one-way system around central car park, sp 'Station Service'. Service Point next to fuel station. Parking: N45°07.176' E004°32.035'. Turn right next to Mairie, sp 'P'. Turn 1st left and designated parking is on the right, signed.

*Local commerce 2 mins. Market Thurs 6am-1pm in central car park. Visited 2011.

3

Euro Relais Junior; Token (ER); May-Sept

Info/Photo: Carol Weaver

ST FELICIEN

| **62** | I9 | | 07410 | N45°05.078' E004°37.718' |

Directions: Place de Haies. From south on D234 turn right just past Gendarmerie into Rue de la Pré Lacour, signed. Aire 30m on right behind Gendarmerie.

*Aire in a small underused car park with recycling bins. Village centre with local commerce 4 mins uphill. Also see 63. Inspected 2014.

6

Euro Relais Junior; €2

ARLEBOSC

| **63** | J9 | | 07410 | N45°02.204' E004°39.145' |

Directions: Place du Marché, off D578. From north on D578 turn right at village boundary, sp 'Place du Marché', 'Poste', 'Mairie' and signed. Service Point at old weighbridge, signed.

*Aire located in large car park with plenty of parking and always likely to have space. Pretty village adj. Inspected 2014.

15

Custom; Toilets down steps

COLOMBIER LE VIEUX

| **64** | J9 | | 07410 | N45°03.967' E004°41.641' |

Directions: D234. From east on D234 turn right just before church, signed. Service Point is immediately behind the church.

*Hells bells - every 15 mins all night! Small rural village with some other parking roadside, but away from church. Inspected 2014.

7; Grass and gravel parking; See 63

Custom

GERVANS

| **65** | J9 | | 26600 | N45°06.546' E004°49.831' |

Directions: Rue de l'École. From N7 turn onto D258, sp 'Gervans Village' and signed. Follow signs through village; narrow, but passable. Best parking 200m past Service Point, next to cemetery: N45°06.614' E004°49.700'.

*Service Point and 1st parking area next to school. 2nd parking is pleasant and has valley views. Inspected 2013.

3+5; Max 24hrs

Custom; Donation

TOURNON SUR RHONE

| **66** | J9 | | 07300 | N45°04.403' E004°49.291' |

Directions: Chemin de Labeaume, off D86. From south follow D86, sp 'Annonay'. Turn off D86 as exit town to north, sp 'P 240 Places' and signed. Aire at far side of car park, signed. Overflow parking: N45°03.829' E004°50.599'. Turn off D86 at river bridge roundabout onto 3.5t restricted road, sp 'Maison Pour Tous' and signed. Follow road along river and turn 1st right, signed. Parking in 1st car park on left, not signed.

*Aire in corner of car park north of town adj to derelict industrial building. Inspected 2014.

10; €5/24hrs; Collected

Euro Relais Junior

ROMANS SUR ISERE | 67 | J9 | 🏭 | 26100 | N45°02.728' E005°03.531'

Directions: Parking Gambetta P3, D532/Avenue Gambetta. Follow sp 'Marques Avenue', designated parking opp Marques Avenue building in centre of road.

ℹ️ Designated parking in popular car park with narrow exit. Main road either side of car park, cars may be parked in designated parking. Secondary school adj. Marques Avenue is an outlet centre with 70 shops open 10am-7pm Mon-Sat. Inspected 2014.

🚐 4; Max 48hrs

🚰 None

CORNAS | 68 | J9 | 🏛 | 07130 | N44°57.609' E004°50.840'

Directions: Grand Rue. Turn off D86 in Cornas, signed. In 10m turn left into car park. Aire immediately on left, signed.

ℹ️ Very convenient for D86, therefore some road noise. Walks on old roads through vines to rear of Aire. Inspected 2013.

🚐 3

🚰 Euro Relais Mini

ST AGREVE | 69 | I9 | 🏛 | 07320 | N45°00.618' E004°23.599'

Directions: D120/Ave des Cevennes. From Lamastre on D533, go straight over roundabout onto D120a, sp 'Le Puy'. Turn 1st right, sp 'P Centre Ville'. Turn left, sp 'P'. Aire in car park on right, signed.

ℹ️ Alt 1061m. Aire in large car park tucked away behind the town centre. The town is agricultural and remote. Market Mon. Inspected 2014.

🚐 10

🚰 Aire Services; Token (3/3); €2.50

COLUMBIER LE JEUNE | 70 | J9 | 🏭 | 07270 | N45°00.676' E004°42.088'

Directions: D209. Service Point located in village square/parking just off D209. Parking at tennis court: N45°00.677' E004°41.958' also adj to D209 as exit village towards Le Crestet.

ℹ️ Rural village with local commerce inc convenience store. Inspected 2012.

🚐 3

🚰 Euro Relais Mini

LAMASTRE | 71 | I9 | ⚓ | 07270 | N44°59.221' E004°34.760'

Directions: Place Pradon. Approach on D534 from Tournon sur Rhône. After passing tourist train on right turn right, sp 'Aire Pique Nique'. Follow road into large car park, Service Point is on the right. To park follow road into additional parking, sp 'P 500'.

ℹ️ Parking in large pleasant car park on grass or gravel. Shallow crayfish river adj with slipway/access. Tourist train runs adj. Town commerce 3 mins. Inspected 2014.

🚐 50 (summer) if overflow parking open; 10 (winter); No parking Mon pm/Tues am (Large market)

🚰 Raclet; Token

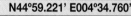

ST ROMAIN DE LERPS | 72 | J9 | 🏭 | 07130 | N44°58.785' E004°47.771'

Directions: D287. Adj to D287 at village boundary by rock terraced parking, signed.

ℹ️ Rural village with historic building. Parking poss but no designated bays. Inspected 2012.

🚐 4; Park adj to road as terraced parking has narrow exit

🚰 Euro Relais Junior; Token (2/1)

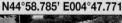

VERNOUX EN VIVARAIS | 73 | J9 | | 07240 | N44°54.149' E004°38.977'

Directions: D14. Exit the town on D14 travelling north. The Service Point is adj to D14 outside Camping Bois de Prat, signed.

ℹ️ Parking is on grass bays separated by hedges just before the campsite barrier. Inspected 2010.

🚐 8; Max 48hrs; Grass parking

🚰 Euro Relais Junior; Token (ER); €2

Info/photos: Keith & Sue Lawrence

LE CHEYLARD | 74 | I9 | | 07160 | N44°54.722' E004°26.451'

Directions: D120, at Super U. From Le Cheylard, take D120 east towards Beauvene. At roundabout turn left to Super U. Service Point in own bay at rear of fuel station and adj to Vulco tyres.

ℹ️ No parking as 2.2m height barrier and 2t weight restriction in car park. Inspected 2010.

🚐 None

🚰 Euro Relais Junior

Info/photos: Keith & Sue Lawrence

PORTES LES VALENCE | 75 | J9 | | 26800 | N44°50.993' E004°52.153'

Directions: D7, at Intermarché. Just off D7 as enter town from south, signed. Service Point in 24hr fuel station, signed.

ℹ️ Supermarket adj. Inspected 2014.

🚐 Poss

🚰 Custom

GRANE | 76 | J9 | | 26400 | N44°45.338' E004°52.061'

Directions: Domaine Distaise, off D104. From Loriol sur Drôme on D104 travel towards Crest/Grane for 3km. The private Aire is on the left down long drive, signed.

ℹ️ Private Aire at fruit and pig farm that also has gîtes. Parking to front on grass, some distant road noise. Fruit, meat, bread and meals avail. Owner's dogs roam free. Inspected 2014.

🚐 10; €2pp/night; Free 1st night for France Passion; Collected; Grass parking

🚰 None; Water €1

LA VOULTE SUR RHONE | 77 | J9 | | 07800 | N44°48.447' E004°47.550'

Directions: D86, ZI Quai Jean Jaurès at Intermarché supermarket. Service Point just past fuel station at rear of supermarket car park.

ℹ️ Supermarket adj. Rhône river across road, lots of unrestricted river parking. Inspected 2013.

🚐 Poss

🚰 Euro Relais Junior; Token (2/1)

PRIVAS | 78 | J9 | | 07000 | N44°43.874' E004°35.585'

Directions: Route des Mines. Exit town on D7, sp 'Villeneuve-de-burg' and signed. Turn left by city wall, signed. Follow road through car park. Aire at bottom of hill, signed.

ℹ️ Aire in a very large gravel area with a remote/undesirable feel. Town 7 mins uphill. Inspected 2014.

🚐 20

🚰 Urba Flux

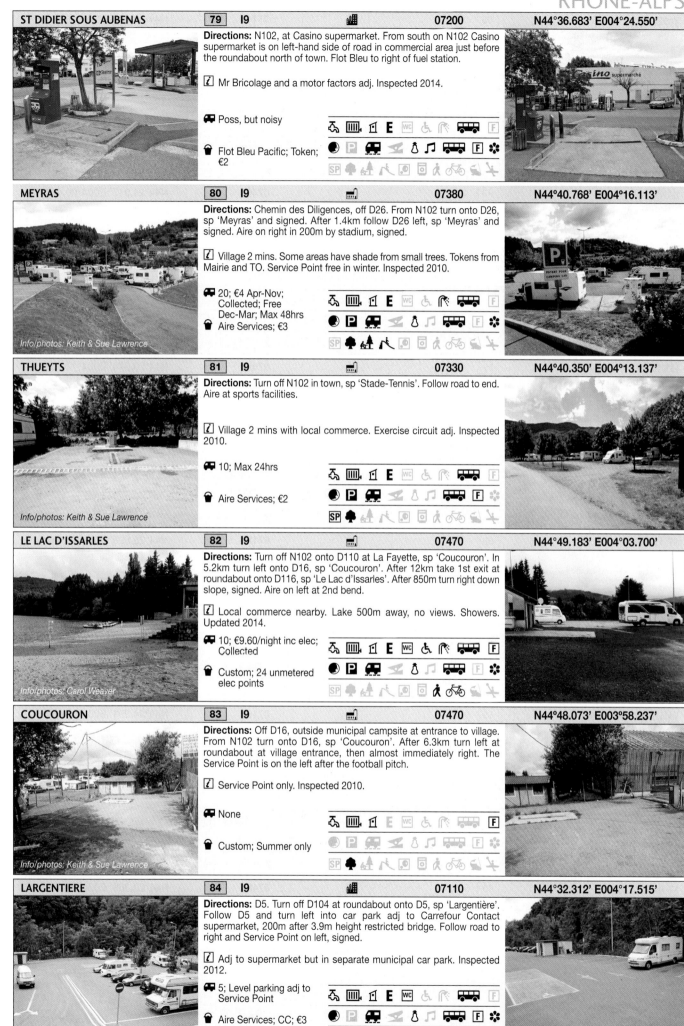

| ST DIDIER SOUS AUBENAS | 79 | I9 | | 07200 | N44°36.683' E004°24.550' |

Directions: N102, at Casino supermarket. From south on N102 Casino supermarket is on left-hand side of road in commercial area just before the roundabout north of town. Flot Bleu to right of fuel station.

Mr Bricolage and a motor factors adj. Inspected 2014.

Poss, but noisy

Flot Bleu Pacific; Token; €2

| MEYRAS | 80 | I9 | | 07380 | N44°40.768' E004°16.113' |

Directions: Chemin des Diligences, off D26. From N102 turn onto D26, sp 'Meyras' and signed. After 1.4km follow D26 left, sp 'Meyras' and signed. Aire on right in 200m by stadium, signed.

Village 2 mins. Some areas have shade from small trees. Tokens from Mairie and TO. Service Point free in winter. Inspected 2010.

20; €4 Apr-Nov; Collected; Free Dec-Mar; Max 48hrs
Aire Services; €3

Info/photos: Keith & Sue Lawrence

| THUEYTS | 81 | I9 | | 07330 | N44°40.350' E004°13.137' |

Directions: Turn off N102 in town, sp 'Stade-Tennis'. Follow road to end. Aire at sports facilities.

Village 2 mins with local commerce. Exercise circuit adj. Inspected 2010.

10; Max 24hrs

Aire Services; €2

Info/photos: Keith & Sue Lawrence

| LE LAC D'ISSARLES | 82 | I9 | | 07470 | N44°49.183' E004°03.700' |

Directions: Turn off N102 onto D110 at La Fayette, sp 'Coucouron'. In 5.2km turn left onto D16, sp 'Coucouron'. After 12km take 1st exit at roundabout onto D116, sp 'Le Lac d'Issarles'. After 850m turn right down slope, signed. Aire on left at 2nd bend.

Local commerce nearby. Lake 500m away, no views. Showers. Updated 2014.

10; €9.60/night inc elec; Collected

Custom; 24 unmetered elec points

Info/photos: Carol Weaver

| COUCOURON | 83 | I9 | | 07470 | N44°48.073' E003°58.237' |

Directions: Off D16, outside municipal campsite at entrance to village. From N102 turn onto D16, sp 'Coucouron'. After 6.3km turn left at roundabout at village entrance, then almost immediately right. The Service Point is on the left after the football pitch.

Service Point only. Inspected 2010.

None

Custom; Summer only

Info/photos: Keith & Sue Lawrence

| LARGENTIERE | 84 | I9 | | 07110 | N44°32.312' E004°17.515' |

Directions: D5. Turn off D104 at roundabout onto D5, sp 'Largentière'. Follow D5 and turn left into car park adj to Carrefour Contact supermarket, 200m after 3.9m height restricted bridge. Follow road to right and Service Point on left, signed.

Adj to supermarket but in separate municipal car park. Inspected 2012.

5; Level parking adj to Service Point

Aire Services; CC; €3

VINEZAC
85	I9	🛏	07110	N44°32.363' E004°19.496'

Directions: Adj to D423. From D104 turn onto D423, sp 'Vinezac'. After 1.8km turn left in village, sp 'Mairie' and 'Stade'. Follow road to left, then right to car park adj to Mairie. Service Point down slope and sharp right into Place du 19 Mars 1962.

ℹ️ Care needed at Service Point as there is an unbarriered kerb on either side. Inspected 2010.

🚐 5

🚰 Euro Relais Junior; €2

Info/photos: Keith & Sue Lawrence

BANNE
86	I10	T	07460	N44°21.917' E004°09.417'

Directions: Parking at church, off D251. Turn off D901 north of St Paul le Jeune onto D251 (restricted to 8m length), sp 'Banne'. Follow road uphill for 3km. Turn right at church, then immediately right again, signed. Aire at base of church.

ℹ️ Aire located at base of church, Hell's bells, on edge of village with panoramic views. Banne, adj, is a Petite Village of Character with a ruined fortification. Small market at church Monday am. Inspected 2014.

🚐 10

🚰 Euro Relais Junior; Token (2/1); €3

LES BORELS - Casteljau
87	I10	🛏	07460	N44°23.974' E004°12.808'

Directions: D285. Turn off D104 onto D252, sp 'Casteljau'. Follow road past campsite then turn right, sp 'Les Borels' and signed. Go straight on then turn left, sp 'Les Borels' and signed, just before 10m length/2.8m width restriction. Aire is 30m on right opp church.

ℹ️ Aire in large car park in centre of peaceful, remote village only 20 mins drive from Gorges de l'Ardèche. Free WiFi. Inspected 2014.

🚐 10

🚰 Euro Relais Junior; Token (2/1)

ST ALBAN AURIOLLES
88	I10	🛏	07120	N44°25.628' E004°18.059'

Directions: Rue Marius Perbost, off D208. From D104 turn onto D208 on southern edge of Maison-Neuve village. After 7.3km, in St Alban Auriolles, turn left into Rue Marius Perbost, signed. Aire on left in 60m at rear of 'Foyer Rural'.

ℹ️ Aire in large car park 1 min from small town commerce. Market Monday am. North of Gorges de l'Ardèche. Inspected 2014.

🚐 20

🚰 Euro Relais Junior; Token (ER); 2 unmetered Cont elec points on wall

VALLON PONT D'ARC
89	I10	⛺	07150	N44°24.291' E004°23.839'

Directions: Chemin du Chastelas, off D390. From south on D290 turn onto D390 at roundabout, sp 'Centre Ville'. After 750m turn right into Chemin du Chastelas, signed. Aire on right in 80m, signed.

ℹ️ Aire 700m from Ardèche river and canoe hire. Tourist commerce 3 mins. Town located on D290 at start/end of Gorges de l'Ardèche. Inspected 2014.

🚐 30; €6/24hrs; CC; Pay at Service Point

🚰 Euro Relais Tall; CC

ST PAUL LE JEUNE
90	I10	🏛	07460	N44°20.369' E004°09.199'

Directions: D901. Turn off D901 in town centre, signed. Service Point to right, parking to left in area set back from main route: N44°20.395' E004°09.194'.

ℹ️ Pleasant well located Aire with parking set away from the main road but in the town centre. Small town commerce adj. Inspected 2014.

🚐 10; Max 48hrs

🚰 Flot Bleu Océane; Token

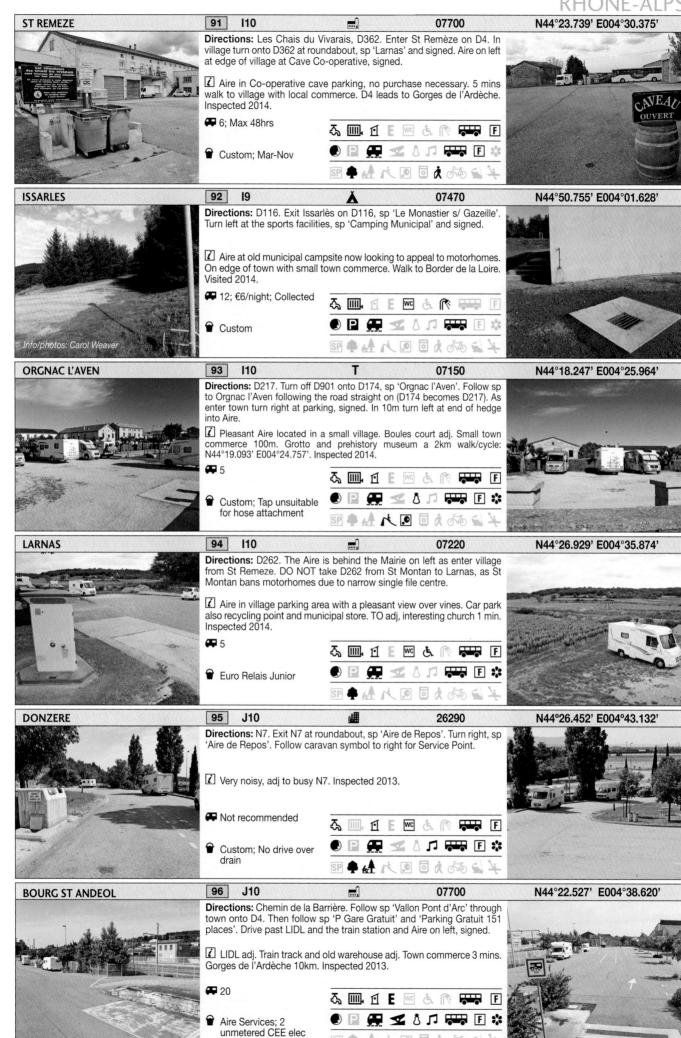

ST REMEZE | 91 | I10 | 07700 | N44°23.739' E004°30.375'

Directions: Les Chais du Vivarais, D362. Enter St Remèze on D4. In village turn onto D362 at roundabout, sp 'Larnas' and signed. Aire on left at edge of village at Cave Co-operative, signed.

ℹ Aire in Co-operative cave parking, no purchase necessary. 5 mins walk to village with local commerce. D4 leads to Gorges de l'Ardèche. Inspected 2014.

🚐 6; Max 48hrs

⛺ Custom; Mar-Nov

ISSARLES | 92 | I9 | 07470 | N44°50.755' E004°01.628'

Directions: D116. Exit Issarlès on D116, sp 'Le Monastier s/ Gazeille'. Turn left at the sports facilities, sp 'Camping Municipal' and signed.

ℹ Aire at old municipal campsite now looking to appeal to motorhomes. On edge of town with small town commerce. Walk to Border de la Loire. Visited 2014.

🚐 12; €6/night; Collected

⛺ Custom

Info/photos: Carol Weaver

ORGNAC L'AVEN | 93 | I10 | 07150 | N44°18.247' E004°25.964'

Directions: D217. Turn off D901 onto D174, sp 'Orgnac l'Aven'. Follow sp to Orgnac l'Aven following the road straight on (D174 becomes D217). As enter town turn right at parking, signed. In 10m turn left at end of hedge into Aire.

ℹ Pleasant Aire located in a small village. Boules court adj. Small town commerce 100m. Grotto and prehistory museum a 2km walk/cycle: N44°19.093' E004°24.757'. Inspected 2014.

🚐 5

⛺ Custom; Tap unsuitable for hose attachment

LARNAS | 94 | I10 | 07220 | N44°26.929' E004°35.874'

Directions: D262. The Aire is behind the Mairie on left as enter village from St Remeze. DO NOT take D262 from St Montan to Larnas, as St Montan bans motorhomes due to narrow single file centre.

ℹ Aire in village parking area with a pleasant view over vines. Car park also recycling point and municipal store. TO adj, interesting church 1 min. Inspected 2014.

🚐 5

⛺ Euro Relais Junior

DONZERE | 95 | J10 | 26290 | N44°26.452' E004°43.132'

Directions: N7. Exit N7 at roundabout, sp 'Aire de Repos'. Turn right, sp 'Aire de Repos'. Follow caravan symbol to right for Service Point.

ℹ Very noisy, adj to busy N7. Inspected 2013.

🚐 Not recommended

⛺ Custom; No drive over drain

BOURG ST ANDEOL | 96 | J10 | 07700 | N44°22.527' E004°38.620'

Directions: Chemin de la Barrière. Follow sp 'Vallon Pont d'Arc' through town onto D4. Then follow sp 'P Gare Gratuit' and 'Parking Gratuit 151 places'. Drive past LIDL and the train station and Aire on left, signed.

ℹ LIDL adj. Train track and old warehouse adj. Town commerce 3 mins. Gorges de l'Ardèche 10km. Inspected 2013.

🚐 20

⛺ Aire Services; 2 unmetered CEE elec points (Not working)

LACHAMP RAPHAEL | 97 | I9 | 73130 | N44°48.648' E004°17.317'

Info/photos: Alan Hoida

Directions: D122. From west on D122 Aire is on right at entrance to village, signed.

i In beautiful area, a short distance from Gerbier de Jonc and Mt Mezenc. Local commerce in village. Visited 2013.

🚐 6

🚰 Aire Services; €2

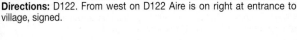

ALBA LA ROMAINE | 98 | I9 | T | 07400 | N44°33.195' E004°35.832'

Directions: Turn off D107 onto D263, sp 'Alba la Romaine'. Turn off D263, sp 'P Obligataire' and signed. Aire in the large village car park.

i Aire located in the obligatory car park adj to village. The town is a labyrinth of streets built of chequered black basalt and white limestone with a ruined castle. Tourist and small town commerce 2 mins. Beau Village. Inspected 2014.

🚐 30; €4/night; Collected

🚰 Euro Relais Junior

AUBIGNAS ★ | 99 | J9 | 07400 | N44°35.236' E004°37.899'

Directions: D363. From N102 turn onto D363, sp 'Aubignas'. After 550m turn left to stay on D363. Stay on D363 following sp 'Aubignas' and signed. Then take sharp left before village into Aire, signed. Service Point behind small building.

i Peaceful Aire in car park with panoramic views of village and countryside, but can be windy. Fortified village 2 mins. Inspected 2014.

🚐 10; €2 minimum donation

🚰 Euro Relais Mini

LES CROTTES/ST THOME | 100 | J9 | 07220 | N44°30.045' E004°38.052'

Directions: D107. Adj to D107 just before entrance to Les Crottes from Viviers. Signed.

i Service Point only. Inspected 2014.

🚐 None

🚰 Raclet; Unmetered CEE elec (Not working)

VIVIERS | 101 | J9 | T | 07220 | N44°28.929' E004°40.765'

Directions: Chemin du Valpeyrouse, in former campsite. Follow D86 through town towards Aubenas, signed. Turn left off D86, sp 'Centre Culturel' and signed. Aire on left in 350m, signed. Hedges restrict access, large motorhomes can only fit on bays nearest entrance or in entrance car park.

i Former municipal campsite with 26 hedged bays, toilet block with cold water showers/sinks. Town commerce and tourist attractions 7 mins. Day parking adj to TO: N44°28.802' E004°41.537'. Inspected 2014.

🚐 26; €6.50/night; Collected; Apr-Oct; Max 7 nights

🚰 Custom; Apr-Oct; Cold water showers; 26 unmetered elec points

VILLENEUVE DE BERG | 102 | I9 | 07170 | N44°34.310' E004°30.703'

Directions: Off N102. Turn off N102 at the D902/N102 roundabout into the Intermarché supermarket. Service Point at the back of the fuel station.

i Supermarket adj. Inspected 2014.

🚐 Poss

🚰 Euro Relais Mini; Token

LE TEIL | 103 | J9 | 07400 | N44°33.079' E004°41.370'

Directions: Allée Paul Avon, off N102. As you exit Le Teil to the east on N102, turn right just before the bridge. Aire 150m on left in what looks like the car park for Restaurant des Allées. Aire behind and to the left of the restaurant.

i Peaceful location, looks like a former campsite. Inspected 2013.

🚐 10

🛏 Custom

MONTELIMAR | 104 | J9 | 26200 | N44°33.907' E004°45.407'

Directions: Chemin du Bois de Laud. In town follow sp 'Valance', then 'Aire de Camping-Car'. Follow signs past E'Leclerc supermarket, fuel station and up hill. Turn right, sp 'Aire Camping-Car'. Aire down slope. Access through credit card operated bollards.

i Commercial Aire. Supermarket 2 mins. Walled city and town centre with small town commerce 5 mins. Updated 2014.

🚐 30; €4.20/24hrs; CC; Max 48hrs; Grass parking

🛏 Urba Flux Tall; Inc; Entry code on receipt

CLANSAYES | 105 | J10 | 26130 | N44°22.161' E004°47.807'

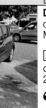

Directions: Aire de Toronne. From St Paul-Trois-Châteaux on D133 turn onto D571, sp 'Clansayes'. Aire on right, signed.

i Commercial Aire in a nice peaceful spot. Swimming pool, €4pp; Showers; BBQ. Rural views. Inspected 2013.

🚐 40; €10-€13/night; Collected

🛏 Custom; Inc; Elec €4

ST PAUL TROIS CHATEAUX | 106 | J10 | 26130 | N44°20.832' E004°46.225'

Directions: Parking Chausy, Lieu-Dit le Courreau. From east on D59 turn off at roundabout by football pitch, sp 'P Chausy 120 places' and 'Stade Municipal'. Turn 1st left and then left again into car park. Well signed.

i Car park adj to pleasant green park. Market adj Tue am, car park oversubscribed at this time. TO adj, historic centre 150m. Inspected 2013.

🚐 20

🛏 Custom

Photo: Keith & Sue Lawrence

ROCHEGUDE | 107 | J10 | 26790 | N44°14.828' E004°49.819'

Directions: D817. Take D117, D11 or D817 into village and turn onto D817 in village centre, sp 'Lagarde-Paréol'. Aire immediately on right.

i Small roadside Service Point and parking area under trees. Inspected 2013.

🚐 5

🛏 Euro Relais Mini

SUZE LA ROUSSE | 108 | J10 | 26790 | N44°17.385' E004°50.887'

Directions: Impasse de la Zone Artisanale. Exit town on D94, sp 'Nyons'. As exit village turn left onto D251, sp 'Bouchet'. In 200m turn right, signed. Service Point immediately on right.

i Service Point only. Inspected 2013.

🚐 None

🛏 Custom

PIERRELATTE | 109 | J10 | | 26700 | N44°22.588' E004°42.194'

Directions: Rue Antoine de St Exupéry. Turn off D458 at roundabout onto D358, sp 'Pierrelatte'. Follow road to roundabout above train track and take the 2nd exit onto D13, sp 'Mairie'. Turn right, and right again and the Service Point is on the right.

Service Point only. Inspected 2014.

Poss on road, car park height barriered

Euro Relais Junior; Token (ER)

GRIGNAN | 110 | J10 | | 26230 | N44°25.198' E004°53.624'

Directions: D541, at Intermarché supermarket. Exit Grignan on D4, then D541 towards Donzère. 600m after town boundary, turn left into the Intermarché supermarket. The Aire is behind the supermarket, signed.

Adj to supermarket with self-service laundry. Grignan town is pleasant but bans motorhomes from parking. Inspected 2012.

10

Euro Relais Junior; Token (ER); No drive over drain

MONTBRISON | 111 | J10 | | 26770 | N44°26.187' E005°01.052'

Directions: D24, near junction with D538. From south on D538 turn left in village onto D24, signed. Aire on right. Service Point is 1.7km away: N44°25.671' E005°01.465'. From Aire travel back to D538 and follow road southeast for 1km. Turn right, sp 'Stade', and Service Point in 550m.

Pleasant village. Aire has a tap by the play equipment. Inspected 2010.

6; At the Mairie

Euro Relais Mini; Token (2/1); €2; 4 unmetered elec points at Mairie

Info/photos: Keith & Sue Lawrence

MIRABEL AUX BARONNIES | 112 | J10 | | 26110 | N44°18.767' E005°05.983'

Directions: Chemin de Grottes. From D538 on northern edge of village, turn into Allée des Soupirs. After 200m turn left and Aire is immediately ahead, signed.

Small Aire. Inspected 2010.

6; Donation; Max 48hrs

Custom

Info/photos: Keith & Sue Lawrence

NYONS | 113 | J10 | | 26110 | N44°21.489' E005°08.315'

Directions: Promenade de la Digue. From north on D538 turn off in town just prior to river bridge, signed. Aire 200m on right. 3.5t weight restriction on D94/D538 river bridge (on approach from south).

Outdoor swimming pool adj, river across road. Inspected 2010.

15; €9/24hrs; Collected; Max 48hrs

Flot Bleu Pacific

Info/photos: Keith & Sue Lawrence

MONTBRUN LES BAINS | 114 | J10 | | 26570 | N44°10.458' E005°26.460'

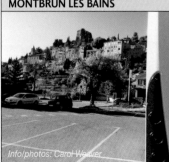

Directions: D542, at Express U. Service Point to the right of the store entrance.

Supermarket adj. Visited 2012.

Poss

Flot Bleu Pacific; €2

Info/photos: Carol Weaver

ST RESTITUT | 115 | J10 | 26130 | N44°19.877' E004°47.455'

Directions: Off D859. North of town turn off D59 onto D859 at roundabout, sp 'St Restitut'. After passing village boundary sign on left, fork right, sp 'Centre Ville', then immediately left into car park, signed. Aire at far end of car park.

i Aire adj to hilltop village. Large caves open to public, follow sp 'Caves Cathèdrale'. Local commerce 1 min. Inspected 2012.

🚐 5

⛲ Custom

MARSANNE | 116 | J9 | 26740 | N44°38.762' E004°52.317'

Directions: D57. Exit village to north on D57, sp 'Mirmande'. Aire on right before village boundary sign, signed. Aire also used by families visiting play area/school.

i On the edge of the village opp school and adj to Aire Naturelle campsite. Play area and exercise trail behind Aire with a ruined fortification beyond. Local commerce 1 min. Updated 2014.

🚐 5

⛲ Custom

DIEULEFIT | 117 | J9 | 26220 | N44°31.215' E005°03.364'

Directions: D540. Approach on D540 from Le Poet-Laval. Turn right into the Super U car park and Service Point is in the far left corner by self-service laundry, signed.

i Supermarket and self-service laundry adj. D538 has lavender/honey/wine producers/sellers offering motorhome parking. Inspected 2012.

🚐 Poss behind supermarket

⛲ Euro Relais Mini; €2; Token (ER)

PUY ST MARTIN | 118 | J9 | 26450 | N44°37.624' E004°58.507'

Directions: Impasse de Fleurs. Turn off D6 in village onto D107, sp 'Manas', 'Mairie' and signed. Turn left at crossroads into Rue de Lavoir, signed. Turn right, signed, then left into Aire.

i Former municipal campsite turned motorhome Aire. Village with local commerce and supermarket 1 min. Inspected 2012.

🚐 20; Donation; Max 48hrs; Grass parking

⛲ Custom

CHAROLS | 119 | J9 | 26450 | N44°35.498' E004°57.259'

Directions: Place Carrovolis, adj to D128. Approach from Cléon d'Andran on D9. Turn left onto D128 at roundabout. In 10m turn right into the adj car park. The Aire is at the far end of the car park.

i Pleasant village Aire with plenty of space. Convenience store adj. Village with local commerce 1 min. Inspected 2012.

🚐 10

⛲ Custom; Elec points (Not working)

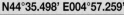

SAILLANS | 120 | J9 | 26340 | N44°41.729' E005°11.633'

Directions: Gîte Rural. From Crest follow D93 to Saillans. At the roundabout turn left, sp 'Centre Ville' and signed. Turn right before town, signed. Follow road for 1km; bumpy, overgrown and single track in places. Turn right at Centre Secours, sp 'Gîte Rural' and signed. Aire in car park behind Centre Secours Pompiers shed, signed.

i Parking adj to river Drôme but no views due to defensive bank. Riverside walk. Small town commerce 5 mins. Inspected 2014.

🚐 30; Max 24hrs; No parking 8pm-6am during periods of flooding

⛲ Euro Relais Mini; Token (ER)

CREST 1 | 121 | J9 | | 26400 | N44°43.554' E005°01.241'

Directions: D538. From west on D104 turn left at traffic lights onto D538, sp 'Centre Ville'. After 600m take 1st exit at roundabout into car park. Long motorhome spaces along right-hand edge of car park, adj to boules club. Service Point across car park. Car park has 3.5t weight restriction.

Historic town on river Drôme with steep cobbled lanes. Laundry 400m in Rue Général Berlier. WiFi. Inspected 2014.

25; €3/24hrs; Collected

Aire Services; CC; €5; Inc overnight fee display receipt

CREST 2 | 122 | J9 | | 26400 | N44°44.297' E005°00.285'

Directions: Adj to D538/D93 roundabout, at fuel station of Casino supermarket. Signed.

Supermarket adj. Inspected 2014.

Poss

Flot Bleu Euro; CC; €2/20 mins

CHICHILIANNE | 123 | J9 | | 38930 | N44°48.741' E005°34.534'

Directions: D7b. Turn off D7 onto D7b, sp 'Chichilianne'. Aire 600m on right adj to D7b.

Remote village Aire with mountain views. D7 goes over Col de Menée (Alt 1457m). Visited 2012.

10; Grass parking

Aire Services; Token

Info/photo: Colin Robinson

DIE 1 | 124 | J9 | | 26150 | N44°45.033' E005°21.983'

Directions: Lieu-Dit Largner. From south on D93 take 2nd exit at roundabout onto D238. After 1km turn left at traffic lights, sp 'Camping Municipal' and signed. Follow sp 'Camping Municipal' to Camping Municipal de Justin. Service Point outside campsite.

Handy Service Point when Die 2 [125] in town is busy or on market days. Inspected 2010.

None

Flot Bleu Océane; Token; €3; May-Sept

Photo: Keith & Sue Lawrence

DIE 2 | 125 | J9 | | 26150 | N44°45.060' E005°22.391'

Directions: Car park 'Aire de Meyrosse' on D238. From south on D93 take 2nd exit at roundabout onto D238. After 600m turn right into car park. Aire straight ahead. Service Point adj to toilet block in main car park.

Busy on Wed/Sat am (market). Historic town with shops and restaurants adj. Inspected 2010.

20; €5/24hrs; Collected

Custom

Info/photos: Keith & Sue Lawrence

VASSIEUX EN VERCORS | 126 | J9 | | 26420 | N44°53.857' E005°22.210'

Directions: D76. From Die follow D518 for 21km over very scenic Col de Rousset (winding road with hairpins but wide enough). Fork left onto D76 and follow road for 8km. Aire on right in very large, open area just north of village.

Alt 1100m. On plateau with excellent views of mountains. Memorial de Resistance 800m. Nice village with local commerce. Updated 2014.

30

Custom

Photos: Carol Weaver

ST JEAN EN ROYANS | 127 | J9 | 26190 | N45°01.200' E005°17.425'

Directions: Rue de la Gare. Approach from north on D76. Go straight over roundabout north of town, signed. In 650m turn right into Rue de la Gare. In 150m Aire on left, signed.

i This is a tranquil location away from the main roads, but just 1 min from commerce. Supermarket 2 mins downhill. Inspected 2012.

🚐 6

⛲ Custom

ST MARCELLIN | 128 | J9 | 38160 | N45°09.316' E005°19.160'

Directions: Blvd Riondel. Enter town from east on D1092. At roundabout turn onto D518, sp 'St Vérand'. Go straight on at traffic lights and in 100m turn right, sp 'P Champ de Mars'. Service Point: N45°09.282' E005°19.073'. Instead of turning right to parking, go straight on and Service Point by recycling bins at corner of square, signed.

i Adj to shaded central square (market Sat 5am-2pm) that has a Germanic maypole. Bars, restaurants and shops, inc LIDL surround the square. Roybon, 15 mins drive, has miniature statue of liberty. Inspected 2012.

🚐 5; Popular town parking adj

⛲ Custom

ST ANTOINE L'ABBAYE | 129 | J8 | 38160 | N45°10.387' E005°13.070'

Directions: D27. In centre of village turn off D27 into large gravel car park to Aire.

i Lovely ancient town adj. Several walks around area; TO has leaflet. Visited 2011.

🚐 12

⛲ Urba Flux Tall; €2

Info/photos: Jean & Ken Fowler

ST HILAIRE DU TOUVET | 130 | K8 | 38660 | N45°18.152' E005°52.821'

Directions: Chemin du Bec Margain. Turn off D30 in village by sports facilities, sp 'Terrain du Foot' and signed. Aire adj to tennis courts.

i Alt 1017m. Village adj with local commerce and convenience store. Visited 2012.

🚐 2

⛲ Custom

Info/photos: Carol Weaver

ST HUGUES DE CHARTREUSE | 131 | K8 | SKI | 38380 | N45°19.029' E005°48.207'

Directions: D57b, at Parking du Cret des Egaux. From St Pierre de Chartreuse take D512 south. After approx 1.5km turn left onto D57b. Follow road for 2km and Aire is on left just before right-hand bend and small 'drag' ski lift.

i Alt 950m. Small rural car park with lovely 360° views. Inspected 2010.

🚐 4

⛲ None

Info/photos: Keith & Sue Lawrence

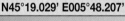

ST PIERRE DE CHARTREUSE | 132 | K8 | SKI | 38380 | N45°20.578' E005°48.743'

Directions: Parking du Couzon. Turn off D512 by church. Take 1st left past the church and the Aire is on the left, sp 'P du Couzon' and signed. Additional parking at base of Télésiége de la Combe de l'Ours chairlift: N45°21.467' E005°49.967'. Turn right off D512 2.2km north of town.

i This Aire was previously located at P Le Bourg. Local commerce 2 mins. Visited 2012.

🚐 50

⛲ Euro Relais Mini; Token

Info/photos: Carol Weaver

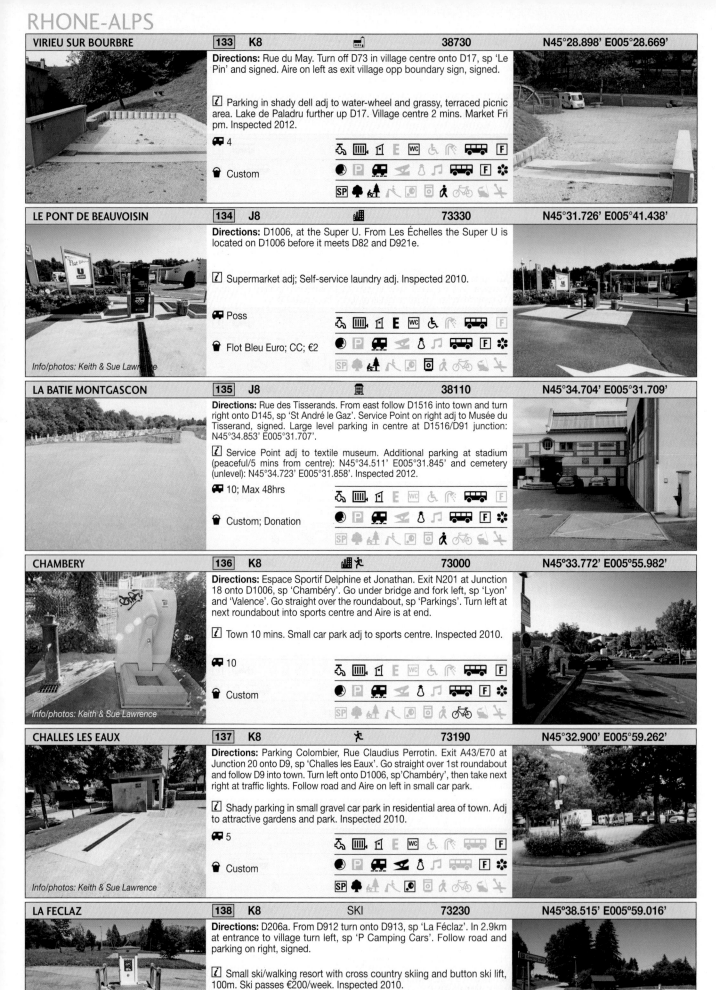

| VIRIEU SUR BOURBRE | 133 | K8 | | 38730 | N45°28.898' E005°28.669' |

Directions: Rue du May. Turn off D73 in village centre onto D17, sp 'Le Pin' and signed. Aire on left as exit village opp boundary sign, signed.

Parking in shady dell adj to water-wheel and grassy, terraced picnic area. Lake de Paladru further up D17. Village centre 2 mins. Market Fri pm. Inspected 2012.

4

Custom

| LE PONT DE BEAUVOISIN | 134 | J8 | | 73330 | N45°31.726' E005°41.438' |

Directions: D1006, at the Super U. From Les Échelles the Super U is located on D1006 before it meets D82 and D921e.

Supermarket adj; Self-service laundry adj. Inspected 2010.

Poss

Flot Bleu Euro; CC; €2

Info/photos: Keith & Sue Lawrence

| LA BATIE MONTGASCON | 135 | J8 | | 38110 | N45°34.704' E005°31.709' |

Directions: Rue des Tisserands. From east follow D1516 into town and turn right onto D145, sp 'St André le Gaz'. Service Point on right adj to Musée du Tisserand, signed. Large level parking in centre at D1516/D91 junction: N45°34.853' E005°31.707'.

Service Point adj to textile museum. Additional parking at stadium (peaceful/5 mins from centre): N45°34.511' E005°31.845' and cemetery (unlevel): N45°34.723' E005°31.858'. Inspected 2012.

10; Max 48hrs

Custom; Donation

| CHAMBERY | 136 | K8 | | 73000 | N45°33.772' E005°55.982' |

Directions: Espace Sportif Delphine et Jonathan. Exit N201 at Junction 18 onto D1006, sp 'Chambéry'. Go under bridge and fork left, sp 'Lyon' and 'Valence'. Go straight over the roundabout, sp 'Parkings'. Turn left at next roundabout into sports centre and Aire is at end.

Town 10 mins. Small car park adj to sports centre. Inspected 2010.

10

Custom

Info/photos: Keith & Sue Lawrence

| CHALLES LES EAUX | 137 | K8 | | 73190 | N45°32.900' E005°59.262' |

Directions: Parking Colombier, Rue Claudius Perrotin. Exit A43/E70 at Junction 20 onto D9, sp 'Challes les Eaux'. Go straight over 1st roundabout and follow D9 into town. Turn left onto D1006, sp 'Chambéry', then take next right at traffic lights. Follow road and Aire on left in small car park.

Shady parking in small gravel car park in residential area of town. Adj to attractive gardens and park. Inspected 2010.

5

Custom

Info/photos: Keith & Sue Lawrence

| LA FECLAZ | 138 | K8 | SKI | 73230 | N45°38.515' E005°59.016' |

Directions: D206a. From D912 turn onto D913, sp 'La Féclaz'. In 2.9km at entrance to village turn left, sp 'P Camping Cars'. Follow road and parking on right, signed.

Small ski/walking resort with cross country skiing and button ski lift, 100m. Ski passes €200/week. Inspected 2010.

40; Pay at TO

Raclet; Token (ER)

Info/photos: Keith & Sue Lawrence

AILLON LE JEUNE

139 K8   73340   N45°36.547' E006°06.266'

Directions: D32a. Turn off D206 onto D32a in Aillon le Jeune by the Mairie and church, sp 'Aillon le Jeune – Station'. Follow road for 2km, around left-hand bend and then straight over roundabout.

i Rural. Lovely countryside. Visited 2012.

🚐 5

🔧 Custom

Info/Photo: Carol Weaver

CHANAZ

140 K8   73310   N45°48.683' E005°47.343'

Directions: Chemin de Cavettaz. Turn off D921 north of Chanaz, sp 'Camping'. Follow sp 'Camping' and the Service Point is in 650m outside the campsite entrance.

i Lots of gravel parking adj but no official motorhome parking. Canoe hire and marina close by. Very pretty tourist village by canal. Visited 2010.

🚐 Poss, when campsite closed

🔧 Aire Services; Token (3/3)

Photo: John and Pat Dunn

Info/Photo: Harry Ridsdale

SERRIERES EN CHAUTAGNE

141 K8   73310   N45°52.843' E005°50.591'

Directions: Off D991. Enter town on D991 and turn off, sp 'Mairie'. Parking beyond Service Point to left of lake.

i Village with local commerce. Adj to small swimming lake. Inspected 2010.

🚐 6; Max 72hrs

🔧 Flot Bleu Fontaine

Photo: Jean & Ken Fowler

ANNECY

142 K8   74000   N45°53.437' E006°08.341'

Directions: Chemin de Colmyr, 1km south of Annecy off D1508 behind car park and P&R at traffic lights. Need to arrive early, busy at peak times. 3.5t weight restriction on access road.

i Very popular Aire opp lake in lovely resort town. Cycle track and footpath adj. Day parking poss at Basillica de Visitation: N45°53.562' E006°07.606'. Updated 2014.

🚐 10; Max 24hrs

🔧 Custom

Photo: goexploremotorhomehire.co.uk

ANNECY LE VIEUX

143 K8   74940   N45°54.433' E006°09.117'

Directions: Rue Centrale. From D909/Avenue du Petit Port, on northern shore of lake, turn into Rue Centrale. Service Point 300m on left.

i Service Point only, but could be useful as access to services at Annecy **142** can be difficult when full. Inspected 2010.

🚐 None

🔧 Custom

Info/photos: Keith & Sue Lawrence

LA BALME DE SILLINGY

144 K7   74330   N45°58.290' E006°01.888'

Directions: D1508, 1km north of village boundary sign by lake.

i By lake. Café adj. Inspected 2010.

🚐 14; €5/24hrs; Apr-Nov; Collected; Max 48hrs

🔧 Custom

Info/photos: Keith & Sue Lawrence

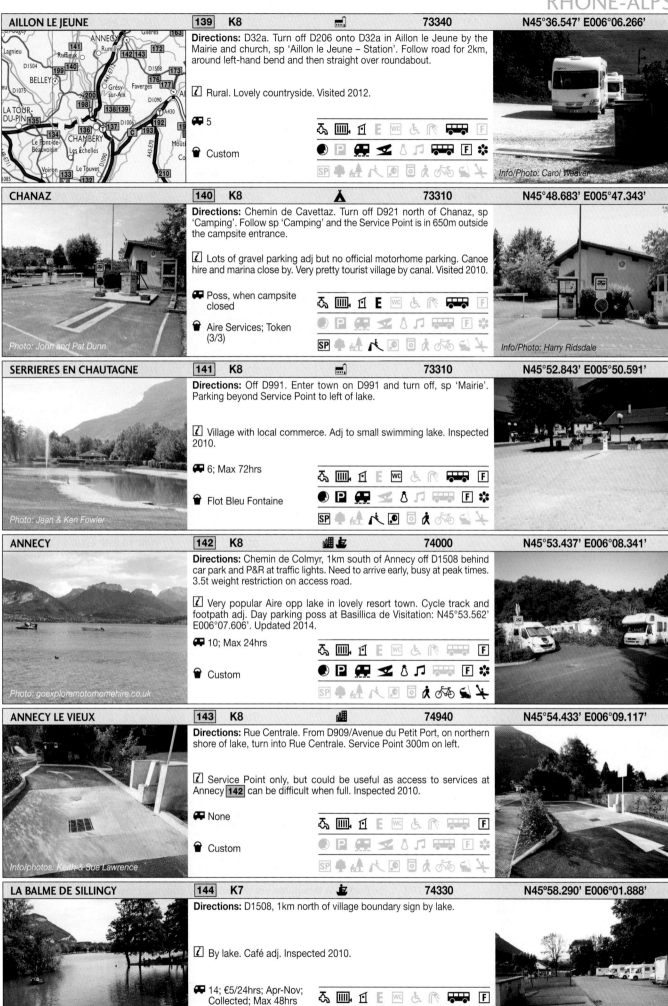

NANTUA ★ | 145 | J7 | 01130 | N46°09.260' E005°35.827'

Photo: Carol Weaver

Directions: D74, adj to lake. Follow sp 'Camping' through town. Turn left, sp 'Aire de Pique Nique' and 'Monument aux Déportés'. Follow road along lake and at next roundabout turn right, sp 'Aire de Pique Nique' and signed. Aire on left in 50m.

ℹ️ Amazing lake/mountain views. Lake swimming (cold). Train line behind Aire has trains during the day only. Town 5 mins, lots of commerce. Updated 2014.

🚐 13; €7.50/night; Collected

🛠 Custom

BELLEYDOUX | 146 | K7 | 01130 | N46°15.331' E005°46.793'

Photos: Carol Weaver

Directions: D13/D33. Adj to the D13/D33 in the village adj to recycling area, signed.

ℹ️ Small village. Inspected 2010.

🚐 3

🛠 Flot Bleu Pacific; Token; €2

BELLEGARDE SUR VALSERINE | 147 | K7 | 01200 | N46°06.420' E005°49.900'

Info/photos: Janet & John Watts

Directions: Place des Frères Zanarelli, off D1206. Exit town on D1206, sp 'Genève'. Cross river and turn right at traffic lights near Gendarmerie, sp 'Borne Camping-Car'. Aire on right at end of road in car park.

ℹ️ Aire alongside river. Small town commerce 4 mins. Updated 2014.

🚐 2

🛠 Aire Services; CC; €3

ST GENIS POUILLY | 148 | K7 | 01630 | N46°15.816' E006°01.814'

Info/photos: Keith & Sue Lawrence

Directions: D984c. Turn off the D984c/D35a roundabout north of town. The Service Point is in the Intermarché supermarket car park, at rear of supermarket building opp Intersport.

ℹ️ Service Point at supermarket. Inspected 2010.

🚐 Poss

🛠 Raclet; Token; €2

MIJOUX | 149 | K7 | SKI | 01410 | N46°22.155' E006°00.133'

Info/photos: Janet & John Watts

Directions: D50. Exit Mijoux on D50, sp 'Le Tabagnoz' and signed. Aire 450m on the left in the woods, signed.

ℹ️ Rural location with woodland views. May feel isolated. Chairlift 500m in village centre with local commerce. Updated 2014.

🚐 10

🛠 Aire Services; Token; €3.50

HAVE YOU VISITED AN AIRE? | GPS co-ordinates in this guide are protected by copyright law

Submit updates
- Amendments
- New Aires
- Not changed

Visit www.all-the-aires.co.uk/submissions.shtml
to upload your updates and photos.

ℹ️ Directions and description.

🚐 Number of parking spaces; Cost per night; Time limit
🛠 Service Point type and details; Payment type; Cost

Take at least 5 digital photos showing
- Signs
- Service Point
- Parking
- Overview
- Amenities

LOISIN | 151 | K7 | | 74140 | N46°16.117' E006°19.002'

Directions: Turn off the D1206/D35 roundabout sp 'Centre Commercial'. The Service Point is in the Super U fuel station.

ℹ️ Supermarket adj. Visited 2012.

🚐 Poss

🚰 Aire Services; Token; €2

Info/photos: Janet & John Watts

LE PRAZ DE LYS - La Savolière | 152 | K7 | SKI | 74440 | N46°08.497' E006°36.278'

Directions: From Les Gets or Tangines on D902 take D307/308, sp 'Praz de Lys'. Aire in 6.5km at entrance to village. Col de Ramaz closed in winter.

ℹ️ Aire 2km from ski lifts and good local skiing, ski bus stop nearby. Village very quiet and Aire free out of ski season. Updated 2014.

🚐 30; €10/24hrs Dec-Apr/mid Jun-mid Sept; CC; 1hr free to use services; Long stay discounts

🚰 Flot Bleu; €2; Elec €2/4hrs (Max 12hrs); 16 elec points

Photo: Andy & Sue Glasgow

SOMMAND | 153 | K7 | SKI | 74440 | N46°09.681' E006°33.293'

Directions: D308. From Taninges take D907 west. At roundabout in Mieussy turn right onto D308. Follow road for 10.5km. After small lake on right, take right-hand fork into large parking area at base of ski lifts. Flot Bleu 500m, turn left after lake, at: N46°09.539' E006°32.959'.

ℹ️ Alt 1413m. Pretty ski village. Good downhill and Nordic skiing. Bars, restaurants and hotel open in ski season. Very quiet in low season, but lovely mountain walks. Updated 2014.

🚐 10

🚰 Flot Bleu Pacific; €2

Photo: Keith & Sue Lawrence

CHATEL | 154 | L7 | SKI | 74390 | N46°15.447' E006°49.773'

Directions: Route des Freinets, off D228a. From northwest on D22 turn right onto D228a in Châtel centre, sp 'Linge' and 'Prés la Joux'. Follow road for 2km and then turn right, sp 'L'Oustalet' with the campsite symbol. Aire in 300m, opp Camping L'Oustalet.

ℹ️ Rural ski resort/summer walking. Access to Portes de Soleil ski area and poss to ski to Switzerland. Inspected 2010.

🚐 12; €6/night; Collected

🚰 Flot Bleu Pacific; €6; Elec €2/1hr

Info/photos: Keith & Sue Lawrence

CLUSES | 155 | K7 | | 74300 | N46°04.145' E006°33.620'

Directions: Rue Joseph Depoisier. Turn off D1205 onto D304, sp 'Taninges'. Follow road straight over 4 roundabouts and cross river bridge. At the next roundabout turn left, sp 'La Poste' and signed. Turn 1st left, sp 'La Poste' and signed. Follow road to end and Aire on left, signed.

ℹ️ Adj riverside car park allows free parking except during market, Thurs noon-8pm. Small town commerce adj. Visited 2014.

🚐 5; No parking Thurs noon-8pm (Market)

🚰 Flot Bleu Euro; CC; €2/20 mins

Info/photo: Gary Watson

LES GETS | 156 | K7 | SKI | 74260 | N46°08.993' E006°39.495'

Directions: Parking Perrières, off D902. Just off D902 at the entrance to the village when approached from Cluses. Aire at bottom of lift. Service Point: N46°08.996' E006°39.411'. From parking turn left, then 1st right.

ℹ️ Superb Aire next to a ski lift, at bottom of ski slope. 800m from village. Pleasant in summer, popular in winter (early arrival essential). Appears free in summer. Updated 2014.

🚐 30; €17/night; Collected; Max 7 days

🚰 Flot Bleu Euro; CC; €4.50

Info/photos: Keith & Sue Lawrence

SAMOENS 1 | 157 | L7 | SKI | 74340 | N46°04.338' E006°42.159'

Photos: Andy & Sue Glasgow

Directions: D254. Exit Samoëns southwest on D4, passing Camping Le Giffre, and cross the river bridge onto D254. Continue for 1.8km to Vercland. The Aire and Service Point are at the bottom of the Vercland ski lift.

i Remote Aire with only a bar/restaurant and chairlift. All other facilities are 3km along D4 in village. See Samoëns 2 | 158 |. Updated 2014.

Poss

Flot Bleu Pacific; €5

SAMOENS 2 | 158 | L7 | | 74340 | N46°04.626' E006°43.154'

Info/photos: Keith & Sue Lawrence

Directions: D4, outside Camping le Giffre. Leave Samoëns and head south on D4. Flot Bleu on right in 700m in roundabout lay-by, opp campsite.

i Service Point only. Updated 2014.

None

Flot Bleu Euro; CC; €5

LA ROCHE SUR FORON | 159 | K7 | | 74800 | N46°03.846' E006°18.780'

Info/photos: Keith & Sue Lawrence

Directions: Parking du Canada. Located at Parking du Canada 200m from town centre, signed. Not suitable for large motorhomes and has very steep, narrow access.

i Pleasant town with 13th century quarter. Inspected 2010.

20

Euro Relais Junior

ST PIERRE EN FAUCIGNY | 160 | K7 | | 74800 | N46°03.555' E006°22.506'

Info/photos: Keith & Sue Lawrence

Directions: D208/Ave de la Gare. Exit A40 at Junction 16 and turn onto D1203, sp 'St Pierre en Faucigny'. At roundabout turn into D19c, sp 'St Pierre en F'. Follow D19c for 1.7km to end, then turn left onto D6. In 100m turn left again, signed, and Aire is on the right in train station car park.

i Some train noise, but trains are electric and don't run at night. Shade from trees in afternoon. Visited 2013.

4; Max 48hrs

Custom; 2 unmetered CEE elec points

LE REPOSOIR | 161 | K7 | | 74950 | N46°00.600' E006°32.180'

Photo: Carol Weaver

Directions: D204. From roundabout on D1205 at Cluses take D4, sp 'Le Reposoir'. Follow road for 11km. Turn left onto D204 in Le Reposoir between church and Mairie. Small sign on map adj to church. Aire on right in approx 150m.

i Alt 980m. Monastère Chartreuse du Reposoir nearby, founded in 1151 AD. Updated 2014.

5

Custom

Photo: Carol Weaver

LE CHINAILLON | 162 | K7 | SKI | 74450 | N45°58.529' E006°27.638'

Info/photos: Keith & Sue Lawrence

Directions: Lieu-Dit Le Chinaillon, off D4. From La Clusaz take D909 north to St Jean de Sixt. At roundabout turn right onto D12/D4, sp 'Le Grand Bornand'. Follow road for 8.2km. At Le Chinaillon take 1st right and follow road past ski lifts to Aire on right.

i Alt 1296m. Service Point signed at Chalet ski lift ticket window, 200m downhill. Updated 2014.

10; Max 48hrs

Custom

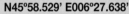

LE GRAND BORNAND | 163 | K8 | SKI | 74450 | N45°56.485' E006°26.178'

Directions: Chemin Rural du Terret à la Broderie. Drive east through town, sp 'Col des Annes'. Turn right onto bridge over stream, sp 'L'Envers de Villeneuve'. Aire on left in 100m, sp 'Le Pessey' and signed.

i Motorhome parking area 10 mins walk from pleasant ski resort with local commerce. Ski bus in season. Updated 2014.

🚐 10; Max 48hrs

⛺ None

Photo: Heidi Hardwick

LES CARROZ D'ARACHES | 164 | K7 | SKI | 74300 | N46°01.517' E006°38.632'

Info/photos: Keith & Sue Lawrence

Directions: Impasse des Sablets. From Cluses take D1205 south and turn onto D6, sp 'Les Carroz D'Arâches'. Follow D6 then D106 for 9.5km. In village centre turn left into Route du Battieu. Follow road round right-hand bend, then left into Impasse des Sablets. Aire opp ski lift.

i For skiing see Flaine 165. Village centre 500m. In winter used as ski bus parking. Inspected 2010.

🚐 Tolerated in summer; Confirm with TO

⛺ Bollard; No drive over drain; 5 unmetered Cont elec points

FLAINE | 165 | L7 | SKI | 74300 | N46°00.274' E006°41.345'

Info/photos: Keith & Sue Lawrence

Directions: From Cluses take D1205 south and turn onto D6, sp 'Les Carroz D'Arâches'. Follow D6, then D106 for 24.8km to Flaine (road full of hairpin bends). Aire in car park P1.

i Alt 1600m. At entrance to car park there is ticket office, toilet and sandwich room with sink and tap. Updated 2014.

🚐 30; €2/12hrs; €5/24hrs; Pay at machine

⛺ None; Do not empty cassette in toilet

SIXT FER A CHEVAL | 166 | L7 | ⚓ | 74740 | N46°03.399' E006°46.783'

Photo: motorhomeandaway.co.uk

Directions: D907. From Samoëns on D907 follow sp 'Sixt Fer à Cheval' and 'Cirque du Fer à Cheval'. Pass through village from west and Aire on right next to river just after end of village sign.

i Pleasant scenic valley setting adj to river on outskirts of Beau Village. Cirque du Fer à Cheval 5.5km further up road. Updated 2014.

🚐 30

⛺ Euro Relais Junior; Token (ER); €4/12hrs; 4 elec points

CHAMONIX MONT BLANC | 167 | L7 | SKI 🏔 | 74400 | N45°54.951' E006°52.171'

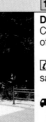

Photo: Carol Weaver

Directions: Parking Grépon, off D1506. Turn off D1506 at roundabout, sp 'P+R Grépon' and 'Aiguille du Midi'. Aire in parking for the Gondola to Aiguille du Midi. Barriered entry, pay upon exit.

i Cable car to Aiguille du Midi, 300m, also has WC. Free bus to town centre at cable car. Updated 2014.

🚐 100; €12.50/24hrs; Or by hr; CC or cash

⛺ Custom; Inc

LE TOUR | 168 | L7 | SKI | 74400 | N46°00.235' E006°56.758'

Info/photos: Keith & Sue Lawrence

Directions: Place du Tour. From Chamonix follow D1506 north for 9km. After Argentière turn right into Route de Montroc, sp 'Le Tour'. Follow road through to Le Tour for 2.3km. Aire in large sloping car park at end of road on both sides of river.

i Snack bar; Ski pass office. Lovely setting with fine views of Mont Blanc and under Le Tour glacier. Updated 2014.

🚐 Tolerated

⛺ None

PLAINE JOUX | 169 | L7 | 🏃 | 74480 | N45°57.033' E006°44.353'

Directions: D43/Route de Plaine-Joux. From Chamonix exit N205 at Junction 22 at Le Fayet and follow D43 north 13km through Plateau-D'Assy to Plaine-Joux. Aire on both sides of road in large parking area before restaurants and paragliding centre.

ℹ Alt 1360m. 2 areas with fantastic views of Mont Blanc. 12 bays on opp side of road without elec. Updated 2014.

🚐 20; €10/night inc Token and showers; Collected

🚰 Flot Bleu Pacific; Token; €3; 8 unmetered elec points; Elec €1.50

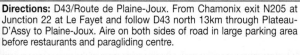

Info/photo: Keith & Sue Lawrence

LES HOUCHES - Chamonix | 170 | L8 | SKI | 74130 | N45°54.942' E006°46.017'

Directions: Aire de la Fontaine, off N205. From N205 exit, sp 'Aire de la Fontaine'. Accessible and signed from both directions.

ℹ Alt 866m. Handy Service Point when enter/leave Chamonix region. Inspected 2010.

🚐 Poss

🚰 Custom

Photo: Keith & Sue Lawrence

Photo: Andy & Sue Glasgow

ST GERVAIS LES BAINS | 171 | L8 | SKI | 74170 | N45°53.250' E006°42.783'

Directions: D909. Signed behind Patinoire (skating rink) in town centre.

ℹ Noisy location. Bins are emptied every morning, park as far away from these as poss! Ski gondola 200m. Updated 2014.

🚐 15

🚰 Raclet; Token; €2

Photo: Carol Weaver

THONES | 172 | K8 | 🏢 | 74230 | N45°52.858' E006°19.275'

Directions: Chemin de Paradis. At D909/D12 roundabout north of town turn onto D12, sp 'Office du Tourisme'. Turn 1st right, sp 'Office du Tourisme', then follow road across river/storm drain bridge and turn left, signed. The parking area is 200m on left, signed.

ℹ Small town nestled amongst the hills. The designated motorhome parking is between trees. Local commerce and LIDL 5 mins. Visited 2012.

🚐 7; Max 48hrs

🚰 None

Info/photos: Heidi Hardwick

UGINE | 173 | K8 | 🏢 | 73400 | N45°44.791' E006°25.034'

Directions: D1508. From west on D1508 turn right into service road immediately after 1st roundabout, signed. Parking in bays on right, Service Point adj to TO.

ℹ Toilets and TO in old railway station building adj. Cycle path to Annecy and Albertville. Inspected 2010.

🚐 17

🚰 Flot Bleu Euro; CC; €2

Info/photos: Keith & Sue Lawrence

LES SAISIES 1 | 174 | K8 | SKI | 73620 | N45°45.749' E006°32.024'

Directions: D218b. From Albertville follow D925 for 16km, sp 'Beaufort' and 'Les Saisies'. Turn onto D218b, sp 'Les Saisies', and follow for 17km passing through Les Saisies. Then at 4th roundabout turn right into Aire, signed.

ℹ Alt 1650m. Mountain Aire in popular family ski resort with Olympic Nordic ski course. Ski info: www.aed-montagne.com. Inspected 2010.

🚐 100; €7.50/24hrs; Pay at machine

🚰 Flot Bleu Pacific; €2

Info/photos: Keith & Sue Lawrence

LES SAISIES 2 | 175 | K8 | 73620 | N45°44.817' E006°32.123'

Directions: D123. From Les Saisies follow D123 uphill for 1.6km, sp 'Quartier de la Fôret'. Service Point on left at bend in road, opp Camping Caravaneige Le Grand Tetras. Signed from Les Saisies. Advise approaching from Les Saisies, not Villard sur Doron.

ℹ️ Service Point only in lay-by on forest road. Inspected 2010.

🚐 None

🛒 Flot Bleu Standard Plus; €2

Info/photos: Keith & Sue Lawrence

FAVERGES | 176 | K8 | 74210 | N45°44.969' E006°17.159'

Directions: D2508/Route d'Annecy. From Annecy take D1508 south for 23km. At roundabout take 2nd exit, sp 'Faverges'. Aire on right in 1.3km just before Carrefour supermarket, sp 'Parking Stade'.

ℹ️ Adj to stadium and supermarket with laundry. Pleasant Aire with nice views. Inspected 2010.

🚐 15

🛒 Custom

Info/photos: Keith & Sue Lawrence

ALBERTVILLE | 177 | K8 | 73200 | N45°40.443' E006°23.828'

Directions: D105. From N90 turn onto D1212. At roundabout go straight over, sp 'Centre-Ville'. After 1.3km turn right at traffic lights, sp 'Venthon'. Cross river and continue up hill on D105 to Venthon. Aire in car park on right, opp cemetery on outskirts of town. Flot Bleu well signed from main road.

ℹ️ Town 5 mins. Conflans is a medieval town worth a visit, 5 mins further up road. Updated 2014.

🚐 6; Max 24hrs

🛒 Flot Bleu Pacific

Info/photo: Keith & Sue Lawrence
Photo: Charlie & Angie Anderson

BEAUFORT | 178 | K8 | 73270 | N45°43.192' E006°34.026'

Directions: D925/Avenue des Sports. From Albertville follow D925, sp 'Beaufort', for 19km. The Aire is at the start of the village on the left in the car park for cross country skiing, next to the fire station.

ℹ️ In pleasant tree clad valley. 700m walk to centre of pretty alpine village with amenities. Lots of walking and cycling from village. Updated 2014.

🚐 7

🛒 Flot Bleu Fontaine

Info/photos: Keith & Sue Lawrence

LA ROSIERE | 179 | L8 | SKI | 73700 | N45°37.482' E006°51.369'

Directions: D1090. Follow D1090 north out of Bourg St Maurice. Aire signed on left just before village, behind Sapeurs Pompiers (fire station).

ℹ️ Alt 1850m. Nice family resort with sunny south facing slopes. Links to Italian resort La Thuile. Ski info: www.larosiere.net. Inspected 2010.

🚐 20; Max 15 days

🛒 Flot Bleu Pacific; Token; €10

Info/photo: Keith & Sue Lawrence
Photo: Andy & Sue Glasgow

BOURG ST MAURICE | 180 | L8 | 73700 | N45°36.210' E006°45.960'

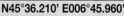
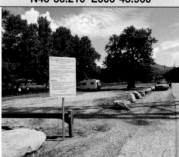

Directions: Lieu-Dit La Regence, off D220. From south on N90 turn right onto D220, sp 'Hauteville Gondon' and 'Gendarmerie'. Follow road for 1km and turn left just before river bridge. Aire immediately on left.

ℹ️ Aire adj to river (no views) with international kayak course. Showers (€1.50) and toilets at kayak centre. Updated 2014.

🚐 20; €6/night; Collected; Max 48hrs

🛒 None

LES ARCS

| 181 | L8 | SKI | 73700 | N45°35.795' E006°47.520' |

Directions: D120, Arc 1600. From Bourg St Maurice on D1090 turn onto D119, sp 'Les Arcs'. Follow road for 13.5km. Then at roundabout take 2nd exit onto D120, sp 'Arc 1600'. Aire on left in 500m.

Views of Mont Blanc; Free ski bus to slopes. Popular campsite 'Le Versoyen' at Bourg St Maurice. Inspected 2010.

10; Tolerated

None

Info/photo: Keith & Sue Lawrence

Photo: Andy and Sue Glasgow

LA PLAGNE ★

| 182 | L8 | SKI | 73210 | N45°30.392' E006°41.205' |

Directions: La Bergerie. North of Plagne 1800 at roundabout junction of D221 and D224 turn onto D221, sp 'Plagne-Centre'. After 1km take 2nd exit at roundabout onto D223, sp 'Plagne-Soleil' and 'P Caravaneige'. Follow winding road for 1.5km. Pass top station of small triple gondola and fork sharp left under high bar.

Nice ski Aire - next to slopes, ticket office 100m. Ideal for intermediates with links to Les Arcs. Inspected 2010.

40

Flot Bleu Pacific; 3 x €0.50

Info/photo: Keith & Sue Lawrence

Photo: Andy & Sue Glasgow

LE PRAZ COURCHEVEL

| 183 | K8 | SKI | 73120 | N45°25.831' E006°37.485' |

Directions: D91a. From north on D91a pass through Le Praz towards Courchevel. Aire on left in Parking Jean Blanc just after bend leaving village. Flot Bleu near entrance; extensive parking amongst cars.

Large level car park with fine views. Village 250m. Ski down to main lifts in village with excellent links to Courchevel/Meribel. Updated 2014.

20

Flot Bleu Pacific; €3

Info/photos: Keith & Sue Lawrence

COURCHEVEL LA TANIA

| 184 | K8 | SKI | 73120 | N45°25.895' E006°36.030' |

Directions: D98. From Moûtiers take D915, then D91a. At Le Praz turn right onto D98 and pass the ski jump. Follow D98 for 1.8km. Aire on left, signed. Service Point 400m further up D98 on right in bus stop/lay-by: N45°25.932' E006°35.736'.

Area being redeveloped, reports suggest Service Point removed. Village 100m. Updated 2014.

6

Flot Bleu Pacific 400m up hill

Info/photos: Keith & Sue Lawrence

LES MENUIRES ★

| 185 | K8 | SKI | 73440 | N45°19.542' E006°32.026' |

Directions: Can approach from north or south on D117/D117a. Turn off roundabout, sp 'Val Thorens' and 'Aire de Camping Cars' (D117/D117a), and travel 1.3km to Aire. Signed and located under Tortollet chairlift. Flot Bleu Park barriered entrance.

Good popular Aire, busy in holidays. Main choice for 3 valleys and the easily reached resort of Val Thorens. Ticket office and free lift to village nearby. Inspected 2010.

74; €10/24hrs; CC

Flot Bleu Pacific; Token; €2; Elec €2/4hrs

Info/photos: Keith & Sue Lawrence

VALLOIRE LES VERNEYS

| 186 | K8 | SKI | 73450 | N45°08.881' E006°25.225' |

Directions: Route du Galibier. Aire located adj to D902 south of Valloire by Verneys ski lift. Enter through PARKNIGHT barrier.

Aire located in the village of Les Verneys at the Verneys ski lift. Local commerce adj. Submitted 2014.

28; €12/night; Discounts for pass holders

Custom

Info/photos: Camping-Car-Park.com

VALLOIRE — 187 — K8 — SKI — 73450 — N45°10.135' E006°25.761'

Directions: Route des Villards/Rue de la Bonne Eau. From south on D902 turn left onto Rue de la Bonne Eau, sp 'Camping'. Follow road downhill alongside river. At end of road Service Point is ahead, slightly to left, outside Camping Sainte Thecle.

i Alt 1385m. Campsite has free snow mini train to slopes. Excellent skiing with 150km of pistes. Inspected 2010.

None

Custom

Info/photos: Keith & Sue Lawrence

ST JEAN DE MAURIENNE — 188 — K8 — 73300 — N45°16.766' E006°20.826'

Directions: Place du Champ de Foire. From south on D1006 turn left onto D77. Turn right at roundabout on D77. After 700m turn right into Rue Jean Jaurés. Go straight over roundabout and Aire in 1st car park on left. Service Point in lower car park.

i Pleasant mountain town with all facilities. Casino supermarket 200m. Updated 2014.

10; Max 48hrs

Flot Bleu Pacific; €4 (2 x €2)

Info/photos: Keith & Sue Lawrence

VAUJANY — 189 — K9 — SKI — 38114 — N45°09.410' E006°04.803'

Directions: Off D43a. From D526 turn onto D43a. After 2km turn left to stay on D43a. After another 2km turn right, sp 'Espace Loisirs' and signed, and follow road to Aire.

i Alt 1250. In large ski area with plenty of ski lifts adj. View of large waterfall opp. Updated 2014.

15

Euro Relais Mini; Token; Elec €5

Info/photos: Keith & Sue Lawrence

ALPE D'HUEZ — 190 — K9 — SKI — 38750 — N45°05.204' E006°04.750'

Directions: East of ski station. From D1091 turn onto D211 and follow road 17km to ski station. At the top follow signs towards the airfield, tennis and Aire. Signed.

i Alt 1860m. Ski resort with good views. 2 good sized Service Points. Tennis courts and golf course adj. Inspected 2010.

75; €10.40/day; CC; Pay at machine

Raclet; Inc

LA LECHERE — 191 — K8 — 73260 — N45°31.180' E006°29.057'

Directions: Parking 3, 'Village 92', Thermal Spa Complex. From south exit N90 at Junction 37, sp 'La Léchère'. Turn left at T-Junction onto D93a. Follow road under N90, cross railway and turn left into Lieu-Dit Château Feuillet. At roundabout take 2nd exit into car park of Thermal Baths.

i Parking at thermal spa, restaurant, café, bar onsite. Riverside walks. Inspected 2010.

19; 48hrs free; 49hrs-21 days €1.50/day

Flot Bleu Fontaine

Info/photos: Keith & Sue Lawrence

AIGUEBELLE — 192 — K8 — 73220 — N45°32.586' E006°18.374'

Directions: Rue des Écoles. From south on D1006 turn right at traffic lights in centre of village into Rue Carret, sp 'Parking V. L. à 50m'. At end of road turn right and the Aire is immediately on left.

i Aire in small car park with some grass parking. Can be busy with lorries, especially market day Tues when best to arrive after 2pm. Railway noise at night. Inspected 2010.

10

Custom

Info/photos: Keith & Sue Lawrence

BOURGNEUF | 193 | K8 | | 73390 | N45°33.165' E006°12.653'

Info/photos: Keith & Sue Lawrence

Directions: D925. From south on D925 turn right at roundabout with D204 into village. Take 1st turning left off D925, sp 'Restaurant Pizzeria' and signed. Follow red, surfaced road in front of pizzeria and parking is in large open area behind boulangerie.

i Parking on edge of village with lovely views of mountains across fields. Boulangerie adj. Inspected 2010.

🚐 10

🚰 Flot Bleu Océane; Elec €2/20mins

SUSVILLE | 194 | K9 | | 38350 | N44°55.487' E005°46.965'

Directions: N85. Service Point at the Casino supermarket fuel station adj to N85.

i Supermarket adj. Updated 2014.

🚐 Poss

🚰 Flot Bleu Euro; CC; €2

LE BOURG D'OISANS | 195 | K9 | | 38520 | N45°03.418' E006°02.077'

Directions: D1091b. Exit town towards river bridge on 1091b and Service Point at the Casino supermarket fuel station on left adj to N85.

i Supermarket adj. Visited 2012.

🚐 Poss

🚰 Flot Bleu Euro; CC; €2

GRESSE EN VERCORS | 196 | J9 | SKI | 38650 | N44°53.500' E005°32.816'

Info/Photos: Sue Thake

Directions: D8d. Turn off D8a in centre of Gresse onto D8d. Aire in 1.5km at end of road, 500m beyond campsite.

i Mountain views. Good walks. Visited 2014.

🚐 5; Max 24hrs

🚰 None; Service Point (pay) at campsite, 500m

LES DEUX ALPS | 197 | K9 | SKI | 38860 | N45°01.401' E006°07.326'

Info/Photos: Heidi Hardwick

Directions: D213. From the bottom of the valley on D213, the Aire is on left just before entering town, sp 'Bus Parking'.

i Small town with commerce 15 mins uphill. Ice skating rink, ski lifts and glacial skiing open all year; free shuttle bus in summer. Area very popular with skiers, snowboarders and mountain bikers. Visited 2012.

🚐 40; €7/24hrs inc elec and water; Collected; Max 7 days
🚰 Urba Flux Tall

LE BOURGET DU LAC | 198 | K8 | | 73370 | N45°39.195' E005°51.772'

Info/photos: Keith & Sue Lawrence

Directions: Outside Camping L'Île aux Cygnes. From south on D1504 turn right onto D14. After 300m turn right into Blvd Ernest Coudurier, sp 'Camping'. Follow road round right-hand bend and Aire at end of road outside campsite.

i Lake nearby but no views. Use of toilets, showers, laundry, private beach. 20 hardstanding pitches plus 10 on grass. Low season free but no services. Updated 2014.

🚐 20+10; €12.33/24hrs in high season; Collected; Max 7 days
🚰 Custom; Mar-Oct

BELLEY | 199 | K8 | 01300 | N45°45.345' E005°40.691'

Photo: Carol Weaver

Directions: Rue de la Poisatte, off D41. Follow sp 'St Germain les P' through village onto D41. Aire is on right by sports facilities, signed.

i Local commerce 8 mins. Lake 2km. Updated 2014.

🚐 8

⛲ Urba Flux; €2 (2 x €1)

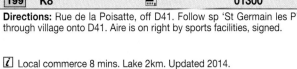

Info/Photo: Brenda & Maurice Cope & Carol Weaver

AIX LES BAINS | 200 | K8 | 73100 | N45°42.309' E005°53.281'

Directions: Ave du Grand Port/D991. Follow sp 'Le Lac-Les Ports'. Aire is on right 200m from the port, sp 'P Le Grand Port' and 'Camping-Cars'. The nearest Service Point is at Camping du Sierroz: N45°42.064' E005°53.165'. Follow the lake south for 700m.

i Popular Aire 200m from the lake, no views. Insufficient space for demand. Nice walking beside lake. Plenty of cafés and bars nearby. Visited 2012.

🚐 16; Max 48hrs

⛲ None; €5 at Camping du Sierroz

Info/Photo: Mike Crampton & Carol Weaver

PONT DU VAUX - St Benigne | 201 | J7 | 01190 | N46°26.220' E004°57.161'

Info/photo: Keith & Sue Lawrence

Directions: D2/Rue de l'Hôpital. From Pont de Vaux take D2 towards St Trivier de Courtes. After 950m turn right at the roundabout. The Aire is at the ATAC supermarket on the right adj to D2. Service Point adj to fuel station.

i Overnight parking on request. Motorhome parking not designated but large car park. Toilets during store hours. Inspected 2010.

🚐 By request

⛲ Euro Relais Junior; Token (ER); €2

Photo: Geoff Myatt

ST TRIVIER DE COURTES | 202 | J7 | 01560 | N46°27.540' E005°04.838'

Info/photos: Keith & Sue Lawrence

Directions: Petit Tour. From south on D975 turn onto D2/Rue des Carrons, sp 'Centre Ville'. At roundabout turn left onto Petit Tour. Sp 'Aire de Repos' in town. Parking on right and water point outside fire station (Sapeurs Pompiers).

i Village adj. Limited services and parking. Old Aire, unlikely to be developed. Inspected 2010.

🚐 3

⛲ Custom

ST ANDRE SUR VIEUX JONC | 203 | J7 | 01960 | N46°09.173' E005°09.116'

Info/photos: Keith & Sue Lawrence

Directions: From Bourg en Bresse head south on D1083. At roundabout turn right onto D117, then 1st left onto D67a, sp 'St Andre-s-Vieux-Jonc'. After 4km turn left into Chemin du Suc. At roundabout take 2nd exit into Chemin du Stade. Aire on left in 200m. Well signed.

i Pleasant, peaceful garden setting with open views to fields beyond football pitches. Inspected 2010.

🚐 3

⛲ Custom

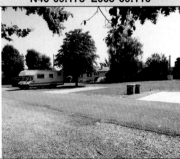

SANDRANS | 204 | J7 | 01400 | N46°03.707' E004°58.347'

Info/photos: Keith & Sue Lawrence

Directions: D27. From south on D2 turn left onto D27 by the church in Sandrans, signed. Follow road for 700m and turn left, sp 'Camping-Pêche'.

i Service Point only adj to fishing lake and campsite. Campsite €9/night. Updated 2014.

🚐 4; Along lakeside; Ask at campsite

⛲ Raclet; Token (2/1); €3

TREVOUX | 205 | J8 | 01600 | N45°56.423' E004°46.018'

Directions: Chemin du Camping. From D933 exit roundabout by river, sp 'Camping'. Service Point on left outside municipal campsite, visible from road: N45°56.405' E004°46.128'. Parking 100m on right, signed.

Aire controlled by municipal campsite. Unrestricted day parking near river 200m. Inspected 2013.

14; €5/night; Pay at campsite

Euro Relais Junior; Token (ER); €2.50; From campsite Apr-Sept

BELLEVILLE | 206 | J7 | 69220 | N46°06.392' E004°45.253'

Directions: Ancienne Ave du Port. Exit A6/E15 at Junction 30, sp 'Belleville'. At roundabout take 1st exit onto D37d. At next roundabout take 2nd exit onto D337, signed. At 3rd roundabout take 2nd exit, Ave de Salzkotten. Go over next roundabout, signed, and turn immediately left, signed. Aire at end of road.

Handy stop for travelling north/south; located between A6/E15 toll motorway and D306/N6 primary route. Under trees. Inspected 2013.

6; Max 48hrs; 11m bays

Custom

BEAUJEU | 207 | I7 | 69430 | N46°09.747' E004°34.420'

Directions: Rue du Stade. Turn off D37 towards Les Dépôts at the village boundary sign, sp 'Le Stade' and signed. Aire at the sports facilities.

Small village with local commerce 4 mins. Woodland walks adj. Visited 2012.

5

Euro Relais Mini; Token (ER)

Info/Photos: Carol Weaver

VILLEFRANCHE SUR SAONE | 208 | J8 | 69400 | N45°58.367' E004°45.082'

Directions: Route de Riottier. Exit A6 at Junction 31.2 then follow sp, 'Plan d'Eau'. The Aire is near the campsite in a riverside park, signed. Enter through PARKNIGHT barrier.

Large commercial Aire adj to River Saône and Bordelan lake. Visited 2014.

103; €12/night; CC; Discounts for pass holders

Euro Relais Junior; Inside; 10amp elec inc

Info/photo: Camping-Car-Park.com

LANSLEBOURG MONT CENIS | 209 | L8 | 73480 | N45°17.066' E006°52.290'

Directions: D1006. From west on D1006 the Service Point is in a lay-by on right as you enter village at 'Lanslebourg' town sign.

Service Point at attractive alpine village. Inspected 2010.

None

Euro Relais Junior; €2

Info/photos: Keith & Sue Lawrence

LA CHAMBRE | 210 | K8 | 73130 | N45°21.784' E006°17.858'

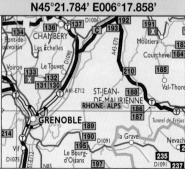

Directions: D76. Exit La Chambre on D76 to north. Turn 1st right after crossing river bridge, sp 'Centre Sportif et Culturel'. Aire 50m, signed.

View of mountains on the edge of town. Small town commerce 10-15 mins. Token from cooperative across bridge. Visited 2014.

9; Max 72hrs

Flot Bleu Pacific; Token; €2

Info/photo: Alan Crocker

MONT SAXONNEX | 211 | K7 | 74130 | N46°03.211' E006°29.068'

Directions: Route de l'Église. Take D4 from Cluses through Scionzier. West of Scionzier turn onto D268, sp 'Mont-Saxonnex'. After 4.5km turn left, sp 'Office du Tourisme' and signed. Aire 100m on left.

i Aire adj to sports facilities in pleasant hilltop village with excellent views. Limited parking opp Service Point adj to play area. Visited 2014.

🚐 Poss

⛲ Custom

Info/photos: Jim Stobart

PASSY | 212 | K8 | 18140 | N45°55.141' E006°42.263'

Directions: D39. Turn off D39 into Super U supermarket. Service Point near car wash.

i Supermarket adj. Useful as close to the main Chamonix-Geneva road. Cheap fuel. Visited 2014.

🚐 Poss

⛲ Flot Bleu; Token/CC; €2

Info/photo: Jim Stobart

VAL D'ISERE | 213 | L8 | SKI | 73150 | N45°27.580' E006°58.220'

Directions: D902. Take D902 from Bourg-St-Maurice (north) and Aire is on right as entering Val d'Isère.

i Alt 1850m. Aire located between two gondolas in a popular ski resort. Surrounding mountains range from 1785m to 3456m high. www.valdisere.com. Visited 2013.

🚐 20; €9/night; Max 3 days; Grass parking; Collected

⛲ Custom

Info/photos: Rob Beggs

LANS EN VERCORS | 214 | J9 | SKI | 38250 | N45°07.463' E005°35.500'

Directions: Route de St Donat. Turn off D531 at roundabout onto D106, sp 'Lans en Vercors'. Turn right, sp 'Massif de l'Aigle' and signed. Aire is in the large car park at the base of the ski lifts, signed.

i Large open parking area near the ski lifts. Visited 2014.

🚐 10

⛲ Custom

Info/photo: David & Sue Thake

Banne

Vicarious Shop

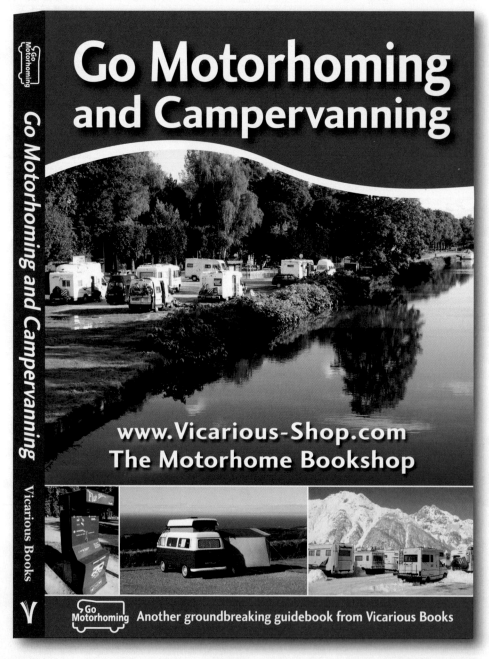

A69 motorway services

St Flour 3

MOTORWAY SERVICE POINTS

Motorway Aires. Do not park overnight at motorway service stations and rest areas!

French motorway service and rest areas often allocate parking with car and caravan signs. The parking areas may look nice, however motorhomes, caravans, trucks and vans are frequently broken into at motorway rest areas. Often the occupants are asleep during the burglary; surely a situation you would not want to be in. The following motorway service areas all have a motorhome/coach Service Point. We have observed that they are often broken, full of rubbish or obstructed by parked trucks. Vicarious Media recommends that you never park overnight at motorway services and rest areas and maintain vigilance at all times when using them.

Town	Map ref.	Grid ref.	GPS	Aire name and location
ATLANTIC				
SAUGON	A	D9	N45°11.330' W000°29.550'	Aire de Saugon Ouest. A10/E5 between Junction 38 and 39a, southbound towards Bordeaux.
SAUGON	A	D9	N45°11.364' W000°29.392'	Aire de Saugon Est. A10/E5 between Junction 38 and 39a, northbound towards Niort.
BORDEAUX	B	E9	N44°38.853' W000°26.160'	Aire des Landes. A62/E72 between Junction 1.1 and 2, northbound towards Bordeaux.
BORDEAUX	B	E9	N44°38.659' W000°26.279'	Aire des Landes. A62/E72 between Junction 1.1 and 2, southeast towards Toulouse.
AGEN	C	E10	N44°11.978' E000°30.367'	Aire d'Agen-Porte d'Aquitane. A62/E72 between Junction 6 and 7. Accessible both sides.
LESPERON	D	D10	N43°56.260' W001°05.400'	Aire du Souquet. N10/E70 between Junction 12 and 13. Accessible both sides.
BAYONNE	E	C11	N43°25.390' W001°35.963'	Aire de Bidart. A63/E80 between Junction 3 and 4, northeast towards Bayonne.
BAYONNE	E	C11	N43°25.306' W001°35.813'	Aire de Bidart. A63/E80 between Junction 3 and 4, southwest towards Spain.
PAU	F	D11	N43°25.262' W000°35.911'	Aire de Lacq-Audejos. A64/E80 between Junction 8 and 9, southeast towards Pau.
LIMOUSIN/AUVERGNE				
ST SULPICE LES FEUILLES	A	F7	N46°18.765' E001°25.052'	Aire de Boismandé Ouest. A20/E9 between Junction 21 and 22, southbound towards Limoges.
ST SULPICE LES FEUILLES	A	F7	N46°18.833' E001°25.223'	Aire de Boismandé Est. A20/E9 between Junction 21 and 22, northbound towards Châteauroux.
LORLANGES	B	H8	N45°20.122' E003°16.338'	Aire de La Fayette. A75/E11 at Junction 21. Accessible both sides.
ST FLOUR	C	H9	N45°01.910' E003°08.095'	Aire de Service du Cantal. D909. Exit A75/E11 at Junction 29 to St Flour. Accessible both sides.

MOTORWAY SERVICE POINTS

Town	Map ref.	Grid ref.	GPS	Aire name and location
MEDITERRANEAN				
LA LOZERE	A	H9	N44°52.177' E003°14.947'	Aire de la Lozère. A75/E11 at Junction 32. Accessible both sides.
AUMONT AUBRAC	B	H9	N44°44.418' E003°17.358'	Aire de l'Aubrac. A75/E11 at Junction 35. Service Point at Simply supermarket.
LE CAYLAR	C	H10	N43°51.896' E003°18.714'	Aire du Caylar. A75/E11 at Junction 49. Accessible both sides.
CAPENDU	D	G11	N43°10.590' E002°32.584'	Aire des Corbières. A61/E80 between Junction 24 and 25, eastbound towards Narbonne.
CAPENDU	D	G11	N43°10.736' E002°32.541'	Aire des Corbières. A61/E80 between Junction 24 and 25, westbound towards Carcassonne.
BANYULS DELS ASPRES	E	H12	N42°34.797' E002°50.785'	Aire du Village Catalan. A9/E15 between Junction 42 and 43. Second Service Point: N42°34.767' E002°50.767'.
CAVES	F	H12	N42°56.993' E002°58.346'	Aire de la Palme. A9/E15 between Junction 40 and 39, northbound towards Narbonne.
CAVES	F	H12	N42°57.047' E002°58.109'	Aire de la Palme. A9/E15 between Junction 39 and 40, southbound towards Perpignan.
NARBONNE	G	H11	N43°12.926' E003°05.633'	Aire de Narbonne-Vinassan. A9/E80 between Junction 37 and 36, northeast towards Béziers.
NARBONNE	G	H11	N43°12.866' E003°05.328'	Aire de Narbonne-Vinassan. A9/E80 between Junction 36 and 37, southbound towards Narbonne.
BEZIERS	H	H11	N43°21.530' E003°20.795'	Aire de Béziers-Montblanc. A9/E80 between Junction 36 and 34, northeast towards Montpellier.
BEZIERS	H	H11	N43°21.609' E003°20.577'	Aire de Béziers-Montblanc. A9/E80 between Junction 34 and 35, southbound towards Béziers.
NIMES	I	I10	N43°52.512' E004°26.888'	Aire de Nîmes-Marguerittes. A9/E15 between Junction 23 and 24, southwest towards Nîmes.
LANCON PROVENCE	J	J11	N43°35.325' E005°11.543'	Aire de Lançon de Provence. A7/E80/E714 between Junction 26 and 28, southbound towards Marseille/Nice.
LANCON PROVENCE	J	J11	N43°35.405' E005°11.510'	Aire de Lançon de Provence. A7/E80/E714 between Junction 28 and 26, northbound towards Lyon.
ROUSSET	K	K11	N43°28.305' E005°38.637'	Aire de Rousset. A8/E80 between Junction 32 and 33, eastbound towards Aix en Provence.
ROUSSET	K	K11	N43°28.079' E005°39.375'	Aire de l'Arc. A8/E80 between Junction 33 and 32, westbound towards Brignoles.
AIRE DE CAMBARETTE	L	K11	N43°25.322' E005°59.480'	Aire de Cambarette. A8/E80 between Junction 34 and 35. In middle, accessible both sides.
VIDAUBAN	M	K11	N43°24.872' E006°27.256'	Aire de Vidauban Sud. A8/E80 between Junction 35 and 36, eastbound towards Italy.
MIDI-PYRENEES				
SEVERAC LE CHATEAU	A	H10	N44°19.839' E003°04.930'	Aire de l'Aveyron. N88. Exit A75/E11 at Junction 42. Accessible both sides.
MONTANS	B	G10	N43°51.786' E001°53.844'	Aire des Issarts. A68 between Junction 8 and 9, northeast towards Albi.
MONTANS	B	G10	N43°51.120' E001°52.831'	Aire de Sanbatan. A68 between Junction 9 and 8, southwest towards Toulouse.
CAPENS	C	F11	N43°20.262' E001°14.742'	Aire du Volvestre. A64/E80 between Junction 27 and 28, westbound towards Bayonne.
AVIGNONET-LAURAGAIS	D	G11	N43°21.311' E001°48.271'	Aire de Port-Lauragais. A61/E80 between Junction 20 and 21. Accessible both sides.
POITOU				
VILLIERS EN PLAINE	A	E7	N46°25.734' W000°30.328'	Aire de la Chateaudrie. A83 between Junction 9 and 10, eastbound towards Poitiers.
VILLIERS EN PLAINE	A	E7	N46°25.828' W000°30.241'	Aire de la Canepetière. A83 between Junction 9 and 10, westbound towards Nantes.

Town	Map ref.	Grid ref.	GPS	Aire name and location
NIORT	**B**	E7	N46°17.777' W000°22.770'	Aire du Poitou-Charentes. A10/E5 between Junction 32 and 33, southbound towards Bordeaux.
BEDENAC	**C**	E9	N45°10.397' W000°19.956'	Aire de Bedenac. N10/E606 between junctions with D145 and D250, southbound towards Bordeaux.
PAMPROUX	**D**	E7	N46°27.275' W000°01.036'	Aire de Rouille-Pamproux. A10/E5 between Junction 30 and 31, northbound towards Angoulême.
PAMPROUX	**D**	E7	N46°27.066' W000°00.956'	Aire de Rouille-Pamproux. A10/E5 between Junction 31 and 30, southbound towards Bordeaux.

RHONE-ALPS

Town	Map ref.	Grid ref.	GPS	Aire name and location
DRACE	**A**	J7	N46°08.649' E004°46.068'	Aire de Dracé. A6/E15 between Junction 29 and 30, southbound towards Lyon.
L'ISLE D'ABEAU	**B**	J8	N45°36.721' E005°12.552'	Aire de l'Isle-d'Abeau. A43/E70 between Junction 6 and 7, eastbound towards Chambry.
L'ISLE D'ABEAU	**B**	J8	N45°36.818' E005°12.729'	Aire de l'Isle d'Abeau. A43/E70 between Junction 7 and 6, northwest towards Lyon.
CHATEAUNEUF	**C**	K8	N45°32.829' E006°09.376'	Aire du Val Gelon. A43/E70 at Junction 23, eastbound towards Italy.
CHATEAUNEUF	**C**	K8	N45°32.898' E006°09.332'	Aire de l'Arclusaz. A43/E70 at Junction 23, westbound towards Chambery.
ST RAMBERT D'ALBON	**D**	J9	N45°16.490' E004°49.576'	Aire de St Rambert d'Albon. A7/E15 between Junction 12 and 13, southbound towards Marseille.
ST RAMBERT D'ALBON	**D**	J9	N45°16.563' E004°49.754'	Aire de St Rambert d'Albon. A7/E15 between Junction 13 and 12, northbound towards Lyon.
PONT DE L'ISERE	**E**	J9	N45°01.237' E004°52.615'	Aire de Latitude 45. A7/E15 between Junction 14 and 13, northbound towards Lyon.
LA BAUME D'HOSTUN	**F**	J9	N45°04.500' E005°12.551'	Aire Porte de la Drôme. A49/E713 between Junction 8 and 9, southwest towards Valence.
LA BAUME D'HOSTUN	**F**	J9	N45°04.291' E005°12.730'	Aire de Royans-Vercors. A49/E713 between Junction 9 and 8, northeast towards Grenoble.
SAULCE SUR RHONE	**G**	J9	N44°43.178' E004°47.276'	Aire de Saulce. A7/E15 between Junction 17 and 16, northbound towards Lyon.
MONTELIMAR	**H**	J9	N44°30.980' E004°46.757'	Aire de Montélimar. A7/E15 between Junction 17 and 18, southbound towards Marseille.
MONTELIMAR	**H**	J9	N44°30.779' E004°46.834'	Aire de Montélimar. A7/E15 between Junction 18 and 17, northbound towards Lyon.
PASSY	**I**	L8	N45°55.304' E006°39.785'	Aire de Passy-Mont Blanc. A40/E25 between Junction 20 and 21, southbound towards Chamonix.

Photo: Keith & Sue Lawrence

Ste Colombe-en-Bruilhois

Photo: Janet & John Watts

Aire de Passy

Lourdes 2

Salins

This list of closed Aires is provided to prevent unnecessary journeys. The Aires have been confirmed closed by inspectors on location. Closed Aires that have no alternative Aire are marked with an X on the mapping. Closed Aires are listed in each region, alphabetically by town name. The map reference number from the edition in which they were published is also provided.

Town	Map number and edition	GPS	Year closed
ATLANTIC			
BERGERAC	54 3rd Ed	N44°50.760' E000°29.275'	2010
BISCARROSSE	145 4th Ed	N44°24.636' W001°10.065'	2013
BISCARROSSE PLAGE 2	148 4th Ed	N44°26.391' W001°14.883'	2013
BRANTOME 2	78 3rd Ed	N45°21.416' E000°39.167'	2010
CAVIGNAC 1	93 3rd Ed	N45°05.964' W000°23.279'	2010
GOURETTE 2	95 4th Ed	N42°57.445' W000°19.837'	2013
JAVERLHAC	2 4th Ed	N45°34.060' E000°33.730'	2013
LE MOUTCHIC	160 4th Ed	N44°59.934' W001°08.431'	2013
LESCAR 2	90 4th Ed	N43°20.025' W000°25.806'	2013
LESPARRE MEDOC	171 4th Ed	N45°18.769' W000°56.733'	2013
MUSSIDAN	60 3rd Ed	N45°02.508' E000°21.137'	2010
MONTPON MENESTEROL	213 4th Ed	N45°01.253' E000°09.601'	2013
PAU	88 4th Ed	N43°17.951' W000°22.581'	2013
PERIGUEUX 1	74 3rd Ed	N45°10.882' E000°43.357'	2010
POUILLON 2	109 4th Ed	N43°35.639' W001°00.942'	2013
PREIGNAC	176 4th Ed	N44°35.125' W000°17.731'	2013
SOUSTONS	126 4th Ed	N43°44.798' W001°19.291'	2013
ST JULIEN EN BORN	136 4th Ed	N44°04.248' W001°13.814'	2013
LIMOUSIN & AUVERGNE			
AYDAT 1	35 3rd Ed	N45°39.630' E002°58.628'	2010
PINOLS	101 4th Ed	N45°03.175' E003°24.760'	2014
SALINS	165 4th Ed	N45°11.492' E002°23.617'	2014
MEDITERRANEAN			
AIGUES MORTES 2	105 4th Ed	N43°33.933' E004°11.733'	2013
ARGELES SUR MER	62 3rd Ed	N42°34.627' E003°02.125'	2010
ARGENS MINERVOIS	52 4th Ed	N43°14.448' E002°45.865'	2013
BOLQUERE PYRENEES 2000 1	22 4th Ed	N42°30.983' E002°03.533'	2013
BORMES LES MIMOSAS	130 3rd Ed	N43°09.317' E006°20.800'	2010
CAIRANNE	132 4th Ed	N44°13.807' E004°55.721'	2013

Town	Map number and edition	GPS	Year closed
CARNON PLAGE 2	94 3rd Ed	N43°33.198' E004°00.590'	2010
DAUPHIN	150 4th Ed	N43°54.034' E005°47.041'	2014
DRAGUIGNAN	53 3rd Ed	N43°31.974' E006°26.976'	2010
FONTCOUVERTE	131 3rd Ed	N45°46.242' W000°32.491'	2008
FONTIES D'AUDE	37 3rd Ed	N43°11.154' E002°27.154'	2012
FREJUS 1	140 3rd Ed	N43°25.238' E006°44.550'	2010
FREJUS 2	141 3rd Ed	N43°25.458' E006°44.264'	2010
HYERES 'LE MEROU'	178 4th Ed	N43°06.550' E006°10.893'	2014
LA BOUILLADISSE	165 4th Ed	N43°23.386' E005°35.912'	2014
LA MOTTE 1	48 3rd Ed	N43°29.457' E006°32.081'	2010
LA REDORTE	95 3rd Ed	N43°14.912' E002°39.520'	2010
LA SEYNE SUR MER	173 4th Ed	N43°06.795' E005°51.469'	2014
LE BARCARES 6	43 4th Ed	N42°47.200' E003°02.283'	2013
LE LAVANDOU	4 3rd Ed	N43°07.458' E006°21.456'	2010
LODEVE	79 4th Ed	N43°44.017' E003°19.083'	2013
MARSEILLAN PLAGE	39 3rd Ed	N43°18.999' E003°32.715'	2010
PELVOUX	200 3rd Ed	N44°52.133' E006°29.100'	2010
PONT DU FOSSE 1	5 3rd Ed	N44°40.075' E006°13.870'	2010
PORT DE BROSSOLETTE	57 4th Ed	N43°10.281' E003°10.846'	2013
PORT ST LOUIS DU RHONE 1	110 4th Ed	N43°23.006' E004°48.439'	2014
PUICHERIC	17 3rd Ed	N43°13.628' E002°37.618'	2010
SABLET	134 4th Ed	N44°11.598' E004°59.695'	2013
SETE BEACH	2 3rd Ed	N43°22.964' E003°38.458'	2010
SIX FOURS LES PLAGES 2	172 4th Ed	N43°04.760' E005°48.587'	2014
ST GILLES	110 3rd Ed	N43°40.337' E004°26.020'	2010
ST MICHEL L'OBSERVATOIRE	147 4th Ed	N43°54.938' E005°42.982'	2014
ST TROPEZ 1	186 4th Ed	N43°16.180' E006°38.054'	2014
STE CECILE LES VIGNES	131 4th Ed	N44°15.078' E004°53.409'	2013
STE MAXIME 2	194 4th Ed	N43°18.474' E006°37.992'	2014
TREBES	98 3rd Ed	N43°12.539' E002°26.798'	2010
MIDI-PYRENEES			
AUZAT	134 4th Ed	N42°45.867' E001°28.833'	2013
BAGNAC SUR CELE	19 4th Ed	N44°40.082' E002°09.475'	2014
CASTELSARRASIN	41 3rd Ed	N44°02.279' E001°06.835'	2012
CASTRES	87 3rd Ed	N43°37.225' E002°15.203'	2012
CUQ LES VIELMUR	62 3rd Ed	N43°38.464' E002°05.846'	2010
GOURDON 1	92 3rd Ed	N44°44.948' E001°22.535'	2010
LISLE SUR TARN	77 3rd Ed	N43°51.708' E001°49.122'	2012
LOURDES 2	161 4th Ed	N43°05.296' W000°03.161'	2014
MARCIAC	164 3rd Ed	N43°31.571' E000°09.759'	2010
MILLAU 1	83 4th Ed	N44°05.695' E003°04.944'	2014
PINSAC	5 4th Ed	N44°51.293' E001°30.719'	2014
POITOU			
AVAILLES LIMOUZINE	61 3rd Ed	N46°07.385' E000°39.626'	2010
BAIGNES STE RADEGONDE	102 4th Ed	N43°19.733' W001°01.933'	2013
BOURG CHARENTE 1	107 4th Ed	N45°40.427' W000°13.461'	2014
BOURG CHARENTE 2	108 4th Ed	N45°40.344' W000°13.677'	2014

CLOSED AIRES

Town	Map number and edition	GPS	Year closed
BOYARDVILLE	157 4th Ed	N45°58.140' W001°14.268'	2014
CHATELAILLON PLAGE 2	159 4th Ed	N46°04.351' W001°05.162'	2014
CHATELAILLON PLAGE 3	160 4th Ed	N46°04.635' W001°05.253'	2014
CONFOLENS 1	79 3rd Ed	N46°00.768' E000°40.047'	2010
DISSAY	44 3rd Ed	N46°42.750' E000°24.810'	2010
FOURAS 1	165 4th Ed	N45°58.894' W001°05.210'	2014
LA PALMYRE 2	69 3rd Ed	N45°41.432' W001°10.610'	2010
LA TREMBLADE	142 4th Ed	N45°45.986' W001°08.343'	2014
LE CHATEAU D'OLERON 1	111 3rd Ed	N45°53.303' W001°12.298'	2010
LES MATHES 1	42 3rd Ed	N45°43.063' W001°08.870'	2010
MERIGNAC	64 3rd Ed	N45°41.687' W000°05.141'	2010
PORT DES BARQUES 2	136 3rd Ed	N45°56.950' W001°05.733'	2010
PORT LES MINIMES	62 3rd Ed	N46°08.533' W001°10.277'	2010
ROCHEFORT 1	39 3rd Ed	N45°56.597' W000°57.518'	2010
RONCE LES BAINS	92 3rd Ed	N45°47.582' W001°09.010'	2010
SAINTES	120 4th Ed	N45°45.300' W000°37.711'	2014
SECONDIGNY	32 3rd Ed	N46°36.274' W000°24.979'	2010
ST GENIS DE SAINTONGE	123 4th Ed	N45°28.785' W000°34.108'	2014
ST JEAN D'ANGELY 1	59 3rd Ed	N45°56.960' W000°32.178'	2010
ST YRIEIX	26 3rd Ed	N45°41.160' E000°08.857'	2010
RHONE-ALPS			
AIGUEBLANCHE	50 3rd Ed	N45°30.169'E006°30.068'	2010
AIX LES BAINS	95 3rd Ed	N45°42.180' E005°53.186'	2010
CHATILLON EN DIOIS	81 3rd Ed	N44°40.952' E005°26.873'	2010
DONZERE (MARKET)	2 3rd Ed	N44°26.600'E004°42.598'	2010
MORZINE	106 3rd Ed	N46°10.456' E006°42.623'	2010
ST CIRGUES EN MONTAGNE	77 3rd Ed	N44°45.351' E004°05.706'	2010
ST DONAT SUR L'HERBASSE	67 4th Ed	N45°07.122' E004°58.301'	2014
ST JUST	94 4th Ed	N44°18.097' E004°36.350'	2014
ST PAUL DE VARAX	71 3rd Ed	N46°05.953' E005°07.761'	2010
ST PIERRE DE CHARTREUSE 1	87 3rd Ed	N45°20.477' E005°49.059'	2010
ST SORLIN EN VALLOIRE	54 4th Ed	N45°17.417' E004°57.250'	2014
TOURNON SUR RHONE 1	28 3rd Ed	N45°04.230' E004°49.716'	2010
VILLARS LES DOMBES	43 3rd Ed	N45°59.572' E005°01.548'	2012

Hyeres le Merou

St Just

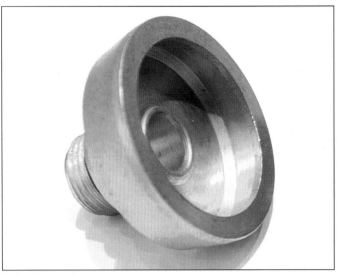

LPG-GPL cup adaptor.

LPG-GPL cup hand gun.

325 LPG fuel stations are listed here. TOTAL kindly gave us permission to publish the addresses on their trade distribution list. In November 2012 TOTAL were supplying LPG to 500 of the 1700 fuel stations across France that sell GPL, as it is named in France. LPG/GPL is available at most motorway service stations and the cup shaped connector is standard across France.

TOWN	GPS	DIRECTIONS
ATLANTIC		
AGEN	N44°10.708' E000°38.004'	Géant. D305 southbound. Take exit for D17/Lacapelete.
AIRE SUR L'ADOUR	N43°43.342' W000°15.874'	Total. D824/103 Route de Bordeaux. 2km north of town.
ARCACHON	N44°39.141' W001°08.819'	Avia. D650/Blvd Mestrezat. 200m from Aire.
BAYONNE	N43°30.290' W001°26.721'	E'Leclerc. D817/D107 roundabout. Northeast of town. Access not ideal for motorhomes over 8m.
BAYONNE	N43°29.543' W001°27.541'	Total. 20 Ave du Marechal Juin. In industrial area bordering northern bank of river L'Adour.
BERGERAC	N44°50.100' E000°26.867'	E'Leclerc. D936/D936e1 roundabout. Southwest of town.
BERGERAC	N44°51.017' E000°29.575'	Total. N21/Blvd Chanzy. East of town.
BERGERAC	N44°49.950' E000°29.800'	Total. N21/Route d'Agen. South of town.
BIDART	N43°25.306' W001°35.813'	Total. Aire de Bidart. A63/E80 between Junction 4 and 3, southwest towards Spain.
BIDART	N43°25.390' W001°35.963'	Total. Aire de Bidart. A63/E80 between Junction 3 and 4, northeast towards Bayonne.
BIGANOS	N44°38.183' W000°57.583'	Auchan. D3e13. South of town in commercial area. LPG pump under 2.95m high canopy.
BILLIERE	N43°18.349' W000°24.186'	Total. D834 roundabout. Take exit for Lons/Route de Bayonne. Northwest of town.
BISCARROSSE	N44°23.417' W001°09.650'	Super U. D652/Ave du Maréchal Lyautey. In centre.
BIZANOS	N43°18.214' W000°19.374'	Total Access. D817/Route de Tarbes. Northeast of town.
BORDEAUX	N44°52.971' W000°33.796'	Auchan. Blvd Aliénor d'Aquitaine. Exit A630/E5 at Junction 4.
BORDEAUX (GRADIGNAN)	N44°47.155' W000°35.734'	Agip. Aire de Thouars Nord. A630/E70 westbound between Junction 16 and 17. South of Bordeaux.
BORDEAUX (GRADIGNAN)	N44°47.172' W000°35.689'	Agip. Aire de Thouars Nord. A630/E70 westbound between Junction 17 and 16. South of Bordeaux.
BOULAZAC	N45°11.138' E000°46.488'	Intermarché. D5/N221 roundabout. Take exit for Zone Commerciale/Hyper U. East of Perigueux.
CASTELJALOUX	N44°19.167' E000°05.600'	Intermarché. Adj to D933. Northeast of town.
CESTAS	N44°44.544' W000°42.435'	Total. Aire de Bordeaux-Cestas. A63/E70 eastbound between Junction 24 and 25.
CESTAS	N44°44.752' W000°42.200'	Total. Aire de Bordeaux-Cestas. A63/E70 westbound between Junction 25 and 24.
DAX	N43°43.032' W001°03.072'	Total. D129/28 Route Georges Chaulet. North of town.
DAX	N43°44.467' W001°01.000'	Total. D824 roundabout. Take exit for C6/Le Hort.

LPG-GPL

TOWN	GPS	DIRECTIONS
EYSINES	N44°53.545' W000°40.058'	Total Access. D1215 roundabout. Take exit D2215/388 Ave du Médoc. West of town.
FUMEL	N44°29.500' E000°58.183'	Intermarché. D710 roundabout. Take exit Ave de Ladhuie/Zone Commerciale de Ladhuie. South of river Lot.
GUJAN MESTRAS	N44°37.001' W001°04.447'	Super U. D650e3/Ave de Césarée, near junction with A660. South of town.
LA TESTE DE BUCH	N44°38.793 W001°09.437'	Elf. D1250/D1251 roundabout. North of town.
LACQ-AUDEJOS	N43°25.300' W000°35.900'	Agip. Aire de Lacq-Audéjos. A64/E80 eastbound between Junction 8 and 9.
LANGON	N44°33.126' W000°15.893'	Total. D116/D8 roundabout. West of town.
LANGON	N44°32.509' W000°15.298'	E'Leclerc. D932e2 roundabout. 1km southwest of town.
LESPARRE MEDOC	N45°18.083' W000°56.043'	Total. D1215/Route de Bordeaux. South of town.
LIBOURNE	N44°53.864' W000°12.524'	Total. D670/Ave du Général Leclerc. Southeast of town.
LORMONT	N44°52.416' W000°30.407'	Total. Rocade Est de Bordeaux. N230/E70 northbound between Junction 26 and 27. Southeast of town.
MARMANDE	N44°30.316' E000°09.032'	Total. D813/84 Route Jean Jaurès. Northwest of town.
MARMANDE	N44°29.333' E000°10.817'	Carrefour. D813 roundabout. Take exit for Hameau de Cramat. Southeast of town.
MARSAC SUR L'ISLE	N45°11.650' E000°39.583'	Auchan. D710e roundabout. West of Perigueux.
MERIGNAC	N44°49.659' W000°40.264'	Total Access. Rue Gutenberg/D106 roundabout. Southwest of town.
MERIGNAC	N44°50.516' W000°39.866'	Total. 127 Ave de l'Yser. Southwest of town.
MERIGNAC	N44°51.003' W000°40.031'	Total. Relais de Gironde. A630/E5 northbound between Junction 10 and 9.
MONTPON-MENESTEROL	N45°00.367' E000°08.550'	Intermarché. D6089/D9 roundabout. Take exit for Centre Commercial.
MUSSIDAN	N45°02.467' E000°21.100'	Super U. D6089 roundabout. Take exit for St Médard de Mussidan. North of town.
OLORON STE MARIE	N43°11.432' W000°37.041'	Total. D936/Ave Charles Mourieu roundabout. West of town.
ORTHEZ	N43°29.114' W000°45.923'	Total. D817/10 Ave Francis Jammes. East of town.
ORTHEZ	N43°29.367' W000°47.800'	E'Leclerc. D817/Route de Bayonne. West of town.
PAU	N43°18.417' W000°22.583'	Avia. D834/17 Ave Jean Mermoz. In centre.
PAU	N43°19.118' W000°22.722'	Total. D834/157 Ave Jean Mermoz. North of town.
PAU (LE LUY)	N43°21.600' W000°23.017'	Intermarché. D834 roundabout. Take exit D716. North of town.
PAU (LONS)	N43°19.767' W000°22.850'	Géant. D834 roundabout. Take exit for Centre Commercial du Mail.
PERIGUEUX	N45°11.849' E000°42.019'	Total. D939/138 Route Pierre Sémard. Northwest of town
PERIGUEUX	N45°11.417' E000°44.150'	Total. D6021/Ave Michel Grandou. Northeast of town.
PESSAC	N44°46.865' W000°38.980'	Total. Ave de Haut Lévèque. Southwest of town near A63/E70 Junction 26a.
POMARET	N44°11.963' E000°30.501'	Total. Aire d'Agen Porte d'Aquitaine. A62/E72 between Junction 6 and 7. Accessible both sides.
PONT DU CASSE	N44°13.606' E000°40.317'	Total. D656/Ave Le Cahors. Southwest of town.
SARLAT LA CANEDA	N44°52.697' E001°13.015'	Avia. D704/Rue du Lot. South of town. Adj to railway bridge.
SAUGNAC ET MURET	N44°21.719' W000°51.072'	Total. Aire de Muret. A63/E5 southbound between Junction 17 and 18.
ST ANDRE DE CUBZAC	N44°58.724' W000°25.881'	Total. Aire de l'Estalot. A10/E5 southbound between Junction 40a and 41.
ST ASTIER	N45°08.702' E000°31.424'	E'Leclerc. D3/Blvd Mal de Lattre de Tassigny.
ST LAURENT SUR MANOIRE	N45°09.021' E000°47.919'	Total. Aire du Manoire. A89/E70 at Junction 16. Accessible both sides
ST MICHEL DE RIEUFRET	N44°38.795' W000°26.255'	Total. Aire des Landes. A62/E72 southbound between Junction 1.1 and 2.
ST-PIERRE-DU-MONT	N43°52.586' W000°30.370'	Total. Ave de St-Sever. Southeast of town.
ST SEVER	N43°46.400' W000°34.033'	Intermarché. D933. North of town.
ST VINCENT DE PAUL	N43°44.451' W001°01.047'	Total. D824 roundabout. Take exit C6/Le Hort. West of town.
ST VINCENT DE TYROSSE	N43°40.000' W001°17.183'	E'Leclerc. D810/Route de Bordeaux. East of town.
STE FOY LA GRANDE (PINEUILH)	N44°50.483' E000°14.633'	E'Leclerc. D936E6/Route de Bergerac. East of town.
TARTAS	N43°50.600' W000°45.650'	Elan. Aire de Champigny. D824. 4km east of Tartas. Accessible both sides.
TERRASSON-LAVILLEDIEU	N45°07.708' E001°19.043'	Total. D6809. East of town.

TOWN	GPS	DIRECTIONS
TONNEINS	N44°24.012' E000°17.906'	E'Leclerc. D813/Ave Pierre Mendés France. North of town.
TRESSES-MELAC	N44°50.416' W000°29.626'	Elf. D936/Ave de Branne, towards Bergerac.
VILLENEUVE SUR LOT	N44°24.242' E000°41.278'	Total. D911/Route de Bordeaux. West of town.

LIMOUSIN AND AUVERGNE

TOWN	GPS	DIRECTIONS
BELLERIVE SUR ALLIER	N46°07.059' E003°24.670'	Total. D2209/22 Ave de la République. East of town.
BRIVE LA GAILLARDE	N45°09.885' E001°30.649'	Total. D1089/90 Ave Ribot. 1km northwest of town.
BRIVE LA GAILLARDE	N45°10.129' E001°33.640'	Géant. D1089/Ave Marie Et Pierre Curie. East of town.
CHAMPS	N46°03.508' E003°06.748'	Total. Aire des Volcans d'Auvergne. A71/E11 between Junction 12 and 13. Accessible both sides.
CLERMONT-FERRAND	N45°47.350' E003°07.070'	Total. D2009/24 Blvd Amboise Bruguière. 1.5km northeast of town.
CLERMONT-FERRAND	N45°48.839' E003°06.545'	Auchan. D2009/Blvd Étienne Clémentel. North of town.
GUERET	N46°10.621' E001°53.899'	Intermarché. N145/E62 at Junction 47 on D4 roundabout.
LAGUENNE	N45°14.740' E001°46.407'	Auchan. D1120/Ave de Coulaud. North of town
LE PUY EN VALEY	N45°02.827' E003°53.583'	Total. N88/Blvd Maréchal Joffre.
MASSERET	N45°32.489' E001°30.506'	Total. Aire de Porte de Corrèze. A20/E9 between Junction 42 and 43. Accessible both sides.
MAURIAC	N45°12.945' E002°20.331'	Carrefour. D681/Rue du Commandant Gabon. 0.25km southeast of town.
MAURIAC	N45°12.865' E002°20.801'	Carrefour. D922/Route d'Aurillac southbound. Southeast of town.
MAURS	N44°42.538' E002°11.763'	Total. N122/Route de Bagnac. Southwest of town.
MONLUCON	N46°20.288' E002°34.041'	Auchan. D745/Ave des Martyrs. West of town. 3.5m height restriction.
MONTMARAULT	N46°19.413' E002°57.855'	Heep. D2371/Route de Moulins. Northeast of town.
PARSAC	N46°11.865' E002°11.130'	Total. Aire de Parsac. N145/E62. 1.5km east of town. Accessible both sides.
RIOM	N45°52.707' E003°06.992'	Carrefour. D6/D6a crossroads. South of town.
ST JUNIEN	N45°53.839' E000°55.215'	Carrefour. D941 roundabout. Exit Ave Nelson Mandela. 1km northeast of town.
ST POURCAIN SUR SIOULE	N46°17.687' E003°17.695'	Total. D2009/Route de Gannat. 1km south of town.
THIERS	N45°50.546' E003°30.879'	Pireyre & Pascal. D2089/Ave du Général de Gaulle. 2.5km southwest of town.
USSEL	N45°32.592' E002°17.843'	E'Leclerc. D157. West of town.
VICHY/BELLERIVE SUR ALLIER	N46°07.055' E003°24.683'	Total. D2209/Ave de Vichy roundabout. East of Bellerive sur Allier.
YZEURE (MOULINS)	N46°33.273' E003°20.191'	Total. D707/28 Route de Lyon. 1km south of town.

MEDITERRANEAN

TOWN	GPS	DIRECTIONS
AIMARGUES	N43°41.752' E004°12.051'	Elf. D6313/Route de la Petite Camargue. 1.5km north of town.
AIX EN PROVENCE	N43°31.704' E005°25.957'	Total. D64/16 Route de Galice. 0.5km west of town.
AIX EN PROVENCE	N43°30.957' E005°27.980'	Total Access. A8/E80 at Junction 31. At roundabout take exit Frejus/Ave Henri Mauriat. 1km southeast of town.
AIX EN PROVENCE	N43°29.049' E005°23.000'	Total Access. D59/Rue Victor Baltard. Between Juncton 3 of D9 and Junction 3 of A51/E712.
APT	N43°52.990' E005°22.870'	Total. D900/Ave de Lançon. 1.5km northwest of town.
ARLES	N43°40.212' E004°37.282'	Total. D35/Ave Bachaga Said Boualem. 1km southwest of town.
ARLES	N43°39.109' E004°40.148'	Total. Aires des Cantarelles. N113/E80 southbound between Junction 7 and 8.
AUBAGNE	N43°17.557' E005°35.606'	Auchan. Chemin des Bonnes Nouvelles. 1km west of town.
AVIGNON	N43°55.928' E004°46.980'	Elf. 1985 Rocade Charles de Gaulle. 1.5km southwest of town.
BEZIERS	N43°19.896' E003°14.875'	Total Access. 1 Ave de la Devèze. 1.5km southeast of town.
BEZIERS	N43°21.260' E003°13.756'	Elf. Ave du Docteur Jean Marie Fabre/Rue de l'Hort de Mgr crossroads. 1.5km northeast of town.
BOUC-BEL-AIR	N43°26.509' E005°23.731'	Total. Aire de la Champouse. A51/E712 southbound between Junction 3 and 2.
BOUC-BEL-AIR	N43°26.022' E005°23.728'	Esso. Aire de Chabauds. A51/E712 northbound between Junction 2 and 3.
BRIANCON	N44°54.234' E006°37.739'	Total Access. N94/10 Ave du Dauphiné. 0.5km northwest of town.

LPG-GPL

TOWN	GPS	DIRECTIONS
CANNES	N43°33.309' E007°00.339'	Total. 57 Blvd du Riou. 0.5km northwest of town.
CANNES LA BOCCA	N43°33.056' E006°57.461'	E'Leclerc. Chemin de la Bastide Rouge/D6007 roundabout. 1km west of town.
CARCASSONNE	N43°12.431' E002°20.140'	Total. D118/Route de Limoux. 0.5km west of town.
CAVAILLON	N43°49.854' E005°03.270'	Total. D973/264 Ave de Cheval Blanc. South of town.
CHATEAU ARNOUX ST AUBAN	N44°05.172' E006°00.494'	Total. D4096/Ave Jean Moulin. 0.5km south of town.
CHATEAUREDON	N44°01.015' E006°12.733'	Elan. N85/l'Hubac et St Jean. North of town.
PORT COGOLIN	N43°15.823' E006°34.653'	Total. D98a/D559 junction. South of town.
COURSAN	N43°12.829' E003°05.390'	Total. Aire de Narbonne-Vinassan. A9/E15 southbound between Junction 36 and 37.
COURSAN	N43°12.961' E003°05.536'	Total. Aire de Narbonne-Vinassan. A9/E15 northbound between Junction 37 and 36.
DIGNE LES BAINS	N44°05.379' E006°14.229'	Intermarché. D19/Ave du Mai 1945 roundabout. South of town.
FOS SUR MER	N43°25.664' E004°57.947'	Elf. N568 northbound. 1km southeast of town.
FOS SUR MER	N43°28.274' E004°54.490'	Elf. N568/ZI Secteur 83. Northwest of town.
FREJUS	N43°26.121' E006°43.489'	Total. DN7/Ave de Verdun. Northwest of town.
FUVEAU	N43°27.948' E005°36.384'	Total. D6. Northeast of town.
GAP	N44°32.479' E006°03.471'	Total. N85/Ave de Provence. 1.5km southwest of town.
GIGNAC LA NERTHE	N43°23.537' E005°15.419'	Total. Aire de Gignac-La-Nerthe. A55 westbound between Junction 6 and 7.
GIGNAC LA NERTHE	N43°23.458' E005°15.500'	Agip. Aire de Rebuty. A55 eastbound between Junction 7 and 6.
HYERES	N43°07.456' E006°08.914'	Intermarché. Ave du Quinzieme Corps. 1.5km east of town.
LA GARDE	N43°08.987' E006°02.050'	Total. Aire de la Chaberte. A57 southbound between Junction 6 and 5.
LANCON DE PROVENCE	N43°35.377' E005°11.596'	Total. Aire de Lançon de Provence. A7/E80/E714 southbound between Junction 27 and 28.
LANCON DE PROVENCE	N43°35.377' E005°11.235'	Total. Aire de Lançon de Provence. A7/E80/E714 northbound between Junction 28 and 27.
LE CAYLAR	N43°51.858' E003°18.727'	Total. Aire de Service à 75. A75/E11 at Junction 49. Accessible both sides.
LE LUC	N43°22.883' E006°18.250'	E'Leclerc. D97. Southwest of town.
LE PONTET	N43°58.619' E004°51.469'	Total. D907/Route de Lyon. 1km north of town.
LES PENNES-MIRABEAU	N43°24.558' E005°19.264'	Elf. D368 ringroad. 0.5km east of town.
LODEVE	N43°43.516' E003°19.380'	Super U. D609. South of town.
MANOSQUE	N43°49.347' E005°47.262'	Total. D4096/Ave Frédéric Mistral. Southwest of town.
MANOSQUE	N43°50.267' E005°48.300'	E'Leclerc. D4096/Blvd du Maréchal Juin. Northeast of town.
MANOSQUE	N43°51.017' E005°49.417'	Auchan. D4096/Route de Volx. Northeast of town.
MARGUERITTES	N43°52.094' E004°26.342'	BP. Aire de Nîmes-Marguerittes. A9/E15 northbound between Junction 24 and 23.
MARGUERITTES	N43°52.502' E004°26.918'	Total. Aire de Nîmes-Marguerittes. A9/E15 southbound between Junction 23 and 24.
MARIGNANE	N43°26.587' E005°13.439'	Total. Aéroport Marseilles Provence. D20d/D20 roundabout. 1.5km north of town.
MARSEILLE	N43°17.165' E005°25.649'	Total. D2/359 Blvd Mireille Lauze. 2.5km east of town.
MARSEILLE	N43°20.969' E005°20.558'	Elf. D5/Chemin du Littoral. 3.5km north of town.
MARSEILLE	N43°19.433' E005°27.199'	Elf. D4/Ave Frédéric Mistral. 4km northeast of town.
MARSEILLE	N43°19.659' E005°21.958'	Total. 99 Route de Lyon. 2km north of town.
MARSEILLE	N43°18.227' E005°24.062'	Elf. 64-70 Blvd Françoise Duparc. In centre.
MARSEILLE	N43°17.518' E005°27.211'	Total. Aire de la Pomme. A50 eastbound between Junction 3 and 4.
MARVEJOLS	N44°33.791' E003°17.520'	Total. D809/38 Ave Theophile Roussel. 1km north of town.
MAUGUIO	N43°37.085' E003°59.312'	Total. D24/Route de Montpellier. 1.5km west of town.
MONTPELLIER	N43°38.095' E003°49.375'	Total. 70 Ave de l'Europe. 3km northwest of town.
MONTPELLIER	N43°35.712' E003°50.889'	Total Access. D65/Ave de Vanières. Southwest of town.
MOUGINS	N43°35.522' E007°02.167'	Total. Aire de Bréguières Nord. A8 southbound between Junction 44 and 42.
MOUGINS	N43°35.377' E007°02.122'	Total. Aire de Bréguières Sud. A8 northbound between Junction 42 and 44.

TOWN	GPS	DIRECTIONS
NARBONNE	N43°10.468' E002°59.552'	Total. Ave Général Leclerc. Southwest of town.
NICE	N43°39.818' E007°12.108'	Total. Blvd Léon Morate at Aéroport de Nice Côte d'Azur. 3km southwest of town.
NICE	N43°40.179' E007°12.994'	BP. Blvd René Cassin. 2.5km southwest of town, near Aéroport de Nice Côte d'Azur.
NICE	N43°42.412' E007°17.544'	Total. 10 Blvd de l'Armée des Alpes. 1.5km east of town.
NIMES	N43°48.609' E004°19.744'	Total. N113/2075 Route de Montpellier. 2km southwest of town.
NIMES	N43°49.304' E004°19.761'	Elf. N106/Blvd Pasteur Marc Boegner. 1.5km southwest of town.
PERPIGNAN	N42°40.673' E002°53.451'	Total. Ave d'Espagne. 1km south of town.
PERPIGNAN	N42°40.089' E002°53.004'	Auchan. D900/Route de Perthus. Southwest of Perpignan.
PERTUIS	N43°40.844' E005°30.028'	Carrefour. D956/Route d'Aix. South of town.
PUGET-SUR-ARGENS	N43°27.995' E006°40.323'	Total. Aire du Canaver. A8/E80 northbound between Junction 37 and 36.
QUISSAC	N43°54.850' E003°59.717'	Vulco. D999/543 Ave de l'Aigoual. North of Quissac.
ONET LE CHATEAU	N44°22.170' E002°35.412'	Total. D988/Route d'Espalion. North of town.
ROQUEFORT LES CORBIERES	N42°59.367' E002°58.339'	Total. D6009/Cambouisset. East of town.
RUOMS	N44°26.563' E004°20.936'	Super U. D579/D557 roundabout. Take exit for ZA de l'Arzallier.
SALON DE PROVENCE	N43°37.961' E005°05.890'	Total. 666 Blvd du Roi René. South of town.
SALON DE PROVENCE	N43°37.150' E005°05.766'	Total. D538/Ave de la Patrouille de France. South of town.
ST MAXIMIN LA STE BAUME	N43°26.836' E005°51.739'	Total. DN7/Route de Nice. South of town.
TOULON	N43°07.027' E005°56.454'	Total. 322 Ave Édouard le Bellegou. 0.5km southeast of town.
TOULON	N43°07.387' E005°56.279'	Total. N97/160 Ave Georges Clemenceau. 0.5km east of town.
VAISON LA ROMAINE	N44°14.525' E005°04.831'	Total. 72 Ave Victor Hugo. East of town.
VENCE	N43°42.908' E007°07.022'	Total. M236/M2 roundabout. South of town.
VILLETELLE	N43°42.971' E004°08.050'	Total. Aire d'Ambrussum. E15/A9 southbound between Junction 26 and 27.
VILLETELLE	N43°42.742' E004°07.886'	Total. Aire d'Ambrussum. E15/A9 northbound between Junction 27 and 26.
VITROLLES	N43°25.252' E005°16.113'	Total. D113. 5km south of town.

MIDI-PYRENEES

TOWN	GPS	DIRECTIONS
ALBI	N43°55.167' E002°07.900'	Total. D988/Ave François Verdier. Southwest of town.
ALBI	N43 55.110' E002 06.435'	E'Leclerc. N88 at Junction 14. Take exit for Bourdès/Rue des Portes d'Albi.
AUCH	N43°39.883' E000°35.500'	E'Leclerc. N124 at junction with N21. Take exit for Roquelaure/Auch-Centre Historique. North of town.
AUSSILLON-MAZAMET	N43°30.535' E002°21.680'	Elan. N112/Blvd du Thoré. 1km north of town.
AUTERIVE	N43°21.792' E001°27.470'	Carrefour. D820/49 Route de Toulouse. North of town.
BAGNERES DE BIGORRE	N43°04.850' E000°08.350'	Total. D935/Ave de la Mongie. North of town.
BALMA	N43°36.580' E001°29.570'	Total Access. D50/Ave de Toulouse. Northwest of town.
BALMA	N43°35.369' E001°30.837'	Total. D826/Route de Castres. 1km southeast of town.
BESSIERES	N43°47.882' E001°36.743'	Super U. D630/Ave de Castres. East of town.
BLAGNAC	N43°38.282' E001°23.416'	Total Access. D2/120 Route de Grenade. Northwest of town.
BLAGNAC	N43°38.480' E001°22.483'	Elf. D902/Voie Lactée northbound. 1km west of town.
BLAYE LES MINES	N44°01.617' E002°09.333'	Super U. D73/N2088/Ave d'Albi crossroads. East of town.
CAHORS	N44°25.467' E001°26.433'	Total. D820/Route de Toulouse. South of Cahors.
CARCASSONNE	N43°21.193' E001°48.386'	Total. Aire de Port Lauragais. A61 southbound between Junction 20 and 21.
CARCASSONNE	N43°21.165' E001°48.587'	Total. Aire de Port Lauragais. A61 northbound between Junction 21 and 20.
CASTELSARRASIN	N44°02.584' E001°06.294'	Total. D813/Ave du Maréchal Leclerc. North of town.
CASTELSARRASIN	N44°03.850' E001°05.833'	E'Leclerc. D813/Route de Moissac. 3km north of town.
CASTRES	N43°37.033' E002°14.650'	Avia. D89/Ave de Roquecourbe. North of town.
CAZAUBON	N43°56.050' W000°03.800'	Elan. D626/Blvd des Pyrénées. East of town.

LPG-GPL

TOWN	GPS	DIRECTIONS
CAZERES	N43°12.650' E001°05.050'	Carrefour. D6/Ave Pasteur. North of town.
CLARAC	N43°06.625' E000°36.820'	Total. Aire des Comminges. A64 between Junction 17 and 18.
CONDOM	N43°57.083' E000°22.267'	Total. D930. South of town.
DONNEVILLE	N43°29.026' E001°32.942'	Carrefour. Aires de Toulouse-Sud. A61 southbound between Junction 19 and 19.1.
DONNEVILLE	N43°29.133' E001°32.976'	Carrefour. Aires de Toulouse-Nord. A61 northbound between Junction 19.1 and 19.
ESTANCARBON	N43°06.764' E000°47.271'	Total. D817. 0.5km north of town.
FIGEAC	N44°36.667' E002°01.667'	Esso. D840/D2/D19 roundabout. North of town.
FOIX	N42°56.883' E001°37.550'	Total. D117. Near N20/E9 Junction 11.
FONBEAUZARD	N43°40.672' E001°25.403'	Total. D4/114 Route de Fronton. 1km west of town.
GOURDON	N44°43.243' E001°22.103'	Elan. D673/Route du Fumel. 2km southwest of town.
LALOUBERE	N43°12.616' E000°04.385'	Géant. D935/Route du Maréchal Foch. South of Tarbes.
LAVAUR	N43°41.762' E001°48.968'	Agip. D87/D112. South of town.
LAVELANET	N42°55.455' E001°50.275'	Super U. D117 roundabout. Take exit for Rue des Pyrénées. Southwest of town.
LECTOURE	N43°54.983' E000°37.683'	Elan. N21. South of town.
LOMBEZ	N43°28.233' E000°55.367'	Intermarché. D626. Take exit onto Ave du Docteur Raynaud. East of town.
LOURDES	N43°05.835' W000°02.295'	Total. Blvd du Lapacca. Near centre.
MONTALZAT	N44°13.966' E001°31.689'	Total. Aire du Bois de Dourre. A20/E9 between Junction 59 and 58. Accessible both sides.
MONTAUBAN	N44°00.267' E001°20.478'	Total. N2020/350 Route de Toulouse. 0.5km southwest of town.
OLEMPS	N44°19.517' E002°33.467'	Super U. D888/D212 roundabout. South of town.
PAVIE	N43°37.000' E000°34.517'	Total. N21/Route de Tarbes. West of town.
PORTET SUR GARONNE	N43°31.492' E001°24.021'	Total Access. D120/43 Route d'Espagne. South of town.
PORTET SUR GARONNE	N43°31.475' E001°23.941'	Elf. D120/106 Route d'Espagne. South of town.
POUZAC	N43°04.857' E000°08.365'	Total. D935/77 Ave de la Mongie. Southeast of town.
REVEL	N43°27.823' E002°00.417'	Elan. D622/Ave de Castres. North of town.
RIEUMES	N43°24.817' E001°06.950'	Carrefour. D28/Route de Samatan. Northwest of town.
SAIX	N43°35.309' E002°11.123'	Auchan. N126/Route de Toulouse. North of town.
SEBAZAC CONCOURES	N44°23.633' E002°36.167'	E'Leclerc. D988. Take exit for Le Comtal Sud et Nord Pôle Commercial. South of town.
SEVERAC LE CHATEAU	N44°19.817' E003°04.850'	Total. Aire de L'Aveyron. N88/A75/E11 at Junction 42.
ST AFFRIQUE	N43°57.483' E002°52.217'	Super U. D999. Take exit for Route Chantefriboule. On west side of town.
ST ALBAN	N43°41.015' E001°25.232'	Elf. D4/16 Route de Fronton. 0.5km southeast of town.
TARBES	N43°14.374' E000°03.632'	Total. D935a/D935b roundabout. On northwest ringroad.
TOULOUSE	N43°39.480' E001°25.175'	Total. D820/353 Ave des États Unis. 3.5km north of town.
TOULOUSE	N43°35.292' E001°25.411'	Total. 7 Blvd Déodat de Séverac. Southwest of town.
TOULOUSE	N43°37.894' E001°28.966'	Auchan. D112/D64d roundabout. 1.5km northeast of town.
TOULOUSE	N43°34.856' E001°23.735'	Total Access. 22 Route St Simon. 2km west of town.
TOULOUSE	N43°35.658' E001°23.836'	Total. A620 southbound at Junction 28.
TOULOUSE	N43°36.032' E001°23.904'	Total. A620 northbound at Junction 28.
VENERQUE	N43°25.700' E001°26.733'	Intermarché. D19/D35 roundabout. South of town.
VIC EN BIGORRE	N43°23.086' E000°03.062'	Intermarché. D6. South of town.
VILLEFRANCHE DE ROUERGUE	N44°21.550' E001°59.182'	Elan. D911. Near D911/D1/D926 roundabout. West of town.

POITOU

TOWN	GPS	DIRECTIONS
BARBEZIEUX ST HILAIRE	N45°27.678' W000°08.545'	Total. D731/D5 roundabout. Southeast of town.
CHASSENEUIL DU POITOU	N46°37.875' E000°21.421'	Total. D910/Route de Paris. South of town.
GEMOZAC	N45°34.549' W000°40.658'	Super U. D732/D6 roundabout. North of town.

TOWN	GPS	DIRECTIONS
LA ROCHELLE	N46°09.405' W001°07.185'	Total. Ave Jean Paul Sartre. East of town.
MONTMORILLON	N46°25.135' E000°51.270'	E'Leclerc. D727. West of town.
NAINTRE	N46°45.234' E000°29.042'	Q8. D910. South of town.
NAINTRE	N46°45.406' E000°29.083'	Intermarché. D23/D910 roundabout. Exit D23/Naintré Centre/Colombiers. South of town.
NEUVILLE DE POITOU	N46°41.079' E000°15.277'	Total. D62. East of town.
NIORT	N46°18.994' W000°28.369'	Total. D811/Ave de la Rochelle. South of town.
NIORT	N46°20.428' W000°23.708'	Elf. D611/Route de Paris. East of town.
NIORT	N46°17.729' W000°22.807'	Total. Aire du Poitou-Charentes. A10/E5 southbound between Junction 33 and 32.
NIORT	N46°17.835' W000°22.297'	Total. Aire du Poitou-Charentes. A10/E5 northbound between Junction 32 and 33.
PAMPROUX	N46°27.177' W000°01.043'	Total. Aire de Rouillé-Pamproux. A10/E5 southbound between Junction 30 and 31.
PAMPROUX	N46°27.089' W000°01.107'	Shell. Aire de Rouillé-Pamproux. A10/E5 northbound between Junction 31 and 30.
POITIERS	N46°36.252' E000°19.944'	Total. D910/Rocade Ouest. North of town.
PUILBOREAU	N46°10.601' W001°06.219'	Total. Aire de Puilboreau. N11/E601/E3 northbound. South of town.
ROYAN	N45°37.907' W000°59.524'	E'Leclerc. N150/Ave du 4éme Zouave. East of town.
RUFFEC	N46°01.260' E000°11.386'	E'Leclerc. D736/Chemin des Meuiers. Southwest of town.
SAINTES	N45°42.183' W000°37.466'	Total. D137/Route de Bordeaux. 2km south of Saintes.
SAINTES	N45°45.384' W000°39.100'	Carrefour. D128/Blvd de Vladimir. Northwest of town.
ST GENIS DE SAINTONGE	N45°29.371' W000°33.951'	Total. D137/Ave de Saintes. North of town.
ST JEAN D'ANGELY	N45°56.667' W000°30.333'	E'Leclerc. D218 roundabout. Exit Centre Commercial/Rue René Cassin.
ST MAIXENT L'ECOLE	N46°24.438' W000°13.537'	E'Leclerc. D8/D611 roundabout. Exit D8/Cherveux. Southwest of town.
TONNAY CHARENTE	N45°57.010' W000°55.599'	Total. D137. 3km east of town.
VILLEGATS	N46°00.060' E000°12.036'	Shell. Aire de L'Eglantier. N10 northbound carriageway. 2.5km south of Ruffec.

RHONE-ALPS

TOWN	GPS	DIRECTIONS
ALBERTVILLE	N45°39.664' E006°22.991'	Total. N90 northbound at Junction 29. South of town.
ALBY SUR CHERAN	N45°49.128' E006°00.261'	Total. D1201/Route d'Aix les Bains eastbound. West of town.
ALLAN	N44°30.889' E004°46.787'	Total. Aire de Montélimar. A7/E15 southbound between Junction 17 and 18.
ALLAN	N44°30.781' E004°46.888'	Shell. Aire de Montélimar. A7/E15 northbound between Junction 18 and 17.
ANNECY	N45°54.558' E006°07.063'	Total. D1501/Blvd de la Rocade. Northeast of town.
BOURG DE PEAGE	N45°02.196' E005°03.242'	Total. D2532N/Blvd Alpes Provence. South of river.
BOURG EN BRESSE	N46°11.328' E005°14.625'	Total. D1075/20 Ave du Maréchal Juin. Southeast of town.
BOURGOIN-JALLIEU	N45°35.675' E005°16.323'	Total. 7-19 Rue de l'Etissey. In centre.
BRON	N45°44.340' E004°54.298'	Total Access. D383/Blvd Périphérique Laurent Bonnevay northbound between D506 and D29.
CALUIRE	N45°48.287' E004°51.556'	Auchan. D48e. Northeast of town.
CEIGNES	N46°06.893' E005°29.434'	Total. Aire de Ceignes Cerdon. A40/E21 northbound between Junction 8 and A42/E611 interchange.
CEIGNES	N46°07.099' E005°29.473'	Total. Aire de Ceignes Haut-Bugey. A40/E21 southbound between A42/E611 interchange and Junction 8.
CEYZERIAT	N46°12.159' E005°17.768'	Total. Aire de Bourg Jasseron. A40/E62/E21 northbound between Junction 7 and 6.
CEYZERIAT	N46°12.177' E005°17.665'	Shell. Aire de Bourg Teyssonge. A40/E62/E21 southbound between Junction 6 and 7.
CHAMBERY	N45°35.584' E005°53.800'	Total Access. N201/E712 northbound at Junction 14.
CLUSES	N46°03.687' E006°33.776'	Total. Ave de la République. West of town.
COMMUNAY	N45°35.458' E004°49.686'	Total. Aire de Communay-Sud. A46/E15/E70 at Junction 17.
COMMUNAY	N45°35.356' E004°49.529'	Total. Aire de Communay-Nord. A46/E15/E70 at Junction 17.
DARDILLY	N45°48.477' E004°46.161'	Total. Aire de Paisy. A6 northbound between Junction 34 and 33.1.
DARDILLY	N45°49.230' E004°45.969'	Auchan. Aire de Dardilly. A6 southbound between Junction 33.1 and 34.

LPG-GPL

TOWN	GPS	DIRECTIONS
DRACE	N46°08.048' E004°45.998'	Avia. Aire de Taponas. A6/E15 northbound between Junction 30 and 29.
DRACE	N46°08.612' E004°46.056'	Total. Aire de Docteuracé. A6/E15 southbound between Junction 29 and 30.
EYBENS	N45°09.117' E005°44.391'	Total. N87/E712 northbound between Junction 6 and 5.
FEURS	N45°44.579' E004°12.447'	Total. D1089/Bigny. West of town after crossing river Loire.
FEYZIN	N45°40.486' E004°50.908'	Elf. D312. West of town near A7 junction.
L'ALBENC	N45°13.177' E005°26.127'	Total. D1092/Route de Grenoble. South of town.
L'ISLE d'ABEAU	N45°36.803' E005°12.797'	Total. Aire de l'Isle d'Abeau. A43/E70/E711 northbound between Junction 7 and 6.
L'ISLE d'ABEAU	N45°36.749' E005°12.555'	Esso. Aire de l'Isle d'Abeau. A43/E70/E711 southbound between Junction 6 and 7.
LA BATHIE	N45°36.733' E006°27.008'	Elan. Aire de Langon. N90 southbound at Junction 34. Accessible from both sides.
LA MOTTE SERVOLEX	N45°36.628' E005°53.194'	Total Access. N201 southbound between Junction 14 and 11. Take exit for ZI Les Landiers Nord.
LA RAVOIRE	N45°34.119' E005°57.777'	Total. D1006/Ave de Chambéry. North of town.
LES HOUCHES	N45°53.901' E006°48.725'	Total. N205/Route Blanche southbound at Junction 28.
LES SALLES	N45°51.279' E003°48.568'	Shell. Aire du Haur-Forez. A89/E70 northbound between Junction 32 and 31.
LES SALLES	N45°51.366' E003°48.860'	Total. Aire du Haut-Forez. A89/E70 southbound between Junction 31 and 32.
LORIOL SUR DROME	N44°45.640' E004°50.282'	Intermarché. N7/D104 roundabout. Take exit for Centre Commercial. Northeast of town.
LYON	N45°44.099' E004°50.361'	Total. 112 Rue de Gerland. In centre.
MACON	N46°17.107' E004°48.470'	Total. D906/Route de Lyon. South of town.
MONTELIMAR	N44°33.317' E004°44.250'	Casino. D540. West of town.
MONTELIMAR	N44°31.970' E004°44.776'	Carrefour. D540a/Route de Marseille. South of town.
MONTELIMAR	N44°31.135' E004°44.708'	Total Access. N7. South of town.
OYONNAX	N46°15.029' E005°38.487'	Total. 174 Cours de Verdun. Southwest of town.
PIERRE BENITE	N45°41.834' E004°49.492'	Total. D15/Blvd de l'Europe. South of town.
PONT DE CLAIX	N45°08.308' E005°42.165'	Total. D1075/D269 crossroads. North of town.
PORTES LES VALENCE	N44°52.034' E004°51.873'	Shell. Aire de Portes Lés Valence. A7/E15 southbound between Junction 15 and 16.
PORTES LES VALENCE	N44°51.937' E004°51.991'	Total. Aire de Portes Lés Valence. A7/E15 northbound between Junction 16 and 15.
ST GENIS LAVAL	N45°40.728' E004°47.529'	Auchan. A450 at Junction 6b. South of town.
ST PRIEST	N45°42.425' E004°59.210'	Total Access. D306/Route de Grenoble. Northeast of town.
SALLANCHES	N45°56.686' E006°37.798'	Total Access. D1205/Ave de Geneve. North of town.
SEREZIN DU RHONE	N45°37.787' E004°49.077'	Total. Aire de Sérézin du Rhône. A7 northbound. Take exit for D312.
SOLAIZE	N45°39.138' E004°50.208'	Elf. Aire de Solaize. A7 southbound. 7km from junction with A46.
ST ETIENNE	N45°26.529' E004°24.579'	Total Access. N488/100 Rue de la Montat. East of town.
ST ETIENNE	N45°27.909' E004°22.670'	Total Access. 11 Ave de Verdun. North of town.
ST JEAN DE BOURNAY	N45°29.933' E005°08.250'	Intermarché. Lotissement du Stade just off D518/Route de Lyon. South of town.
ST RAMBERT	N45°16.542' E004°49.752'	BP. Aire de St Rambert d'Albon. A7/E15 northbound between Junction 13 and 12.
ST RAMBERT	N45°16.681' E004°49.508'	Total. Aire de St Rambert d'Albon. A7/E15 southbound between Junction 12 and 13.
ST VALLIER	N45°11.700' E004°48.855'	Total. N7/Ave de Québec. 2km north of town.
VALENCE	N44°56.572' E004°51.571'	Avia. D533/Ave Gross Umstadt. Northwest of town.
VALENCE	N44°56.412' E004°54.491'	Total Access. 41 Blvd Gustave André. East of town.
VALENCE	N44°55.188' E004°52.675'	Total Access. D2007n/162 Ave de Provence. South of town.
VILLARS	N45°28.557' E004°20.661'	Auchan. D201. North of town.
VIZILLE	N45°04.979' E005°45.912'	Total. N85/D5 roundabout. North of town.
VOIRON	N45°21.515' E005°35.537'	Total. D592/5 Ave du Docteur Valois. South of town.
VOREPPE	N45°16.686' E005°37.456'	Total. Aire de Voreppe. A48/E713 northbound at Junction 12.
VOREPPE	N45°16.635' E005°37.363'	Agip. Aire de l'Ile Rose. A48/E713 southbound at Junction 12.

INDEX

INDEX

INDEX

M

N

O

P

INDEX

INDEX

The French Aires situation is constantly changing and customer feedback has proven vital in keeping the guide up to date. Photographs are essential because they provide the supporting evidence we need to confirm that your submissions are accurate. The truth is that Submissions without photos are like reading a book in the dark. Filling in a submission form onsite is best practice because you are unlikely to remember everything, however it is essential that you record GPS coordinates onsite. The best way to keep an accurate record is with your digital camera by following this photographic checklist.

Take photos of the:

• Parking area from several angles
• Surrounding area from several angles
• Service Point showing all working parts/sides
• Close-up of the payment slot to identify token or payment type.
• Close-up of the electricity points and trip-switches to identify plug type and amperage
• Designation signs and information boards, including close-ups of text.
• Also take GPS coordinates onsite

Please name photos by the town name, region, and the person's name to be credited if they are published.

You can submit your text and digital photos online at www.All-the-Aires.co.uk/submissions.shtml. We cannot process printed photos, but they are still useful as record shots.
If you have lots of submissions and photos burn them to disk and post them to:

Vicarious Media
62 Tontine Street
Folkestone
CT20 1JP

Considerable thanks goes to the Aire Heads who have provided photographs and information about the Aires they have visited. Some of the Aire Heads are listed below:

Al Green, Alan and Pam Wallace, Alan Hoida, Alan Potter, Ann Beck, Anna Mills, Barry Mills, Bob Weddell, Brenda & Maurice Cope, Carol Weaver, Caroline Winter, Chris de Wet, Chris Hamson & Margaret Chmielewski, Chris Thomas, David Abbott, David Hayward, Diana and Michael Adams, Dot Palastanga, Fiona Beattie, Gary Watson, Gerda Noordhoek, Graham Vaughan, Heidi Hardwick, Ian & Chris, Ian Cooper, Ian Coull, Ian Jackson, Ivan wadsworth, J Miller, Janet & John Watts, Jean & Ken Fowler, Jim Stobart, John Dunn, John Pipe, John Watts, Joy & Bob Podesta, Jytte Jakobsen, Karen Evans, Linda Wilson, Lisette Johnston, Lynne Watson, M G Thorne, Marguerite Brown, Mark Francis, Martin & Joanne Rennie, Mary Hayes, Mary Seddon, Mr and Mrs SA Matterson, Mr I E Buechse, Mrs J Westwood, Patricia Houghton,Paul Newman, Paul Sparks, Paul, Julia & Alice, Peter Hesketh, Phil & Julie Hutchins, Robert Horan & Jennifer Payne, Robin Culverhouse, Rod & Liz Sleigh, Rod Poxon, Roger Quigley, Roy France, Sally & Peter Moorhouse, Sally Bethell, Steve Brindle, Sue Thake, Tim Ellwood-Wade.

Please use this form to update Aires information in this guide. If the Aire is already listed, complete only the sections where changes apply. Please write in capital letters and circle appropriate symbols.

Town/Village:

Region:

Road name/number:

Date Visited:

Surroundings:

	Coastal		Rural		Farm	SKI	Sking		Marina
	Residential		Village		Park		Day parking	!	Warning
	Urban		Riverside or lakeside		Campsite	T	Tourism	R	Recommended

Please circle 1 or more symbols as appropriate

Page Number: Postcode – if known:

Number of Spaces:

Time limit: Cost:

Parking symbols:

	Overnight parking possible		Hard surface		Large motorhomes
P	Designated motorhome parking		Sloping	F	Free of charge
			Illuminated		
			Noisy		

Please circle 1 or more symbols as appropriate

Service Point type: Cost:

Payment/Token type:

Sanitation symbols:

	Water	E	Electric hook up		Showers
	Grey water disposal	WC	Toilets	F	Free of charge
	Toilet disposal		Disabled toilet		Open all year

Please circle 1 or more symbols as appropriate

Leisure Information Symbols:

SP	Shaded parking		Children's play area		Marked cycle route
	Green space suitable for dogs/children		Boules		Fishing
	Picnic tables/benches		Washing machine		Boating (unmotorised)
			Walking - path or trail		

Please circle 1 or more symbols as appropriate

Please turn over

AIRE/LPG SUBMISSION FORM

Directions - Brief, specific directions to Aire/LPG:

GPS Coordinates:

Information - Brief description of location and amenities:

Name and email or address - so information can be credited:

Your feedback is vital to keep this guide up to date. Fill in this form whilst you are at the Aire. Please name photos with the town name, region, and the name you want credited if they are published. Please submit your text and digital photos online at **www.All-the-Aires.co.uk/submissions.shtml** or post your completed forms and CDs of photos to **Vicarious Media, 62 Tontine Street, Folkestone, CT20 1JP.** You can print off more forms at **www.All-the-Aires.co.uk**

Please include at least five photos showing the parking area in different directions and close-ups of any signs. Photograph the service point showing working parts, and the token slot, so that we may identify the token type, don't forget the grey drain. Submissions without photos are like reading a book in the dark. We cannot process printed photos, but they are still useful as record shots.

Thank you very much for your time.

By supplying details and photographs you are giving unrestricted publication and reproduction rights to Vicarious Media Ltd.

Please use this form to update Aires information in this guide. If the Aire is already listed, complete only the sections where changes apply. Please write in capital letters and circle appropriate symbols.

Town/Village:

Region:

Road name/number:

Date Visited:

Surroundings:

	Coastal		Rural		Farm	SKI	Sking		Marina
	Residential		Village		Park	☼	Day parking	!	Warning
	Urban		Riverside or lakeside		Campsite	T	Tourism	R	Recommended

Please circle 1 or more symbols as appropriate

Page Number: Postcode – if known:

Number of Spaces:

Time limit: Cost:

Parking symbols:

	Overnight parking possible		Hard surface		Large motorhomes
P	Designated motorhome parking		Sloping	F	Free of charge
			Illuminated		
			Noisy		

Please circle 1 or more symbols as appropriate

Service Point type: Cost:

Payment/Token type:

Sanitation symbols:

	Water	E	Electric hook up		Showers
	Grey water disposal	WC	Toilets	F	Free of charge
	Toilet disposal		Disabled toilet		Open all year

Please circle 1 or more symbols as appropriate

Leisure Information Symbols:

SP	Shaded parking		Children's play area		Marked cycle route
	Green space suitable for dogs/children		Boules		Fishing
			Washing machine		Boating (unmotorised)
	Picnic tables/benches		Walking - path or trail		

Please circle 1 or more symbols as appropriate

Please turn over

AIRE/LPG SUBMISSION FORM

Directions - Brief, specific directions to Aire/LPG:

GPS Coordinates:

Information - Brief description of location and amenities:

Name and email or address - so information can be credited:

Your feedback is vital to keep this guide up to date. Fill in this form whilst you are at the Aire. Please name photos with the town name, region, and the name you want credited if they are published. Please submit your text and digital photos online at **www.All-the-Aires.co.uk/submissions.shtml** or post your completed forms and CDs of photos to **Vicarious Media, 62 Tontine Street, Folkestone, CT20 1JP.** You can print off more forms at **www.All-the-Aires.co.uk**

Please include at least five photos showing the parking area in different directions and close-ups of any signs. Photograph the service point showing working parts, and the token slot, so that we may identify the token type, don't forget the grey drain. Submissions without photos are like reading a book in the dark. We cannot process printed photos, but they are still useful as record shots.

Thank you very much for your time.

By supplying details and photographs you are giving unrestricted publication and reproduction rights to Vicarious Media Ltd.

Please use this form to update Aires information in this guide. If the Aire is already listed, complete only the sections where changes apply. Please write in capital letters and circle appropriate symbols.

Town/Village:

Region:

Road name/number:

Date Visited:

Surroundings:

Coastal	Rural	Farm	SKI Sking	Marina
Residential	Village	Park	Day parking	! Warning
Urban	Riverside or lakeside	Campsite	T Tourism	R Recommended

Please circle 1 or more symbols as appropriate

Page Number: Postcode – if known:

Number of Spaces:

Time limit: Cost:

Parking symbols:

Overnight parking possible	Hard surface	Large motorhomes
P Designated motorhome parking	Sloping	F Free of charge
	Illuminated	
	Noisy	

Please circle 1 or more symbols as appropriate

Service Point type: Cost:

Payment/Token type:

Sanitation symbols:

Water	E Electric hook up	Showers
Grey water disposal	WC Toilets	F Free of charge
Toilet disposal	Disabled toilet	Open all year

Please circle 1 or more symbols as appropriate

Leisure Information Symbols:

SP Shaded parking	Children's play area	Marked cycle route
Green space suitable for dogs/children	Boules	Fishing
Picnic tables/benches	Washing machine	Boating (unmotorised)
	Walking - path or trail	

Please circle 1 or more symbols as appropriate

Please turn over

AIRE/LPG SUBMISSION FORM

Directions - Brief, specific directions to Aire/LPG:

GPS Coordinates:

Information - Brief description of location and amenities:

Name and email or address - so information can be credited:

Your feedback is vital to keep this guide up to date. Fill in this form whilst you are at the Aire. Please name photos with the town name, region, and the name you want credited if they are published. Please submit your text and digital photos online at **www.All-the-Aires.co.uk/submissions.shtml** or post your completed forms and CDs of photos to **Vicarious Media, 62 Tontine Street, Folkestone, CT20 1JP.** You can print off more forms at **www.All-the-Aires.co.uk**

Please include at least five photos showing the parking area in different directions and close-ups of any signs. Photograph the service point showing working parts, and the token slot, so that we may identify the token type, don't forget the grey drain. Submissions without photos are like reading a book in the dark. We cannot process printed photos, but they are still useful as record shots.

Thank you very much for your time.

By supplying details and photographs you are giving unrestricted publication and reproduction rights to Vicarious Media Ltd.

Please use this form to update Aires information in this guide. If the Aire is already listed, complete only the sections where changes apply. Please write in capital letters and circle appropriate symbols.

Town/Village:

Region:

Road name/number:

Date Visited:

Surroundings:

⚓ Coastal	⌂ Rural	🚜 Farm	SKI Sking	⛵ Marina	
🏛 Residential	🏘 Village	🏃 Park	☼ Day parking	! Warning	
🏢 Urban	🚣 Riverside or lakeside	⛺ Campsite	T Tourism	R Recommended	

Please circle 1 or more symbols as appropriate

Page Number: Postcode – if known:

🚐 Number of Spaces:

Time limit: Cost:

Parking symbols:

⬤ Overnight parking possible	🚐 Hard surface	🚌 Large motorhomes
P Designated motorhome parking	◣ Sloping	F Free of charge
	🌡 Illuminated	
	♫ Noisy	

Please circle 1 or more symbols as appropriate

🪣 Service Point type: Cost:

Payment/Token type:

Sanitation symbols:

🚰 Water	E Electric hook up	🚿 Showers
⬛ Grey water disposal	WC Toilets	F Free of charge
🚽 Toilet disposal	♿ Disabled toilet	✵ Open all year

Please circle 1 or more symbols as appropriate

Leisure Information Symbols:

SP Shaded parking	🤸 Children's play area	🚲 Marked cycle route
♣ Green space suitable for dogs/children	🎯 Boules	🎣 Fishing
🌲 Picnic tables/benches	◉ Washing machine	🛶 Boating (unmotorised)
	🚶 Walking - path or trail	

Please circle 1 or more symbols as appropriate

Please turn over

AIRE/LPG SUBMISSION FORM

Directions - Brief, specific directions to Aire/LPG:

GPS Coordinates:

Information - Brief description of location and amenities:

Name and email or address - so information can be credited:

Your feedback is vital to keep this guide up to date. Fill in this form whilst you are at the Aire. Please name photos with the town name, region, and the name you want credited if they are published. Please submit your text and digital photos online at **www.All-the-Aires.co.uk/submissions.shtml** or post your completed forms and CDs of photos to **Vicarious Media, 62 Tontine Street, Folkestone, CT20 1JP.** You can print off more forms at **www.All-the-Aires.co.uk**

Please include at least five photos showing the parking area in different directions and close-ups of any signs. Photograph the service point showing working parts, and the token slot, so that we may identify the token type, don't forget the grey drain. Submissions without photos are like reading a book in the dark. We cannot process printed photos, but they are still useful as record shots.

Thank you very much for your time.

By supplying details and photographs you are giving unrestricted publication and reproduction rights to Vicarious Media Ltd.

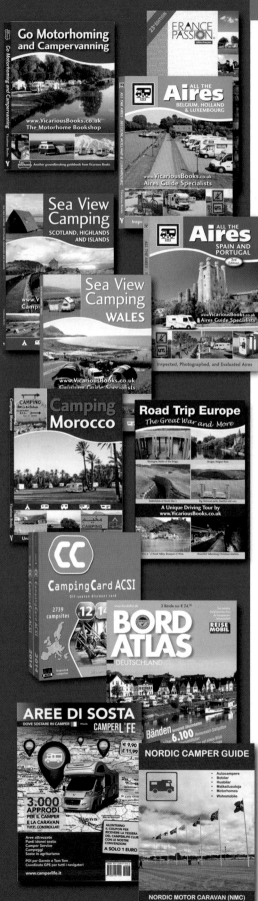

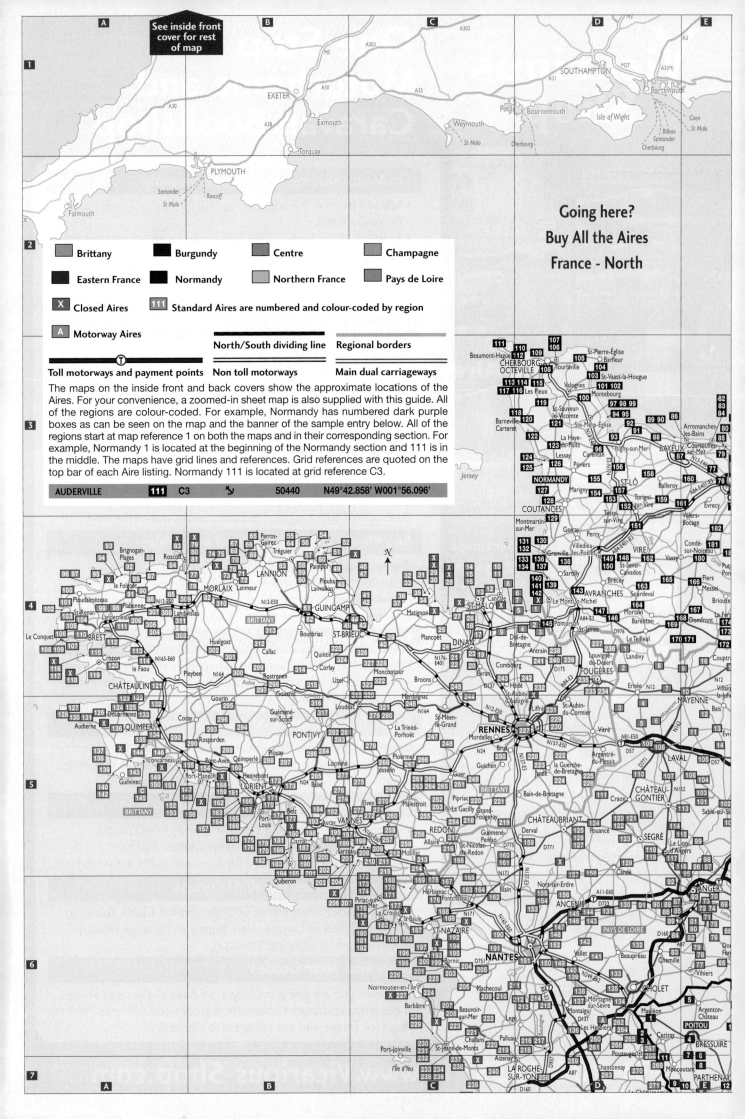

See inside front cover for rest of map

Going here?
Buy All the Aires
France - North

Legend:

- Brittany
- Burgundy
- Centre
- Champagne
- Eastern France
- Normandy
- Northern France
- Pays de Loire
- X Closed Aires
- 111 Standard Aires are numbered and colour-coded by region
- A Motorway Aires
- North/South dividing line
- Regional borders
- T Toll motorways and payment points
- Non toll motorways
- Main dual carriageways

The maps on the inside front and back covers show the approximate locations of the Aires. For your convenience, a zoomed-in sheet map is also supplied with this guide. All of the regions are colour-coded. For example, Normandy has numbered dark purple boxes as can be seen on the map and the banner of the sample entry below. All of the regions start at map reference 1 on both the maps and in their corresponding section. For example, Normandy 1 is located at the beginning of the Normandy section and 111 is in the middle. The maps have grid lines and references. Grid references are quoted on the top bar of each Aire listing. Normandy 111 is located at grid reference C3.

| AUDERVILLE | 111 | C3 | ⚓ | 50440 | N49°42.858' W001°56.096' |